The Daily T

EVERYDAY LAW

AVIVA GOLDEN

HarperCollins*Publishers*

In memory of
my parents, Liebe and Michael Jacobson,
and my brother, Joshua Jacobson

HarperCollins*Publishers*
Westerhill Road, Bishopbriggs, Glasgow G64 2QT

The Collins website is www.collins.co.uk

First published 1994
Second edition 1996
Third edition 2000
Fourth edition 2003

© 2003 The Daily Telegraph and Aviva Golden

Reprint 10 9 8 7 6 5 4 3 2 1 0

ISBN 0-00-714621-3

A catalogue record for this book is available from the British Library

Typeset by Davidson Pre-Press Graphics Ltd, Glasgow G3

Printed and bound by William Clowes Ltd, Beccles and London

CONTENTS

PREFACE

Nobody can be expected to know all the law – but ignorance of the law is no defence.

Armed with *Everyday Law* you will, at least, have a sporting chance of finding out what you need to know: there is more law in these pages than you will find in the mind of the wisest lawyer. Indeed, the legal adviser who keeps this book in a desk drawer will never be caught out by the client who wants to know if he can keep his luxuriant ponytail while serving food in a delicatessen or who wonders if she has been overcharged when buying a cheap flight on the Internet. Do you need a licence to look after your neighbour's puppies while he is on holiday? Who can you sue if the office prankster pulls your chair away as you are sitting down? What happens if you signal left and turn right? How much can you be fined for breaching an anti-social behaviour order? Just enquire within.

Just as valuable are the directories of useful organisations, complete with phone numbers and – new in this edition – websites. What, pray, is the Pyramus and Thisbe Club? It's website – *www.partywalls.org.uk* – gives us the clue. And is it only the alphabet that makes neighbours of the Noise Network and Office of the Deputy Prime Minister?

Law students used to ask Lord Denning, the famous judge, not to create any new law until the exams were over. The pace of legislative change these days, thanks not least to the Human Rights Act, means that only the latest edition of a work like this will do.

But Aviva Golden has not rested on her well-earned laurels, merely updating a word here or a figure there. There are new chapters on *Growing Old* and *Providing for your Retirement*, subjects of increasing importance as we live longer and find that our pensions are worth less (though not, we hope, worthless). Her book is worth buying for its expanded chapter on *The Legal System* alone.

And what makes this more than just a work of reference is the author's personality, always present though never intrusive. Chapters begin with a lively introduction to the issues, explaining why the law is as it is and setting factual advice into a broader context. This is a book that can be read for pleasure as well as profit – and that's not something you can say about many works of legal scholarship. *Everyday Law* should find a place in every home.

Joshua Rozenberg
Legal Editor
The Daily Telegraph

ACKNOWLEDGEMENTS

4th Edition

I am so pleased to acknowledge the unstinting help, thoughtfulness, and support from my colleagues and friends who worked on the preparation of this edition.

The present book contains additional chapters which deal with the law in relation to the elderly: Victor Gersten wrote the original text for the chapter entitled *Growing Old*, while Eileen O'Grady supplied the text for *Providing for your Retirement*. I am much in their debt.

With regard to the existing chapters, Jean Campbell undertook the updating of the chapters on *The Countryside, Pets, Goods and Services, Death – Before and After*, and the chapter on *Accidents*. Rona Epstein worked on the *Children* chapters, as well as having researched and written the additional section on Special Educational Needs in *Children (Part 2)*. Eileen O'Grady updated the chapters on *The Legal System, Buying and Selling your Home, Neighbours,* and *Working for a Living* (employment law having grown to such an extent that we now have two chapters on the subject instead of one). I must thank Dr Patrick Campbell who gave valuable assistance to the section on *Psychiatric treatment and committal procedures* (under the Mental Health Act) in the chapter on *Growing Old*.

The Directories are their own testimony to Judith Samson's careful research. They now also provide the reader with web addresses in almost all instances.

My colleagues at the Islington Legal Advice Centre are actively engaged in providing legal help to those most in need of it. I am privileged to share time and space with them.

I am not able to express my gratitude to all the people by name in the various organisations, press sections, government departments, university faculties, and NGOs, who were so ready to assist with the questions which I put to them in the course of preparation of the fourth edition. I was struck again and again by their helpfulness in searching out information or discussing the text to ensure accuracy in response to my e-mail or telephone queries.

Masoud Gerami, managing director of Context Legal Systems, is generous – as always – in allowing unrestricted use of the Justis databases for research purposes. From time to time, I also called on the expertise of his editorial staff. I was also very fortunate in being able to use the online service of the *Estates Gazette* for the chapters on property law. My thanks to Henry Everett, the *EG*'s legal editor, and to his team.

The partnership with Telegraph Books has been a significant factor in the success of *Everyday Law*. I would like to express my appreciation to Alex Stitt, Director of Telegraph Enterprises, and Morven Knowles, publisher of Telegraph Books.

The editing of the book by Monica Thorp provides a safety net for all of us. Her deep involvement in the subject matter – as well as her concern for every aspect of this major undertaking – provide both a happy collaboration and a much-needed reassurance.

Edwin Moore of HarperCollins, who has always championed the book, is both enthusiastic publisher and valued friend.

Ann Hand began work on the *Motoring* chapter for this edition. Ann had been involved, with evident pleasure, on all previous editions of this book. Sadly she died just as the page proofs were being published.

At home, Jacky Carby gave me kind and cheerful backup in my office. And my husband never wavered in providing support of all kinds, both in encouraging me to get the job done and in his confidence that I would be able to do so.

AUTHOR'S NOTE

Please note that the law in this book is applicable to England and Wales only. I have endeavoured to state the law at the date of going to press. However, this can only present a snapshot of a moving image. With every day that passes, the law undergoes subtle – and sometimes dramatic – changes both in the courts of law and in Parliament.

The text and the examples cited are there to illustrate a principle. In every case, principles have to be applied to the particular facts. Thus the contents do not point to a conclusion or outcome in any specific case and are not a substitute for a full consideration of all the relevant facts and law in any given situation by a trained legal advisor. While every endeavour is made to be accurate, the information – of necessity – reflects the generalised nature of the publication.

Further, neither the author nor the publishers intend to render a professional service with this publication, nor are they liable for any error or omission in the book; for any use to which the contents are put; or for any loss arising therefrom.

Both author and publishers regret that they are unable to answer readers' individual queries.

The directories

At the end of the chapters, you will find a directory of relevant organisations. The family law directory on page 109 is a combined one for all the first four chapters. The property law directory on page 215 is a combined one for chapters six and seven. We have endeavoured to ensure that names and addresses are correct at the time of going to press.

If any organisation would like to be considered for inclusion in one or other of the directories in future editions of the book, a letter should be sent to the Reference Department, HarperCollins Publishers, Westerhill Road, Bishopbriggs, Glasgow G64 2QT.

Readers are asked to note that some organisations give advice only to their own paid-up members; some organisations provide information but do not offer advice or handle complaints; some organisations respond to written queries only and cannot answer over the telephone. Several of the organisations listed offer publications and leaflets, while a few have library facilities. Do check which organisations are member-based only.

Most directory entries now carry web addresses. If you do not have access to the Internet, do try your local library as you are likely to find very helpful assistance there. An internet café is another option.

Inclusion of an organisation in the directories or in the text does not indicate that we endorse any particular product, publication, or advice.

As far as the religious organisations are concerned, for detailed information on the requirements of any particular faith we advise you to contact someone connected with that faith.

Do note that some religious organisations are faith-led and offer advice only to their own adherents.

Aviva Golden 1 May 1996, November 1998, April 2000 and December 2002.

The tables in the Motoring chapter on pages 485, 497 and 505 are reproduced with the permission of the Controller of Her Majesty's Stationery Office and are to be found in the Highway Code. The law's view of stages of growing up, at the end of the chapter *Children (Part 2)*, is based on information in the booklet *At what age can I...?*, published by the Children's Legal Centre.

1 SETTING UP HOME
Marriage and Cohabitation

If we look around us, perhaps the most striking social change we would notice in the past century has been in the sphere of personal relations. Today no lawyer could categorically state, with the certainty of a Victorian judge, that marriage is 'the voluntary union for life of one man and one woman to the exclusion of all others'.

On the contrary, the law and the lawmakers recognise how much has changed in family life. The statistics of present day England speak for themselves: more than a million couples each year choose to live together rather than to marry; gay couples are increasingly succeeding in their campaign for legal recognition; one in three children today is born to unmarried parents; more and more children are being brought up in single-parent households; and among the number of couples who do get married, one in every three of them will seek a divorce.

Even under review is the hitherto binding assumption that, when discussing marriage, we are discussing a union between two persons who were born a male and a female. A civil ceremony for gay couples has been initiated in London, and the right of transsexuals to marry has been endorsed by the European Court of Human Rights in a landmark judgement (see section 1.2.2 below). In response the UK government has announced that draft legislation is to be published allowing transsexuals, after due enquiry, to marry 'in their acquired gender'.

The formalities relating to marriage are surprisingly complicated – particularly if we contrast them with the simple procedure involved in an undefended divorce (see chapter on *Divorce*, section 3). Nonetheless both marriage and divorce do require a legal process and confer a defined legal status unlike the informal arrangements that many couples of today choose instead.

The need to bring the procedures for marriage more up to date and more in line with the nature of modern society has led to a White Paper: *Civil Registration: Vital Change*. This is dealt with at the end of the chapter. These proposals, once they are brought in to effect, are intended to cover religious marriages as well.

Again, nothing could have seemed more basic than the concept of parenthood itself – from both the biological and the social points of view. Yet today, when we talk in terms of a child's 'natural' parents, we must also consider the legal implications of artificial insemination, *in vitro* fertilisation, and surrogate motherhood. The scale of the impact of science on today's social and moral climate – with new developments and techniques including the possibility of cloning and the creation of 'designer' babies – generates new complexities in the bio-ethical debate.

It is not surprising then that one of the most striking features in the field of family law in the past decade is the extent to which the legal establishment has moved in recognising a wide definition of the 'family'.

In a case which concerned a woman's application to succeed to her deceased partner's estate, the judge said that in considering the question of whether the couple had in fact been 'living as husband and wife', a court had to take into account 'the multifarious nature of marital relationships'. While this case dealt with the specific issue of the intestacy rules, the broad view it takes of relationships is not without significance in the larger context. (See also the chapter on *Death – Before and After*, section 8.5.)

In another case on the law relating to succession to a protected tenancy, the rights of a same-sex partner came to be decided in the House of Lords. As the word 'family' was used in a number of different senses, some wider and some narrower, how was it to be interpreted in this particular case? Did 'family' mean only a legal relationship of blood, a legal ceremony of marriage, or a legal adoption? No longer so. Over the years, the courts have come to be flexible in applying the word 'family', their Lordships stated. It should no longer be applied 'only to legally binding relationships'. Since then, the Court of Appeal has gone one step further, also in a case of rights of succession of a same-sex partner. In their role as protector of minority rights, the judges stated, a surviving partner of a homosexual union was to be treated in law as the spouse of the deceased. (See also the chapter on *Landlords and their Tenants*, section 8.1.2.)

So family relationships are being broadly rather than narrowly defined by the courts. Nonetheless, concern at family breakdown – however defined – is being expressed at every level of society. In November 1999, the Lord Chancellor's Department announced the setting up of a new advisory group, including advisors from other government departments, the Office for National Statistics, and the voluntary sector, to consider strategies for the support of marriages and other relationships. A number of initiatives have followed on this announcement, as outlined in a document *Moving Forward Together* issued by the Lord Chancellor's Department, as well as the allocation of increased funding for marriage and relationship support for 2002–2003. However, the effectiveness of government intervention in areas as private and as sensitive as these has yet to be gauged.

It is not the purpose of this book to take sides in any debate but to endeavour to state the law in a rapidly changing social environment and to acknowledge that family law has to take account of the dramatic shifts in our established patterns of family life. Of course, this is far more easily said than done. The issues raised are highly charged and very complex. How far must the law adapt to these changing patterns? Or rather, to what extent should it impose its own pattern of what is 'desirable' in family life? Can conflicting ideologies on what constitutes family values be bridged at all? Are the courts the right place in which to try to build these bridges? Given the speed of change of family and social *mores*, it is no wonder that profound difficulties arise – for those who have to make the laws, for those who have to implement them, and for those who have to turn to the courts for assistance. No wonder, too, that the law can sometimes appear helpless in the face of these problems, some of which it has to confront and to settle, as best it may, on a daily basis.

There is yet another dimension. The Human Rights Act 1998 has incorporated the European Human Rights Convention into English law. A fundamental Article of the Convention states that 'everyone has the right to respect for his private and family life'. The Article goes on to say that there should not be any 'interference by a public authority with the exercise of this right' except

a) in accordance with the law,
b) where necessary in a democratic society,
c) where called for in order to protect health, morals, and the rights and freedoms of others.

The Human Rights Act 1998, brought into force in October 2000, has profoundly affected the way in which judges view the cases brought before them. Application of the Act is also evolving all the time. For example, the European law on human rights had a direct bearing in the case cited above, where same-sex partners were held to be regarded as spouses rather than family members.

Note: A DIRECTORY of organisations and other bodies which provide support or information on many aspects of family law can be found at the end of Chapter 4 on page 109.

This chapter looks at:

- who can get married
- the engagement
- marriage formalities
- effects of marriage
- cohabitation agreements
- proposals for change: Civil Registration.

1   WHO CAN GET MARRIED?

1.1   Determining who is a 'single' person

The law stipulates that in order to marry, every person must:

a) be unmarried (for definition of a single person see section 1.1.1 below)

b) be over the age of 16

c) want to marry someone of the opposite sex

d) not be closely related to their future spouse

e) agree to the marriage (i.e. it must be a 'voluntary union').

1.1.1   An unmarried person

Every marriage in this country must be a monogamous union, i.e. it must be between two single persons. The law regards you as a single person if:

a) you have never been married at all; or

b) you have been married before but that marriage has:

    i. been dissolved (through recognised divorce proceedings)

    ii. ended with the death of your spouse, or

    iii. been annulled (as void).

1.1.2   Someone who has been through a recognised divorce

A divorce is recognised in this country if it is obtained in a civil court according to the law of England. Thus divorces which are obtained in England in purely religious proceedings are not recognised.

☞   *You and your husband are Orthodox Jews who have always lived in London. You have agreed to his request for a divorce and have obtained a divorce according to Jewish law (a get). You are told that you have to go through civil divorce proceedings if you wish to remarry here.*

    That is correct. A *get* on its own would not entitle you to remarry under the laws of England.

Do note, however, that the converse is also true. Under the Divorce (Religious Marriages) Act 2002, a civil court can refuse to grant a decree absolute if the couple have not already been through the divorce procedures required by their own religion.

However, a divorce obtained abroad is recognised provided:

a) the parties are domiciled there; and

b) it was obtained in proper proceedings recognised under the law of the country where the divorce proceedings took place. The proceedings can be religious or civil provided that they are formally held and are conducted under set rules.

1.1.3   A widow or widower (including presumption of a former spouse's death)

There may be difficulties if you need to establish the death or disappearance of a former spouse before you can remarry. To assist in such cases, the law 'presumes' that a spouse is dead if all contact has been lost with him or her for seven years and you have no reason to believe that he or she is alive.

☞   *Your husband left you several years ago to live abroad. You have never heard from him and all your endeavours to trace him have failed. Someone has suggested that your husband may even be dead. You now want to remarry. What can you do?*

    If your husband has not been heard from for seven years you can petition the courts to dissolve your first marriage on the grounds that he is 'presumed to be dead'. You would have to show the court that there were persons who would probably have heard from him had he still been alive and that they have not heard from him. You would also have to show that you have made proper enquiries as to his whereabouts.

    If he has been out of touch for less than seven years, you would have to go further and to show positive evidence as to why you think he may be dead (e.g. a suicide note although no body has been found). In any event, you might have grounds for divorce on the basis of a five-year separation (see chapter on *Divorce*), if he has been away for that long.

1.1.4   Someone whose previous marriage has been annulled

You are also in law a single person if your previous marriage has been annulled (see section 1.3 below).

1.1.5   The question of polygamy

Difficulties can arise in our multi-ethnic society where some groups accept polygamous unions which are not accepted by the law of England. For example, you might marry a foreigner in this country and then discover that he already has a legal wife, since under the laws of his own country, it is legal for a man to be married to more than one woman. As far as your own marriage is concerned, it is void in English law.

In certain circumstances, however, the courts will recognise a polygamous union, entered into abroad, according to the law of the country where both the parties were domiciled.

1.1.6   Summary

Anyone who has been married once before cannot remarry in this country until the law regards him or her as single once again. In other words, monogamy is still the guiding principle of the institution of marriage according to the law of England – for the purposes of marrying here.

1.2   Other necessary qualifications to meet

In addition to insisting that marriage can only take place between two single people, the law insists on several other necessary criteria before two people can marry.

1.2.1   Age requirements

You must meet the age requirements:

- any single person can get married over the age of 18
- if you are aged between 16 and 18, you must obtain parental consent
- a marriage where one of the persons is under the age of 16 is absolutely void.

If someone marries between the ages of 16 and 18 without parental consent, their marriage is voidable (for the difference between 'void' and 'voidable' marriages, see sections 1.3.1 and 1.3.2 below).

Who must consent to a marriage of a child aged 16 to 18?:

- the parents, or
- the guardian, or
- the court.

☞   *You are 17-years-old and are desperate to marry the man of your choice. However, your parents thoroughly disapprove of him and refuse to consent to the marriage. You are so determined that you make a false statement to the superintendent registrar that you are 18 in order to get a licence (see section 3.2.1(d)). Three weeks later you get married. Now your parents state that your marriage is void. What is your position?*

   Your false statement has not invalidated your marriage (see section 1.3 below). However, giving false information to the superintendent registrar of marriages is a serious criminal offence.

The sensible alternative would have been to apply to court to ask its permission to marry. The court can dispense with parental consent and give its own consent to your marriage if you can persuade the magistrates that your parents, by withholding their consent, are acting unreasonably.

☞   *You are 17 and wish to get married. You live with your mother, who separated from your father when you were ten. She is quite agreeable to your proposed marriage. You received occasional visits from your father for the first couple of years after your parents split up, but he has been out of touch with you since. Do you need his permission too?*

   The law on this issue is not clear; if your mother has sole parental responsibility for you only her consent would be necessary. If your father and mother have joint parental responsibility then you might have to seek your father's permission (for Parental Responsibility see the chapter on *Children (Part 1)*). In any event, you could apply to a magistrates' court to dispense with your father's consent.

1.2.2   Intention to marry someone of the opposite sex

The law specifies that the parties must be male and female, 'one man and one woman'. So there cannot be a legal marriage of a couple who are homosexual. However it may be possible to register a partnership of a same-sex couple, under the scheme introduced by the Mayor of London, if at least one partner lives in London (see the website at *www.lpr.london.gov.uk* or phone the helpline for an information pack: 020 7983 6536).

Problems also arise with transsexuals who wish to marry. As far as the present law in the UK is concerned, every person's sex is determined at birth and as entered on their birth certificate. Thus even if a person has undergone a sex change, there cannot be a valid marriage in this country to someone of their former sex.

However, once again this issue has been raised in the European Court of Human Rights. It ruled that while it was for the UK to determine the conditions under which a person should be granted legal recognition as a transsexual, as well as formalities applicable to their future marriage, there was no justification for barring transsexuals from enjoying the right to marry under any circumstances. Since then, the UK government has announced that it is committed to legislating as soon as possible to give transsexual people their Convention rights.

1.2.3   No marriage can take place between close relations

How is relationship defined?

There are many degrees of relationship in which intermarriage is forbidden by law. These relationships are usually grouped into two categories:

a) blood relations (*consanguinity*)
b) non-blood relations but where the relationship is so close that a ban on intermarriage is still imposed (*affinity*).

Note: an adopted child is generally treated in law as a blood relative.

1.2.3(a)   Consanguinity

A man cannot marry:

- his daughter
- his mother
- his sister
- his niece
- his granddaughter
- his adopted daughter.

A woman cannot marry:

- her son
- her father
- her brother
- her nephew
- her grandson
- her adopted son.

1.2.3(b)   Affinity

In general a man or woman cannot marry:

- a stepchild
- a son- or daughter-in-law.

However, in the affinity category, the prohibitions on intermarriage are not always absolute.

☞ *After the sudden death of your wife, you found it difficult to cope with your job as well as having to look after your two small children. Your wife's sister, who is a divorcee, came to live in your house to assist you with the housekeeping. You have now fallen in love with her and you both decide that you would like to get married. What is the position?*

An Act of Parliament allows brothers-in-law and sisters-in-law to marry.

So marriages in the affinity category can be allowed in certain, tightly circumscribed circumstances: for example, a step-parent can marry a step-child – provided only that the step-child:

- has not been brought up as a 'child of the family' (*see also Children (Part 1) section 3.4*), and
- is over 21.

1.2.4   The marriage must be voluntary

Where a person has gone through a ceremony of marriage because of coercion, the law holds that that person has not given proper consent to the marriage. Among certain ethnic and religious groups, it is common practice for the parents to arrange marriages for their children. Is an arranged marriage regarded as a 'voluntary union'?

In general, the law does not interfere with arranged marriages. However the issue has become a problem when there is a conflict between the wishes of the parents and those of the child. If the conflict is grave, the courts may be called upon to assess the point at which parental and social pressures overstep an acceptable limit and become unacceptable duress. The distinction to be drawn, not always an easy one, is between an arranged marriage and a forced marriage. Thus the courts have found instances of duress where there is:

- a threat of injury to life or liberty, or
- a child is threatened with expulsion from home and community.

In one case, the court was to asked to intervene where parents had taken their 17-year-old daughter abroad so that she could be married against her will. The judge said: 'Child abduction is still child abduction when both parents are the abductors and the child is very nearly an adult.' He called on social workers and schools to be more interventionist in implementing their duty of care in protecting girls in such instances while being aware of the need to be sensitive to the needs of ethnic minorities in which arranged marriages are common practice.

1.3   Marriages which can be annulled

1.3.1   Void marriages

Certain marriages are regarded in law as absolutely void. In other words the marriage – in the eyes of the law – has never taken place at all.

Marriages are absolutely void where:

- one of the parties is under the age of 16
- the parties are closely related (see section 1.2.3 above)
- one of the parties is not a single person, i.e. the marriage is bigamous or polygamous (see section 1.1.5 above)
- the parties are regarded in law as being of the same sex (see section 1.2.2 above).

1.3.2   When are proceedings for annulment instituted? The question of voidable marriages

Certain marriages are regarded in law as valid until they are annulled. These are 'voidable' marriages and, in the eyes of the law, they can be annulled on the petition of either party.

On the whole these proceedings are retained to meet the needs of those who have objection to divorce proceedings and who have grounds for annulment. The number of such petitions is on the increase.

1.3.3   Grounds for annulment

In order for a court to annul a voidable marriage, a person would have to show one of the following grounds:

- the marriage has not been consummated
- the husband or wife had not understood the nature of the ceremony in other words, he or she got married through a mistake (such as not knowing that it was a ceremony of marriage)
- the marriage was to someone of unsound mind
- the marriage was to someone with VD (now generally referred to as sexually transmitted disease).

2   THE ENGAGEMENT

2.1   Breach of promise?

Today an engagement is not a precondition of a marriage although couples often do make a public, formal announcement of their engagement.

At one time, an engagement was considered a binding legal contract. If you broke off an engagement, you could be sued by your ex-fiancé(e) for 'breach of promise' to marry. Today this is no longer so.

Thus whatever heartache their decision to part entails, people who are engaged are absolutely free to change their minds if they decide not to marry after all. They need not fear a court action!

☞ *You lived abroad and became engaged to your fiancé in a foreign country where engagement is regarded as a binding legal agreement. You both now live in England. After a time, you decide to break off the engagement. Your ex-fiancé threatens to sue you. What is your position?*

An agreement to marry is not legally enforceable in the English courts – wherever the engagement took place. It might still be actionable abroad however.

2.2   Problems if an engagement falls through

Although there is no action for breach of promise, legal disputes do arise between an engaged couple who decide to part. These disputes usually concern property and gifts.

2.2.1   The engagement ring

Certain clear rules of law govern the question of the return of an engagement ring. It is regarded as an outright gift – unless it can be shown to be a family heirloom.

☞ *Your fiancé has given you a very expensive engagement ring but the engagement has since been broken off by mutual agreement. Are you under a legal obligation to return the ring?*

The answer is that an engagement ring is presumed to be an absolute gift so that there is no obligation to return it. The same rule applies to birthday or Christmas gifts which your fiancé may have given to you – or you to him.

☞ *Your fiancé has given you a very valuable engagement ring which is a family heirloom, having once belonged to his great-grandmother. The engagement is broken off by mutual agreement. Are you under a legal obligation to return the ring?*

Again the presumption is that an engagement ring is intended to be an outright gift. However, where your fiancé can show – as in this case – that the ring is intended to remain in his family, you may be obliged by law to return it.

2.2.2   Other expenses

Weddings today can be very expensive and involve an outlay of thousands of pounds. What is the position if the wedding is cancelled? In addition, the couple may have gone to the trouble and expense of putting a down-payment on a flat or house. What happens to their deposit if they decide to call the whole thing off?

In each case, the question will turn on the contract into which the parties have entered.

☞ *You have each put down money on the asking price of a flat where you were intending to live after your marriage. A great deal of expense has been incurred for your forthcoming wedding. The bride's father has hired the hall and paid a deposit to the caterers and the band; the groom's family have paid for a honeymoon in the West Indies. Family and friends have already sent gifts. The wedding is called off and you blame each other. What is the position?*

2.2.2(a)   The wedding expenses

With regard to the expenses incurred for the wedding, such as the deposit on the hall or the catering costs, the money may well be lost.

Recovery of the money would depend on the terms of the contract on making the arrangements. It would always be prudent to ask, specifically, in dealing with caterers and others, what would happen in the event of a cancellation.

Do scrutinise the terms of contract: in one case, the Office of Fair Trading intervened where the cancellation fees were extremely high and made no allowance for the catering company to take steps to mitigate its loss in the event of a cancellation (in other words, for the catering company to try to arrange another event for the same date). Other terms were also altered in this case, e.g. where the company refused to take responsibility for damage caused by its employees (see OFT *Bulletin 19, Unfair Contract Terms*).

Can you obtain insurance cover against calling off the party?

In the scenario above, the wedding was entirely called off. Insurers are unlikely to cover a change of heart. However, in other circumstances, a bride or groom may fall ill, have to cancel arrangements, and not be able to fix another date for their planned wedding for many months. Enquiries should be made from certain specialist insurers who have policies which carry cover against cancellation of wedding arrangements in these circumstances.

2.2.2(b) The honeymoon

With regard to the cancelled honeymoon, most people take out insurance to cover the sudden curtailment of holiday plans. Such policies usually deal with illness or bereavement.

Note: certain insurers will also cover cancellations of weddings that have been planned to take place abroad (see section 3.7 below).

2.2.2(c) Property

With regard to the question of the flat, rights to it are governed by the law of property, as well as by statute. The Matrimonial Proceedings Act 1970 states that the same rules apply to interests in property between formally engaged couples as between husband and wife. For details of evidence of an engagement see section 2.3.1 below.

On the face of it, each partner should be entitled to a share in the property equivalent to the sum of money which has been expended on it. But other factors will come into account, such as the name or names in which the down-payment was made, any arrangements for a mortgage, and whether contracts on the flat had been exchanged with the seller.

Note: in spite of the provisions of the Act, the courts do not have the same extensive powers to make arrangements for the sharing out of the property of an engaged couple who then break up, as they have for that of a married couple who decide on a divorce.

In any transaction where there is an intention to purchase property jointly, both parties must seek legal advice.

2.2.2(d) Wedding gifts

Another question arises. What about the expenses of other people? For example, guests might have spent money on gifts which they have already despatched only to learn that the wedding is cancelled.

The couple are probably obliged to return to their senders those wedding gifts already received. The law implies a condition that the presents were sent in the event of a marriage taking place; that condition having failed, the guests are entitled to the return of their gifts.

2.3   Problem of harassment when an engagement falls through

Persons who are, or have been, in relationships are protected in law against harassment and molestation.

Situations may arise where an engaged or formerly engaged couple are in a dysfunctional relationship. In such a case, the law protects one person from being molested by the other (see below, section 5.3, for issues relating to domestic violence and molestation. See also the chapter on *Divorce*, section 9.3, for protection against harassment).

☞   *You have broken off your engagement with your fiancé. He now keeps pestering you by calling at your home early in the morning and late at night. Recently he has started to call round at your place of work as well, upsetting you and your colleagues. You wonder what you can do.*

Under the Family Law Act 1996, the court has powers to prevent one person from molesting another. These powers, under the Act, apply to 'associated persons' who include persons who are engaged or, who formerly have been engaged. However, the court will need evidence of an engagement (see section 2.3.1 immediately below).

For protection against molestation and harassment from someone who is not considered to be an 'associated person' because he or she has not been in a relationship with the victim, but who is threatening a stranger by e.g. stalking, see the chapter on *Divorce*, section 9.

2.3.1   Evidence of an engagement

This can comprise:

- evidence in writing
- an engagement ring
- some form of ceremony witnessed by others assembled to act as witnesses.

3   **MARRIAGE FORMALITIES**

For a marriage to be valid, a licence and a formal ceremony are necessary.

3.1   **The preliminaries**

3.1.1   **Simplifying the law?**

The preliminary formalities necessary before a couple can get married are surprisingly complicated. They are also outmoded. Many of the rules which regulate these preliminaries were first formulated in the eighteenth century and were primarily designed to protect wealthy heiresses from making clandestine – and unsuitable – marriages.

Recommendations have been made for simplifying the law so that everyone could readily understand the rules and regulations which govern the ceremonial aspects of marriage. Thus far, however, some changes have been enacted in relation to premises to be approved by local authorities for civil marriages (see section 3.4.3 below), and to the form of words used in the ceremony, and, in particular, in relation to the notice/residence period (see section 3.4.6(b) below). For details of further changes proposed to these procedures, see section 7 below. In the following sections, we deal with the law as it exists at the time of writing.

3.1.2   **Who can give authorisation for a marriage?**

Authority to license marriages is given to priests of the Anglican church and to civil officials (the superintendent registrar of marriages of each district). Every couple, therefore, must first obtain either religious or civil authorisation to marry, or publish banns in an Anglican church, before they can go through a wedding ceremony.

3.2   **Religious ceremonies**

Religious ceremonies are categorised according to whether they are solemnised by:

- the Anglican Church including the Church in Wales, or
- Jews or Quakers (for whom special rules apply under the Marriage Act 1949) or
- some other recognised denomination or religion.

We live in a multi-denominational, multi-ethnic society. The fact that different rules apply to different religious groups has increased the pressure for change in these rules. The proposed changes to the preliminaries to marriage, as well as to its ceremonial aspects, are intended to minimise these distinctions.

3.2.1   **Church of England: licence to marry**

One in three of all religious marriage ceremonies takes place in the Church of England.

There are four ways to effect the necessary preliminaries for an Anglican marriage. Only one of these may be used. Thus in order to obtain consent to get married in the Church of England, you must either:

- publish banns, or
- obtain one of the following:
  i. a common ecclesiastical licence
  ii. a 'special' licence, also from the ecclesiastical authorities
  iii. a superintendent registrar's certificate from the civil authorities.

(a) Publishing banns

'Banns' are the announcement of the names of the couple who intend to marry, and an appeal for possible objections. Banns have to be read aloud ('published') in the church of the parish where the couple are resident. If they are resident in different parishes, the banns must be read in each parish church, in one or other of which the ceremony must take place.

☞   *You and your husband-to-be live and work in the same parish in London. However, you decide you want to get married in a church in the village where your mother-in-law lives as she is not very mobile. Where should the banns be read?*

   In this case, the banns will have to be read in the church in which you intend to get married as well as in the church of the parish in which you are resident. The priest needs seven days' notice in writing from both parties before he can read the banns. He has to read them in 'an audible manner' in his church on three successive Sundays.

If there is no objection from a member of the congregation, the marriage can take place at any time up to three months after the third reading of the banns. Any objection to the marriage must be voiced publicly in church by a member of the congregation after the banns are read. The banns are then void.

Do note: the purpose of the banns is clearly intended to ensure publicity for the intended marriage. But because of a demographic changes in the community – where groups are more amorphous and more transient – the Church has accepted proposals for church/state preliminaries which would entail a greater involvement of the civil authorities (see below, section 3.2.1(d)).

Provided, therefore, that you do not intend to conceal your identity, you can publish the banns under a name by which you are generally known.

☞   *You are known as Miss Roberts after the name of your stepfather although the name on your birth certificate is Smith (your father's name). You publish your banns under the name of Roberts. Are they still valid?*

The answer is 'yes', provided there has been no attempt to conceal your identity.

(b) Common licence

This dispenses with the banns and is granted by the bishop of the diocese. You must make a sworn statement in writing [an *affidavit*] that there is no impediment to the marriage, that any necessary parental consent has been given (see section 1.2.1 above), and that you have resided in the parish for 15 days.

Once granted, the licence to marry takes immediate effect and remains valid for three months. It must specify the church in which the wedding is to take place. In general the church authorities advise this procedure for a marriage between a foreign person and a British subject or between two foreigners who wish to get married in a church of the Church of England.

(c) Special licence

This is issued by the Archbishop of Canterbury and dispenses with the residence period of 15 days. A special licence is considered a privilege and not a right. It might be applied for if, for example, one of the couple were seriously ill. To apply for such a licence, an application form must be obtained from the Faculty Office, 1 The Sanctuary, Westminster, London SW1P 3JT). You are advised to approach your local minister where the service is to be held and who should support your application (see also *www.facultyoffice.org.uk*).

Note: addresses for the issue of common licence and special licence by the ecclesiastical authorities appear in the DIRECTORY on page 109.

(d) Proposed change

In July 2002, the General Synod of the Church of England endorsed a report, *The Challenge to Change*, which would entail a joint system of Church/State preliminaries.

The minister would enquire whether there was any impediment to the marriage and collect the relevant information which would then be sent to the civil registrar. The civil authorities would then have the task, as well as the legal responsibility, of checking its accuracy and displaying the notice locally or via the Internet. An announcement could still be made in church, 'similar in spirit to the current practice of calling banns' but this would no longer be a legal requirement (see also section 7 below).

(e) Superintendent registrar's certificate

It is usual for a wedding in the Church of England to take place after publication of the banns or after obtaining a licence from the church authorities (above). There is thus generally no need to involve the civil authorities. However, an Anglican wedding can take place via the civil route after a superintendent registrar's certificate to marry has been obtained.

The procedure is as follows:

a) The parties must give their notice to the superintendent registrar of the district in which they must have resided for at least seven days before giving notice. Notice must be given in person;

b) They must make a solemn declaration (not an affidavit) that:

- there are no lawful impediments to their union
- they meet the residential requirement

and (in the case of persons between 16 and 18) that:

- their parents have consented.

Do note: in addition, both parties have to declare their nationality and provide identification evidence requested by the Superintendent Registrar.

If the parties live in different districts, then notice must be given in each district.

The notice, written into the notice book, is also displayed in the superintendent registrar's office for 15 days on a notice board to which the public have access. At the end of that period – provided there has been no objection – the superintendent registrar's certificate is issued. The marriage can take place on the sixteenth day. The certificate is valid for 12 months.

3.2.2   Divorced persons who wish to remarry in the Church of England

The Anglican Church regards marriage as a union for life. As a result, where either party to a marriage is a divorced person a remarriage, until very recently, could not be solemnised in a Church of England church. This rule did not apply to marriages which have been annulled.

A working party, commissioned by the House of Bishops, issued a report, *Marriage in Church after Divorce*, which proposed that the Church's law-making body, the General Synod, should allow for the remarriage of divorced couples in church under exceptional circumstances. These proposals were accepted in July 2002 and represent a major change in Church policy. They have now come into effect.

The Bishops are finalising advice to their clergy on how to deal with applications from those of their parishioners who are divorcees and who wish to remarry.

3.2.3   Right to refuse

In spite of the changes stated immediately above, ministers can act according to their own conscience and refuse to permit marriage of divorcees in their parish church.

☞   *You have recently decided to get married for a second time having been divorced from your first husband. You attend church regularly. You obtain a superintendent registrar's certificate and approach your minister to ask whether he would solemnise your marriage. He refuses. Can you prevail upon him to change his mind?*

The answer is 'no'. He is not obliged to solemnise the marriage of a person whose first spouse is still alive.

3.2.4   Need to observe other rules

Other stipulations to a Church of England wedding are also laid down by law: an Anglican wedding must take place:

- in an unlocked church
- between the hours of 8 am and 6 pm
- with two witnesses present during the ceremony

(see section 3.5 below for the application of these rules to other wedding ceremonies – religious and civil).

3.3   Other denominations and religions

If you belong to a denomination or religion other than the Church of England you must first obtain permission (either certificate or licence) from the civil authorities in order to marry.

There are four ways of meeting the civil requirements, only one of which need be used:

- a superintendent registrar's certificate (see section 3.2.1(e) above)
- a superintendent registrar's certificate with a licence. A single waiting period has been introduced of 15 days after notice has been given.

However, for those seriously ill or otherwise confined, special provisions apply:

- under the Marriage Act 1983 and
- under the Marriage (Registrar General's Licence) Act 1970.

3.3.1   Formalities: Jews and Quakers

Weddings for Jews and Quakers can take place anywhere and at any time under the Marriage Act according to their own practices. The marriage is solemnised by a person designated for the purpose after the issue of a civil licence.

3.3.2   Formalities: other denominations and religions

3.3.2(a)   Civil certificate and registered building

In addition to the need to obtain a civil certificate (see section 3.2.1(e) above), marriages for denominations and religions other than Jewish or Quaker must take place in a registered building or chapel.

3.3.2(b)   Solemn declaration according to civil procedure

Not only is a civil licence required, but at some stage of the proceedings, the person designated to officiate at the ceremony must use the same form of words as is used in a civil ceremony (see *Solemn declaration* section 3.4.1 below).

3.3.3   Possible source of friction

It is clear that different rules apply to different religious groups and denominations. Legislation in an area as sensitive as marriage can cause resentment among groups who are not accorded the same treatment as others in law. For acknowledgement of these difficulties and the government's intention to iron out differences, see below, section 7, *Civil Registration: Vital Change.*

3.4   Civil ceremonies

The General Register Office issues a leaflet for general guidance: *Getting Married – A Guide to Weddings in England and Wales.*

A Home Office paper, *Supporting Families*, has proposed that superintendent registrars give more information to couples including making available marriage preparation packs and giving couples information on pre-marriage support services.

3.4.1   Solemn declaration

Marriages in a register office or approved premises (see section 3.4.4 below), as well as marriages of faiths other than Anglican, Jewish or Quaker, require a solemn declaration from both bride and groom according to the civil form:

* that they know of no impediment to their union
* that they call upon those present to witness that they take each other as lawful wedded wife and husband.

The two witnesses present then sign the register; this is a requirement in all cases (see section 3.5.1 below).

3.4.2   Presence of registrars

A superintendent registrar and the registrar must both be present at a civil wedding.

3.4.3   Choosing your venue

Until recently the premises in which you could marry by civil procedure were confined to municipal buildings designated for this purpose – 'the register office'.

A White Paper proposed that for those who wanted it, a civil marriage ceremony should offer more interesting and varied venues. These proposals were enacted in the Marriage Act 1994. Under the Act, local authorities can now 'approve' premises for the solemnisation of marriages, and must keep available a register of approved premises.

Remember: local authorities can continue to solemnise marriages in standard register offices.

3.4.4   Nature of approved premises

The 1994 Act had a two-fold purpose:

* to broaden the scope and range of buildings available for marriage ceremonies
* to maintain the solemnity of the ceremony itself.

So, by law, the venue must be 'seemly and dignified', and the building must be:

- regularly available to the public for marriage ceremonies
- secular, thus excluding any recent or continuing connection with religion or religious practice.

The room must be:

- a distinct part of the premises and
- separate from any other activity on the premises at the time of the ceremony.

In addition no food or drink may be sold or consumed in the room in which the ceremony is to take place for an hour beforehand – nor during the ceremony itself.

Premises approved so far include, in the main, stately homes and hotels.

Note: marriages cannot take place in a temporary structure such as a marquee or in the open air.

3.4.5 Nature of ceremony

Under the present more relaxed rules, the couple can choose to arrange for a reading, music or additional words to form part of the ceremony. The law stipulates that the content must be secular, and must meet with the prior approval of the superintendent registrar of the district in which the approved premises are situated.

Note: however, the ceremony must still conform to standard procedures in the following regards:

- there must be a solemn declaration (see 3.4.1 above)
- there must be both the superintendent registrar and registrar present (see section 3.4.2 above)
- there must be two witnesses (see 3.5.1 below).

3.4.6 Other requirements

For a civil ceremony, you will need to give formal notice of your marriage to the superintendent registrar of the district in which you live.

You must both give notice in person – no one can do it in your stead.

If you and your partner live in different districts, you will each need to give notice to the superintendent registrar of your particular area. Even, if you are both resident in the same district both of you need give the notice.

Notice can be given either by certificate or by licence.

Note: do check beforehand on the documentation you are required to bring with you.

3.4.6(a) Certificate

The procedure for obtaining a superintendent registrar's certificate has been outlined in section 3.2.1(e) above.

This certificate or the licence (see immediately below) will validate the ceremony if you marry in another district (see section 3.4.7 below).

3.4.6(b) Licence

In order to obtain a licence, either you or your partner must have lived in the registration district for a minimum of seven days before you can give notice. Your partner also needs a 7-day residence period.

Do note: from 1 January 2001, changes proposed to the marriage law in the Immigration and Asylum Act 1999 came into effect. These provisions provide for a single 15-day notice period and require both parties to the marriage to give notice in person. Both of you must declare your nationality.

3.4.7 Choosing your marriage venue

Under the Marriage Act 1994, you no longer have to marry in your district. If you decide to marry in a stately home or other such venue in another part of the country, you can now do so, although you have to give formal notice to the superintendent registrar of the district in which you live (see section 3.4.6 above).

In addition, you have to contact the superintendent registrar of the district in which you wish to marry. He or she will then be able to make a provisional booking so that you can ensure that you will be able to have both the venue and date of your choice.

Note: a licence or certificate to marry is valid for 12 months. However, you could make a provisional booking more than twelve months beforehand with the superintendent registrar of the district in which you wish to marry.

The superintendent registrar will give you precise information about the fees that will be charged for their presence at the ceremony, which are set by the local authority, as well as the schedule of fees charged for use of the premises. Of course these will vary with the premises, e.g. a smart London hotel will charge more than a working farm.

3.5   Other rules: religious and civil ceremonies

The rules concerning witnesses to the ceremony of marriage, the buildings in which such ceremonies can take place, and the hours during which they can take place, were drawn up to ensure that marriages cannot take place in secret.

3.5.1   Witnesses

All marriages – without exception, be they religious or civil – require two witnesses to the ceremony. The witnesses need not know the couple.

3.5.2   Buildings

All marriages, except those according to the practices of Jews and Quakers, must take place in a building registered or approved for that purpose. Where someone is so sick as to be housebound, then special procedures are allowed for.

3.5.3   Hours

All marriages, again those of Jews and Quakers excepted, have to take place between the hours of 8 am and 6 pm. These rules are expected to be relaxed in due course (see section 7 below).

3.5.4   The marriage certificate

After every ceremony, civil or religious, the marriage is entered on the marriage register and signed by two witnesses. The couple are entitled to a copy of the certificate. Extra copies, if required, can be obtained from the register office.

3.6   Marrying abroad

In this section, we are not dealing with persons who marry abroad because one or other spouse is a foreign person or lives abroad. We are dealing, instead, with English persons, domiciled here, who choose to marry abroad. Certain problems can arise if your wedding takes place abroad, among them being that you can find yourself bound by the laws of the country in which you have got married (see section 3.6.1 below).

☞   *You are planning your wedding and have read in a magazine that you can get married abroad. The idea of getting married in an exotic location really appeals to you and you want to find out more about it. You wish to know whether there are any legal snags of which you should be aware.*

Specialist travel agencies publish brochures which arrange for wedding ceremonies in a host of countries from the Far East to the Mid-West of the United States. The brochures are usually very detailed and are quite specific as to the documentation required for each country, as well as for residence requirements.

With regard to the legal issues, a marriage that is valid by the laws of the country in which it has taken place is regarded, generally speaking, as a legally binding and valid marriage in this country.

3.6.1   Problems which might arise

If both parties are domiciled in England, the marriage also has to be valid by the law of your domicile, i.e. England. For example, a marriage would be invalid here if one of the parties was under-age or the couple were too closely related to each other. Such a marriage could be a valid marriage in the country in which it took place, but it would not be regarded as valid here.

Other questions also arise. Would you be bound by the laws of the country in which the wedding ceremony has taken place? For example, you might choose to have a wedding ceremony abroad and only subsequently discover that, according to that country's marriage laws, a husband can administer (i.e. take charge of) his wife's property. That could land you in a very awkward situation.

In one celebrated case, it transpired that the 'marriage' in question had never even taken place. The ceremony itself was not a valid marriage ceremony even by the law of the country in which it had taken place.

Note: it is essential to seek legal advice on these issues. To make absolutely sure that your marriage would be governed – for all future purposes – by the laws of England, you might have to arrange to go through a civil ceremony in the British Embassy in the country which you have chosen for your wedding venue.

4   EFFECTS OF MARRIAGE

4.1   The effects

'Being married' confers a definite legal status on both husband and wife. This status affects many aspects of their lives and can last for the rest of their lives. It confers rights and duties on them both, stemming from their 'common home and common life'. Moreover, the change in their legal status takes place from the moment that they marry.

At one stage, a husband and wife were even regarded as one person in law. That person was the husband! A wife's legal personality was said to have 'merged' into his.

Over the past hundred years, there have been significant changes to the law in an endeavour to free wives from this legal doctrine which was described in the House of Lords as anachronistic and offensive. A wife is no longer her husband's chattel and a marriage should be regarded in law as a partnership of equals.

In general, questions of status, rights and duties concern the following:

4.1.1   Duty to live together

Husband and wife have a duty to live together. Of course, they are free to leave if the marriage proves unhappy. However, if one spouse leaves the other for good, this can be a factor in showing that the marriage has irretrievably broken down (see chapter on *Divorce*).

4.1.2   Duty to maintain

Spouses have a duty to maintain one another. Again it is usually only on divorce that this element of marriage takes on legal significance. Its significance is great, however. Along with responsibility for caring for their children, the duty to maintain one another can survive even the break-up of a marriage. It also can lead to protracted legal battles on divorce when all other issues between the couple have been settled.

4.1.3   Sexual relationship

Husband and wife are expected to have sexual relations. Failure to consummate a marriage can be grounds for annulment (see section 1.3.3 above).

Take note: the sexual act must be voluntary and the wife must consent to it. A husband can be charged with rape if he forces himself on his unwilling wife.

4.1.4   Fidelity

Husband and wife are expected to be faithful to one another; adultery is still a main fact in showing the irretrievable breakdown of a marriage (see chapter on *Divorce*).

4.1.5   Common surname?

The wife can take her husband's surname but she is not under a legal duty to do so. A wife's right to use her husband's surname survives his death and even a divorce from him. It is unusual for the husband to take his wife's name though he can do so if he wishes. Occasionally, couples adopt both surnames.

If a wife does change her name to her husband's surname, she can do so informally, simply by using his name. However, married women have to inform institutions such as banks or building societies of their change of name, and could expect to be asked to produce their marriage certificates.

☞ *You intend to take your husband's name from the day that you get married. You have made plans to spend the honeymoon abroad. Can you apply for a passport in your married name before the wedding day?*

The answer is 'yes'. You can apply for a British passport which can be post-dated with your married name although you will not be able to use your passport until the actual day of the wedding. In order to make the application, which can be at any point up to three months before you get married, you have to get two forms from the Passport Agency: Form PD2, which must be completed by the person who will be conducting the ceremony, and a correctly completed standard application form. You can opt either to be issued with a new standard 10-year passport and surrender your present passport or you can have your current passport updated with your husband's name. The Passport Services also issue an explanatory leaflet (ask for leaflet PD1).

4.1.6   Joint assets

Matrimonial property such as the family home or family income are regarded as an 'asset' of the marriage.

Nonetheless, under English law, property owned by either spouse before the marriage does not become owned jointly, in other words there is no 'community of property' between husband and wife as exists in certain other legal systems. For example, if a wife inherits her mother's house after she has married, she can then dispose of it, sell it, leave it in her will to her children or to her favourite charity without consulting her husband. It remains her sole property throughout her lifetime.

Thus property or money which is acquired by the spouses individually during the marriage is not common property, as the example of the inherited house makes clear. However, if the marriage breaks down, this seemingly clear doctrine, i.e. that there is no community of property in English law, becomes less clear-cut. Inroads have been made into the principle because the courts have such very extensive powers under statute to intervene, where there is a dispute in divorce proceedings over 'who gets what'. The judges have at their disposal wide-ranging court orders which enable them to redistribute assets, whether owned by the husband or the wife in a manner that they think is 'fair and reasonable'.

Not only does property such as the matrimonial home, as well as family income, become an 'asset' of the marriage but, on its breakdown, other meaningful assets can become subject to court orders in the court's endeavour to reach an equitable division between the parties (see chapter on *Divorce*, section 6.3).

Another important exception to the doctrine that there is no community of property in English law is found in the intestacy rules. These allow a surviving spouse to inherit a large proportion of an estate where the deceased husband or wife left no will: see section 4.1.9(c) below and, in particular, the chapter on *Death – Before and After*, section 7.

4.1.6(a)   The matrimonial home

Irrespective of questions of whether she owns or part-owns the family home, a wife was given the right to occupy the matrimonial home under the Matrimonial Homes Act 1983. This right of occupation under earlier legislation is now re-enacted in the Family Law Act 1996, where the right to occupy and register it as a charge – so that it is valid against third parties – is now called 'matrimonial home rights'. See also the chapter on *Divorce*, section 8.1. This right of occupation applies to the matrimonial home only, although other property may be subject to a court order in a final divorce settlement.

(These issues are discussed in greater detail in the chapter on *Divorce*.)

4.1.6(b)   Pledging the matrimonial home

There have been a number of cases which have involved a husband who has persuaded his wife to pledge the matrimonial home with his bank against his business debts.

☞ *Your husband has run into financial difficulties in his business. He has asked you to come to the bank with him to sign a guarantee to the bank for extra funds for his business. The bank has asked that your family house, which you own jointly with your husband, should be given as collateral for the loan and has prepared forms for you to sign to that effect. You are reluctant to sign but are very anxious not to let your husband down.*

You must take legal advice. The courts have taken a protective attitude towards married women in these circumstances. They have recognised that while the pattern of family life has changed and that some women can exert their independence, others are vulnerable to their husband's influence.

The overriding consideration for the courts is whether a woman who appears to be acting in a way which is to her manifest disadvantage, is given an opportunity to exercise an independent judgement before committing herself to giving their home as collateral for her husband's debts. Banks or other lenders should be aware of the potential for undue influence whenever a wife offers to stand surety for her husband's debts by pledging the matrimonial home. In order to obviate emotional pressure, they are under a duty to:

- have an interview alone with the wife
- explain to her what acting as a surety entails
- warn her of the risks to the property
- ensure that she seeks independent advice.

Lawyers who are consulted by the wife are also under a duty:

- to advise on the nature of the charge
- to satisfy themselves that the wife is free from her husband's 'undue influence'
- not to proceed further with the transaction if they take the view that it is not in the wife's interests.

4.1.7   Common parenthood

Husband and wife automatically acquire parental responsibility for the children of their marriage. This aspect is discussed more fully in the chapter on *Children (Part 1)*, but it is worth noting that parental responsibility covers such basic concerns as decisions over the children's religion, education, consent to marriage etc.

If the parents separate, of course, the courts can be asked to alter the relationship between parent and child: for example, the courts can determine the question of how much contact a divorced father or mother should have with their children although both will be expected to continue to share parental responsibility. The obligation to maintain their children survives a marriage breakdown.

4.1.8   Tax position of husband/wife

In 1990, the tax laws were changed so that husband and wife now have separate tax identities. Instead of the married man's allowance, a married couple's allowance was introduced which was transferable between the spouses. This in turn has been replaced by a system of tax credits.

Gifts between husband and wife are not liable to capital gains tax.

4.1.9   Questions arising on spouse's death

The death of a spouse raises many questions concerning married status. These issues are discussed in detail in the chapter on *Death – Before and After*. It is just worth noting the following at this stage:

(a) Pensions

If you are a married man or woman, you may be entitled to a pension on the death of your spouse.

(b) Position under will

If you inherit under your spouse's will, you are entitled to take your share of the estate free of inheritance tax.

(c) Intestacy

If your spouse dies without a will, the position of the surviving spouse is well protected by law. He or she will be entitled to the major share of the estate, if not all of it. As most people do not make wills, this safeguard for provision of the surviving spouse under the intestacy rules is of considerable importance.

4.2   Marital confidences

Secrets, and other confidences of married life shared between husband and wife, are protected by law. In an era of 'kiss and tell' journalism, the legal principle of protecting husband–wife confidentiality is clearly under strain, however. Confidentiality clauses are sometimes inserted into divorce agreements where either party fears that their former spouse might disclose secrets and generate unwanted publicity.

Nonetheless, the courts have made it clear that confidences between husband and wife are to be protected to a greater degree than those which might arise in 'transient relationships'.

4.3   Questions of nationality and immigration

In general, issues of nationality have become so difficult that if you are in any doubt as to your status or that of your spouse, you would be well advised to seek legal advice. A UK resident is allowed to bring his or her spouse into this country after receiving clearance to do so. A UK resident is also entitled to bring his fiancée or her fiancé into this country.

4.3.1   Arranging for your spouse or fiancé(e) to enter the UK

Your spouse can join you in the UK under rules which allow the husband or wife, or the fiancé(e) of a person who is settled here permanently to enter the country. However, clearance must be obtained abroad before you can come and join your partner here. Initial clearance for spouses is for one 'probationary' year during which the Home Office will wish to satisfy itself that the marriage is still subsisting, among other matters.

Do note: according to a recent White Paper, the probationary period will be extended for two years for spouses to match that for unmarried couples (see section 5.1.6 below).

The White Paper also proposes that if you have already been married/cohabiting for more than five years, you can apply for entry clearance without having to go through the probationary period.

The rules are intended to prevent bogus 'marriages of convenience' to UK residents, where such marriages are intended to get round the immigration laws. Thus in order to issue you with an entry clearance certificate to enter the UK as an affianced person or as a spouse, the immigration authorities have to be sure that you and your spouse intend to live together as man and wife – in other words, that you are not going to part immediately after the ceremony.

Other requirements have to be met, e.g. satisfactory financial status, satisfactory accommodation provision, and documentation of proof of marriage. In the case of an engaged couple, there will need to be evidence that the couple know each other. Entry clearance for fiancés is usually for six months and they have to get married during this time unless there is a very good reason to postpone the ceremony.

☞   *You came to England having been sent here by your firm which has a head office in the United States. Within months of your arrival, you met someone you wish to marry here in the parish church of your future husband. You wonder what your position is with regard to the immigration authorities.*

People who have entered the country but get married once they are here can apply to stay on as a spouse, but again would have to go through the probationary year successfully before being able to stay permanently. For the marriage formalities for non-nationals, see section 3.4.6(b) above.

Do note: a completely different set of rules for family members applies within the European Economic Area (EU plus Iceland, Norway and Liechtenstein). For information on free right of movement in the UK for these nationals, see *www.index.homeoffice.gov.uk*.

For information advice generally and application forms, telephone the Immigration and Enquiry Bureau: 087 0606 7766.

The Joint Council for the Welfare of Immigrants issues a Factsheet (*Factsheet Number 1*) and also runs a helpline – see DIRECTORY on page 109.

Do take heed: immigration is the focus of a great deal of public and political concern. The rules are complex and liable to change so couples are strenuously urged to consult a professional adviser as to the best course of action for entry clearance into the UK.

5   COHABITATION

5.1   The legal effects

Despite the common misconception, there is no such thing as a 'common law marriage'. Either one is legally married or one is not. Of course, many cohabiting couples do regard themselves as married to all intents and purposes – and look on the absence of legal formalities as a mere detail. However, in the eyes of the law, a cohabiting couple is regarded, in several respects, as two single people. About a million couples cohabit and many of them have children. The fact that they are usually considered as two single individuals – as far as the law is concerned – entails certain clear consequences.

5.1.1   No legal duties

Whether or not they are married, couples still care for one another, support one another and are faithful to each other. However, in the case of a cohabiting couple, these duties are not legal ones. Hence, if they separate, the law does not generally impose duties upon them – except where there are children involved (see section 5.1.1(b) below). A Civil Partnerships Bill, intended to regulate financial and other matters between cohabiting couples was introduced into Parliament but appears to be in abeyance at the time of writing.

(a) No duty to cohabit

Either partner can leave the other at any time to marry someone else, without having to go through any formal legal procedures whatsoever in order to separate.

(b) No duty to maintain

There is no duty to maintain one another. Thus, there are no proper legal structures, in the event of a break-up of the relationship, whereby the courts can adjust the assets of the partnership to take care of a partner who is financially hard hit by the separation. This is in striking contrast to the position of married couples in the event of their divorce (see the chapter on *Divorce*). However, the position with regard to the children of the relationship is different; an obligation to maintain the children is legally enforceable (see immediately below). Under the Child Support Acts (see the chapter on *Children (Part 1)*, section 2.2), an element of maintenance is calculated for the person with care of the child. This is not intended to be the same as maintenance for a divorced spouse.

5.1.2   Effect on children

At present, parental responsibility for a child whose parents are not married to each other is given to the mother.

However, since the passing of the Children Act 1989, greater emphasis is laid on the notion of parenthood. The position of the unmarried father is thus improved by law. Mother and father can enter into a 'parental responsibility agreement' which would place them in a similar position to that of married parents to share fully the responsibility for their children.

☞   *You are living happily with your partner and you are shortly expecting your first child. You would like him to share parental responsibility with you. How can this be arranged?*

The steps entail a formal declaration on a prescribed form, in front of witnesses. The form must then be registered at the High Court (see chapter on *Children (Part 1)*, section 2.13, for details).

5.1.2(a)   Duty to maintain

If a couple do have children and then separate, the 'absent' parent, often the father, is under a legal duty to maintain the children until they reach the age of 17 (see the chapter on *Children (Part 1)*).

5.1.3   Effect on assets

There are cases where the courts have established that one partner is to be given a share in assets which a couple own together. However, this share is generally based on the concrete facts of the couple's individual contributions. For example, a partner would be entitled to share in the assets where he or she has contributed to the purchase of a car, paid money into a joint bank account, put down a deposit on a house or flat, or helped to pay off the mortgage. So if you do have a financial share in the bank account, car or house along with your boyfriend or girlfriend, that share is not based on a question of what is 'fair' or 'right' or 'just' when you split up. It depends on your own financial contribution.

5.1.3(a)   A fallacy: the 'common law marriage'

The term 'common law marriage' is utterly misleading because:

a) there is no such thing in law as a common law marriage; and
b) it wrongly denotes that 'common law spouses' have rights in law which they do not, in fact, have.

5.1.3(b)   Buying a home together

The courts have dealt again and again with the issue of the division of a home which has been bought by two people who have chosen to live together rather than to marry.

The questions which the court will try to answer are:

a) Has there been any agreement or understanding as to how the property is to be shared?
b) Has one partner relied on that agreement to his or her detriment?

If there is no agreement, then the court has to ask whether there have been direct contributions to the purchase price, either as a lump sum or as regular contributions to the mortgage.

If there is no agreement and no direct money contribution, then the courts examine the broader issues:

- has there been a common intention that the property would be shared by both partners as their common home?
- who has put work into it, such as redecorating?
- was the work funded from a joint account?
- who paid for the food and household expenses?

In seeking to answer these questions the courts are endeavouring to reach some sort of solution in a situation where they have no direct powers to divide the assets of cohabitees. But how much cheaper and simpler it would be if the questions need not be posed before the courts at all!

Thus, as far as property rights are concerned, you are best advised to ensure that a joint venture which includes setting up and purchasing a home together has proper legal safeguards.

Take heed: consult a solicitor (see also below section 6.3.1 and *Divorce*, section 10).

The Law Commission, which was due to publish a consultation paper on the property rights of home-sharers, has found the task too difficult to encompass in a 'one size fits all' formula.

Remember: although these rules generally work against women, men too can be disadvantaged by them.

5.1.3(c)   The present position

In the event of a split-up, as we have seen above, the courts do not have the same wide powers to deal fairly with the couple's house or flat as they have with the property of a divorcing couple. Sometimes the judges have had to resort to legal doctrines which were never intended to fit such situations and will try to find a 'trust' in favour of one partner who has put a lot of hard work into a property. On the whole, though, this is poor protection.

Certain countries have passed legislation to deal with property disputes in what they call *de facto* relationships. We have no such laws in England.

Note: a live-in partner has no right to occupy the family home under the divorce legislation (compare the position of the wife, see section 4.1.6(a) above; and see the chapter on *Divorce*).

☞ *Your boyfriend persuaded you to move into his flat. You agreed to pay half the mortgage instalments and you did so until the birth of your first child when you stopped working. After that, you looked after the baby, did the housework, and spent a great deal of time on doing up the flat. Your boyfriend now insists that you and the baby must leave the flat, which he says he intends to sell. He is quite agreeable to pay maintenance for his child. Can you insist on staying on in the flat?*

a) You have no automatic rights of *occupation* under law. In order to assert any rights of *ownership*, you would have to show that when you moved in and agreed to pay your share of the mortgage instalments, your name was entered on the title deeds.

b) Alternatively, you would have to show that your solicitor drew up a trust deed in which your boyfriend declared that he held a share of the property in trust for you.

c) Otherwise you have the task of persuading the court to imply a trust in your favour.

d) Your solicitor should establish whether the property is registered with the Land Registry and enter a caution to warn an intending buyer that there is a conflict over your property rights.

e) Under the Children Act 1989, the court has been given power to make a property transfer 'on behalf of a child'.

f) The Family Law Act 1996, in the section which deals with family homes and domestic violence, gives the courts power to order occupation rights to cohabitees. However, it still does draw a distinction between the married and the unmarried. It also draws a distinction between those who have a share of the property and those who do not.

As far as partners, rather than spouses, are concerned, a person who is entitled in law to some share of the property, that is, he or she is a joint tenant or a joint owner, can ask for an occupation order. For a person who is not so entitled, an occupation order can be granted for six months with a further extension for another six months. The courts also now have the power to transfer a tenancy from one partner to another.

Do take heed: in all cases, the court will examine the circumstances and housing needs of the parties concerned. After taking these and other factors into account, the court must then assess 'the balance of harm' for the parties in dispute between making or not making an order.

5.1.4   Tax position

The tax position of a married woman has been altered so that her position now much more closely resembles that of a single woman (see section 4.1.8 above). However, there are still important differences between the taxation position of a cohabiting couple and that of a married couple:

• they cannot take advantage of the taxation rules that ensure that gifts between husband and wife are free of capital gains tax

• they cannot take advantage of the fact that on the death of a spouse, the other spouse inherits free of inheritance tax.

5.1.5   Effect on intestacy

As we shall see in the chapter *Death – Before and After*, most people do not make wills. So it is very important to note that when a husband or wife dies, leaving no will, the other spouse is entitled as of right under the provisions of the intestacy rules to receive something from the estate. When you are not married however, your position can be very different (see chapter on *Death – Before and After*, section 7.2).

5.1.5(a)   Pensions

Bereavement benefits from the State are not available to the surviving partner of a cohabiting couple – no matter how long-standing the relationship.

☞ *You and your partner have been together for several years. You are an employee of a multinational firm. You belong to a company pension scheme and would like to ensure that your partner will benefit from it. What can you do?*

You would have to sort out the position with regard to nominating your partner as beneficiary of an employee pension scheme. A spouse benefits automatically from these schemes but a cohabitee does not. Whether or not the trustees of the scheme will accept your nomination is a matter that you would have to ensure. It is also very important to check the terms of a private pension scheme.

5.1.5(b) Wills

Persons who live together are advised to make wills to ensure that their partner will receive under their estate. If the relationship breaks down, a will would then have to be revoked. In cases of divorce, a will is automatically revoked (see chapter on *Death – Before and After*, section 6.4).

5.1.5(c) Intestacy

A surviving partner can claim against the estate of his or her deceased cohabitee, if it can be shown that immediately before the death, that partner was maintaining the other, i.e. was 'making a substantial contribution towards his or her maintenance in money or money's worth'. In other words, survivors have to show that they have been dependants.

☞ *You have been living with a 54-year-old divorced man for several years. You were talking of getting married but have never got round to formalising the relationship. You also have heard your partner talking of making a will but you do not know if he ever got round to it. Your partner has recently died of a sudden heart attack. You live in his house and you learn from the solicitor, appointed by your partner's children, that they want the house sold. What are your rights, if any?*

You may be able to establish some rights if you make a claim under the Inheritance (Provision for Family and Dependants) Act 1975. You would need to consult your own solicitor and would have to establish that you have not received 'reasonable financial provision' from his estate, and that you are in need. See also chapter on *Death – Before and After*, section 8.5.

5.1.6   Nationality and immigration issues

A concession has been made within the immigration rules to unmarried partners for leave to enter the UK to join a person in the UK. The requirements for leave to enter are that:

- the couple must have been living in a relationship akin to marriage for two years or more; and
- they are unable to marry under UK law (for example, because they are homosexual, or because they are still married to someone else in the country from which they come, but divorce is not permitted there).

The partner will be allowed to stay for two years initially. For the purposes of this concession, same-sex partners are treated the same as heterosexual partners.

The White Paper proposes that unmarried couples will no longer need to show a legal impediment to marriage, and if cohabitation has lasted for more than five years, there will no longer be a requirement of a probationary period.

Note of caution: specialist advice should be sought from an immigration lawyer or from an advice agency dealing with immigration matters.

5.1.7   Confidentiality

As we have seen, the law has imposed a duty of confidentiality on husband and wife. The question is whether this principle would include live-in partners or other friends to whom secrets have been told in confidence.

☞ *You tell a very close friend of the sexual problems in your relationship with your live-in girlfriend. You make it clear to her that the information is imparted only in the strictest confidence. Soon afterwards, you hear from someone else that your friend is intent on selling the information to a newspaper. Can you stop publication?*

In a similar example, the court stated that there was a case against someone who tried to sell information to a newspaper, as well as a case against the paper's editors. The information, the court stated, had been received on the basis of confidentiality which ought to be protected. As we have seen above, however (section 4.2), principles of confidentiality are more honoured in the breach than in the observance.

Confidentiality which may arise in a 'transient relationship' is not to be equated with that accorded to husband and wife, the court has recently stated.

5.1.8   Maintenance and remarriage

Under the present law of divorce, either spouse can be awarded maintenance in the form of periodical payments. These payments cease on remarriage. However, if a former spouse cohabits with a new partner, but does not actually marry him or her, these payments continue (see also chapter on *Divorce*, section 7.2.4).

5.2   Surnames

There is nothing in law to stop you taking your partner's surname, either informally or by deed poll. However, even if you call yourself by your partner's surname, and you refer to yourself as a 'Common Law Wife' or a 'Common Law Husband' the term still has no meaning in law.

5.3   Where the law treats cohabitees as husband and wife

Having outlined the differences in how the law regards husband and wife from how it regards a cohabiting couple, it is important to note the following:

a) Victims of domestic violence are entitled to protection under the law, whether or not the couple are married. However, although the rules are more streamlined under the Family Law Act 1996 and the two orders which the courts can make – viz. an occupation order and a non-molestation order – are available to a wider range of people than married couples alone, the judges are nonetheless obliged to take into account additional factors such as the 'nature of the couple's relationship'. The court will also take into account the fact that the couple have not given to each other the binding commitment of marriage. Orders for unmarried couples can also be more limited in duration in certain cases. In all cases of domestic violence, you must seek help. (See chapter on *Divorce*, section 9 and also the DIRECTORY on page 109.)

b) With regard to secure tenancies, a couple who 'live together as husband and wife' are entitled to security of tenure under council housing as are husband and wife (see chapter on *Landlords and their Tenants*). A same-sex partner, too, can be regarded as a spouse or as a member of the original tenant's family for the purposes of succeeding to a council tenancy (see the chapter on *Landlords and their Tenants*, section 8.1.2).

c) Certain social security benefits are available for live-in couples, as well as for parents and children, irrespective of marital status.

d) Most importantly, as we have seen, a duty to maintain the children of the relationship is imposed – irrespective of marriage, divorce, cohabitation or relationship breakdown.

e) Cohabitees who pledge their home to secure the debts of a partner are as vulnerable to emotional pressure as spouses. So when they act as sureties, they must be given the same safeguards as a wife in similar circumstances (see section 4.1.6(b) above). In these cases, however, which can cover both homosexual and heterosexual couples, the bank must be aware of the relationship whereas in the case of a husband and wife, the relationship is taken to be self-evident.

f) Under the Fatal Accidents Act, dependent cohabitees who have lived with their partner for two years may be entitled to damages on his or her death (see chapter on *Accidents*, section 11.5).

g) For the purposes of assessing means under the community legal funding rules (formerly legal aid), a partner's income may be taken into account (see chapter on *The Legal System*).

h) In limited circumstances, a partner's income may be a factor in assessing maintenance under the Child Support Acts.

i) Where an unmarried couple seek fertility treatment together and the man has given consent in writing, a child born as a result of such treatment can be considered the child of the couple, although the man will have to establish parental responsibility by agreement or court order as would any other unmarried father.

Under the Parental Leave Directive, an employer must give time off from work in order to deal with a crisis at home for 'dependants'. A dependant includes a partner or cohabitee (for more details, see chapter on *Working for a Living (Part 2)*, section 1.3.4(k)).

The Children and Adoption Act allows cohabiting couples the opportunity to adopt a child (see chapter on *Children (Part 2)*, section 2.1).

6   AGREEMENTS

Certain countries have enacted legislation to deal with property and other matters which concern a cohabiting couple who then split up. As there are no such laws in this country, the question then arises whether cohabitees should enter into their own agreement to protect themselves in the event of a breakdown in their relationship. At the same time, some, including government ministers, have argued that even couples who are in fact contemplating marriage or are already married should enter into contracts or agreements to avoid possible litigation at a later stage.

6.1   Contracts between married couples

At common law, a husband 'administered' his wife's property. In effect, a woman no longer owned property once she married. This effect of marriage was removed in 1882 by the Married Women's Property Act. Today, property which a woman owns before she marries remains her property during the subsistence of the marriage. However, the doctrine that there is no community of property in English law may have little application once a couple are in the process of divorce proceedings. As the chapter on *Divorce* demonstrates, in deciding on the spouses' needs and in endeavouring to reach an equitable division between them, the courts have the power to make extensive property and financial adjustment orders. These orders can extend to the assets of either party although the matrimonial home only is subject to certain rights of occupation.

Do note: while the courts consider all the circumstances of each case, the welfare of any children of the marriage is put first.

In view of the court's wide powers to share out the family assets, few couples enter into agreement on what would happen in the event of a divorce between them. Certain of the legal difficulties of such agreements are also dealt with in section 6.2 below.

A consultation exercise regarding government proposals to make 'pre-nuptial agreements' legally binding found that the responses in favour and against were almost equally divided.

6.2   Cohabitation agreements

When an unmarried couple part, as we have seen, the courts do not have power to adjust their assets. Should the couple enter into an agreement to pre-empt a situation which could arise in the event of the breakdown of their relationship?

With regard to cohabitation agreements, there are immediate problems under the law of contract. In brief, when parties enter into a contract, both sides have to offer something towards the contract. For example, an employee will offer his labour and the employer will offer a monthly salary. The 'something' that each side offers is called the 'consideration' for the contract. In an agreement to cohabit, it would be difficult to define the consideration, other than on the basis of a sexual relationship, which the law may not accept as a valid contractual basis.

Marriage, on the other hand, paradoxically enough is described among other things in law as a 'contract'. It is a contract with so many peculiar features that the label tends to mislead rather than to illuminate the true position of husband and wife. Which other contract, for example, is intended to last a lifetime?

6.3   Scope of agreements

A crucial argument against cohabitation agreements or agreements between husband and wife does not stem from problems to do with definition, however. Circumstances change so dramatically in people's lives that few of the issues which the couple decide upon beforehand might assist them in a crisis.

How could one draw up an agreement to cover all contingencies? One or other partner might become unemployed or sick; they may have children; an elderly relative might move in. It is difficult enough to handle such events after they take place. The consensus seems to be that a judge would have to be given very wide latitude to take into account changes in circumstance. Therefore an agreement entered into before marriage (a 'pre-nuptial agreement') could only be a pointer to a final disposition of the couple's assets but not be the determining factor. In effect, that is the present position: a judge can pay heed to a pre-nuptial agreement but is not bound by it.

6.3.1   Property rights

The complications which can arise when two people buy a home with the intention of living in it together but then split up, have been dealt with in section 5.1.3(b) and (c) above.

Most important: try to ensure that you enter into a carefully considered and drawn-up agreement as to your respective rights concerning:

- how much money you have contributed
- how much you intend to contribute e.g. to mortgage payments, household bills and insurance
- your share in the property
- other property you might own.

(See also the chapter *Buying and Selling your Home*, section 4, for considerations of buying as joint tenants or as tenants-in-common.)

6.3.2   Mediation

Rather than protracted and expensive litigation in the event of marriage or partnership breakdown, the emphasis today lies in a different direction altogether. Concerted efforts are being made, by the legislators and the legislated alike, to take family law out of the domain of the courts as much as possible. The focus is presently on mediation – with the assistance of legally aided and trained mediators (see the chapter on *Divorce*). It is increasingly felt that people must be helped to resolve their own difficulties as much as possible rather than have solutions imposed upon them. However, the take-up of couples who sought mediation rather than the advice of a solicitor, proved a disappointment, and the government decided not to implement core provisions of the Family Law Act in relation to divorce on the grounds that the Act failed to meet its objectives in assisting couples to stay together and minimising acrimony. Provisions of the Family Law Act relating to mediation funding (now subsumed into the Funding Code for the Community Legal Service), domestic violence, and also ancillary relief, remain in force, however (see the chapter on *Divorce*, section 2.2).

(See also the DIRECTORY on page 109 for more details of organisations which provide information or assistance.)

7   CIVIL REGISTRATION: VITAL CHANGE

The civil preliminaries to marriage are to undergo significant changes according to a White Paper published in January 2002 (available on the website of the Office of National Statistics *www.statistics.gov.uk/registration*). This sets out the proposals to improve and modernise the civil registration service in England and Wales, and covers the registration of births and deaths, as well as marriage.

Certain significant features of the present procedures for registration of marriage will be retained. For example, it will remain essential that couples should give notice in person, that they should have an habitual residency of seven days preceding registration, and that the ceremony should remain dignified and seemly (see above sections 3.4.4 and 3.4.6). The 15-day waiting period is also to be retained.

7.1   Preliminaries

However, the government intends to bring current arrangements more into line with present-day requirements in the light of the far-reaching social, as well as technological, changes in our daily lives. Proposals are as follows:

- couples will be able to choose where they can give notice to the Registrar
- information will then be entered on to a central database
- the Internet will be used to ensure publicity for the proposed marriage although some link with the locality will be retained (currently a notice of marriage is displayed in the Register Office of the district where the bride or groom lives)
- once the necessary checks have been completed and the required 15 days' waiting period has elapsed (see section 3.3 above), the couple will be given a document to confirm that the ceremony can go ahead

- this same document will then be used to confirm that the marriage has taken place, to be signed by bride and groom, as well as the person who conducts the ceremony
- this will then be returned to the local registration service.

7.2   The ceremony itself

These changes are also intended to move the focus of the ceremony from place to person:

- the marriage will be conducted by appointed 'celebrants' who will negotiate time and place with the couple
- national standards will set out criteria to ensure that the solemnity and dignity are maintained
- the various religious groups will appoint their own ministers so that the current distinctions, which are enshrined in the Marriage Act, will be minimised (see section 3 above).
- the restrictions on hours will be lifted so that marriages may take place at any time
- a far greater choice of venue is envisaged
- couples will be able to obtain a 'commemorative certificate'; but in general, it is hoped to reduce the number of paper certificates (see immediately below).

7.3   A record of life events

The proposed registration service is intended to bring together information on the registration of births, marriages, and deaths which is currently held in piecemeal fashion. It is hoped thereby to compile – over time – a sequence of 'life events'. This information could also be used in conjunction with other services such as social security and probate.

7.4   Time-scale

A start has already been made on bringing about the legislative changes for implementing the reforms outlined in the White Paper. Implementation is expected to be phased in over some years, commencing with the necessary statutory basis to be in place by 2004.

2 DIVORCE AND SEPARATION

By the end of the 1960s, it was felt that it was no longer in the public interest to try to keep alive marriages that were to all intents and purposes dead. The modern divorce law was thus introduced. For the first time 'irretrievable breakdown' became the sole ground of divorce. In the event the law emerged as a somewhat uneasy compromise. While it stated that irretrievable breakdown was the only ground for divorce, it also perpetuated some requirements from earlier divorce legislation, known as 'matrimonial offences', such as adultery or desertion, one of which still has to be alleged in a divorce petition (see section 1.3.1 below for the 'five facts').

Until the recognition of irretrievable breakdown, the law had insisted upon an 'innocent' party and a 'guilty' party in divorce proceedings. A 'guilty' spouse could not petition for a divorce; an 'innocent party', on the other hand, could only obtain a divorce after proving to the court that a 'matrimonial offence' had been committed against him or her.

Since the introduction of the present legislation which governs divorce, the number of divorces has risen dramatically. As at present, the rate of divorce – after having dropped slightly in 2000 – again increased in 2001. Strenuous endeavours have been made to alter the law relating to divorce, but the conflicts inherent in the issues cannot be easily reconciled. If society respects the institution of marriage, should the law try to preserve it? If so, how? Is there any purpose served by keeping people locked into marriages which they do not want? How should the law encourage reconciliation between warring spouses? Or must it rather endeavour to make their parting as painless and as 'conciliatory' as possible? To what extent should these issues be taken out of the hands of the lawyers and judges and the process become a non-judicial one? Can mediation services be insisted upon by legislation to supersede the role of the courts? The Family Law Act 1996 contained far-reaching proposals to answer some of these questions. The Act saw its purpose as encouraging stable relationships and marriage support was coupled with greater support for cohabiting couples.

Mediation was given great prominence by the Act and, indeed, the implementation of some of the provisions dealing with the role of mediation were soon put in to force (see section 2.2 below). Although the Family Law Act 1996 tried to settle some of the thorniest issues, the results of pilot studies into its workings in practice proved disappointing. This, in turn, led to an abandonment of the provisions of the Act dealing with substantive changes to the law of divorce. Thus those provisions of the 1996 Act which are operative concern domestic violence, occupation of the matrimonial home, mediation and public funding (subsumed into the Community Legal Service Funding Code), as well as certain orders for financial relief.

An initiative to cut costs and, in particular, to deal with cases where mounting expenses of divorce litigation are in danger of outstripping the assets of the couple involved is dealt with below in section 6.1.2. A 'family law protocol' has been devised by the Law Society, in conjunction with other concerned bodies, to deal with divorce, domestic violence and, in addition, financial settlements involved in matrimonial and cohabitation disputes. The protocol is to be used to make procedures uniform and to endeavour to take some of the stress and bitterness out of proceedings. By taking a less hostile approach, it is also hoped to curtail lawyers' costs.

Mediation, in particular, is seen as a way of resolving disputes over children and family finances more speedily, more cheaply and with less acrimony than by going to court. Funding is therefore available for mediation in cases where couples, willing to accept mediation as an alternative, are eligible to receive public funding.

Judicial concern has been expressed, in particular, at the lack of predictability in reaching financial settlements. While the courts have powers to try to tailor the outcome to the individual case (see section 6 below), there is a growing view that the elasticity thus provided to the judges should be curtailed in favour of more ascertainable outcomes. However, there is no likelihood of such reform within the foreseeable future.

In relation to the children of separating spouses, under the Children Act 1989, parents in divorce proceedings are actively encouraged to take matters into their own hands and make their own decisions regarding their children's future. The courts' interventionist role has been confined (see section 5.2.1 below).

Another striking change in the course of the last decade is that since April 1993 maintenance applications for children have also no longer been a matter for the courts in general. Under the Child Support Acts, the task of determining such applications for maintenance passed to the Child Support Agency (see chapter on *Children (Part 1)* section 2.2). The courts only deal with maintenance matters in certain clearly defined circumstances (see section 5 below).

The hope is that these changes would lead to less litigation and to less heartache. There is no certainty that they are doing so.

Do note: Leaflets are available from the county courts and the Internet on the procedures entailed in making application for a divorce. See also Community Service Leaflets, *Divorce and Separation* (CLS, leaflet No. 3) and *Family Mediation* (CLS, leaflet No. 24). The Lord Chancellor's Department has also made available leaflets for children whose parents are in the process of divorce. These are intended for children of 5-years-old and upwards. Also two leaflets have been issued to assist parents in explaining the family breakup to their children: *www.lcd.gov.uk/family/divleaf.htm.*

In this chapter we look at:

- seeking a divorce
- seeking an amicable solution – reconciliation and mediation
- procedure – an outline
- changes to the law
- the children of the marriage
- sorting out family assets on divorce
- the court orders: maintenance
- the family home
- domestic violence
- when cohabitees split up.

1   SEEKING A DIVORCE

1.1   Is there 'irretrievable breakdown'?

Husbands and wives, as we have seen in the chapter on *Setting up Home*, have many obligations to one another. In particular they are expected to live together and to support one another.

An absolute decree of divorce makes the couple into two single persons again for all legal purposes. They are, of course, then free to remarry. Most of their mutual obligations fall away.

However, their obligation to support one another remains despite a divorce. Hence the number of factors which the court must take into account in trying to distribute the family assets. (For the issue of imposing a 'clean break' between the couple, see section 6.4 below.)

Another primary obligation remains unalterable. Where a husband and wife have children, they are both responsible, as father and mother, for their children until these reach the age of maturity (usually 18).

1.2   Jurisdiction

The first issue, for any couple who wish to divorce, is to establish whether the court has jurisdiction to hear their case. In other words, the question is: can they bring divorce proceedings?

If a husband or wife wishes to divorce the other spouse, he or she:

a) must have been married for a minimum of a year; and

b) must be domiciled in this country, i.e. England is regarded as their home. The petitioning spouse must also have been resident in England for six months before the date on which proceedings are brought;
   or

c) the petitioning spouse must have been habitually resident in this country for twelve months (see also section 1.2.2 below).

1.2.1   The marriage must have lasted for a minimum of a year

No petition for divorce can be presented to the courts before the expiry of one year from the date of the marriage. This is an absolute bar. In some difficult situations this one-year bar can cause problems.

☞   *Three months ago, you married a woman 20 years younger than yourself. You find that not only are your personalities totally incompatible but she is having affairs with other men and bringing them into your house. One of her boyfriends threatened you when you protested at his presence in your own home. You feel that a year is a long time to wait in the circumstances. You wonder what you can do?*

You can petition for judicial separation within the year (see *Judicial separation*, section 1.4 below). Otherwise you must wait for the first year of marriage to elapse before you can petition for divorce. However, when you are able to present the petition at the end of your first year of marriage, it can be based on events occurring in the course of that year.

Where there is violence in the home, or the threat of violence, you can apply immediately to court for an order to exclude the other spouse (see *Domestic violence*, section 9 below).

1.2.2   Living in the UK

Generally speaking, you must be domiciled in this country to petition for divorce here, i.e. you must regard England as your home. In addition to your domicile, you also must have resided in England or Wales for six months before you can begin proceedings here. Otherwise you can petition on the basis that you have lived here for twelve months preceding your petition for divorce.

1.2.3   When can a court refuse to hear divorce proceedings because of domicile or residence issues?

A court can order a halt to proceedings for divorce in England if it would be better for the case to be heard in another country. The usual test which the courts apply is to decide 'with which country the parties are most closely associated'.

However, as far as the EU is concerned (Denmark excepted), where there are divorce proceedings commenced in different Member States, a binding rule will apply that only the court where the proceedings were originally initiated must deal with the matter; all other courts must refuse to do so.

☞   *You are an English woman married to a French husband. You separated from him a year ago and have lived in London since then. You wish to petition for a divorce here but your husband has informed you that he has instructed a lawyer in Paris where proceedings have already begun. You wonder what you can do.*

If you petition the English court, it will halt the proceedings until such time as it confirms the jurisdiction of the court in Paris. If such jurisdiction is indeed established and the proceedings are already under way in France, the UK court will decline to hear your petition. For the question of legal aid abroad (see chapter on *The Legal System*, section 3.6.4).

1.3   Grounds for divorce

There is only one ground for granting a decree: the marriage must have broken down irretrievably (Matrimonial Causes Act 1973). Ostensibly, therefore, a divorce is no longer based on a matrimonial 'offence'.

Note: the spouse who asks for a divorce is the *petitioner*; the other spouse is the *respondent*.

1.3.1   The five facts – the matrimonial 'fault'

However, the court must be satisfied that the marriage has broken down irretrievably and that there is evidence of one or more of the following five facts:

- that the respondent has committed adultery and the petitioner finds it intolerable to live with the respondent (see section 1.3.1(a))
- that the respondent has behaved in such a way that the petitioner cannot reasonably be expected to live with the respondent (see section 1.3.1(b))

- that the respondent has deserted the petitioner for a continuous period of at least two years immediately preceding the presentation of the petition (see section 1.3.1(c))
- that the parties to the marriage have lived apart for a continuous period of at least two years immediately preceding the presentation of the petition and the respondent consents to a decree being granted (i.e. two years' separation plus consent of the other spouse). This is known as the 'no fault' ground (see section 1.3.1(d))
- that the parties to the marriage have lived apart for a continuous period of at least five years immediately preceding the presentation of the petition (see section 1.3.1(e)).

Statistics show that about 70 per cent of divorces are awarded on the grounds of unreasonable behaviour and adultery (the classic matrimonial offences). About 18 to 25 per cent of all divorces are on the basis of a fact of 'no fault', i.e. that the couple have been separated for two years and both partners consent to the divorce.

So despite the fact that there is only one ground for divorce, i.e. irretrievable breakdown, the law lays down two separate requirements: irretrievable breakdown and one of the five facts as evidence of the breakdown. Thus, without necessarily intending to, the law lays stress on the unhappiest aspects of a marriage. It requires the parties to cite them as one of the five facts in their petitions for divorce in order to give the petition credibility.

1.3.1(a)   Adultery plus intolerability

Adultery is defined as heterosexual sex between one spouse of the marriage and some other person who is not the other spouse. There must be penetration, so 'heavy petting' does not constitute adultery. Because the law specifies a heterosexual act, a gay or lesbian sexual act cannot constitute adultery.

☞ *You are a married man and you learn from your wife that she is involved in a lesbian relationship. You both feel that the marriage has irretrievably broken down and agree that you should petition her for an undefended divorce.*

You cannot base the petition on adultery because your wife's relationship with someone outside the marriage is not a heterosexual one. However, you could petition on some other ground, for instance, two years' separation with consent if you leave home, or on the 'unreasonable behaviour' ground (see sections 1.3.1(d) and 1.3.1(b) below).

To prove adultery, an admission by the respondent and co-respondent or circumstantial evidence generally suffices. The courts do not inquire into the evidence closely in undefended petitions.

The co-respondent need not be named in the petition.

☞ *Your wife has committed adultery with the husband of a close family friend. You do not want to name him as co-respondent because of the unhappiness it will cause his family. You are told that because you know the identity of the co-respondent, his name must be given in the divorce petition.*

This is no longer the case; even where the co-respondent's name is known, it does not have to be cited.

Evidence of fathering a child outside the marriage would be certain proof of adultery. However, the court will only order blood tests to establish paternity in limited sets of circumstances. These would not usually include someone's wish to prove adultery in divorce proceedings.

☞ *An unmarried woman who works in your husband's business is about to have a baby. You have been suspicious for some time that there is a relationship between your husband and this woman. You think that he could be the father of her child. You would like to have DNA testing done when the baby is born in order to ascertain whether your suspicions are correct.*

A court will not order blood tests to establish adultery. However, if the court took the view that it was in the child's interests to know his or her true identity, then tests may be ordered (see chapter on *Children, (Part 1)*, section 2.15).

'Intolerability' is an additional factor required in a petition alleging adultery. It was introduced because it was felt that an occasional 'fling' should not be sufficient to bring marriages to an end. There had to be something more: so the petitioner must not only prove adultery but must also show that he or she can no longer live with the other spouse. The two requirements are separate so that the 'intolerability' need not be linked to the adultery.

☞ *Your husband, whom you married five years ago, admitted that he committed adultery with a woman called Jane. After a few weeks' separation, he has returned home, saying that the affair is quite over. You wish to rebuild your marriage. However, since his return, your husband has been telephoning another woman called Mary and has gone out at night without telling you where he is going. You find his behaviour intolerable even though he assures you that he and Mary are not having an adulterous relationship.*

You would be entitled to petition for divorce. Even though his adulterous affair with Jane is over, his past affair and present behaviour satisfy together the requirements of the law.

1.3.1(b) Behaviour

This ground is pleaded where one spouse has behaved in such a way that the other cannot reasonably be expected to live with him or her – taking into account all the circumstances as well as the personalities of the parties.

There has been a range of case law on the subject of 'behaviour' and whether the other spouse could reasonably be expected to put up with it. The courts have examined instances of where one spouse was emotionally or sexually unresponsive; where one partner was financially irresponsible; where a husband treated his wife like a child.

In a recent case, the wife alleged that her husband's behaviour had been highly critical, undermining and controlling, and that he showed lack of respect, insight, and warmth, as well as having gone in for publicly humiliating her. As a result she suffered depression and nervous strain and had lost her self-confidence and self-esteem. The court held that the test of whether or not a wife could live with her husband (or he with her) was only objective in part. There was no single category of behaviour which qualified as unreasonable but all behaviour could be taken into account.

Take care: one set of circumstances cannot automatically be applied to another case in a divorce petition: every case, as every unhappy family, has its own particularity.

A court is not supposed to 'rubber stamp' divorce petitions. On the other hand, it does not wish to make pointless inquiries into conduct once one spouse has declared that the marriage is at an end. In all such cases it is a matter of fact and degree. A course of conduct made up of a number of incidents and over a period of time is often cited on this ground.

☞ *Three years ago you married a man many years older than yourself. He has subjected everything you do at home to a constant stream of criticism. You live in an atmosphere of disapproval which is profoundly undermining. You would like to petition for divorce but cannot bring any grave allegation against your husband such as violent behaviour. You also do not think he would consent to a divorce.*

In the circumstances, the court is likely to view your petition sympathetically on the grounds of your husband's behaviour.

☞ *Your wife has petitioned for a divorce on the ground that the marriage has irretrievably broken down. The facts which she alleged in her petition concerned your behaviour. She stated that she could not reasonably be expected to live with you. She alleged that your enthusiasm for DIY interfered with your life together and caused you to neglect her. You feel that her allegations are trivial. You wonder how closely the court is likely to inquire into the reasons for the failure of your marriage.*

A petition based on behaviour should be able to substantiate its claims, and a court is expected to consider the issues involved.

However, in certain circumstances, the courts have accepted that a series of seemingly trivial acts can add up to unreasonable behaviour.

1.3.1(c) Desertion

The petitioner must show that he or she has been deserted for a continuous period of at least two years immediately preceding the presentation of the petition.

1) There must be a clear evidence of a separation.

Note: separation means two separate households; it does not necessarily mean that each spouse lives under a separate roof. For example, if a couple cannot afford separate accommodation, they may continue to live in the same premises but lead quite separate lives.

2) There must be a clear intention to desert the other spouse; for example, if a separation is involuntary through imprisonment or because of an overseas posting, the necessary intention to desert is missing.

3) The petitioner does not consent to the desertion. This distinguishes desertion from the 'no fault' ground of two years' separation with consent.

4) There must have been no just cause for the desertion. In other words, if a husband or wife petitions for divorce on the ground of desertion, the court will wish to establish whether it was their own behaviour which caused the other spouse to leave home.

☞   *Your wife has become extremely suspicious of you and is convinced that you are committing adultery although this is not the case. She spies on you at every opportunity, listens in to your phone calls, and rummages through your briefcase and your clothing. You are beginning to find her behaviour impossible to tolerate and are thinking of leaving home. You would like to know whether you would be deserting your wife in these circumstances.*

It may well be that a court would find that you were being driven from your home by her behaviour, in which case your wife would be the 'deserting' spouse.

5) There must be satisfactory financial provision for the deserted spouse.

1.3.1(d)   Separation for two years with consent

This is the closest that the law approaches to a divorce by mutual consent. Either spouse can apply after they have lived apart for a continuous period of at least two years immediately preceding the presentation of the petition. The petitioner must show that the respondent consents to a decree being granted.

Consent entails:

• proper information
• proper documentation
• proper procedure.

☞   *You have lived abroad for three years and have received a form from your wife's solicitors in England asking you to acknowledge 'service' of her petition for divorce [i.e. that the petition has been served on you]. You write back on your own notepaper acknowledging the receipt of this letter. You wonder if you have now 'consented' to the divorce.*

The court will refuse to accept that this is specific consent. A proper procedure must be followed and you must acknowledge service of the petition on a prescribed form (see section 3.1.1 below).

1.3.1(e)   Separation for five years

Once husband and wife have lived apart for a continuous period of five years, a petitioner can be granted a divorce without having to show that the other spouse consents to it.

However, there is a proviso that, if the financial arrangements are not reasonable, the respondent can raise an objection.

1.4   Judicial separation

In 2001, the number of petitions for judicial separation fell to 535. These petitions are based on the same five facts as are necessary for a petition for divorce but there is no need to show irretrievable breakdown of the marriage.

There is no need to wait for one year to elapse to petition for judicial separation as is the case with divorce. The effect of judicial separation is to end the duty of husband and wife to cohabit with one another. It does not end the marriage. Where there are religious objections to divorce, a decree of judicial separation can be an alternative.

Note: the provisions for financial arrangements between spouses (see section 6 below) apply to judicial separations in the same way as they apply on divorce.

If there is a formal separation agreement or a decree of judicial separation there cannot be desertion. The duty to cohabit has in fact been legally terminated by such a decree. If there is no duty to cohabit, there can be no desertion.

2   SEEKING AN AMICABLE PARTING

2.1   Reconciliation

In all the provisions of the law relating to the five 'facts' which have to be shown in addition to irretrievable breakdown, there are in-built reconciliation provisions. In effect, these provisions allow for a period of up to six months in which the parties can make an attempt at reconciliation. If in the event, the reconciliation fails, the six-month reconciliation period of grace will not jeopardise their legal position in subsequent divorce proceedings.

The reconciliation provisions apply for a single period of up to six months or for periods which do not total more than six months.

☞   *Your wife has told you that she is in love with another man. You persuade her that she should give the marriage another try particularly for the sake of the children. You then live together for three months but she says that she cannot continue in the marriage. She leaves home. Again you prevail on her to return but this time she only stays for a few weeks.*

The fact that you have lived with your wife on and off for a period of less than six months – since you learned of her adultery – does not affect your legal position if divorce proceedings ensue. In earlier times, once a man took a wife back (and vice versa) after learning of adultery, he was considered to have 'condoned' the adultery and so lost the right to petition for a divorce.

In addition a solicitor acting for a petitioner has to certify that he or she:

* has discussed the possibility of reconciliation; and
* has made sure the parties know where they can seek guidance if they sincerely desire reconciliation.

The court can also adjourn proceedings to give the parties further time to decide whether they genuinely wish to make another attempt at sustaining their marriage.

Note: a list of organisations which provide marriage counselling as well as mediation and services is found at the end of Chapter 4 under DIRECTORY on page 109.

The matters discussed above under the term 'reconciliation' concern an attempt by both spouses to live together again as husband and wife.

The Family Law Act 1996 broadened the approach to reconciliation attempting to make it an integral part of the steps to bolster and shore up a failing marriage.

2.2   Mediation services

Mediation, on the other hand, is directed towards different goals and is not intended to effect a reconciliation. Rather it is intended to make parting easier and resolve issues by agreement. A mediator's role is to sort out some of the difficulties between spouses or cohabiting partners with regard, in particular, to arrangements for children and family finances.

2.2.1   Extension of mediation services

Mediation is seen as a way of assisting couples to assist themselves in reducing bitterness and acrimony once they have made the decision to part. They are to be helped in reaching agreement over their disputes rather than having their disputes 'judged'. The conviction determining the legislation is that agreements which parties reach themselves are more likely to be kept than agreements imposed by outsiders.

The Family Law Act 1996 incorporated a far greater use of mediation services, which are funded, where the relevant criteria are met, by the Community Legal Services Fund [formerly legal aid] (see section 4 below). These provisions relating to mediation are now part of the Funding Code and have been extended to all of England and Wales as from 22 December 2000.

Certain solicitors' firms and mediation bodies can provide publicly funded mediation once they have met the standards set by the Legal Services Commission and have entered in to a contract with the Commission. They must abide by a code of practice which covers such matters as, for example, confidentiality. Any member of a couple who is eligible for funding is eligible for mediation in disputes for which publicly funded mediation is available and where mediation is suitable to the dispute.

Indeed someone who wishes to apply for public (legal aid) funding for most family proceedings and who approaches a solicitor, must (subject to certain exceptions) be directed to a recognised mediation body. Suitability for this form of dispute resolution will be assessed with regard to all the circumstances. In particular it must be possible that mediation will take place without either party being influenced by fear of violence or other harm.

In the usual course of events, public funding for proceedings will be refused unless the applicant has first attended such a meeting with a mediator. The meeting can be attended either separately or jointly by both parties. However mediation is not compulsory and if it subsequently breaks down because, for example, one side is unable to mediate, a form will be returned to the applicant's solicitor who will then make an application for public (legal aid) funding and start afresh.

Pilot studies into the use of mediation services as envisaged by the substantive changes in the Family Law Act have proved disappointing. However, the government has reiterated that its commitment to mediation was unaffected by its decision not to implement the main body of the Act.

It is hoped that over a period of time couples will see for themselves that mediation is an option which might assist them to resolve the issues between them more amicably, more quickly and more cheaply than by court proceedings. Making funding available to them for mediation in cases where they would receive public funding for proceedings is viewed as a means of fostering that goal.

3   CURRENT DIVORCE PROCEDURE: AN OUTLINE

In undefended petitions both spouses accept that the divorce will go ahead; in defended divorces one spouse resists the petition and seeks to raise a defence against it (see section 3.2 below).

3.1   Special procedure: undefended divorces

A special procedure was introduced to deal with undefended divorce petitions. The statistics show that this procedure is the normal practice. Petitions are before a District Judge who then announces the decrees by number if the proper requirements have been met.

There have been consistent calls for reform to this procedure (see section 4 below).

3.1.1   Standard forms

There are standard forms available from law stationers, the courts and HMSO. The procedure follows a set pattern:

a) the petition must be filled in
b) it must enclose a statement of the arrangements for the children
c) it must be sent to the registrar of the divorce county court
d) there must be sufficient copies for the other parties (e.g. a named co-respondent)
e) the respondent will receive his or her copy from the court
f) so will any other of the parties involved
g) the respondent must acknowledge service i.e. must send a reply, also on a prescribed form, that the petition has been received
h) the respondent must make clear that he or she has no intention to defend
i) the documents are examined by an official of the court (the divorce registrar)
j) s/he then certifies that the facts of the case are proved
k) the judge pronounces the decree nisi in open court
l) the decree is made absolute on application by the petitioner.

The Lord Chancellor's Department issues helpful leaflets. (For initiating a petition, see Leaflet 1, *About Divorce*.) See also 'note of warning' in section 3.1.3 below.

3.1.1(a)   Where there are children – 'Statement of arrangements'

☞   *You would like to proceed with a divorce petition on the grounds of adultery and your husband has indicated that he will not defend the petition. You have two children from the marriage aged 10 and 6. You wonder if there are any further procedures entailed.*

The court will require a 'statement of arrangements' as far as the children are concerned. This entails providing the following information:

- the children's names
- dates of birth
- their present address
- the schools which they attend
- the arrangements which have been made/agreed for their future care.

Do note: you must also include information, where appropriate, if your children have any special health or educational needs and/or whether social services have been involved in their welfare.

For the procedure regarding financial arrangements on divorce, see section 6.1.2 below.

3.1.2 Funding available in the divorce process

Help with forms and procedure entailed in undefended divorce procedure (but not usually full public funding) can be available from solicitors and advice agencies, contracted with the Legal Services Commission, under a scheme known as Legal Help (see also chapter on *The Legal System* on meeting the legal aid requirements). Public funding for mediation and for legal representation is available for disputes relating to children, as well as contested matters concerning finances and property – provided that all the other criteria, including the means test, for receiving funding are met.

3.1.3 D-I-Y divorces

Couples may handle their own divorce proceedings. This is usually possible in the most straightforward situations where no children are involved, the marriage is short and the parting is amicable.

Do note: divorce forms can be obtained via the Internet with guidance on how to fill them in.

Note of warning: if there are children to the marriage, or financial or property matters to be sorted out, it may be inadvisable to tackle these on your own (see chapter on *The Legal System* for sources of advice, information and the question of public funding).

3.2 Defended divorces

The respondent who intends to defend a divorce petition must file an answer to the allegations.

Among other matters which can be raised is the issue of financial hardship. For example a court is not allowed to make an order in cases of desertion, if no adequate provision is made for the deserted spouse (see section 1.3.1 above). Usually, fewer than 100 divorces are defended each year.

A decree nisi is pronounced in open court. A decree absolute follows after an interval of six weeks.

4 CURRENT SITUATION OF THE LAW

The present state of divorce law was viewed as unsatisfactory both with regard to the substantive law, i.e. the actual basis on which divorce is granted, and to the 'special procedure'.

4.1 Repeal of Part II of The Family Law Act 1996

The Act had a controversial passage through Parliament. Its intention was to reform the law of divorce on many fronts. Its proponents strongly believed that the institution of marriage ought to be supported as much as possible and that divorce was not to be undertaken lightly. At the same time, they wished to ensure that if there has to be a divorce, it should not be a painful and costly legal process. Certain provisions of the Act, that had been expected to come into force in the year 2000, were repealed after disappointing pilot schemes and an interim report which stated that the substantive proposed changes to the law failed to meet objectives in helping couples to resolve their problems.

Thus the sole ground for divorce remains irretrievable breakdown; the five facts indicating 'marital fault' (see section 1.3.1 above) still have to be shown. The present requirement that one year must elapse before proceedings can begin also stands.

4.1.1 Mediation and The Family Law Act (in force)

The Family Law Act, as we have seen, placed particular stress on mediation. The initial meetings should begin by pointing the couple towards mediation, and further directions for mediation can be given at other stages in the procedure.

Another radical change is that funding for family mediation services comes, at least in part, from the Community Legal Services Commission [formerly the Legal Aid Board]. This provision covers England and Wales as part of the Funding Code of the Legal Services Commission (see section 2.2.1 above).

4.1.2   Domestic violence and the provisions of The Family Law Act (in force)

This was originally the subject matter of a separate Bill but, after opposition, some of its provisions have now been incorporated into The Family Law Act 1996 and are also presently in force (see also section 9 below).

5   CHILDREN

It is the duty of the court to have regard to all the circumstances in a divorce petition, and the first consideration must be the welfare of any child of the family under the age of 18.

5.1   The Children Act 1989

Children of parents who live in amity do not need the law's guidance. The underlying intention of the Children Act 1989 is that even when there is marital breakdown, the law should not be called upon to intervene. Parents should continue to care for and to have responsibility for their children until they reach the age of 18. As far as possible parents should make their own decisions. Thus the court's role has been reduced. It can only intervene if it decides that to make an order for a child would be better than to make no order at all.

The orders are:
- residence orders
- contact orders
- specific issue orders
- prohibited steps orders.

(These orders are discussed in detail in the chapter on *Children (Part 1)* section 3.1.2.)

5.1.1   Financial relief under the Matrimonial Causes Act 1973

In the next section, we shall deal with the orders which are available to the court to distribute the spouses' assets on a divorce. These orders are available for the benefit of the children of the family too. The orders last until a child's 18th birthday. For children over 18, provision is made where a child is receiving further education or there are other circumstances which warrant special provision, e.g. disability. In deciding whether to grant an order and, if so, for how much, the court takes into account all the circumstances, including:

a) income, earning capacity and property and other financial resources, including those available in the foreseeable future, of the child
b) the parents' financial needs
c) the child's financial needs
d) any physical or mental disability of the child
e) the manner in which the child was being or was expected to be educated or trained.

5.1.2   Financial relief under the Children Act

Under the Children Act 1989 wide-ranging powers are given to the court for orders which can be made for the benefit of a child. Orders can be made for periodical payments, lump sums, and transfers of property. The powers under this Act, unlike those under section 5.1.1 above, do not depend upon divorce proceedings. They are thus available to children of unmarried parents. Day-to-day maintenance was intended to be determined under the Child Support Acts.

5.2   Child Support Acts

The Child Support Act 1991 took away from the courts the role of deciding on questions of financial support for children to a large extent. The courts will only be called upon to decide such issues in limited circumstances, for example when there are special grounds or when a parent seeks 'topping up' of the maintenance awarded under the Act (see section 5.2.1 below).

Children's maintenance is now assessed by the Child Support Agency (CSA). (See chapter on *Children (Part 1)*, section 2.1.)

In an endeavour to meet the criticism of the Act, which was regarded as working unfairly, another Child Support Act was passed in 1995 (see chapter *Children (Part 1)*, section 2.2.2). Further changes to the system are expected to deal with renewed criticism of the workings of the formula for assessing maintenance.

5.2.1   The court's jurisdiction

The courts will no longer make orders for maintenance for children in divorce proceedings except where:

- they exceed the amount assessed by the CSA, or
- there are special grounds put forward such as educational needs.

In addition:

- the court will still have jurisdiction to make orders for stepchildren and other 'children of the family' (see section 5.2.2 below)
- the court will still make orders for lump sum and property adjustment orders for children
- the court will make orders for disabled children.

5.2.2   Step-children

Financial Orders are still to be made by the courts for the 'children of the family'.

☞   *You are a wealthy woman who married some years ago. Your husband had two children by his former marriage and you have effectively brought them up. You are now in the middle of rather acrimonious divorce proceedings and your husband states that you have assumed responsibility for his children so he will be applying for a financial order against you on his children's behalf. You wonder what your legal position is.*

The court must weigh up whether you in fact assumed responsibility for the children's maintenance. If you did, the court must establish the extent to which you were responsible for them, and for how long you met that responsibility. It will then take into account their father's liability to maintain them. If it does make an order, it must state that you are not the children's mother.

5.2.3   Who can apply

Any person with whom a child is resident under a residence order can apply to court for maintenance (see the chapter *Children (Part 1)*, section 3.1.2, for a *residence order*).

☞   *Your wife left you and your two children to live in another town. You are unable to care for the children and continue to work so, as a result, they both live in your parents' house, i.e. with their grandparents. Costs of their keep are mounting and your parents would like some additional support from your wife.*

If the children are living with their grandparents under a residence order, then the grandparents can apply to court for financial provision.

6   SORTING OUT FAMILY ASSETS ON DIVORCE

6.1   Duty to support continues

The duty of husband and wife to support one another and for both to maintain their children continues despite a divorce. Thus even in undefended petitions, quite separate proceedings can and do take place over maintenance and the family home.

While 'big money' cases attract the headlines, for the usual run of couples who are in the process of divorce the problem is that there may not be enough 'in the kitty' for both of them to maintain their standard of living, ensure separate accommodation for two households, adequate provision for the children while they are young, and also provision for the divorcing spouses in their old age. In general their only capital asset of any worth is the matrimonial home and this is dealt with separately below, see section 8. Pension sharing on divorce is also dealt with below (section 6.7.8).

6.1.1   Need to sort out amicable arrangement

While each spouse should receive independent legal advice where necessary to guard their interests, the parties' main endeavour should be to sort out their financial affairs as amicably as possible.

The costs of litigating over 'who gets what' can eat up assets very effectively. In that case, the whole family may lose more than any individual family member is likely to gain from a protracted dispute.

In a recent case, a couple pursued an action where the total estimated value of their assets was £127,400. Legal costs which included an appeal to the House of Lords on how they should divide those assets were in excess of £128,000. Although both sides were funded by the [then] Legal Aid Board, the Board had a charge on the assets to recover its expenditure if it decided to enforce it. The House of Lords stated that by the time the case had reached the Court of Appeal, it had been considered by five differently constituted tribunals. The issue, in broad terms, concerned whether the wife's housing needs or those of the husband should have priority. To allow successive appeals in the hope of producing an answer which accorded with perfect justice, their Lordships stated, was to kill the parties with kindness.

(See DIRECTORY on page 109 for mediation organisations which assist in trying to mitigate acrimonious disputes over property and related matters on divorce.)

6.1.2   Ancillary relief – how best to tackle it

Ancillary relief is the technical term for the financial arrangements which couples make when they divorce. In order to reduce the cost, expense and delay that litigation can entail, as well as in an endeavour to reduce legal costs which can be disproportionate to the value of the assets at stake, a new procedure came into force on 5 June 2000. A 'family law protocol' has been devised by the Law Society, in conjunction with other concerned bodies, to deal with divorce, domestic violence, and also financial matters involved in matrimonial and cohabitation disputes. It is intended to make procedures uniform and to endeavour to take some of the stress and anguish out of such proceedings. By taking a less hostile approach, it is also intended to cut costs.

The intention of these reforms, above all, is to enable the couple and the court to focus on the facts most relevant to the dispute. To this end the procedure is designed to:

- identify the issues which are important to the couple
- encourage them to reach agreement
- reduce unnecessary cost, delay and personal distress
- ensure people understand at every stage how much money they are spending on taking forward their case; and
- curb exhaustive and unnecessary disclosure of financial information.

The key to these improvements is 'active case management' so that a case is dealt with in ways which are proportionate to the amount of money involved; the importance of the case; the complexity of the issues; and the financial position of each party.

Among the features of the scheme are:

- cases are to be judge-led
- disclosure of information is to be controlled
- strict timetabling is to be imposed; and
- spouses are to be encouraged to resolve their disputes through court-led mediation conferences instead of continuing litigation.

6.1.3   Tax and divorce

A very important factor is the parties' tax position on divorce. Specialist advice should always be sought.

6.2   What are the assets of a marriage?

On the breakdown of a marriage, everything which has been earned or owned during the marriage is considered part of the assets of the marriage. These can all be redistributed on divorce. Assets can include present and future earnings; savings; property owned separately; the family car; holiday cottage or boat; expectations under a will in certain circumstances; and even the family pet!

6.3   Court's wide powers

The court has very wide powers indeed to redistribute the assets of the spouses (see section 6.7 below). This is known as the court's 'discretion'. Its task is to try to reach a fair and just division in all the circumstances of each individual case.

Do take heed: because of the courts' very wide discretion, while it is easy to enunciate general principles, it is very difficult to predict what outcome will be reached in any particular case.

- The circumstances of each case are to be taken into account so that every case is dealt with individually on its merits
- past cases are not necessarily a guide to present decisions
- children come first in any financial arrangements on divorce (see section 5 above).

The court has at its disposal the following powers:

a) to deal with capital assets
b) to deal with money payments
c) to order a sale to meet the above payments.

Money payments can be ordered to be paid by one spouse to the other and these payments can be secured upon his or her own property. The court can also order lump sum payments or make property adjustment orders whereby it can order a transfer of property, generally the matrimonial home, from one spouse to the other. It can also order a sale of property, to meet the financial orders it has already made. The court will endeavour to reach what it regards as an equitable arrangement. At the same time, it strives to be reasonable and to take all circumstances into account. The court will want a statement of the general nature of the means of each party, signed by themselves or by their solicitor (see also section 6.1.2 above).

The court will also assess the question of a party's 'needs' (see section 6.7 below).

Do take note: 'needs' are relative. The wife of a pop star will be seen as having greater 'needs' than the wife of a man who is on a modest salary so that available resources are a factor in their own right. Indeed, even when interpreted generously and called 'reasonable requirements', a spouse's immediate needs would not necessarily determine the division of assets as recent cases show.

In one case, the House of Lords stated that, self-evidently, fairness required the court to take in account all the circumstances. It was also self-evident that the factual circumstances in which the courts exercised their powers varied enormously. The legislation itself was intended to deal with all applications for financial settlements, whether they originated from a poverty-stricken couple or from multi-millionaires.

While there is power in the court to 'tailor a bespoke solution' to the individual case before it, there has been considerable concern expressed at the lack of predictability in the search for the goal of a fair outcome. Pending new legislation, however, to alter the current position, the courts are left with these discretionary powers in trying to reach a reasonably fair outcome; the judges also have to reflect changing social values and expectations since the Act was passed 30 years ago.

6.4   A clean break

The duty of husband and wife to support one another does not end on divorce. In principle, their duty to maintain remains. However there have been inroads on this principle.

In particular the court must consider whether it would not be better to impose a clean break on the couple. This is seen as a desirable alternative to long-term support. Today the court has the power to impose a clean break in divorce proceedings – whether or not husband or wife wants it. It is obligatory for the courts to consider the question of ending one spouse's financial dependence on the other, once the marriage itself has come to an end.

6.4.1   Difficulties in practice

Obviously, the principle is easier to state on paper than implement in practice. Circumstances vary so much from household to household that it is difficult to lay down anything except the broadest of rules:

- If the marriage has been short-lived
- if the parties to it are still young
- if there are no children involved
- if there is sufficient capital for one spouse (generally the husband) to 'buy out' the other spouse's maintenance needs

the courts will generally want to see a clean break between the parties.

☞   *You are a 25-year-old woman, married to a wealthy man. The marriage lasted only eighteen months and you have not had any children. You kept on your flat which you owned before you married, and rented it out. In your application for ancillary relief to your divorce petition, you have asked for secured payments as you do not need a lump sum to purchase accommodation. Your lawyer has told you that the court can impose a clean break whether or not you have asked for it and whether or not you would consent to it. You want to know if this is correct.*

The answer is 'yes'. The courts now have the power to impose a clean break even if one of the parties is unwilling to accept it.

Generally, it is fair to say that the clean break principle has been more honoured in its breach than in its observance. For example, the courts have stated that a settlement of the matrimonial home on the wife until the children reach the age of 18 does not offend against the clean break principle.

Further, since the relevant Family Law Act provisions came into force in November 1998, property orders are no longer final. The court can consider a second application by either spouse for an additional capital sum. A 'clean break' may no longer mean what it says.

☞   *When you divorced, your husband paid you a lump sum and arranged for you to receive periodical payments, which were expected to cover your needs as well as to represent your capital requirements for the future. You have now heard that he has become an instant millionaire as a National Lottery winner. You feel that it is inequitable that you should not receive a share of his good fortune.*

The court has the power to order a capital sum and/or discharge the periodical payments. The court will still consider all the circumstances of the case in deciding whether a lump sum is justifiable. In the present case, it may be relatively easy for the court so to decide. But in other cases, there would be some reluctance to order a spouse, perhaps years after a divorce, to make a radical re-structuring of capital to meet a new application of this kind.

6.5   Achieving a fair outcome

In very general terms, if a clean break was not ordered, the court used to calculate on the basis of the 'one-third rule', i.e. the wife gets one third of the combined income – exclusive of maintenance for the children.

However, in a recent case, the House of Lords stated that there should be 'no bias in favour of the money-earner and against the home-maker and child-carer'. It was the court's duty to reach a fair outcome, their Lordships stated. The yardstick, where applicable, should be equality of division although each case must, of course, depend on its facts.

Since then the Court of Appeal has reiterated that judges should avoid 'any discriminatory appraisal of the traditional role of the woman as home-maker and of the man as bread-winner and arbiter of the destination of family assets for the next generation. A calculation of what would be the result of equal division was 'a necessary cross-check against such discrimination'. Nonetheless, issues such as 'conduct' and 'contribution' may still be taken into account in order to decide whether or not equality of division is appropriate in any particular case.

6.6   The role of the welfare state

State benefits have been an ever-increasing factor in assessing financial arrangements. The social security legislation is outside the scope of this book, but its importance in overall terms cannot be over-emphasised.

Thus the legal principle which underlies financial arrangements on divorce is that spouses are expected to maintain one another and both are expected to maintain their children. This principle applies as much to feckless or devious spouses as to responsible and caring ones. However, there is no doubt that while the courts accept that the burden of maintenance should not be taken out of individual hands and placed on the State, they also must accept that – in practice – this is what often happens. Fierce debate rages – particularly in today's economic climate – on the extent to which the benefit system is seen as a factor in family disintegration.

The Child Support Acts (see section 5.2 above) are indicative of a change of policy to make parents rather than the State bear the burden of supporting children in family breakdown.

6.7   Factors which the court takes into account in making its orders

6.7.1   Income, earning capacity, property and other financial resources of each party to the marriage – what they have and what they may expect

This is the totality of the family's available resources. Calculations are based on wage slips of gross income less other contributions such as NIC, superannuation, and trade union dues. The court will assess a couple's true income and will look beyond what the parties may say about their position in order to establish precise figures.

☞   *You allege that the salary statements of your wife, who is suing you for divorce, give an inadequate idea of her true income. She receives a company car, free travel and travel insurance, belongs to a BUPA scheme paid for her by her employers, and is given cash bonuses. You also understand that she is due for a substantial salary increase.*

These are legitimate matters to be taken into account in assessing her income and earning capacity.

In assessing earning capacity, the courts take into account the earnings a spouse would obtain on the open market. This means taking into account such factors as age, job experience, opportunities for employment etc. For example, a woman who worked before she got married but did not work throughout her marriage, would have her earning potential assessed accordingly.

Other matters to be taken into account would be expectations under a will or a family settlement. While the courts have taken these matters into account in the past they will always be circumspect about them. Evidence which would be an invasion of privacy will not be allowed.

☞   *Your husband is the only son of an 85-year-old mother. She is a woman of considerable means and you understand that he is to be her sole heir. You would like to receive evidence of her will.*

The court will not order a relative to give evidence in these circumstances. However, this does not mean that your husband's expectations on his mother's death will necessarily be ignored in the court's assessment.

☞   *When your father-in-law died, he left the life interest in his estate to his widow but, after her death, his estate is to go to your wife, from whom you are now divorced. The estate includes a very substantial house and grounds, as well as a shares portfolio.*

You are currently out of work and have no capital assets of similar magnitude.

The court may make an order during your mother-in-law's lifetime that the property (or some of it) be transferred to you on her death.

6.7.2   Financial needs, obligations and responsibilities; now or in the near future

This covers all outgoings such as food, fuel, clothing etc. If either spouse has set up home with another partner or intends to remarry, then that second family's needs will also be an important factor in the computation.

☞   *You have recently left your husband and moved in with your partner who works as a stockbroker. Your husband states that your partner should now provide for you.*

While the court will take into account your partner's means, it will not order him to provide for either you or for any children from your marriage.

6.7.3   Standard of living before breakdown of marriage

The parties are not expected to be put in the position that they would have been in if the marriage had survived. Two separate households cannot cost the same as one. In the case of very wealthy people, however, an adjustment might be made to approximate the standard of living which would have been expected had the marriage survived.

6.7.4   Age of each party and duration of the marriage

The court has to take into account factors such as how old the parties are; for example, a young person may need less support than an elderly one.

The duration of the marriage is also relevant. A very short union might well lead to the imposition of a clean break where there are no children involved. Of course, a short marriage might have been preceded by a long period of cohabitation.

☞ *Your wife and yourself cohabited for five years before marrying but thereafter soon split up. She says that the period of cohabitation is to be taken into account in assessing the duration of the marriage.*

The court has a duty to consider all the circumstances of the marriage. So the meaningfulness of a period of cohabitation will be assessed in terms of the actual situation at the time. e.g. whether before you got married you had children together or bought a house together etc.

6.7.5   Physical or mental disability

If either spouse suffers from a disability or serious illness, this will obviously be factor in assessing the proportionate shares in the division of a family's assets on divorce.

6.7.6   Contributions to the welfare of the family including any contribution by looking after the home or caring for the family

6.7.6(a)   Wide interpretation of 'contribution'

It is important to note that 'contribution' under this heading includes looking after home and/or children.

The significance of this has recently been restated. Judges are not to look at traditional roles but to take into account the totality of the circumstances within the marriage while it lasted.

However, looking after home and children does not exclude other contributions, for example to a family business – whether made directly or indirectly.

☞ *You and your husband came to this country as poor immigrants from Eastern Europe. You both decided to set up a small bakery business on money which your husband borrowed from a bank. It involved your working unsociable hours together with him for several years. The business is now a flourishing chain of cafés and patisseries. Your marriage has now broken down but you feel that the financial settlement should take your contribution to the business into account.*

The court is very likely to hold, as the business partnership was a reality, that you are entitled to a share of the assets in the business for your contribution to its exceptional success.

In fact, the House of Lords has stated that if a husband and wife by their joint efforts over many years – his directly in his business and hers indirectly at home – have built up a valuable business from scratch, the claimant wife ought not to be confined to the court's assessment of her 'reasonable requirements' and leave the husband with the much larger share.

6.7.6(b)   'Contribution' of both spouses to home and children

This heading of 'contribution to family welfare' is generally seen as intended to protect a wife on divorce. It can assist a husband too, however.

☞ *You married a well-to-do woman whose family provided you with the matrimonial home. However, during the marriage, you worked hard as a commercial traveller and made strenuous efforts to keep the family together. You feel that your endeavours are entitled to credit when it comes to assessing shares in the house which you and your wife have agreed to sell.*

The court is likely to give a sympathetic hearing to your case for your contribution to be taken into account.

6.7.7   The conduct of each of the parties if, in the opinion of the court, it would be unfair to disregard it

In settling financial claims, the courts do not want to investigate the relative behaviour of spouses. An allocation on this ground, it is felt, would mean inquiring into guilt or blame for failed marriages. This in turn would lead to the court imposing financial penalties for supposed misbehaviour in the course of an unhappy marriage. However, there may be cases where it would affront a sense of justice for an award to be made to one spouse at the expense of the other.

The legal phrase is that conduct must be 'obvious and gross' before a spouse should be deprived of financial provision. Cases where conduct has been taken into account include physical violence, the dissipation of family assets, instances where the husband has abducted the children, and dishonesty. But even in extreme cases, the amount of relief may be reduced rather than altogether refused, depending on the court's view of the conduct in question.

6.7.8 The value of any benefit e.g. a pension, which that party will lose the chance of acquiring

The question of pension rights is a very vexed one. Pensions could represent a considerable aspect of family investment in the long term. For a couple who divorce late in life, the value of lost pension rights for one of the spouses can mean the difference between relative comfort and penury. Moreover, if a former spouse dies, the survivor can lose the prospect of bereavement benefits once there has been a divorce (see chapter on *Death – Before and After*, section 2.1.1).

Do note also: the question of pension sharing on divorce is dealt with in further detail in the chapter *Providing for your Retirement*, section 5.

At the same time, there are difficulties in trying to put an actual value in today's terms on the projected value of future pension rights, which can depend on so many incalculable factors. Prevailing market conditions can, in a short space of time, cut large swathes from a seemingly comfortable pension provision. Then again, a person's circumstances can change dramatically – even from one day to the next. A wealthy person, earning a substantial salary, may find him- or herself unexpectedly redundant, or suffering from a debilitating illness.

The review of the whole area of pension rights on divorce has gone on for several years and has been the subject of successive legislation.

1) Under the Pensions Act of 1995, an ex-wife could be awarded a share of her husband's pension from the date of his retirement. The power was little used and the pension still belonged to the paying spouse. Thus there was always the risk that even if a person was awarded intended retirement income, it would be lost if the ex-spouse died.

Do take heed: in these circumstances it may be possible to make a claim against the estate as a dependant of the deceased (see chapter on *Death – Before and After*, section 8.8). If you are asked, on a divorce settlement, to renounce all claims against an estate, you would no longer have this right, so do take legal advice.

2) The Family Law Act 1996 allowed for a 'pension adjustment order' which the court may award in marital proceedings, enabling a former wife to obtain a share of her husband's pension. This provision has not been brought into force.

3) The Welfare Reform and Pensions Act was passed in 1999 and does allow for pension-sharing on divorce. This provision came into force in 1 December 2000 but is not retrospective. It enables some or all of the rights of a pension to be transferred from one divorcing spouse to the other at the time of divorce. It means that those rights will belong to the person to whom they have been given irrespective of the circumstances of the ex-spouse. It is hoped thereby that fairer settlements can be reached and will enable divorcing couples to achieve a 'clean break' financial independence from each other. Pension-sharing will not be compulsory and it will still be possible to offset pension rights against other assets.

In fact, a recent survey found that many divorcing couples were reluctant to consider pension-sharing because of concern about the complexity of such arrangements and the difficulty of obtaining actuarial values. Nonetheless, couples should examine all the options with their legal advisors so that they can make an informed choice.

Do note: the court will not allow a party to a divorce to go back on a decree nisi to take advantage of the pension-sharing provisions unless both parties consent to such a procedure.

7   THE COURT ORDERS

7.1 Immediate action

The court has the power to order one party to a divorce to pay to the other reasonable sums at any time after the filing of a divorce petition. These orders can begin immediately. They are known as 'orders pending suit'.

☞ *Your husband has filed for a divorce and you have been served with papers. You are very concerned that he should keep up the payments for your son's university education while long-term arrangements are made.*

The court can make an order which will take immediate effect until the divorce is finalised. For example, it can order monthly payments for your son's benefit if it feels that is necessary in all the circumstances of the case.

7.2   Court orders

The court can make *financial provision orders* which cover periodical payments and secured periodical payments; and can also order that a lump sum be paid by instalments.

The court can also make *property adjustment orders* which generally cover a transfer of property, e.g. the matrimonial home, but could include shareholdings or other investments.

7.2.1   Periodical payments

Periodical payments are regular sums usually ordered to be paid on a monthly basis. These can be secured or unsecured. Problems can arise in enforcing unsecured payments.

7.2.2   Secured periodical payments

The court has the power to take steps in advance to ensure that a spouse will receive the payments it orders. Of course, this would only be applicable where there are capital assets which can be charged, such as an ex-spouse's home, or where there are income-producing assets, such as a savings account, or shares.

☞ *You have petitioned for a divorce and your husband has been required to pay you a monthly sum in maintenance. You understand that he is now talking of going to Australia to make a fresh start and you are concerned that you may not be able to secure the maintenance ordered. What can you do?*

You can approach the court to ask that the maintenance payments be secured on your husband's assets. Alternatively, you can ask for a lump sum instead of regular payments.

A secured charge can be limited in time and the property or assets charged can revert – free of the charge – to the person against whom the order was made, or to his estate.

☞ *You received £5,000 per annum as a secured periodical payment from your ex-spouse. You now hear that he has died. You would like to know what your position is.*

It will depend on the terms of the order. An order such as this might only last for as long as either you or your husband are alive, or it might survive your husband's death. If you are likely to lose the benefit of the order, you might be able to make a claim out of his estate under the Family Provision legislation (see chapter on *Death – Before and After*, section 8.4).

Note: a husband's life can be insured to protect these sums.

7.2.3   Lump sum

A lump sum is used:

- to transfer the matrimonial home to one or other spouse (see section 8 below)
- to replace periodical payments
- to compensate for the loss of the home
- to 'buy out' the wife's maintenance payments
- where enforcement is going to be difficult (e.g. where an ex-spouse may emigrate or dissipate the assets).

It is self-evident that an order for a lump sum will only be available where there are assets to meet it.

☞ *You have a flourishing photography business which you run from home. Your wife is suing you for divorce and is asking for a lump sum to compensate her for the fact that she has to find alternative accommodation. The only way you can meet her demand is to sell your house which will put you out of both home and business.*

The court will not put you in a position where you stand to lose your home and jeopardise your business. However, it will enquire whether it could reasonably expect that you might be able to raise a loan to pay a lump sum which would assist your wife in finding accommodation.

Do take note: since the end of 1998, when certain provisions of the Family Law Act were brought into force, the court has had power, on the application of an ex-spouse who has been receiving maintenance or has been given a lump sum, to order a second transfer of capital (see section 6.4.1 above).

7.2.4   When do orders for maintenance cease?

Orders for maintenance generally cease on the remarriage of the spouse who receives them, or on his or her death. They also cease on the death of the spouse who is making the payments except in certain cases of secured payments (see section 7.2.2 above).

☞   *Your husband has made a generous offer of maintenance on your divorce. However, he has specified that the payments are to cease after three years as he expects that you will have returned to paid employment within that period. You wonder what your position is.*

The court is entitled to specify a date on which the payments will end. Generally, depending on the terms of the court order, you could apply to vary the order so as to extend the three-year period if necessary, but you would have to do so before the due date expires.

7.2.5   Obeying the court's orders

Ensuring payments for maintenance is a recurring problem. It is estimated that in about half the cases, payments are not made without enforcement procedures. These can include:

- attachment of earnings orders (where the employer pays the ex-spouse directly out of earnings)
- a court order that a standing order be set up

or as a last resort

- a summons under the Debtor's Act which could involve the defaulter going to prison.

7.2.6   Disposal of assets

Of course some people would rather dispose of their assets altogether than have to hand them over to an estranged husband or wife. Thus, the courts also have the power under the Matrimonial Causes Act to ensure that a spouse does not transfer his or her property to someone else or shift it outside the country in order to defeat a claim for matrimonial relief.

The courts' powers to prevent a disposal of assets can be used either:

- pre-emptively
  or
- after the disposal has taken place

provided that the the question of intention, i.e a deliberate act to thwart the court's orders, can be shown.

7.2.6(a)   Pre-emptive measures

☞   *You learn that your wife intends to set up an elaborate trust fund which would in effect strip her of all her assets prior to your divorce. You wonder what you can do?*

You can ask the court for an injunction to freeze her assets pending settlement.

7.2.6(b)   Setting aside transactions which have already taken place

The court can order that a transaction be set aside after it has taken place provided a petitioner can show:

a) that it would directly affect the financial relief he or she might expect, and
b) the intention behind the transaction was to diminish the assets available for possible distribution.

☞   *Your ex-husband has set up an offshore bank account and has transferred all his existing bank balances into the new account.*

If you can show that you would be entitled to financial provision from these particular funds or that the setting up of the accounts would otherwise affect what you were entitled to receive, you could ask for the transaction to be set aside. Of course, the more complicated the transaction – such as one that involved an offshore base – the more difficult it may be to enforce any order you might obtain from the court.

8   THE FAMILY HOME

This is usually the family's greatest asset in financial terms. Even more important, it provides a roof over the family's head. Children's interests as we have seen, generally take priority. So a decision on who will have the family home – whether in the short or long term – must always take account of children's needs.

These orders must not be viewed in isolation from questions of financial relief dealt with above. For example, a court can reduce or terminate monthly payments to make up for the capital involved in a transfer of the matrimonial home from one spouse to another.

A necessary precaution: a spouse in divorce proceedings should take immediate steps to protect his or her rights of occupation. Do seek legal advice on this.

8.1   The Family Law Act 1996 and matrimonial home rights

For many years now, a spouse has been able to occupy the family home and register this right as a land charge. Under the Family Law Act 1996, these rights are called 'matrimonial home rights'. In effect, these rights mean that whether or not the spouse has any title to the property, he or she nonetheless has a right not to be evicted or excluded from the house except with leave of the court. It also means that these rights can bind third parties (see also chapter on *Buying and Selling your Home*, section 1.2.3).

For example, your husband owns the matrimonial home. He borrows money on it from a moneylender. Provided your right has been registered, you cannot be evicted from the house, if your husband defaults on his debt, unless there is a court order to that effect.

On the basis of matrimonial home rights, too, the court can make an indefinite occupation order (see section 9.2 below).

Do take careful note:

* These rights do not apply to any home e.g. a home which has not been and was not intended by the spouses to be the matrimonial home. (However, in relation to asset-splitting on divorce, other property will be considered in relation to redistribution, see above section 6.2).
* Matrimonial home rights do not apply to cohabitees.
* The procedures for registering a notice in respect of matrimonial home rights was laid down by a set of rules in 1997 – the Land Registration (Matrimonial Home Rights) Rules. It is outside the scope of this book to provide details of the procedure.

8.2   Who owns the family home?

To answer this question, one must look at the title deeds. Usually property is registered in the names of both husband and wife so that they own it jointly; otherwise it will be registered in the name of one of the spouses only.

Nevertheless, whoever owns it, the court can make an order with regard to the matrimonial home. In an endeavour to ensure fairness to the family as a whole, it can transfer the entire property to a spouse, particularly a mother with young children, usually on certain stringent conditions. The court can order an outright sale, or it can postpone a sale so that the capital is tied up for years (see section 8.2.2 below).

8.2.1   Who can live in it?

In general, rights of occupation are registered as a notice in the Land Registry or as a land charge on the title deeds to property. This gives a right of occupation in law under the Family Law Act 1996 irrespective of ownership.

The court will then deal with the question of the long-term disposition of the matrimonial home.

8.2.2   The orders available to the court

As we are all too well aware, a house in today's market is a fluctuating asset. This makes long-term solutions by the court, as much as by the parties themselves, particularly difficult.

The court, as we know, has the widest discretion in sorting out the assets of the spouses.

With regard to the family home, there are usually three types of order:

- immediate sale and division of proceeds
- transfer of house into the sole name of one spouse
- postponement of the sale of the house till a later stage.

8.2.2(a) Postponement of sale until children grow up

The courts can order that the matrimonial home should be occupied by the spouse who has the children living with him or her. It could then be sold when the youngest child turns 17.

While this was at one time seen as a satisfactory solution to housing needs it is now realised that it can be a recipe for problems at a later stage.

☞ *Your wife was granted an order by the court that she should remain in the house after divorce until the youngest child was 17. The children were then 12, 9 and 7. Ten years have passed and your youngest child is now about to leave home. You are in a quandary as the house has fallen into considerable disrepair over the past three years, and your ex-wife is in her mid-fifties and depressed at the prospect of the last of her children leaving home. She also does not wish to move. On the other hand, you need some capital at this stage of your life. Can she ask the court to vary the order?*

It would be helpful if you could work out some arrangement between you on the best way of dealing with the problem of the house. Do ensure that you each take legal and accountancy advice.

8.2.2(b) Postponement of sale until wife's circumstances change

There is another type of order which the courts use in postponing the sale of the house on divorce proceedings. One spouse can have the use of the home (with the children) until such a time as he or she remarries, cohabits with someone else, or dies – whichever is the soonest. Then it must be sold and the proceeds divided up.

Again, this solution may create as many problems as it solves.

☞ *Your husband divorced you. You are presently living in the home with your two small children of the marriage. The court has ordered that you are to live there until you remarry or cohabit with someone else. The children are receiving maintenance from your ex-husband. You have recently met another man and have formed a deep relationship with him. He is very attached to the children and you want him to move in with you. You cannot move into his accommodation as it is unsuitable for a family. You are fearful of losing either your boyfriend or your home. You would like some advice.*

Perhaps you and your boyfriend could raise the capital to buy out your ex-husband's share of the home. Alternatively, you may be able to ask the court to vary the order to work out some compensatory arrangement for his share of the capital asset.

Remember: the court will certainly take into account the pooling of resources on your cohabitation although it has no actual power to make an adjustment to your partner's finances or to order him to contribute capital towards any buy-out.

8.3 Orders for sale

The court has the power to order the sale of property to meet the obligations of its orders listed above.

8.4 Rented accommodation

A tenancy can be just as much a property right as outright home ownership.

Under the matrimonial legislation, the spouse of a secure tenant has rights of occupation as long as the marriage subsists. However, the divorce law also allows for a transfer of the tenancy from one spouse to another on a divorce. The court can transfer a contractual tenancy even where there is a covenant prohibiting assignment (see also chapter on *Landlords and their Tenants*).

Do take note: the 1996 Family Law Act made important changes with regard to tenancies for an unmarried couple and the courts can order a transfer of tenancy in the cases of cohabitees too.

The following tenancies can be transferred:

- a protected tenancy or statutory tenancy within the Rent Act 1977
- a secure tenancy under the Housing Act 1985
- an assured tenancy within the Housing Act 1988
- an introductory tenancy within the Housing Act 1996.

☞   *For several years your partner has rented a pied-à-terre in London where he stays on the days when he works there. For the rest of the time, the two of you live in accommodation in Reading. You are in the process of leaving him and are looking for a job in the City. You would like to know whether you can ask the court for an order transferring the tenancy of the London flat to yourself.*

The answer is 'no'.

For a court order, the property must be the matrimonial home in the case of spouses or must be the home in which you and your partner lived together as husband and wife.

Warning note: this area of law is extremely complex. If there is any change in your married circumstances which could jeopardise your position in a rented house or flat, do seek proper advice.

9   DOMESTIC VIOLENCE

9.1   Unsatisfactory state of the law

Unfortunately, the laws governing the protection of victims of violence in domestic disputes were seen as most unsatisfactory and extremely complicated. Among other matters, they turned on:

- whether a couple was married or not, and
- which jurisdiction was invoked i.e. whether a person turned to a magistrates' court or a county court for assistance.

The Family Law Act 1996 contained provisions to make the law on domestic violence more uniform and to streamline procedures. New provisions became immediately effective. They include a right to apply to court for an order to occupy the family home, which applies to spouses and also to cohabitees in certain circumstances. The Act also provides for non-molestation orders which can be made available to children and others provided they satisfy the court of the need for such an order (see 9.3 below). These two main orders are available in all courts which deal with family proceedings.

Thus the Family Law Act 1996, Part IV, was intended to provide a single set of remedies to deal with domestic violence, to replace the existing ones, with the aim of achieving better protection for its victims. Primarily the remedies comprise two orders: occupation orders and non-molestation orders (see further section 9.3 below). However, because of the seriousness of the issues involved and the difficulties of dealing with domestic violence (which is both secretive and widespread), another review of present legislation is presently under way.

Outside the confines of the legislation, strenuous endeavours are also being made by targeted police action, other government agencies, and social and volunteer workers to deal with the problem of domestic violence.

For a list of organisations to turn to in case of need, see DIRECTORY on page 109.

9.2   Occupation orders

When the court issues an occupation order, it is effectively deciding who is allowed to occupy the family home. It can also order the other party to leave the property altogether and even its vicinity. If, for example, a couple live in a block of flats, and provided the circumstances justified such a step, one of them could be ordered not only to leave the flat but to be excluded from a 'defined area' in which the flat is situated.

9.2.1   Who can apply?

Those entitled to apply include spouses and ex-spouses, partners and ex-partners.

1) You can apply for an occupation order if you already are entitled to occupy the property (in legal terms, you have beneficial rights in the property such as co-ownership) or have registered you matrimonial home rights (see section 8 above) in the property:

You can also apply against anyone who is an 'associated person': an associated person can include not only your ex-spouse or ex-partner but can extend further to include relatives.

☞   *You and your husband are in the process of divorce. He has become abusive and threatening. You have been living in the matrimonial home which you jointly own and you have registered your rights in it. Your husband's 10-year-old son, by his first marriage, lives in the house as well as your mother-in-law who has taken sides against you. You would like to have an occupation order which would exclude them from the house.*

When you apply for an occupation order, the court will consider all the circumstances of the case, including:

- the housing needs and resources of all the parties and their children
- their financial resources
- the likely effect of an order on your and your husband's health, safety and well being and that of his child
- the conduct of the parties.

The court will then operate a 'balance of harm' test and endeavour to ascertain whether you, as the applicant for the order, or your husband and his family (the 'associated persons') against whom the order is sought, would suffer greater harm if the order is (or is not) made. The court must make an order if the balance of harm tilts in your favour.

The court will weigh carefully the competing needs of you yourself, your husband, your stepson and your mother-in-law.

Do note: the court's powers in such cases are very wide. It can decide your interest in the house and that of your husband. It can make an order that you can occupy some or all of the house and the terms on which that occupation can take place, e.g. in relation to outgoings. It can also determine the length of time for which the order should last.

On the other hand, the courts have seen the power to exclude a party from his or her own home as 'draconian' and only to be used in exceptional circumstances.

2) You can apply for an order if you do not have any rights of occupation. If you are a former spouse, and have no rights to occupy, in addition to the considerations outlined above, the court will also consider the length of time since you ceased to live together; the length of time since there was a divorce; and whether there are any current proceedings between the parties.

3) If you are a partner or former partner with no existing right to occupy the property, you can apply for an occupation order.

☞   *You moved into your partner's house with two young children. You are now pregnant and your partner says that he wants you to leave. You have no rights in the house but also have nowhere to go. You want to know whether you can apply for an occupation order.*

Where you have no rights of occupation and were not married, the court will not only consider the factors above, but additional factors such as:

- the nature of your relationship – including the fact that you have not given each other the commitment involved in marriage
- whether there are children involved and whether you have any children together with your partner
- the length of time which you have been together
- the existence of any current legal proceedings, e.g. for financial relief.

The court will then go on to consider the 'balance of harm', but is not under a duty to make an order. If it does make an order in your favour, it can only be for six months and can be renewed only once more.

Note of warning: even this brief analysis of the provisions of the Family Law Act 1996 indicates the complexity of the law so, in all cases of need, do seek informed help and advice.

9.2.2   Tenancies

Under the Housing Act 1996, charitable housing trusts and other social landlords can commence actions for possession to assured and shorthold tenancies where a partner, or a member of his or her family, has left the property and is unlikely to return, because of violence or threats of violence from the other partner.

9.3   Non-molestation orders

A non-molestation order prevents one person from molesting another or a relevant child. It can prohibit molestation in general, or particular behaviour, e.g. pestering by abusive letters.

A wide range of people can apply – including not only spouses but cohabitees and others who live in the same household; engaged or formerly engaged couples; and relatives. So for example, if your daughter separates from her husband and returns to your home, you too would be entitled to ask the court for an order if the husband's behaviour amounted to molestation. The order can extend to a defined vicinity.

The phrase 'those who live in the same household' does not include lodgers, tenants or employees. It also would not include, for example, an ex-spouse who started on a course of conduct which amounts to molestation.

☞ *Your partner divorced his wife many years ago and lived alone thereafter. You met him at a conference recently and he has now moved into your flat. His ex-wife has started to ring you in the middle of the night and to make pestering calls while you are at work.*

You would not be able to invoke the non-molestation regime in such a case. The orders above apply only to persons who are, or have been, in a relationship. Further molestation under the Family Law Act 1996 only applies to those who have lived in the same household so in your case, the conduct of which you complain is clearly excluded from the scope of a non-molestation order.

The Protection from Harassment Act 1997 was passed to protect against so-called 'stalking'. For the purposes of the Act, there must be a course of conduct which amounts to harassment. In general, the Act's purpose was directed against strangers who stalk and put their victim in fear. While undoubtedly the Act has been invoked in domestic disputes that was not the intention behind the legislation.

☞ *You are a successful disc jockey at a club. One of your female fans has been pestering you. Of late, she has been seen lurking outside your front door. She has also been writing letters which you find very disturbing as the letters contain veiled threats against you and the members of your family. You would like to take action before her behaviour gets out of hand.*

Although the term 'harassment' itself is not defined, victims of an obsessive admirer (or hater) need to show that the stalker has pursued a course of conduct that causes alarm or distress.

9.4   Protection of children

Until the Family Law Act was passed, when someone was suspected of abusing a child in the family home an emergency protection order or care order was made under the Children Act 1989 (see the chapter *Children (Part 2)*), to remove the child for his or her protection, with all the upheaval that entailed. Now, the provisions of the Family Law Act amend the Children Act to enable the court to place an exclusion order on the person suspected of abuse so that it is he or she who will be removed from the home – and not the child.

9.5   Powers of arrest

The court has powers to attach a power of arrest to an occupation or non-molestation order where there is violence or the threat of violence. The police will then have power to arrest if the order is breached. This power gives significant added force to the orders under the Family Law Act to provide proper protection for victims of domestic violence.

9.6   Undertakings

☞ *Your ex-partner has sought a non-molestation order against you because you have written daily letters begging her to return to you. You do not intend to harm either her or your child but have been trying to prevail upon her. Lately you have been appearing regularly on the doorstep of your former home.*

When a non-molestation order is applied for, you can give the court an undertaking not to pursue the course of conduct which your ex-partner finds upsetting, e.g. you can undertake not to go within a certain distance of your house.

No power of arrest can be attached to an undertaking.

9.7   Community Legal Services Funding

In order to get community legal services funding [formerly legal aid], you would have to satisfy the capital and income tests, as well as the 'merit' test, i.e. that your case, on the face of it, is worth pursuing (see the chapter on *The Legal System*, sections 3.1 and 3.2, as well as above, section 3.1.2). Priority is given to cases which involve domestic violence.

9.8   Possession procedures

Under the Housing Act 1996, section 149, there is a new ground for possession of rented property where one partner of a couple, or a member of the partner's family, has left the property because of violence or threats of violence from the other partner. This ground does not apply to private landlords (see also the chapter on *Landlords and their Tenants*).

10   WHEN COHABITEES SPLIT UP

Despite the numbers of cohabiting couples, their status in law differs fundamentally from that of married couples (see also the chapter on *Setting up Home*).

The law of divorce reflects certain profound legal assumptions about the marital relationship – in particular, a duty to maintain the other spouse. This duty survives even breakdown of the marriage – hence the detailed provisions on ancillary relief (see section 6 above).

In cohabitation, on the other hand, no such assumptions are made. As a result the courts do not have the powers to deal with the family assets of a cohabiting couple who split up that they have when a married couple get divorced. In fact, of course, the situations of both couples may be identical in other ways: there may be children, there may be a deserted partner who needs somewhere to live. However, they are treated differently in law.

Do note: the Family Law Act 1996 contains provisions which strengthen the position of cohabitees.

10.1   Who owns the house?

The answer to this question is usually determined by the names on the title deeds.

In contrast to the situation in a divorce, when a cohabiting couple splits up the court has no statutory power to make a property transfer order – unless there are children involved. Thus as between the couple themselves, legal ownership of the property is the definitive factor when they split up (see the chapter on *Setting up Home*, section 5.1.3(b)).

In dealing with property matters, legal advice must always be sought.

10.1.1   Joint ownership

If the property is in joint names, the usual division is on a 50/50 basis. With regard to the position of a person with whom a child of the family is resident, however, see section 10.1.4 below.

10.1.2   Title deeds in one name only

What happens if a cohabitee whose name is not on the title deeds wants to claim part-ownership or some other interest in the home? The task is made very difficult; the law presumes that whosoever has his or her name on the deeds is the owner.

Doctrines have been developed in order to mitigate the rigour of the law but these would apply as much to two friends who share a flat or house as to a couple who might have been living together for years as man and wife.

A cohabiting partner who wants to claim, as of right, a share of a house which is in one name only must prove to the court's satisfaction:

a) that at the time the home was purchased there was an intention to benefit both parties
b) that the person making a claim also made a contribution to the purchase in money or money's worth
c) that he or she has lost out as a result of that action.

10.1.3   Who can live in the home?

There are no matrimonial home rights which you can register. This is in striking contrast to the position of a married spouse under the Family Law Act 1996.

However, property transfer orders can now be made for children under the Children Act 1989 (see section 10.1.4 below).

The court also has the power to make an occupation order in favour of a cohabitee but the duration of the period is limited and the court's considerations of the circumstances of the relationship are again extensive (see section 9.2 above).

For the position of a tenant, see section 8.4 above. For the position in case of domestic violence, see section 9.

10.1.4   Claims on behalf of children of cohabitees

Under the Children Act 1989, a parent can apply for a financial order for a child. The term 'parent' extends to parents who are not married to each other. There is a wide range of orders available including an order to make a lump sum or to transfer property. Thus an order can apply to a family home or to a local authority tenancy. The home – belonging to either parent – could be set up on trust for the parent with whom the child is living until the child's 18th birthday.

10.1.4(a) Home ownership

Thus, under the Children Act 1989, claims can be made on behalf of children for a property transfer against the other parent for the benefit of a child.

A court can make a transfer of property order which can directly benefit the children of the family. In effect, this would give an indirect benefit to the other partner as well. Thus an unmarried parent may have rights of occupation, for example, conferred on him or her with regard to the family home.

☞ *You and your boyfriend live in a house which belongs to him. You have had two children together. He now wants to end the relationship and bring his new girlfriend into the house. You and the children have nowhere to go.*

Under the Children Act, the court can make property orders. It could, for instance, depending on the circumstances and the view the court takes of them, determine that the house should be held in trust for the benefit of the children until they reach the age of 18.

10.1.4(b) Rented accommodation

In the case of local authority accommodation, a parent can apply for the transfer of the tenancy under the Children Act for the benefit of the child.

10.2   Maintenance

A cohabitee has no right to claim maintenance from his or her partner on separation. Obviously this too can lead to grave injustice when the couple may have been living as man and wife for many years and have brought up a family together.

10.3   Parent 'with care'

Maintenance must be paid for and on behalf of the children however. The question of applications for maintenance against an 'absent parent' under the Child Support Acts is dealt with in the chapter *Children (Part 1)* (sections 2.2.1 and 2.2.2). Maintenance for the child includes an element for the person with care of that child.

3 CHILDREN (Part 1)
A Parent's Rights and Duties

At first glance, it would seem that the law has little to do with the upbringing of a child. Parents, after all, are nature's protectors of their children and have their wellbeing most at heart. How can parents' responsibilities be defined in legal terms? And when would it be necessary to think in such terms?

In fact, as we shall see, the law intervenes from the first day of a child's life. Moreover, throughout childhood, the law endeavours to watch over the welfare of children at every turn. Children are regarded as vulnerable, open to exploitation, in need of education, and in need of protection from themselves and from others. Thus, as far as children's day-to-day lives are concerned, their activities are governed by a battery of legislation – not always appreciated by young persons themselves!

Only gradually does the law allow children to assume adult 'rights', according to age.

Thus, although we tend to think that a child 'becomes' an adult on his or her 18th birthday, growing up is a very complicated process as far as the law is concerned (see *The legal stages of growing up*, at the end of the chapter *Children (Part 2)* at page 107).

With regard to the role of parents, the law generally steps in when things go wrong. For example, parents have a legal duty to protect their child; if they fail to do so and neglect their child, other authorities will take charge.

In the sphere of children's welfare, the law has made strenuous efforts to move with the times. Along with legislation, a general awareness has developed that children too have 'rights'. Children's views are heeded now in the courts when possible. No longer is it just a matter of the courts or others in authority deciding what is 'best' for the child. See section 2.11 below.

The Human Rights Act 1998, which came into force in October 2000, has impinged on family law and children's rights generally, particularly as the provisions of the Act are directed towards public authorities such as local councils or the NHS (see also the chapter on *The Legal System*). The extent of the Act's impact will only become clear with time but should not be underestimated.

In this chapter we look at:

- parental responsibilities
- unmarried parents
- when parents split up.

1   PARENTAL RESPONSIBILITIES

Attitudes to parent–child relationships have changed. For many centuries the common law had assigned a legitimate child – for all legal purposes – to the father's sole authority. Now no longer has a married father absolute authority over his child. Parental responsibilities are shared equally between married father and mother (see section 1.2 below).

According to the Children Act 1989, parental responsibilities mean 'all the rights, duties, powers, responsibilities and authority which a parent has by law' in relation to a child and to the child's property.

Where the parents of a child are married to each other, all parental responsibilities are shared between the mother and the father. Even if they subsequently divorce, so that their child lives with only one parent, the other parent still has continuing responsibility for the child.

In the case of unmarried parents, the mother is entitled to all parental responsibilities in law unless the parents themselves or the courts decide that they should be shared between father and mother.

Until recently, the law spoke of 'parental rights' – now it refers to 'parental responsibilities'. This is more than a mere change of terms; it reflects a distinct shift in perception of the relationship between parent and child. The concept of 'rights over' your son or daughter is quite a different one from that of 'responsibility for' them.

Moreover, the views of children themselves are increasingly taken into account (see section 2.11 below).

1.1   Landmark legislation

1.1.1   The Children Act 1989

The Children Act 1989 was passed so that the law relating to children would be more in keeping with modern views. It was also intended to make uniform the multiplicity of laws governing the legal position of children. It was also hoped to ensure, as far as possible, that the courts' structure would be more 'family-friendly' (i.e. less adversarial) and that trained personnel would deal with issues involving children and the law.

The central assumptions of the Children Act are that:

- the welfare of children is the paramount and overriding factor in any decision which the courts take on their future
- children are entitled to the love and care of both parents, irrespective of whether both parents live at home with them or not
- delay in arrangements for children can have tragic consequences
- parents who separate should decide for themselves as far as possible – without the court's intervention – on the best arrangements for their children
- the courts should have a range of flexible orders at their disposal in dealing with children
- proceedings should be simplified in everyone's interest
- local authorities which deal with children at risk or in need must do so – as far as possible – in partnership with parents
- the courts should only intervene after deciding that intervention would be more beneficial for the child than non-intervention.

The success or failure of the Act depends – as it is intended to – on the parents involved just as much as on the courts, welfare officers, social workers, lawyers and judges. Criticisms of the workings of the Act since it was passed, over a decade ago, have focused on the fact that there is an over-emphasis on the need to keep families together. Thus even in situations where children are in need or at risk, parents' rights have prevailed, at times to the detriment of the children themselves.

The Act made sweeping and fundamental changes in both the private and public law aspect of child care.

1.1.2   The Child Support Act 1991

As we have seen in the chapter on *Divorce*, parents are liable to maintain their children while these are minors. In cases of broken homes, that liability was imposed by the courts of law although in practice the State often had to bear the cost of maintaining children of lone parents.

The Child Support Act 1991 was brought in to change the whole approach to child maintenance. The courts were no longer to act as the collectors of children's maintenance; that task was now to be given to a new body set up for the purpose, the Child Support Agency. It is run by the Department of Social Security with centres throughout the country. For further details see section 2.2 below.

1.1.3   Maintenance matters still dealt with by the courts

The following matters are outside the scope of the Child Support Acts:

a) maintenance for step-children
b) maintenance for children who are too old to be qualifying children (i.e. who are 19 or over and in education or training)

c) maintenance to be paid in addition to what has been assessed by the CSA

d) maintenance to meet related expenses of a child's education

e) expenses associated with caring for a disabled child; the court can make an order for this to supplement the CSA's assessment.

1.2   The nature of parental responsibilities

1.2.1   When do they begin?

In general parental responsibilities begin at birth.

A pregnant woman is not responsible in law to her unborn child for her lifestyle; in other words, even if harm were to come to the foetus from her behaviour, she cannot be prevented from smoking or drinking too much, or from taking drugs. However, if she has a car accident because, for example, she drives negligently, and her baby is born handicapped as a result, the child could bring an action against her. That would be the responsibility of the insurers.

A father cannot take steps to prevent the mother of his child from terminating her pregnancy.

☞   *Your wife is pregnant but says that she does not want the child. She feels that she has good, legal grounds for an abortion. You are desperately keen to have the child and wish to prevent any harm coming to it. What can you do?*

You would not be able to stop the abortion in this case provided your wife could fulfil the legal/medical grounds for terminating her pregnancy; nor can an unmarried man stop his girlfriend from proceeding with an abortion.

1.2.2   Notice of birth

A notice of every birth must be given by a person in attendance at the birth, such as doctor or midwife, to the district Medical Officer of Health within 36 hours.

1.3   Registering the birth

The birth of every child must be registered within 42 days of birth with the Registrar of Births and Deaths of the sub-district in which the birth took place.

From October 2002 babies receive an NHS number when their birth is registered. The number, which is 10 digits long, is printed on to birth notification notices produced by the Child Health unit for the area where baby is born. Midwives are responsible for requesting numbers for babies they have just delivered.

The government announced new proposals in January 2002 on ways to register births, e.g. via the Internet, over the phone, or in person at any Register Office. The intention is to modernise the service and bring benefit to the community e.g. to those living in rural areas. The proposals also cover new services such as 'baby naming' (a non-religious celebration of the birth of a child). New parents will also be given information on support and advisory services relating to births. The changes are expected to be in place by the end of 2004 (see *Civil Registration: Vital Change* at *www.statistics.gov.uk/registration*).

1.3.1   Married parents

Where parents are married, it is usually the father or mother who registers the birth. A leaflet (Form 362) is issued to the mother in hospital.

The information to be supplied to the Registrar includes:

• the date and the place of baby's birth
• the sex of the child
• the baby's name.

Arrangements can be made to register a child even if you are no longer in the district in which the birth took place.

☞   *You leave the district where your baby was born. Do you need to go back to it in order to register the birth?*

The answer is 'no'. You need not return to the district in person. You could go to any registrar of births in England and Wales to give details. The mother or father, as well as the registrar, must sign a declaration. This is then sent to the registrar of the sub-district where the birth took place. However, there is still a legal duty to register the birth within 42 days.

1.3.2   Unmarried parents

In 2001, over a quarter of million children were born to unmarried parents; they account for 40% of live births in the UK.

Where fathers and mothers are not married to each other, the mother has the sole duty and power to register their child's names.

If the father wishes his name to appear on the birth certificate, then the procedures vary and either:

a) the father and mother must attend together at the Registrar's office;

or

b) if the father cannot attend, he must make a statutory declaration of paternity (see also 1.3.4 below). This a pro-forma form which must be completed in the presence of a solicitor and must be produced to the Registrar. The mother must make her own declaration that he is the father;

or

c) if the father attends the office, the mother can make a statutory declaration, also on a pro-forma form and completed in a solicitor's presence, acknowledging the father's paternity. The father must give this declaration to the Registrar. He must then make his own declaration;

or

d) where mother and father have entered into a Parental Responsibility Agreement (see section 2.13.1(a) below) or there is an appropriate court order granting him parental responsibility, this must be produced to the Registrar.

Do note: there is no obligation for an unmarried mother to register the father's name if she does not wish to. That part of the register can be left blank.

☞   *You fell pregnant and your boyfriend left you. You have since given birth to a little girl. You do not wish to include any details of her father on the birth certificate.*

No details need be given of the unmarried father if the mother so wishes. (For the father's on-going liability to support the child, see below section 2.2.)

If, however, circumstances change, and there is a reconciliation between you and your boyfriend, it will be possible to apply for a form for the re-registration of your daughter to include her father's details. You must apply on form GRO 185 (see immediately below).

Although there is no time limit for re-registration, parents are advised that it is in their best interest to re-register as soon as they can.

1.3.3   Re-registration

By re-registering you can add the natural father's details to a new record of your child's birth. The new record will then take the place of the original entry in the register, and a new birth certificate can be issued (see section 1.3.6 below).

Do note: future birth certificates are then issued from the new record.

Either the mother or father, or both, can apply where:

• the child was born in England or Wales
• the parents were not married to each other at the date of the birth and since that date have not married each other
• the existing registration does not show the father's details.

You and the father must give information jointly for the new entry at the register office for the district in which your child was born.

If you cannot attend together then one of you must produce either a statutory declaration of paternity (see immediately below) or a parental responsibility agreement or a court order.

You can change the child's forename within 12 months of the original birth registration. If you wish to change your child's surname, you must apply to the Registrar (see also section 1.3.8 below). For further information, you can telephone the Re-registration section on 0151 471 4806.

1.3.4   Father's declaration of paternity

As we have seen above, special rules apply if the unmarried father cannot be present to register the birth.

☞   *Your boyfriend is a serviceman who is about to be sent abroad shortly before you are to give birth to his child. It is unlikely therefore that he will be able to be present to sign the register with you. Both of you are very concerned that his name should appear on the register. What can you do?*

An acknowledgment of paternity cannot be made until the birth has taken place. Your boyfriend must sign a special statutory declaration of paternity (the form is available from the local registry office) and his signature can be witnessed by his senior officer. If on the other hand, he is in the UK, he must sign the form and have it witnessed by a solicitor, JP, or notary public. For details on the procedure for obtaining a Parental Responsibility Agreement, see section 2.13.1(a) below.

1.3.5   Parents subsequently marrying

Where a child is born to parents who are not married to each other, but who subsequently marry, they should let the Registrar have the necessary information with a view to obtaining the re-registration of the birth of that child. The form to be used is LA1.

☞   *When your daughter was born, you were not married to her father because he was married to another woman at the time. Your personal details on the birth certificate appear under your maiden name, in which your daughter was also registered. Since then your boyfriend has divorced his wife and you intend to marry each other soon. You would both like to alter the birth certificate so that you and your daughter are registered in her father's name.*

Once you are married to the father of your child, you can apply to have the birth re-registered in your married name. You would have to produce her original birth certificate, your marriage certificate, the re-registration form (LA1), plus any additional documentation that may be required for authorisation, to the Registrar General.

Your daughter's surname may also be altered to that of her father but application will have to be made to the Registrar (see section 1.3.3 above).

1.3.6   Changes for the future

The Government announced in 1998 their intention to change the law so that unmarried fathers signing the birth certificate jointly with the mother would acquire parental responsibility without further formality. The change will not be retrospective. The Children and Adoption Act 2002 is due to come into force in 2004. The Act will change the law so that an unmarried father will acquire parental responsibility where he and the mother register the birth of their child together. It will still be possible for unmarried fathers to make a parental responsibility agreement or apply for a parental responsibility order as now.

1.3.7   Issue of birth certificate

After the birth has been registered, a short birth certificate is issued free of charge. It would suffice for most purposes (e.g. applying for a passport) but a full birth certificate, containing all the details of the register entry, is also available. This can be purchased at the time of registration or at any time afterwards, as can copies of the short birth certificate.

1.3.8   Naming a child

Parents give the child both surname and forename, the latter usually for life. The custom, although not the law, in the case of married parents, is that the child is given the father's surname. The names are registered at the time of the registration of the baby's birth. If the parents are married, both their names must be registered. (For the status of an unmarried mother with regard to registration, see above, section 1.3.2.)

Where the parents are not married, the mother can give the child any first name and any surname she wishes.

☞ *You are expecting a baby soon and have broken up with your former boyfriend, the baby's father. He has denied that the child is his and does not want the child to be given his name. You are hoping for a reconciliation and would like the child to have his father's surname, perhaps as a last name or perhaps as a middle name. Can you do that without your former boyfriend's consent?*

Yes, you have complete freedom to choose your child's forename, middle name(s) and surname.

However, you cannot fill in the box on the registration form citing your former boyfriend as the child's father without his consent.

If the reconciliation takes place, then the father's details can be entered by the appropriate re-registration procedures (see section 1.3.3 above).

1.3.8(a) Can you change a child's name?

Changing a name on a birth certificate:

a) *Forename:* if you wish to change your child's forename, this can be done within 12 months of the original registration, either on production of a baptismal certificate under the new name or on a form available from the registrar.

b) *Re-registration:* Where a child is born to parents who are not married to each other, but who subsequently marry, they should then inform the Registrar with a view to obtaining the re-registration of the birth of that child. The child may then acquire the father's name unless there are reasons not to, e.g. a court order forbidding the change of name.

c) *Consent:* If, in the case of married parents, the child is given the father's surname, the mother cannot apply to have the child registered under her name unless with the father's consent. Over the years, the courts came to feel that a unilateral change of a child's name, for example to the name of a step-parent, was a serious matter. Both the legislation and the decisions of the courts reflect this view.

Under the Children Act 1989, a child's name cannot be changed without the consent of persons who have parental responsibility for the child – usually both mother and father.

If one of the persons with parental responsibility withholds consent, application will have to be made to court to give its consent. The court will scrutinise such an application very carefully indeed to see if it is in the child's best interests (see section 3 below on Orders available to the court).

☞ *You divorced your husband in December 1998 when your little girl was three and she came to live with you under a residence order from the court. The child has very regular contact with her father. You recently remarried and changed your name to that of your second husband. You are now expecting another baby. You would like your daughter to have the same surname as yourself as you think it will be easier for her to integrate into her new family. Can you do so at will?*

Under the Children Act, as we have seen, you cannot change your daughter's surname to that of your second husband without her father's consent or consent of the court. That was an automatic condition attached to the fact that the court allowed her to live with you under the residence order. You thus have two choices. You could discuss it with her father and seek to persuade him that it is in your daughter's best interest to have the same name as her half-brother or sister. You can assure him that you do not wish to take this step in order to sever the relationship or weaken the links between him and his child.

If you cannot persuade him, you could apply to court for permission for the name change but you may find it difficult to persuade a judge that you have a sufficiently strong case.

However, in very exceptional circumstances the courts have agreed to change a child's surname even without the consent of one of the parents.

☞ *Your child was born when you were living happily with her father, and you registered his name as her surname. Later you split up and the feeling between you is very bitter. You wish to change her surname so that it is the same as yours, but your ex-boyfriend refuses to give his consent. What can you do?*

The courts have said that there have to be very good reasons to allow a change of surname without the permission of both parents. In one case the court did allow the change against the father's wishes: in that case he was a notorious criminal serving a very long sentence, and the court ruled that there was a real risk of the child, as he grew up, identifying with a criminal underclass because he had his father's surname.

Each case is looked at individually, and only in exceptional cases will the courts allow a child's surname to be changed in the absence of agreement by both parents.

Reasons given for changing or seeking to change a child's name based on the fact that the name should be the same as the parent making an application do not generally carry much weight with a court. In particular, where parents were once married to each other, the fact of the marriage is considered important and there would have to be strong grounds to change from the father's surname once your child had been registered with it.

In one case, the Court of Appeal held that adolescent children should keep their father's name though they wished to use their stepfather's name (see also section 2.11 below).

A court will take into account many factors including those which could arise in the future as well as the present. In all cases the welfare of the child is the paramount consideration.

2 OTHER RESPONSIBILITIES

Notifying the authorities of the birth of your child, and registering his or her birth with the names you have chosen, are the very first formal steps to be taken. Other parental responsibilities are outlined below.

2.1 Duty to protect

There is a duty to protect a child from harm. This duty is enforced with criminal sanctions. A child is not to be ill-treated, neglected or abandoned, under the Children Act 1933. A parent is guilty of neglect if he or she fails to provide a child with adequate food, clothing, medical aid and lodging.

Note: this law is now over 70-years-old; there are calls to reform it.

The 'home alone' case of a mother who left her 2-year-old daughter alone when she went to work is an extreme example of neglect under this heading. (See also *Children (Part 2)*, section 5.1.3).

It is also a criminal offence for anyone over the age of 16 to allow a young child in a room with an unguarded open fire or any other heating appliance liable to cause injury and an injury ensues.

2.1.1 Duty on others who care for a child

If someone over the age of 16 wilfully neglects, assaults, ill-treats or abandons a child in his or her care, that too is a criminal offence.

This does not mean, however, that a young person under the age of 16 may not look after a child.

☞ *You have asked friends and neighbours to recommend a babysitter. You have received the recommendation of a 14-year-old schoolgirl who seems level-headed and sensible. You have been told that no person under the age of 16 is allowed to baby-sit by law. Is that correct?*

The answer is 'no'. There is no specific age at which a person may be left alone in charge of a child. The law specifies, however, that if anyone over the age of 16, who has a child in his or her charge, wilfully neglects the child, that person is guilty of a criminal offence.

Thus a person under 16 cannot be held responsible for anything that happens to a child left in his or her care. For that reason, the NSPCC advises that parents should ensure that only over-16s should baby-sit.

2.1.2 Looking after children for profit

Many working parents leave their children with others to care for them. As far as possible, the law tries to ensure that childminders and those who run nursery schools are fit and proper people to take care of children. Anyone who looks after more than one child, for profit, for more than two hours per day, must be registered with OFSTED who have a duty to inspect and ensure that the person is suitable for such employment. A list of childminders registered with OFSTED is maintained by every local authority and is available for your area on request.

In one case a mother left her baby with a registered childminder. The baby suffered severe injury at the hands of the minder. The local authority officer had assured her that it was safe to leave her child with the minder although he was aware that there had been an earlier incident when another baby had suffered injury in the same woman's care. The court ruled that the local authority was liable to the mother because of its negligent assurances that her child would be safe. However, merely putting a name on a register did not – of itself – carry any assurances as to safe care.

Reforms have been put in place for the regulation system of childminders by transferring the responsibility to a new register of early-years child care inspectors under the Care Standards Act 2000. From September 2001 OFSTED has become responsible for the registration of childminding and day care in England. People wishing to register as a childminder should telephone OFSTED on 0845 601 4771. Parents seeking childcare should visit *www.childcarelink.gov.uk.*

ChildcareLink has details of local Children's Information Services on 08000 960296.

Do note: although the Department of Health issued guidelines on smacking and childminders some years ago, many local authorities have a 'no-smacking' policy in place for their registered childminders.

☞   *You prefer not to send your nine-month old baby to a childminder now that your maternity leave has expired and you are returning to work. You would prefer to employ a live-in nanny.*

Be vigilant: nannies are the only childcarers not registered and regulated and therefore parents who wish to employ a nanny must make checks themselves, e.g. to ensure that their prospective nanny has no previous criminal convictions, points on her driving licence etc. Even if you employ a nanny through a reputable recruitment agency, you are also advised to check thoroughly certificates, references, and passport.

For useful guidelines on employing a nanny and the checks to ensure your child will be safe in his or her care, contact the Professional Association of Nursery Nurses (PANN) at *www.pann.pat.org.uk.*

2.2   Duty to maintain

The duty to maintain children does not depend upon the marital status of the parents. At the very least, a child must be fed, housed and clothed. This duty applies whether parents are married, whether they have been married and are now divorced, or whether they have never been married at all.

The Child Support legislation was introduced to provide maintenance for children with 'absent parents'. It stipulates how maintenance is to be assessed and also allows for appeals against assessment. Even if an unmarried father has no parental responsibility for his child, he still has a legal duty to maintain the child.

2.2.1   The Child Support Act 1991

Under the Child Support Act 1991, each parent of a 'qualifying child' is responsible for maintaining him or her.

(a) The 'qualifying child'

A child qualifies for maintenance under the Child Support Act if one of its parents does not live at home. In other words he or she has an absent parent.

(b) The absent parent

An 'absent parent' is the one who does not live with the child at home. The status of an absent parent does not depend on whether the parents are married.

(c) The person with care

The term applies to the person who has the daily care of the child.

Note: although the absent parent is usually the father and the person with care is usually the mother, this need not always be the case.

(d) Ambit of the Act

If a parent with care of the child of a marriage or partnership which has broken down, claims benefit, then the Benefits Agency will automatically inform the CSA.

However, if parents split up and no benefits are being claimed, then it is at either parent's discretion to notify the CSA.

Note: the Act applies where both parents are normally resident in the UK. The courts will deal with cases where an absent parent or a person with care lives abroad. (For other matters still dealt with by the courts, see section 1.1.3 above.)

(e) How the assessment is made

Lone parents on social security benefits are sent an application form automatically. They have to fill in the form and, in particular, supply information so that an absent parent can be identified and traced. Refusal to supply the information will have to be justified by showing good reason – such as fear of violence.

Figures from the Child Support Agency show that 90 per cent of parents who apply to the CSA provide details of the non-resident parent.

A child support officer is entrusted with the task of making the assessment.

(f) How the assessment is calculated

The assessment is calculated according to a formula which takes into account:

- the maintenance needed for the children
- the income available to each parent after their own personal expenses have been set off against their net income
- the assessable income then left after the set-off. It is from that assessable income that the maintenance requirement is taken.

(g) Element of maintenance for carer

The assessment includes an amount for the person who has care of the child based on income support rates. This particular provision has caused a great deal of resentment as it is seen as an 'adult' maintenance payment.

(h) Appeals

Periodic reviews are built in to the Act based on fresh information from the person with care or from the absent parent. There can also be a review after a change of circumstances. If dissatisfied with a decision, an absent parent can apply for a review to a different child support officer.

There is a basic right of appeal to a Child Support Appeal Tribunal. There are 50 appeal tribunals throughout the country.

(i) Criticism of the Act

The Act evoked a great deal of public outcry. The application of the formula was seen as too rigid.

The particular charges against the Act were:

- that long-standing agreements between ex-partners were being overturned
- that fathers who started second families, bought second homes etc., were finding themselves unable to finance commitments made before the Act came into force
- that caring fathers were being penalised as 'soft targets' while feckless fathers, who are more difficult to track down, were not being dealt with.

2.2.2   The Child Support Act 1995

This Act was intended to:

- remedy certain criticism of the original Act
- provide for a more flexible interpretation of it
- give greater discretion to those administering the formula for assessing maintenance.

Under the 1991 Act no discretion was available and the formula was rigidly applied. To achieve these goals, the 1995 Act introduces the concept of a 'departure direction'.

2.2.2(a) Departure direction

This enables either the person with care or the absent parent to apply to the Secretary of State for a 'departure direction'. The applicant must show that it is 'just and equitable' to give the departure direction, which can lead to an increase or decrease in the amount of child support maintenance.

The direction will be given in three situations:

a) where the applicant has 'special expenses' which could not have been taken into account when the original assessment was made
b) where there is a court order or agreement transferring property as a result of which maintenance payable for children is less
c) where a parent artificially reduces his or her income.

Note: the Act was intended to meet the criticisms levelled at the 1991 Act, but it added yet another layer of bureaucratic complexity to the workings of the scheme, and so has itself come under criticism. It is now intended that child maintenance should be calculated according to a fixed percentage of disposable or net income (see below, section 2.2.3).

2.2.2(b) Guidelines to a departure direction

'Special expenses' include expenses of travelling to work; costs of maintaining contact; costs of supporting another child in a new family; debts incurred in the previous relationship.

Note: these guidelines and examples are not intended to be exhaustive.

With regard to transfers of capital assets, the Act is yet another attempt to deal with the question of the transfer of the family home in settlement of all financial claims including child maintenance. These settlements will be examined in a departure direction to establish whether the effect of the transfer has been 'properly reflected' in the current assessment.

Remember: if you are refused a departure direction, you can appeal to a child support appeal tribunal.

2.2.3 Changes in the future

(a) Present failings in the system

According to the Department for Work and Pensions, many parents are still not fulfilling their responsibilities. It is estimated that about one million children should benefit from the child support system while only about a quarter of that figure are receiving maintenance payments. And of those who do receive regular maintenance, about 60 per cent are not receiving the full amount assessed for them.

Further, about 90 per cent of staff time is used in working out the assessments according to the formula, which leaves only 10 per cent of resources available to track down parents who are failing to keep up with their payments.

(b) Introduction of a new system under the Child Support, Pensions and Social Security Act 2000

Because of the complexity and the time involved in working out the formula, a new system of assessing child support is to be gradually phased in. This will involve a flat levy on net income, i.e. after deduction of tax and national insurance etc., as follows: 15 per cent for one child; 20 per cent for two children; and 25 per cent for three children. Lower rates will apply where there is a second family to support, and there will be a sliding scale for those on lower incomes. At the time of writing, it is expected that this system will begin during the summer of 2003.

Fines will be introduced for anyone who refuses to provide information to the CSA, or who supplies false information. Other sanctions are also being looked at, e.g. withdrawal of driving licences.

In light of past experience there is understandable concern as to whether the introduction of a simplified system will necessarily lead to one which is also fairer and therefore more acceptable.

Do note: new cases will be assessed under this system from summer 2003; existing cases will transfer at a later date.

2.3   Keeping discipline

Parents generally insist on certain behaviour from their children although in some families discipline will be much stricter than in others. It is important to note in this context how much society as a whole has moved away from accepting corporal punishment as the answer to a recalcitrant child.

☞   *You have recently remarried and there is a running conflict between your teenage daughter and her stepfather. He has lost his temper with her frequently and has lately begun to hit her too. She states that she will not be punished or hurt in this way and is going to complain to the police.*

If force is used against a child by a parent or someone in the role of a parent, the child may invoke the protection of the law. It is all a matter of degree.

English law allows parents to use 'reasonable chastisement'. The problem is how to define and delimit chastisement which can be regarded as reasonable.

In a similar case, where a stepfather repeatedly hit his stepson with a garden cane, the boy took his case to court which ruled that the stepfather had the law on his side to inflict reasonable chastisement. Where action would otherwise be an assault, a parent had a perfectly good defence if it was merely the 'correcting of a child by its parent, provided that the correction be moderate in the manner, the instrument and the quantity of it'.

The boy then appealed against this decision to the European Court of Human Rights (this case is known as *A v. UK*). The European Court unanimously ruled that 'reasonable chastisement' was not a defence in these circumstances. It was the duty of the law to provide protection to children and other vulnerable persons. Article 3 of the Convention on Human Rights had been breached which stipulated that 'No one shall be subjected to torture or to inhuman and degrading treatment.'

In response to the ruling, the government issued a consultation paper 'Protecting Children, Supporting Parents', to canvass the views of the public on whether the physical punishment of children by their parents should be made unlawful. In the light of the consultations, the government instructed the courts that when it considers a defence of 'reasonable chastisement', the law must be read together with Article 3 of the Convention, and must take into account the case of *A v. UK*. In deciding what is reasonable chastisement the court will have to take into consideration the following factors:

* the nature and context of the punishment
* its duration
* its physical and mental effects; and in some instances,
* the sex, age and state of health of the victim.

Injuries to a child which are more serious than red marks or bruises that last only a few days are not acceptable, and could not be defended as 'reasonable'. Any injuries to the head were unacceptable, as were a wide range of other harsh punishments such as shaking etc. (see the Department of Health document LAC 94/23).

There are various organisations and Help Lines available to be contacted – for parents, step-parents, and children who need assistance if there is a fraught situation (see DIRECTORY at the end of the next chapter, page 109).

A parent's 'right' to punish his or her child cannot be passed on to another member of the family except those *in loco parentis*. In one case an elder brother administered a beating to his younger brother and claimed that he did so on their father's behalf. The courts held that this was unlawful.

Note: for the issue of corporal punishment in relation to schools, see *Children (Part 2)*, section 3.5.1.

It is only too clear that children are vulnerable to excessive punishment wherever they are. Cases have occurred where children who have been taken into care, on the grounds of need or of being at risk – in other words, some of the most vulnerable of all children – have been subjected to unlawful punishments such as 'pindown' in local authority homes.

2.4   Medical treatment

2.4.1   Allowing treatment

The general rule: parents are entitled to give consent to medical treatment for their children up to the age of 16. A child over the age of 16 can consent to any surgical, medical or dental treatment without his or her parents' consent.

However, delicate and difficult problems have arisen.

2.4.2   Refusing treatment

What if a parent refuses consent to treatment which the doctors consider necessary for the child's welfare? Parents may refuse on religious grounds or for some other reason – such as not wanting the doctors to inflict suffering on the child.

☞   *You are very worried about the baby of your brother and his girlfriend, because you know that the mother is HIV positive and that against medical advice she is breastfeeding the baby. The parents have refused to allow the baby to be tested to see whether he is also HIV positive. What can be done to protect the baby?*

In a recent case where a mother who was HIV positive refused to allow her baby to be tested, the court decided that it would overrule the parents' wishes.

The court took the view that the child's welfare is paramount, and the medical need of the baby to be tested was an overriding issue.

In certain cases where a parent has refused to allow a blood transfusion for a sick child, the court has made the child a 'ward of court' (see *Children (Part 2)*, section 2.4) and given consent to treatment.

The conflict between doctor and parent can go the other way too – in one case, the mother wanted her child to remain on a life support system while the doctors felt it was not in the child's interests to continue treatment. The courts overrode the mother's views and left the ultimate decision to the doctors.

In another case, where doctors and relatives had clashed over the resuscitation of a 12-year-old boy, the Court of Appeal held that doctors had to endeavour to seek a consensus with parents on the best course of treatment for the child. Where no resolution to a conflict could be reached over treatment in serious cases, the matter should be taken to the courts.

2.4.3   Child's own choices

2.4.3(a)   What if a child is under 16 but wants to consult a doctor or consent to treatment without involving parents?

A landmark decision decided that:

• where a child has sufficient understanding and intelligence and can understand the nature of the treatment being proposed, then he or she can consent to treatment.

The case concerned advice given by the (then) Department of Health and Social Security to doctors allowing them to advise on contraception for girls under 16 if the circumstances warranted it. Mrs Gillick, a mother of five daughters, all under 16, challenged the DHSS advice and her case went all the way to the House of Lords. The Law Lords decided that it would be most unusual for a doctor to advise a child on contraceptive matters without the knowledge and consent of her parents.

However, parents do not have an absolute veto on such matters. In certain circumstances, a doctor may be in a better position to judge issues of medical advice and treatment most conducive to a child's welfare. Further, a child who had sufficient understanding and maturity to grasp what was involved could give a valid consent. Understanding varies with the complexity of the issues but does not turn on a fixed age.

The Children Act has since enshrined the principle of listening to children's views in regard to critical matters in their lives (see section 2.11 below).

Note: the fact that doctors may be in a better position than parents to judge medical issues is applicable to boys under 16 as well as to girls.

2.4.3(b)   What if a child wants to refuse treatment?

It would appear that in a life-threatening situation, a doctor can get the court's sanction to override the wishes of the child. This does not seem to be age-dependent; in a recent case an anorexic girl, aged over 16, was ordered to have treatment against her wishes.

In another situation, a mother won a case in the High Court that her 'extremely attractive' mentally handicapped daughter, aged 28, should be sterilised despite the fact that the mother's application was opposed by the Official Solicitor on behalf of the girl. The Court of Appeal has since overruled this decision on the ground that the understandable concerns of a caring mother were insufficient to tilt the balance towards major irreversible surgery.

In the first case which had sought the court's approval for sterilisation of a male patient, who was regarded as mentally incapable of giving consent, the court stated that the considerations and best interests, in the case of a man, were not identical to those in respect of a woman. This was not a matter of equality of the sexes but a balancing exercise on a case-by-case basis for persons who are unable to make their own decisions. In refusing the application the court stated that there was no evidence to suggest that having the operation would have any effect on the care that the patient received and nor would it allow him any greater freedom. If his situation were to change in the future that would be the time to seek the court's reappraisal of the patient's best interests.

Do note: if you have a child who shows mental health problems such as depressive illness, sometimes legal measures are needed to safeguard his or her health. The appropriate steps to be taken are outlined in the chapter on *Growing Old*, section 8.3.

2.4.3(c)   Non-parental consent

What if you are looking after children in their parents' absence, and consent to medical treatment is needed?

☞ *Your sister has gone abroad on a motoring holiday and left her 15-year-old daughter in your charge. Your niece falls and breaks a leg in a school hockey match and needs surgery to reset it. The doctor asks you to sign a consent form.*

> In this case, the girl herself could consent if she is not too upset. As far as your position as aunt is concerned, the Children Act 1989 specifically gives parental responsibility, which includes the right to consent to medical treatment, to people who have temporary charge of a child.

The situation might be different if you had to consent to elective treatment, i.e. treatment which a patient could choose to have or not, such as the removal of a tooth under anaesthetic. You would be advised in such circumstances to await the parents' return.

Again the age of the patient is a very material factor in elective treatment; a girl or boy of 15 might be able to consent whereas a much younger child would have to show that he or she clearly understood the issues involved in letting a doctor or dentist treat him or her.

2.5   Emigration, nationality and passport matters

Parents can decide together to take the child out of the UK. However, a parent's right to act alone is limited. Where a child lives with one parent under a residence order, that parent can take a child abroad for a period of up to one month; for a longer period, every person with parental responsibility must give written consent. If they refuse, consent of the court must be obtained.

2.5.1   Emigration

☞ *You have recently married for the second time and your second husband is Canadian. You would like to settle in Canada with him, taking your two children by your first marriage. Their father objects. What can you do?*

> If you cannot get the father's written consent, you would have to apply to court for an order to settle this specific issue ('a specific issue order', see section 3.1.2 below). The court would weigh the advantages to the children of a new life against the fact that they would lose touch with their natural father. The views of older children would also be taken into account.

2.5.2   Nationality and passport

A child born in the UK is automatically a British citizen provided that at the time of the birth one or both of the parents is a British citizen or is settled in the UK without time-limit restriction. This applies where the parents are married.

Children under 16, including newborn babies, need their own passport when travelling abroad, even with their parents. Children already on their parents' passports can continue to travel on them until they are 16 or until the passport expires or needs amendment (because, for example, your child's name has been changed).

☞ *You need to travel to the United States to visit an ailing relative. Your baby is just 2 months old and you must take her with you. You wonder what sort of photograph you will need to be lodged with your application for your daughter's passport.*

You will need two photographs taken against a white background. As your baby is still very young, her head can be supported and a parent's hand can also be in the picture. The main concern is that the features are clear.

The passport will be issued for five years but you can have another photograph inserted during its validity period if you wish.

☞ *Your son will turn 16 shortly. He is currently on your passport and you intend that he should accompany you on a holiday in Spain.*

His details will need to be removed from your passport. With the application for a passport for him, therefore, you must enclose your passport which will be returned to you after the deletions have been made.

2.5.2(a)   Signature – parents

A passport form has to be signed by the parents until a child reaches 18.

Where the parents are married, section 9 of the form must be completed and signed by a parent or person with parental responsibility.

☞ *Your nephew aged 12 is at school in England while both his parents live abroad. He stays with you and your family. He needs a passport to visit his parents during the school holiday.*

As the boy is living with you, you should be eligible to sign the form as the person who has parental responsibility for the child. Do check the situation with the passport agency, however, which has set up an integrated website and national call centre operational from 1 March 2000: tel: 0870 521 0410 or at *www.ukpa.gov.uk.*

Where the parents of the child are unmarried, consent must be given by the child's mother, unless the father has a parental responsibility order or agreement.

2.5.2(b)   Signature of a child

The signature of a child of 12 and upwards is required on the passport application form, which is completed by the parent. Children of 16–17 may complete their own application, but the signature of a parent is also required.

2.6   Choosing religious upbringing

Parents are generally said to have the 'power' to determine their child's religious upbringing. Indeed such a right would seem to be self-evident along with all the other rights, duties, and responsibilities which accompany parenthood.

In today's pluralistic, secular society, parents may choose to bring their children up as non-believers.

Note: there is a general requirement under the Education Acts that schools must provide religious education (see *Children (Part 2)*, section 3.4.3, *Religious education*).

As far as the law is concerned, religion as an issue in a child's upbringing also arises:

- in cases of adoption
- in cases of fostering
- where there is conflict between the parents e.g. over a specific issue which concerns the child, e.g. wanting to have a boy circumcised for religious reasons.

One such case arose in 1999. The father sought a specific issue order that the mother of his son, who was a non-Muslim, should have the boy circumcised. However, the Court of Appeal held that it was the duty of the courts in such cases to consider first the welfare of the boy rather than the parents' religious wishes. In the present case, the boy was to be brought up by his mother in a non-Muslim environment and it could not be in his best interests to have a circumcision performed against her wishes. Circumcision was an effectively irreversible surgical intervention.

In general, the court held that both parents should consent in respect of important decisions such as having their son circumcised and, where there was a conflict between them, the matter should be referred to the courts to resolve the issue.

Although the courts have intervened where they feel that a child may be brainwashed by an undesirable set of beliefs, in general it is not the duty of the courts to sit in moral judgement on people's religious beliefs.

☞ *You discover that your ex-husband is taking your six-year-old daughter to meetings of a revivalist sect on the weekends that he has access to her. You are very unhappy about it as you fear that the child is being indoctrinated with the sect's beliefs. You have talked to him about the problem but to no avail. He stoutly maintains that there is freedom of religion in this country. What can you do?*

You would want to avoid the child becoming embroiled in a conflict in court over religion between two estranged parents – although the courts have taken such matters up in the past. You might try to arrange for her father to have contact on days other than those on which meetings are being held.

If it were to go to court, you could seek a 'specific issue order' that the child should be brought up in your own religion – but you would have to persuade the judge that such an order would be better than no order at all and was in the child's best interests.

Alternatively, you could apply for an order which would prohibit her father from taking your daughter to the meetings (a 'prohibited steps order'). Again the court would weigh up the issues very carefully in your daughter's interests before making any order at all.

Note: where certain sects have been outlawed for dubious practices and beliefs, the courts will take a stronger view in protecting children against them.

2.7 Appointing guardians

Parents who have children under 18 may be anxious about what would happen to them in the event of their death. They can appoint guardians for minor children in their wills. In other words, the guardian takes the place of the deceased parent in the child's life. (This is discussed fully in the chapter *Death – Before and After*, section 9.)

2.8 Consenting to adoption

The issue of parental consent to adoption is discussed in the next chapter, *Children (Part 2)*, section 2.1.1.

2.9 Consenting to marriage

a) Marriages of children under the age of 16 are not allowed at all
b) Marriages of minors between the age of 16 and 18 need parental consent
c) Over-18-year-olds are free to marry without parental consent.

Note: issues of consent for the marriage of minors will be found in the chapter on *Setting up Home*, section 1.2.1.

2.10 When parental responsibility ends

Parents who have parental responsibility for their child cannot abrogate it. In other words, you cannot give up responsibility unilaterally for as long as the child is a minor.

A child attains majority at the age of 18. At that age parental responsibility formally ceases. Many court orders last until a child is 16 or 17. However, if a child is in further, full-time education, a parent can be called upon to support his or her child beyond the age of 18.

Under a Parental Responsibility Agreement, parental responsibility can be brought to an end by an order of the court on the application of:

- any person who has parental responsibility for the child
- the child – provided the court has given the child permission to make the application (see section 2.11 immediately below).

The list at the end of the next chapter (page 107) sets out the ages at which a child's activities are legally allowed (or proscribed). Apart from the 18-year threshold, parental responsibility will also cease:

- when a minor marries
- when a minor is serving in the armed forces
- by court order.

2.11   Listening to a child's views

As we have seen, a most important feature of the Children Act is its emphasis on giving children their own voice. This is not age-dependent. Rather, the court's duty is to pay heed to the views of children provided that they have sufficient understanding and maturity to understand the issues at stake. Thus although parents still have responsibility for their children, a young person of sufficient understanding can put his or her views to the court in matters which affect their welfare or well-being. For example, they can ask the court to decide that:

- an absent father should visit them
- a parent should pay for their full-time education over the age of 18
- contact with their natural parents by adopted children should be resumed
- a move into a boyfriend's family should be allowed, because life at home is so intolerable
- they should not have to leave the country
- they may change their surname, as there is a compelling reason why they wish to do so.

For example, in one case children in care sought to change their surname from that of their father to that of their maternal family after allegations against the father of physical and sexual abuse. A criminal prosecution against the father was pending at the time of the application. The girls' mother had died. The Court of Appeal reiterated that a judge hearing such an application should give careful consideration to the wishes, feelings, and needs of the child and should also give 'searching scrutiny' to the motives and objectives of the person (in this case the girls' father) who opposes a child's application.

Do remember: children can apply to court themselves. To do so, they need leave of the court to make application for an order. Permission will only be granted if the court is sure that the child has sufficient understanding.

To obtain permission, children must have a solicitor or other legal advisor prepared to act on their behalf and apply for community legal funding [formerly legal aid] if needed. See the DIRECTORY on page 109 for agencies which can help and advise a child who wants to take legal action.

2.12   Parental responsibility – unmarried parents

In the case of parents who are not married to each other, the mother alone has legal responsibility for the child.

However, under the Children Act 1989, if an unmarried mother agrees, parental responsibility can now be shared by the father of her child. Parental responsibility can also be shared between the mother or father and a partner in the case of same-sex couples.

2.12.1   Status of child

As far as the child is concerned, the law has moved steadily in the direction of equating the status of a legitimate and an illegitimate child. The stigma has been removed as far as illegitimate children's own rights in law are concerned. For example if a parent of an illegitimate child dies and does not leave a will, the child can inherit under the laws of intestacy (see chapter on *Death – Before and After*).

2.12.2   Status of mother

However, the Children Act 1989 still draws a very clear distinction between the parental responsibility of married and unmarried parents. That very fact means that not quite equal treatment is accorded to a child whose parents are not married to each other. In particular the status of the mother is the cardinal indicator of the different approach of the law. All parental responsibility is given to the mother at the birth of the child if she is not married to the child's father. This position is not irrevocable, however (see *Status of father*, section 2.12.3 below).

There is no obligation for an unmarried mother to register the father's name if she does not wish to. That part of the register can be left blank.

If she does want to register the name of the father, this can be done at their joint request and they generally must both be present to sign the register.

These issues are discussed in detail in the section on registering a baby's birth, see section 1.3.2.

2.12.3   Status of father

The position of an unmarried father is not quite the same as that of a married father, as we have seen. However, his position has been strengthened by recent legislation (see above, section 1.3.6 for the Adoption and Children Act 2002) as well as by the attitude of the courts:

- he can assume parental responsibility with the mother's consent
- he can obtain parental responsibility by marrying the mother (see section 1.3.5 above)
- if the mother does not consent, an unmarried father can apply to court and ask for a Parental Responsibility Order so that he then has a right to be involved in all major matters concerning his child.

So although the position of an unmarried father has improved under the Act, he still does not have the same status in law as a married father unless he takes steps to acquire it.

Note: legislation soon to be in force will confer parental responsibility on an unmarried father as a matter of course if his name appears on the birth certificate (see also section 1.3.3 above).

2.13   Acquiring parental responsibility

An unmarried father can acquire parental responsibility with the mother's consent, [a 'parental responsibility agreement'] or by consent of the court [a 'parental responsibility order'].

2.13.1   Acting with the mother's consent

Under the Children Act 1989, if an unmarried mother agrees, parental responsibility can now be shared by both parents.

☞ *Your girlfriend is expecting your first child. You have been living together for some years and have a happy, stable relationship. Although you are not married, you would like your relationship with your child to approximate to that of a married father as much as possible. What can you do?*

You can sign a Parental Responsibility Agreement with the mother's consent.

2.13.1(a) The Parental Responsibility Agreement

Under section 4 of the Children Act 1989, where mother and father agree, they can enter into a Parental Responsibility Agreement. The Agreement has to be in this prescribed form (obtainable from law stationers). The form must include details of both parents, who must declare that they both agree that the father should have parental responsibility for the child.

The form must be signed by each parent in the presence of a witness, who must be a JP, a justice's clerk or an authorised court official. The mother must bring along the child's full birth certificate, plus evidence of her identity showing a photograph and signature (e.g. a passport). The father will also need evidence of his identity showing photograph and signature. The Agreement is legally binding on both mother and father so advice from either a solicitor or another adviser is urged before signing.

The Agreement must then be filed with two copies at the Principal Registry, Family Division of the High Court, First Avenue House, 42–49 High Holborn, London WC1V 6NP. The Agreement is then recorded and a copy sent to each parent.

Note: it is not effective until it has been received and recorded at the Principal Registry of the Family Division.

2.13.2   If the mother does not consent

A father who is not married to the mother of his child can apply to court for a parental responsibility order.

The court's duty is to act in the child's best interest. Generally speaking, a child's interest is best served by the involvement of both natural parents. Indeed that is the philosophy behind the Act unless there are very strong contra-indications such as fear of violence or abuse.

On a father's application to the court for an order for parental responsibility, the court will weigh his commitment to the child and the child's attachment to him. If the court is satisfied, an order in his favour may perhaps be made even against a mother's objection.

Note: no two cases are the same. It is difficult to predict how the court will weigh a father's application. So in all cases, do seek legal advice.

2.14   Duty to maintain

Every father is obliged by law to maintain his child. This duty is enforceable whether or not the father has parental responsibility and whether or not he is involved with his child's life or upbringing.

See section 2.2 above.

2.15   Proving paternity

If a mother asserts that a certain man is the father of her child and he is therefore liable to maintain her child, this assertion may have to be proved in a court of law. Applications to courts for declarations of paternity were generally heard in 'affiliation proceedings' when a mother applied to court for maintenance for her child and the alleged father resisted the claim. Blood tests could be inconclusive. DNA 'fingerprinting', on the other hand, has made proving the truthfulness or otherwise of an assertion of parentage much more certain.

Today, where a mother is on benefit, notification is made to the Child Support Agency for child support. She will have to give the name of the father except in certain cases where to do so could lead to harm. If the putative father denies parentage, a court can be asked to determine the paternity issue. If a man refuses to have a test, the court can draw inferences against him from his refusal.

In two recent cases, it was the father who asked for a blood test to determine the paternity of the child. In each case the mother refused her consent. The court declared that it had no jurisdiction to compel the parent with care of the child to give consent to have a sample taken of the child's blood, unlike in cases of necessary medical treatment. The court stated that the present legal situation of being unable to insist upon a blood test was not satisfactory as knowledge of paternity was increasingly seen as of prime importance to children. Under new Regulations, the courts are empowered to order tests on a putative mother or father, as well as ordering a sample on a child under 16, if it is in his or her best interests.

In a recent case a man who believed he was the father of a child applied to the court asking it to order DNA testing – the mother had refused. He cited the Human Rights Act, Article 8, the right to a private and family life. The court ruled that the child's right to know for certain who his father was should be the deciding factor and ordered the tests.

In another case the court also ruled that twins be tested against the wishes of their mother, who had refused testing on the ground that if her ex-lover was found to be the father of her twins, it would break up her marriage. The ex-lover had brought the case under the Child Support and Pensions and Social Security Act 2000 which allows compulsory testing. The court's view was that it was more important to remove doubt over who was the father than abide by the mother's wishes.

Under the Child Support Act 1995, there is the power to recoup the cost of the fees for the DNA test from the person established by the test to be the father.

The courts will not order a test:

- to satisfy a suspicion of adultery; or
- where it would be against the child's best interests.

In one case, where a married woman gave birth to a baby, a DNA test showed that her husband was not the father of her child. The man with whom she was having a love affair at the time that she conceived, refused to take a blood test on an application by the CSA to the court. The judge said that where a putative father declined to give a blood test when ordered to do so by a court, he did so 'at his peril'. Accordingly an inference was drawn from that refusal that he was the child's father.

2.15.1   Retrospective testing?

The courts will order a DNA test to take advantage of genetic fingerprinting even though an earlier blood test proved inconclusive.

☞ *You are a married man. A child was born to a woman friend of yours in 1995. She alleged that you were the father of her child and that you were liable to pay maintenance – a claim which you strenuously denied. You took a blood test which proved inconclusive. The mother's claim against you was dismissed. She has now sought to reopen the case and asked the court to order a DNA test. You want to know whether she is entitled to reopen the case.*

The answer is 'yes'. There is no rule against retrospective DNA fingerprinting. And if you refuse to take another test, the court can draw an inference from your refusal.

2.16   Child's nationality

Where the parents are unmarried, only the mother's nationality or settled status is relevant with regard to the child's nationality under English law.

3   WHEN PARENTS SPLIT UP

3.1   Private law

Private law applies when children remain with one or other parent or a relative, e.g. a grandparent, on the break-up of their parents' relationship. Private law is the law between private individuals. Public law in relation to children (see *Children (Part 2)* section 1) applies when the state intervenes by, for example, taking children into care.

In general the Children Act 1989 stresses the need of continuing responsibility of both parents for their child(ren) so as to lessen the impact on the child of the departure of one of the parents. Thus a most significant aspect of the Act is that both parents are still expected to take an active role in bringing up their children despite separation or divorce.

However, the law can only help couples to help themselves. It can only endeavour to assist them in reaching an amicable agreement on the future of their children's wellbeing. Personal issues are not really meant for litigation – particularly where children are involved.

The DIRECTORY at the end of the next chapter has an extensive list of organisations which exist to help parents and children in situations of family conflict.

3.1.1   Main features of the Act

a) The welfare of the child will be the paramount consideration in decisions on the child's future.
b) Any delay in deciding that future will be considered prejudicial to the child.
c) The court must pay regard to a principle known as the 'non-intervention principle'. In other words it should only make an order on behalf of a child when it is sure that a court order would be more helpful than no order at all.

3.1.2   Orders available to the court under the Children Act 1989

- *Residence orders:* orders which decide with whom the child should live. Most importantly, a residence order also gives parental responsibility to those who have the child living with them but who are not necessarily the child's parents (for example, grandparents). This means that parental responsibility can be split amongst several people.
- *Contact orders:* orders to the person with whom the child lives to allow visits from the person named in the order, or to allow other contact (e.g. by letter or telephone). This would apply most frequently in cases where a father lives away from his child but wishes to maintain contact.

- *Prohibited step orders:* orders which prohibit certain steps being taken in relation to the child without consent of the court (for example, taking a child abroad on a permanent basis).
- *Specific issue orders:* orders which decide specific questions which have arisen in connection with the child's upbringing (for example, whether or not to have medical treatment, or to change schools).

Note: the court can issue any order in a child's interest – not necessarily the order which was applied for. The orders last until a child turns 16.

☞   *Your two children, age 9 and 11, live with you but have seen their father on a regular basis since your divorce two years ago. He has now moved, and lives abroad, and they spend part of each holiday with him and his new partner. He says that he wants his 11-year-old son to go to a special school for musically gifted children because he thinks he has great potential as a musician. You do not agree. You think the local school is providing a stimulating curriculum, your son has music lessons after school, he is happily settled at the school where he has made friends and you do not want him to have to change schools. Can your ex-husband force you to change your son's school?*

Your ex-husband can apply to the court for a specific issue order, namely for your son to attend the school of the father's choice. The court will look at all the facts of the case, including the wishes expressed by the child. In a recent case the court ruled that there were good reasons for the divorced father to wish his child to attend a particular school, against the mother's wishes, and allowed a specific issue order requiring a change of school. In that case, the father lived in France and wanted his child to attend the Lycée in London so that his son would be able to speak French when he visited his relatives during school holidays.

3.1.3   Intentions behind the Act

The intentions behind the Act are to encourage:

- a non-adversarial approach in deciding on the future of children
- the love and care of both parents towards their children
- use of a flexible range of orders so that there should no longer be a question of children being 'won' or 'lost' in court battles
- both parents sharing responsibility for their children in all crucial matters
- involvement of other relatives in a child's life.

3.2   Court's checklist

In order to decide whether an order would be justified, the court must consider the following checklist:

a) the wishes and feelings of the child
b) the child's physical and emotional needs
c) the likely effect on the child of any change in his or her circumstances
d) the child's sex, background, and characteristics which the court considers relevant
e) any harm which the child has suffered or is at risk of suffering
f) how capable each of his parents or any other person is of meeting the child's needs
g) the range of powers available to the court under the Children Act 1989.

3.3   Who can obtain an order?

Any person with parental responsibility can apply for an order – i.e. parents or guardians. So can any person with a residence order in their favour (grandparents, for example, may have the child living with them under a residence order). An unmarried father can apply for an order even if he does not have parental responsibility.

Children themselves can apply to court for permission for an order to be made in their favour. Their views and feelings must be taken into account in any event. See *Listening to a child's views*, section 2.11 above.

Anyone with an interest in the child's welfare can ask the court for permission to apply for an order. People who could use this provision would include grandparents, step-parents, former partners, other relatives such an aunt, uncle or cousin, and even friends.

☞ *Your son and his girlfriend had a child four years ago, and you are devoted to this little girl. Unfortunately the couple have split up and the child has moved away to another part of the country with her mother, and no longer sees her father or any of his relatives. Someone you know told you recently that the mother has started to drink heavily, and sometimes leaves the little girl on her own. You are desperately worried, what can you do?*

You need to see a solicitor with a view to asking the court for permission to apply for an order for contact between your grandchild and yourself. If you feel you can help by seeing your grandchild regularly and can offer help in a delicate and difficult situation, the court may well grant your order. Remember that the court must have the child's welfare as their paramount consideration. Bear in mind also that mediation can be an effective way forward rather than taking a case to court. See the chapter on *Growing Old*, as well as the chapter on *The Legal System* which also provides sources of help and advice.

3.4 Who are the orders for? (child of the family)

The orders relate to a 'child of the family' and includes anyone brought up as a family member. This feature is particularly important today where there are so many step-families involving children from previous relationships.

☞ *When your husband married you, he was a widower and was living with his young son, then aged six. You lived with your husband for four years, during which time you cared for, and looked after his son. You and your husband have now separated. You quite understand that the boy should remain with his father but you would like to continue seeing him even though you have left the family home. However, your husband is hurt and angry and says that he refuses you any contact with the child. Is there anything you can do?*

Contact orders under the Act are made in relation to a 'child of the family'. It includes any child who has been treated by both husband and wife as a child of the family and clearly includes your stepson in your case. You would have to persuade the court that it is in the child's interest to make an order so that you continue to keep in touch with him. (For assistance in these cases, see under DIRECTORY at end of next chapter.)

3.5 Family assistance orders

A probation officer or local authority social worker can be appointed by the court to advise, assist, and befriend any parent or guardian of the child, or any other person with whom the child lives, or with whom the child has contact. The orders are usually made as a means of providing social-work support to families experiencing difficulties after separation or divorce. It is the only court order available in private law proceedings through which social work support can be provided.

A family assistance order can also apply to a child in need of assistance. However, these orders can only be made in 'exceptional' circumstances.

☞ *Your wife has suddenly left you and your two children, and has gone to live abroad with another man. You are now in the throes of an acrimonious divorce and are in a great deal of distress but want to make every effort to keep the children at home with you and not have to put them into care.*

It would seem that a family assistance order might help you in your circumstances although there is no definition of what qualifies as exceptional circumstances. As one judge stated: 'almost every case can be described in some way as exceptional'.

These orders are intended as a short term help only. An appointment only lasts for six months.

3.6 The most suitable order

In all cases, the court can make any order which it feels most suits the case before it. In other words, even if you apply to court for a particular order, you may find some other order made on your child's behalf. For example, you might apply to court for a specific issue order that your child should go to a certain school. The court may think it best for the child to issue a prohibited steps order that the child cannot be removed from its present school.

3.7   Mediation services

Mediators presuppose that there will be a separation but try to make it less painful (see DIRECTORY on page 109). In particular, mediation is used in order to avoid and/or mitigate parental quarrels over the future of their children.

☞   *You and your husband have agreed to separate but much bitterness remains and certain key issues, such as the children's future and whether or not to sell your joint home, are unresolved. You have seen your own solicitor and your husband has contacted his own solicitor. You feel that a more conciliatory approach, primarily for the children's sake, must be tried. You feel it is too late for marriage guidance because it is help with the separation you most need, not with the marriage which is beyond retrieval. What can you do?*

Under the present position, mediation services, comprising specially trained lawyers and mediators, audited for their quality of service by the Legal Services Commission, can work in conjunction with couples, helping to sort out such difficulties. It is hoped that in a marriage or partnership breakdown, couples will see mediation as a positive and less stressful alternative to litigation.

Community legal funding is now available for accredited mediation services. Consult the DIRECTORY for help on how to find a mediator in your area.

See also chapter on *Divorce*, section 2.2.1.

3.8   Which parent?

There are factors which the courts have applied in the past to settle the contentious and painful issue of whether children should live with their mother or father. Although the Act was intended to transform the nature of family proceedings, some of the factors in these cases will, no doubt, apply in the future. The court must consider:

- the personality and character of each parent
- the desirability of a mother caring for young children, although this will not necessarily weigh to the exclusion of all other factors
- the need to preserve stability in a child's life and provide continuity of care
- the need to keep brothers and sisters together.

A High Court judge stated in the Court of Appeal that the days had gone when mothers could assume they were the ones who should care for the children. In the past decade the growing equality of the sexes had resulted in fathers being much better equipped to take on child rearing, if necessary on their own.

3.9   No delay

Until 1991, a divorce could not be made final until the court had considered arrangements for children of the marriage.

Today under the Act, delay is seen as harmful to a child's welfare. The court must only postpone the decree if it needs time for further consideration in the interests of the child.

It will also impose a timetable on proceedings so that parents and children have issues decided as speedily as possible. Children's futures are not to be kept hanging in the balance while others wrangle over them. However, despite the Act's good intentions, delay has continued to be an increasing matter for concern in proceedings involving children. It is hoped that other civil procedure rules, designed to speed up the court process, will have an impact on this aspect of family law as well.

3.10   Maintaining contact

The courts have increasingly taken the view that it is in the child's best interests to maintain contact with the birth father. It has wide powers to make orders and conditions to facilitate such contact.

3.10.1   The court's view

The child's welfare is the paramount consideration.

☞   *Your estranged partner has insisted that you should not have personal contact with your child. You have accepted the situation for the time being in the hope that her quite irrational antipathy to your presence will dissipate with time. However, you would like to send the child cards and presents and receive some photographs. Your ex-partner has refused, saying that she cannot be made to do anything against her wishes.*

The courts are most unlikely to heed her wishes in this regard where the request is for indirect contact. They have stressed that parents who looked after their children on a day-to-day basis should not think that the more intransigent, unreasonable and uncooperative they were the more likely they were to get their own way.

Where parents were separated and the child was in the care of one of them, it is generally in the child's interests to have contact with the other parent.

With regard to direct contact, although judges can commit a mother to prison for contempt of court for failure to comply with an order giving the father contact with his children, such a procedure was only to be used as a last resort. The Court of Appeal stated that one of the thorniest problems for the courts to cope with was an irrational and unjustifiable hostility by one parent against the other which also alienated the children. The courts had become 'sadly familiar' with the issue and when a contact order was made, the problem then arose as to how the court should respond when it was openly defied. However, coercive powers could not only fail to maintain the link between father and child but there was a risk that committal proceedings might exacerbate the poor relationships which already existed.

Guidelines were laid down for judges in such situations so that all other steps were to be exhausted before the weapon of committal was used.

3.10.2   Domestic violence

In cases where a father is asking for contact which the mother is refusing on the grounds that there is a history of domestic violence, the courts have been given new guidelines. These require the court to consider any allegations of violence and decide, if such allegations are found to be true, whether any contact will be in the interests of the child. Fathers guilty of violence will only be allowed contact with their children where the safety of the child and of the residential parent can be secured before, during and after any such contact. The court should obtain a report from a children and family reporter (appointed by the court) on the question of contact if this is necessary to safeguard a child's interests. The children's wishes and feelings must be ascertained. The court may order treatment as a precondition to contact and can specify whether and if so how the contact should be organised.

☞   *Your ex-boyfriend is often drunk but says he loves his daughter and wants to see her. Although he has threatened violence, he has never hit you or your child. Nonetheless, you are afraid that if you allow visits his behaviour may become out of control. Can you refuse to allow him to visit?*

If he applies to the court for a contact order, the court will make enquiries to establish the facts of his previous behaviour (alcohol abuse and/or violence). The courts are concerned that one parent should not alienate the affections of the child against the other parent and it has a range of options depending on its view of the facts.

The court may make an order that any direct contact with the child should be supervised and/or that the father should undergo treatment for alcohol abuse and anger management. Generally, the courts have been reluctant to see all contact between parent and child severed. Thus, the court may make an order for indirect contact (letters, presents etc) so that some relationship is maintain between child and father.

You are advised to seek legal advice on how best to proceed in order to do the best for yourself and your child. Do establish if there is a contact centre in your vicinity (see immediately below).

3.10.3   Contact centres

Contact centres are available to enable estranged parents to meet their children in a neutral atmosphere. There are 280 such centres and information on their locations can be obtained from the National Association of Child Contact Centres (see DIRECTORY on page 109) which also assists persons who wish to set up a centre in their own area.

4 CHILDREN (Part 2)
THE STATE'S RIGHTS AND DUTIES

In this chapter we look at those circumstances in which the State can take a more active role in your child's life. A situation at home may lead to an entirely voluntary approach by parents to their local authority – for example where a mother falls ill and wants to have someone reliable to look after her child either as a foster carer or childminder. But State intervention can also come about as the result of a more extreme situation, generally where a child is at serious risk of harm and needs care of a very different sort. Thus we cover the steps that may have to be taken by social workers to protect children in danger – even against the parents' wishes.

It has to be stressed, however, that the 'private' and 'public' aspects of legal rights and obligations in relation to children do not fall into neat categories. Nor are they intended to. To take one example: local authorities not only provide schooling but must also endeavour to involve parents in determining school policy, for example, through parent governors.

Again, in relation to marital breakdown, which falls into the realm of private law and is dealt with in the preceding chapter, *Children (Part 1)*, the court can take whatever steps it thinks fit in the circumstances of each individual case: for example, in dealing with a dispute over children between individual parents, the court may decide that it is in the child's best interests to make a care order in favour of a local authority.

Finally, the chapter touches on situations in which a child may get involved in the criminal law, and draws attention to new initiatives in the administration of youth justice and in tackling youth crime.

The Human Rights Act 1998, which came into force in October 2000, has changed the legal culture. Judges are duty-bound to assess whether there is a human rights dimension in the cases before them. Of necessity, this element has a significant impact on the sphere of family law, in particular with regard to family proceedings, and to the duties of local authorities in dealing with children at risk of harm or already in their care (see below section 1.1.1 and the chapter on *The Legal System*, section 6).

In this chapter we look at:

- when parents fail
- other parents and carers
- education
- special educational needs
- children and crime.

1   WHEN PARENTS FAIL

1.1   Public law

Under the heading of 'public law', we will deal with situations in which a local authority intervenes in a child's life.

1.1.1   Duties of local authorities

The duties placed on the local authority by the Children Act 1989 are manifold. Among them are requirements to:

- maintain a list of childminders, foster parents and nurseries (information received from OFSTED as the registering and inspecting body)

- take care of children 'in need' in its area (see section 1.2 below)
- protect children in danger
- provide accommodation in children's homes
- take children into care.

In the past, the local authorities have been found to be both:

- too officious in taking children away from their parents and putting them into care on mere suspicion of wrongdoing or abuse
- failing in their duty to children who have slipped through the net and have suffered terrible harm and even fatal injury as a result of local authority dereliction of duty.

The Children Act 1989 was intended to assist local authorities to work in conjunction with parents. It was hoped to avoid some of the worst difficulties of the past. Thus, hopes placed on the Act were very high.

The Human Rights Act 1998 makes it unlawful for a public authority to act or fail to act in a way incompatible with a right enshrined in the European Convention of Human Rights. In the present context, it is the right of an individual to respect for his private and family life that will matter most.

Thus, if a local authority takes a child away from his parents, this would be an infringement of this right unless it can be shown that there is justification for the action, e.g. to protect a child's health, morals, or freedom (among other justifications). Doubtless a child's best interests will continue to override other concerns, such as the parents' wishes. Nonetheless the emphasis on parental involvement in local authority decisions is likely to be enhanced now that the Act is in force.

The Human Rights Act will also strengthen the position of children who are, or have formerly been, in care and who feel that their situation was mishandled by the authorities – for example, that their placement in a foster home, or a series of foster homes, had caused them harm.

1.2   Children in need: orders available

The orders in the Children Act are intended to cover a wide range of situations. They are also intended to give a local authority sufficient flexibility for it to be able to make appropriate and measured responses to the problems it encounters. Orders are directed to 'children in need'. This phrase is given a wide definition i.e. a child is in need if he or she is 'unlikely to achieve or maintain ... a reasonable standard of health or development'.

It is interesting to note from the definition that not only is a child's physical well-being covered but 'development' relates to a child's emotional and psychological needs as well.

However, uncertainty about when to investigate allegations of harm and when to take care proceedings has been a consistent problem in enforcing the child protection legislation.

New guidance for assessment of children in need and their families has been prepared after having been jointly developed by several relevant government departments. It has been issued to NHS staff, social services, the police and teachers among others. It is intended to help these professionals make clear judgements about whether or not a child is in need, is suffering or is likely to suffer significant harm, what action to take, and by which services. A copy of the guidance is available at this website: *www.doh.gov.uk/scg/cin.htm*.

1.2.1   Types of orders

The orders available under the Children Act 1989 are:

- child assessment order
- care order
- supervision order
- education supervision order (see below, section 3.6.3)
- emergency protection order.

Note: under its domestic violence provisions, the Family Law Act 1996 introduced a non-molestation order, to prevent a person from molesting a person or child in the same household. If emergency action is needed to protect a child, a suspected abuser can be removed from the home under a non-molestation order. Children under 16 can themselves apply for an order with the court's permission (see also chapter on *Divorce*, section 9).

All these orders, except the education supervision order, are dealt with below (see sections 1.3–1.6). First, however, we must examine some of the tasks imposed on a local authority under the Act:

- it has a general duty to take care of children 'in need'
- it is required by law to work with families of children in need
- it has a specific duty to investigate cases where a child suffers or is likely to suffer significant harm
- it must enter a child's name on the Child Protection Register if he or she is at risk.

Child Protection Registers are kept by local authorities on an inter-agency basis to pool information on children who may be in danger of harm, and to assist social services in considering whether to bring proceedings for a care order. Entries relate to 'physical injury', risk of neglect, and sexual abuse.

1.2.2   General duty

Each local authority has a general duty to safeguard and promote the welfare of children within its area who are in need, and so far as is consistent with that duty, to promote the upbringing of such children by their families.

1.2.3   Need to work with families

As far as possible the Act seeks to avoid the powers which allowed local authorities to take over responsibility from a child's parents and to transfer it to themselves. Its prime concern is to give children in need, as well as their families, the support that they require. Family ties between parents and children are to be fostered, wherever possible, not severed; care provided by a local authority is to be given in partnership with parents – not in opposition to them.

1.2.4   Specific duty to investigate

Where a local authority has reasonable cause to suspect that a child in its area is suffering or is likely to suffer significant harm, it must make enquiries necessary to decide whether to take any action to safeguard the child's welfare.

The National Society for the Prevention of Cruelty to Children is the only voluntary organisation specifically named in the Children Act and given the statutory powers to take legal action to protect a child who is being abused or is at risk.

1.3   Assessment order

This order is not intended:

- to take the place of the old place of safety order
- to be a care order
- to be used in emergencies. (For emergency situations see section 1.6 below, *Children in danger.*)

However, there are cases where a local authority may have reasonable grounds to suspect that a child is at real risk of suffering harm. It may find that those looking after the child do not co-operate when it tries to establish the true position.

An assessment order therefore is intended:

- to cover a situation where there is some ground for suspicion that the child could come to harm
- to enable the local authority or the NSPCC to have a medical or psychiatric examination made of that child.

The child need not be removed from home for an assessment. Removal can be permitted under the Act if the person who has care of the child fails to produce him or her for assessment. The court must be satisfied that:

- there are reasonable grounds for suspecting that the child is suffering significant harm or is at risk of suffering significant harm
- an assessment is needed of the state of the child's health or development or the way in which he or she is being treated, in order to establish whether the child is suffering or is likely to suffer significant harm; and
- it is unlikely that such an assessment will be made in the absence of a court order.

The court must always decide on the basis that:

- the child's welfare is paramount
- making an order would be better than not making an order.

The order lasts seven days.

Note: the court can issue an emergency protection order (see section 1.6 below) on the evidence before it.

1.4   Care order

Care orders apply to cases where a local authority takes a child into care and assumes parental responsibility for the child. Thus any residence order for the child is terminated. The child is taken from home and placed either in a local authority home or with local authority foster parents.

A care order can only be made by court order. The court must be satisfied:

- that the child is suffering or is likely to suffer significant harm (i.e. ill-treatment or impairment to health or development), and
- that harm results from lack of reasonable parental care; or
- that the child is beyond parental control.

Note: the responsibility of the parents of a child in care continues as well, so that a local authority cannot:

- free a child for adoption or
- appoint a guardian.

The local authority also has parental responsibility for the child under care.

Care orders may also be issued in other circumstances, for example:

- in divorce proceedings
- when a child is involved in criminal proceedings.

Important note: under the Crime and Disorder Act 1998, where a court is satisfied that a child has failed to comply with the requirement of a child safety order, the court can make a care order under the Children Act 1989. For details of these orders, see below, section 5.2.5(b).

Care orders can last until a child is 18 but cannot be made for a child over 17.

In a significant decision and by a majority of three to two, the House of Lords ruled that a child could not be taken into care under a care order unless a real possibility existed that the child would suffer significant harm at the hands of his or her parents or carers. To convince the court that it should make the order there had to be more than just suspicion: there had to be facts.

The uncertainty which has surrounded a local authority's duties to take care proceedings and to investigate allegations of harm has led to the issue of revised guidelines (see above section 1.2).

1.5   Supervision order

This order appoints a supervisor who has the duty to advise, assist and befriend the child. Such an order usually lasts a year. A supervisor can apply to extend the order but its maximum duration is three years; on the other hand, a care order, as we have seen, can last till a child is 18.

1.6   Children in danger

Note: a local authority, concerned about a child in a situation of danger or distress, does not have to wait for harm to have actually occurred to the child.

CHILDLINE, the national free helpline, exists for children in trouble. The number is 0800 1111. The number for children in care to ring is 0800 884 4444.

1.6.1   Emergency protection order

A local authority can apply to court for an emergency protection order – which replaces the former place of safety order. The order only lasts eight days. Although it can be extended for another 7 days, only one extension may be granted.

The court must be satisfied that:

- significant harm has occurred or could happen
- action is necessary because social workers are being denied access to the child to check on the child's health and welfare and there are fears that the child cannot be seen, in circumstances in which significant harm could occur.

The court can make:

- an order for parental contact
- an assessment order for a medical or psychiatric examination.

1.6.2   Who can apply to court for any of the above orders?

1.6.2(a)   Assessment, care or supervision orders

Only a local authority or the NSPCC can apply to court for an assessment order, a care order, or a supervision order.

1.6.2(b)   Children in danger – emergency protection orders

Applications for emergency protection orders can be made by:

- local authorities
- the NSPCC
- any other concerned applicant.

a) In making application to court for an emergency protection order, *a local authority* has to show that:

- it has been making enquiries on the child's behalf
- its enquiries into the child's wellbeing are being frustrated, and
- access to the child is required as a matter of urgency.

b) *The NSPCC* must show that:

- it has been making enquiries which have been frustrated
- access to the child is required as a matter of urgency
- it has reasonable cause to suspect that a child is suffering or is likely to suffer significant harm.

c) *Any other applicant* must show that:

- he or she has reasonable cause to believe that the child is likely to suffer significant harm if not removed.

1.6.3   Reports by concerned friends or neighbours – confidentiality

Apart from applying for an emergency protection order, a concerned friend or neighbour can approach the court to make a child a ward of court (see *Wardship* below, section 2.4).

If you suspect that a child is being neglected, ill-treated or abused, you can report your suspicions to the local authority or the NSPCC. The NSPCC Helpline number is 0808 800 5000. Confidentiality is ensured.

☞ *You suspect the family in the next-door flat is abusing their child. You want to report the case to the NSPCC but do not want it known to the parents that you have taken this step. Can you insist that your name will not be divulged in any subsequent proceedings.*

   The answer is 'yes'.

1.6.4   Who can apply for release from an order?

- the parents
- the child – provided he or she is of sufficient understanding and maturity
- any other person with parental responsibility
- any person with whom the child was living immediately before the making of the order.

1.6.4(a)   When to apply?

An application to discharge an emergency protection order can be made after 72 hours.

1.6.5   Court's considerations

In making any of the above orders, the court is obliged to observe its statutory duties. It must decide that:

- an order would be in the child's best interest
- it is better to make an order than to make no order at all
- delay is prejudicial to a child's best interests.

1.6.6   Improving support for children in care

A number of initiatives are being taken to improve support for children in care. It has been found, for example, that education of 'looked after' children is inadequate, with up to 75 per cent of children leaving care without a single qualification. Truancy and exclusions also affect a disproportionate number of children in care.

Again, once children leave care aged 16 or 17, too many have to fend for themselves. Arrangements are being put in place in order to improve the chances of these children and to endeavour to prevent homelessness and unemployment among them. The numbers involved are considerable: during 2001 some 6,800 young people aged 16 or older left care.

When a child in care reaches 16, Social Services have to appoint a 'Personal Advisor' for the child who will keep in touch with the child and make sure s/he has the help they need.

Once a child reaches the age of 18 a Care Order will automatically end. However, Social Services should still offer help, for example with finding somewhere to live, until the young person is 21-years-old. In October 2001 new rules came into force about help on leaving care. The new rules aim to:

- promote and maintain relationships after leaving care, and prepare the young person to be ready to leave care (providing guidance on health, budgeting, domestic skills, personal and relationship skills)
- to provide help with housing
- to help in a crisis and offer personal support
- help the young person fulfil her/his potential in education, training and employment.

When a child in care turns 16, Social Services will appoint a Personal Advisor who, together with the young person, will draw up a Pathway Plan which will cover issues such as education and accommodation. If the young person leaving care wants to go into full-time education, Social Services must support him or her both with housing (if needed) and money. An information website has been set up for children in care: *www.carelaw.org.uk*. It covers a range of topics including contact, adoption, education, crime, and leaving care, among other issues. The topics are dealt with in a question-and-answer format.

1.6.7   'Looking after' children by local authority: no compulsion

There are many reasons why children are taken into care. The orders dealt with above concern State intervention from outside the family. However children can be looked after by a local authority on a voluntary basis where it is felt that it would promote the child's welfare. For example, if a parent is ill or otherwise cannot provide the child with proper accommodation or care, a parent can approach the local authority to make application to court for a care order on the child's behalf.

The parents retain responsibility for the child and can remove the child at any time from the accommodation. The local authority is under a duty to:

- ascertain the child's wishes
- ascertain the parents' wishes
- ascertain the wishes of any other relevant person.

The child's age and understanding, religion, racial origins and cultural and linguistic background must all be taken into account.

The most important aspect of looking after children in this way is the so-called 'family placement' i.e. foster parenting (see *Other parents* below, section 2).

☞ *Your wife recently died. Your teenage daughter was very difficult during her mother's illness, and she has now become uncontrollable. You feel you can no longer cope and that she needs the kind of care which you just cannot give to her. You would like to consider the possibility of fostering.*

You can apply to the local authority which will then investigate the entire family situation. Your daughter's views will also be taken into account.

Note: it is open to the court to provide for some other form of order, such as a supervision order which will entail a social worker or probation officer befriending and assisting a child to help over a present crisis (see *Supervision order* above, section 1.5). It can also make a family assistance order (see *Children (Part 1)*, section 3.5).

2   OTHER PARENTS AND CARERS

2.1   Adoption

Adoption is the total and legal transfer of a child from one set of parents to another set of parents. It is intended to terminate the child's existing legal relationship and to give all parental responsibility to the adopting parents. Adoption procedures are strictly controlled by legislation and the child's new status is given formal recognition by the court. Even a new birth certificate is entered into the register in place of the child's original birth certificate.

Until now adoption was governed by the 1976 Adoption Act which all agree has become outdated.

The Adoption and Children Act 2002 which received Royal Assent in November 2002 is intended to modernise the legal framework for adoption. It aims to increase the number of potential adoptive parents in order the reduce the numbers of children in foster and other care. The new law hopes to encourage more people to come forward to adopt, by:

* providing an adoption support service
* enabling single people to adopt
* setting up an independent review mechanism for applicants who consider that they have been unfairly turned down as adopters.

At present only married couples or single people can apply to adopt a child, but under the new Act both unmarried couples and same-sex partners will be able to adopt.

Parents who wish to adopt are carefully vetted by an adoption agency or the local authority acting as an adoption agency. They are usually:

* childless couples or
* step-parents or
* a natural parent, such as the unmarried father of a child.

In 2000, there were 2,800 orders for adoption made in the courts. Of these, about 50 per cent were step-parent adoptions.

(At the end of this chapter, there is a DIRECTORY of organisations which give information or advice on adoption issues.)

Where there is a complete severance of all ties between children and natural parents, the child's new family is expected to take their place, as well as the place of other relatives.

☞ *You are unmarried and have given full agreement to the adoption of your baby girl aged three months. However, your mother, the child's grandmother, wishes to maintain contact with the child. What is her position?*

A natural grandmother would have to make application to the court for a contact order and would have to persuade the court that it would be in the child's best interests for contact to be maintained. The court would also take into account the views and feelings of the adopting parents.

Local social services authorities and other adoption agencies are being encouraged by the government to maximise the use of adoption as a choice for children who are in care and to improve their current practices which have been seen as unduly restrictive.

New guidelines have been set which state that adoption has been regarded for too long as the last and least acceptable option.

Certain practices that local authorities have insisted upon for their vetting procedures have been deemed 'misguided' – for example, discounting prospective parents who were over 40, or were deemed to be the wrong colour, or who smoked; or paying undue attention to the belief of social workers that the natural family must be kept together even at the expense of the child's best interests.

Do note: local authorities are under a duty of care to warn adoptive parents of any particular problem that might affect the relationship between them and the child; for example, in one case the local authority was found negligent because it had failed to inform the adoptive parents that a child suffered from a hyperactive condition that made him impossible to control.

2.1.1   Conflicts of interest

The court's role is generally to give formal recognition to the change of status of an adopted child. However, conflicts do arise between a local authority which has a child in care and wishes to free it for adoption, and the child's natural parent(s). The court thus becomes the final arbiter in disputes where the natural parents – usually an unmarried mother – refuse to agree to an adoption. An adoption agency can submit that the parents are 'unreasonably withholding their consent' and ask the court to override the parents' wishes.

These are some of the most difficult and painful cases which a court has to deal with. The guidelines at present are that the court must view the case in terms of whether a 'reasonable' parent would see that adoption is in the long-term best interests of the child.

In one case where a mother sought to have her baby boy returned to her after he had been with his prospective adopters for nearly three months from birth, the judge said that it was one of the most heartfelt cases which had called for his decision. Inevitably his judgment was going to hurt someone very much. By the time of the hearing the child was about to have his first birthday and it would be too traumatic for him to return to his mother. The dispute was between two good families but the judge concluded that a 'reasonable mother' in the present circumstances would give her consent to the adoption.

In relation to adoption proceedings, birth parents who seek community legal funding [formerly legal aid] have to meet less stringent requirements: for example, their need to be legally represented is more readily realised, and the threshold 'merit test' which they have to cross is also lower than in other cases (see chapter on *The Legal System*, section 3.1).

2.1.2   Adoptions from abroad

In this country a couple who wish to adopt a child from another country must go through the proper channels for inter-country adoptions.

Over the years, it has been acknowledged that while there are currently hundreds of successful adoptions from overseas each year, there were other cases where people avoided the screening procedures and brought children into the UK even when they had been assessed as unsuitable as adoptive parents.

In 1999 the Adoption (Intercountry Aspects) Act was passed which is aimed at ensuring that inter-country adoption only takes place when it is in the best interest of the child. The Act gives effect to the 1993 Hague Convention on Protection of Children and Co-operation.

It makes it an offence to bring a child into the UK to be adopted by people who have no authority to do so, unless they are relatives.

The Act is also intended to stop adoption-trafficking by creating a statutory basis for inter-country adoption and enables children adopted from overseas to enjoy the same legal status as children adopted in the UK.

Adoption societies are to be allowed to provide inter-country adoption services and it is not acceptable practice to deny parents assessment on the grounds that an agency does not agree with inter-country adoption.

The Registrar General, provided that he has sufficient particulars, can register a foreign adoption in the Adopted Children Register.

☞ *You have seen pictures on television of the plight of orphan children in Romanian orphanages. You and your husband are childless and wish to adopt one of these children. You want to go through all the proper channels and wonder where you should begin with your enquiries.*

All local authority social services have an adoption service. This should include assessment of would-be parents wishing to adopt from overseas as well. You should contact your local authority, therefore, in the first instance although it may then refer you on to another agency, such as a voluntary adoption agency. It should not be a factor that you do not share the same ethnic or cultural background as the children from your country of choice (see circular LAC (98) 20).

There is also a HelpLine for Overseas Adoptions: 0990 168 742.

2.1.3   Re-establishing contact – child and natural parents

2.1.3(a)   Access to birth records

At the age of 18, adopted children now have access to their original birth records so that they can establish their original parentage.

There are limitations:

* for adoption before 1975, counselling is obligatory
* information against the public interest can be withheld.

See the DIRECTORY for organisations that give counselling and advice on re-establishing contact with your natural parents.

2.1.3(b)   Adoption Contact Register

Relatives of a child who has been adopted can record their details in a register if they wish to resume contact. These details will then be passed on, provided that the adopted person – in turn – has indicated that he or she wishes to resume contact. There are agencies which will help, in particular the Children's Society and the Post-Adoption Centre. Relatives can also seek help in tracing adopted children through Families in Time (see DIRECTORY on page 109).

2.1.3(c)   Making contact – the new law

Under the Adoption and Children Act 2002 birth relatives will have the statutory right to ask an adoption support agency to make contact with sons, daughters, brothers and sisters who were adopted when they were children.

The adoption support agency will be able to:

* obtain information from the adoption agency or the Registrar General which will help it to trace the adopted person
* inform the adopted adult of the application from the birth relative
* ask the adopted adult if he or she is prepared to give their consent for their identity to be passed to the birth relative.

If the adopted adult gives consent, his or her identity is to be disclosed to the birth relative. If the adopted adult does not give his or her consent, it must not be disclosed.

This system would apply to adoptions made before the Adoption and Children Act comes into force.

Information may be obtained via the Department of Health website: *www.doh.gov.uk.*

The amendments do not:

* give a right to birth parents to make direct contact with the adopted adult or adopted child
* give birth parents the right to the information maintained by the Registrar General in the Adopted Children Register.

☞ *You have heard about a new law to allow birth relatives contact with adopted children. You were adopted and have no wish to be in contact with your birth family. You are now very worried that you may be contacted against your wishes and feel that this would be a violation of your right to privacy. What can you do?*

Many adopted people are pleased that these proposals will mean they meet birth relatives. Others, like you, are worried about what the new law could mean. You need not be afraid that you will have to face unwelcome contact with any member of your birth family. Information will only be released with your consent and if you do not consent, no information will be disclosed to any birth relative. However you can make your position clear in advance by writing to the Registrar General (Adoptions Section) Smedley Hydro, Trafalgar Road, Southport, Lancs, giving details of your name, your date of birth and your adoptive parents' names and ask the Registrar General to note your views.

On the other hand, you might like to consider whether there are any circumstances in which you would like information about your birth family, e.g. to be advised of significant genetically important medical information or to learn of a bequest from a will. You can make the relevant bodies aware of this. Contact NORCAP (see DIRECTORY) for more help and advice.

☞ *You have been told by a relative that your mother gave up a baby girl for adoption five years before you were born. Your mother has now died and there are no relatives who can tell you anything about your sister. You would like to contact her. What can you do?*

There are agencies which will help, in particular the Children's Society and the Post-Adoption Centre. Another support group is Families in Time (see DIRECTORY). There is a bulletin board for people seeking contact on a website *www.adoption-net.co.uk*.

NORCAP (National Organisation for Counselling Adoptees and Parents) will offer advice and support, telephone 01865 875000 (see DIRECTORY). You can post a notice about your search on *www.cl.cam.ac.uk/newslist/alt.adoption.html* by clicking on alt.adoption.searching.

2.1.4   Changing adoption patterns

Unmarried mothers now receive state support to bring up their babies. The stigma which attached to having children out of wedlock has also largely gone. Termination of unwanted pregnancies is also generally made available. As a result, fewer and fewer babies are placed by their mothers for adoption soon after birth. Thus children who are available for adoption are likely to be older, and therefore ties with their birth parents may already be strong. Consequently, while the legal status with their families may be altered irrevocably, the psychological links may remain more unyielding to change. Moreover, as we have seen, about half the annual number of adoptions now take place between children and their step-parents.

Thus the concept of a total legal severance of ties between adopted children and their natural parents is no longer always apposite. These changing needs and patterns are reflected in the continuing debate on how best to legislate for adoption procedures.

2.2   Guardians

Parents who have children under 18 may be anxious about what would happen to them in the event of their death. They can appoint guardians for minor children in their wills. In other words, the guardian takes the place of the deceased parent in the child's life. (This is also discussed in the chapter *Death – Before and After*, section 9.)

2.3   Fostering

A child can be cared for by others under a private arrangement. Notice of such an arrangement must be given to a local authority. Under the Children Act 1989, a private fostering arrangement applies when a child is:

* under the age of 16
* living with others (excluding parents, someone with a parental responsibility order, or a relative) for a period of longer than 28 days.

Payment is not a necessary factor.

The Act excludes many situations, such as where a child is in boarding school. The fact that relatives are excluded too means that common domestic arrangements, such as grandparents looking after a child, do not fall within the Act.

If a private fostering arrangement does apply, the local authority can visit the foster parents and inspect their accommodation. However, the most common fostering arrangements are those in which a local authority takes a child into care and places him or her with foster parents rather than in a local authority home.

2.4   Wardship

2.4.1   What is wardship?

Wardship over children is a power of the court, used in very special circumstances, to transfer to the court all responsibility for a child's life. That child then becomes a 'ward of court'. The child must be a minor, i.e. under 18. No major step can be taken with regard to the child, once he or she has been made a ward of court, without permission of the court.

2.4.2   When is wardship used?

A wardship application is made to court when there is an urgent need to protect a child's interests. It has been used in life-threatening situations, e.g. when doctors wanted to turn off the life-support machine of a dying infant. It has also been used while deciding the question of sterilisation of a mentally retarded girl.

However, wardship has been invoked in other circumstances, such as to ensure the proper supervision of property belonging to a child, or to prevent a child from being abducted from home.

The 1989 Children Act is intended to cut down on wardship applications; for example, local authorities are no longer able to apply to make a child a ward of court in order to take a child into care. Where a local authority does apply to court for wardship, it has to obtain the court's permission which will only be granted if the local authority can show that:

- the other orders available to it under the Act will not achieve the necessary results and
- the child will suffer significant harm if not warded.

In general the courts have stated that wardship will not be granted where an issue can be settled by its powers under the Children Act.

2.4.3   Procedure

Although anyone can apply for wardship of a child – for example, a non-relative such as a doctor or social worker – an applicant must have a genuine interest in the child's welfare. Wardship takes effect immediately, even before a judge hears the case. The hearing must then take place within three weeks.

2.5   In need of care from 'carers' – protection for children

As we have seen, the Children Act tries to impose standards on those whose job it is to look after children. However, abuses do take place both within the family and outside it.

The problems are manifold: changing social patterns and attitudes, lack of public resources, conflict between the necessity for state protection of children and the undesirability of intrusive interference in family life. Where requirements are made too onerous – for foster parents or childminders, for example – how can local authorities enforce them? Difficulties in legislating and then in implementing the legislation are only too clear.

Note of warning: the depressing litany of public inquiries into abuse in children's homes (for example, the Waterhouse Report into abuse in children's homes in North Wales) indicates only too clearly the difficulty of ensuring that the vulnerable in our society are properly looked after by those employed to do so. Safeguards and procedures against employing child molesters and other abusers to care for children are in place, and are being strengthened all the time in the light of recommendations in the various reports. Under the Protection of Children Act 1999, a Consultancy Index has been drawn up which lists those who are unsuitable to work with children. Henceforward employers will be obliged to check the names of anyone seeking employment which entails regular contact with children against the list which is held by the Department of Health and the Department for Education and Skills. However it is doubtful that any system of controls can be devised which prevents undesirable people from ever penetrating the screening.

Therefore and in addition, every social services authority should put in place a Children's Complaints Officer who is not a line manager of residential staff. An independent advocacy service for any child in care who wishes to have it is also being put together under a government programme.

A National Care Standards Commission was set up in April 2002 to regulate children's homes, among other care homes, and will inspect care services and work to national standards. It can be contacted at *enquiries@ncsc.gsi.gov.uk* or at its website (also see DIRECTORY).

Do note: the courts have no power to supervise council childcare plans once they have been agreed to by the courts. Indeed, the House of Lords has recently ruled that judges are not empowered to interfere with the way that local authorities discharge their parental responsibilities under a care order.

They should ensure that the care plan is specific, and councils should present to the courts a reasonably clear picture of the likely way ahead for the children in care for the foreseeable future.

3   EDUCATION

3.1   Parent's duty to educate

By law, from the age of 5 to 16 all children must receive compulsory full-time education. Moreover, children are legally entitled to receive education which is suitable to their needs and aptitudes. The past decades have seen a mass of legislation in the educational field. The latest major piece of legislation is the School Standards and Framework Act which was passed in 1998 and which deals with the following:

- parent representation on the LEAs
- categories of schools
- admission procedures
- pupil exclusions
- setting up education action zones
- identification of failing schools, i.e. schools which are unlikely to give pupils a proper standard of education.

A single curriculum authority, the Qualification and Curriculum Authority, has taken the place of the earlier body. See section 3.4.1 below. (See also DIRECTORY.)

3.2   Schools' changing role

One of the main purposes of the new legislation was to give parents greater preference and more information over their children's education.

3.2.1   Parental preference

Parents should be able to make informed choices about the schools in which their children are taught.

3.2.2   Information on offer

The local education authority must produce a booklet of information on schools in its area, including the number of pupils to be admitted in each school and the basis for selection so that the admissions policies of all schools in their area are clear to parents.

Each school must produce its own prospectus, which must include:

- school aims
- subjects offered
- other activities and clubs
- discipline and other measures.

Each board of governors must produce an annual report including:

- names of governors
- address for contacting school
- information about next parent-governor elections
- details of complaints and appeals procedures
- school budget.

Inspectors' reports of full inspections must be published. Schools must publish a 'league table' of results of all passes at GCSE and A level. Independent schools (i.e. schools outside the state sector) are included in these tables. Since 1997, the LEAs have been obliged to publish performance tables of primary schools.

3.2.3   Open enrolment

All classes must be filled with the optimum number of pupils. Class level numbers have been set as targets in a strenuous effort to reduce numbers of children in a single classroom, and this may affect your child's chances of entrance to the school of your choice.

However, your child is entitled to a place unless the class is filled to capacity with pupils who have a stronger claim.

3.2.3(a)   Enrolment appeals

If there are more applicants than places, the local education authority, or the governors, must apply their own rules on who may be enrolled into the school. If your child is refused a place you can appeal to an admission appeal panel set up for the purpose.

The composition of the committee and its procedure varies from authority to authority. However, in an endeavour to introduce greater transparency and openness for parents, admission appeal panels must be independently constituted from other admissions authorities.

☞ *The time has come for your eldest child to transfer to secondary school. You have studied the school prospectuses for the local area, as well as the LEA secondary transfer booklet. You have discussed the merits of the different schools with other parents and you have made a number of visits to the various schools on your shortlist. You now have decided on the school to which you want to send your child. It is some distance from your home. When you make application, you are told that the school enrolment is full. What can you do?*

Legally, you have a right of appeal. In the case of a voluntary or foundation school, the admission authority may be the governing body. Your appeal will be heard by an admission appeal panel which must be independent of the admissions authority itself, i.e. the local education authority or individual school. If you can persuade the panel of your case and it feels that your reasons are compelling, it can overrule the local education authority or governors.

The procedure differs slightly from one local education authority to another as the law gives them some autonomy in organising the appeals procedure. The Council of Tribunals has issued a code of practice, which the committees should follow and which is available for the guidance of LEAs. In addition, in making their decision the admission appeal panel must follow the statutory guidelines drawn up by the Secretary of State for Education and Skills.

A Department of Education and Skills study showed that parents were confused by the new admission rules. Their children were often denied a place at their choice of school, and the aggrieved parents consequently appealed. Indeed, the number of appeals has grown considerably, with 90,700 appeals lodged in 2000–01. About one-third of the appeals were decided in the parents' favour.

Under the School Standards and Act 1998, school admission authorities are under a duty to comply with parental preference except in circumstances where to admit the child would prejudice the provision of efficient education or use of resources. Difficulty in meeting parental preference may also arise:

- by reason of compliance with the limit on infant class sizes
- where the preferred school is a voluntary aided or foundation school and admission would be incompatible with the preservation of its religious character
- where the school is wholly selective by high ability or aptitude
- where the child has been permanently excluded from two or more schools (at least one exclusion must be after 1 September 1997) – this does not apply to children who have been reinstated after exclusion
- where admission would be incompatible with co-ordinated admission arrangements covering two or more maintained schools.

3.3   Schools' structure

3.3.1   School governors

The recent reforms in education have given a great deal of authority to school governors. Strenuous efforts are being made to encourage parents and civic-minded people in the community to put themselves forward in the role of governor.

3.3.2   Role of head

The role of the headteacher has changed with all the reforms which have been introduced. Heads have to liaise with the governing body, the LEA and the parents, and they can now only exercise their powers over curriculum, staffing, discipline, finance and admission of pupils in conjunction with the governors and in co-operation with them.

The head sets the standards of school behaviour and makes the rules accordingly. He or she alone has the sole power to exclude or expel a pupil (see section 3.5.2 below) but there are rights of appeal thereafter to the governing body.

3.3.3   Role of parents

The increased involvement of parents in their children's education has been encouraged by recent legislation.

Parents are represented by their own governors on the school governing body.

In addition, under the School Standards and Framework Act, local authorities must ensure that there are parent-governor representatives on their main education committees. These parent-governor representatives have both speaking and voting rights, and must be elected by all current parent governors within the LEA.

A circular (13/99) defines their role, among other matters, as:

- acting as a voice for parents in the area by representing to the local authority their main concerns
- liaising with other parent-governor representatives in the area
- communicating to parents the local authority's discussions and decisions on education.

Parents will also be called upon to sign home–school agreements which set out the school's ethos, as well as policies regarding attendance, discipline, homework, and other information. The Department for Education and Skills website contains information on home–school agreements at *www.dfes.gov.uk*. These agreements are intended to ensure that parents understand what they can expect from the school, while the school, in turn, can rely on parental commitment. Matters in the agreement include:

- regular, punctual attendance
- homework guidelines
- discipline
- anti-bullying policies
- educational standards.

All parents are expected to sign a declaration in support of the agreement.

☞   *You are told that you should sign a home–school agreement by the City Technology College which your child is hoping to attend. You are eager to co-operate but wonder what the legal position is if either your son or you yourself inadvertently breaches one of its clauses, such as how much time is to be spent on homework each night.*

   The agreement is there to spell out to parent and child that both they and the school have obligations as well as duties. However, the agreement does not have binding legal force. These agreements are also not to be used in admissions procedures.

At the DfES website (see above) there is a site called Parents Centre. It contains information on pre-school, choosing a school, curriculum, assessment, learning at home, learning support, and education after the age of 16. As we have seen above (section 3.2.2), parents are entitled to certain information by law. They have a right to appeal or complain on many issues (see *Where parents can turn for help*, section 3.7 below).

3.4   School syllabus

3.4.1   National curriculum

A national curriculum of core subjects has been laid down. It applies to children aged from 5 to 16. The three core subjects are English language, mathematics and science. The eight foundation subjects comprise design and technology, history, geography, art, music, and communication technology. A modern language is taught in secondary schools.

From September 2000 a national non-statutory framework was introduced for the teaching of personal, social and health education (PSHE) for 5 to 16-year-olds (see also 3.4.4 below).

Citizenship has been introduced as a foundation subject for 11 to 16-year-olds from September 2002. There will also be a non-statutory framework for the teaching of Citizenship at key stages 1 and 2.

All aspects of the curriculum are kept under review by the Qualification and Curriculum Authority (see DIRECTORY).

Physical education remains compulsory across all key stages, and competitive games remain compulsory for all 5 to 14-year-olds.

3.4.1(a)   Standard attainment tasks

On the basis of this curriculum, children have to perform Standard Attainment Tasks (SATs). These are compulsory in English, mathematics and science at ages 7, 11, and 14.

3.4.2   Records

The school must keep a 'profile of attainment' for each child of how he or she performed in the SATs.

A 'Record of achievement' is compiled for each pupil from the first day of school to the last and covers a broad range of matters and not just test scores.

Schools must publish league table results of examination passes.

3.4.2(a)   Access to records

Parents wanting access to school records on their child must approach the head or the board of governors.

3.4.3   Religious education

Every pupil must receive religious education under the Education Act 1988 and take part in a daily act of religious worship. Emphasis is laid on the mainly Christian traditions of this country. At the moment, each LEA draws up its own curriculum within general guidelines laid down by the Department for Education and Skills.

Although the religious tradition of this country is mainly Christian, the syllabus is generally expected to include teaching on the other principal world religions. Children can be withdrawn from assembly on request of the parents on the grounds of conscience. Teachers are also permitted to refuse to teach RE. Pupils who practise other religions can receive their own religious education – apart from the rest of the school – if groups of parents approach the school and alternative teaching can be arranged.

Pupils themselves cannot opt out of RE classes.

☞   *Your teenage son has asked his form teacher whether he can be excused RE on the ground that he does not believe in the existence of God. The teacher has refused. What is your son's position?*

It is only the parents who can request the withdrawal of their children from RE classes.

3.4.4   Sex education

School governors can decide whether the school should give sex education lessons. Pupils are to be encouraged to 'have due regard to moral considerations and the value of family life' in sex education classes.

Parents are entitled to ask for their children to be withdrawn from sex education lessons except insofar as the instruction forms part of the national curriculum e.g. in science classes.

☞ *Your 14-year-old daughter, who goes to the local comprehensive school, receives sex education lessons. You would like to have some idea of what she is being taught. You also understand that the school uses an educational video on sex education. You wonder whether you can ask to view the video?*

You should approach the head and explain the nature of your request and why you are making it. You should receive a sympathetic response. You could also approach the board of governors. Independent complaints committees exist, set up by the local education authorities, to whom you can turn if you are still not happy with the outcome. You can also withdraw your child from the class altogether.

In fact, a survey has shown that one in four schools has failed to draw up a policy document on sex education classes. However, the national curriculum framework for personal, social and health education (PSHE) (see also section 3.4.1 above) is intended to help pupils deal with 'difficult moral and social questions'. In the interim, and in part as a result of attempting to legislate on educating children about homosexual and other relationships ('Clause 28' debate), guidance on sex and relationship education was issued by the DfES in March 2000.

3.5   School discipline

A statement of school rules should appear in the prospectus issued by the school, and, under the School Standards and Framework Act 1998, the governing body and head teacher are responsible for good behaviour and discipline. However the Act also gives the LEA a residual power to take whatever steps are thought necessary to prevent or put right a breakdown of discipline.

3.5.1   Corporal punishment

As a result of a free vote in the House of Commons, corporal punishment was made illegal in all schools. However, staff are allowed to use physical force to restrain pupils:

- in order to prevent a child from committing an offence
- where there is an immediate danger of personal injury either to someone else or to the child involved
- where there is an immediate danger to property.

These rules apply both during teaching sessions and otherwise, e.g. during playtime.

3.5.2   Exclusions and expulsions

Only a head teacher has power to exclude a child from a state school.

The head must take reasonable steps to inform the parents without delay of the reasons for the exclusion and how long it is likely to last. The head may not exclude a pupil for one or more fixed periods which result in the pupil being excluded for more than 45 school days in any one school year. During the period the pupil is excluded from school, work should be set and it should be marked. A head may not exclude a pupil for an indefinite period. However a power exists to exclude a pupil from a school permanently. Parents are entitled to express their views to the governors or to the independent appeal panel, which can order a reinstatement either immediately or by a particular date. The head is obliged to reinstate at their direction.

If a head has decided to exclude for a longer period than five days, the governors and the LEA must be informed. If a pupil is permanently excluded from any school, the local education authority has the duty to provide other suitable education. This may be a place in another school, or the local education authority could place the pupil in a local special educational unit (sometimes called a Pupil Referral Unit or PRU), or provide home or individual tuition. Current figures are that 9,956 children attend PRUs full-time.

3.5.2(a)   Appeal Process

If your child is excluded for a fixed-period exclusion or a permanent exclusion, you have the right to make representations to the Discipline Committee which is made up of school governors. If the Discipline Committee upholds a permanent exclusion, you have the right to appeal to an Independent Appeal Panel. There is very detailed DfES guidance on exclusions which is available at *www.dfee.gov.uk/circulars/10-99.*

An exclusions advice line (0808 8000 327) is run by the Advisory Centre for Education (ACE) on weekday afternoons who also provide an information pack about school exclusion. For further information about the service call the ACE Information Line on 020 7704 9822 (also see DIRECTORY).

Exclusion should not be used for:

- minor incidents such as failure to do homework or bring dinner money
- poor academic performance
- lateness or truancy
- pregnancy
- breaching school uniform policy including hairstyle or wearing jewellery
- punishing pupils for the behaviour of the parents – for example, by extending a fixed-period exclusion until the parents agree to attend a meeting.

If a child is excluded, there is an automatic right of appeal to the school governors or the independent appeal panel.

☞   *Your 15-year-old child has been excluded from his school for 10 school days. You feel it is most unfair because the incident involved another boy who was clearly the ringleader. That child has also been excluded. You would like to appeal and your son would like to attend the appeal hearing.*

As a parent you should be given written notice of rights to appeal against the exclusion. You should also be given a time limit in which you must reply in writing setting out the grounds of your appeal.

Parents can attend the appeal and will be given guidance on how to present their case. You can be accompanied by a friend and you may even be represented. However, a pupil under the age of 18 has no right to attend the appeal.

If the parents of the other boy also wish to appeal, the two appeals may be considered together as they relate to the same incident.

The Court of Appeal has stated that parents are entitled to know what is being said against their child and that, in all fairness, parents should have access to damaging evidence to which an appeal panel or governing body also has access.

According to statistics from the DfES, the data for 2000–01 shows that of 9,135 permanent exclusions, 314 appeals were found in favour of the parents.

3.5.3   School security

This acute problem has been much highlighted by the tragic events of the last few years.

There are two aspects to the problem:

- attacks on teachers from children within and without the school premises
- attacks on children from outsiders entering school premises.

At the same time, by their very nature, schools are places where parents, staff and children have to come and go – usually at set hours but sometimes outside these hours. The difficulties are exacerbated by the fact that schools can be built over a large area with many entrances to the grounds.

Schools are resorting to different methods of trying to police their premises, in certain cases employing professional security staff.

3.6   Other problems

3.6.1   Bullying

The subject of the school bully has received a lot of attention in the media of late. There have been tragic instances of children driven to extremes by the fear of having to face their school 'friends' either in the school playground or on journeys to and from school.

Under the 1998 Schools Standards and Framework Act, a head teacher is under a statutory duty to take measures to prevent bullying amongst the pupils.

Bullying takes many forms: physical assault, insults, mockery, ostracism, or racial or sexual abuse.

☞ *Your child has returned home at the end of the school day obviously upset. You notice that his school books have been defaced and that his jacket is torn. He refuses to tell you what has happened but he is a retiring boy and you fear that he may be the victim of school bullies. What can you do?*

The first thing would be to try to get the child to talk to you, but if you are unsuccessful, you may persuade him to talk to another relation or family friend. You should also approach the class teacher in person. Second, ask to see the school's anti-bullying policy which all schools should have. It is a document that sets out how the school deals with incidents of bullying. You have a right to know about this policy, which is for parents, and what they can do, as much as for staff and pupils.

Second, if your child confides in you, keep a log listing the details of every incident. This should be discussed with the child's teacher or the headteacher if the bullying is repeated. The child's teacher could be asked to keep an eye on the child. Particularly vulnerable times for children who are victims of bullies are when they are not actually under direct supervision, but are moving from class to class or are in the playground. You might suggest to the head that the school governors appoint a member of staff as counsellor whom children can approach.

Much material has been prepared for class lessons and discussions on the subject of bullying. Do ascertain whether such material is available in your son's particular school.

If your fears about bullying are confirmed, and the school is not dealing with the problem in a satisfactory way, you should make a formal complaint to the board of governors.

In cases of bullying that involve violence or even the threat of violence, an anxious parent can always turn to the police.

In boarding schools, problems of bullying and harassment can be exacerbated because a child is far from home.

Note: the school's 'behaviour policy' should set out the steps to counter bullying, as well as racial and sexual harassment. Anti-bullying strategies should also cover break and lunch times. Governors should regularly review the anti-bullying policy. Pupils should be encouraged to report bullying to older pupils or staff. The prospectus should explain how to report bullying and how staff investigate. All staff should be alert to bullying and act quickly. Schools should record all racial incidents. Parents and governors should be told about them and about any action taken.

ACE *www.ace-ed.org.uk/advice.html* has a useful list of topics including bullying. They report that some schools have successfully tackled the problem of bullying by various means, such as organised discussion, drama workshops, or a 'Bullying Box' where pupils can secretly report any bullying.

The DfES has advice on its anti-bullying website: *Don't Suffer in Silence* at *www.dfes.gov.uk/bullying*.

(For further information on organisations to turn to for assistance, see DIRECTORY.)

3.6.2   Truancy

Truancy has become an increasing problem.

The School Standards and Framework Act 1998 gives power to the Secretary of State for Education to require governing bodies to have annual school attendance targets.

Many parents are at work and are not in a position to ensure that their child is attending school regularly. As they are obliged by law to ensure that their child is in full-time education, they may find themselves in a situation in which they can be prosecuted and even fined (see section 3.6.2(a) below).

☞ *You are a single parent and work during the day. You were upset to receive a letter from the headmaster stating that your 14-year-old son has been absent from school for some days. You were not aware of the fact that he had been playing truant. You have since heard that the educational welfare officer will be paying you a call at home.*

You should try to establish the reason for the truancy – it may be because of bullying or harassment so that your son may be in need of help. You might consult the LEA or the head, about possible transfer to another school. Plans have been put forward for the parents to be given pagers in cases of children who are playing truant on a regular basis; you could approach your school to enquire whether this is an option.

The educational welfare officer can issue a school attendance order. If your child still does not attend school regularly, in compliance with the order, a local authority can apply to court for an education supervision order (see section 3.6.3 below).

Electronic monitoring may also be introduced for consistent non-attenders.

3.6.2(a) Sanctions against parents

Parents can be prosecuted and fined for the persistent truancy of their children. Until recently, parents could be fined up to £1000 for the persistent non-attendance at school of their child.

Since 1 March 2001 the government changed the situation with regard to truancy by imposing a maximum fine for persistent truancy of £2,500 per parent per child, i.e. £5000 per two-parent family with one child. In addition, under the government's new powers, parents can be forced to attend court when their children consistently play truant, or face arrest, facing a criminal offence with up to three months' imprisonment as punishment if guilty.

In May 2002 a mother's imprisonment made the headlines: she was sentenced by magistrates in Oxfordshire to 60 days' imprisonment for failing to ensure that her daughters, aged 13 and 15-years-old, attended school regularly.

In addition to these measures, the Crime and Disorder Act of 1998 (see below section 5.2.4) has introduced several new orders that could be put in place where children consistently fail to go to school – in particular, parenting orders, which can involve a condition that the parent escorts the child to and from school. In addition the police have been given powers to pick up suspected truants and take them back to school or to other premises. They have no power to arrest or detain the child.

3.6.2(b) Prevention better than cure

Because of the link between truancy, bullying, exclusions and crime, certain schools are to be given funds to invest in projects which will endeavour to get through to children 'who are on the cusp of criminal behaviour' so as to get them back on track. Preventative strategies are to be put in place to tackle disaffection in the classroom with pupil support and mentoring programmes and improved home–school liaison with parents.

3.6.3 Education supervision order

This is an order under the Children Act 1989. The ground for such an order is that 'the child ... is of compulsory school age and is not being properly educated'.

If a child is subject to a school attendance order which is being disobeyed, or is registered at school but not attending regularly, it is assumed that he or she is not being properly educated.

The courts must use the Checklist (see *Children (Part 1)* section 3.2) before issuing an education supervision order and must decide that to issue an order is better than no order at all.

An application to the court must be made by the LEA and both child and parent must be given notice of the application and of the court proceedings. They are entitled to legal aid where appropriate.

If the court is satisfied that your child is not being properly educated, it will appoint a supervisor. It will be the job of the supervisor to befriend and assist the child in his or her difficulties at school.

3.7 Where parents can turn for help

Under the 1988 Education Act parents have a specific right of appeal to the governors or the LEA.

Note: parents can go beyond the local education authority too.

Section 68 of the Education Act 1944 provides that the Secretary of State can be called upon to intervene where a parent's complaint shows that the LEA or the governors have acted unreasonably. The Secretary of State also has the power to order the governors or the LEA to carry out a duty which they have failed to do.

3.8   School structure

3.8.1   New features

The School Standards and Framework Act 1998 established three new categories of mainstream school – community, foundation, and voluntary schools – from September 1999. The categories were largely self-chosen and most former grant-maintained schools became either foundation or voluntary schools.

3.8.2   City Technology Colleges

These are independent schools set up by the then Department of Education in conjunction with commercial and industrial sponsors in urban areas. The CTCs are intended to provide a broad curriculum but with a particular emphasis on technology. They are run by City Technology Trusts.

3.9   The private sector

In the independent sector, the relationship between parent and school is governed by the contract between them. This covers matters including fees, syllabus, discipline etc.

In a recent case, parents of a child who was expelled from an independent school wanted to use the procedures laid down in the Education Act to appeal against expulsion. The court said that the parents could not resort to the public law in a purely private arrangement with the school.

It is not known to what extent the Human Rights Act will impact on an area of private law in a situation such as this. The Act is directed against public authorities. If, however, a child or adult is able to bring their case to the courts at all, then they may be able to argue that the law itself is incompatible with the human rights legislation and is therefore failing to protect them.

3.10   Home-based education

Note: education is compulsory, schoolgoing is not.

☞   *You decide you no longer want to send your child aged 10, who is a gifted chess player, to school. You are a former headteacher and a chess player of note and feel that, in the circumstances, your child would be better educated at home. Are you entitled to withdraw him from school?*

The Education Act 1996 states that it is the duty of parents of school-age children to ensure that they receive efficient full-time education 'either by regular attendance at school or otherwise'. So in fact, while the parents' duty to ensure that their children are being educated is enforceable by law, this education can be 'at school or otherwise'.

Further, the education which every child receives has by law to be efficient, full time, and suitable to his or her needs, age, ability and aptitude.

Educating children at home has seen an increase over recent years as popular schools become over-subscribed and pressure on places grows correspondingly. Parents are able to compare school results and may opt to take their children out of school altogether rather than send them to a school which is 'failing'.

It is estimated that 50,000 children now learn at home. A new scheme called notschool.net provides computers and support for 13 to 15-year-olds who are out of the school system for a variety of reasons such as persistent truancy, illness etc. Suitable children are recommended by schools to the LEA which draws up a shortlist. The selected teenagers are the on the roll of notschool.net which introduces them to the online learning system. More information can be obtained from *enquiries@notschool.net.*

There are organisations which give advice and support to parents who wish to educate their children at home (see DIRECTORY and also the website: *www.education-otherwise.org*).

4   EDUCATING CHILDREN WITH SPECIAL NEEDS

Concerns about a child's education and progress are amongst the most distressing problems for both children and their parents. Yet learning problems are common – about one child in six finds he or she needs help at some stage of schooling. Most such problems are handled in ordinary schools by the class teacher, but about one child in fifty may have problems which need more specialised expertise and more long-term provision.

4.1   What are Special Educational Needs (SEN)?

A child has special educational needs (SEN) if he or she has a learning difficulty which calls for special educational provision to be made for him or her. Thus children are considered to have a learning difficulty if they have a significantly greater difficulty in learning than the majority of children of their age, or have a disability which prevents them from making use of educational facilities of a kind generally provided for children in schools within the area. For example, a child may have difficulties due to:

- a mental or physical disability
- a problem with sight, hearing, speech or communication
- emotional or behavioural problems
- difficulties in an area of school work such as reading, writing, speaking or understanding numbers.

4.2   The Law

The law on special education is contained in the Education Act 1996 amended by the Special Educational Needs and Disability Act 2001. There is also a considerable body of case law on the issue.

LEAs, schools and pre-school settings should work together to ensure that special educational needs (SEN) are identified early. The SEN Code of Practice came into force in January 2002. It gives guidance to LEAs on their duties concerning the education of children with special needs and how those needs should be met. It specifies as follows:

- most children with SEN will be educated in mainstream schools or settings
- the views of the child should be sought and should be taken into account
- parents have a vital role to play in supporting their child's education and their views should be taken into account
- children with SEN should be offered full access to a broad, balanced and relevant education including an appropriate curriculum for the foundation stage and the national curriculum.

For further information, see also *www.dfes.gov.uk/sen/documents/The_Code.htm*.

☞   *Janet was dyslexic from an early age. At the age of 12, she was referred by her head teacher to the school psychological service because of poor progress in reading and writing. The educational psychologist tested her and stated that there were no specific weaknesses although her reading age was that of a child aged seven. Janet was given special needs teaching in English and maths but the psychologist failed to diagnose her dyslexia. She subsequently played truant at school and was unemployed thereafter for years. She would like to claim damages against the local education authority on the grounds of negligence and their failure to carry out their statutory duties in diagnosing and dealing with her educational difficulties.*

In a similar case, the House of Lords held that when an educational psychologist was specifically called in to advise in relation to the assessment of a specific child, knowing that the child's parents and teachers would follow that advice, then a duty of care could arise.

A similar duty could apply to teachers to monitor the needs and performance of their pupils.

Do note however: each case turns on its facts and the view that the court takes of them. The judges are likely to examine such claims closely to ensure that they are not exaggerated and do indeed have a valid basis.

4.3   Identifying children with special educational needs (SEN)

4.3.1   Pre-school children

Local education authorities have a duty to identify those children in their area who will need special educational provision. Children from 2 years of age to 19 are covered. However, this does not mean that the majority will require a Statement (see section 4.4.2 below).

For children under two the position is that the LEA has a duty to identify and provide for special needs if requested by the parents.

☞   *Your sister is worried about her little boy who is 22 months old and does not speak. She is also concerned that he does not respond in social situations. She has asked her GP and the Health Visitor, and both have said that he appears to be able to hear normally and there is nothing to worry about. What can she do?*

She could approach the local education authority and ask to have her child assessed by an educational psychologist. If the boy has SEN they can be assessed and provision can be made for him to have special education and other special help. She can also ask her GP to refer the child to a speech and language therapist.

4.3.2   School age children

If parents are concerned about a child's progress, they should raise the issue with the child's class teacher and the head teacher. The school will assess the child and, if the school believes that a child needs special help, there are a number of options.

School Action: this provides additional support to the child above that given through normal classroom teaching, but is from within the school's resources. The school decides what help is needed and prescribes this on an Individual Education Plan (IEP). At a later stage, if further help is needed, the school will provide.

School Action Plus: that is, after an IEP review meeting, the school consults with the parents and decides that advice from external specialists is required.

4.4   What if extra support is not enough?

Where there is significant cause for concern, the law has provided for a special assessment of the child's needs (Education Act 1996). The purpose of the assessment is to enable the LEA to decide whether the child has special education needs, what those needs are, and how those needs should be met. A Statement (see section 4.4.2 below) can follow the assessment, depending on its outcome.

4.4.1   Assessment

The decision to make an assessment can be triggered by a formal request (in writing) by a parent, or a formal request by a headteacher or a pre-school provider, or a referral by another agency such as a health authority or social services. If a headteacher or nursery head requests a statutory assessment, the authority must respond.

Either the parents or the school may ask the LEA for a statutory assessment of a child and the LEA must agree to make one if:

- no assessment has been made in the last six months
  and
- it considers that it is necessary to make such an assessment.

Where parents have asked an LEA to make an assessment, the LEA must say within six weeks whether or not it will make such an assessment. Where an LEA decides to assess a child for a Statement, it must give the parents a proposed or draft Statement within a further ten weeks, that is, within sixteen weeks of the parents' first asking for an assessment.

The LEA will make an assessment based on evidence from the school and the parents, with advice from educational, medical, psychological and social services, and any other agency that may have useful information about the child's progress. As a result of the assessment the LEA will decide whether it needs to make a Statement (see 4.4.2 immediately below).

4.4.2   Statement of special educational needs

If, after the assessment, the LEA decides that it should make a Statement of special educational needs, it must follow the procedures set out in the Education Act 1996 and in the Education (Special Educational Needs) Regulations 2001. Parents must be sent a copy of a proposed Statement. In the Statement, the LEA must set out its view of the special educational needs of the child. The name and address and other details of the child and the parents are set out in Part 1, with a list of all the child's learning difficulties (Part 2). The Statement must say what special educational provision the LEA thinks will be suitable to meet those needs (Part 3). The LEA will first issue a proposed Statement which says what type of school the LEA thinks will be appropriate for the child (Part 4), but with the name of the school left blank. This is to allow the parents to state their preference. Education at home is also a possibility: if the parents want to educate the child at home and the LEA considers this to be appropriate, the LEA will give details of the provision that it believes to be suitable for the child. (For Home Education help and advice see the DIRECTORY).

Parts 5 and 6 specify the non-educational needs which the child may have, e.g. for transport, and how those needs may be met. Do seek advice if you are uncertain that a Statement includes all the elements required.

Parents who are embarking on this process should obtain a copy of the booklet 'SENT ahead' published by the Independent Panel of Special Education Advisers (IPSEA): tel. 01394 382 814; The Tribunal Service, tel. 01394 384 711, or at: *www.ipsea.co.uk* (see also DIRECTORY).

The LEA must send the parents a copy of the final Statement which specifies a named school and give them written notice that they have a right of appeal to a Tribunal. The time limit for making an appeal is two months from the date they receive the LEA's decision.

4.4.3   Reviewing the Statement

Parents may ask the LEA for a review under the 1996 Education Act if they want to amend any aspect of Parts 2, 3 or 4 of the Statement. LEAs have the power to review a Statement at any time during the year. All Statements must be reviewed each year. An annual review may lead to changes in a child's Statement. This may be because, for example:

- the child's needs may have changed significantly
- the LEA may decide that different kinds of extra help are necessary
- the child may have to move to a different school.

Where an LEA proposes to make changes following a review, it must send the parents an amendment notice that sets out the details for the proposed changes and explains the reasons. Parents have a right to appeal to the SEN Tribunal (see section 4.7 below) against any change made by the LEA to the description of the child's SEN, the types of help to be provided and the name of the school to be attended.

4.4.4   Refusal to assess

It should be noted that the LEA can and often does refuse a parental request for a statutory assessment. The parent can then appeal to the Special Educational Needs and Disability Tribunal (see section 4.7 below).

The law also includes protection for parents who do not want their child to be assessed (or later, after assessment, to have a Statement). Thus, there is a right of appeal to the Tribunal against a decision to assess as well as against one not to assess.

4.5   Which school?

Most children with Statements are taught in ordinary schools. It has been government policy for many years to include children with special needs in mainstream schools if at all possible. The Special Educational Needs and Disability Discrimination Act 2001 gave parents a stronger right to a place in a mainstream school for their child. Where the parents wish a place in an ordinary (mainstream) school, this can be refused only where the education of other children would suffer or if the child's needs could not be adequately met. Unless the parents ask for special school education the LEAs have a duty to educate in mainstream schools where this is possible.

The decision as to whether a mainstream or a special school would be best for a child can be very difficult. Parent-partnership services are advice and information services which are arranged by LEAs for parents of children with special educational needs. The Services organise the recruitment and training of Independent Parental Supporters (IPS) to meet the needs of parents in their area. Parents should ask the LEA for their help in making contact and then use the Services and the IPS. The IPS may, for example, help to arrange for the parent to visit possible schools. There is also information about Ofsted reports at local libraries or the Ofsted website: *www.ofsted.gov.uk.*

Parents have a right to express a preference for a particular special school, which may be maintained (that is funded by the LEA), non-maintained or independent.

Will the wishes of the parents always be followed? No, not always. If the parents ask for a school outside the LEA where they live, they need to make a case for what that school could provide over and above what would be available in their own LEA. The law says that the LEA must name the maintained school that parents prefer unless the school is unsuitable for the child or the child's attendance would be incompatible with the efficient education of other children in the school or with the efficient use of the LEA's resources.

☞ *Christopher's parents expressed their preference to their local education authority, in the borough of Y, that he should be educated at a special school, outside its boundaries in the neighbouring borough of X. The request was refused on the ground that it would undermine the efficient use of resources to do so; in fact, it would cost the borough council of Y several thousand pounds a year more to send Christopher to a school maintained by the borough of X than at a school maintained by Y's own local education authority. The parents argued that 'resources' should not be considered only in relation to those of the home authority but overall.*

In a similar case, the House of Lords stated that although there was a right to express a preference that did not mean that the consideration concerned resources generally. The scheme for the provision of special educational needs was for children for whom the local education authority was responsible, i.e. for those children who were in their own area.

When parents express a preference for a particular school, the LEA will consider that school's suitability for the child. The LEA must consult the governors of the parent's preferred school; the LEA has the final decision on which school to name in the Statement.

A court has ruled that 'an appropriate school' specified in a Statement meant appropriate to the child's education in a wide sense and was not confined to his special educational needs. It reached its decision in a case in which a dyslexic boy had begun attending a private school at his parents' expense. Once his educational needs were assessed by his LEA, it named a different school in the Statement of Needs. It was argued on behalf of the boy that a transfer to the other school would be detrimental to his educational progress. The court agreed and stated that what was 'appropriate' had to take into account work actually undertaken – such as syllabuses and courses already embarked on – as well as the difficulty that such a move would cause for the boy.

In order to help parents decide which school is right for their child, it is worth referring to voluntary organisations, some of which are listed in the DIRECTORY. Others are listed in a booklet published by ACE (see DIRECTORY) entitled *Children with special needs: sources of help.*

4.6   Complaints

Parents have a right to complain about the way a school is meeting a child's needs, the way the LEA is arranging for the child to be helped, or the length of time it has taken to assess or statement the child. It is always best to contact the school informally to discuss any problems or complaints concerning the school's approach to the child to try to sort out any problems. If that doesn't resolve the issue the parents should ask for a copy of school procedures for making complaints about SEN. If these discussions leave unresolved issues, the parents may consider using the SEN disagreement resolution process. The LEA must set up a disagreement resolution service in which issues concerning education will be looked at by an independent panel, with the child's welfare and needs being the primary consideration.

4.7   The right to appeal

Parents have a right to appeal to an independent tribunal against decisions affecting their child's education, for example to arrange for the child to be a pupil in a mainstream or a special school. The Special Educational Needs and Disability Tribunal hears these appeals. The Tribunal's decision on the facts is final but there is a right of appeal on a point of law. The Tribunal has produced a booklet, *How to Appeal*, which contains an appeal form and guidance notes. It can be obtained by phoning 01325 392 555. There is a two-month time limit for making an appeal which starts to run when the LEA gives its final written decision.

A parent can appeal if the LEA:

- will not carry out a formal assessment of a child's SEN; or
- refuses to issue a Statement of the child's SEN.

If the LEA has made a Statement or has changed a previous Statement the parent can appeal against:

- the parts which describe the child's SEN (Part 2) and set out the special educational help (Part 3) that the LEA think the child should get; or
- the school named in Part 4 of the Statement; or
- the LEA not naming a school in Part 4.

A parent can also appeal if the LEA:

- refuses to change the school named in the child's Statement, if that Statement is at least a year old (but parents can only ask for an LEA-maintained school, that is, one that is funded by the LEA); or
- refuses to reassess the child's SEN if the LEA has not made a new assessment for at least six months
- decides not to maintain the child's Statement; or
- decides not to change the Statement after reassessing the child.

Parents can appoint a representative or may conduct the case themselves. There can be more than one representative if the Tribunal agrees. Free legal help from a solicitor may be available for those who qualify, as this is means-tested. This would be provided via the Legal Services Commission [formerly Legal Aid]. See also the chapter on *The Legal System*, section 3.1 concerning the priority given to cases involving the welfare of children. Information is also available at *www.justask.org.uk*. The hearing normally takes half a day, and the Tribunal usually writes to the parents within 10 working days of the hearing with its decision. Both parties (that is, the LEA and the parents) may apply to the Tribunal for the decision to be reviewed on one or more of four grounds:

1) The decision was wrong because of an error by Tribunal staff
2) A party who failed to appear had good reasons for absence and his/her evidence would have been relevant
3) There was an obvious error in the decision
4) The decision is not in the interests of justice.

The Tribunal which reviews a decision may alter the decision, or revoke it, or order a rehearing before the same or a different Tribunal. If parents have asked for a review but after the review they are still not satisfied, they can appeal to the High Court, but only on points of law. The Tribunal's decision on the facts is final. Appeals must be started within 28 days from the date of the Tribunal's decision. Advice from a solicitor or a voluntary organisation would be very helpful (see the DIRECTORY and also the chapter on *The Legal System* for where to turn to for advice and assistance).

4.8   What happens when a child turns 16?

Education for young people with SEN does not stop at 16. If both parents and the LEA agree that the school which the child attends can continue to meet the young person's needs then the Statement should be maintained after the 16th birthday.

☞ *Your son was assessed and a Statement made of his special educational needs when he was 10-years-old. At age 16, the local education authority decided to cease to maintain that*

Statement. You wonder what you can do as you feel he should have the chance for further education.

In a similar case, the court ruled that a parent could appeal to the Special Educational Needs Tribunal (see section 4.7 immediately above).

Where the young person is transferring to an LEA-maintained 16–19 institution (such as a college of further education or a sixth-form college), the LEA must amend the Statement by 15 February of the calendar year of transfer. If the young person wishes to attend a further education or sixth-form college or training centre, there will be a Young Person's Transition Plan setting out the aim of continuing their education outside school. Under Section 140 of the Learning and Skills Act 2000 the Connexions Service (see section 4.8.1 immediately below) must undertake an assessment of the young person's needs in the final year of school and identify suitable provision for that young person's continuing educational needs. The Connexions Service works with the local Learning and Skills Council (see DIRECTORY) to ensure that there will be provision for the young person when he or she transfers. If on the other hand, the young person chooses to seek employment, he or she would then cease to be a responsibility of the LEA.

4.8.1 The Connexions Service

This service for all 13 to 19-year-olds gives priority to those young people at greatest risk of not making a successful transition to adulthood. A network of Personal Advisers (PAs) provide particular services for young people with SEN. PAs link in with specialist support services and also sometimes work directly with young people in schools. The Service's responsibilities stem from the legal duties of the Secretary of State for Education under the Learning and Skills Act 2000.

4.8.2 Setting up a trust for a disabled child

If you, as a parent of a disabled or handicapped person, wish to set up a trust out of your estate to take care of their future needs, please turn to the chapter on *Death – Before and After*, section 4.1.4.

4.8.3 Mediation

A mediation service is available for schools, colleges and universities to resolve disputes with parents of disabled children or disabled students. The service is run independently from the Disability Rights Commission by Mediation UK (see DIRECTORY).

5 CHILDREN AND CRIME

5.1 Crimes against children

All the crimes which may be committed against adults may also be committed against children. They may be assaulted, robbed or murdered. However, in this section we deal briefly with specific crimes which may be committed against children.

5.1.1 Abduction

With the number of failed marriages and the present general state of flux, the abduction of children by estranged parents is a growing and grave issue. Most abductions are carried out by fathers.

Newspaper and other reports testify to the heartbreak of the parents involved. The traumatic effects on the children involved can only be guessed at. The headlines refer to child abduction as 'tug-of-love' but the end result is human misery.

There are complex legal issues involved, particularly in view of the fact that the problem of child abduction often crosses international borders. If you are fearful of a possible abduction, legal advice should be taken as a pre-emptive measure whenever possible.

There are organisations to advise and assist at every stage. The National Council for the Abducted Child (Reunite) is on hand to give advice and has a network of lawyers who have had experience in this field. The UK has signed up to two international agreements which facilitate co-operation in the search for missing children: the European Convention on the Recognition and Enforcement of Decisions on Custody, and the Hague Convention which 55 countries have signed (some of which are also party to the European Convention). The Lord Chancellor's Department (see DIRECTORY at the end of this chapter) has a special unit to deal with child abduction to Hague Convention countries and issues a booklet entitled *Child Abduction – Advice to Parents*.

Where a child is living with someone under a residence order, the child cannot be taken abroad for longer than a month without leave of the court or without the consent of the other parent, a guardian, or any other person who has parental responsibility for that child. However, where there is a genuine fear of abduction, a prohibited steps order (see *Children (Part 1)*, section 3.1.2) can be issued by a court to prevent a parent with a residence order from taking a child abroad even for the month normally allowed.

You do not have to wait for the worst to happen before you can act. If you have genuine grounds to fear that your child might be abducted, there are immediate steps which you can take.

☞ *You are divorced from your American husband who has regular access to your 3 year-old-son. Both your ex-husband and yourself live in London and he has never indicated in any way to you that he is thinking of taking the child away from you.*

However, you learn from mutual friends that he has been making threats to that effect. You wonder if there are any steps that you can take to forestall any such eventuality. The child was registered on your passport before the new regulations came into effect that all children in the UK must have their own passports; see Children (Part 1), section 2.5.2.

1) You must consult a solicitor.
2) Try to ensure that there is a third party present at all meetings between your child and his father. This could be made a condition of his visits by court order.
3) You can also try to ensure that the father surrenders his passport to a solicitor as a condition of his contact with your son.
4) If you are unable to achieve a surrender of the passport, you must keep all documents concerning your son (such as birth certificate) to prevent, if possible, the father using them to have his son's name placed on his passport as he is not a British citizen.
5) You can write to the US Consulate, explaining the position and requesting that your son's name should not be included on his father's passport or asking that a passport should not be issued to the child. You cannot compel a foreign consulate to heed your request.
6) Where fears are well-grounded, application can be made to court for a prohibited steps order to prevent a UK passport being issued to your child on the father's application.
7) If there is immediate danger of abduction abroad, the police can circulate a child's name at ports and airports.
8) In addition, you should keep a photo of your ex-husband, details of his passport if you have them, and any other information which could assist in tracing him if such a need arose.

5.1.2 Sexual offences

The law is concerned to protect young persons against sexual advances of those adults, including close family members, who would seek to take advantage of their youth and inexperience. Indeed most cases of child abuse take place in the child's own home.

It is an offence for a man to have sexual intercourse with a woman he knows to be his daughter, sister or granddaughter. The offence of incest applies also to a half-sister.

Sexual intercourse with a girl under the age of 14 is an offence.

In a recent case, a 15-year-old was convicted of inciting a 13-year-old girl to commit an act of gross indecency with him. He had honestly believed that she was over 14. The House of Lords, in allowing his appeal, stated that the offence could not be committed unless the offender knew or believed that the girl was under-age.

It is also an offence to have sexual intercourse with a girl under the age of 16 ('the age of consent').

There is a defence to a charge of unlawful sexual intercourse with a girl aged 13–16 where the man is:

• under 24

and he can show that:

• he had reasonable cause to believe that the girl was over 16.

The age of consensual sex for both sexes is 16. However, it is an offence for any person who is in a position of trust and is over 18 to have sex with a person under 18. A 'position of trust' is statutorily defined under the Sexual Offences (Amendment) Act 2000.

5.1.2(a) Indecent assault

A child under the age of 16 cannot in law give any consent which would prevent an act from being an indecent assault. For example, a 15-year-old boy might welcome sexual advances from an older woman but his consent would not prevent her acts from being indecent assault.

Child sexual abuse is often accompanied by other forms of abuse such as neglect and physical cruelty. (For issues of confidentiality, see section 1.6.3 above.)

The Crime and Disorder Act 1998 introduced a sex offenders' register in order to protect children against known abusers.

5.1.3 Neglect

We have seen that any person who is over the age of 16 and who wilfully neglects or ill treats a child in his or her care commits a criminal offence (see *Duty to protect*, in *Children (Part 1)*, section 2.1).

5.2 Crimes committed by children

If a child commits a criminal offence, several rules apply.

5.2.1 Criminal age

Children under 10 cannot be charged with a criminal offence. However, if they have done something wrong which would be a criminal offence in an adult, the social services may institute proceedings. These could involve the child being taken into care in the most serious instances.

Under the Crime and Disorder Act 1998, Child Safety Orders can be imposed on children under 10 by both the police and the social services (see below section 5.2.5(b)).

Local authorities can also impose child curfew schemes in their area to deal with children under 10 on the streets at night. However, to date, this power has not been used.

There is no longer a rule that a child aged between 10 and 14 who commits an offence must be shown to have a 'criminal mind', i.e. that the child could tell the difference between right and wrong.

Until 1993, a boy aged under 14 was deemed incapable of rape. However, the law has now been altered so that a boy aged 10 or over can be found guilty of the offence.

5.2.2 Safeguards

Special rules apply to juveniles aged between 14 and 17. The rules cover the type of court in which they can be charged – called youth courts; procedures governing police questioning; the giving of evidence; and also safeguards against publicity.

Where a grave crime is involved, a child can be remanded in custody. Remittal is to the local authority to provide accommodation, which can be secure accommodation if the circumstances warrant it.

On the whole, there is a strenuous endeavour to keep children out of the criminal justice system.

There are now new powers available to magistrates in the case of juveniles who are guilty of repeated offences. Now they can be electronically tagged if they breach their bail conditions and re-offend. The aim is to keep control of offending behaviour while at the same time avoiding a sentence in a Young Offenders Institution which is to be kept for only the most serious offences. The electronic tag will help keep the youngster at home at times when they might otherwise be out getting up to mischief.

5.2.3 Parental responsibility

Under the Criminal Justice Act 1991, parents can be made responsible for the fines of their children as well as for compensation orders imposed on them. The means of the parents would be taken into account and the fine imposed accordingly.

Under the same Act, a parent can undertake by means of 'recognisances' to take proper care of a child under 16 and exercise proper control over him or her. Recognisances are fixed up to a maximum of £1,000. If a parent refuses consent, a fine of £1,000 can be imposed. Again the means of the parent are taken into account.

A parent can appeal to the Crown Court from an order of a magistrates' court, and to the Court of Appeal from a Crown Court order.

Under the Criminal Justice and Public Order Act 1994, parents can be bound over to ensure that their children comply with a community sentence passed on them. For example, the parents might have to ensure that their child attended an attendance centre.

5.2.4 Crime and Disorder Act 1998

This Act introduced a number of changes to the Youth Justice system, in particular it replaced the system of cautions, which were considered to be ineffective, with a system of reprimands and warnings.

It also allows for a number of other orders to be imposed on children which would cover antisocial behaviour, and for protection of children under 10 by means of a child safety order.

New structures have been put in place, notably a Youth Justice Board and 'youth offending teams' having a multidisciplinary approach, to deal with juvenile offenders.

'Parenting orders' can be imposed on parents who fail to carry out their responsibilities, instead of a binding-over order (these orders are dealt with below, section 5.2.5(e)).

5.2.5 Orders available

There is a range of orders available depending on the type of action which is felt appropriate to the child's age and/or misdeeds. Some of these are outlined below. All the orders, after being introduced by pilot schemes, became available nation-wide from 1 June 2000. Other orders include:

- a reparation order, which lasts three months, and is intended to bring home to the offender the 'cost' of his offence (not just in money terms) to the public at large, as well as to the victim
- an action plan order, which also lasts for three months under an intensive programme, for the rehabilitation of the young offender or to prevent him committing further offences
- a detention and training order, for an offender who requires a custodial sentence
- a referral order, a new order for 10 to 17-year-olds who plead guilty and are convicted for the first time. Young offenders are referred to a Youth Offender Panel and a contract is agreed which is aimed at discouraging re-offending. The contract also contains elements of reparation to the victim or to the community, and a programme of education, help or treatment to address the offending behaviour and the reasons for it. Orders are made for a minimum of three and a maximum of twelve months. It is important to note that if the referral order is completed the sentence becomes spent and does not result in a criminal record.

5.2.5(a) Antisocial behaviour orders

Antisocial behaviour orders are community-based orders which can be used against an individual or several individuals (for example, members of the same family who are harassing their neighbours) whose behaviour causes alarm, harassment or distress to others (see also chapter on *Neighbours*, section 2.6.3). It aims to deal with serious, but not necessarily criminal, antisocial behaviour by those aged 10 and above.

Under the Crime and Disorder Act 1998, both the police and local authorities can apply to the court for an antisocial behaviour order in consultation with each other. An antisocial behaviour order can be made in respect of children of the age of 10 upwards but is more likely to be used for older children, say 12 to 17-year-olds, who are thought capable of this type of behaviour without adult involvement.

The courts can decide whether or not to impose a parenting order in conjunction with this order (see section 5.2.5(e)), after taking into account family circumstances. Either the police or a local authority can make application to the court for an antisocial behaviour order.

The minimum duration of an antisocial behaviour order is two years, and breach of such an order will be considered a criminal offence which could involve a fine of up to £5,000 and a period of detention of up to five years' imprisonment depending on the age of the culprit and the seriousness of the breach. Some schools, acting with the parents' agreement, have sent unruly pupils letters which warn them that the council is considering applying for antisocial behaviour orders against them. This has acted as a warning and brought home to the youngsters the need to curb disruptive behaviour like stealing from the school or damaging school property. It is of course essential that the school and the parents work together to deal with such problems.

5.2.5(b) Child safety orders

Child safety orders are aimed at preventing children under 10 from becoming involved in criminal or antisocial behaviour.

A child safety order may be imposed in three circumstances:

1) where a child has committed an act which would be a criminal offence if the child were over 10-years-old
2) where required to prevent the child from participating in criminal or antisocial behaviour
3) where a child has breached a local child curfew notice (see below).

A child who is placed under a child safety order will be put under the supervision of either a local authority social worker or a member of a youth offending team who will provide the child with protection, support and control and, it is hoped, act to prevent further bad behaviour.

A child safety order is usually imposed for three months, but may be imposed for up to 12 months.

Failure to comply with a child safety order can lead to a child being made subject of a care order (see above section 1.4).

5.2.5(c) Reprimands and warnings for young offenders

This system replaces the old system of cautioning for young offenders.

Depending on the seriousness of the offence, the police have three choices; they can issue:

• a reprimand; or
• a warning; or
• they can bring full criminal charges.

Reprimands and warnings must be given to persons under 17 in a police station in the presence of an appropriate adult, usually a parent, foster carer, or social worker.

In order for the police to issue either a reprimand or a warning, four criteria must be met:

• there must be sufficient evidence of the person having committed a crime
• the young person must admit the crime
• he or she must have no previous convictions
• it must not be in the public interest for the young person to be prosecuted.

A young person will effectively have only one chance at each stage; once a reprimand has been given, the next offence will lead to a warning and a further offence will lead to a charge and prosecution unless there are exceptional circumstances.

Once a young person has been given a warning, he or she will automatically be referred to a youth offending team who will assess the offender and draw up a programme aimed at preventing him or her from re-offending.

5.2.5(d) Youth Justice

The aim of the legislation with regard to young offenders is to establish a local structure of teams and services to deal with them. To this end, it has established a Youth Justice Board to ensure the youth justice system in local areas is working effectively.

Each local authority is under a duty to ensure that there are adequate youth justice services in their area. These services include the following:

• provision of appropriate adults during police interviews
• bail support
• supervision of community sentences.

The Youth Justice Board monitors the actions of youth justice services nationally.

5.2.5(e) Parenting orders

These are designed to help and support parents whose children have offended or committed antisocial behaviour.

The orders can be put in place in four different circumstances:

- when the court makes a child safety order
- when the court makes an antisocial behaviour (or sex offender) order
- when a child or young person has been convicted of an offence
- when a child is in breach of certain sections of the Education Act 1996 with regard to regular school attendance.

Once made, a parenting order can consist of two elements:

- a requirement on the parent or guardian to attend counselling or guidance sessions for up to three months
- requirements encouraging parents or guardians to exercise control over the child by, for example, ensuring that he or she attend school. These requirements can last for up to 12 months. Failure to comply with a parenting order can result in a fine. Parents can also be bound over to exercise proper care over a child aged 10 or over who has committed an offence so as to prevent her/him from re-offending. Failure to comply can result in a fine of up to £1,000.

5.2.5(f) Local child-curfew schemes

These can be put in place by the local authority to deal with children under the age of 10 unsupervised on the streets at night. The upper age limit of children who may be the subject of a local child-curfew has now been raised to 15. The section gives the police power to act in such circumstances and places a duty on social services to investigate any breach of the curfew notice. No such order has been used and it would appear unlikely that this provision will be used at all.

5.2.5(g) Power for the police to remove truants

The police have the power to take any child they believe to be of school age, who does not have lawful authority to be absent from school, back to school. The child must be in a public place for the police to be able to do this.

5.2.5(h) Drugs and youth offending

Drug misuse is strongly associated with offending. Many juveniles commit offences such as muggings and burglaries to fund a drug habit. If you suspect that drugs are playing a part in your youngster's misbehaviour or criminal activities, do turn to the various sources of help. Help is available from the free national helpline run by Parentline Plus on 0808 800 2222 (see DIRECTORY). The National Drug Prevention Alliance at *www.drugprevent.org.uk* can offer help and support. There is also a system of mentors where older teenagers are matched with younger children in difficulties and supply help and guidance: *www.mentors.org.uk.*

6   PROPOSED CHANGES IN THE LAW

There are new laws in the pipeline with the aim of protecting children from sex offenders. Children under 13 will not be capable in law of giving consent to any form of sexual activity. Any sexual intercourse with a child under 13 will be charged as rape. There will be new rules about contact with children on the Internet, and stronger protection against child prostitution.

THE LEGAL STAGES OF GROWING UP

Education

Age 5   You become of compulsory school age.

Age 16   You can leave school. Pupils can leave school on the last Friday in June in the school year in which they reach the age of 16.

             Subject to certain exceptions, you are entitled to apply for access to your school records.

Age 18   You alone are entitled to access to your school records.

Age 19   All young people are entitled to full-time education up to the age of 19, either at school or college.

Financial

Age 5   You have to pay child's fare on trains, buses and tubes in London and on buses in most other areas.

Age 7   You can open and draw money from a National Savings Bank account.

             Some banks might let you open an ordinary bank account in your own right if they think you fully understand banking transactions.

Age 15   You can open a Post Office Girobank account, but you'll need a guarantor – someone who will be liable for your debts.

Age 16   You have to pay full fare on trains and on buses and tubes in London. You might have to pay full fare in other areas.

             You can buy Premium Bonds.

             You can enter into legally binding contracts.

Employment

Age 14   You can get a part-time job, but there are restrictions – e.g. you cannot work for more than two hours on a school day or on a Sunday.

Age 14–16 You can work five hours a day during the school holidays, but may not work for more than 25 hours per week.

Age 16   You can work full-time if you have left school.

             You can join most trade unions.

Health

Age 16   You have to pay prescription charges unless you are in full-time education, pregnant, in receipt of income support, on a low income or in certain other circumstances. You have to pay for a sight test and for glasses unless you are in full-time education, you or any other member of your family are in receipt of income support or on a low income, or your eyesight is constantly changing. You also have to pay for certain dental treatment if you are not in full-time education.

             You can consent to surgical, medical or dental treatment, including the taking of blood samples; and also choose your own doctor. You may not be able to refuse treatment, however. See *Children (Part 1)*, section 2.4.3(b).

Age 18   You have to pay for dental treatment unless you are still in full-time education, or pregnant, or certain other circumstances apply.

Rights and Obligations

Age 5   You can see a U- or PG-category film at a cinema unaccompanied. In London you probably cannot do this until you are 7. In practice, a cinema manager has complete discretion over admission.

Age 12   You can buy a pet (see also chapter on *Pets*, section 1.1).

Age 14   You can go into a pub but you cannot buy or drink alcohol there.

Age 15   You can see a category-15 film or rent a category-15 video.

Age 16   You can get a National Insurance number.

You can probably leave home without your parents' or guardian's consent.

You can consent to sexual intercourse; this now applies to both sexes.

You can marry with parental consent. (See chapter on *Setting up Home*, section 1.2.1.)

A boy can join the armed forces with parental consent.

You can apply for your own passport, but one parent must give written consent. You do not need parental consent if you are married or in the armed forces. Below 16, a parent must apply for a separate passport for you (for rules with regard to who signs a passport application, see *Children (Part 1)*, section 2.5.2(a)).

You can have beer, cider or wine with a meal in the restaurant or other room used for meals in a pub or hotel.

You are legally responsible for a child left in your care and can be held criminally liable if you ill-treat him or her (see *Children (Part 1)*, section 2.1.1).

You can buy a lottery ticket, cigarettes and tobacco.

Age 17   A care order can no longer be made on you, nor can you be received into care.

You can hold a licence to drive most vehicles apart from medium and heavy goods vehicles.

You can buy or hire any firearm or ammunition.

If you are a girl, you can join the armed forces with parental consent.

Age 18   You reach the age of maturity – you are an adult in the eyes of the law.

You can vote in local and general elections.

If you are an adopted child, you can look up your birth details (see section 2.3.1(a) above).

You can serve on a jury.

You have complete contractual capacity so you can own land, buy a house or flat, apply for a mortgage, sue and be sued in your own right. You can act as an executor or administrator of a deceased person's estate.

You can open a bank account or a Post Office Girobank account without your parents' signature. You can apply for a passport without your parents' consent.

You can make a will.

Note: If you are in the armed forces or a marine or seaman you can make a will under the age of 18.

You can buy and drink alcohol in a bar.

You can join the armed forces without parental consent.

You can bring an action for personal injury which occurred before you were 18, within 3 years of your 18th birthday (see chapter on *Accidents*).

You can see a category-18 film. You can buy a video that has been given a certificate for viewing by adults only. Certificates will state that a video is suitable for viewing by children of a specified age.

Age 21   You can become an MP or local councillor.

DIRECTORY
Family Law

Action for Sick Children
National Children's Bureau
8 Wakley Street
London EC1V 7QE
Tel. 020 7843 6444
www.actionforsickchildren.org

Adoption UK
Manor Farm
Appletree Road
Banbury
Oxon OX17 1LH
Tel. 01295 660 121
www.adoptionuk.org

The Association of Workers for Children with Emotional and Behavioural Difficulties
Charlton Court
East Sutton
Maidstone
Kent ME17 3DQ
Tel. 01622 843104
www.awcebd.co.uk

Boys' and Girls' Welfare Society
The BGWS Centre
Schools Hill
Cheadle
Cheshire SK8 1JE
Tel. 0161 283 4848
www.bgws.org.uk

The Brandon Centre
(formerly London Youth Advisory Centre)
26 Prince of Wales Road
London NW5 3LG
Tel. 020 7267 4792
www.brandon-centre.org.uk

British Agencies for Adoption and Fostering
(BAAF)
Skyline House
200 Union Street
London SE1 0LX
Tel. 020 7593 2000
www.baaf.org.uk

British Association for the Study and Prevention of Child Abuse and Neglect
(BASPCAN)
10 Priory Street
York YO1 6EZ
Tel. 01904 613605
www.baspcan.org.uk

Child Abduction Unit
The Lord Chancellor's Department
81 Chancery Lane
London WC2A 1DD
Tel. 020 7911 7047
www.offsol.demon.co.uk

Child Accident Prevention Trust
4th Floor
18–20 Farringdon Lane
London EC1R 3HA
Tel. 020 7608 3828
www.capt.org.uk

ChildLine
2nd Floor
Royal Mail Building
Studd Street
London N1 0QW
Tel. 020 7239 1000 *(admin)*
or
ChildLine
Freepost 1111
London N1 0BR
(Freephone) 0800 1111
For children in care:
Tel. 0800 884444
(Minicom) Tel. 0800 400 222
www.childline.org.uk

The Children Panel
The Law Society
Ipsley Court
Redditch
Worcestershire B98 0TD
Tel. 020 7242 1222 or
0870 606 2555
www.lawsociety.org.uk

Children's Legal Centre
University of Essex
Wivenhoe Park
Colchester
Essex CO4 3SQ
Tel. 01206 873820
www.2.essex.ac.uk/clc

Children's Rights Alliance for England
94 White Lion Street
London N1 9PF
Tel. 020 7278 8222
www.crights.org.uk

The Children's Society (England)
Edward Rudolf House
69–85 Margery Street
London WC1X OJL
Tel. 020 7841 4400
www.childrenssociety.org.uk

Child Support Agency
(Enquiry Line) Tel. 08457 133 133
www.dss.gov.uk/csa

End Physical Punishment of Children *(EPOCH)*
77 Holloway Road
London N7 8JZ
Tel. 020 7700 0627
www.childrenunbeatable.org.uk

Families in Time
(helps relatives trace adopted children)
36A-37A Myddleton Street
London EC1
Tel. 07741 190 000

Grandparents' Association
Moot House
The Stow
Harlow
Essex CM20 3AG
Tel. 01279 444964
www.grandparentsfederation.org.uk

Kidscape *(campaign for children's safety)*
2 Grosvenor Gardens
London SW1W ODH
Tel. 020 7730 3300
www.kidscape.org.uk

National Association of Child Contact Centres
Minerva House
Spaniel Row
Nottingham NG1 6EP
Tel. 0115 948 4557
www.naccc.org.uk

The National Care Standards Commission
St. Nicholas Building
St. Nicholas Street
Newcastle upon Tyne NE1 1NB
(Helpline) Tel. 0191 233 3556
www.carestandards.org.uk

National Child Protection Helpline *(NSPCC)*
Tel. 0800 800 5000

National Children's Bureau
8 Wakley Street
London EC1V 7QE
Tel. 020 7843 6000
www.ncb.org.uk

National Children's Centre
Brian Jackson House
New North Parade
Huddersfield
West Yorkshire HD1 5JP
Tel. 01484 519988
www.nccuk.org.uk

NCH Action for Children
85 Highbury Park
London N5 IUD
. Tel. 08457 626 579
www.nch.org.uk

National Early Years Network
77 Holloway Road
London N7 8JZ
Tel. 020 7607 9573
Email: info@neyn.org.uk

National Society for the Prevention of Cruelty to Children *(NSPCC)*
42 Curtain Road
London EC2A 3NH
Tel. 020 7825 2500
(Child Protection Helpline) Tel. 0800 800 5000
www.nspcc.org.uk

National Youth Advocacy Service
99-105 Argyle Street
Birkenhead
Wirral
Cheshire CH41 6AD
Tel. 0151 649 8700
(Children's Helpline) Tel. 0800 616 101
www.nyas.net

National Youth Agency
17–23 Albion Street
Leicester LE1 6GD
Tel. 01162 853 700
www.nya.org.uk

National Family and Parenting Institute *(NFPI)*
430 Highgate Studios
53-79 Highgate Road
London NW5 1TL
Tel. 020 7424 3460
www.nfpi.org

National Organisation for Counselling Adoptees and Parents *(NORCAP)*
112 Church Road
Wheatley
Oxon OX33 1LU
Tel. 01865 875 000
www.norcap.org.uk

Post-Adoption Centre
5 Torriano Mews
Torriano Avenue
London NW5 2RZ
Tel. 020 7284 0555
(Advice Line) Tel. 020 7485 2931
www.postadoptioncentre.org.uk

Reunite – National Council for Abducted Children
Child Abduction Centre
PO Box 24875
London E1 6FR
Tel. 0116 2555 345
www.reunite.org.uk

Trust for the Study of Adolescence
23 New Road
Brighton
East Sussex BN1 1WZ
Tel. 01273 693311
www.tsa.uk.com

Voice for the Child in Care
Unit 4 Pride Court
80–82 White Lion Street
London N1 9PF
Tel. 020 7833 5792
or
Suite G15
Redlands
3–5 Tapton House Road
Sheffield S10 5BY
Tel. 01142 679 38
Email: info@vcc-uk.org

Who Cares Trust *(campaigning magazine for children in the care system)*
Kemp House
152 City Road
London EC1V 2NP
Tel. 020 7251 3117
www.thewhocarestrust.org.uk

Young People's Consultation Service
Tavistock Centre
120 Belsize Lane
London NW3 5BA
Tel. 020 7435 7111
(Direct Line) Tel. 020 7447 3787
www.tavi-port.uk.org

Youth Access
1A Taylors Yard
67 Alderbrook Road
London SW12 8AD
Tel: 020 8772 9900
Email: admin@youthaccess.org.uk

EDUCATION

Advisory Centre for Education *(ACE)*
1c Aberdeen Studios
22 Highbury Grove
London N5 2DQ
Tel. 020 7354 8321
(Freephone) 0808 800 5793
www.ace-ed.org.uk

Advisory Unit: Computers in Education
(independent organisation for support for educational computing in schools)
112 Great North Road
Hatfield
Herts AL9 5JZ
Tel. 01707 266 714
www.advisory-unit.org.uk

The Boarding Schools' Association
Grosvenor Gardens House
35–37 Grosvenor Gardens
London SW1W 0BS
Tel. 020 7798 1580

Boarding School Survivors
6 Chester Court
Lissenden Gardens
London NW5 1LY
Tel. 020 7267 7098
www.bsv.co.uk

Campaign for Real Education
18 Westlands Grove
Stockton Lane
York YO31 1EF
Tel. 01904 424 134
www.cre.org.uk

Campaign for State Education *(CASE)*
158 Durham Road
London SW20 0DG
Tel. 020 8944 8206
www.casenet.org.uk

Careers Research and Advisory Centre *(CRAC)*
Sheraton House
Castle Park
Cambridge CB3 0AX
Tel. 01223 460277
www.crac.org.uk

Department for Education and Skills
Sanctuary Buildings
Great Smith Street
London SW1P 3BT
Tel. 020 7925 5555
www.dfes.gov.uk

Education Otherwise
PO Box 7420
London N9 9SG
www.education-otherwise.org

English Schools' Athletics Association
26 Newborough Green
New Malden
Surrey KT3 5HS
Tel. 020 8949 1506
www.esaa.net

Home Education Advisory Service
PO Box 98
Welwyn Garden City
Herts AL8 6AN
Tel. 01707 371854
www.heas.org.uk

Independent Schools Careers Organisation
12A Princess Way
Camberley
Surrey GU15 3SP
Tel. 01276 21188
www.isco.org.uk

Independent Schools Council
Grosvenor Gardens House
35–37 Grosvenor Gardens
London SW1W 0BS
Tel. 020 7798 1500
www.iscis.uk.net

National Assembly for Wales
Schools Administration Division 3
Crown Building
Cathays Park
Cardiff CF10 3NQ
Tel. 02920 825111
www.wales.gov.uk

National Association of Governors & Managers
(NAGM)
Suite 1
Western House
Smallbrook Queensway
Birmingham B5 4HQ
Tel. 0121 643 5787
www.nagm.org.uk

National Confederation of Parent–Teacher Associations *(NCPTA)*
18 St. John's Hill
Sevenoaks
Kent TN13 3NP
Tel. 01732 748 850
www.ncpta.org.uk

Office of the Schools Adjudicator
Vincent House
2 Woodland Road
Darlington DL3 7PJ
Tel. 0870 0012468
www.schoolsadjudicator.gov.uk

The Qualification and Curriculum Authority
(formerly National Curriculum Council)
83 Piccadilly
London W1J 8QA
Tel. 020 7509 5555
www.qca.org.uk

The Qualification Curriculum and Assessment Authority for Wales *(ACCAC)*
Castle Buildings
Womanby Street
Cardiff CF10 1SX
Tel. 02920 375400
www.acccac.org.uk

Service Children's Education (UK)
(advice and helpline for service families)
Trenchard Lane
Upavon
Pewsey
Wiltshire SN9 6BE
Tel. 01980 618244
www.sceschools.com

Service Children's Education
(for schools overseas)
HQSCE
Building 5
Wegberg Military Complex
BFPO 40
www.sceschools.com

State Boarding Information Service *(Stabis)*
The Pupil Wellbeing and Transport Team
Department for Education and Skills
Mowden Hall
Staindrop Road
Darlington DL3 9BG
Tel. 01325 391272
www.stabis.org.uk

EDUCATION OF CHILDREN WITH SPECIAL NEEDS

ACE Centre
(for young people with communication difficulties)
92 Windmill Road
Headington
Oxford OX3 7DR
Tel. 01865 759800
www.ace-centre.org.uk

ACE Centre North
(technologies for disabled people)
Broadbent Road
Watersheddings
Oldham
Lancs OL1 4HU
Tel. 0161 627 1746
www.ace-north.org.uk

Action on Entitlement
17 Cumberland Road
Richmond
Surrey TW9 3HJ
Tel. 020 8948 1746
www.aoe.org.uk

After 16 – what's new?
(website for disabled teenagers and young people)
www.after16.org.uk

Birth Defects Foundation
(incorporating In Touch Trust)
BDF Centre
Hemlock Way
Cannock
Staffs WS11 2GF
Tel. 08700 707020
www.birthdefects.co.uk

British Computer Society Disability Group
c/o BAE Research
West Hanningfield Road
Great Baddow
Chelmsford
Essex CM2 8HN
Tel. 01245 242 950
www.bcs.org/disability

Centre for Studies on Inclusive Education *(CSIE)*
Room 2S 203
S Block
Frenchay Campus
Coldharbour Lane
Bristol BS16 1QU
Tel. 0117 344 4007
www.inclusion.uwe.ac.uk

Contact a Family
209 City Road
London EC1V 1JN
Tel. 0808 808 3555
www.cafamily.org.uk

Council for Disabled Children
8 Wakley Street
London EC1V 7QE
Tel. 020 7843 1900
www.ncb.org.uk/cdc.htm

Disability Alliance
Universal House
88 Wentworth Street
London E1 7SA
Tel. 020 7247 8776
www.disabilityalliance.org.uk

Disability Law Service
39–45 Cavell Street
London E1 2BP
Tel. 020 7791 9800
www.dls.org.uk

Education of Children with Special Needs
2 Woodland Road
Darlington DL3 7PJ
Tel. 0870 001 2468

HE Special
(Home Education of Children with Special Needs)
www.he-special.org.uk

Independent Panel of Special Education Advisers
6 Carlow Mews
Woodbridge
Suffolk IP12 1DH
Tel. 01394 382 814
(Tribune Appeals Advice Line) 020 8682 0442
www.ipsea.co.uk

Learning and Skills Council
Cheylsmore House
Quinton Road
Coventry CV1 2WT
Tel. 0870 900 6800
www.lsc.gov.uk

Mediation UK
Alexander House
Telephone Avenue
Bristol BS1 4BS
Tel. 0117 904 6661
www.mediationuk.org.uk

MENCAP
123 Golden Lane
London EC1Y 0RT
Tel. 020 7454 0454
www.mencap.org.uk

National Association of Gifted Children
Suite 14
Challenge House
Sherwood Drive
Bletchley
Milton Keynes MK3 6DP
www.nagcbritain.org.uk

National Association for Special Educational Needs *(NASEN)*
NASEN House
4 Amber Business Village
Amington
Tamworth
Staffs B77 4RP
Tel. 01827 311500
www.nasen.org.uk

National Federation of Access Centres
Hereward College
Bramston Crescent
Tile Hill Lane
Coventry CV4 9SW
Tel. 02476 461 231
www.hereward.ac.uk

Network 81
(support for parents in assessment and statementing)
1–7 Woodfield Terrace
Stansted
Essex CM24 8AJ
(Helpline) Tel. 0870 770 3306
www.network81.co.uk

Parents for Inclusion
Unit 2
70 South Lambeth Road
London SW8 1RL
Tel. 020 7582 5008
www.parentsforinclusion.org

RADAR
(Royal Association for Disability and Rehabilitation)
12 City Forum
250 City Road
London EC1V 8AF
Tel. 020 7250 3222
www.radar.org.uk

Rathbone Special Education Advice Line
4th Floor
Churchgate House
56 Oxford Street
Manchester M1 6EU
Tel. 0800 917 6790
www.rathbonetraining.co.uk

SKILL
(national bureau for students with disabilities)
Chapter House
18 Crucifix Lane
London SE1 3JW
Tel. 0800 328 5050
www.skill.org.uk

POLICY AND MEDIATION

Courts Family Division
Principal Registry
First Avenue House
42–49 High Holborn
London WC1V 6NP
Tel. 020 7947 6000
www.courtservice.gov.uk

The Family Law Bar Association
2nd Floor
2/3 Cursitor Street
London EC4A 1NE
Tel. 020 72421289
www.barcouncil.org.uk

Family Mediation Service
(Northumberland & Tyneside)
MEA House
2 Ellison Place
Newcastle NE1 8XS
Tel. 0191 2619212
www.nch.org.uk

Family Policy Division
Lord Chancellor's Department
54–60 Victoria Street
London SW1E 6QW
Tel. 020 7210 1212
www.lcd.gov.uk

Family Rights Group
The Print House
18 Ashwin Street
London E8 3DL
Tel. 020 7923 2628
www.frg.org.uk

Family Service Units
(offices nationwide)
207 Old Marylebone Road
London NW1 5QP
Tel. 020 7402 5175
www.fsu.org.uk

Institute of Family Therapy
(includes couple therapy)
Family Mediation Service
24–32 Stephenson Way
London NW1 2HX
Tel. 020 7391 9150
www.instituteoffamilytherapy.org.uk

Mediation UK
Alexander House
Telephone Avenue
Bristol BS1 4BS
Tel. 0117 904 6661
www.mediationuk.org.uk

National Family Mediation
Star House
3rd Floor
104 Grafton Road
London NW5 4BD
Tel. 020 7485 8809
www.nfm.u-net.com

National Organisation for the Counselling of Adoptees and Parents *(NORCAP)*
112 Church Road
Wheatley
Oxfordshire OX33 1LU
Tel. 01865 875000
www.norcap.org.uk

One Plus One
(a marriage and partnership research charity)
The Wells
7–15 Rosebery Avenue
London EC1R 4SP
Tel. 020 7841 3660
www.oneplusone.org.uk

Relate
Herbert Gray College
Little Church Street
Rugby CV21 3AP
Tel. 01788 573241
www.relate.org.uk

Solicitors' Family Law Association
PO Box 302
Orpington
Kent BR6 8QX
Tel. 01689 850 227
www.sfla.org.uk

UK College of Family Mediators
Alexander House
Telephone Avenue
Bristol BS1 4BS
Tel. 0117 904 7223
www.ukcfm.co.uk

PARENTS

Families Need Fathers
134 Curtain Road
London EC2A 3AR
Tel. 020 7613 5060
www.fnf.org.uk

Fathers Direct
Herald House
Lamb's Passage
Bunhill Row
London EC1Y 8TQ
Tel. 020 7374 2966
www.fathersdirect.com

Fostering Network
87 Blackfriars Road
London SE1 8HA
Tel. 020 7620 6400
www.fostering.net

Gingerbread
(guidance for single parents and children)
1st Floor
7 Sovereign Close
Sovereign Court
London E1W 3HW
(Free Advice Line) Tel. 0800 018 4318
www.gingerbread.org.uk

National Council for One Parent Families
255 Kentish Town Road
London NW5 2LX
Tel. 020 7428 5400
(Helpline) Tel. 0800 018 5026
www.oneparentfamilies.org.uk

NEWPIN
(provides support for parents of children under 5 with emotional difficulties)
Sutherland House
35 Sutherland Square
Walworth
London SE17 3EE
Tel. 020 7358 5900
www.newpin.org.uk

Parentline Plus
520 Highgate Studios
53–79 Highgate Road
London NW5 1TL
Tel. 020 7284 5500
(Freephone Helpline) Tel. 0808 800 2222
www.parentlineplus.org.uk

Parents for Children
41 Southgate Road
London N1 3JP
Tel. 020 7359 7530
www.parentsforchildren.org.uk

The Rights of Parents
(explains laws governing parents' rights)
www.yourrights.org.uk

DOMESTIC VIOLENCE

Careline
Tel. 020 8514 1177

Refuge
(24-hour national crisis line)
Tel. 0870 599 5443

Samaritans
(National helpline)
Tel. 08457 909090
www.samaritans.org.uk

Shelterline
Tel. 0808 800 4444
www.shelter.org.uk/housingadvice/shelterline/
index.asp

Victim Support
Tel. 0845 30 30 900
www.victimsupport.com

Welsh Women's Aid
Tel. 02920 390 874
www.accac.org.uk

Women's Aid
(National helpline)
Tel. 08457 023 468
www.womensaid.org.uk
(see also under National Society for the Prevention
of Cruelty to Children)

Women's Link
(an accommodation advice service for women)
Room 417–419
London Fruit and Wool Exchange
Brushfield Street
London E1 6EL
Tel. 020 7248 1200
www.womenslink.org.uk

GENERAL

Citizens' Advice Bureau
(National Association)
115–123 Pentonville Road
London N1 9LZ
Tel. 020 7833 2181
www.nacab.org.uk

Child Support Agency
Tel. 08457 133133
www.dss.gov.uk/csa

European Court of Human Rights
Council of Europe
F67075
Strasbourg Cedex
France
Tel. 00 333 88 412 000
www.echr.coe.int

Foreign & Commonwealth Office
King Charles Street
London SW1A 2AH
Tel. 020 7270 1500
www.fco.gov.uk

**Foreign & Commonwealth Office Consular
Department**
Old Admiralty Building
Whitehall
London SW1A 2AF
Tel. 020 7270 1500
www.fco.gov.uk

General Register Office
(Births, Deaths & Marriages)
The Family Records Centre
1 Myddleton Street
London EC1R 1UW
Tel. 020 8392 5300
www.frc.gov.uk
(see also Office for National Statistics)

**International Social Service of the
United Kingdom** *(ISS)*
Cranmer House
39 Brixton Road
London SW9 6DD
Tel. 020 7735 8941
Email: issuk@charity.vfree.com

Joint Council for the Welfare of Immigrants
115 Old Street
London EC1V 9RT
Tel. 020 7251 8708
www.jcwi.org.uk

Law Centres Federation
(offices nationwide)
Duchess House
18–19 Warren Street
London W1P 5LR
Tel. 020 7387 8570
www.lawcentres.org.uk

The Law Society
113 Chancery Lane
London WC2A 1PL
Tel. 020 7242 1222
www.lawsocity.org.uk

Legal Aid Board
(see Legal Services Commission)

Legal Services Commission
85 Gray's Inn Road
London WC1X 8TX
Tel. 020 7813 1000
www.legalservices.gov.uk

LIFE
(pregnancy, birth, DSS benefits, post-adoption counselling)
LIFE House
Newbold Terrace
Leamington Spa
Warwickshire CV32 4EA
Tel. 01926 421587
www.lifeuk.org

London Friend
(helpline for lesbians and gay men)
86 Caledonian Road
London N1 9DN
Tel. 020 7837 3337
www.londonfriend.org.uk

National Association of Councils for Voluntary Service *(NACVS)*
3rd Floor, Arundel Court
177 Arundel Street
Sheffield S1 2NU
Tel. 01142 786636
www.nacvs.org.uk

Office for National Statistics
Smedley Hydro
Trafalgar Road
Birkdale
Southport PRO 2HH
Tel. 01704 569824
www.statistics.gov.uk

The Passport Agency
London Passport Office
Globe House
89 Eccleston Square
London SW1V 1PN
(National calls centre)
Tel. 0870 521 0410
www.passport.gov.uk
Offices also in Belfast, Durham, Glasgow, Liverpool, Newport and Peterborough

The Prince's Trust
18 Park Square East
London NW1 4LH
Tel. 0800 842 842
www.princes-trust.org.uk

RELIGIOUS ORGANISATIONS

Baptist Union of Great Britain
Baptist House
PO Box 44
129 Broadway
Didcot
Oxfordshire OX11 8RT
Tel. 01235 517 700
www.baptist.org.uk

Catholic Marriage Care
Clitherow House
1 Blythe Mews
Blythe Road
London W14 0NW
Tel. 020 7371 1341
www.marriagecare.org.uk

Church of England
General Synod Enquiry Centre
Church House
Great Smith Street
London SW1P 3NZ
Tel. 020 7898 1000
www.c-of-e.org.uk

Churches Together in England
27 Tavistock Square
London WC1H 9HH
Tel. 020 7387 8413
www.churches-together.org.uk

Court of the Chief Rabbi *(Beth Din)*
Adler House
735 High Road
North Finchley
London N12 0US
Tel. 020 8343 6270
www.jewish.co.uk/bethdin.php3

Evangelical Alliance
186 Kennington Park Road
London SE11 4BT
Tel. 020 7207 2100
www.eauk.org

Free Churches Council
27 Tavistock Square
London WC1H 9HH
Tel. 020 7387 8413

Hindu Centre
Radha Krishna Temple
5–7 Cedars Road
London E15 4NE
Tel. 020 8534 8879

Jewish Marriage Council
23 Ravenshurst Avenue
London NW4 4EE
Tel. 020 8203 6311
www.jmc-uk.org

London Buddhist Centre
51 Roman Road
London E2 0HU
Tel. 020 8981 1225
www.lbc.org.uk

London Central Mosque Trust Ltd
Islamic Cultural Centre
146 Park Road
London NW8 7RG
Tel. 020 7724 3363
www.iccuk.org

Methodist Church
Central Hall
Storeys Gate
London SW1H 9NH
Tel. 020 7222 8010
www.c-h-w.com

The Registrar
The Court of Faculties of the
Lord Archbishop of Canterbury
(marriage licences)
1 The Sanctuary
London SW1P 3JT
Tel. 020 7222 5381
www.facultyoffice.org.uk

Religious Society of Friends *(Quakers)*
Friends House
173–177 Euston Road
London NW1 2BJ
Tel. 020 7387 3601
www.quaker.org.uk

Seventh-Day Adventist Church
Stanborough Park
Watford
Hertfordshire WD2 6JP
Tel. 01923 672251
www.adventist.org.uk

The United Reformed Church
86 Tavistock Place
London WC1H 9RT
Tel. 020 7916 2020
www.urc.org.uk

United Synagogue *(Orthodox)*
Adler House
735 High Road
North Finchley
London N12 0US
Tel. 020 8434 8989
www.unitedsynagogue.org.uk

See also:

The British Humanist Association
47 Theobald's Road
London WC1X 8SP
Tel. 020 7430 0908
www.humanism.org.uk

The National Secular Society
25 Red Lion Square
London WC1R 4RL
Tel. 020 7404 3126
www.secularism.org.uk

The Salvation Army *(UK Headquarters)*
101 Newington Causeway
London SE1 6BN
Tel. 020 7367 4500
www.salvationarmy.org.uk

The Samaritans *(Headquarters)*
The Upper Mill
Kingston Road
Ewell
Surrey KT17 2AF
Tel. 020 8394 8300
(Helpline) Tel. 08457 909090
www.samaritans.org.uk

5 DEATH –
BEFORE AND AFTER

When someone dies, the partner or close relatives have to deal with a multitude of practical matters as well as coping with their emotions. This chapter sets out what must be done. In the short term, the death must be registered, arrangements must be made for the funeral, and the immediate day-to-day expenses of dependants must be provided for. In the longer term, after these urgent matters have been dealt with, the affairs of the deceased person must be settled. This means that someone must take charge of his or her property, personal possessions, debts, business, and so forth, which the law calls by the portmanteau term 'the deceased's estate'.

In this chapter you will find a guide to the formal procedures which have to be gone through when someone dies, and also a detailed explanation of the duties of whoever takes charge of the deceased person's estate depending on whether or not a will was made – and how their responsibility for winding up the estate must be discharged. This includes the payment of the debts of the deceased and taking care of the property in the estate during the winding up process. Then, after the debts have been paid, the residue of the estate must be distributed to those entitled to inherit: this in turn depends on whether or not there is a will. If there is not, the law lays down who benefits from the distribution.

If someone is disappointed by the terms of a will, or their expectations of inheriting are defeated, they may be able to challenge the will. Alternatively, they may be able to obtain some maintenance out of the estate if no provision was made for them by the will or by the general rules for distribution in the absence of a will.

We all also have not only to think about the death of others, but to anticipate our own demise sooner or later. For most of us, the overriding concern is for our surviving families. How will they manage financially? Who would look after any young children? Would the elderly be provided for and protected? Not surprisingly perhaps, many people tend to avoid thinking about such potential problems. A will enables you to decide exactly who will take charge and who will benefit after your death. Although general rules do exist to cover situations where there is no will, the general rules may not suit your particular circumstances or preferences. For example, the rules favour a surviving spouse of the deceased, which may not be entirely appropriate if the deceased has young children from a previous marriage, or was in a long-term relationship with someone whom he or she never married. This chapter also tells you what will happen to your property if you do not make a will, and explains the advantages of making a will and the procedure for doing so.

Finally, we also look at problems of how to protect minors.

Thus this chapter deals with:

- registering the death
- immediate financial problems
- the deceased's affairs
- before death – preparing for the inevitable
- making sure a will is effective
- when a will can be challenged
- when there is no will – intestate succession
- provision for dependants
- protecting minors.

1   WHEN YOU HAVE TO DEAL WITH A DEATH

1.1   Registering the death

When you register a death you are playing 'an important role in the protection of human life'. Registration is a legal process. It gives finality to a person's life and constitutes an essential step in assisting relatives to deal with the loss. Possession of the death certificate enables them to go on to attend to other urgent tasks, such as proceeding with the funeral arrangements, and dealing with the deceased's estate. In addition, registrars may be in a position to provide information on financial assistance, or on how to establish probate (these issues are dealt with in the course of this chapter).

A death must be registered within five days. (This can be extended if the coroner is involved – see section 1.2). There is no fee for registration (but a death certificate costs £3.50). Registration procedures are outlined below.

1.1.1   The medical certificate

Where a death was due to natural causes, the doctor who was treating the deceased will provide (without charge) a medical certificate of the cause of death, together with instructions on how to register the death in the subdistrict where it took place. If the body is to be cremated, two doctors must sign a certificate – but the first doctor will instruct the second doctor who can see the body in the chapel of rest or at the mortuary.

If the deceased was being treated in hospital, the doctor may ask the next of kin for permission to conduct a *postmortem* examination, to investigate exactly how death came about.

The doctor must have seen the patient within the fortnight preceding the death. If there was no doctor attending the deceased, a coroner may issue the certificate.

☞   *Your husband suffered a mild heart attack when he was 45-years-old. Fifteen years then passed and he appeared absolutely fit and healthy for his age. You find him collapsed at the top of the stairs in your home and, by the time you have called the ambulance, he has died from a massive coronary.*

   If your GP is not prepared to sign the certificate because he had not seen your husband within the fortnight, your husband's death will be reported to the coroner who, in this case, will certify the death as having been from natural causes.

1.1.2   The death certificate

Generally, you must register the death within five days with the Registrar of Births, Marriages and Deaths in the area in which the death took place. The address will be listed in your local telephone directory under Registration of Births, Marriages and Deaths.

Take along the medical certificate of the cause of death. You will be required to provide the full names of the deceased person, and any other names that he or she has been known by, including the maiden surname of a woman who has been married; his or her date and place of birth; their most recent occupation, and, if the person who has died was a married woman, her husband's full name and occupation. It will also be necessary to confirm the date and place of death. Other questions will be asked about the date of birth of the surviving spouse, and information about the state pensions and allowances that the person was receiving, including war pensions. The NHS insurance number will be requested, and the deceased's medical card should be surrendered if it is available. However, if this number is not known and the medical card is not available, there is no need to worry.

The death is recorded in a register of deaths, and a certified copy of the entry is called the *death certificate*. The registrar will issue a certificate for the burial of the body which can then be handed over to the funeral director as generally speaking the funeral cannot proceed without it. Cremation cannot take place without the certificate. A certificate for sending to social security will also be issued to the person registering the death. This form serves a dual purpose; details of the death are given on one side and the other side is the application for the relevant claim forms. (See section 2.1.1 below.)

Note: as copies of the death certificate will be needed for the will and for dealing with the deceased's property (in particular for making claims on life insurance), ask for several copies of the certificate at the same time. This also reduces the costs.

1.1.3 When you are unable to attend the local register office

☞ *You took a day return to London when your great-uncle died. After seeing to various matters in his flat and contacting his solicitor, you went to the local office to register his death. There were others in the queue ahead of you and you had to leave to catch your train before you could be attended to. You wonder what the procedure is for registering his death from your home town of Walsall.*

The person registering the death does not have to attend the register office in the district where the death occurred but can make a formal declaration giving all the details required in any registration office. This will then be passed on to the registrar for the district where the death occurred, who will issue the death certificate and any other documents.

Do note: the procedures above are likely to change, the changes to be phased in after 2004. For an outline of the new procedures, see section 1.1.6 below.

1.1.4 Stillborn babies

A baby is stillborn if it is born dead after the 24th week of pregnancy.

☞ *Sadly for Mary-Anne, her baby boy was born dead in the 28th week of her pregnancy. A midwife was present at the time. Mary-Anne would like to give the baby a funeral service and to give him a name. She would like to know if this is possible and what the procedures are for registration.*

As the baby is stillborn (born dead after the 24th week of pregnancy) Mary-Anne will be given a Medical Certificate of Stillbirth signed by the midwife. She must give this certificate to the registrar. Registration of a stillbirth can take place at any registrar's office.

Mary-Anne will receive a Certificate for Burial or Cremation and a Certificate of Registration of Stillbirth, which can include, at her request, the baby's first name provided it has been recorded on the register. At Mary-Anne's request, she can also get certified copies of the entry of stillbirth.

With regard to a funeral service, this can be arranged either through the health authority or by the parents themselves to accord with their wishes, religious or otherwise.

A support group, the Stillbirth and Neonatal Death Society (SANDS) can offer parents information and advice (see DIRECTORY).

Do note: if no doctor or midwife attended the stillbirth or examined the baby's body, the mother must sign Form 35 which is obtainable from the registrar.

1.1.5 Miscarriage

If a pregnancy terminates at under 24 weeks, this is known as a miscarriage. There is no need to register a death in this case.

1.1.6 Proposed changes to certfication procedure

In the light of the Harold Shipman case, and the scandal at Alder Hey, the Home Office has been reviewing the current procedures of certification of deaths. It was felt necessary to reassure the public that burial and cremations could not take place without a more efficient and answerable system in place for investigation. This review, together with one in to the coroner system, will be expected to lead to a more stringent legislative framework for registration.

In addition, in a White Paper – *Civil Registration: Vital Change*, issued in January 2002 – the government proposed to make a more active use of IT systems so that relatives who have to register a death would be able to do so by telephone or via the Internet, provided proper safeguards are in place. It is also proposes a central database, with data exchange between doctors, coroners and registrars so as to 'ease the burden on the bereaved'. In addition:

- The persons eligible to register a death will include a 'life partner', as well as an executor, to take account of changing patterns of family life

- Use of the Welsh language is to be extended
- The same information will be recorded for men and women, e.g. inclusion of marital status and name and occupation of deceased's spouse
- There will be a new provision for registration of certain deaths at sea
- Procedures for the registration of stillbirths will be altered and, among other matters, registration can take place within one year; and persons eligible to provide the information will be extended.

The legislative changes for the White Paper are expected to be in place in 2004, and the new system to be phased in thereafter.

At present full details of how to register the death are at *www.statistics.gov.uk/nsbase/registration/regering_death.asp*. Alternatively, these can be obtained from your local registry office, or telephone 0151 471 4805.

1.2   Coroners

A doctor, the police, or the registrar must ask a coroner to investigate any death that has taken place:

- in consequence of accident or injury
- in consequence of industrial disease
- in consequence of sudden and unexplained events
- under anaesthetic or while undergoing surgery
- while in custody.

Coroners also investigate cases of apparent suicide. The widow or widower or the next of kin must be told if an inquest will be held. If the process may be lengthy, an interim certificate from the coroner confirming the death will be recognised for National Insurance and social security purposes.

Note: all deaths of foreigners who die in this country are reported to the coroner.

A coroner may arrange for a *postmortem* examination without asking permission from the next of kin.

☞ *Your sister is killed in an accident while hang-gliding. You feel that the hang-gliding school she attended was not taking all proper safety precautions. You understand that there will be a postmortem as well as an inquest i.e. a public enquiry into the death. You want to be informed of the outcome in both cases.*

You should tell the coroner if you want to be present, or to be represented, at the postmortem. Relatives are able to have a doctor of their choice present when the postmortem is carried out. For the position of a relative at an inquest, see section 1.2.2 below.

The Home Office has published a model Coroners' Service Charter which tells you what standards of performance are to be expected in the coroner service and what to do if something goes wrong. It also published a leaflet: *The Work of the Coroner*, available from the coroner's office, police stations, council offices etc. You can also contact the Coroners Section of the Home Office (see DIRECTORY).

1.2.1   Identifying the body

If a death occurs unexpectedly or in macabre circumstances (e.g. a suicide, murder or road accident), it may be extremely distressing for a relative or acquaintance to be asked to view the body in order to identify the deceased. There appears to be no legal rule which compels someone to do this against their will. However, there is a general legal obligation not to actually obstruct the police or the coroner in the performance of their duties.

1.2.2   Inquests

If the coroner establishes that a death is not due to natural causes, an inquest must be held. If an inquest is to be held, the coroner must inform beforehand the widow or widower of the deceased or, if there is no surviving spouse, any other next of kin. If the deceased has nominated personal representatives (see section 3.2 below) who are not his or her surviving spouse or next of kin, then they must also be informed of the hearing of the inquest.

Relatives and spouses are entitled to be legally represented at the inquest although only limited legal funding is available for this purpose. (See chapter on *The Legal System*, section 7.6.) Other persons may show that they have an interest in the inquest, for example an employer or trade union officer if the death was related to an accident at work. Relatives (and others, with the coroner's approval) are entitled to question witnesses at the inquest although questions must be restricted to the medical nature and circumstances surrounding the death.

The coroner is limited to ascertaining the cause of the death – it is not his function to attribute fault. Where the coroner refuses to hold an inquest (for example, because he has concluded that an inquest would not reach a different conclusion as to the cause of death from that reached at the *postmortem*), his decision can only be challenged by going to court by way of judicial review. This is not an appeal in the usual sense, and you would have to show that the coroner has misdirected himself in law or that his factual conclusion is irrational.

In one case the relatives of the deceased blamed his death on the fact that an ambulance that was called after he suffered an asthma attack took 30 minutes to arrive. If it had arrived within 10 minutes the deceased's death might have been prevented. The coroner decided after the *postmortem* that the death was due to natural causes. Although the relatives objected vigorously, the coroner was entitled to refuse to hold an inquest in these circumstances (see also *Accidents* chapter, section 9.5).

All inquests must be held in public and may be reported in the press. The coroner will usually try to prevent highly personal details from emerging – for example, suicide notes and personal letters will not be read out unless they have to be.

A funeral can be held even before the inquest is concluded, with the permission of the coroner.

The Home Office is currently reviewing the role of coroners, and proposals for reform of the procedures are likely.

1.3   Organ donation

If the deceased wanted his organs or body to be donated for transplant or medical research, the medical certificate of death must first be obtained.

Inform the doctor as soon as possible, since organs deteriorate rapidly (e.g. corneas from the eye must be taken within 12 hours of death).

If the whole body is to be donated, contact the anatomy office of your nearest medical school. For general enquiries, contact HM Inspector of Anatomy at the Department of Health (tel. 020 7972 4342). It is a good idea to discuss with your relatives your wishes in advance; see section 4.1 below.

In addition to mentioning the donation in a will, donors should also complete a form of authorisation to be kept with the will or with the donor's other papers. This can be witnessed by a member of the family as a sign of their agreement, and by the persons named as executor in the will. The forms can be obtained from HM Inspector of Anatomy, Room 316, Wellington House, 135–155 Waterloo Road, London SE1 8UC.

The medical school will take responsibility for cremation of the remains after the body has been dissected. The type of religious service desired can be specified by the next of kin, who may also wish to be present.

1.3.1   Donor cards

Donor card application forms are available from doctors' surgeries, hospitals, post offices and libraries. It is also possible to register as a donor when applying for a driving licence.

Ideally, those who wish to donate organs should register as potential donors with the NHS Donor Register (P.O. Box 14, Patchway, Bristol, B534 8ZZ). Registration can be cancelled or altered at any time. An organ donor card is available in post offices and in doctors' surgeries. Carrying such a card will save valuable time if the donor dies suddenly, as a will may not be looked at for some days.

Funeral arrangements need not be delayed if an organ donation is accepted.

1.3.2   Relatives' consent

☞ *Your 19-year-old son died suddenly in a cycle accident. He carried a donor card but you would like to know what your legal position is.*

Relatives will be asked to consent. It is unlikely that the medical team would override their wishes even though the deceased expressed willingness to act as a donor. In law, it seems that it is only the deceased's willingness which is required, so if there are no next of kin, or they do not object, the transplant will go ahead. See also section 1.3.3 below.

1.3.3   Coroner's consent

If a death has been reported to a coroner, his consent is necessary for removing an organ for donation. However, as noted at 1.3.4, recent evidence shows that not all hospitals have advised the coroner of their intention when removing organs from small children who have undergone *postmortems*.

1.3.4   Retention of organs without consent

The current form for agreement to hospital *postmortems* states that 'tissues may be retained for diagnostic, teaching and research purposes'. The understanding was that relatives were asked to sign a form giving permission which states that they 'do not object' to the retention of organs for these purposes. In late 1999 evidence revealed that a number of hospitals have retained organs removed from children who underwent *postmortems*, without either the knowledge or the consent of the parents. After investigation into the practice, procedures have now been altered.

1.3.5   Proposed 'opt out' system for organ donation

There is a national shortage of organs needed for transplant and research purposes and proposals have been made whereby organs could be taken for donation in any case unless the person had registered an objection to the use of his organs. This would replace the current system, described above, under which a person who agrees to the use of his organs after his death, carries a donor card. A survey, carried out in July 1999, showed that a majority of the public did not support such a scheme and no firm proposals for its introduction have yet been introduced.

1.4   Death abroad

☞ *Your parents retired to Spain some years ago. Your mother, who has just died, had always expressed a wish to be buried in England.*

1) Deaths abroad must be registered in the country where they occurred according to local formalities.
2) If possible, the death should also be registered with the British consul. This will enable a death certificate to be obtained in this country from the Coroners section of the Home Office (see DIRECTORY on page 151).
3) The British consul should give you advice about the procedures for bringing the body home.
4) You should also obtain an authenticated translation of the foreign documents: the death certificate or equivalent will be needed in order to bring the body through British Customs.
5) You will also need the death certificate to obtain a certificate of 'No Liability to Register' from the registrar of the district in which your mother's funeral is to take place.

It will nearly always be cheaper to have a local burial than to bring a body back to the UK. A compromise solution would be a local cremation, if available. The ashes can then come back to this country, but get the foreign crematorium to furnish you with a certificate.

If a death abroad occurs during a package holiday, the tour operator and the travel insurers should provide assistance.

1.5   The funeral

1.5.1   The deceased's wishes

Sometimes the will contains instructions about the funeral or cremation, so check if this is the case. If there is a will, the executor has the right to decide whether there will be a burial or a cremation, whether the will expresses a particular wish or not. If there is no will, the next of kin should decide.

It is also important to check whether the deceased had already made arrangements for his or her own funeral, or carried funeral insurance.

1.5.1(a) Cremation

Over 70% of funerals in the U.K. are followed by a cremation rather than a burial. A survey has found that the average cost of a burial in 2000 was £2,046, while for a cremation it was £1,215.

Muslims and Jews may have religious reasons for preferring burial, Hindus for preferring cremation. There is no legal reason why a cremation should not take place after a burial, or why the ashes of the deceased should not be buried after a cremation.

Cremation, like burial, may not proceed if the body needs to be retained for a *postmortem* or for the coroner (see above, section 1.2).

1.5.2 Arranging the funeral

Funeral directors should provide you with price lists and written estimates. If there is to be a religious service, contact the appropriate minister of religion. The funeral director should advise you on this, and on the formalities for cremation. A religious service is not required by law.

The Office of Fair Trading has launched on-line advice for people arranging a funeral. See *www.oft.gov.uk*. Useful information is also available at *www.uk-funerals.co.uk*.

It was reported that complaints to the independent Funeral Ombudsman doubled between 1997 and 2001, and doubled again in 2001. The funeral industry shut down the independent ombudsman in September 2002, so that customers with complaints must now look for redress to the conciliation schemes run by the trade bodies of the industry itself. These trade bodies are the National Association of Funeral Directors, tel. 0121 711 1343; the National Society of Allied and Independent Funeral Directors, tel. 01279 726 777; and the Funeral Standards Council, tel. 029 2034 3554.

1.5.2(a) Alternative arrangements

i. It is also possible to arrange a burial without the help of a funeral director, with arrangements being made direct with the crematorium or cemetery and minister of religion if desired. A coffin can be purchased from an undertaker, or made. A large estate car or van will be needed to transport the coffin and 4 to 6 people to carry it. Some funeral directors will assist in do-it-yourself funerals by supplying a simple coffin and dealing with the documentation.

ii. In some areas it is possible to arrange a 'green' funeral using biodegradable coffins and doing away with headstones. The funeral director or local authority should be able to advise if this is available from the Natural Death Centre (see DIRECTORY). The Centre also publishes information on-line and a handbook.

iii. A 'virtual memorial garden' can be set up on the Internet.

See also *Public service funerals*, section 1.5.4 below.

1.5.3 Paying for the funeral

If you arrange the funeral you are responsible for payment. If the deceased left enough assets or cash, you may be able to claim reimbursement out of the estate for reasonable funeral expenses. Some pension schemes provide a lump sum to help with funeral expenses, or the deceased may have been a member of a burial or cremation society, or have taken out insurance to cover the costs. The National Association for Pre-Paid Funeral Plans is based at the National Association of Funeral Directors (see DIRECTORY).

The deceased's bank account is frozen on death (unless it is a joint account), so if you cannot pay and you cannot find sources of income among the deceased's papers, a claim can be made on the DSS Social Fund (which may subsequently claim recovery from the deceased's estate); alternatively ask at your local council offices about help for the funeral. They too may subsequently claim reimbursement from the deceased's estate. (In general, a grant under the Social Fund will be made only to a person considered to be responsible for the funeral who is in receipt of a means-tested benefit and has savings below a certain level, so it is advisable to check if you qualify before making arrangements.)

1.5.4   Public service funerals

Local authorities and hospitals will provide free funerals for people without relatives. This is particularly relevant to persons who may have resided in long-stay psychiatric hospitals where there is difficulty in tracing next of kin. These used to be known as paupers' funerals but are now called public service funerals. In such cases there is now erected a memorial or plaque to record the deceased.

2   IMMEDIATE FINANCIAL PROBLEMS

2.1   Help in coping

There are various ways in which dependants may seek help if they are in urgent need. A bank loan may be available if it is only a matter of time before funds are released from the estate; or a pension fund of which the deceased was a member may offer benefits. Social security is available to tide over problems.

☞ *You are an only son, a student at university. Your father died when you were young and your mother did not remarry. Your mother, who was a successful businesswoman, has died suddenly. You understand that you are the sole heir. Until now you received a monthly sum from her personal bank account, but this account is frozen and you are therefore without funds. Her affairs are being well taken care of by a firm of solicitors who have been appointed as her executors, but they cannot make payments out of the estate immediately. What can be done?*

If the estate is substantial, you should approach the bank together with the solicitors to arrange a loan to tide you over until your mother's estate is sorted out.

2.1.1   Turning to social security

Assistance is available in various forms for grieving relatives who also may have to cope with the financial impact of their loss.

☞ *You married many years ago and received a weekly housekeeping allowance from your husband. He died after a road accident and you find yourself in financial difficulties. In fact you are in need of immediate income support. Your husband was still working as an employee of an engineering firm when the accident happened. He has left no will. You know that he once took out a life insurance policy and you have found the policy document.*

To alleviate your immediate financial problems, you will have to apply for social security. Contact the Department for Work and Pensions, or your local Jobcentre Plus or Pension Service office. Leaflet CAT1 is a catalogue of the leaflets available.

Bereavement payment is a one-off payment of £2,000 available for immediate needs. Bereavement allowance is a weekly benefit payable to the surviving spouse who is over 45 at the deceased's death without dependant children, for 52 weeks following the death. Widowed parent's allowance is a weekly benefit for those bringing up dependent children. If you are over the state pension age when your spouse dies you may also get extra retirement pension based on the deceased's national insurance contributions. All these are available to both men and women.

Booklets GL14 and NP45 will advise you about bereavement allowance and bereavement payments. Leaflet SERPSSSL1A deals with the state-earnings-related pension scheme. Detailed leaflets are also available on income support (IS 20 and MIGIL). You may also be entitled to the Working Families Tax Credit — contact *www.inlandrevenue.gov.uk.*

For a possible claim under the Fatal Accidents Act, see chapter on *Accidents*, section 11.5.

You will need a certificate of registration of death (Form BD8) which is for social security purposes only. There is a claim form on the back of the certificate which you must fill in and give to your social security office. However, even if there is a delay in obtaining FormBD8, you must still contact the office and make your claim as soon as possible. Your Social Security office provides information and help with form-filling.

Do note: bereavement allowances are not payable:

- if you have been divorced from the deceased
- if you remarry, or if you live with a partner as though married, subsequent to your spouse's death
- if you never legally married your deceased partner
- if you are in prison or are being held in legal custody.

Do take advice: as the rules and regulations are complicated – relating to your age when bereaved as well as to your own and your spouse's contributions among other matters – and, as very strict time limits apply to appeal against a decision, you are urged to seek advice from a qualified advisor.

Other immediate relief available from social security may be in the form of industrial death benefit (for industrial accidents), retirement pensions and war pensions.

2.1.2   Pensions and insurance

If you find yourself bereaved, you must also check with the employers of your late spouse regarding his or her occupational pension scheme and find out who are the trustees of the pension fund. You will have to approach the trustees to establish whether you are entitled to receive the benefit of his or her pension. If the deceased was retired and had cashed in the funds in a personal pension fund on retirement, depending on its terms there may be no provision for continuing to pay after death.

Life or accident insurance policy, if taken out for the benefit of an heir, may provide for payment direct to you. Otherwise money payable from life policies falls into the deceased's estate. This means it will only be paid out when the personal representatives have obtained letters of administration. See sections 3.2 to 3.4 below. See also chapter on *Growing Old*, section 3.4.1 and 3.4.2.

2.1.3   Joint bank accounts

Personal accounts are frozen on death. Joint accounts can be operated provided that both signatories are not required to sign every cheque.

☞   *You and your live-in partner operated a joint bank account. He has died suddenly and your landlord is pressing for the rent. You know that his business account is frozen but would like to pay the rent from the joint account.*

You can operate the joint account provided it only required a single signature. The money in the account is not then considered part of the estate.

2.1.4   Insurance: cars and household

It is most important to note who is the main policyholder on the car and household insurance in the event of a death.

2.1.4(a)   Car

If the policy is in the deceased's name this means that no one else may be able to drive his or her car until a new policy document is issued. Where there are no other named drivers, but a car is insured 'for any driver', the insurers regard other drivers as driving the car with the policyholder's consent. Such consent, naturally, ceases on death.

☞   *You and your late wife owned a family car. She always attended to the insurance on the car. You are concerned that the insurance on the car was in her name as the main policyholder, although you were named as a driver in the policy.*

You may not be able to drive the car until the insurance policy is changed for you to become the main policyholder.

☞   *You return to your home town to visit your ailing elderly father. You have been driving his car to visit him in hospital when his condition worsens and he dies.*

The insurance on the car may not cover you to continue to drive it; nor will it protect the car against theft. You must inform the insurers of the death as soon as possible and ask them to hold you covered while fresh insurance is arranged.

2.1.4(b) Household

Important: you must notify insurers immediately. Check whether a household contents policy lapses on death. Leaving a house unoccupied with valuable possessions could be a breach of a household policy in any event, and alternative insurance may have to be arranged.

2.1.5 Housing

See sections 7.4 and 7.5 below.

3 THE DECEASED'S AFFAIRS

3.1 Who to tell and why

3.1.1 The deceased's papers – finding out if there is a will

In all cases, the first thing to establish in dealing with a deceased's estate is whether or not there is a will.

☞ *Your uncle, who had no children of his own, died after a long illness. Your aunt is so upset that she has been unable to deal with her late husband's affairs. She asks you to assist in sorting out his papers. She says that she is sure that he left a will as he made changes to the will while he was in hospital. She also says that you will find a shotgun locked in a steel cupboard in the study, for which he had a firearms certificate.*

Go through the personal papers left by the deceased. Check with his bank and with his past and present solicitors whether they hold his will. It might also have been deposited for safe custody with the Registry of the Family Division of the High Court. See also section 6.1.1(a) below, and section 3.1.6 on guns.

3.1.2 NHS equipment

Return any NHS equipment lent to the deceased (such as a wheelchair).

3.1.3 Sending back official documents

Other official documents should be sent back to the issuing office, with a note about the date of death.

3.1.3(a) The passport

The deceased's passport should be returned to the passport office.

3.1.3(b) The driving licence

The driving licence should be returned to the DVLA Swansea.

3.1.4 Checking with insurers

See section 2.1.4 above.

3.1.5 Tax office

Inform the deceased's Tax Office about the death as soon as possible. Leaflet IR45, on what to do about tax when someone dies, is available from *www.inlandrevenue.gov.uk*.

3.1.6 Guns

It is an offence to keep a gun without a firearms certificate. Your uncle's certificate is no longer valid once he has died, so hand over the shotgun to a registered firearms dealer for safekeeping (they have special authority for this) pending the settlement of the estate.

3.1.7 Bank direct debits and standing orders

Check all direct debit mandates and standing orders; these cease on death if paid through a bank account in a deceased's sole name. Bills for basic services such as telephone, gas etc., may have been paid in this way.

3.1.8 Credit cards

Make sure that all credit cards are returned with notice of death to the card companies to avoid fraudulent misuse.

3.2 The personal representatives

These are the official representatives of the deceased who 'wind up the estate'.

In one sense, all the deceased's affairs come to a halt at the moment of death; just to cite a single example, bank accounts in his or her sole name are automatically frozen. In another sense, all the affairs of the deceased's estate survive; for example the debts of the deceased still have to be paid.

So someone has to take charge of an estate and sort out all matters relating to it, i.e.:

- to take care of the deceased's property
- to pay outstanding debts and taxes
- to ascertain which persons are entitled to what is left (they are called *beneficiaries*)
- to ensure that the beneficiaries are given their proper share in due course.

This is a position of great responsibility, and also involves a fair amount of work, not all of it straightforward.

'Personal representatives' is a generic term which includes both *executors* and *administrators* (see below).

3.2.1 Distinction between executors and administrators

The question of who that 'someone' is whose duty it is to take charge of an estate hinges on whether or not there is a will.

a) If you leave a will, you can decide whom to appoint as your executors who will take charge of your affairs after your death.

b) If you do not leave a will, the next of kin will have to take charge. They are not called executors but are referred to as administrators of the deceased's estate.

There need be only one executor or one administrator. Two executors are usually appointed in a will in the event that one might be unwilling or unable to take on the role. If both take on the role they act together. Even if the tasks are undertaken unevenly, both are legally responsible. A will can name up to four executors.

Take note: although executors can act on behalf of an estate unofficially from the death of the person who appointed them, administrators cannot act until the grant of 'letters of administration' (see section 3.4 below).

In most cases, the executors are also the beneficiaries of the estate; for example a husband or wife will appoint the surviving spouse and/or their children as their executors and beneficiaries who will then wish to wind up the estate as quickly and as cheaply as possible.

3.2.2 A word of caution

Take heed: if you deal with any of the property of a deceased person without any authority to do so, you can be liable to penalties. See section 3.3.1 below.

3.2.3 Obtaining authority to act – probate

If the deceased leaves a will which names executors, the executors must apply to the Probate Division of the High Court for the grant of probate. This gives them official authority to act on behalf of the estate. If you are named and are prepared to act as executor, the procedures for obtaining a grant of probate are set out in a helpful booklet, *How to obtain probate*, produced by the Court Service and obtainable from the Probate Office (see DIRECTORY) and from the probate website at *www.courtservice.gov.uk*.

If there is no will, the administrators of the estate will be granted 'letters of administration' by the same Probate Division.

Both grant of probate and grant of letters of administration are referred to by a generic term: *grant of representation*.

☞ *Your grandfather lived with you until his death. He made you sole heir and executor of his estate. As far as you are aware, his only assets were a small savings account in a local building society. You wonder what steps you need to take.*

If the estate is worth less than £5,000, probate is not legally required, but a bank or building society holding the deceased's account may require such a document before releasing the funds; however, they may be satisfied with production of a death certificate. The certificate alone is likely to be sufficient where there was a joint account which is to be transferred into the name of the survivor. Probate is necessary where the deceased had property or land, or owned stocks or shares, or where he or she left assets outside of England and Wales.

Once this procedure is over, the will is a public document open to inspection by the public.

Help at hand: the addresses of the Probate Registries are listed in Booklet PA2. You will be assigned your own probate interviewing officer to deal with you and handle your application to minimise difficulties. Note, however, that their role ends once you are granted probate, and probate officers do not assist in administering the affairs of the estate.

3.2.4   Inheritance tax

If the net value of the assets left by the deceased is more than £250,000 (for 2002–2003; the figure may change), the personal representatives are personally liable to pay inheritance tax on the estate. They must send an account to the Inland Revenue within three months of first acting as personal representatives, or within 12 months of the death, whichever is the later date.

The responsibilities of the personal representatives are set out in Booklet IHT/4, available at *www.inlandrevenue.gov.uk*.

As with lifetime gifts between spouses (see chapter on *Setting up Home*, section 4.1.8), if the entire estate goes to the surviving spouse, then no inheritance tax is payable. Bequests to registered charities are also exempt from inheritance tax.

☞   *You are nominated as executor of your stepmother's large estate. You are not able to afford the likely inheritance tax bill and would like to know what you should do.*

You may have to borrow money to pay the inheritance tax. However, you can claim reimbursement out of the estate when you have received the grant of representation (see section 3.2.3 above). Forms IHT 44 and IHT 205 are the relevant forms.

3.3   Acting as executor

There is no legal compulsion to take on the task of executor if named in someone's will.

☞   *A very close friend asked you whether you would be prepared to act as his executor at a time when he was terminally ill. He said that it would be a simple matter of dealing with his property and personal effects. You agreed to his request and he has named you as sole executor in his will. Now that he has died, you would like some advice on taking on the task.*

If you are named as executor in a will you are under no legal compulsion to accept the role, even if before the death you promised your friend you would do so. Indeed, in certain circumstances, you should be wary of accepting the role of executor, however honoured you may feel that you were nominated by your friend.

If the friend was himself acting as the executor in someone else's estate at the time of his death (perhaps, for example, he was winding up his wife's estate and died before completing the task), you would have to complete that role, as well as winding up your friend's own estate. You should also take legal advice before accepting the nomination as executor if:

- you were your friend's business partner at the time of his death; or
- he was still running his own business; or
- he had substantial overseas assets (which might render you personally liable for inheritance tax on their value to the UK revenue authorities).

3.3.1   Taking on the job

If you start acting as an executor you will be regarded as having accepted, so do not begin dealing with the property of the deceased until you have made up your mind (except for urgent matters such as feeding pets, making emergency repairs or disposing of rubbish which could become a health hazard).

Take heed: if you get it wrong, you could be sued by lots of different people. For your own protection, it is well worth while seeking the advice of a solicitor – the costs of which will come out of the estate.

3.3.2 Remuneration and expenses

It is wiser not to become executor of an estate with few assets and many debts. Even if the estate is not bankrupt, if it is fairly large and complicated it may take a lot of your time, and although you will be able to recoup expenses from the estate you cannot charge for your time and trouble (unless the will so specifies, or all the beneficiaries agree). For the position of banks or lawyers acting as executors, see section 4.1.1 below.

Out-of-pocket expenses are always paid out of the estate.

Note: unless payment has been specified in the will, if an executor or administrator is to be paid for acting in the winding up of an estate, all the beneficiaries must agree in writing by a formal document. In this case, it requires a *deed under seal*. A mere informal written agreement to pay executors for their time and trouble is not enough.

3.4 Appointing an administrator

3.4.1 Letters of administration

Letters of administration must be obtained where the deceased did not leave a will, or left a will but failed to name his executors. Persons who obtain a grant of letters of administration from the Probate Registry are known as the *administrators*. They then take over the deceased's estate, dealing with it in the same way as executors.

☞ *Your late brother has left a will but has not named any executors in it. You have been approached by his live-in partner, who asks you to act as executor. You are quite ready to accept. However, you are not quite sure of your legal position.*

If there is:

- *no executor named in the will, or*
- *no will at all*

then a grant of letters of administration will be issued by the Probate Registry to next of kin.

This is in a prescribed order of priority (see Booklet PA2) based on the closeness of family relationship. A brother will be appointed as personal representative after:

- surviving spouse (which is not applicable in this case); then
- children; then
- parents.

3.4.2 Children of parents not married to each other

Children of parents who are not married to each other are not discriminated against; they can act as administrators if their parents die without a will and they can inherit in the same way and proportion as children of parents married to each other.

☞ *You have lived with your partner for many years and have had two children by him. He has now died intestate. You would like the children to act as administrators of the estate but have been told by a friend that, because they were born out of wedlock, they are not entitled to act. Is this so?*

The answer is 'no'. For the purposes of the order of priorities of appointment of administrator, the children are your partner's next of kin. The fact that you and he were not married is not relevant to the children's status with regard to acting for his estate.

The order of priorities (above) relates solely to the question of who can act as administrator of an intestate estate. There are different rules for who can *inherit* under an intestacy (see section 7 below).

If the whole estate is worth less than £5,000 then a grant of representation may not be necessary (see Booklet PA2).

3.5 Dealing with the deceased's property

3.5.1 Property in the UK

Once the grant of representation has been issued, the personal representatives can administer the property of the deceased in England and Wales. If there is property in Scotland or Northern Ireland, there is no need to obtain separate confirmations or grants of representation.

Conversely, if the deceased died in Scotland or Northern Ireland, confirmation or grant of representation should be obtained in the country of death, and this will be recognised in England and Wales.

3.5.2 Function of personal representatives

The function of the personal representatives is to take control of the deceased's property and land, as well as cash and personal effects:

a) They must keep records
b) They must, of course, keep this property quite separate from their own
c) They must take reasonable care of the property
d) They can take out insurance for this purpose.

They will have to give a rough valuation of the house or flat which the deceased owned, to the probate registry. This figure will subsequently be checked by a valuation officer of the Inland Revenue.

Shares are valued as at the day before the date of death. The figures are easily checked from the Stock Exchange Daily Official List.

3.5.3 Taking legal advice

You can instruct a solicitor, accountant, or bank to deal with winding up the estate. Their fees can be substantial, so ask first. If the deceased's affairs are straightforward, a layperson can deal with them. Booklets are available on how to go about it. You may wish to do it yourself and only take advice if problems arise (see below).

When you should consult a solicitor:

- if the estate involves the transfer of ownership of a house or flat
- if the estate involves rented property, and the rights of a secure or protected tenant to remain in occupation are at issue
- if there are assets of the estate outside of England and Wales
- if there are children under 18
- if there is a second family involved, e.g. children and stepchildren, with competing claims
- if the estate appears insolvent
- if the deceased was running a business
- if the estate is very large and it would be complicated to administer
- if there is a problem in tracing some of the beneficiaries who might have a claim on the estate
- if the will might have been tampered with – either by the testator or some other person
- if there are likely to be claims against the estate by dependants for whom the will did not make provision
- if the validity of a will is open to question
- if the deceased was killed in an accident in circumstances where his relatives may make a claim for damages under the Fatal Accidents Act (if, for example, he or she was killed in a car crash or work accident); see also *Accidents* chapter, section 11.5
- if the deceased owned or rented agricultural property.

Note: this list is not exhaustive and is intended for guideline purposes only.

A will sometimes directs that the executors should use the services of a named solicitor or accountant. This is not binding on the executor, who can choose to consult someone else.

Executors can claim reimbursement of legal fees from the estate. See also section 3.3.2 above.

3.5.4 Insuring the estate

See section 2.1.4 above for the insurance position immediately the death occurs.

Insurance is always advisable for personal representatives, and since they can be held personally liable to make up any losses caused to a beneficiary or creditor of the estate, they should make sure any valuables are lodged securely with a bank.

☞ *Your co-executor has absconded with some valuable jewellery which your mother-in-law left in her will to her sister. You have been told that you are now personally responsible for making up the loss. You want to know if this is correct.*

The answer is 'yes'. You are legally responsible for the actions of your co-executor.

3.5.5   Keeping accounts

At each stage a careful and accurate record should be kept of what is done as you can be called upon to account for your administration by persons interested in the estate, or by the court.

Warning note: executors are urged to open a separate bank account, known as the 'executor's account', in order to keep a careful record of all payments in and out of the estate and to obviate any confusion with the executor's personal affairs.

3.5.6   The deceased's business

If the deceased ran a business, the personal representatives do not have the power to carry on the business except for the purpose of selling it as a going concern. They should see a solicitor if the deceased was a partner in a business or ran his own business through a limited liability company.

3.5.7   The deceased's creditors

The personal representatives are responsible for paying taxes and satisfying debts due by the deceased, out of the assets in the estate. They may advertise for claims from creditors, allowing at least two months for claims to be lodged before paying out to the beneficiaries. Assets may have to be sold to raise cash in order to settle the debts, but beneficiaries under the will (if there is one) may have an interest in particular assets. The order in which assets should be disposed of is laid down by law.

3.5.8   When the estate is insolvent

If there are insufficient assets to pay debts and taxes, the estate is insolvent, i.e. the estate is bankrupt. It must then be administered in accordance with a particular procedure specified in the Administration of Insolvent Estates of Deceased Persons Order (SI 1986 No. 1999, obtainable from HMSO). For example, after paying the expenses of the funeral and administration, and arrears which the deceased owed on social security and pension fund contributions, tax claims by the Inland Revenue must be paid before debts due to ordinary creditors.

Secured creditors such as mortgagees will rely on their security and sell the mortgaged property to recover payment. If the correct procedure is not observed, the personal representatives may become personally liable to creditors.

The next of kin are not liable to pay the deceased's debts, if he or she left insufficient assets to pay them.

If the will gives a specified amount as legacies to X and Y, if there is not enough property left they will only get a proportion according to how much remains in the estate after the deceased's debts have been paid; the persons named in the will to get the rest of the property will then receive nothing.

3.5.9   Paying the beneficiaries

If there are assets left over after paying expenses, taxes and debts, the personal representatives must distribute them in accordance with the will. If there is no will, or no valid will, or the will disposes of only part of the assets, the law prescribes who is entitled to share in the assets of the deceased (see *Intestacy*, section 7 below). The Office of National Statistics has a service for tracing individuals, known as Traceline, which may help to locate beneficiaries whose address is not known. See *www.statistics.gov.uk/registration/traceline/help.asp*.

The personal representatives are not obliged to pay out legacies or distribute the assets of the estate to beneficiaries until one year has elapsed since the death. This is known as the 'executor's year'. Thereafter it is desirable to distribute as soon as possible although the timing will depend on the complexity of the deceased's affairs.

4   BEFORE DEATH: PREPARING FOR THE INEVITABLE

The choice is between leaving a will or dying intestate.

A valid will ensures that we can determine what happens to our property after our death. If we do not make a will, in other words if we die intestate, the law determines how our property will be distributed, to whom, and in what proportion.

4.1   Whether to make a will

As explained above, without a will, assets and belongings will be distributed on death according to the law of intestacy (dealt with in detail in section 7). The intestacy laws benefit blood relatives in the order of proximity, but charities and close friends get nothing.

Good reasons exist, therefore, for choosing to make a will:

a) to revoke a previous will
b) to appoint guardians or set up trusts for property you are leaving to your minor children (although guardianship can also be done less formally – see section 9.4 below)
c) to nominate executors and trustees
d) to make gifts to individuals and charities, and to provide for pets
e) to prevent family squabbles about who takes what
f) to plan, with professional advice, the distribution of your estate so as to minimise inheritance tax and capital gains tax
g) to leave instructions about your funeral or cremation, or to leave your organs for research or transplant. But as the will may not be seen till after the funeral, except possibly by the executors, it is a sensible precaution for you also to tell your family and proposed executor about your wishes in this regard (see section 1.3 above on the matter of donating organs).

Note: when you make a will, it is also advisable to sign an enduring power of attorney (see chapter on *Growing Old*, section 8.2.2).

If you need to deal with property situated outside England and Wales, or have family links abroad, where a different system of law and tax will be applied, it is better to make a separate will for that country. Take legal advice about this.

4.1.1   How to go about making a will

Any solicitor will prepare a will for you. The fees can vary from as little as £50 at a High Street solicitor, up to several hundred pounds, depending on:

• the size of the estate and
• the complexity of the will itself.

Do ask beforehand about legal charges; most solicitors will give you an approximate figure.

If you do not want to consult a solicitor, there are inexpensive customised will-making services available.

In addition:

• various charities such as Oxfam or Help the Aged offer a will-making service
• banks and some life insurance companies offer a will-writing service
• there is no legal reason why you should not simply write out a will yourself or use a ready-made will form from a legal stationer (but see section 4.1.2. below).

Forms and advice on preparing a will are now available from various sites on the Internet as well.

Note: if you nominate as executor a bank or similar organisation, or a solicitor or accountant, the will usually includes a clause that they will charge for their professional services (cf. section 3.3.2 above). Their fees can make very substantial inroads into the amount of the estate available for the beneficiaries. Professional fees for acting as executor can be challenged, if the beneficiaries regard them as excessive. You could approach the Law Society to look at the final bill.

4.1.2   Home-made wills

Take heed: it is a risky business to try to make a will without some kind of advice. Many home-made wills turn out to be invalid for one reason or another. If they are invalid, then the deceased's wishes can be thwarted and the estate will be distributed according to the intestacy rules.

For example, a pre-printed will form may contain a flaw such as omitting to warn that a beneficiary should not be a witness. Customers who buy such a form may have their wishes defeated by the error, whereas obtaining legal advice should prevent such a problem.

4.1.3 Negligence

As there is no licensing or training requirement anyone can set up in business offering a will-making service. Reputable will-making services carry indemnity insurance against negligence, as solicitors do. However, not all services have insurance. You will then have no proper safeguard, so do check.

A solicitor instructed by a client to draw up a will owes a duty of care to the client. If he negligently fails to carry out this professional obligation the will may be invalid.

Disappointed beneficiaries who therefore failed to inherit under a will have been able to sue solicitors who were professionally negligent – for example, if they did not ensure that the will was properly witnessed, so that it was ineffective. If the solicitor delayed in preparing the will after receiving the instructions, so that the testator died before the will was signed, whether the solicitor was negligent or acted with due diligence may depend on such factors as the health or age of the intending testator. However, if the client could not have complained about the way the solicitor handled the matter, neither can any beneficiary.

In one case a solicitor, in drawing up a new will, under which the deceased intended to leave her share in a property to her niece, did suggest that it would be advisable to check how the property was held, but failed to take further simple steps to avoid a problem from arising. Because of that failure, the property in question did not pass to the intended beneficiary and the solicitor was held responsible for the consequences of that negligence.

Do note: these cases are exceptional; do not generally expect to make up for your disappointed hopes by suing the solicitors involved!

Note too: the courts can correct obvious errors, such as a mis-spelling of the name of a particular property which the deceased intended to leave to a relative.

4.1.4 Obtaining community legal services funding [formerly legal aid] for drawing up a will

Provided that you meet the requirements laid down which entitle you to community legal services funding (see chapter on *The Legal System*), legal help will be funded for advice and for the preparation of a will:

- for testators aged 70 years or over; or
- for a disabled person within the meaning of section 1 of the Disability Discrimination Act 1995; or
- for the parent of a disabled person as defined above who wishes to provide for that person in a will; or
- for the parent of a minor who is living with only one parent and that parent wishes to appoint a guardian for the minor in his or her will.

☞ *Your grandchild, aged 10, lives with you under a parental responsibility order from the court as both parents live abroad. You are aged 65. You wish to appoint a guardian in your will for the child and wonder if you are eligible for funding for legal help.*

For the purposes of the provisions for legal funding, a 'parent' includes any person with parental responsibility for the child.

☞ *You and your wife have a child with Down's syndrome and you worry about her future. You would like expert legal assistance in case an accident befalls either of you and you daughter would be left alone.*

In this case, you can apply to see whether, in your financial circumstances, you are eligible for legal funding, i.e. State help towards payment of legal fees in drawing up a will best suited to her needs.

Certain organisations such as MENCAP can provide advice on how to set up a trust for a handicapped person out of an estate.

In any event, you should always take advice if you wish to leave money or property to someone who is physically disabled and is in consequence not self-supporting, or to someone with a mental handicap who is incapable of taking decisions about his or her affairs. A solicitor or other adviser can advise you about the desirability of setting up a trust in these circumstances.

Remember: if the legatee is receiving social security or local authority benefits, your legacy may leave him or her no better off. When a legacy causes a change in the financial circumstances of the beneficiary, a means test may lead to the loss of these benefits.

4.1.5 Informal wishes

If after someone's death a letter or note is found among their effects stating that certain objects should be given to particular persons, this has no legal effect unless it complies with the requirements for making a will. It would be unlawful for the personal representatives to pay regard to it unless all the beneficiaries and creditors agree. (See also section 5.3.1 below.)

4.1.6 Wills – tying up property for the future

On the whole the courts do not look kindly on the idea that property should be tied up for the benefit of future generations. This is known as the rule against perpetuities.

☞ *Clare's son has just got married. She would like to draw up a will which would ensure that her family home goes to any future grandchildren as she feels that her son and daughter-in-law are well provided for.*

The rule against perpetuities exists to restrict how far one generation can control the passing of property at the expense of the succeeding generation.

The two possible perpetuity periods are:

- a life or lives in being plus 21 years; or
- a specified period of up to 80 years.

These rules are complex and as Clare is considering tying up her estate in order to benefit any future grandchildren, she should consult a solicitor so as to avoid possible pitfalls which could result in some of her bequests becoming invalid. The Law Commission has proposed some simplification of the perpetuity rules, but these are unlikely to affect Clare's position.

4.2 Other ways to dispose of property – gifts in contemplation of death

An individual may wish to make a gift during his or her lifetime, with the intention of ensuring that the recipient will receive the gift after the donor's death. Such a gift is said to be 'made in contemplation of death'.

4.2.1 How to make the gift

The gift must be clearly made in the donor's lifetime.

☞ *Your mother, who knows she is terminally ill, gives you the key to her jewellery box. She tells you that she wants you to have her jewellery after her death. Three days later she dies.*

You can keep the jewellery and it does not fall into the estate for distribution under your mother's will, if she left one, or on intestacy if she did not.

In one recent case an elderly woman told her nephew that she intended to transfer certain shares to him. She signed the transfer form but died before doing anything further about it. The court held that the gift of the shares was valid.

4.2.2 Gift at any time

In a recent case, a father realised he was terminally ill. He said to his son from his hospital bed 'You can keep the keys of the car; I won't be driving it any more.' It was held that it was a gift in contemplation of death and the other beneficiaries under the father's will could not claim that the car was part of the father's estate.

However, a gift made in contemplation of death can be revoked at any time during the lifetime of the donor.

☞ *Three days after giving you the key to her jewellery box and telling you that she wants you to have her jewellery after her death, your mother quarrels with you. She forces open the jewellery box and gives her jewels to her sister. Soon afterwards, she dies.*

This is a clear indication that your mother revoked her gift to you of the jewellery. It now belongs to her sister. Again it does not belong to the estate after your mother's death.

4.2.3 Gift must be completed

Any gift must be 'completed' before death.

☞ *At the same time as your mother gives you the jewellery, she gives your brother a cheque for an equivalent amount. She dies before he has deposited the cheque.*

The money represented by the cheque was not a 'completed' gift. Your brother has no claim for that amount – as distinct from any other claim he may have as a beneficiary.

4.2.4 Buildings and land

Note: gifts in contemplation of death can apply to house property as well as to personal possessions.

☞ *Your friend owns little except his house. He has made no will, but while dying in hospital, he tells you that the house is yours. He gives you the keys to the house and tells you where you will find a box in which he kept the title deeds to the property. He gives you the key to the box as well. After his death, his relatives claim the house under the intestacy rules. You want to know whether the gift is valid.*

In a similar case, the court held that the person who received the keys and the title deeds from her dying friend was entitled to the house despite the relatives' claims.

Note: it is possible that a gift 'made in contemplation of death' cannot be made in contemplation of suicide.

4.2.5 Distinguished from ordinary gifts – the 'seven-year rule'

Gifts made in contemplation of death, which are only intended to take effect on death, are not to be confused with gifts made in a donor's lifetime which are intended to take effect immediately. These gifts are a device to avoid inheritance tax and can be made up to the current nil band of £250,000 inheritance tax threshold. If the donor dies within seven years of the gift, the gift attracts inheritance tax on a sliding scale after three years; but if the donor survives for longer than seven years, the gift is inheritance-tax free. These are known as partially exempt transfers (PETS). To be effective you must transfer the property in its entirety.

☞ *You own a flat in Brighton which you rent out. You want to make a gift of the flat to your only daughter, Cynthia, in order to avoid her having to pay inheritance tax both on your own home and on the flat, at a later stage.*

You cannot expect to receive rent from the flat after you make it over to Cynthia. In other words, you cannot part with the flat and at the same time reserve the benefit of it for yourself in the form of rental income.

Note: it is always advisable to seek the assistance of a lawyer or accountant if you are concerned about inheritance tax.

5 MAKING SURE A WILL IS EFFECTIVE

Your will cannot be made effective on your death unless it complies with the formalities prescribed by law.

5.1 Formalities

The *testator* or *testatrix* (the maker of a will) must be aged over 18. Members of the armed forces who are under 18 can also make a valid will.

The will must be in writing. It need not be in English to be valid, if the testator is more familiar with another language.

The will should be clear and legible, though it does not have to be typed. It should not be written in pencil. (For your convenience, keep a copy of the will; this copy need not be signed.)

5.1.1　Signatures

The will should be signed by the testator *at the end of the document*. This is most important. A signature at the top of the will could be challenged.

The will must be signed by at least two witnesses. They and the testator must all be in the same room at the same time *throughout* the signing session. This fact should be stated in the will, and the date should be inserted.

☞　*You call in two neighbours to witness your will. They are in the room with you while you sign it but one of them refuses to sign unless she reads the will first. She says that otherwise her signature will not be valid.*

　　The witnesses do not have to read the document. They do not even have to know that the document is a will, as long as they know that they are there to witness your signature.

Below the testator's signature the witnesses should then write their usual signatures, and add their addresses and occupations or descriptions.

5.1.2　Who can be witnesses

The witnesses must not be persons who are benefiting under the will. They also cannot be married to persons benefiting under the will.

☞　*Your two sons are to be your sole heirs under your will. You know that neither of them can witness your signature but your daughter-in-law is visiting you and you want to ask her to act as a witness, together with a neighbour.*

　　A person married to someone benefiting under the will cannot act as a witness.

If the testator is very elderly or infirm, one of the persons acting as witness should be a doctor, who should examine him first to make sure he understands what he is doing and its implications. The doctor should be asked to keep a record of the examination.

If the testator is too weak to sign, then even a mark will do provided it is made in the presence of the doctor who is acting as witness.

The solicitor who prepared the will can be a witness.

5.2　Where to keep the will

Deposit the signed will in a safe place, perhaps with your solicitor or your bank. It is also possible to deposit a will at any Registry of the Family Division of the High Court. It is advisable that you tell your executor and family where you have put the will, so that delay in tracing it is avoided. (They will not be able to see it until after your death.)

5.3　Reviewing the contents of the will regularly

The provisions of your will should be reviewed every five years or as your circumstances change or there are changes in the value of your possessions. You must certainly consider making a new will when major family events occur, such as marriage, divorce, the birth of a child, or the death of someone close to you. (For the effect of such events on an existing will, see *Revocation of will*s in section 6.4 below.)

5.3.1　Minor amendments and codicils

For a minor amendment to your will, you can consider making a codicil.

Codicils are used for the purpose of making changes to a will where there is no necessity to rewrite the whole will. Two witnesses must witness the signature to the codicil which must be signed and dated in the same way as a will. The codicil is then attached to the will.

Do state that the rest of the will is unchanged, in the codicil's opening sentence.

☞　*You named two executors for your will but one of them has since died and you would now like to name someone in her stead. Otherwise your will is unchanged. You call in two friends to witness the signing of the codicil and one of them asks whether it is necessary for you to have the same witnesses to your signature of the codicil as witnessed your original will.*

　　The answer is 'no'. Provided you have two witnesses to the codicil they need not be the same two people who witnessed your signature to the original will, but see section 5.1.2 above.

A letter or memo setting out the testator's wishes will have no legal force although if the beneficiaries agree to abide by its terms and inform the personal representative to that effect, the courts will give effect to such an agreement. A codicil is the simpler and safer way of making sure minor amendments have full legal force.

5.4   Soldiers' and seamen's wills

In certain emergency situations individuals can make a valid will without complying with any of the above formalities. These are called 'privileged wills' and are as effective after the individual's death as a formal written will. The only persons who can make such wills are soldiers on actual military service or mariners while at sea (even if they are under 18). They can even make their will orally, as long as they intended by the statement to dispose of their property on death.

☞   *Edward, a bomb disposal expert, is injured while carrying out a security operation in England. He gasps out to his comrade: 'If I don't make it, make sure my girlfriend Anne gets all my stuff'.*

This is a valid privileged will, and remains so even if Edward recovers and leaves the army. It remains valid until he makes a new will or he revokes it.

Note: the armed forces normally require recruits to make a formal will when joining up.

6   WHEN A WILL CAN BE CHALLENGED

If certain people are dissatisfied with the outcome – either through having been left out of the will or because the intestacy rules have excluded them – they are able to challenge these arrangements.

Note: challengers are not limited to dependants which are described below.

6.1.1(a)   Inspecting the will

There is now a Probate Records Centre in Birmingham, which replaces the previous system whereby probate documents were stored in district registries throughout England and Wales.

Members of the public can go to any registry in England and Wales and ask to read a copy of a will for £5. This service is also to be made available electronically. Addresses of registries can be obtained at *www.courtservice.gov.uk/wills_probate/ADDRESS.htm.*

6.1.1(b)   Time Limits

Beneficiaries or anyone else wishing to challenge a will can only do so within six months. [Check the website of the Office of National Statistics for whether there is a will.]

6.1.2   Revocation

It may be claimed that the will was no longer valid because the testator had changed his mind, i.e. the will had been revoked. (See also sections 6.4.2 and 6.4.3 below.)

In a recent case, the testator had made a will disinheriting his daughters. After a reconciliation, he instructed his solicitors to prepare a new will leaving £9,000 to each of them. However, the solicitor delayed preparing the new will and the father died in the meantime. The daughters could not challenge the will disinheriting them even though their father had clearly changed his mind. But in these circumstances, they successfully sued the solicitors for negligence.

6.1.3   Mental incapacity

It may be claimed that the deceased did not know or understand what he or she was doing, or its effect, when making the will. See also section 6.5 below.

6.1.4   Undue influence or fraud

It may be claimed that the deceased was subject to undue influence or fraud when making the will.

6.1.5   Failure to provide for dependants

It may be claimed that the deceased failed to make reasonable provision for a dependant. See section 8 below.

6.2   Costs of challenge

Where legal proceedings are brought to challenge a will, the executor may insist that the beneficiaries indemnify him against the cost of defending the action, before he accepts office. The court will not necessarily order the costs and expenses of the proceedings to be taken out of the estate.

6.3   Reasons for failure of testator's intentions

Even if a will has left you a legacy, various factors may operate to prevent you from receiving the benefit.

6.3.1   Insolvency

If the estate was insolvent, all the assets are used up in paying creditors.

6.3.2   Terms of the will

A gift will also depend on the terms of the will.

☞   *In her will your sister left you 'the diamond brooch given to me by our mother'. It now appears that your sister sold the brooch some years before her death.*

You will not be able to receive the diamond brooch and cannot claim anything from the estate in lieu of the brooch. If she had simply left you 'a diamond brooch' the executor must buy one out of the assets of the estate, provided they are sufficient.

☞   *Your uncle's will states that his collection of porcelain should be sold. He directs his executors to buy you a sports car from the proceeds. The executors inform you that the money raised from the sale of the porcelain falls short of the amount needed to buy even the cheapest sports car.*

By the terms of the will, the sale of the porcelain must realise sufficient to buy the car; if it does not, the bequest fails and the proceeds from the sale of the porcelain fall into the balance of the estate – the *residue*.

In one case the testator's will divided his estate between the National Children's Home and the National Canine Defence League, the latter's half-share being made subject to the condition that the League looked after his domestic pets for the remainder of their lives. At the time of the testator's death all the pets had already died. As it was therefore impossible for the League to fulfil the condition, it lapsed, and the half-share went to the League unconditionally.

6.3.3   Rectification

If a will is so expressed that it fails to carry out the testator's intentions, it may be possible to apply to court have the will rectified. This has to be done within six months of the grant of the letters of representation, and is only possible where there was a clerical error in the will or the person drafting it failed to understand the testator's instructions.

☞   *Lewis was sent a draft will by his solicitor, which included a provision that certain family members could not benefit under the will during the lifetime of their parents. Lewis read the draft and instructed the solicitor to delete this provision, but the solicitor inadvertently failed to remove it from the final version of the will signed by Lewis. After Lewis's death the court permitted rectification of the will by deletion of the contested provision.*

Very convincing evidence will be required to persuade the court to rectify. Do take independent legal advice as soon as possible.

6.4   A will that has been revoked

A will may be revoked by an act of the testator – e.g. by making a later will or destroying a will. Sometimes the law regards a will as revoked automatically, either in whole or in part.

6.4.1   By marriage

A will is automatically revoked by operation of the law (i.e. without any act on the testator's part) if the person who made the will ('the testator') subsequently gets married. The will is revoked in its entirety.

☞ *Your husband made a will leaving his estate to you, whom he also named as executrix. After 25 years of marriage, he divorced you and remarried. He died three months later.*

In this case, the whole of his will was revoked by his remarriage, so that the estate will be divided according to intestacy, with his second wife taking the lion's share as surviving spouse.

However, you could make a claim under the family provision legislation. The court will weigh up all the circumstances, taking into account your present needs, and the kind of settlement you received when you were divorced (see section 8 below).

This 'revocation by marriage' applies except where a will states that it is made 'in contemplation of marriage'. For example, a couple who intend to honeymoon abroad decide to make wills before their wedding 'in contemplation of marriage'. In that case, their wills are valid.

Note: the birth of a child or grandchild does not revoke an existing will. However, it clearly requires consideration to be given to the making of a new will or codicil.

6.4.2 By a later will or codicil

A will is generally revoked by a later will, usually by express words, such as 'This is my last will and testament and I hereby revoke all former wills.'

However, not all later wills expressly revoke earlier ones. If there are no words of express revocation, the effect of the later will depends on its terms, inconsistency with the earlier will, and the implications which flow from the existing wills.

☞ *Your father left two wills, the second will having been made about a year after the first one. The later one does not expressly revoke the earlier will and the terms of both wills are similar except for one specific gift. In his first will he left £1,000 to his housekeeper, whom he has since dismissed; the gift is omitted in the second will. You are the sole executor and beneficiary. You would like some advice.*

The gift to your father's former housekeeper would no longer be effective.

If a later will does not expressly revoke an earlier one, it can do so by implication. It depends on the terms and whether the second will contains provisions inconsistent with the first one.

If the two wills are not inconsistent, and there is no express revocation of the earlier will in the later, they will both be effective and have combined effect.

If a couple agreed to make mutual wills leaving their property to each other or their children, then after the death of the first, the survivor's ability to make different arrangements by a new will may be limited. A solicitor should be consulted in these circumstances.

6.4.3 By destruction

Clearly a will is revoked if the testator destroys it. Only actual physical destruction – e.g. burning it, or cutting it up – is a revocation, and then only if it is done intentionally by the testator or, if by someone else, in his presence. Striking out pages, by drawing a line through the words, is insufficient; but cutting out the signatures, or crossing them through so thickly that they cannot be made out, operates as a revocation.

☞ *You understand that your cousin telephoned her solicitor and asked him to destroy her will. He properly advised her that she should destroy it herself, and posted it to her. She has since died and you have found her will among her papers, heavily scribbled on and with the word 'Cancelled' written at the top. The will can still be read, although with difficulty, as can the signatures. You would like to know whether the will is valid.*

In all cases where the validity of a will is open to challenge, it is advisable to consult a solicitor. However, in a case similar to this one, the court held that where the will and its signatures could still be read, it was valid.

6.4.4 By divorce

If the testator gets divorced after the date of the will, the will is partially revoked; the will remains valid but any appointments of the former spouse as executor, and bequests to him or her, are deleted as though the former spouse had died on the date of the divorce. Separation without divorce has no effect on the will.

☞ *Your mother made a will naming your father as co-executor with her brother. She left your father two-thirds of her estate, with the other third going to you. Thereafter she divorced your father. She has recently died and you would like to know the present position.*

As a result of the divorce, your father, as your mother's ex-husband, has to be left out of account in dealing with her estate – both as legatee of the two-thirds of her estate and as co-executor. As a result you will receive one-third of the estate under the will, and the other two-thirds will devolve as on intestacy (see section 7 below), with her brother acting as the sole executor.

If your father cannot support himself, he could apply for family provision (see section 8 below).

It is particularly important to note that where a testator has appointed his spouse as guardian of any minor child of the testator, this appointment is also revoked if their marriage ends in divorce.

☞ *Steve, a widower with two young children, married Tracy. In his will he named her as guardian. Steve divorced Tracy five years later. He died when both children were still under 18.*

The appointment of Tracy as guardian lapsed on their divorce. If Steve had wanted to ensure that she should continue to be guardian despite the divorce, the will should have made that clear.

6.5   Mental incapacity

For wills to be valid, testators must have known and understood what they were about at the time of making the will. If they subsequently become senile or mentally ill this does not revoke an earlier will. Under the Access to Health Records Act 1990, the executors or administrators of the deceased's estate, and any person who may have a claim arising out of the death, can apply to the health authorities to be given access to the deceased's health records.

A valid will can be spiteful or eccentric, unexpected or capricious – this fact alone does not cast doubt on the testator's mental capacity. All that is required is that testators have the capacity to understand the nature of a will, the extent of their property and the claims on their bounty of their relatives and friends.

If the will was made when the testator was very elderly or was known to have suffered from mental illness, a doctor may have been asked to witness the will, and if so may have kept a record of the testator's state of mind at the time. (See also the chapter on *Growing Old*, section 8.)

If the testator suffered from a mental illness at the time of making the will this does not necessarily reflect on his ability to understand what he was doing. But if the symptoms did influence the provisions of the will it will not be valid. For example, if the testator suffered from a delusion about one child of the family, whom he therefore disinherited, the will may be set aside. If the delusion affects only a portion of the will, only that portion may be declared inoperative.

A situation analogous to lack of capacity arises where there is a suspicion that the testator did not understand or approve the will he signed. If this can be proved, the will is invalid.

☞ *Nina, a wealthy, infirm and frail widow of 91, lived in a nursing home run by Mr and Mrs Smith. A letter signed by Nina was sent to solicitors she had never consulted previously, asking them to draw up a will leaving her estate to Mrs Smith. They sent the will to her, which she signed. The solicitors did not see Nina personally, and during visits to Nina by her relatives Mr or Mrs Smith were always present. After Nina's death her relatives challenge the validity of the will.*

Given the highly suspicious circumstances the court is unlikely to find that Nina knew and approved the contents of the will when signing it.

(See also section 6.7 below.)

6.6   Undue influence and fraud

Where the testator was persuaded to make a will in particular terms – such as leaving large sums to a religious sect – this will not invalidate the will unless the testator was subjected to excessive pressure or coercion. The mere fact that the beneficiary was in some position of authority or influence over the testator (as doctor, priest or solicitor, for instance) raises no presumption that excessive pressure was used.

☞ *James, after a marriage of many years to Celia, separates from her and starts a relationship with Beth. Beth, with whom James is obsessed, persuades him to make a will leaving his substantial property to her to the exclusion of his wife and children.*

On James's death the will is valid. (However, Celia and the children can claim family provision out of the estate – see section 8 below.)

6.7   Statutory wills for the mentally impaired

A person who lacks the understanding to make a valid will may still possess some property. The court can be asked under the Mental Health Act to make a will for the patient, in such terms as the patient might be expected to have intended if of sound mind. Such a will must be sealed by the Court of Protection before probate can be granted, but need not have been so sealed before the death of the testator.

In 2001 the Public Guardianship Office replaced the previously existing Public Trust Office to manage the assets of the mentally incapacitated (see DIRECTORY and chapter on *Growing Old*, section 8).

7   WHERE THERE IS NO WILL: INTESTATE SUCCESSION

Only about one in three of the population bothers to make a will at all. Many others may intend to do so but just do not get round to it. In such cases, whether they wish it or not, they are relying on the rules of distribution of their estates under the intestacy laws. These laws, generally speaking, are designed to follow a deceased's own wishes: in other words, the law assumes that people who leave no wills would wish their estate to benefit their closest relatives.

However, since the intestacy rules were drawn up there have been noteworthy changes in home ownership patterns: about 70% of houses are now owner-occupied today, compared with only about 30% forty years ago. This fact, taken together with the marked increase in the numbers of people who have pensions and life insurance, as well as owning property, means that the intestacy rules, intended to act as a safety net, can instead sometimes work in an arbitrary and unfair way.

7.1   Who inherits?

Intestate succession in England and Wales proceeds in accordance with the diagram overleaf. If there is no surviving relative, the estate will go the Crown. If you think you may be entitled to inherit the estate of a deceased relative, check the government website dealing with this: *www.bonavacantia.gov.uk*.

The law requires that persons in a more remote category (see diagram on page 145) can only inherit if the previous category of persons all died before the testator.

Alan dies intestate. His only surviving relatives are an uncle, Bryan, and Bryan's son Colin. If Bryan disclaims the inheritance, because he would prefer the estate to go to Colin, the disclaimer will not have the effect of benefiting Colin: instead, the estate will pass to the Crown because the only person entitled to inherit has waived his right to do so.

7.2   Who is a 'spouse' of the deceased?

As we can see from the diagram, the surviving spouse is given the first £125,000 of an estate where there are children (and £200,000 where there are no children). Therefore the definition of a 'spouse' is critical for the purposes of division.

The spouse is only treated as having a right to inherit under these rules if he or she survived the deceased by 28 days. If husband and wife are involved in a car accident in which the husband is killed outright and the wife is fatally injured, living on for another five weeks, she will inherit from her husband's estate and it becomes part of her estate. However, if she dies after only 10 days, she does not inherit from him, and in this case only the property which belonged to her before the date of her husband's death forms her estate.

Remember: under the laws of intestate succession, property left by a deceased person is distributed according to set general rules. As a result they can have unintended consequences.

☞ *You parted from your wife and contact between you and her just about ceased once your only son was grown up. You were never formally divorced, however. Your son now tells you that she has died intestate. He says that by law you are entitled to all her personal possessions, as well as a share in her estate up to £125,000. Thereafter you have a 50 per cent share in the life interest in the remainder, with your son having the other share. He feels that this is most unfair in view of the fact that he has been living with his mother all the time, while you, in fact, had deserted them to live with another woman for the past 15 years.*

Under the intestacy rules, the estate will be divided as stated by your son. If you and your wife had divorced, on the other hand, you would not have received anything from her estate.

In the present case your son could apply under the laws for family provision (see section 8) but he would have to show that he was dependent on his mother at the time that she died.

7.3   Who is a child of the deceased?

Under the intestacy rules, the children who qualify are:

- legitimate and illegitimate children
- adopted children; but
- *not* stepchildren.

☞ *When you were 6-years-old your mother married for the second time. Your stepfather was a very wealthy man who has recently died. His will failed because it did not comply with the legal formalities of making a will. A friend tells you that you are entitled to a share of an estate as a 'child of the family'. You wonder if this is correct.*

The answer is 'no' – you are not entitled to share in your stepfather's estate. However, if you can show that your stepfather was maintaining you at the time of his death and that you were dependent on that maintenance, you could apply under the law which makes family provision for dependants (see section 8).

A grandchild will not inherit if a child of the deceased (the parent) is alive, even if the parent is prevented by law from receiving the inheritance.

In one case Edmund was murdered by his son Fred. Edmund left no will. Fred was disqualified from inheriting because of the crime. But Fred's children could not inherit because Fred was still alive, and therefore Edmund's estate would go to the next category of beneficiaries (see diagram). The same would apply if, without being the murderer, Fred for any reason disclaimed his share of the inheritance after Edmund's death.

7.4   Property issues

In all matters concerning property, do seek legal advice.

Notes to the diagram for intestate succession

1) 'Spouse' means a person to whom the deceased was married at the date of death, even if separated or estranged. A cohabitee, however long the relationship, has no right to inherit on intestacy. So for the purposes of the rules of intestacy, 'spouse' includes a separated or estranged spouse but not a divorced spouse.

2) 'Child' includes an adopted child and an illegitimate child, but not a stepchild or the child of a cohabitee and another person.

3) The children of any one of these will inherit in their place.

☞ *John, who dies without leaving a will, is survived by two nieces – the children of his predeceased sister Diana – and by his uncle Harry.*

The entire estate will be shared between the nieces, who take the place of Diana and thus exclude the category to which Harry belongs.

4) Boxes X, Y and Z: see section 7.4.2 below.

Intestate succession

7.4.1 The matrimonial home

The outline below only lists the general rules which apply to inheriting property on an intestacy. A Community Legal Services directory also lists a wide variety of legal advisors for each area (see chapter on *The Legal System*, section 1.1).

7.4.2 Owner-occupied property

Under the law of intestacy the surviving spouse of the deceased (most often the widow) is not necessarily entitled to the matrimonial home unless it was jointly owned:

- If the house was jointly owned then the survivor normally acquires it automatically in addition to his or her share of the estate as detailed above.
- If the house is mortgaged, and it passes to the surviving spouse under a joint ownership, mortgage repayments must be kept up to avoid repossession. Many people take out insurance (either life insurance or endowment policies) to pay off all or part of the mortgage on the matrimonial home. Do check all policy documents (see also chapter on *Growing Old*, section 3.4).
- If the house was in the name of the deceased alone, and its value is less than the statutory entitlement (see boxes marked X, Y and Z on the diagram on page 145), the survivor can insist that it goes towards that entitlement.
- If the house was in the name of the deceased alone, and it is worth more than the statutory entitlement, the survivor can only claim it as his or her share if he or she has other assets out of which the excess can be paid.

☞ *You are recently widowed and would like to continue to live in the family home which was in your husband's sole name. You have no children. Your husband died without leaving a will and the house has been valued at £300,000.*

You are only entitled to £200,000 out of the estate and your in-laws would be entitled to the balance. Therefore if you wish to keep the house, you would have to find the £100,000 to pay them the excess.

7.4.3 Rented property

Remember: never negotiate with a landlord without first getting legal advice.

If the first-dying spouse was named as the tenant under the lease, check the wording to see whether the death automatically brings the lease to an end.

If the landlord knows of the tenant's death, but continues to accept rent from the surviving spouse, he may be accepting the survivor as the tenant in place of the deceased.

Note: where there are two persons who can succeed to the tenancy – for example, a surviving spouse and another member of the tenant's family, then the spouse takes preference.

Rights of succession are granted to protected tenants under the Rent Acts. These include:

- the surviving spouse
- a cohabitee who was living with the original tenant as his or her wife or husband
- a person who was a member of the original tenant's family and who was living with him or her for a period of two years immediately before the original tenant died.

A member of a couple, who had been a partner in a longstanding and faithful homosexual relationship, has been held to be a spouse and/or member of the deceased's family for the purposes of succeeding to the tenancy.

These rules do not apply where a member of the family is a successor already. The rules are dealt with in greater detail in the chapter on *Landlords and their Tenants*, section 8.

7.5 Cohabitees

7.5.1 Position on intestacy

Take heed: a cohabitee has no entitlement on intestacy, but may be entitled as a dependant (see under *Provision for dependants*, section 8 below).

7.5.2 Occupation of property

With regard to house ownership, the position for cohabitees is much less favourable than for a surviving husband or wife. If the home was not jointly owned, but was in the name of the first-dying, the cohabitee cannot claim any share in it unless (s)he made a substantial contribution to its acquisition or improvement.

For the position where property is rented, see chapter on *Landlords and their Tenants*.

8 PROVISION FOR DEPENDANTS

Provision is available to a limited group of people – whether or not the deceased left a will.

Note carefully: the law limits those who can challenge the division or sharing out of an estate on the ground of dependency to a narrow class of people.

(See section 6 above for details of other grounds for challenging a will: for example, that it is invalid.) On the question of dependency, the class of people who can challenge a will is confined to those who might have expected something from an estate through their relationship with the deceased, but who have been left in need.

It is the relationship with the deceased, plus dependency on him or her, that gives a legal opportunity to make such a challenge.

8.1 Who can apply

In 1975 the Inheritance (Provision for Family and Dependants) Act was passed to ensure that a limited class of dependants of a deceased person – those with a legitimate expectation of receiving something on his death – could be provided for out of a deceased's estate.

8.1.1 Relationship with deceased plus dependency

The Act applies both:

- where the rules on intestacy (see above) fail to provide for such a dependant, and
- where the deceased made a will which did not make any adequate provision for his dependants.

In either case an application can be made to the court.

8.1.2 Time limits

Note: the application must be made within six months from the date of grant of representation to the personal representatives.

8.2 Gifts during the deceased's lifetime

The deceased may have given away assets during his lifetime precisely in an attempt to defeat the legitimate expectations of his family. Persons who received such gifts from the deceased less than six years before his death may have to return their value to the estate to meet claims under the Act.

8.3 Reasonable maintenance

When considering these applications, the court is not trying to decide what would have been a fair apportionment of the estate, nor whether it was unreasonable or unjust of the deceased not to have left something to one of the applicants. Instead, the court will consider objectively what is reasonable maintenance for the applicant, taking into account the size of the estate and the needs of the applicant.

8.4 The surviving spouse

Only the surviving spouse of the deceased may be entitled to more than reasonable maintenance. Other applicants – if successful – will get simply what is reasonable for their maintenance. This is a much more restrictive test.

☞ *Your husband has left you nothing in his will even though he was a wealthy man. You have been advised to claim under the family provision scheme. You wonder how the courts assess the position of a widow in these circumstances.*

The claim of the spouse is for such financial provision as it would be reasonable for her to receive in all the circumstances irrespective of what is required for her maintenance. This is to be adjudged at the time of the court hearing and not at the time when the will was made.

In one case the deceased had left his wife an annuity of £150 per week, which was reasonable provision at the time when he died, but the judge decided that it was inappropriate by the time the matter finally came to court, and he substantially increased the amount.

If the estate is large she will be awarded substantially more than she needs to maintain herself – and is unlikely to get less than she would have received on divorce. If the marriage was a fairly long one she may even get at least half the estate.

Apart from a surviving spouse, the following persons can apply to court under the Act:

- a cohabitee
- an ex-spouse
- a child
- a person who was supported by the deceased.

8.5   Cohabitees

Legislation has enhanced the rights of a cohabitee to claim from a partner's estate.

A person who was cohabiting with the deceased for a period of at least two years up to the date of death can claim reasonable maintenance from the estate. The couple have to have been cohabiting as 'husband and wife'. The amount awarded will depend on the needs of the cohabitee.

The court will also take into account:

- the duration of the relationship
- the age of the cohabitee
- his or her contribution to caring for the deceased's family and looking after the home.

A couple will be considered to have been living 'as husband and wife' if, in the opinion of a reasonable person, that was the nature of their relationship. A court has held that a couple were indeed living as husband and wife in a case of a couple in their 50s, who moved in together and lived companionably for 10 years with the man going out to work and the woman responsible for the running of the household. The Crown had claimed that they had not lived as husband and wife since they did not share a bedroom, did not have sex and had agreed to contribute equally to household running expenses. The judge said that in considering the question of whether a couple were living as husband and wife, a court must take into account 'the multifarious nature of marital relationships'. This indicates a broader interpretation of the legislation dealing with intestacy.

8.6   The ex-spouse

As the financial claims may have been settled on divorce, it is only in very exceptional cases that an ex-spouse will get anything extra under the 1975 Act.

☞ *At the time of your divorce from your husband, you were running a very successful estate-agency business. You opted for a 'clean break' settlement with him as your maintenance was met out of your own earnings. Since then, however, your business has had to be wound up. Your ex-husband has now died leaving his estate to his second wife and their children. You would like to make a claim on the estate.*

This is a situation where the court may well take the view that notwithstanding the divorce, your circumstances have altered in such a way as to entitle you to a share of the estate.

Do take heed: you are advised not to renounce all claims against an estate as part of a divorce settlement (see chapter on *Divorce*, section 6.7.8).

8.7   Children

A 'child of the deceased' includes an illegitimate child or a child adopted by the deceased.

'Reasonable provision' here will depend on the circumstances; a minor or young person may get the costs of completing education or training, if the deceased was paying for this during his lifetime, whereas an adult child who is able to earn, or is being adequately supported by a spouse, is unlikely to succeed in an application – even if help would be welcome (and even if the deceased failed to fulfil his financial responsibilities when the child was a minor).

In one recent case, where the deceased was survived by his wife and the adult son of a former marriage who was a longstanding drug addict, the court ruled that the deceased's legal obligation to maintain his spouse outweighed the purely moral obligation owed to the son.

If there are special circumstances, even an able-bodied adult child may succeed, e.g. if (s)he gave up work to care for the deceased during illness, or ran the deceased's business unpaid.

A person treated by the deceased as his/her child, such as a stepchild who was being supported by the deceased, is treated in the same way as a child by blood.

8.8   Persons who were supported by the deceased

Dependants of the deceased may include cohabitees, elderly relatives etc. In fact, any person who was receiving a degree of regular maintenance from the deceased, whether or not a relative and whether or not living in the deceased's household, could be eligible. Cohabitees who do not meet the requirements of the new legislation (see section 8.5 above) may be able to claim under this head.

The most common situation here is where two people – e.g. friends or relatives – share a home and expenses, and the owner of the home dies without making provision for the survivor.

For the deceased to have provided rent-free accommodation is in itself a significant contribution towards maintenance, especially in the case of an OAP.

☞ *Several years ago, Sonia, a well-off widow, invited an old cousin, Rose, to share her house. Knowing Rose was struggling to make ends meet, Sonia paid most of the expenses. Rose took care of the house, and when Sonia's health deteriorated, Rose nursed her devotedly through a long terminal illness.*

After Sonia's death, Rose finds that Sonia has left everything (including the house) to her children, who argue that Rose was not a dependant but was in fact 'paying' Sonia for her board and lodging by what she did for Sonia.

In such a case, the court may well take the view that loving care and attention were not 'payment', and Rose may possibly be entitled to reasonable maintenance out of the estate.

Note: 'maintenance' out of an estate could in some cases include a share in the home.

In another case, a mother who looked after her severely brain-damaged daughter from birth until the latter's death, giving up employment to provide that care, was held to be a dependant of the daughter and could therefore claim maintenance from the estate.

9   APPOINTING A GUARDIAN

If you have minor children, the appointment of a guardian should always be considered. You should then decide whether the guardian is to be appointed to act as such:

- jointly with the surviving parent, or
- only after the death of both parents.

9.1   Who can appoint a guardian

The mother of a child can appoint another person to be guardian to the child after her death. If she was married to the child's father at the time of the birth, the guardian will act jointly with the father after her death unless she specifies that the guardian should only act after the father's death.

The father of a child has the right to appoint a person to be guardian to the child if:

a) he was married to the child's mother at the time of the child's birth, or

b) he was given 'parental responsibility' for the child by a court order; or

c) he entered into a 'parental responsibility agreement' with the child's mother in statutory form (see the chapter *Children (Part 1)*, section 2.7).

Unless the father specifies that the guardian's appointment is to take effect only after the death of both parents, the guardian appointed by the father will act jointly with the mother.

9.2   Appointment by will

If you are making a will, the appointment of a guardian should be made in the will, with the formalities prescribed for all wills as set out above (section 5.1). If you then change your mind and want to appoint someone else, you could do it by codicil.

☞ *You are a single man. You and your former girlfriend have a little boy. She made a will nominating you as guardian of the child in the event of her death. You parted and she married another man. You now learn that she has died and her mother is caring for your son. You tell the grandmother that you are the child's legal guardian but she disputes this. What is your position?*

1) Your girlfriend's will, including the nomination of you as guardian, is automatically revoked on her marriage (see section 6.4.1 above).

2) However, if you had entered into a parental responsibility agreement in the legal form, you would have become guardian of your son on her death. The agreement (unlike the will) is not revoked by her marriage. A parental responsibility agreement can only be revoked by a court of law.

3) Her husband, who is your little boy's stepfather, does not become a guardian on her death unless his wife had appointed him to this capacity.

Do note: the guardianship can only take effect if there is no one else with parental responsibility for the boy.

As to community legal funding [formerly legal aid], see section 4.1.4 above.

Note: the appointment of a guardian can be revoked by making a new will or codicil or even informally. The informal revocation must be in writing, and signed and dated.

Further, under legislation, if the person appointed to be guardian was married to the person appointing, and they subsequently divorced, the appointment as guardian lapses automatically (unless the appointment specifies otherwise), provided the person appointed was not a parent of the child or someone with parental responsibility for the child. A formal re-appointment after the divorce should be made if this is what is wanted.

9.3   Informal appointment

If you do not wish to make a will, perhaps because you are satisfied with the statutory scheme for intestacy, or because you have insufficient assets to be worth the bother and expense, it is also possible to make an informal appointment of a guardian.

The only formalities required are that:

a) the appointment must be in writing
b) it must be signed
c) it must be dated.

There is no *legal* requirement for witnesses, but it may be a sensible precaution to have at least one witness to your signature, who, after seeing you sign, should write his usual signature below yours with his address and occupation.

The informal appointment can be revoked by:

• a later will; or
• the destruction of the written appointment by the person making it; or
• a new informal appointment of a guardian by the mother or father.

DIRECTORY
DEATH – BEFORE AND AFTER

Age Concern England
(National Council on Ageing)
Astral House
1268 London Road
London SW16 4ER
Tel. 020 8765 7200
www.ageconcern.org.uk

Age Concern Cymru
4th Floor
1 Cathedral Road
Cardiff CF1 9SD
Tel. 02920 371 566
www.accymru.org.uk

The British Association of Cancer United Patients
(BACUP)
3 Bath Place
Rivington Street
London EC2A 3JR
Tel. 0808 800 1234
www.cancerbacup.org.uk

The British Humanist Association
47 Theobald's Road
London WC1X 8SP
Tel. 020 7430 0908
www.humanism.org.uk

British Organ Donor Society
Balsham
Cambridge CB1 6DL
Tel. 01223 893636
www.argonet.co.uk/body

Centre for Policy on Ageing *(CPA)*
25–31 Ironmonger Row
London EC1V 3QP
Tel. 020 7253 1787
www.cpa.org.uk

The Child Bereavement Trust
Aston House
High Street
High Wycombe
Buckinghamshire HP14 3AG
Tel. 01494 446 648
www.childbereavement.org.uk

The Compassionate Friends
53 North Street
Bristol BS3 1EN
(Helpline) Tel. 0117 953 9639
(Admin) Tel. 0117 966 5202
www.tcf.org.uk

Court of Protection
Public Guardianship Office
Archway Tower
2 Junction Road
London N19 5SZ
Tel. 020 7664 7000
www.guardianship.gov.uk

The Cremation Society of Great Britain
2nd Floor
Brecon House
16/16a Albion Place
Maidstone
Kent ME14 5DZ
Tel. 01622 688292
www.cremation.org.uk

Cruse – Bereavement Care
126 Sheen Road
Richmond
Surrey TW9 1UR
Tel. 0870 167 1677
www.crusebereavementcare.org.uk

Cruse Cymru
Ty Energlyn
Heol Las
Caerphilly CF83 2WP
Tel. 02920 886 913
Email: cruse.cymru@care4free.net

The Foundation for the Study of Infant Deaths
Artillery House
11–19 Artillery Row
London SW1P 1RT
Tel. 020 7235 0965
(Cot Death Helpline) Tel. 020 7235 1721
www.sids.org.uk

General Register Office *(England & Wales)*
Family Records Centre
1 Myddleton Street
London EC1R 1UW
Tel. 020 8392 5300
(Certificates) Tel. 020 7233 9233
www.frc.gov.uk

Help the Aged
207-221 Pentonville Road
London N1 9UZ
(Admin) Tel. 020 7253 0253
(Seniorline) Tel. 0808 800 6565
www.helptheaged.org.uk

Home Office
Coroners Section
Room 972
50 Queen Anne's Gate
London SW1H 9AT
Tel. 020 7273 2888
www.homeoffice.gov.uk

National Association of Bereavement Services
2nd Floor
2 Pinchin Street
London E1 1SA
Tel. 020 7709 9090

National Association of Funeral Directors
618 Warwick Road
Solihull
West Midlands B91 1AA
Tel. 0121 711 1343
www.nafd.org.uk

National Association of Memorial Masons
27a Albert Street
Rugby
Warwickshire CV21 2SG
Tel. 01788 542264
www.namm.org.uk

National Association of Widows
48 Queens Road
Coventry CV1 3EH
Tel. 024 7663 4848
www.widows.uk.net

The National Secular Society
25 Red Lion Square
London WC1R 4RL
Tel. 020 7404 3126
www.secularism.org.uk

The Natural Death Centre
6 Blackstock Mews
Blackstock Road
London N4 2BT
Tel. 020 8208 2853
www.naturaldeath.org.uk

Office of National Statistics
(including Overseas Registration Section)
Smedley Hydro
Trafalgar Road
Birkdale
Southport PR8 2HH
Tel. 0151 471 4801
www.statistics.gov.uk

Probate Department Principal Registry
Family Division
First Avenue House
42–49 High Holborn
London WC1V 0NP
Tel. 020 7947 7000
(Personal applications)
Tel. 020 7936 6983
www.courtservice.gov.uk

Society of Allied and Independent Funeral Directors
Business Centre
4 Bullfields
Sawbridgeworth
Herts CN21 9BD
Tel. 01279 726777
www.saiflink.org

Stillbirth and Neonatal Death Society *(SANDS)*
28 Portland Place
London W1B 1LY
(Helpline) Tel. 020 7436 5881
www.uk-sands.org

Terence Higgins Trust
52–54 Grays Inn Road
London WC1X 8JU
Tel. 020 7831 0330
(Helpline) Tel. 0845 1221 200
www.tht.org.uk

Voluntary Euthanasia Society
13 Prince of Wales Terrace
London W8 5PG
Tel. 020 7937 7770
www.ves.org.uk

See also Religious Organisations in Family Law Directory, page 109.

6 LANDLORDS AND THEIR TENANTS

Some of the most basic terms of English property law, such as 'freehold' and 'leasehold', go back to feudal times. Land, and the buildings on it, lasts longer than we ourselves do – hence the need for formality in dealing with or 'conveying' property. Clearly, owning, dealing in, or renting property are quite different from owning, dealing in, or renting our other possessions. Moreover, buying a flat or house is usually the most expensive transaction we ever undertake and paying rent or a mortgage is usually the most expensive item in any budget. It is a debt that can also last upwards of 25 years.

However, despite the fact that property law dates back centuries, it is not immune to change. It reflects the pressures of the times as does any other body of law. The most recent and striking example of such change is the Commonhold and Leasehold Reform Act 2002. The purpose of commonhold is to set in place a satisfactory scheme of owning and managing property to overcome the problems of the leasehold system. First and foremost, with the passing of time, a lease itself get shorter and therefore loses value. Commonhold is intended to transfer the benefit enjoyed by freeholders, namely that they own their property in perpetuity, to the long-leaseholder.

Second, commonhold is intended to overcome the difficulty with regard to enforcing positive covenants. A positive covenant (e.g. to keep a property in a good state of repair) cannot be enforced against interdependent, although not necessarily physically connected, freehold properties. Until now, leasehold was the only existing scheme for owning land and enforcing positive covenants. As we see below (section 2.1), the terms of the lease put an obligation on landlords and tenants to do or refrain from doing certain acts [i.e. they are bound by the covenants in the lease]. The covenants also obligate those who buy from the tenant, and are thus enforceable for the length of the lease.

Third, the Commonhold and Leasehold Act 2002 introduces extensive reform into the requirements for long-leaseholders to purchase the freehold of their flats or to extend their leases (see further below sections 10 and 11).

Fourth, the Act makes significant changes to the way properties are to be managed and run (see below section 12).

Another example of the way in which property law changes with changing social needs and attitudes is the steady liberation of rented accommodation from the laws that were intended to give security to tenants. The driving force behind this legislation is a clear policy decision to encourage the private rental sector of the property market.

Other examples of policy decisions which have determined the present course of property law can easily be found: for instance, the 'Right to buy' legislation which allowed tenants in the public sector to buy their own homes. This has much altered the position of local authorities as landlords. The issue, however, is again under scrutiny in view of the current lack of affordable housing.

On the whole, these laws have been passed piecemeal to reflect very different political and ideological approaches to property-holding. At the same time, all the legislation has been superimposed on the system of landholding developed under the common law with its ancient roots.

Today, therefore, all common-law property principles must be read as subject to overriding Acts of Parliament. For example, under common law, a tenant must leave the premises when a lease expires. Much of statute law, however, lays down requirements which a landlord must meet before he may recover his property from the tenant.

As a result of these and other factors, property law should be regarded as a job for experts.

In this chapter, we focus on the landlord and tenant aspects of property law. The issues involved in buying and selling your home are dealt with in the next chapter, *Buying and Selling your Home*.

In the field of landlord and tenant relationships, as with other aspects of property law, it cannot be over-emphasised that you are entering a minefield of legal complexity. If you are uncertain of your rights – whether as landlord or as tenant – you must seek informed advice.

Indeed, the Law Commission has published radical proposals for a total overhaul of the law governing residential lettings in order to simplfy and rationalise the current system.

In this chapter we look at:

- some fundamental aspects of the landlord and tenant relationship
- covenants between landlord and tenant
- renting in the private sector
- public sector accommodation
- protection from harassment and eviction
- the resident landlord
- assignment and subletting
- death of a tenant
- buying a long leasehold
- buying the freehold
- extending your lease
- managing agents and service charges.

Do note: a DIRECTORY of organisations that assist and advise on property law matters is on page 215. The Office of the Deputy Prime Minister produces a range of booklets on such topics as the rights of tenants, landlords' rights, letting a room in your home, regulated tenancies, notices to leave, and eviction. These are available from ODPM Free Literature, PO Box No 236, Wetherby, LS23 7NB, tel: 0870 1226 236.

1 SOME FUNDAMENTAL ASPECTS OF THE LANDLORD AND TENANT RELATIONSHIP

1.1 Similarity in diversity

There are many kinds of lease. They may cover business premises which might comprise several city blocks; council houses in the public sector; flats bought on long leases; private rented accommodation which could consist of no more than a bedsitter; vast agricultural estates or small-holdings.

However, all forms of lease have several factors in common which distinguish them from owning your own home. These factors also distinguish *leases* from *licences* which are generally a mere permission to use premises in a particular way or for a particular time.

1.2 Outlines of the relationship

a) A lease always entails at least two parties: a landlord and a tenant. A landlord grants to the tenant the exclusive use of property on certain conditions and for a certain time. There can, of course, be joint tenants and joint landlords; or subtenants.

b) A lease is thus bound by a time limit: this can be for a week, a month, a year or a fixed period of years. The longer the period, say 999 years, the more the lease resembles absolute ownership. However, the obligations under the lease (called *covenants*, see section 2 below) – of both landlord and tenant – still have to be observed. Indeed, long leaseholds have been an effective way of ensuring that property is kept up and maintained to standard. If you own your house you cannot be bound by a covenant to paint the outside of it, as restrictive covenants can only be negative (see the chapter on *Neighbours*, section 7.1). If, on the other hand, you have taken out a lease on a property your landlord can and usually does insist on your maintaining the property as one of the terms in the lease. A new system of owning property, known as 'commonhold' is intended to overcome this difficulty.

c) An essential aspect of a lease is the need for exclusive possession. This is dealt with more fully in section 1.5.2 below. In return for being granted possession for a fixed term or a periodic term, i.e. on a weekly, monthly or yearly basis, the tenant must pay rent to the landlord. Again, the amount is infinitely variable, from a token amount for ground rent, say a peppercorn or £100 per annum on a long leasehold flat, to hundreds of pounds per week for furnished residential accommodation. Rent can also be in the form of services in exchange for accommodation.

d) Both landlord and tenant are bound by a complex network of duties and obligations, called covenants, which are found in all leases. Some of these covenants may be implied by law (i.e. the law 'writes' the covenants into the lease, even if the parties fail to do so themselves; see section 2 below on *Covenants*).

e) When a lease expires, the property which comprises the lease must go back or 'revert' to the landlord (a landlord is sometimes called a 'reversioner' for this reason).

f) However, as we all know, the position of a tenant is protected by legislation to a greater or lesser extent depending on the type of lease. This means that instead of the property reverting to the landlord, the tenant of rented accommodation may be able to stay on, i.e. his entitlement is ensured (see below, section 3.4).

If a tenant on a long lease (i.e. usually one of over 21 years) wishes to leave, he is usually entitled under the terms of the lease to sell the remainder of his lease. Under general circumstances, a landlord cannot reasonably refuse permission for the sale. For example, having bought a flat 10 years ago on a 75-year lease, you could sell the 'remainder of the term', i.e. the 65 years of the lease which is still left to run. This sale for the remainder of the term of the lease is called an 'assignment' (see below, section 7). The person to whom the tenant sells will step into his or her shoes and be bound by the covenants of the lease.

A landlord is entitled to ensure, however, before he or she agrees to the assignment of a lease, that the new tenant will be in a position to perform those covenants. For example, the landlord will want to be certain that the tenant is sufficiently credit-worthy to honour obligations with regard to payment of rent (see also section 7 below).

In the same way, a landlord can sell his reversion. The new landlord is then also bound to the tenant under the covenants of the lease.

In other words, persons can change – whether as landlord or as tenant – but the lease continues. (In exceptional cases, there may be essentially personal covenants between landlord and tenant. These would not bind future landlords and tenants.)

Under the Landlord and Tenant Act 1987, a landlord who intends to sell the freehold of a block of flats had to offer the 'right of first refusal' to the tenants. This meant that they could choose whether or not to purchase the freehold themselves. This obligation on the landlord's part, however, was more honoured in the breach than in the observance and tenants found themselves at a severe disadvantage faced with a new, and sometimes unscrupulous, landlord. As a result changes were enacted to tighten up on this particular obligation and to penalise landlords who tried to get round it.

Under the Housing Act 1996, landlords commit a criminal offence if they fail to serve notice on their tenants. If tenants wish to buy, the landlords have to enter into a binding contract with them within a specified time.

Do note: a lease that had 50 or fewer years to run has been a depreciating asset. It was therefore seen as inequitable that persons who owned leases, principally on flats, should lose out in this way, as successive years of their lease run out. As a result of government intervention, therefore, it is now possible to extend your lease provided minimum requirements are met (see section 11 below).

g) Freehold and leasehold property comprise what is known as an 'estate in land'. This means that they are both forms of land ownership defined in terms of their duration. Both, therefore, require written formalities in their acquisition and in subsequent dealings with them.

1.3 Distinction between leasehold and freehold property

Having outlined the common factors of a lease, it is easy to highlight the contrast with freehold property – also in outline. The characteristics of freehold property are that:

- it does not involve two parties; the property belongs to the owner, therefore there is no reversion
- it does not have time limits on its ownership
- rent is not payable.

1.4 Where the lines are blurred

1.4.1 Limitations on ownership

Nothing in property law is simple: while one can state in bald outline the clear distinction between outright ownership of one's own home on the one hand, and renting one's home or buying it on a long lease on the other, there are nonetheless limitations on owning one's own home too. Legislation – to some extent – has also led to an erosion of the clear distinctions between the two forms of property-holding with their roots in antiquity, namely freehold and leasehold. Since then, a new form of owning and managing property has been introduced by statute, namely *commonhold*.

a) Absolute ownership is not what it seems; there are all sorts of limitations on the property: for example, it can be compulsorily acquired under the planning laws.
b) The leasehold reform Acts allow conversion to freehold status on certain conditions. Meeting these conditions has also been made progressively easier by legislation. In particular, under the Leasehold Reform Housing and Urban Development Act 1993, and the present Commonhold and Leasehold Reform Act 2002, long leaseholders are able to acquire the freehold to their properties on certain conditions and in certain circumstances (see section 10 below).
c) Even with freeholds, there may still be rights against the property in the form of easements or restrictive covenants (see chapter on *Neighbours*).
d) A new form of owning property has been brought into being by the government which would provide flat-owners with greater means of participating in the freehold interest in their own homes and a system for the fairer and more efficient management of their buildings as a whole. This form of ownership is called 'commonhold' (regulations are expected to be put in place for the implementation of these changes). See also sections 10 and 11 below.

1.5 Distinction between lease and licence

Instead of leasing property, you may wish to use it – or only be allowed to use it – in a limited way. In other words, you will not be granted a lease by your landlord but only a *licence*.

A licence, like a lease, can entail the payment of rent and be limited in time. So how does a lease differ from a licence?

Among other differences, a licence does not usually give exclusive possession of property (see section 3.2.2 below).

1.5.1 The need for a clear distinction

The distinction between a lease and a licence is of critical importance. If you have a lease, you will generally have some form of protection – in particular, you may be able to stay on in the premises when your lease expires. Licensees never have this protection; they have to leave once their licence is revoked although the landlord must still get a court order for eviction. They are thus still protected against harassment and against being unlawfully turned out of the premises (see section 5).

In order to get round the protection which the law gives to tenants on a lease, where the landlord has to prove certain grounds before getting a court order (see section 3 below), landlords have resorted to the ruse of calling a lease 'a mere licence'. With the shift in legislation towards greater incentive for landlords and less security for their tenants, no doubt this ruse will be less used. Nonetheless, the distinction between a lease and a licence remains crucial to the rights of both landlords and tenants under their agreement.

1.5.2 Exclusive possession

A tenant has exclusive possession of the premises which are leased to him or her. A licensee generally does not.

☞ *You are a single woman occupying the double room of a flat in which there are two other single bedrooms. The 'landlord' made it clear when letting you into possession that if he can find a couple to take over the double bedroom, you will have to move into one of the single bedrooms. He now states that you are occupying the double bedroom under licence only. You wonder what your position is.*

You are a mere licensee as you would not be able to assert a right to a double bedroom. The position might have been different if you occupied it with your boyfriend (see section 3.2.2 below).

1.5.3 Does it matter what your landlord calls your agreement?

The answer to this question is a resounding 'no'.

The courts will look at the substance of the agreement, and not at the label which the parties give to their agreement. There have been many attempts by landlords to get round the security-of-tenure provisions of the Rent Acts by calling their agreements with their tenants 'licences'. This has singularly failed to wash with the courts. Unfortunately, however, the lines between lease and licence can get blurred. There is no all-embracing test and each case is determined on its facts to see on which side of the line an agreement falls. For the courts, the critical issue is to seek to establish whether the essential hallmarks of a tenancy are present, i.e. exclusive possession; a time limit; and the payment of rent (see also immediately below, section 1.5.4).

1.5.4 Other forms of licence

Other forms of licence exist even when an occupier of the premises may have exclusive possession.

For example a caretaker in a block of flats who is provided with a flat for his own use is generally only a licensee. But in all cases, the surrounding circumstances are taken into account to determine whether there is a tenancy or a licence to occupy.

Examples are also found in the public sector, where local authorities license housing associations to allow persons into short-term property (usually property earmarked for redevelopment) in exchange for rent. As the housing association is only a licensee, it was generally thought that the temporary occupiers are also only licensees.

However a recent case in the House of Lords has altered the legal position the other way. The landlords in that case were a Housing Trust which provided short-term accommodation for the homeless. The Trust had use of a block of flats owned by a local authority which had given it a licence to use the property for temporary housing. The tenant entered into an agreement with the Trust that the 'occupation was for short-life accommodation on a temporary basis'. The tenant's property comprised one of the flats in the block which was offered to him 'on a weekly licence'. The agreement between the Trust and the tenant went on to state that the property had been acquired on licence from the council pending its development and 'is offered on condition that you will vacate on receiving reasonable notice from the Trust ...'. The tenant complained that the Trust had not carried out the repairs that it was required to do under the landlord and tenant legislation. The Trust in turn gave him notice to quit. In the event, the House of Lords stated that the agreement had the hallmarks of a tenancy:

a) exclusive possession
b) a limit of time
c) payment of a weekly rent.

The facts that the Trust performed a socially valuable function and that it had agreed with the council that it was itself a licensee only, could not affect the outcome of the case.

☞ *You have been offered work as an assistant to the gardener on a landed estate. You are provided with a cottage in the grounds for your exclusive use. The accommodation is nominally rent-free but this fact is taken into account in the way that your wages are calculated. You wonder what your status is in law. Would your employer, for example, be able to ask you to leave the cottage at a moment's notice? You are also concerned about the gas boiler in the cottage as it seems in need of a service.*

Accommodation may be provided rent-free in return for a person providing services e.g. as a gardener. This can constitute a tenancy, but very often it is a mere licence.

Nonetheless, where a licence to occupy exists, you are entitled to a notice to leave the premises [called a 'notice to determine the licence'] even if you are a mere licensee. The notice must be in writing and must be given at least four weeks before the date of termination. Furthermore, your employer would have to get a court order for possession before you could be evicted.

With regard to the gas boiler, the obligation to observe safety regulations, which applies to landlords (see below, section 2.1.8(a)) applies to premises occupied for residential purposes whether under a licence or under a tenancy agreement.

Other situations exist where there is only a licence to occupy and not a tenancy. For example, if a property owner has unlimited access, to clean a room or provide other services such as doing the laundry, on a regular and meaningful basis, the person who occupies is generally a mere licensee. However, the courts will disregard services which are just 'window-dressing' in order to get round the provisions of the Rent Acts.

1.5.5   Landlord living on the premises

Generally, where a landlord lives on the premises together with his tenant, the tenant occupies the property as a licensee only. For the rules governing resident landlords, see section 6 below.

2   COVENANTS

Note: even if certain covenants are not written into the lease (although they usually will be), the landlord and the tenant are still obliged to perform them. They are covenants which the law will imply as duties in the landlord and tenant relationship. These *implied covenants* are considered to be so crucial that the lease would not be effective without them.

No other covenants are implied by law apart from those listed below.

In general, *express covenants* (those written into the lease) still take precedence over implied ones – but not invariably. See section 2.1.4 below.

2.1   The landlord's implied covenants

2.1.1   Covenant for quiet enjoyment

This covenant generally relates to interruption of the physical use of the premises. The interruption must be substantial.

☞ *You have taken out a lease on one of the four flats in a converted house. Your flat is periodically flooded from the flat above. It transpires that the landlord has converted the flats so badly that the drains are totally inadequate for their purpose. The insurers tell you that you will have to leave your flat for several months for proper work on the drains to be put in hand.*

In such a situation, quite apart from the question of nuisance (see chapter on *Neighbours*), the courts would be entitled to hold that the landlord is in breach of his covenant for quiet enjoyment.

However, breach of a covenant for quiet enjoyment does not apply to mere temporary inconvenience.

☞ *You have taken out a lease on one of the four flats in a converted house. You have explained to the landlord that you are buying the flat because of its peaceful situation. The landlord lives on the premises and decides to convert two of the flats into a large family-sized flat for himself. There is noise and disruption which you find difficult for your working and living conditions. You wonder if he is in breach of his covenant for quiet enjoyment of your own property.*

The answer is probably 'no' – although in all such issues, it is a matter of fact and degree.

The covenant also does not apply to noise which is quite outside the landlord's control, e.g. noise from the street.

In a recent case tenants complained that the sound insulation in their building was so poor that they could hear their neighbours' everyday activities. They wanted the building soundproofed in order to allow themselves greater privacy – whether they were cooking, watching TV, or making love. The House of Lords stated that the 'covenant for quiet enjoyment' meant that a landlord would not substantially interfere with the tenant's lawful possession of the property. Thus excessive noise could constitute an interference in breach of the covenant in certain cases.

Read literally, the words seemed very apt. The flats were not quiet and the tenants were not enjoying them. However, the words could not be read literally. The covenant looked to the future and not to things that had happened before the tenancy was granted – notwithstanding that there might be continuing consequences for a tenant.

In the present case the building was constructed in 1919 and the tenants had to take the property in the condition in which it had been built. Although there was an inherent structural defect, it was one for which the landlord had no responsibility. The tenants were attempting to use the covenant for quiet enjoyment to oblige their landlord to improve the premises, not merely repair them. The House of Lords rejected such an obligation. Further, the normal use of a residential flat could not possibly constitute a 'nuisance' about which the other tenants could complain (see also chapter on *Neighbours*, section 4).

2.1.2 Covenant not to detract from the value of the lease

This covenant, spelled out in legal terms, is the covenant of the landlord 'not to derogate from his grant'. In effect, it means that a landlord cannot grant you a lease and then take action which in effect detracts from what he has already granted to you under your lease.

☞ *You have a flat with a terrace and an outside staircase leading to a communal garden. Your landlord intends to build a conservatory which would entail removing the staircase. You wonder what the position is.*

Your landlord may be in breach of his covenant by detracting from the value of the lease which he has granted to you. However, you would have to look at the terms of your lease very carefully to see what the landlord's rights might be.

☞ *You rent a furnished flat with a forecourt for parking for two cars which you and your wife use as you are a two-car family. Lately your landlord has allowed a van to park in the grounds which effectively blocks the space for one of your cars. You feel that you are not getting the use from the premises which you expected.*

If your lease specified that you were entitled to the forecourt parking for your own exclusive use, then you are in a position to claim that your landlord is breaching the terms of the lease. In a similar case, the court held that where a landlord failed to prevent his tenants parking in such a way as to interfere with the rights of another tenant, he had 'adopted' the nuisance and had derogated from their grant.

Again, it very much depends on the rights which you have under your tenancy agreement, as well as other circumstances.

In another case, there were parking spaces for 12 or 13 cars in the forecourt of a block of flats and the residents competed for these spaces on a 'first come, first served' basis. Thereafter the landlord restricted the area to three or four spaces but on the same basis of competition. The court held that the landlord's action had substantially interfered with the claimant's enjoyment of her rights as tenant.

2.1.3 Fitness of premises – repairs

In short-term lettings, (i.e. generally under seven years) there is an implied covenant that the premises should be fit for habitation.

Note: this covenant is overlaid with statutory law which imposes on the landlord an obligation to keep premises in repair. See also the second paragraph of section 2.1.4 immediately below.

Under the Landlord and Tenant Act 1985, the landlord is responsible for repairs to:

- the structure and exterior of the property
- baths, sinks, basins, and other sanitary installations
- heating and hot water installations

- (in cases of flats or maisonettes) other parts of the building or installations under the landlord's control whose disrepair would affect the tenant
- other repairs depending on the terms of the tenancy agreement.

☞ *You are renting a terraced house. You have serious problems as the house itself is damp and the roof leaks. Some of the drains are blocked and the electric sockets blow frequently. The state of the premises, you feel, is injurious to your health. Your frequent complaints to your landlord are unavailing. You wonder what you can do.*

You must contact the environmental health office based in your local authority neighbourhood office. An environmental health officer will visit you and check out the complaint. The EHO can serve a notice on your landlord obliging him to carry out specified repairs within a given period of time. If there is no compliance the landlord can be prosecuted and the works carried out by the local authority which will then recoup the costs from the owner.

If your landlord is itself the local authority which is being neglectful of its duties to carry out repairs, you must complain to the Local Government Ombudsman.

When a long leasehold is being purchased, a lease will usually contain express terms on the landlord's duties to maintain the premises. The outlay is usually recovered from the long leaseholders under the lease in the form of service charges (see below, section 9).

The Law Commission has made proposals to simplify and modernise the law regarding repair and maintenance of rented property in the private sector. It found that the present law is both obscure and outdated. The proposals follow upon a survey that established that more than one-fifth of private rented accommodation is unfit for human habitation. Both landlords and tenants should be placed under much more stringent requirements to take proper care of premises. The law of waste (see section 2.2.3 below) should be abolished and new obligations imposed.

At the time of writing, the position is that some of the Law Commission's recommendations have been welcomed by the government. Legislation is awaited to introduce a new 'housing health and safety rating system' in place of the current housing fitness standard. The new system would measure and identify risks to health and safety in rental property with a duty to take action where risks are unacceptable. A strengthened enforcement regime would also be introduced.

☞ *You are injured by falling over a broken paving stone in the private road which leads to your block of flats and have been told that it will be several months before your injury heals and you can return to work. Before your accident, you had written to your landlord's managing agents twice regarding the need to repair the pathway, but nothing was done. You do not have the means to sue your landlord for damages and wonder whether you could apply for legal aid [now called community legal services funding].*

On the whole, personal injury claims are now outside the legal aid system. However, where a tenant is hurt through a landlord's failure to repair, legal aid can be made available to pursue a claim provided that all the other eligibility criteria for public funding are met (see chapter on *The Legal System*, section 3.1.1).

Do note: a tenant can make a claim against a landlord that he should repair premises, in the small claims court (see the chapter on *The Legal System*, section 1.2.1) where the claim is under £1000 (see also the chapter on *Accidents*, section 1.1.1).

2.1.4 When an implied covenant conflicts with a lease's express covenant

If there is a contradiction between a covenant implied by law and the express terms of your lease, then the express terms generally prevail. For instance, a landlord may wish to build a tarred roadway past your block of flats to serve his neighbouring block: if your lease allows him to reserve a right of way, then he will be allowed to do so – in other words, he can 'derogate from his grant' because the lease allows him to do so.

Note: a landlord cannot contract out of certain repairing covenants imposed by law. Where he is under a statutory duty to keep premises in repair, he will not be able to write a term into the lease which will allow him to evade his legal obligations.

A landlord cannot regain possession of residential accommodation without a court order unless the tenant leaves willingly.

2.1.5 'Small print regulations'

The Office of Fair Trading has drawn up extensive guidance to help ensure that good faith and fair dealing do apply in standard or *pro forma* agreements between landlords and their tenants. The guidance is intended for agreements for both assured and assured shorthold tenancies which are the most common form of rentals in the private sector (see further below, section 3).

Do note: the legal terminology is confusing, referring to both assured and assured shorthold tenancies which apply to different types of agreement. For the sake of clarity, we will refer to 'shorthold tenancies' here and below.

2.1.5(a) How do the regulations apply?

They apply to standard terms, i.e. terms that have not been individually negotiated.

The terms must be fair.

2.1.5(b) What is the test of fairness?

This is generally defined as a requirement of good faith and of fair and open dealing. Openness requires that the terms should be expressed fully, clearly, and legibly, and contain no hidden pitfalls or traps.

A tenant may not be required to understand every word of the contract, but should be given the opportunity to examine all the terms so that he or she can understand what they are agreeing to.

☞ *You have been presented with a tenancy agreement which states that your landlord will not be responsible for repairs 'unless notified of them immediately'.*

Your work takes you abroad for periods of time and you are concerned that you may breach this provision unintentionally.

A term which frees a landlord from all responsibility towards a tenant who fails to complain immediately, or even within an excessively short period of time, could be in breach of the fair terms regulations depending on the view which the court would take of the wording of the term.

Do note however: tenants can be required to notify the landlord as promptly as reasonably possible if a repair is needed in order to prevent further damage.

2.1.6 Terms considered potentially unfair

The guidance sets out a range of situations and clauses which could be considered unfair. Examples are:

- if you have to pay for repairs which are, in fact, the responsibility of the landlord (e.g. repair to the drains)
- if the landlord is entitled to enter the property without proper notice (other than in an emergency)
- if the landlord can determine how much of the deposit (s)he should withhold at the end of the tenancy
- if the agreement imposes excessive penalties for rent arrears.

Do note: this list is not exhaustive.

2.1.7 Do the regulations apply to all terms?

'Core' terms are excluded from the regulations. These are terms which state:

- the rent
- the details of the property
- the length of the tenancy.

However, do note: even with regard to core terms, the tenant must read and understand them. Plain vocabulary alone would not necessarily meet this requirement. If the term is illegible or hidden away in small print as if it were unimportant this could be viewed as 'unfair'.

Do they apply to all agreements?

☞ *Your job requires you to go abroad for six months. A friend of yours has recently sold his cottage in the country and is negotiating the purchase of a house in London. You offer to sublet your London flat while you are away. You buy a standard lease agreement from a law printers.*

The regulations would probably not apply as you are a private landlord and you are not 'in business'. You would be advised, however, to study the terms of your standard lease agreement to see that they conform to the OFT guidelines.

You can obtain a leaflet from the OFT: 0870 60 60 321, or speak to the helpline at 08457 22 33 99.

2.1.8   Safety regulations

Special regulations apply to the safety of private-sector accommodation.

2.1.8(a) Gas regulations

With regard to the installation and fitting of gas appliances, landlords are under a duty to keep and maintain all appliances and installation work in a safe condition. The regulations are extensive in scope and include the following duties on the landlord:

- to ensure that gas fittings and flues are maintained in a safe condition
- to carry out annual checks
- to keep a record of the inspections
- to use only an installer registered with CORGI.

Note: the landlord is not responsible for the tenant's gas appliances.

The Gas Safety Advice Line number is 0800 300 363.

☞ *You have just become a tenant in a furnished flat. You are concerned about the safety of the gas fire in the lounge. Your landlord assures you that the fire is safe and that he carries out regular annual inspections.*

Under the regulations, tenants are to be issued with a copy of the safety check record within 28 days of the check having been carried out. New tenants are entitled to a copy before they move in to the premises.

The landlord must ensure that the check has been carried out within one year before the start of your lease. If however, the gas fire has been installed for less than 12 months, the next check should be 12 months from the installation date.

The Health and Safety Executive issues a free leaflet: *A guide to landlords' duties: Gas Safety (installation and Use) Regulations 1998* (tel: 01787 881165, or HSE Books, PO Box 1999, Sudbury, Suffolk, CO10 6FS).

2.1.8(b) Furniture regulations

In response to outbreaks of fire, particularly in rented accommodation, safety regulations were passed to deal with certain very dangerous materials being used in upholstery. Today it is an offence for a shop to sell furniture which does not comply with the current safety regulations that set levels of fire resistance for domestic upholstery and other furnishings.

Landlords must ensure that all furniture supplied in all let accommodation must comply with these safety requirements.

2.1.8(c) Electrical appliances

There is no regulation that all electrical appliances need an annual inspection. However, landlords have to ensure that such appliances are safe. Examples given include worn plugs and overloaded circuits, but the regulations would apply to other appliances including heaters, television sets etc.

2.2   The tenant's implied covenants

2.2.1   To pay the rent

There is usually an express clause in the lease concerning payment of rent. In any event, such a clause would be implied into a lease. If a tenant fails to pay rent, the landlord is usually entitled to seek possession of the premises (for details, see also section 3.7 below).

Note: we usually associate payment of rent with payment of money. However, premises can be let in exchange for services – for example, you could be the tenant of a house attached to a private school in return for acting as school caretaker. Your services must be measurable, in the sense that they have a financial value, to establish a tenancy, though, and the terms of the agreement must be made clear, i.e. that you are not a mere licensee but a tenant (see section 1.5.4 above).

2.2.2   To pay certain charges

(a) Long leases

In long leases (i.e. generally more than 21 years) a tenant may be obliged to pay service charges. This again is generally an express covenant found in most leases (see section 12 below).

(b) Short-term lettings

If a short-term letting does not so expressly provide, it would generally be an implied term that the tenant should pay for ordinary outgoings such as electricity or gas bills.

It is axiomatic that the more specific a lease is with regard to such matters, the less scope there is for disagreement. For example, it is generally agreed that, in furnished lettings, the tenants should pay the council tax. That is still no reason, however, why the lease should not specify that the tenant is obliged to make this payment.

2.2.3   Not to 'commit waste'

As we have seen, a fundamental doctrine of landlord and tenant law is that the property 'reverts' to the freeholder when the lease expires. The tenant, therefore, is under a duty, implied by law, not to take any action which would diminish the value of the premises on their reversion to the landlord. For example, you may rent a cottage with wooded grounds on a long lease. You would be liable, as tenant, if you cut down the trees or demolished a wing of the cottage. Again, like so many matters in law, it is a matter of fact and degree. The actions described above are positive actions which are clearly harmful to the landlord's interests. But what if a tenant is merely neglectful or forgetful?

☞   *You go away for a Christmas break and omit to empty the water tanks. There is a sudden freeze, and you return to find the premises flooded after a thaw. Your landlord says that you are liable for the damage. You wonder what your position is.*

The court will consider the terms of your lease and the type of your tenancy (for example, whether you are a weekly tenant or in the house for a longer term) as well as for how long you left the premises empty. The terms of the landlord's insurance policy will also be relevant. In one case, it was held that a two-day break during a very cold spell was not sufficient to make the tenant liable for ensuing damage.

2.2.4   To allow the landlord to enter the premises

It is reasonable that if a landlord is responsible for maintaining the premises and keeping them in repair, he should be allowed to view them to establish whether repairs are necessary. He should give the tenant reasonable notice of his intention to view the premises. However, in the case of an emergency, for example a power failure, the landlord should be allowed to enter without notice.

2.3   Other covenants usually found in leases – express terms

This section deals with some covenants which are often – but not always – expressly written into a lease. In any event, they will not be implied into a lease by law.

2.3.1   Covenants concerning use

Some leases will contain clauses which forbid the tenant to use the premises in a certain way. For example, a lease in a residential block of flats will usually have a covenant against using the flat for business purposes.

2.3.2   Covenants controlling assignment

This is dealt with in section 7 below. In general terms, a landlord often insists that his permission should be sought and obtained before a tenant can let someone act as tenant in his or her stead.

2.3.3   Insurance

Leases generally provide that the landlord will insure the premises. In long leaseholds (i.e. over 21 years), the insurance premiums are usually recoverable from the tenants on a proportionate basis as part of the service charges.

2.3.4 Terminating a tenancy

Leases usually contain clauses which allow a landlord to regain the premises in certain circumstances – for example, where a tenant fails to pay rent, or uses the premises in a way which the lease does not permit, e.g. uses residential property for business purposes [i.e. in 'breach of the user covenant']. In legal terms, the lease is 'forfeited' and the landlord can 're-enter' – subject always to the laws which protect tenants against eviction (see below, section 5). Restrictions are coming on the capacity of landlords to use forfeiture proceedings for non-payment of service charges (see section 12 below).

3 RENTING IN THE PRIVATE SECTOR

This section applies to property which is let on a:

- weekly
- fortnightly
- monthly or
- yearly basis; or
- for leases of less than 21 years.

(For leases of 21 years and over, see section 9 below.)

For many years now, the government has been anxious to promote private-sector lettings. It was felt that the main obstacle to developing the private rental market was the fact that landlords were reluctant to let their properties because of:

- the difficulties in ensuring that tenants vacated their premises when their leases expired; and
- the difficulties in ensuring a market rent for their properties.

In other words, laws which had been passed to give protection to tenants militated against the private rental market.

Thus, in order to encourage landlords to let privately, legislation was passed to enable landlords to recover their premises more easily.

Most importantly in this connection, a new form of rental was established – known as shorthold – which gives tenants a very minimum of security. (This is dealt with below, see section 3.6.)

Note of warning: in general the law on private-sector lettings is a very complex area. It is difficult not only for the unwary but even for those who think they know their business! The courts resound to litigation between landlords and tenants locked in bitter dispute over their rights. It is for this reason, too, that legislation has been introduced to avoid the creation of secure tenants through inadvertence (see below section 3.6).

Do make sure: always insist on a written agreement when you are entering into a rental agreement. For consideration of unfair terms in pro forma agreements (see section 2.1.5 above).

3.1 The Housing Acts of 1988 and 1996

In 1988 a Housing Act was passed which was specifically intended to ease the landlords' position. That Act determined private-sector lettings of residential accommodation after 15 January 1989. All new lettings entered into after that date were governed by the Housing Act 1988. Its provisions are now subject to the amendments found in the Housing Act 1996.

These provisions nonetheless co-exist with earlier legislation, in particular the Rent Act 1977, which had quite different policy goals: its concern was to protect the position of the tenant. This chapter focuses primarily on the 1988 and 1996 legislation as it applies to private-sector lettings today.

Under the Housing Act 1988, there were two types of tenancy:

- assured tenancy
- shorthold tenancy.

These two types of tenancy are retained by the Housing Act 1996 although the procedure for creating them has been altered.

Do note: the legal terminology is confusing, referring to both assured and assured shorthold tenancies, which are different types of agreement. For the sake of clarity, we will refer to 'shorthold tenancies' here and below.

Note also: rules have been introduced to streamline possession proceedings for these two types of tenancy. Under the procedure, district judges will be able to grant the landlord a possession order without a court hearing, if the tenant is unlikely to have a defence (see section 3.7 below).

3.2 Some general principles

For all residential tenancies, irrespective of the piece of legislation under which they are created, certain basis rules are applicable.

The law requires that there must be a 'letting of a dwelling house as a separate dwelling'; and:

* it must be let under a lease and not on a licence
* the tenant must be an individual, i.e. company lets have no protection
* the dwelling house must be occupied as the tenant's only or principal home
* it must not be a tenancy specifically excluded from protection by the Acts (holiday lettings on certain conditions, for example, are specifically excluded from protection).

All of these points will be dealt with below.

3.2.1 It must be a dwelling house let as a separate dwelling

The term 'dwelling house' has been given the widest interpretation. It must be a fixed abode where a tenant can sleep, cook and eat. These have been considered the basic activities for which we use our living space. Thus 'dwelling house' covers, for example, a permanently moored boat or even a well-fitted out beach hut.

☞ *In a recent case, a landlord sought possession from two people who were living in single rooms in a long-stay hotel. They asserted that their rooms were let as separate dwellings so that they were protected tenants under the Rent Acts. The landlord argued that there were no proper cooking facilities in the rooms and so they could not constitute a 'dwelling'. Thus the question facing the courts was whether, in these days of fast food restaurants and take-away meals, proper cooking facilities are an essential pre-requisite of a dwelling house?*

No, answered the House of Lords. Each case depends on its own facts. Where someone occupies a room as his home, it is a dwelling irrespective of his eating and rudimentary cooking arrangements.

3.2.2 What does 'let as a separate dwelling' mean?

The requirement that the accommodation is let as a separate dwelling means that each tenant must have exclusive possession of his or her living area.

To be a tenant, you must have exclusive possession of the premises which are let to you. It does not mean you have to rent a whole flat or a whole house. You can have exclusive possession of a single room, such as a bedsitter.

☞ *You have rented a room in a flat with your boyfriend. You have both signed an agreement with the landlord. You have a double room and there is one other single bedroom which is occupied by another tenant. You share the kitchen and bathroom with the other tenant and you all use the communal lounge.*

You and your boyfriend can claim that you have exclusive possession of the double bedroom.

(See also section 3.2.1 above).

3.2.2(a) Difficulties which can arise in practice

Problems frequently arise in regard to exclusive possession. As we have seen, a tenant can have exclusive use of a bedroom but the other areas of the house such as the bathroom will be shared. (For the position where there is a resident landlord, see section 6 below.) There may be other arrangements with the landlord – for example, that he can require a tenant to move out of one room and into another. We are back to a problem we have encountered before, viz. is the letting a lease or a licence? (See above, section 1.5.2.) Hence the importance of ensuring that the agreement reflects the true position between landlord and tenant.

3.2.2(b) Company lets

Company lets are excluded from the provisions of the Rent Acts, hence the regularity with which advertisements appear in newspapers stating that 'company lets only' will be accepted. The company rents the accommodation, and its employee who lives there is a mere licensee.

3.2.3 Occupied as the only home or as a principal home

A tenant who has moved out of the dwelling house cannot claim protection of the Rent Acts. He or she is no longer occupying it as their principal home. However, protection is not withheld if an absence is short relative to the time which the tenant has lived in the premises. Again it becomes a matter of fact and degree.

☞ *You are the tenant of a flat in which you have lived for a number of years. Your employers send you abroad for three months. During this time, you do not sublet the flat and you continue to pay rent.*

You have not jeopardised your position with regard to protection vis-à-vis your landlord.

However, the flat must be your only, or your principal, home. A person cannot have two main homes. If you work in London during the week and live in a rented flat, returning to your country cottage at weekends, you will have to persuade the court that the rented flat represents your principal home.

3.2.4 Position on divorce

As part of a divorce property settlement, a court can usually assign a lease or tenancy from one spouse to the other, subject to an existing order, e.g. to pay rent arrears.

For the circumstances in which the court may assign a tenancy in cases where a relationship between an unmarried couple breaks down, see chapter on *Divorce*, section 8.4.

3.3 Encouraging private lettings under legislation

There were two particular aspects of the earlier landlord and tenant legislation which have been addressed by legislation. The one concerned the type of tenancy, and the other concerned rent. Both were intended to make the renting out of property a desirable option for new landlords. Possession procedures were modified and changes were introduced into the mortgage market to make it easier to buy housing for investment purposes.

Thus the way in which tenancies could be created was substantially altered and simplified, and the latest legislation to this effect is found in the Housing Act 1996.

Basically two types of tenancy can be created at present in the private rented sector: assured tenancies or shorthold tenancies. All new tenancies are automatically shorthold, under the 1996 Act, unless the landlord specifies his intention to create an assured tenancy.

3.3.1 Rent

'Regulated' rents still apply to most tenancies which came into existence before the 1988 Act. They were governed by the 'fair rent' procedure.

3.3.1(a) The 'fair rent' procedure

Under earlier legislation, rent was registered as a 'fair rent' in a register maintained by the local authority. It was determined by various factors, such as location and type of accommodation. However, it was not a market rent and was not fixed according to whether or not there was a shortage of properties in the area. If either landlord or tenant regarded the level of rent as not 'fair', there was an appeal to the rent assessment panel of the area (now known as the Residential Property Tribunal Service). Its decision was final except on a point of law. Moreover, an application for an increase or decrease could be made only after two years from the last registration.

The 'fair rent' procedure was seen as a deterrent to private-sector lettings.

On 1 February 1999, new rules were introduced to the fair rent procedure for the calculation of increases. Increases are limited to the application of a formula linked to the Retail Prices Index (RPI) and the House of Lords has since held that the rules are valid.

3.3.1(b)   The present procedure

Under the 1988 Act, with regard to an assured tenancy, a landlord can serve a notice, on a prescribed form, giving notice of a new rent. This notice can be served when the lease expires. Alternatively the lease itself can have included a term for a regular rent increase.

If the tenant refers the rent to a rent assessment committee, presently known as a a Residential Property Tribunal, it must consider the rent the letting would get in an open market.

Note: the tenant of an assured tenancy can only take the rent issue to a tribunal when the lease expires.

Do take heed: the tribunal may decide that the proposed rent is too low. Thus the tenant is taking a risk in making the appeal.

Different rules apply for rent assessment for a shorthold tenancy.

☞ *You rented a flat on a shorthold basis when you were relocated to London by your firm. You felt at the time that your landlord was asking an excessive amount in rent but you had no point of comparison and felt that you had no alternative but to accept. You now discover, after three months, that the rent is way out of line with other properties in the area.*

As a shorthold tenant, you can take the matter to a residential property tribunal. However, there is a deadline. You must do so within six months of the beginning of the original tenancy.

The committee will only consider the rent if it is 'significantly higher' than the landlord ought to receive – in other words, if it is excessive.

3.4   Tenancies: regaining possession

As we have seen, two main types of tenancy are currently in existence. The question of regaining possession of the premises depends on which type of tenancy exists:

- an assured tenancy allows the tenant to remain in the property unless the landlord can show the court that he has grounds for possession (see 3.4.1 immediately below)
- a shorthold tenancy gives minimum security for the tenant, who can be required to leave after six months, provided that the landlord has served two months' notice in writing (see section 3.6 below).

3.4.1   An assured tenancy

3.4.1(a)   The notice

A landlord can only get possession if he obtains a court order. In general, a court cannot make a possession order unless the landlord has served a proper notice on the tenant as specified by regulation, or the court dispenses with the need for a notice.

3.4.1(b)   Meeting the grounds for possession

The landlord can only obtain a court order for possession of a dwelling house under an assured tenancy, if he can prove one of 16 grounds specified in the 1988 Housing Act. On grounds 1–8, the court must order possession. On grounds 8–16, on the other hand, the court must be satisfied that not only has the ground been proved but that it is *reasonable* to grant possession. In other words, on one of those grounds, the court may order possession.

Note: an additional ground for possession was added by the 1996 Housing Act (see section 3.5.2 below).

3.5   The grounds

There are 17 grounds for obtaining possession.

3.5.1   Mandatory grounds

Grounds 1–8: the court must order possession if the landlord proves one of them. There is no need to show 'reasonableness'.

Ground 1:

- the landlord lived in the premises at some time as his principal home; or he or she desires to use it in this way at some future date

- he or she gave notice to the tenant in writing at the beginning of the tenancy of an intention to return at some stage; and
- that landlord now wishes to return.

The landlord may be able to use this ground even if he or she wants to sell the house, provided it was previously used as his or her only or principal home.

Ground 1 also applies if someone acquires the property as an inheritance or as a gift from a landlord who already had a right to rely on this ground. It does not apply, however, to someone buying the property after the tenancy has already begun.

Note: it can apply to the spouse of the landlord.

☞ *You and your wife let your only home when you were relocated by your firm. You inform the tenant in writing that it is your principal home and that you intend to return to live in it. Your wife is very unhappy with the relocation and wants to return home to live there with the children. You want to know what is your position.*

On these facts, it would seem that the court would give you possession on ground 1.

Ground 2: A mortgagee of the property wishes to obtain possession in order to exercise its power of sale with vacant possession. Again, notice of the fact that the property was mortgaged should be given by the landlord to the tenant at the beginning of the tenancy.

Note: if you buy a property on a mortgage and then let it to a tenant, you may be in breach of your mortgage agreement. You must get permission from your building society or bank before you let it out to others.

Ground 3: The house is usually used for holiday lettings. A landlord can let a property to the tenant who does not want it for a holiday for a fixed term not exceeding eight months provided that:

- the tenant was informed that it would be required for letting for four months (usually the summer period) after the eight-month period, and
- the house had been let as a holiday home in the year before the tenancy began.

Ground 4: The premises belong to an educational institution which normally lets them to students, and which wants the premises back again for this purpose.

Ground 5: The premises are normally used by a minister of religion and they are required again for this purpose.

Ground 6: The landlord intends to demolish the whole or a substantial part of the dwelling and the works cannot be carried out with the tenant in occupation.

Ground 7: The person residing in the premises after the death of the tenant is not entitled to succeed to the tenancy (see below: *Death of a tenant*, section 8, and see also chapter on *Death – Before and After*).

Ground 8: There are arrears of rent which exceed:

- eight weeks if rent is payable weekly or fortnightly
- two months if rent is payable monthly
- three months if rent is payable quarterly
- three months if rent is payable yearly.

3.5.2 Discretionary grounds

In these cases the court may order possession on one of these grounds if it thinks it reasonable to do so:

Ground 9: Suitable alternative accommodation is available for the tenant if an order for possession is granted.

Ground 10: Some rent is in arrears but not for the length of time set out in ground 8 (above).

Ground 11: There is persistent delay in paying rent which is lawfully due.

Ground 12: There is a breach of the tenant's obligations.

Ground 13: There is deterioration of the property through the tenant's waste or neglect by the tenant or any person living with the tenant.

Ground 14: The tenant, or anyone residing with the tenant, or even visiting the tenant:

- has caused or is likely to cause a nuisance or annoyance to someone living in or visiting the locality; or
- has been convicted of using the property or allowing it to be used for immoral or illegal purposes; or
- has committed an arrestable offence in the property or in the locality.

A landlord can start court proceedings immediately he has served notice on the tenant that he wants to repossess his property on this ground.

Ground 15: The tenant, or anyone living with the tenant, damages the landlord's furniture.

Ground 16: The tenant was an employee of the landlord and the employment has come to an end.

Ground 17: Under the Housing Act 1996 a new ground was added, namely that:

- the landlord was persuaded to grant the tenancy on the basis of a false statement knowingly or recklessly made by the tenant or a person acting at the tenant's behest.

3.6   A shorthold tenancy

This form of tenancy provides the tenant with very little protection. There is no need to give notice stating that a shorthold tenancy is being established, although the landlord must give the terms (commencement date, rent payable, etc.) in writing.

However, a landlord must serve at least two months' notice, in writing, on the tenant to leave the premises, and still has to apply to court for an order if a tenant does not leave willingly.

A landlord must be granted a court order if a tenant refuses to leave after expiry of the tenancy. There is no need to prove any of the grounds above.

The situation would differ, however, if you wished to bring the tenancy to an end before the end of its term and you are not prepared to wait for the expiry of the notice period.

☞   *You own two adjoining flats for rental purposes. In the one flat you have a longstanding tenant who has never caused you any difficulties. You recently installed a new tenant into the second flat on a shorthold tenancy for one year. You now have received several complaints that he is disturbing his neighbours because of his racist abuse and his threats of violence against his partner. You would like to have him leave the premises forthwith.*

If your tenant cannot be persuaded to moderate his behaviour, you can make an application to the court for possession, either on the ground of breach of covenant in his lease for causing a nuisance, or on ground 14 above. It will depend on the view that the judge takes on the evidence before him as to whether, in the circumstances, your application should be granted.

Other grounds do exist for claiming possession from a tenant before the six-month expiry date; in some cases, e.g. non-payment of rent, the court must grant possession. In other cases, such as the example outlined above, it will depend on the court's discretion.

3.6.1   The main elements

The tenancy may be for a fixed term, e.g. a year less one day, or it can run on from one rent period to the next; but the landlord, under normal circumstances, cannot regain his property before the first six months have expired.

As a result, therefore, all tenancies in the private rented sector are now shorthold tenancies unless the landlord has served a notice on the tenant before the beginning of the tenancy that it is not intended to be a shorthold tenancy. This significant change was introduced to ease the lot of landlords. Some landlords had intended creating shorthold tenancies so that they would automatically receive back their properties (subject to notice) at the expiry of the term, but found that they had instead created assured tenancies through procedural oversight.

3.6.2   Continuing the tenancy – no need for new notice

If the same landlord and tenant wish to continue on the same terms with reference to the same premises, the shorthold tenancy will continue.

3.6.3 Excluded tenancies

Certain tenancies are excluded from the provisions of the Acts, in particular, tenancies which began before 15 January 1989.

Several grounds are set out in the legislation, for example those which concern 'resident landlords' (see below, section 6).

Other grounds include:

- holiday letting of the property
- very high- or very low-rental property (there are specified limits)
- property granted to students

(this list is not exhaustive).

Do note: tenancies in the public sector are also excluded (see section 4 below).

For protection of tenants, see also below, *Protection from harassment and eviction*, section 5).

3.7 Accelerated possession procedure

Rules are in force which deal with possession proceedings for assured and shorthold tenancies. The rules are intended to streamline possession proceedings in certain cases and enable a judge to make a possession order on written application without necessarily requiring the parties to attend in court for a hearing. Where anti-social behaviour is involved, special powers are to be introduced for 'fast track' possession orders.

3.7.1 In the case of an assured tenancy

If a landlord wishes to recover possession of a dwelling house on grounds of:

- landlord occupation
- former holiday occupation
- former student letting
- occupation by a minister of religion

and provided the tenant has been given proper notice, the landlord can file all the relevant information with the court together with his application for possession. The information required is stipulated in the rules and must be on a prescribed form. The landlord must also serve a copy on the tenant.

A tenant has 14 days in which to make a reply.

If there is no reply, the landlord may make a written request for a possession order.

If there is a reply the judge can:

- make an order after considering the reply, or
- fix a day for a hearing.

Note: on 15 October 2001, new procedures came into force with regard to case management of all possession claims.

3.7.2 In the case of a shorthold tenancy

The rules apply where a landlord intends to recover possession when the tenancy has come to an end.

Note: the accelerated procedure can only be used to recover possession. It cannot be used if there is another action by the landlord against the tenant as well, for example for non-payment of rent.

4 PUBLIC SECTOR ACCOMMODATION

The local authorities' position as landlords has undergone dramatic changes in the past decades. Their powers in relation to planning and compulsory acquisition have remained largely the same; their duties to provide homes for the homeless and the needy have grown as the requirements of our changing society have to be met. However, the actual housing stock has been diminished through the 'right to buy' legislation and the current limitations on local government finance.

Since 1988, local authorities have also transferred all or part of their housing stock to new landlords, know as Registered Social Landlords (RSLs), for example, housing associations. These transfers can only take place where the majority of tenants support the move. As these RSLs are not subject to the same financial constraints as local authorities, it is hoped that changes will be to the benefit of the tenants, e.g. that repairs are carried out more quickly.

4.1   How housing is allocated

Each council allocates its rental property to persons who make application for a council house according to a set of criteria. Priority is given, for example, to an applicant who has spent a long time on the waiting list; to single-parent families; and to personal factors such as health or disability, etc.

4.2   Security of tenure – the general rules

In general, council tenants are secure tenants. There are certain exceptions however. Among them are the following:

a) Licensees on short-term lets.

b) Employees: residential accommodation can be let as part of a contract of employment, e.g. to members of the police or fire services. The criterion is whether the accommodation is necessary for an employee to be able to carry out his duties properly. Tricky questions sometimes do arise concerning whether or not the accommodation was really needed for employment purposes. For example, the headmaster of a school may live as a tenant in a property owned by the local authority on or near school grounds. He may resist possession proceedings on the ground that he is a secure tenant; alternatively he might wish to exercise the right to buy the premises which is available to public-sector tenants.

c) Certain others on short-term lets, such as homeless persons or job seekers.

d) Tenants on 'introductory tenancies'.

4.3   Tenant's rights

Under the Housing Acts, most tenants have security of tenure. This means the right to remain in the premises for the tenant's lifetime and also allows for succession after the death of a tenant (see below, section 8).

However, the Council can gain possession of premises from a secure tenant in certain circumstances and on certain grounds, although in general the Council can only gain possession of its premises by court order and it must persuade the court that it is a reasonable order for the court to make.

4.3.1   Grounds for possession

Among the grounds for possession are the following:

- rent arrears or some other breach of tenancy (for example, a council might prohibit the keeping of pets that could harm the property or be a nuisance to other residents; a persistent breach of this condition, by e.g. keeping a barking dog locked in your flat, might result in a possession order)
- causing or likely to cause a nuisance or annoyance to other occupiers, as well as to others in the locality; conviction for an offence in the locality; nuisance or annoyance caused by the tenant's visitors
- allowing the premises you occupy, or the common parts, to fall into a state of disrepair
- obtaining the tenancy by means of a false statement
- exchanging the tenancy and taking a premium on the exchange
- misconduct, where the tenant occupies the premises in connection with employment
- the premises were given to the tenant as a temporary measure while repairs were carried out to his or her usual dwelling house.

Note: this list is not exhaustive.

Under the Housing Act 1996, new grounds for possession were introduced in addition to extending the nuisance ground (see above). It was found that the existing legislation was inadequate to combat antisocial tenants who, even if few in number, could make life unbearable for an entire neighbourhood.

The Act makes provision for 'introductory tenancies' at the option of the local authority. Such tenancies are probationary for the first year. If the local authority wishes to repossess within that period, it does not have to make out a ground for possession to the court.

It also introduces a new ground where one partner of a couple, or a member of the partner's family, has left the property because of violence or threats of violence from the other partner and is unlikely to return.

In addition, the government has urged local authorities to take advantage of a type of order known as an antisocial-behaviour order, under the Crime and Disorder Act 1998, which is intended to create safer communities by dealing with threatening and criminal behaviour (see chapter on *Neighbours*, section 2.6.3).

☞ *You are aware that your next-door neighbour's teenage son seems to have some very undesirable friends whose demeanour menaces you as you go in and out of you house.*

☞ *You also have cause to believe that drug trafficking is taking place among these young men. You are anxious to report the matter to the police and to the landlord of the estate but do not wish to become a target of their aggression in the future.*

   The Housing Act 1996, as well as the system set up for antisocial-behaviour orders, allows you to report your anxieties anonymously. The authorities can then use a 'professional witness' to collect evidence and present it in court so as to spare you victimisation.

4.3.2   Suitable alternative accommodation

An order for possession is *mandatory* (i.e. the court must order possession) if one of the following grounds is established. However, the Council must show that it can offer suitable alternative accommodation once the order comes into effect. The grounds are that:

* the premises are overcrowded
* the landlord has to demolish or reconstruct the premises and cannot do so without gaining possession of them
* the whole estate is to be disposed of and vacant possession must first be obtained
* the tenant occupies the accommodation from a charity – such as a charitable housing trust – and the tenant no longer meets the purposes of the charity. For example, a charity might have been set up to provide special facilities for tenants with mobility problems but you no longer need such facilities.

4.3.3   Some other categories for possession

There are certain cases where, in order to get possession, the Council must prove:

a) that it is reasonable to evict, and
b) that suitable alternative accommodation is available.

In other words the court has a discretionary power; compare section 4.3.2 (above) where the court must order possession in the circumstances. In cases of this sort:

a) the tenant was, for example, formerly an employee of the Council and the premises were needed for a new employee, or
b) the premises were adapted for a person with a disability and let to a disabled person who no longer lives there.

☞ *Your husband was handicapped and was housed by the Council in accommodation adapted to meet his disability. He has since died and you have succeeded him to the tenancy (see below, section 8.2). You have now been told that the Council requires the premises for someone else with a disability but can offer you accommodation elsewhere.*

   Provided the accommodation is suitable, the Council has good grounds for possession in your case.

In cases where a surviving occupant succeeds to the tenancy but the premises are considered too large for one person living alone, the Council might wish to move him or her to smaller premises. For example, you and your late husband occupied a two-bedroomed council flat. You have succeeded to the tenancy. The Council may decide that a one-bedroomed flat now suffices for your purposes. See section 8 below, *Death of a tenant*.

4.3.4 Suitable alternative accommodation

The court will take into account all sorts of factors with regard to the accommodation such as present facilities, locality, and proximity to amenities. It will also take into account the needs of the tenant relating to age, employment etc.

5 PROTECTION FROM HARASSMENT AND EVICTION

There are two forms of protection against harassment and eviction:

- criminal prosecution
- civil action for damages.

5.1 Harassment

Harassment is any action likely to interfere with the peace or comfort of the residential occupier or any member of his or her family. It also covers withdrawal of services reasonably needed for residential occupation. In short, it is any action deliberately intended to make an occupier:

- give up the property or
- feel too intimidated to exercise his or her legal rights.

Examples of harassment include:

- changing the locks
- uttering threats and using other forms of intimidation
- disrupting basic services
- accumulating rubbish on the premises
- removing light bulbs in common parts.

Note: victims of harassment can include licensees who do not have protection of Rent Acts. The statutory provisions apply to 'all lawful residential occupiers'.

Usually criminal prosecutions for harassment and/or eviction are brought by the local authority.

5.1.1 Civil actions for damages

The courts can award significant sums to tenants who have been unlawfully put out of their dwellings.

Damages can be obtained by tenants or by mere licensees if they prove unlawful eviction. Damages for their goods can also be claimed.

Awards can be very high to deter unscrupulous landlords. In one case a tenant who was forced out of her bedsitter was awarded £31,000 in compensation. Her landlord had woken her at 2 am to ask for rent, played loud music, come into the bathroom when she was using it, and changed the locks when she fled the place. While she was out of the premises he then smashed her belongings.

5.1.2 Injunctions

A tenant can apply to court for an order (an injunction) to stop the unlawful action. If the landlord breaches the injunction, he is then liable for contempt of court.

5.1.3 The landlord's defences

The landlord has certain grounds on which to make a case that his action either was lawful or, in the case of reinstatement, is no longer unlawful.

5.1.3(a) Reinstatement

If a landlord is being prosecuted for unlawful eviction or sued for civil damages, he can offer to reinstate the tenant so that the action against him will be dropped. However, merely handing a tenant a key to the front door is insufficient. There must be a genuine reinstatement to the premises together with the tenant's possessions. It is no use inviting a tenant to go back to a room which has been totally wrecked. Of course, it can be difficult to enforce such orders.

5.1.3(b) Genuine belief that the tenant has left

A landlord might be able to persuade the court of his genuine belief that a tenant has left.

☞ *Your tenant has been several weeks in arrears with her rent. All attempts to contact her are to no avail. Other tenants tell you that her post is accumulating outside her corridor. You decide to change the lock to the flat and put her goods into storage. The tenant returns after a three-month trip abroad and threatens to sue for unlawful eviction.*

A court will take heed of your defence to her claim and assess its genuineness in the light of the circumstances of the case.

5.2   The need for a court order to evict

If premises are let as a dwelling and the tenancy comes to an end but the person occupying it continues living there, the owner can only recover possession by commencing court proceedings.

Court proceedings can begin only after a valid notice to quit has been given to the tenant and the period of the notice has expired. For the accelerated proceedings in assured and shorthold tenancies, see section 3.7 above.

5.2.1   Valid notice

A notice is only valid if it is given in writing at least four weeks before the date on which it is to take effect. The grounds on which it is being brought must be set out (see section 3.5 above).

5.2.2   Excluded licences or tenancies

There is no need for a court order where:

- the occupier shares accommodation with a resident landlord or with a member of the landlord's family. They must live in the same premises. If your landlord only uses a room in your flat occasionally, you share the accommodation but he does not live there
- it is a holiday let
- no rent is being paid (i.e. occupation is rent-free).

However, even in these cases, although a court order is not required, reasonable notice is required and, most importantly, no harassment can be used to get the occupier out of the premises.

6   A RESIDENT LANDLORD

A letting of a property cannot be on an 'assured tenancy' basis if the landlord is 'resident'. What is a *resident landlord* for the purposes of the 1988 Act?

6.1   Some general rules

a) The property rented by you must be part of the same premises in which the landlord lives. Thus it could be a single flat in which you both live. Where the flat is part of a purpose-built block, your landlord can be resident if, for example, he has a long lease on a three-bedroomed flat in which you rent one of the bedrooms and your landlord and his son occupy the other two rooms. It is perfectly clear that he is a 'resident' landlord for the purposes of the Act.

Do take note, however: if you live in a flat in a purpose-built block of flats and your landlord lives in another flat in the same block, he is not a resident landlord.

b) The landlord must be an individual (not a company).
c) The landlord must have resided in the same building since the commencement of the tenancy.
d) He must use the premises as his home.
e) He must be in continuous residence. (This does not mean he has to stay there every night.)

☞ *You rent a flat in central London with two bedrooms – one of which the landlord reserves for himself. He has two homes, one of which is in the country about 100 miles away. He uses the London accommodation two nights per week. He wants you to quit the premises when your lease expires on the grounds that he is a resident landlord. You dispute this.*

In all such cases, it is a matter of fact and degree. There is nothing to stop a landlord having two homes if he has reason to be in London on those particular nights of the week. He also does not have to be in residence every night of the week. If he reserved one room as an office, however, which was only occasionally used, you could assert that he is not a resident landlord.

6.1.1   If a 'resident landlord' sells the property

The new landlord can continue 'residence' provided:

a) he moves in within 28 days; or
b) he notifies the tenant in writing of his intention to move in within 28 days and
c) he moves in within six months.

6.1.2   If a resident landlord dies

A successor has two years in which to move in.

Note: the issue of whether or not there is a 'resident' landlord also applies when tenants seek to buy their freehold (see below, section 10).

7   ASSIGNMENT AND SUB-LETTING

7.1   What is an assignment?

A tenant may be allowed to 'assign' the whole of the remainder of his lease in the tenancy. For example, you rent a property on a three-year lease, and you spend a year living there. Your firm then wants to send you abroad for a year and you therefore wish to dispose of your lease for the remaining two-year period. You must establish whether you have a right to assign the property, i.e. whether you can let another tenant take over in your stead.

7.1.1   Absolute prohibition

A lease may have an absolute prohibition against assignment by the tenant. Such a clause may well fall foul of the Unfair Contract Terms Regulations (see 2.1.5 above).

7.1.2   Qualified prohibition

More generally, a lease has a qualified prohibition against assignment, i.e. a tenant may assign if he or she has the landlord's consent. The landlord's consent is not to be unreasonably withheld. Under the Landlord and Tenant Act of 1988, a landlord has to:

* answer within a reasonable time
* give reasons why he withholds his consent
* give his reasons in writing.

☞ *You wish to assign the remainder of your two-year lease to a friend of yours. Your landlord has to consent to the assignment. She refuses her consent in writing within a couple of weeks on the grounds that your friend has failed to supply adequate references for credit-worthiness.*

All a tenant's covenants have to be performed by a new tenant on an assignment. Therefore it is reasonable for a landlord to enquire whether the person you are proposing in your stead will be able to pay the rent.

7.1.3   Unreasonable withholding of consent

What happens if a landlord refuses consent to assign and the tenant thinks the refusal is being unreasonably withheld?

A tenant can apply to court for:

a) a declaration that the landlord's consent is being unreasonably withheld
b) damages.

7.1.4   No prohibition against assignment

The lease may have no prohibition at all against assignment and, in such a case, a tenant is free to assign.

7.2   Enforcing covenants against others

A landlord, as we have seen, expects a tenant, on assignment, to perform all the covenants in the lease.

7.3 Sublettings

7.3.1 What is a subletting?

A subletting takes place if a tenant lets his property for less than the remainder of his term. For example, if you have a three-year lease and you go abroad for a year, and let your property for the year that you are away, that will be a subletting. The terms of the lease will generally contain a covenant which specifies whether or not there can be a subletting. If the lease does allow a sublet, it may be on terms; for example, the landlord's consent.

A subletting also applies to a let of part of your premises. For example, you rent a two-bedroomed flat and you only occupy one of those rooms. You decide to rent out the other room. Before doing so, you must check the terms of your lease; many residential leases contain an absolute prohibition against subletting part of the premises.

Note of warning: if you assign your lease, you will lose assured tenancy protection. You will not be able to claim that the premises are your principal home once you cease to occupy it. The same warning must be borne in mind for a sublet – where it will be a matter of fact and degree. For instance, if you sublet the whole premises while you go on holiday or for a stint of work elsewhere, you may keep the protection. If you cease to occupy the premises, you will probably lose it. However, you will not lose your status if you sublet part only of the premises – provided your lease allows you to do so.

Note: it is advisable to check with your insurers. Even if your landlord insures the building and the subtenant insures his or her possessions, you will want to insure your own possessions too – such as carpets, curtains, kitchen equipment etc.

8 DEATH OF A TENANT

Take note: the rules governing succession to tenancies in both the private and the public sector are complicated; different succession rights apply to Rent Act tenants, assured tenants (private and housing association tenants), and secure (council) tenants. Do seek legal advice when you are faced with a death in the family and the deceased lived in rental accommodation.

The Law Commission has made proposals to modify and simplify succession rules: see their website: *www.lawcom.gov.uk* (via the link to the Library) for the Consultation Paper No. 168.

The outline of the present law below illustrates the complexity of the issues.

8.1 Private sector

8.1.1 An assured tenant under the 1988 Act

8.1.1(a) Periodic tenancy

If a tenant who rents property on a 'periodic' basis (i.e. from week to week, month to month or for some other period which is not fixed in advance (see 8.1.1(b) *Fixed-term tenancy* below) then dies, leaving a spouse or cohabitee who lived with the tenant as husband or wife and who was resident at the time of the tenant's death, then the landlord has no grounds for possession. The survivor can continue to live in the premises.

Note: there is one important proviso to the above right of succession. The tenant cannot himself or herself have been a successor. In other words, if you succeed to a tenancy as the widow or widower of a tenant, and then remarry, your second spouse cannot succeed to a periodic tenancy.

If there is no survivor as defined in law, the landlord is advised to approach the executors or the adminstrators of the estate to establish how much time would be needed to clear the property for re-letting. In the meantime, the estate is liable for the rent and other costs until such time as the property is vacated. Because of these liabilities, it is advisable to sign a deed of surrender to take effect as soon as possible. In the absence of such a deed, the landlords can ask the court to terminate the tenancy.

8.1.1(b) Fixed-term tenancy

If a tenant dies who has a fixed-term tenancy (i.e. a tenancy for a period which has been fixed in advance, for example, for 15 years), and this has not expired, the balance of the tenancy will pass to a beneficiary either under a will or on an intestacy. The landlord cannot recover the property in these circumstances but s/he can apply to the executors of the estate or to the administrators for the rent and other charges in the meantime.

8.1.1(c) Shorthold tenancy

☞ *You moved into your boyfriend's flat which he rented on a shorthold tenancy for a year. He died very suddenly and your landlord has now given you two months' notice that he requires possession at the end of the term. You wonder what you can do?*

Your landlord has an automatic right to repossess and you have no succession rights. If you remain on in the flat, you are liable to pay the rent. You can apply to your landlord that you should become his tenant in your partner's stead and try to negotiate with him accordingly.

Do ensure that you enter into a written agreement which conforms to the principles of fairness in its terms (see above, section 2.1.5(b)).

8.1.2 Different rules apply to tenancies under the Rent Act 1977

If the original tenant dies leaving a spouse or cohabitee in the house, that survivor will become a statutory tenant and can remain in occupation. If the original tenant dies and there is no surviving partner, another member of the tenant's family is entitled to an assured tenancy which will be governed by the 1988 Act.

In a decision on succession rights to protected tenancies, the House of Lords held that the survivor of a same-sex relationship could succeed to an assured tenancy as he had lived with his deceased partner 'as a member of his family'.

Since then the Court of Appeal has held, in a decision hailed as 'groundbreaking', that cohabiting gay couples have the same rights as heterosexual couples to succeed to a tenancy after the death of a partner. The words that the couple were to be either husband or wife or living together 'as his or her wife or husband' had to be read to mean 'as if they were his or her wife or husband.' Therefore a survivor of such a relationship becomes a statutory tenant with all the rights that that entails.

Another interesting decision concerned the right of a child to succeed to a secure tenancy.

☞ *Mary, at the age of 13 years, came to live with her grandmother in a house which she rented under a secure tenancy. Three years later the grandmother died. The landlord argued that Mary could not succeed to the tenancy as she was still a minor.*

In a similar case, the Court of Appeal ruled that there was 'ample reason to conclude that minor children were not non-persons in the law of landlord and tenant let alone the law of property generally. The modern tendency of the law was to recognise that children were indeed people' and in the court's view, a minor could clearly succeed to a tenancy held by a deceased secure tenant.

If the successor dies, a second successor can take over if:

- he or she was a member of the family of both the original tenant and the first successor; and
- he or she lived with the first successor for at least two years prior to the first successor's death.

8.2 Public sector

If a tenant is a secure tenant in public sector accommodation, as most tenants generally are (see section 4 above), then family members can inherit on the death of a tenant.

8.2.1 Spouse (including cohabitee)

A wife or husband of the tenant (including a cohabitee) can inherit provided it was his or her main home (see however the Court of Appeal decision above in relation to same-sex couples, section 8.1.2).

8.2.2 Other members of the family

Another member of the family of the deceased tenant may succeed to the tenancy provided he or she had lived with the tenant for 12 months before the tenant died. There is no need to prove that they lived in only one property throughout those 12 months; for example, two brothers may occupy a council flat, and then arrange to exchange the flat for another one. Shortly after they move the tenant dies. The brother can succeed him provided that their total residence together was for 12 months or more in council property.

A person cannot inherit from a council tenant where that tenant was already a successor.

Do take heed: In view of the complexity of the overlapping legislation, the variety of personal factors to be taken into account, and the ever-evolving case law, in all instances of a death of a tenant, you are strenuously advised to seek legal advice.

9   BUYING A LONG LEASEHOLD

For the purposes of landlord and tenant law, a long leasehold is one that generally extends for 21 years or more.

As we have seen, a lease is a formal document which sets out the duties, rights, and obligations of both landlord and tenant.

9.1   Need for care

Great care must always be taken in purchasing a long leasehold. In fact the complexities are such that, although in some ways you are buying something 'less' than a freehold, you are also buying something 'more' than a freehold in other ways. You are bound to a landlord by terms, obligations and duties specified in your lease. These can be onerous.

You are committed to paying service charges which may increase with great rapidity. Your decisions are no longer your own – not only with regard to the fact that you now have a landlord. You also have to take into account the wishes and needs of all the other long leaseholders. For example, a decision can be taken by the other tenants that the whole block needs repainting. This will cost something in the region of £100,000. You might prefer to spend your share of that sum in renewing the carpets in your own flat. You may find yourself short of money and not wish to spend anything at all – nonetheless, you will be bound to pay your contribution.

A lease for a long-leasehold purchase will usually contain express terms on the landlord's duties to maintain the premises. The outlay is usually recovered from the long-leaseholders under the lease (see section 12, *Managing agents,* below).

This is one of the areas in landlord and tenant law which generates much heat. Lessees have suffered on the following counts:

- their landlords have neglected their premises
- their landlords have charged exorbitant amounts for necessary works
- the managing agents do not fulfil their tasks
- the landlords have carried out unnecessary works.

9.1.1   Service charges

Service charges are amounts payable for 'services, repairs, maintenance or insurance or the landlord's costs of management'.

With regard to those charges:

a) the landlord is not supposed to make a profit
b) they must be reasonably incurred; lessees can refuse to pay excessive amounts
c) when building work in excess of £50 per flat or £1,000 per block is to be carried out, two estimates must be obtained. A 'section 20' notice must be sent to all residents giving them one month to convey their views
d) service charges cannot be recovered after 18 months unless there has been proper notice
e) a residents' association is entitled to request copies of the estimates and of management accounts. (For a fuller discussion, see below, section 12.)
f) service charges include the cost of insurance cover which the landlord is obligated to arrange.

9.1.2   Neglect of premises

Blocks of flats were sometimes allowed to fall into disrepair. A landlord might have appointed managing agents who did not perform their duties properly. What were tenants to do? Both with regard to service charges and concerns over neglect of premises, major changes have been enacted to ease the position of tenants. Jurisdiction to deal with these matters was transferred to the Leasehold Valuation Tribunals (see also below, sections 10–12).

10   BUYING THE FREEHOLD

An understandable concern for those owning property on a long lease is that leases depreciate or 'waste' with time (i.e. as the years go by, the lease's term, and with it its value, diminishes).

Another problem of the leasehold system is that landlords do not always carry out their duties. Of course, some landlords do ensure that their premises are well managed. Tenants receive an annual bill for service charges which are kept to a reasonable level; the managing agents, if appointed, carry out their duties efficiently.

However, considerable difficulties arise in practice, as we all know. Legislation has endeavoured in piecemeal fashion to deal with these problems, particularly issues of management.

Then, an Act was introduced in 1993 which took matters much further. The purpose of the legislation was to assist tenants who wished to buy the freehold of their flats so as to ensure that their properties were being run to their own standards; in other words empowering long-leaseholders through 'enfranchisement'.

Further significant reforms to the 1993 Act have been introduced by the Commonhold and Leasehold Reform Act 2002 which amends the qualifications of leaseholders wishing to enfranchise, as well as enhancing their powers to manage their own affairs.

Do take heed: the 2002 Act is to be phased in over a period of time. A public consultation process is in progress for a number of the Act's main provisions. Thereafter the appropriate regulations will have to be drafted. Only then will we know the full details, and only later still will we be able to gauge how they work out in practice.

At present the only operative clauses of the Act (at the time of writing), are those that deal with enfranchisement (dealt with in this section), and lease extension (see section 11 below). Thus far, too, they only apply to England.

In all cases, in important transactions such as these, leaseholders are urged to seek professional advice as to the best course of action – particularly in the light of overlapping legislation.

10.1   Long leaseholds – flat dwellers

Under the Leasehold Reform Housing and Urban Development Act 1993, long-leaseholders who qualified were able to acquire the freehold to their properties on certain conditions. This was a group action. However, individual leaseholders who qualified were able to renew their leases for a further 90 years (see below, section 11) if they chose not to go in for enfranchisement.

There are certain features of the 1993 Act worth noting at the outset. It is helpful to read them in the context of subsequent changes introduced recently by the Commonhold and Leasehold Reform Act 2002:

a) The ability to buy the freehold altered the relationship between landlord and tenant to a significant degree
b) The legislation was very complex.

Note: although the Leasehold Reform Act constituted a largely new field of legislation to both landlords and their tenants, as well as to their professional advisers, a number of blocks of flats successfully acquired their freeholds through the procedure.

10.1.1   The terminology

qualifying tenant: certain conditions were laid down before a tenant could 'qualify' for either enfranchisement or lease extension (these involved length of residence, willingness to participate in a group action etc);

qualifying building: certain conditions were laid down before a building could qualify (involving length of lease, proportion of business to residential premises etc);

residence test: the residence test could be either:

a) continuous residence, or
b) a number of years' residence in the previous ten years; in addition the property had to be occupied as a main or principal residence;

'marriage value': this is the potential increase in value that results from the freehold and leasehold interests being joined together;

low rent: a level of rent, calculated by means of a complicated formula of assessment, under which the original lease was granted;

enfranchisement: the acquisition by a group of tenants of the freehold to their block of flats, or the acquisition by a single householder of the freehold to a house which was on a long leasehold;

lease extension: the option of an individual tenant to extend his or her lease for a further 90 years;

'nominee purchaser': generally a nominee company set up by the tenants to act as the purchaser.

10.2 General observations

Under the 1993 Act, leaseholders were given two basic rights subject to conditions: to club together to buy the freehold, or to extend their individual leases.

The Commonhold and Leasehold Reform Act 2002 on the other hand, is intended – in the long term – to provide a different system for the ownership of flats, as well as of other interdependent buildings, provided that they share services and common parts. It will apply in particular to new developments, although existing leaseholders who have already bought their freehold could convert to commonhold provided that they all agree to do so.

The Act also makes significant changes to the existing leasehold legislation for those leaseholders who cannot convert to commonhold or do not wish to do so. We are concerned with this aspect of the Act below.

For enfranchisement, both the tenants and the buildings in which they live have to meet certain conditions.

10.3 The qualifications (from 1993 to 2002)

- At least two-thirds of the flats had to be long leaseholds (more than 21 years at the time that the leases were granted)
- at least 90 per cent of the floor space of a block had to be residential
- there had to be a 'low rent' if the lease was less than 35 years
- fifty per cent of the leaseholders had to use the flat as their main residence for a year
- two-thirds of the qualifying tenants, occupying at least half of all the flats in the building, had to agree to make the purchase
- if a block was converted and had fewer than five flats there could be no resident landlord on the premises.

10.4 Preparation and timetable

Once the tenants qualified in terms of numbers, residence etc. and the building itself met its qualifications, the Act specified an elaborate timetable which involved the following:

- Assessment of the purchase price
- Instruction of professional advisers
- Establishment of the finance fund
- Ascertainment of the nominee purchaser
- Service of the initial notice
- Follow up on the procedures and timelimits as laid down by Statute.

Do note: these procedures are dealt with in detail in a booklet available from LEASE or online at *www.lease-advice./org.cegsmenu.htm*. The booklet also makes clear the extent to which there are transitional arrangements which cover both the 1993 and 2002 Acts.

10.5 The present qualifications – 2002

Criticism of the 1993 Act focused on the following:

- The required percentage of qualifying tenants was too high
- The residence test was difficult to apply
- The valuation process entailed heavy costs for the tenant
- The 'marriage value' worked to the advantage of the landlord
- The valuation date was uncertain and also worked to the landlord's advantage.

Although much of the Commonhold and Leasehold Reform Act still needs to be implemented, those sections of the Act dealing with certain aspects of enfranchisement, with lease extension, and which amend the 1993 Act (see above) have been put in to force. In particular, those criticisms outlined above have been addressed.

Do note however: thus far implementation of these provisions apply to England only.

10.5.1 Qualifications for Tenants

Among the many significant changes are the following:

* There is no longer a residence test
* Only 50 per cent of leaseholders need participate instead of the present requirement of two-thirds.

10.5.2 Qualifications for Buildings

* The building must contain two or more flats and at least two-thirds of those flats must be held on long leases (i.e. an original term exceeding 21 years)
* There is no longer a 'low rent' requirement
* Three-quarters of the building must be residential (as opposed to commercial)
* Special rules apply to converted property with four or fewer flats where the landlord or an adult member of his family has lived in one of the flats.

10.5.3 Valuation

* The valuation date is to be set at the date on which the notice claiming enfranchisement is sent to the landlord by the tenants in a group action
* There is no 'marriage value' payable where leases have more than 80 years to run
* Compensation, however, will be payable to the landlord, for example, if he loses a potential for development
* Where 'marriage value' is payable and has been assessed, the amount is to be divided equally between tenants and landlord.

10.5.4 Company Requirements (RTE company)

At present, tenants can effect an enfranchisement through a nominee purchaser. They must also go through the procedures stipulated (see section 10.4 above), paying particular heed to both the timetable and to the transitional arrangements. Readers are advised to consult the booklet issued by LEASE which also can supply lists of solicitors and surveyors who have been involved in the statutory procedures, although LEASE does not recommend any particular professsional advisors.

However, once the provisions of the new Act are in force, leaseholders will have to set up a 'Right to Enfranchise' (RTE) company which would serve notice on the landlord of the intention to enfranchise. This will be a private company limited by guarantee, the memorandum and articles of which will be prescribed by government regulations. The intention is to simplify the manner in which tenants can buy the freehold by standardising the company procedures involved. Nonetheless, a degree of flexibility will be maintained to deal with any unique feature of a development.

The membership of the company will be restricted to all the unit-holders within the development, i.e. each separate property (for example each flat in a block of 15 flats) will be called a unit and its owner will be the unit-holder. All unit-holders will have two interests in the property of the commonhold:

a) a direct interest in the units, for example the flats, which they own and
b) a company members' interest in the commonhold company [to be known as the commonhold association] which owns the common parts. There will be no landlord.

In order to protect tenants from being excluded, the RTE company would have to serve a notice inviting all qualifying tenants to become company members. The notice would have to provide an estimate of price and costs.

For details of the consultation process in drafting regulations which would govern the setting up of an RTE company, contact the Commonhold Team at the Lord Chancellor's Department (see DIRECTORY on page 215).

11   EXTENDING YOUR LEASE

The 1993 Act empowered tenants to enfranchise, as we have seen above. However, it also gave tenants an additional right to extend their leases by 90 years. Lease extension involved less expense and the complications were fewer. At the same time, the Act was intended to provide an alternative – apart from enfranchisement – of prolonging the life of a long leaseholder's 'wasting asset' which was often his home.

However, again criticism was directed at the unnecessarily restrictive nature of the requirements which tenants had to meet before they could extend their leases.

11.1   Qualification for extension under the 1993 Act

To qualify for extension there had to be:

a) a lease requirement:

- a lease for more than 21 years
- a lease at a low rent

b) a residence requirement:

- the tenant must have lived in the flat as his or her main or only home, for three years; or
- the tenant must have lived there for a total of three years in the preceding ten.

11.2   Lease extension under the 2002 Act

- The residence test is abolished (however, see the note below)
- The low rent requirement is abolished
- There must still be an original lease of 21 years or more.

Do note: tenants must have owned the lease for two years before they can qualify for a lease extension.

11.3   What the tenant must pay

The valuation of the premises in the light of a lease extension is a critical factor both for the tenant who stands to gain, and for the landlord, who stands to lose:

- A tenant will have to compensate the landlord for the reduction in the value of the landlord's interest as a result of the new longer lease (i.e. the loss due to the additional 90 years before the landlord can expect the surrender of the flat at the end of the term of lease) plus
- Half the 'marriage value' (only payable on leases with less than 80 years to run)
- Compensation for other losses, such as development value
- Loss of ground rent
- The landlord's reasonable costs of dealing with the lease renewal.

From the above outline alone, it is clear that the valuation process is a difficult and uncertain one. You are strenuously advised therefore to seek professional advice.

The Leasehold Advisory Service sets out the legislative basis, the general methods and principles involved, and the role of a professional adviser in its booklet: *Valuation for Lease Extension* (see DIRECTORY on page 215; the information is also available online).

11.3.1   The 'trigger' notice

Once a qualifying tenant has a valuation in hand, he or she can then serve notice on the landlord of their intention to extend their lease. This in turn triggers the timetable as laid down by statute.

11.3.2   What happens in event of a death?

The 2002 Act has clarified the position with regard to the position after the death of a long leaseholder.

☞   *Your father owned a flat with a lease of 50 years to run. He wished to take advantage of the lease-extension provisions and had been in contact with his solicitor about the matter. He then unexpectedly died in August 2002. You are his sole heir and executor. You wonder what the legal position is.*

A new power has been given to personal representatives of a deceased tenant under the Act. You have the right to a new lease, provided your father qualified for a lease extension immediately before he died. The right is exercisable for a period of two years starting from the date of the grant of probate or letters of administration (see chapter on *Death – Before and After*, section 3.4).

12   MANAGING AGENTS

Do note: the sections below should be read in the light of the additional statutory powers given to tenants to take over management functions from the landlord without having to prove fault. These provisions have yet to be brought into force (see section 12.3 below).

12.1   Appointment of managing agent

Under the Landlord and Tenant Act 1987, a tenants' association may serve a notice on the landlord asking to be consulted on the appointment of a managing agent. The landlord has to reply to such a notice by giving:

a) the name of the person he intends appointing
b) a list of the duties which the landlord intends the managing agent to fulfil on his behalf
c) an opportunity for the association to make their comments on the appointment.

12.1.1   Employment of managing agent

A residents' association is entitled to serve a notice on a landlord concerning a managing agent who is already being employed for their premises. The landlord has to reply stating the obligations which the agent is carrying out on his behalf; and giving a reasonable period for the association to comment on the manner in which the agent has been discharging those obligations and whether it is desirable that he should continue to do so.

12.1.2   Code of conduct for managing agents

The Leasehold Reform Housing and Urban Development Act 1993 gave the Secretary of State authority to approve a code of conduct to promote 'desirable practices' in the management of residential property. Among other matters, the code provides for:

a) resolving disputes between landlord and tenant
b) ensuring competitive tendering for works in connection with the property
c) administering money paid for service charges.

The standards set by the code are also relevant to determining whether management is 'efficient and effective' if a management audit is carried out (see below, section 12.2).

12.1.3   Failing to comply with the code

However, if the manager fails to comply with the code, this will not, of itself, make him or her liable for any proceedings. Such failure can be used in evidence, however, if proceedings arise and tenants wish to have another managing agent appointed by a Leasehold Valuation Tribunal (see below, section 12.2.3).

12.2   Management audit

The Act also makes provision for a management audit. If two-thirds of the qualifying tenants agree, they can appoint a surveyor or accountant to carry out an audit to determine whether

• there is efficient and effective management and
• their service charges are 'being applied in an efficient and effective manner'.

12.2.1   'Qualifying' tenants

Tenants can qualify for the purposes of appointing an auditor if they

• have a long lease and
• pay service charges.

12.2.2   Costs

The tenants will have to pay the costs of the audit. Furthermore, if the landlord incurs costs in making copies of documents etc. available to the auditor, the landlord is 'not precluded' (as the Act primly puts it) from recouping these costs from the service charges.

12.2.3   Service charges – need to inform

The management-audit provisions follow upon earlier legislation which provide for the need to inform tenants of their service charges. Under the Landlord and Tenant Acts 1985 and 1987, tenants are entitled to:

- be informed of how the figure for the service charge is reached
- inspect accounts and receipts
- be consulted concerning major works which cost over £1,000, or £50 per flat multiplied by the number of flats – whichever is the greater
- be shown at least two estimates of the works
- be certain that their service charges are held in trust.

Because excessive charges can be an area of great conflict, the Housing Act 1996 specifies that a tenant can apply to a Leasehold Valuation Tribunal (LVT) for a 'certificate of reasonableness'. He or she can also apply to determine whether insurance premiums are excessive. The fees for a hearing at an LVT are set at a reasonable level and tenants are not liable for costs if they lose their case.

Further, tenants can also apply to an LVT to appoint a manager, provided that they can show unreasonable service charges, a failure to comply with a code of conduct, or a failure to meet the lease's obligations and the tribunal is satisfied that it would be just to grant the order.

12.3   Service charges under the Commonhold and Leasehold Reform Act 2002 – leaseholders' new rights

The 2002 Act introduces a number of changes to leaseholders' rights with regard to service charges and introduces new rights to challenge unreasonable charges.

Landlords will have to furnish annual accounting statements regarding:

- sums paid into a service charge fund
- standing in credit of the service charge fund
- costs incurred by the landlord.

Do note: leaseholders will be able to withhold service charges if this requirement has not been met.

In addition:

- Landlords will have to give leaseholders a summary of their rights and obligations regarding the service charges with the accounting statement
- Leaseholders will be entitled to inspect documentation relating to the accounting statements within 21 days of their request, as well as to take copies at reasonable cost
- Leaseholders will be able to challenge service charges before an LVT even if the amount has already been paid to the landlord, provided that the amount has not been agreed or admitted
- Landlords will have to hold service charges funds in designated separate client accounts and furnish proof to this effect; and leaseholders can withhold service charges if there are reasonable grounds for believing that the landlord is not complying with this requirement
- Leaseholders can inspect the insurance policy for the insurance of their building; and they will be able to take copies of the insurance policy
- The existing definition of 'service charge' will be extended to cover improvements, and allow it to be further extended by regulations, if necessary
- Leaseholders can challenge unreasonable administration charges payable under a lease.

The Act aims to simplify and strengthen the rights that leaseholders have to be consulted, by:

a) ensuring that landlords consult leaseholders before entering into contracts for more than a period of 12 months which are for more than a prescribed sum (subject to certain exceptions, which will be prescribed by regulation following consultation). Failure to consult where required would mean that the amount in excess of the prescribed amount could not be recovered from leaseholders;

b) introducing new powers which will allow procedures to be followed where landlords are required to consult on major works (an existing requirement). The new Act will give a power to set the 'prescribed amount' in regulations (landlords do not have to consult on major works which cost less than the prescribed amount). Failure to comply would mean that the amount in excess of the prescribed amount would be irrecoverable.

The Act also introduces a new right for tenants subject to an Estate Management Scheme to challenge the reasonableness of charges levied under that scheme at an LVT.

12.3.1 The 'right to manage'

This is a new power, which is to be given to tenants by the Commonhold and Leasehold Reform Act 2002 to manage their own block without having to prove fault on the landlord's part or without the need to buy the freehold.

Do note: the provisions in the Act which relate to the right to manage require detailed regulations which have yet to go through a public consultation exercise. Thereafter the regulations will require drafting before coming in to force.

12.3.2 The criteria

- The building must be self-contained and contain at least two flats
- Two-thirds of the flats must be held by long leaseholders, i.e. those who bought leases of 21 years or more; and
- No more than 25 per cent of the internal floor areas (excluding common areas) are to be in non-residential or business use.

12.3.3 The Right To Manage company (RTM)

A private company must be set up by the tenants, and limited by guarantee: the Right To Manage Company. All qualifying tenants would not only be entitled to be members, but must be specifically invited to participate.

A formal notice must then be served on the landlord, who will also have a share in the RTM company.

The company's articles and memorandum will be governed by regulations, and provisions which are inconsistent with the regulations will have no effect.

A claim notice will then be served upon the landlord and a managing agent, if any, of the tenants' intention to take over the management functions through the RTM company.

Thereafter the steps must follow the statutory procedures as laid down in the Commonhold and Leasehold Reform Act 2002. For details concerning the public consultation exercise on the RTM company, contact the Commonhold Team at the Lord Chancellor's Department (see DIRECTORY on page 215).

7 BUYING AND SELLING YOUR HOME

In the chapter on *Landlords and their Tenants*, you can see that the law regards transactions which involve the buying and selling of property as different from other transactions which involve the buying and selling of ordinary goods. Most importantly, the law insists on certain formalities in buying and selling land embodied in a process known as 'conveying' property, or conveyancing.

This is because different transactions in a single property may have taken place over centuries. Thus each house, and the plot of land on which it is built, has its own history. That history will determine whether the property is freehold or leasehold, is registered or unregistered, unencumbered or encumbered with other people's rights over it.

Because of the complexity of the tasks involved in buying and selling property, as well as the sums of money entailed, people generally use professionals, such as conveyancers and surveyors, to assist them. Their duties will vary according to the terms of their contract although certain procedures are generally standardised.

The scale of the commitment alone involved in owning our own home should ensure that we use reliable professional persons wherever necessary and that we ensure, as far as possible, that they – in turn – exercise the care expected of them. Indeed the more we can understand of the negotiations and transaction in advance, the better position we are in to know that our own interests are being safeguarded. After all, buying or selling our home is usually the biggest financial transaction we ever undertake and entering into a mortgage entails us in a large debt which can last 20 to 25 years – a substantial part of any adult lifetime!

Concerns have been expressed at the way in which such major transactions may be conducted to the detriment of the consumer. Some of the anxiety surrounds how the deals are financed; others voice doubts over technical matters, in particular that the conveyancing process itself is both tardy and fraught with delay for both buyer and seller.

The year 2002 was a landmark year for the enactment of legislation which concerns property law. For centuries, land in this country was held by either leaseholders or freeholders. Now a 'third way' of owning and managing property has been introduced, viz. *commonhold*. The Commonhold and Leasehold Reform Act 2002 intends to give the benefit to leaseholders enjoyed by freeholders, that is the right to own their property in perpetuity. It is also intended to give those who live or work in separate but inter-dependent properties that share common parts, the right to enforce positive covenants (such as to keep your property in good repair). The term 'common parts' covers a broad spectrum, from just a common entrance and stairwell, or a shop with a storehouse on another plot, to a considerable area such as an estate with its own roads, communal gardens, and a separate garage block. Eventually, it is hoped that all new property developments (e.g. a block of flats, a shopping precinct or a housing estate) will adopt the commonhold concept.

Many of the aspects of the Act are under consultation at the time of writing, particularly with regard to the company set-up which is to run the commonhold association for each property development (see section 1.5.3 below). The Act represents a truly critical break with the past and with our unique property laws, and only in practice will we be able to tell its effects in both the short and the long term.

Another significant statute is the Land Registration Act 2002. It is hoped that electronic conveyancing introduced by this Act will streamline and speed up the process of home transfers. Within a decade contracts, transfers, leases and mortgages could be replaced by virtual documents. Instead of handwritten signatures the relevant documents could incorporate electronic signatures and lawyers could have direct access to Land Registry records in order to view a client's title and input new data. We will have to wait and see whether the Act fulfils expectations. The test will be whether it saves time and money and whether it operates effectively and safely (see also section 5.8.2 below). The Land Registry's consultation exercise on the detailed planning of the system is expected to be concluded in the summer of 2003.

New technology is already being used to improve conveyancing practice: the online National Land Information Service (NLIS) draws together information about land from a variety of sources to provide a one-stop shop for anyone carrying out searches and enquiries. It is also possible to access Land Registry records through Land Registry Direct which provides details of 18 million registered titles and allows you to order official copies and to carry out electronic searching.

The NLIS is in the first year of operation – over a quarter of a million searches of all types have been processed so far. Over 1,500 solicitors and conveyancing firms have signed up to the new service.

In this chapter we deal with the following:

- choosing a home – the basic information
- employing professional services
- raising finance
- minding the pitfalls
- selling your property.

1   CHOOSING A HOME – THE BASIC INFORMATION

The factors which will influence your choice are manifold: you may be looking for a home because you are relocated in your job; you may have moved in with a partner; you may be wanting to start a family, or to retire. Property transactions may also be prompted by circumstances directly connected to legal issues, such as a death or divorce, which are dealt with elsewhere in this book.

In all cases, however, your choice should be governed by what you can afford. Would-be purchasers are thus generally advised to go first to the lending institution of their choice to establish whether they could be given a 'loan in principle' and, if so, for what amount. This assists greatly in setting limits to the price range at which they can comfortably afford to buy (see *Raising the finance*, section 3).

1.1   Getting to know the locality

Again your choice will generally be determined by the reason for your purchase: if you need to get to work, accessibility may be a main consideration. If you are moving because of your children's needs, you may be attracted by the reputation of the schools in the neighbourhood.

Note: always remember that localities vary even within a very narrow area. Your house may have greater value if it is in one street rather than another; if it is at the end of a terrace rather than in the middle; and so forth.

There are several ways of trying to find a property. The suggestion is to use all of them: going to local estate agents (see section 2.1 below); reading the local papers; speaking to people in the area which you have chosen, e.g. local shopkeepers, publicans, or even residents in a street which you have visited. A new and increasingly popular way of trying to establish details of a locality, in order to save legwork and unnecessary effort in your investigations, is via the Internet (see section 2.8 below). You can establish property prices, the availability of local schools and how they fare in school league tables, and council tax rates as well as crime and health statistics, before making visits to your chosen area.

1.2   Registered or unregistered land

As stated in the introduction, land carries with it its own history. Not all land in England and Wales is yet registered. However three-quarters of property is 'registered property' i.e. registered at the Land Registry. This is a body which was set up in 1925 to keep a register of ownership.

The Land Registry Index Map indicates which properties are registered and which are not. It is necessary to inspect this Index Map to establish whether or not a particular property is registered and, if it is, to obtain the title number of the property.

For a fee, the Land Registry will provide the name and address of the registered owner and/or will provide a copy of the register and/or the title plan.

The Land Registry has changed its policy on requisitions, cancellation and the rejection of applications for registration as a result of customer criticism that it should take a firmer line when applications are not lodged in good order. The Registry has produced two leaflets to help customers with the new procedures which can be downloaded from *www.landreg.gov.uk*.

1.2.1 Registered land

The register is in four parts, comprising:

- *the property register* – which describes the property
- *the proprietorship register* – which registers the name of the proprietor [owner]
- *the charges register* – which contains mortgage details and restrictive covenants; it also contains charges, e.g. under the divorce legislation (see chapter on *Divorce*, section 8.1)
- *the filed plan* – which shows the location of the land and its boundaries (see, however, section 1.4 below, as well as the chapter on *Neighbours*, section 3).

The Land Registry will issue a certificate stating who is the registered proprietor. This is proof of ownership and the title is guaranteed by the State.

This certificate becomes the *title deeds* to the property. The Land Registry issues a number of explanatory leaflets, in particular Leaflet 15, which is a guide to the information it holds and how to obtain it.

All land is due to be registered by law. Whether or not a property is registered can be established by contacting the Land Registry for that area. The form is obtainable from the Land Registry (Form 096) and has to be filled in and sent to the Land Registry. The service is free of charge.

☞ *You have seen a very desirable house in a rural location. You think that you may be able to afford to buy it and wish to proceed with the transaction. You were introduced to the ostensible owner of the house through a mutual friend. This friend now tells you that the person you are dealing with may not be the true owner of the property. What do you do?*

You can write to the Land Registry of the area to enquire whether the property is registered. If you are not satisfied with the reply, or if the property is not yet registered, you would be well advised to seek legal advice before proceeding any further (see also section 4.1.2 below).

1.2.2 Unregistered land

Where you are interested in a property that has not been registered, you can only establish who owns it through a search of the title deeds – a task generally entrusted to your professional adviser.

The owner of unregistered land will have a bundle of deeds which form a record of previous sales, mortgages and other dealings with the land. However, if the land is mortgaged, the lender will normally hold the deeds as security for their loan. There is usually no public record of the information contained in the deeds.

However, in Middlesex and the Yorkshire Ridings, Deeds Registries were set up prior to land registration which kept records of certain land transactions, but the deeds were registered against the names of the parties involved, rather than by address. To make a search of a Deeds Registry you need to know the name of the current owner of the property.

The Land Charges Department maintains a record of restrictive covenants, rights and mortgages relating to unregistered land. These are registered against the name of the land owner at the time the entry was made, rather than against the land or property (see section 1.2.3 immediately below).

If you want to find out about a restrictive covenant registered before you bought your property, you need to search against the name of the owner at the time the covenant was registered.

1.2.3 Establishing the interests of other people in a property

The Land Charges Register documents the charges [i.e. other people's interests in the property] on unregistered land. These include a bank charge on the property to secure its loan, as well as certain other charges, notably the right of a wife to occupy the matrimonial home in the event of a marriage break-down, now known as matrimonial home rights (see chapter on *Divorce*, section 8.1). It may also document restrictive covenants and other rights, e.g. right of way on the property – and also bankruptcy searches against the vendor and registration of judgment against him or her, if any.

1.3   Freehold or leasehold

The purchase of a home today is generally on a freehold basis. This gives you an 'absolute' title (right) to the property, in other words, you own both the house and the ground it stands on. No one has a title which is 'superior' to yours, i.e. can override yours. Freehold property is contrasted with leasehold property where, if you buy on a lease, there is a landlord above you who owns the freehold. (For the distinction between leasehold and freehold property, see chapter on *Landlords and their Tenants*, section 1.3.). In general, flats are bought on a long lease; their purchase is discussed in the chapter on *Landlords and their Tenants* in section 9.

However, as we shall see, the word 'absolute' can be misleading. Other people may have rights over your property even when you buy as freehold owner. A clear example is the right of a lender, such as a building society or bank to which borrowers 'charge' the property as security for their loan. This right entitles the lender to repossess if borrowers fail to meet their financial obligations (see section 3 below).

But there are other interests which may affect your absolute title: for example,

* a neighbour may have a right of way over your property;
  or
* your estranged wife may be living in the house with your children.

See also 1.4 immediately below.

1.4   Rights and liabilities

In theory, as a freehold owner you can do what you wish with your property, e.g. you can live in it or rent it out without anyone's permission. It can be left to a person named in your will. You can decide whether or not to spend the money on improvements or maintenance. You may want to change the internal layout of the house or to change the layout of the garden. You may decide to put up a wall or fence or build a garage on the land.

In practice, however, the rights of a homeowner are much curtailed.

You will be liable to:

* the planning authorities for any development of your property in breach of planning laws
* the local authority for any offence under the Environment Acts – e.g. you cannot let your property fall into such a state of disrepair as would endanger the wellbeing of others
* the planning authorities if you decide to use your property in an unauthorised way – e.g. to use some of the rooms as a clinic
* previous owners, if you have undertaken certain restrictive covenants, e.g. a covenant against subdividing the plot of land
* next-door neighbours if they have, for example, a right of way over your land
* the building society or the bank which lent you money to buy the property (their vested interest in the property maintaining its value is clear)
* the local authority if you were in breach of building regulations even for internal changes to your home (see also the chapters on *Neighbours* and *The Countryside*).

☞ *You have recently bought a house and you are intent on using the strip of land at the side of your property to build a garage. You have been told that this does not constitute 'development' under the planning legislation. You begin to dig the foundations. Your next door neighbour approaches you and says that he has been using that strip of land as a short cut to the field at the back of both your houses. You wonder whether you should continue with your plans despite his objections.*

You may have a serious problem on your hands. The question of a right of way of others over your property should have been brought to your attention before you purchased the property. You would be well advised to ask your conveyancer to check again the documents of title, in particular the information received from the seller before you completed your purchase, and the Land Registration documentation (see also sections 4 below and 1.2.1 above).

1.5   Estate management

Certain residential developments have estate management schemes in order to ensure that the standard and amenities of the estate are maintained – for example, that the properties are regularly redecorated and the common parts are decently maintained. They may include a duty to contribute to the upkeep of roads on the estate.

The schemes may be sustained by long leaseholds or by corporate management. See sections 1.5.1 and 1.5.2 below.

A new system of landholding, viz. commonhold, has been introduced in order to deal with the question of the maintenance of interdependent, freehold property; see section 1.5.3 below.

1.5.1   Long leaseholds

These are usually for very extensive periods such as 999 years. Nonetheless, each purchaser of a home on the estate becomes, in effect, a leaseholder and is not a freehold owner. This is because leases are generally used as a means to ensure that covenants in the lease can be regularly enforced. For example, the freehold owner of a house cannot be compelled to paint his property at regular intervals. However, when you buy a property on a long lease, covenants in the lease, such as an obligation to redecorate the outside, or to mow your front lawn, are enforceable against you.

1.5.2   Corporate management

This is another means to achieve the same goal, viz. to ensure that the external appearance of an estate, and the individual properties in it, are well maintained. A management company is set up with each property owner holding a share in the company. That share cannot be sold to anyone other than another purchaser of a property on the estate.

The houses are freehold, but the owners covenant with the management company to keep their properties in good repair. There are usually other covenants, too, such as not using the premises for business purposes, not putting up signboards, etc.

Each shareholder undertakes to pay the management company a service fee to be levied annually in accordance with audited accounts. In turn, the management company undertakes to maintain the common parts, such as communal gardens, lighting etc.

1.5.3   Commonhold

The Government enacted measures in 2002 for a new form of landholding, to be known as 'commonhold'. This is an entirely new concept of owning and managing property in this country although it does exist in other jurisdictions.

The Act envisages that each separate entity in commonhold property will be called a unit. It might be a flat, a house, a shop, or a development containing more than one kind of unit, e.g. shops on the ground floor with flats above. The owner of each unit, known as the unit-holder, will have a share in a private company limited by guarantee, known as the commonhold association. Thus the unit-holder will have two interests in the property: the direct interest in the unit which he or she owns, e.g. a house on an estate, and a company member's interest in the commonhold association that owns the common parts, which could include the roads, garage block etc.

The scheme resembles freehold ownership in that it gives to the unit-holder:

- a title in perpetuity, and
- freedom from a landlord.

The commonhold association will own those parts of the development that will not be separately owned, and the association will be run by a private company limited by guarantee. It would be possible to add to or to diminish the size of the development by purchase or sale of common parts, and the documents for the companies would be subject to memoranda and articles of association with some flexibility allowed for unique features in a particular case. At the time of writing a consultation process is under way seeking views on the setting up, running and ending of a commonhold scheme, according to a press release of the Commonhold Team in the Lord Chancellors Department (for details see DIRECTORY on page 215).

Apart from the benefit of owning property where time is not a factor (i.e. the disadvantage of leases is that they run out in time), the intention behind commonhold is also to overcome the problems which exist because positive covenants, e.g. a requirement to maintain the outside of a property to a requisite standard, or to repair a wall, cannot be imposed upon freehold owners. The only way this could be done before the Act was by selling property on long leases and making charges for maintenance a term in the lease. Commonhold is intended to be available for all forms of interdependent developments but for those where former leaseholders have already acquired the freehold to their properties, there will have to be 100 per cent agreement for conversion (see chapter on *Landlords and the Tenants*, section 10.2).

For the distinction between positive and negative covenants, see the chapters on *Neighbours*, section 7.1 and on *Landlords and their Tenants*, section 2.1.

1.6   Buying a newly built home

Each major developer offers its own schemes to attract buyers of 'new build' homes and it is not the purpose of the section to discuss these schemes. However, while certain elements in conveyancing will remain the same, e.g. investigation into rights of way or title, there are other elements which are specific to the transactions involved in buying such houses. Particular heed should also be paid to the question of boundaries when buying a home in a new development (see section 4.5.1 below).

1.6.1   Guarantees

New homes come with a guarantee which provides insurance against major damage arising from structural defects. The normal guarantee period is 10 years.

Note of warning: it is important that you study the terms of the insurance carefully.

* You should refer to the policy of insurance itself when you do so and not just to the policy summary
* you should take note of the policy limitations, e.g. buyers are still under obligation to maintain and repair their properties.

1.6.2   Better access to new homes – the Disability Discrimination Act 1996

Guidance has been issued by the Government to help house builders and local authorities to implement new building regulations to improve access to new homes. The extension of the building regulations requires the provision of easily accessible entrances to new homes. Steps up to and into homes pose the single greatest barrier to access for wheelchair users and people with limited mobility. The guidance suggests design solutions for overcoming this whilst minimising the risk of water entering the building and avoiding conflict with the other aspects of the building regulations. The measures will require that properties have wider doorways and others features to accommodate not only wheelchairs users, but the elderly and mothers with pushchairs.

Further, under the Disability Discrimination Act 1996 it is against the law for a seller of property to discriminate unreasonably against the disabled, for example by discouraging their presence by offering property at a higher price. However, vendors are not required to make adjustments to their properties to make them accessible to the disabled.

2   EMPLOYING PROFESSIONAL SERVICES

2.1   Estate agents

The seller employs the estate agent (this is dealt with in section 5 below as well as in the chapter on *Goods and Services*, section 5.7). As a buyer, therefore, you are not strictly 'employing' an estate agent when you go into his office and ask for particulars of the house you may be interested in purchasing. Nonetheless, your relationship with the estate agent does have legal implications.

2.1.1   Particulars of property

An estate agent will generally have prepared particulars (or details) of the property. These will include, among other matters, an indication of the size of the rooms, and will generally point to special features of the house and/or garden.

The law has become more rigorous in making demands on estate agents to curb the extravagance of their language.

2.1.1(a) The criminal law

Under the Property Misdescriptions Act 1991, an estate agent is liable to be prosecuted if he or she misdescribes a property, that is, makes 'a misleading statement ... in the course of estate agency business'.

2.1.1(b) Printed particulars and disclaimers

However, for those people who might buy on the basis of a misleading statement, it is probably more important to establish whether you can sue for damages than whether or not the agent is guilty of a criminal offence.

It is established law that an estate agent owes a 'duty of care' to a seller in discharging his duties. After all, it is the seller who is going to pay him his commission (see also *Selling your home*, section 5 below).

However, at this stage, we are concerned with the position with regard to a buyer who goes ahead with a purchase on the basis of misleading particulars. Does the agent owe him a duty of care too?

☞ *You have seen a house with a lovely stretch of ground attached. The estate agent tells you that the ground is about an acre in extent. The written particulars repeat this measurement. In fact the grounds are only about half an acre. However, on the basis of the representation, and without undertaking an independent survey, you buy the property. You discover your mistake and sue the agent for damages.*

> In a case, with very similar facts, the appeal court decided that the estate agent could rely on the disclaimer which appeared below the printed particulars.

These disclaimers are usually in standard format and state that the agent takes no responsibility for the description of the property, which is for guidance only. It is for the purchaser to satisfy himself of the accuracy of the particulars which are not guaranteed and do not form part of any contract.

2.1.1(c) Misconduct by Estate Agents

The Director General of Fair Trading can bar from estate agency work anyone who has been convicted of certain specified offences such as fraud or other dishonesty or violence; or who has committed racial or sexual discrimination in the course of estate agency work; or who has failed to comply with the requirements placed on estate agents by the Estate Agents Act 1979.

'Estate agency work' means introducing to someone else a person who wishes to buy, sell or lease land or property, and being involved in negotiating the subsequent deal. The work must be in the course of business but does not include acting as a letting agent.

A single case of malpractice can result in being banned. One case was brought by a firm of estate agents, who claimed that two of its own employees had made a secret arrangement with a potential buyer. The two were to receive £5,000 each for recommending an offer of £950,000 to the seller and misrepresenting the details of the offer to him. After the contracts had been exchanged, but before completion, the property was advertised for auction by the purchaser, with a reserve price of £1 to £1.2 million. It was in fact sold for £1.2 million before the auction, generating a profit to the purchaser on the resale of £250,000 less expenses and stamp duty.

The Court of Appeal held that a single such misrepresentation was sufficient to amount to undesirable practice under the law.

Note: this ruling should ensure greater protection for consumers. The Office of Fair Trading should be able to take more effective action to ban or warn rogue estate agents (see also 2.1.7 below).

2.1.2 Negotiations

The agent's task goes further than merely showing you various properties.

☞ *You have been dealing with a firm of estate agents for some months while you search for a new house. You have been put on their mailing list and have been taken to view several properties by the agent. You have now found the house you are looking for and you would like to make an offer.*

> The agent will get in touch with the seller and will have a very good idea of the price which the seller will accept. Your offer should be made to the agent and can be made orally. If you put it in writing, your letter must be headed 'Offer Subject to Contract' .

☞ *You suggest a price to the agent but can tell from his response that he thinks the offer is on the low side. You are concerned that he will not pass the offer on to the seller.*

An agent is obliged by law to pass on to a seller all offers which are made to him unless they are below the seller's stipulated minimum price.

2.1.3 Deposits

Agents do sometimes ask for an initial deposit after you have made an offer which the seller has accepted in principle.

☞ *The agent asks you for a ten per cent deposit of the agreed price as an indication of your seriousness about an offer you have made on a house. You want to know whether to hand over the money.*

Agents, acting for the seller, can ask for a deposit. You may be advised to pay it to the agent. However, do note:

- the money should be kept in a clients' account
- it must be returned to you if the deal does not go through (unlike a deposit paid on exchange of contracts (see below)
- you must consult your conveyancer before agreeing to hand over any money.

The sum suggested of ten per cent in the example above is too large in any event; a maximum of five per cent should be sufficient as evidence of your serious intentions.

2.1.4 Other estate agency services

Estate agents are often in a position to offer to find an institution willing to lend money as an advance on property purchases (see *Raising the finance*, section 3 below). There is no reason why you should not take advantage of such an offer if it suits you.

If, on the other hand, it does not suit you, for example because you already have the finance arranged, then you ought to decline the offer. The level of service which you can expect should not be affected by the fact that you have turned down these services from the estate agent.

Certain estate agency chains are themselves part of the overall business of big lenders such as banks or insurance companies. However, the tie-in of mortgages to insurance, as a system of 'one-stop' shopping, has been criticised as not always providing the client with a sufficiently free choice (see, for example section 3.3.3 below).

2.1.5 Mailshots

Estate agents are under a duty when encouraging people to use their services, to do so in a way which is not misleading or unethical.

☞ *You have put your house on sale with a local firm of estate agents, ABC. You now receive an unsolicited letter from another local estate agency, XYZ. The letter states that it has several purchasers who are expressly intent on buying a property in your street. When you ask for details of these would-be purchasers, it transpires that it is mere advertising hyperbole.*

Marketing letters and canvassing material are governed by the Control of Misleading Advertisement Regulations 1988. Mailshots should not convey a false impression, as in this case, that certain persons have registered an interest with the estate agency to purchase property as described in the letter.

2.1.6 Cold-calling

If an estate agent sends you unsolicited details of a property in which you might be interested, he cannot later claim a fee if you decide to purchase the property.

☞ *An estate agent, Derek, sent a letter, by way of a cold-calling exercise, to a would-be purchaser, Sandra, with information about a property that might be of interest. The letter set out the fees payable to Derek in the event of a successful sale. When she received the letter, Sandra viewed the property, made an offer, and bought it. Derek then claimed for his commission fee.*

In a similar case, the Appeal Court held that the information provided in a cold-calling letter was 'past consideration' that could not support a contract between an agent and a subsequent purchaser. The letter could not be read as an offer to provide information in return for a fee if a sale went ahead. There was no sufficiently clear offer to be accepted and no agreement had been made.

2.1.7 Complaining about an estate agent

Although an estate agent's contract is with the seller, if you have a complaint, either as a buyer or as a seller, you should first try to resolve it with the agency or through its professional association (if the firm is a member of one). It the matter still cannot be settled, contact the trading standards department of your local council.

There is also an Ombudsman for Estate Agents who will consider a complaint and has the authority to award compensation, if the case merits it.

Warning: not all estate agents are members of the scheme so do check carefully about an agent's membership before entering into a contract.

The Office of Fair Trading (OFT) has the power to ban an estate agent from estate agency work. In a recent case, an individual was banned after being convicted of conspiracy to defraud. After considering representations, an adjudicator appointed by the Director of Fair Trading determined that the estate agent was unfit to carry on estate agency work.

The Director of Fair Trading stated that the ban demonstrated that the OFT will use its powers where there is evidence of the need to do so in order to protect the housing market.

2.1.8 OEA Code of Practice

The Ombudsman for Estate Agents (OEA) was set up in 1998 to increase the opportunity for dissatisfied house buyers and sellers to have access to a free, fair and wholly independent complaints procedure. As at May 2002 a total of 2,489 offices from 12 corporate estate agencies, and 1,737 offices from 753 independent firms had signed up to the scheme.

On 28 October 2002, the Office of Fair Trading (OFT) announced a new code of practice agreed with the OEA. The provisions of the code are mandatory on member agencies and it has received the personal endorsment of the Director General of Fair Trading.

This is the first stage of a two-stage process towards achieving full OFT approval. The OFT will monitor the code and evaluate its effectiveness. The OEA has to show that it safeguards and promotes consumers' interests before it receives full approval.

At the time of writing much work is still required to implement the new code but the OEA plans to achieve full implementation in the first quarter of 2003.

One of the most significant changes is that access to independent redress is specifically included within the new code, thus distinguishing it from the codes of other bodies within the estate agency sector.

2.1.8(a) How will your complaint be dealt with?

The OEA can only deal with a complaint against one of its members and you must go through the in-house complaints-handling procedure of the member agent concerned before the OEA will start to investigate your complaint. This is to give you and the agent a chance to try and resolve the problem between yourselves.

If you cannot reach a settlement independently, the OEA will send you a complaint form and some guidance notes to help you to frame your complaint. A case officer will then review your complaint and his or her conclusions are seen by the Ombudsman himself.

The Ombudsman will always consider, and actively promote and support, any opportunity for a mediated settlement. If the agent has made you a goodwill offer by way of settlement, which you have rejected, the Ombudsman will consider whether the offer represents appropriate compensation for your complaint.

Note: if the estate agent has already made you a financial offer by way of settling your dispute, that offer lapses if you refer your complaint to the OEA. It may or may not be reinstated. The Ombudsman will come to an independent judgment on the matter.

If the Ombudsman agrees with your complaint he can make an award of up to £25,000.

Members of the OEA scheme have agreed to abide by any award made provided that you accept it in full and final settlement of the complaint.

If you are dissatisfied with the Ombudsman's recommendation, your legal rights have not been restricted in any way and you still have recourse to the courts or any other avenue of redress.

2.2 Surveyors

Any person who buys a house should not just be tempted by its appearance. In fact, any recent redecoration could hide a multitude of faults! If you borrow money to finance the purchase, a lender will insist upon a survey for his own valuation purposes (see 2.2.1(a) below).

In giving instructions to your own surveyor, do make crystal clear your requirements of what you expect from the property.

☞ *You saw the house of your dreams in the heart of the countryside. There appeared to be only one question-mark over the transaction – the house was about 15 miles from Gatwick airport. You wanted to be reasonably sure that the property was not seriously affected by noise from passing aircraft overhead, so you specifically asked the surveyor about aircraft noise.*

In his report, the surveyor reassuringly wrote that although some planes would inevitably cross the area, it was unlikely that the property would suffer greatly from noise. Soon after moving in you discover that the property is not far away from a navigation beacon, that aircraft stack up during busy periods waiting to land, that they frequently pass directly over the house, and their impact on the tranquillity of your 'dream home' was marked.

You wonder what your position is.

The court would agree that the surveyor had been negligent. However, the argument, in a similar case, concerned whether the buyer was entitled to damages for inconvenience and discomfort – instead of the pleasure and peace of mind he expected when he moved in to his new home.

The House of Lords accepted that the general rule was that a claimant could only recover for financial loss. However, where a professional person undertook a specific obligation to exercise reasonable care to investigate a matter (in this case aircraft noise) which was important to the customer, he or she was under a duty to carry out that investigation thoroughly.

In the present case, the surveyor could have carried out his instructions by checking the position with Gatwick. Had he been informed of the true position, the claimant would not have bought the property. He was accordingly entitled to damages for the distress and loss of enjoyment he suffered – and continued to suffer – as a result of the purchase.

2.2.1 Different types of valuation and survey

There are five different types of survey which are generally available for potential homebuyers.

2.2.1(a) Mortgage valuation report

A building society or other lender will insist upon its own valuation to establish whether, if the borrower defaults, the property will realise the amount of the loan on a sale.

Although the buyer pays for the surveyor's services, the primary purpose is to protect the lender. The lender often shows the contents of the report to the buyer but is not obliged to do so. The buyer is generally warned that the purpose of the valuation of the house is a limited one and is told that it may be prudent to obtain a more detailed report (section 2.2.1(b) immediately below).

Nonetheless, it is accepted that buyers, particularly at the cheaper end of the market, often do rely on the valuation report although it ordinarily involves no more than a brief inspection. If the valuation is free you may not get to see a copy of the report.

Note: it is also accepted law that the surveyors – even though instructed by the building society – owe a duty of care to the buyer to carry out their inspection with reasonable skill and care and not overlook any obvious defect.

2.2.1(b) House Buyer's Report and Valuation

This is a more thorough report, containing more detail and information, than a mere valuation for a lender's purposes mentioned above. It also costs more though the fee is still moderate. It is presented in a standard easy-to-follow format and clients can see a copy of the blank form beforehand.

Should the House Buyers' Report reveal a serious problem, a buyer should not proceed without a structural survey.

2.2.1(c) Structural survey

This is used where the buyer requires the most rigorous survey of the property. As a general rule such surveys are only really necessary for properties over 100-years-old or which are in a bad state of repair.

☞ *You have recently seen a house which is more than three hundred years old. You have been told by a friend, who is a builder, that it is likely to need underpinning to support the front beams.*

You would be well advised to pay the extra cost involved in obtaining a structural survey before proceeding with your purchase.

Specialists can also be called in for reports on problems such as woodworm, tree roots or rising damp.

2.2.1(d) Environmental survey

This is a more limited type of survey which analyses whether the house you are interested in is built on a site that may pose a health or environmental hazard.

2.2.1(e) Energy audit

This rates the energy efficiency of the house and suggests improvements. It may be included as part of a homebuyer's report or building survey.

2.3 Conveyancers

Solicitors or licensed conveyancers are involved in various stages of the house-buying process and generally act for:

- the seller
- the mortgage lender
- the buyer.

(For further details on licensed conveyancers, see section 2.5 below.)

2.3.1 Acting for the parties

1) Often the buyer uses the same solicitor as the one used by the lender to arrange the loan. While it does lead to a saving in costs, it can also lead to a situation where a conflict of interest may arise. For example, if you use a firm of solicitors which is regularly used by a big mortgage lender, such as a building society, the solicitors might be more concerned to protect the interests of their bigger client than your own interests. However, in other cases, the lenders themselves have sued the solicitors for failing to pass on to them information which would have influenced their decision on whether or not to grant a loan to a particular borrower.

2) Quite often, you will be buying one house and, at the same time, selling your present home. You will no doubt use the same conveyancer to effect both transactions so that the two deals can be tied up simultaneously.

3) It is definitely not advisable to use the same person or firm to act for buyer and seller of the same property. A dispute could arise with the seller, and you would want your conveyancer to act in your interests alone.

4) You can do your own conveyancing yourself but this is only advised in the most straightforward of circumstances.

☞ *You have a friend who is a designer. He says that he did his own conveyancing when he bought his house and is happy to assist you in the transfer of the flat which you intend buying. He says that he will charge you only a small fee.*

While buyers can do their own conveyancing (although this is not advised with leasehold property), you should not pay anyone, other than a solicitor or licensed conveyancer, to do it for you.

2.3.2 Instructions

If you have seen a house which you wish to purchase, you will then in all likelihood instruct your conveyancer to act for you. This entails setting the agenda: see section 2.3.3 below.

Beware: there is no binding agreement with the seller until you actually exchange contracts. You might, however, endeavour to enter into a 'lock out agreement' for a short period (see section 5.4 below).

2.3.3 Setting the agenda

2.3.3(a) Fees

Do establish a fee with your conveyancer in advance. It is always a good idea to ascertain what the fee will cover, e.g. disbursements etc. It may be a fixed fee but is usually on a percentage basis of the price of the transaction.

Conveyancers have been steadily reducing their fees so that it would be in your interest to shop around. However, in a transaction which involves so much money, you should not sacrifice quality of service for the sake of small savings.

2.3.3(b) Timetable

Conveyancing is generally considered a slow process, but it need not be one. If you are in a hurry to exchange contracts and to complete, do give your conveyancer a firm indication of time scale.

Certain searches can be accelerated, for an extra charge, by the local authority.

The time taken to buy a house could be cut substantially under government plans for electronic conveyancing introduced by the Land Registration Act 2002. This is intended to help curb 'gazumping', i.e. the practice whereby a seller agrees a sale at one price but subsequently accepts a higher offer from a different purchaser before exchange of contract. This can not only be profoundly disappointing but also costly in wasted solicitor's and surveyor's fees, etc.

It is also hoped that electronic conveyancing will enable obstacles to be identified in the transaction because all the relevant information on a particular house purchase would be on computer and available to all interested parties.

Where a client neither needs a mortgage nor requires a survey, a solicitor can achieve a swift deal between receiving instructions to buy a property and the exchange of contracts. In such a case, the seller's solicitors must have all the papers ready, including an updated local search.

Take heed: obtaining a search certificate from the local authority as soon as the property is put on the market may not always be that helpful. By the time an acceptable offer is made that search may no longer be relevant and the cost of the search wasted.

See also section 5.7.

2.3.3(c) Additional precautions

Try to think ahead about matters which might cause problems at a later stage. Prevention is always better (and cheaper!) than cure. Many of these issues are dealt with in section 4 below.

An obvious matter to ensure is, for example, that you receive from the seller's conveyancer a list of fixtures and fittings which go with the purchase. You do not want to have a wrangle at a later stage with the seller over whether or not he was entitled to remove the light fittings prior to completion, or the rose bushes!

'Fixtures and fittings', which usually are included in a sale, must be distinguished from 'chattels', which are usually not included (see section 5.2.3 below).

2.4 The conveyancer's tasks

2.4.1 Carrying out searches

2.4.1(a) The preliminary enquiries

These involve:
- checking on the title of the seller (see section 4.1.2 below)
- obtaining a local land charges search
- obtaining answers from the seller on the property information form (PIF) – see section 5.2 below.

Many of these procedures are today standardised to make the process of conveyancing easier. The Law Society has its own national scheme, using procedures and documentation for this purpose known as TransAction (the Seller's Property Information Form).

2.4.1(b) Ensuring that you are in funds

Your conveyancer must ensure that the mortgage offer from the building society or bank has been approved and is ready for take-up on exchange of contracts.

Warning notice: never rush into a transaction on the say-so of a broker that the mortgage is 'sure to be OK'. You must have an approved offer of the loan in writing before proceeding to exchange contracts – unless you are one of the lucky few who would have the cash to pay for the property in full if the mortgage is refused.

2.4.2 Drawing up a binding contract

Generally, your conveyancer will receive a draft contract forwarded to him from the conveyancer for the seller. Amendments can be made to it if need be and these must be sent back for approval. This process can take time.

Note of warning: it is very important to ascertain exactly what you are buying: questions of boundaries etc. are dealt with in section 4.5 below.

Since 1989, for a contract for the sale of land to be binding

- it must be written
- the written document must contain all the particulars
- it must be signed by both parties or
- identical documents must be signed by each party (the *exchange of contracts* – see immediately below).

However, in some circumstances an agreement can be binding even if it is not made in writing. The Appeal Court has ruled that it would enforce an agreement under which the purchaser of a house promised, only orally, to grant an interest in the property to another in exchange for his materials and services as a builder. The court took the view that although social policy wished to simplify conveyancing by requiring the certainty of a written document, that should not allow unscrupulous behaviour to prevail.

2.4.3 Exchange of contracts

Once each party signs and the contracts are exchanged, the contract becomes irrevocable.

Do note: Your solicitor can sign on your behalf. A deposit of ten per cent is immediately payable. A completion date will be set in the contract for the balance of the purchase price.

2.4.4 Insurance

As soon as contracts are exchanged, you become responsible for the property. If it burns down or is vandalised between exchange and completion, the risk and the loss will be yours. So you must ensure that your solicitor has arranged insurance cover for the buildings and/or any contents from the moment of exchange onwards. The Association of British Insurers issues helpful leaflets (see Property Law DIRECTORY at the end of this chapter).

Remember: this does not entitle the vendor to do what he likes with the property! He is considered as holding it in trust for you and must take proper care of it on your behalf until completion.

2.4.5 Liaison with the lenders

It is your conveyancer's task to draw up an account in preparation for completion and to ensure that the funds, from the bank or building society, have been transmitted into a client account. In turn, the conveyancer undertakes to the lending institution that the funds will only be applied for the purposes of that particular mortgage transaction.

2.4.6 Completion – the point at which the property changes hands

This will take place on the date specified. It involves the buyer handing over the balance of the purchase price and receiving the title deeds.

You are legally bound to complete the transaction. If you do not do so, the seller can retain the deposit. In certain cases, you may also find that the seller can use other legal weapons against you by suing for:

- specific performance, i.e. the court can order you to complete; or
- damages for a sum equivalent to the purchase price.

2.5   Licensed conveyancers

Licensed conveyancers undertake the same tasks as solicitors in relation to transferring property. They are also covered, as are solicitors, by professional insurance, and are governed by a professional code of conduct.

If you wish to find a licensed conveyancer practising in your area, you can write to the Council for Licensed Conveyancers (see Property Law DIRECTORY at the end of this chapter).

2.6   Auctioneers

Property can be bought at auction (see also chapter on *Goods and Services*, section 4.5).

It is essential beforehand to:

- have the property surveyed before the auction
- inspect the documents at the offices of the conveyancer to the seller, including the preliminary answers to the Law Society Conditions of Sale and a local land charges search
- arrange finance.

Once the hammer falls on your bid price you are committed to the purchase.

This involves paying:

- ten per cent of the price there and then
- the balance within 28 days.

2.7   Negligence

Professional negligence claims involving surveyors and the legal profession are dealt with in the chapter on *Goods and Services,* section 5.6.

It is just worth noting here, therefore, that:

- solicitors are most often sued over failures in standard and routine conveyancing tasks, according to a survey of the Council of Mortgage Lenders
- surveyors tend to be sued for failure to report on a defect in the property and, in general by the lending institutions where the market is in decline, for over valuation.

☞ *Your surveyor failed to point out to you certain defects in the property which you purchased.*

You wonder what the relevant date is for the purposes of bringing an action for professional negligence. Is it the date on which the contracts were exchanged or when completion took place?

If you wish to sue on the basis of a negligent valuation report, your right to bring an action begins on the date when contracts were exchanged. That is considered the date when you acted on the report and suffered damage.

2.7.1   Time limits for professional negligence claims

The six-year period of time within which an action for professional negligence should be brought starts to run from the date when contracts are exchanged.

In one case, the purchasers exchanged contracts on a flat in Portsmouth relying on a valuation report written by a chartered surveyor. The report had been commissioned from the firm by the building society which was arranging a mortgage with the purchasers. After completion, defects came to light which the purchasers alleged should have been described in the report but were not. The Court of Appeal ruled that their action for damages was statute-barred because the writ was issued more than six years after completion, whereas time started to run from the date when contracts were exchanged.

The court stated that although the purchaser only received the property – in the sense of a legal estate – on completion, nonetheless he obtained a very real interest in the property on exchange – for example, he had to insure it (see section 2.4.5 above).

2.7.2 Settling disputes without going to court

All qualified surveyors should belong to a professional association such as the Royal Institute of Chartered Surveyors (RICS) (see DIRECTORY for details).

RICS has a complaints procedure and an arbitration scheme which is simpler and cheaper than going to court. You and the surveyor each prepare a report and the property is re-inspected if necessary. You can claim up to £50,000 if the property is shown to have a defect which means that it is worth less than you paid for it. The arbitrator's decision is legally binding on you both.

Note: this does not affect your right to redress in the courts if you are not happy with the arbitrator's recommendation, although you will need to show good reason why you think the award is wrong.

2.8 The Internet

With the development of new technology it is now possible to find your new home on the Internet. There are now many websites offering this and other connected services.

These 'one-stop' facilities can provide some or all of the following:

- an electronic search system allowing solicitors to process land- and other searches more quickly and easily
- a user-friendly public website, from which properties for rent or sale can be advertised
- conveyancing, surveying, mortgage and insurance products
- information on sellers' packs and mortgages, as outlined in the Government's homebuying and selling proposals
- a databank of demographic and other information, such as house prices and school league-tables, to assist buyers in moving house.

Solicitors' firms also offer interactive, online conveyancing, often at set fees. DIY conveyancing is also available online (see chapter on *The Legal System*, section 1.1.5).

3 RAISING THE FINANCE

Every purchaser has to decide for him or herself the most important matter of all, that is, how much to spend. A budget should be drawn up and both long-term and short-term expenditure calculated, to be set against the buyer's capital and income.

3.1.1 How much to borrow?

For a sole borrower, the lender will generally lend up to three times gross income. Thus if you have a salary of £20,000 per annum, you could expect a loan of £60,000, although with the low interest rates in recent years it is not unheard of for loan up to four or five times annual salary to be granted.

Mortgage lenders will take into account a partner's income. In such a case, the ratio will be two and a half times the joint income.

Note: these are only approximate figures: lending terms depend on a host of factors, personal to the borrower (e.g. job prospects) and particular to the property (e.g. its age, location and condition).

The Council of Mortgage Lenders' (CML) website has a mortgage repayment calculator which you can access online at the website: *www.cml.org.uk*.

There is also a range of leaflets which they have available on borrowing for mortgage purposes, notably, *You and Your Mortgage: The Mortgage Code* and *Mortgage Indemnity: A Borrower's Guide*.

3.1.1(a) The Mortgage Code

The CML produces a Mortgage Code which sets out the key commitments of both lenders and mortgage intermediaries on the marketing of mortgages. It also deals with advertising, advice on helping you to choose a mortgage, and the level of service provided.

3.1.1(b) European Code of Conduct

The European Code of Conduct officially came into effect on 30 September 2002. It is a voluntary initiative which was coordinated by the European Mortgage Federation together with other European Credit Sector Associations, representatives of consumer bodies and officials at the European Commission.

As the European Code is based on the UK's Mortgage Code, any UK lender which subscribes to the UK Code already substantially complies with the majority of the provisions of the European Code. However, a new feature of the European Code is that subscribers are required to provide an Information Sheet (ESIS) designed to help you compare different products across the EU.

An important part of a new regulatory regime for the UK, developed by the Financial Services Authority, is the provision to customers of a pre-application illustration (PAI). This sets out how a particular mortgage product would apply to the individual customer and the exact cost involved. The PAI should meet the requirements of the ESIS which – due to delay – will only be in force in 2004 (see also immediately below).

3.1.1(c) Regulated mortgage contracts

At present, the majority of secured loans made by CML members either exceed £25,000 or are for a purpose which is exempt from the provisions of the Consumer Credit Act 1974. They are currently, therefore, unregulated by that Act. However a significant number of them will, in due course, be regulated by the Financial Services Authority as 'regulated mortgage contracts'. The expected date for such regulation coming into force is October 2004 (see also section 3.2.1 below).

3.1.1(d) Co-ownership

With the continuing increase in house prices, many people simply cannot afford to buy a home solely out of their own income. However, they may decide to do so with a friend, or they may have money from a parent. More usually, however, the income of a partner forms an indispensable element in calculating how to repay a mortgage.

Note of warning: there can be considerable difficulties involved in a joint purchase – whether with a partner or a parent. Some are discussed in section 4.1 below. See also the chapter on *Setting up Home*, section 5.1.3(b). Liability for a mortgage can be both joint and individual.

3.2 The lending institutions

There was once a much clearer distinction between banks and building societies in relation to loans for housing. Banks lent money for all sorts of reasons; building societies lent money for house purchase. Today the distinction can be much less clear cut in certain instances. The banks have taken to arranging mortgages while many building societies have turned themselves into banks.

The most important factor for a would-be purchaser is making the calculations that go into making a commitment. You must decide which is the best deal for your circumstances. You may need the advice of your solicitor or accountant before reaching a decision. There are many options available today, such as fixed-term rates, variable rates etc. but a discussion of these is beyond the scope of this book.

There is no doubt that if you are in steady employment and a 'good risk' from the lender's point of view, you are likely to be in a position to shop around for an advantageous loan.

Note of warning: watch out for penalty payments if you want to pay off your mortgage before the agreed date (see, in particular, the criticism levelled at the lending institutions, section 3.2.2 below).

3.2.1 Mortgage advice and other lending institutions

In addition to banks and building societies, mortgage loans can be arranged through finance houses, insurance companies, and certain specialist mortgage firms.

Lenders have been severely criticised in recent years for the way mortgages have been sold and for the quality of the advice they give, and it was hoped that the £490-billion mortgage sector would be brought under statutory control. After months of consultation the Financial Services Authority (FSA) was given the task of regulating the sale of mortgages and improving the information given to the country's 11 million homebuyers.

Following the Treasury's decision in December 2001 to extend the FSA's powers to include mortgage advice, from October 2004 firms that sell many types of mortgages will need to be authorised by the FSA. The stated intention is to make sure that you get clear, comparable information on mortgages and that where you get advice you are recommended a suitable mortgage. This will underpin and largely accord with the current Mortgage Code.

Firms that will need authorisation include banks, building societies, specialist lenders and mortgage intermediaries.

The new rules will cover mortgages taken out by an individual or trustee which are a first legal charge on the borrower's property. The property must be located in the UK and must be at least 40% occupied by the borrower or immediate family. The final form of the rules is expected to be published in Spring 2003.

Note: the rules will not apply to second charge loans, most 'buy-to-let' arrangements and loans to companies.

Further note of warning: extra protection is proposed for consumers buying higher-risk mortgages such as equity release mortgages for older consumers (which the FSA calls lifetime mortgages). (See chapter on *Growing Old*, section 4.3.)

3.2.2   Information to customers

The choice and range of mortgage products has not always proved as helpful to customers as should be expected. The Banking Ombudsman (now part of the Financial Ombudsman Service, see 3.2.5(a) below) , in common with the Office of Fair Trading, suggested a 'best advice' obligation on the part of the lending institutions to assist borrowers in making a free and informed choice. Mortgage contracts are often difficult to understand and were described as being 'written in arcane legalese'. As a result of surveys and pressure from consumer organisations, further weight was given to calls for mortgages to be regulated by the Financial Services Authority (FSA) rather than by a voluntary scheme and self-regulation (see also section 3.2.1 immediately above).

The advice – as always – is to shop around to obtain the best deal for your own particular circumstances and avoid being pressured into a deal which you might well regret in time. The pressure is particularly marked at the time of writing because the property market has been so buoyant. However, even just a small downturn could lead to serious difficulties.

Note of warning: because there have been so many mergers between societies and banks in recent years, you may find yourself in a position where the lender of your choice has been taken over by another company.

☞ *You consulted your financial adviser before you bought your first home. He suggested a small building society as the one offering the most advantageous terms for your particular circumstances. Three years later, you find that the company has been taken over. You wonder what you can do.*

Every mortgage contract gives the lender the right to assign the mortgage to another company. In the circumstances, you can either carry on with the existing company or enter into a new mortgage with another lender – which may involve extra administration costs.

3.2.3   Loan 'in principle'

It is generally best to approach your lending institution at a very early stage. You will then be able to ascertain how much it will be prepared to lend you 'in principle'. You can then enter the housing market knowing the range of property prices you will be able to afford.

Lenders need to have details of income from an employer or accountant (for the self-employed) in order to agree in principle to a loan.

The terms, of course, can only be properly agreed upon once the lender is sure that the property you wish to purchase will be adequate security for the money lent.

Mortgage and credit lenders are required to give clear, comparable information about the products they offer. Warnings such as 'Your home is at risk if you do not keep up repayments on a mortgage or other loan secured on it' should be shown in all precontractual information on mortgage offers.

Banks and building societies have also been criticised for the way in which they vary interest rates for 'captive' borrowers and savers. While the Office of Fair Trading states that it cannot seek to set the level of interest rates or to stop them from being varied, it has set out guidelines to limit the freedom of institutions to act to the detriment of its customers. Typical 'lock-ins' concern mortgage redemption penalties which a borrower must pay if he or she wishes to switch to another lending institution, although this has become progressively easier in a competitive market.

Take extra care: it is only when your solicitor or conveyancer receives the mortgage offer in writing that you should proceed with exchange of contracts.

3.2.4   Rights and obligations of the lender

When borrower and lender enter into a mortgage deed, the lender takes a legal charge over the property. This provides security for the loan in case the borrower defaults on the mortgage repayments. The Council of Mortgage Lenders, which represents most lending institutions in this country, has issued a statement of policy that they are 'in the business of providing homes for people, not for taking their homes away'. Repossession of a mortgaged property will only be considered as a last resort.

Note: although the housing market was experiencing an almost unprecedented surge in 2002, official figures nonetheless show that during the first quarter, 16,484 mortgage possession actions were entered (not all of which resulted in a re-possession order being made). On the other hand, data from CML shows that mortgage arrears and re-possessions fell again in the first six months of 2002 as the combination of low unemployment and interest rates and rising property prices continued to create a favourable environment for home owners. This situation is not expected to continue indefinitely.

3.2.4(a) Court order

A lender must apply to court for an order for possession even where a borrower is clearly in default. Even then the court exercises a discretion to adjourn the grant of possession orders to allow the parties to reach some other financial accommodation. It must give the borrower a 'reasonable period' to pay off the current instalments as well as the arrears (see below).

3.2.4(b) Negligent advice

A professional lender has a duty not to act negligently when giving advice to borrowers who are not experienced business people.

Furthermore, where there may be emotional pressure – for example where a partner is asked to use their home as security for a loan or overdraft for a spouse or cohabitee – the dangers of losing their home must be explained.

Do remember: the lender has to ensure that the person involved has received independent legal advice (see the chapter on *Setting up Home*, section 4.1.6(b)).

3.2.4(c) Obligations on sale

If the lender does repossess the property under a court order and proceeds to sell it, there is an obligation to:

- get the best price 'reasonably obtainable'
- account to the borrower if the proceeds of sale exceed the debt, thus if there is a surplus, the balance must be refunded to the borrower.

☞ *You were unable to pay your mortgage instalments after you were made redundant. You moved in with your in-laws and the house was left vacant for a while. Its condition deteriorated. The building society repossessed the property, finally selling it at a very low price and, in your view, certainly not the 'best price reasonably obtainable'. You feel that if some repairs had been carried out, the house would have fetched more money. You wonder whether you have a case against the building society.*

A lender cannot dispose of a property at any price. However, it has no obligation to 'nurse' the property before a sale, by, for example, putting it into repair.

3.2.4(d) Time Limits

Your mortgagee [i.e. the bank or building society] has 12 years within which to bring a claim for the principal sum owed from the date when you default on your covenant to pay.

☞ *You lost your job and defaulted on your mortgage payments. Your lender repossessed and sold your house but it was unable to recover the full amount you owed. You are now being sued for the shortfall. However you believe that their action against you is time-barred because your lender's claim was replaced by a an implied contractual obligation on you to repay that shortfall. As a result, the six-year time limit for bringing an action of this kind has expired. Are you right?*

In a similar case the Administrative Court decided that the lender's right to sue to recover its debt arose when the borrowers failed to meet their mortgage payments. The fact that the lender exercised its power of sale and discharged the mortgage did not mean that the mortgage debt did not have to be paid. The covenant to pay was not cancelled along with the legal charge. Therefore your lender will probably be entitled to claim the balance of the principal sum owed. However the general, shorter six-year limitation period will apply to any claim for interest.

3.2.5 The borrower's obligations and rights

Primarily, the borrower is expected to repay the loan according to the terms of the agreement. In today's world, however, where property-owning can become an onerous obligation, paying mortgage instalments can become too much for some – no matter how carefully they made their calculations before buying their homes.

3.2.5(a) Failure to pay

The mortgage companies strenuously advise their customers to contact them immediately they become aware that they may run into difficulties. Sometimes, alternative arrangements can be set in place – before the outstanding repayments on the capital, as well as the incremental interest, grow too large. For example, the lender may defer the term, or capitalise the interest owing.

The law provides that a borrower should be given a 'reasonable period' to pay off the arrears as we have seen above (section 3.2.4(a)).

What is a 'reasonable period' for this purpose? In one case in the Court of Appeal, it was held that the borrowers were entitled to the same period as the mortgage then in existence, which still had 13 years to run. The case was hailed as a breakthrough for borrowers in difficulties. However, the court will not make the same order if the value of the property is so low that the building society would be unlikely to realise its security; or if the borrower is unlikely to take proper care of the property; or if the borrower would be unable to meet any of the repayments to be made.

Do note: The building societies had their own Ombudsman who has now merged with the Banking Ombudsman and the Insurance Ombudsman (together with the Ombudsmen involved in the personal investments and pensions) into: The Financial Ombudsman Service, South Quay Plaza, 183 Marsh Wall, London E14 9SR: tel. 08450 801 800 or *www.financial-ombudsman.org.uk.*

3.2.5(b) Negative equity

If the property market were to fall, borrowers could find themselves in a position where the amount that they have borrowed will exceed the value of the property which they have bought. This would mean that they could not sell their present property even if it no longer suited their needs at all. Building societies and other lenders have put forward various plans to the government to rescue those in the 'negative equity' trap. One arrangement is that borrowers can carry their mortgage forward to a new purchase without, of necessity, having to pay off their previous loan.

In all cases, do approach your lender who will probably assist you as far as possible (see also section 3.2.5(c) below).

3.2.5(c) Voluntary repossession

You may feel that there is no way you can pay your debt, and decide to 'hand over the keys' to your lender.

Warning: if you do that you are still obliged to make your mortgage payments and pay any arrears and interest until the property is sold. This is not such a problem when property is in demand during a property boom but it can be a real problem when the market is not so buoyant.

After a lender takes a property into possession, interest will generally continue to be charged on the mortgage loan until the property is sold. There will also be other costs charged to the mortgage account, including estate agents' costs in selling the property, and legal costs.

The Legal Services Commission (see DIRECTORY) produces a leaflet, *Losing your Home*, which sets out your rights if you face losing your home.

3.2.5(d) Other terms of the agreement

A mortgage contract has many clauses to protect the interests of the lender. For example, there is usually a clause which prohibits the borrower from letting the property unless by express agreement. It is clear that if a mortgage lender has to repossess and sell up, it does not want to find a tenant, of whose presence the lender was unaware, installed on the premises.

A borrower has to take reasonable care of the property too, because otherwise the lender's security for the loan is placed in jeopardy.

Consent has to be obtained for alterations.

3.2.5(e) Rights

Despite the lender's legal charge on the property, it is clear that someone who buys a property with a mortgage is 'owner' in other respects. For example, a borrower has the right to sue someone who trespasses on their property, or to apply for planning permission to develop it.

3.3   Insurance

Apart from strict criteria for buildings insurance, a lender will usually require some form of life insurance to cover the borrower in the event of death. Obviously, it is in the interests of the borrower, too, as it safeguards his familial dependants. Independent advice must be sought on the terms of such policies, as well as on the different kinds of policy available, e.g. straight life assurance or endowment assurance – to name but two of those most commonly used.

3.3.1   Mortgage insurance guarantee

If a loan on a property exceeds 75 per cent, the lender may ask for a one-off premium on a mortgage insurance.

Note of warning: this policy protects the lender and not the borrower. Only the lender can claim from the insurance company for the balance of the loan if the borrower defaults. Moreover, in a recent case, the insurance company was then allowed to claim the money from the borrower that it had paid out to the lending institution.

3.3.2   Mortgage Payment Protection Insurance (MPPI)

If you take out a mortgage with a high-street lender you are likely to be offered MPPI which covers mortgage repayments if you are prevented from working because of accident, sickness or unemployment. Since your home is at risk if you cannot keep up the payments, it is easy to sell this type of insurance but it may not necessarily be the best option. MPPI can be very expensive with three levels of cover: unemployment only, accident and sickness only, and accident, sickness and unemployment in a single policy. The cost of cover you choose is based on the size of your mortgage payments.

Now that the FSA has taken over regulation of mortgage lending, mortgage advisers may have to provide borrowers with much clearer details about MPPI products which may encourage home buyers to explore other options such as income protection and critical-illness cover.

Do take advice from an independent financial adviser and consider all the options before taking out mortgage protection insurance.

3.3.3   Mortgage tie-in deals

New moves to break the compulsory link between mortgages and home insurance deals have been announced by the Department of Trade and Industry. Legislation will be introduced to stop consumers being forced to take out insurance policies linked to a mortgage. Some mortgages offering a low start-up interest rate come with compulsory buildings or contents insurance. The insurance does not have to be competitively priced because the borrower cannot shop around for a better deal. Many borrowers can also be put off from looking for different insurance by the fee their current lender might charge if they go elsewhere.

3.4   The 'chain'

Even if you have found the house which you want to buy and have agreed with the owners on the price, you may find that they are not in a position to finalise because they are part of a 'chain'. In other words, they cannot conclude any deal because the people they intend to buy from are also waiting on the outcome of their negotiations on their own purchase. Thus all the links in the chain are equally weak in such a case.

Remember: you are ill-advised to try to break out of this situation by taking out a bridging loan from a bank in order to conclude your purchase. You would be letting yourself in for an open-ended transaction by having to complete on your new home before you can sell your present one. See section 5.7 below for details of the 'seller's pack' which is intended to speed up the process of home-buying.

3.5   Your tax position

There is a close interrelationship between owning a home and your tax position. Specialist advice needs to be sought on issues such as mortgage relief, as well as the position of capital gains tax (which might arise if you sell your home) and inheritance tax. These topics, however, are outside the scope of this book.

4   MINDING THE PITFALLS

The warnings against getting involved in a property where there are existing or potential problems cannot be made too loud or too clear. No matter how much you fall in love with the house, how much you think it ideal for your purposes, the purchase can spell future misery for you and your family if certain fundamental issues are not resolved before you make an irrevocable commitment to buy.

Do remember: you will not only have to wrestle with these problems while you live in your house, but they can also make your house unsaleable if you decide to move.

Thus you must satisfy yourself that the issues are resolved to your satisfaction before you exchange contracts.

(Some of the problems have been discussed in the chapters on *Neighbours, Landlords and their Tenants*, and *The Countryside*, so will only be mentioned below.)

4.1   Title

The question of who buys and who sells property is of paramount importance. Title is the determining factor to undisputed ownership. Where the issue is not made clear from the beginning, disputes can and do arise.

4.1.1   Who buys

You may be buying a property in your sole name. Generally speaking, however, today people buy a home together with a partner or family member (see also chapter on *Setting up Home*).

Sharers must establish their own position before going in for a property venture with another person – even one involving a close family member, as when an elderly person decides to sell up, buy a house with her child and move into a 'granny flat'. (See chapter on *Growing Old*, section 4.5.)

You must both decide how the property is to be registered. Do seek legal advice so that you can make a proper and informed choice as to which of the two methods of co-ownership of the property, i.e. as *joint tenants* or as *tenants-in-common*, would best suit your present and future circumstances.

Note: these are archaic terms to reflect co-ownership, and are not to be confused with 'tenants' or 'tenancy' in leases.

4.1.1(a) Joint tenants

This is usually the basis on which a husband and wife choose to buy the matrimonial home. The property is then owned jointly, i.e. in equal shares. If either person dies, the other share passes automatically to the survivor who then becomes the sole owner of the property.

However, a joint tenancy can be severed during the parties' lifetime. This converts it into a tenancy-in-common (see immediately below).

4.1.1(b) Tenancies-in-common

In this case, each co-owner owns a separate share in the property. It can be, but does not have to be, an equal share in the property, e.g. it can reflect the value of what each party has contributed to the purchase price.

If one tenant-in-common dies, his or her share of the property will be dealt with according to the will if there is one; otherwise it will be dealt with under the intestacy laws (see chapter on *Death – Before and After*).

Note of warning: in all cases, make sure that you have decided on the best course of action for yourself. Do ask your legal advisor to draw up a trust deed setting out the terms of ownership even though this may involve you in a small extra cost. It will still be cheap compared with possible litigation if a dispute between you and your partner or co-owner should arise.

4.1.2 Who sells?

This issue should be comparatively straightforward – it is the owner with registered title who sells the property (see also section 5 below).

However, problems do arise concerning ownership which sometimes only reveal themselves either at the point of sale or, for an unfortunate purchaser, at a later date.

> *You bought a one-bedroomed flat from a developer for yourself and your wife as first-time buyers two years ago. The flat is one of several in a converted Victorian house. Your flat is on the ground floor where, in order to make room for the kitchen and bathroom, the developer built an extension. Your wife is now expecting a child and you wish to sell. You have found a buyer but his conveyancer asserts that the ground on which the extension was built did not belong to the developer when he sold the flat to you. Instead it belongs to the next door property.*
>
> *In a similar case, the unfortunate couple had to stay on in the one-bedroomed flat for years before they could finally get proper title to sell their flat. They successfully sued the solicitor who had acted for them in the purchase.*

The question of title also involves other people with a possible interest in the property, e.g. a divorced spouse.

There may also be charges over the property – sometimes people borrow money from a building society to buy a house, and then take out second, and even third loans secured by further legal charges over the property.

Title is also closely tied to the question of vacant possession (see immediately below).

4.2 Vacant possession

You may have reached agreement with the owner of the property on your purchase and are happy to proceed with the deal. However, unknown to you, there may be other people living in the house who have a right to be there and have no intention of leaving on request.

For obvious reasons, a lending institution is reluctant to lend unless there is vacant possession. It is therefore for you and your conveyancer to ensure that the property will be empty on the day on which you plan to move in. To be absolutely certain of this, you must ensure that any occupant who has a right to be on the property is also made a party to the contract of sale.

Do remember: live-in family arrangements, in particular, have to be scrutinised. For example, there may be a seemingly informal arrangement that your vendor's mother lives in a granny flat in the garden of the property which you have just bought. You should not assume, however, that just because the seller is moving out, she intends to do so too. It may also be discovered, too late, that she has certain rights to occupy.

4.3   Easements, planning controls, and restrictive covenants

Land and buildings can involve:

- other people's rights to, over, and under your property
- existing and future plans for your area, e.g. road-building schemes.

All these matters must be investigated to your satisfaction before you proceed. (Change of use is dealt with in the *Neighbours* chapter, section 7.3.1.)

4.3.1   Private rights

As most of these matters are taken up in detail in the chapters on *The Countryside* and *Neighbours* (section 7.2), they are just mentioned below as a reminder to the unwary!

Private rights can involve:

- rights of way
- riparian rights
- mining rights
- gaming rights
- rights to maintain and/or repair fences and hedges
- rights to light
- restrictive covenants which curtail the uses to which you can put your house or land, such as a restrictive covenant against building on the plot of land which you have purchased and intended to develop.

4.3.2   Local authority plans and designations

These can involve:

- compulsory purchase orders
- road schemes
- tree preservation orders
- conservation area designation
- building preservation orders
- drainage
- listed building designation.

Do remember: planning regulations can also affect you in other ways.

Note: from 1 April 2002 a standard form of drainage enquiry for use in property conveyancing was introduced (CON29DW) which must be submitted to the relevant water company rather than the local authority.

1) If there has already been an alteration or extension to a property which you wish to buy, you must make sure that the proper planning permission was obtained at the time.

In one case, a couple bought a house with a one-bedroomed bungalow in the grounds. They were told by the estate agents and the seller's solicitor that planning permission had been obtained when the bungalow was built. These statements were made on the authority of the seller. After they bought the property, the local planning authority ordered the couple to demolish the bungalow because, in fact, it had been put up without planning permission.

2) If you intend buying a property with a view to developing it or changing its use, you should obtain planning permission beforehand. At the very least, you should receive an informal answer from the planning officer as to whether there would be any objection in principle and at the outset to planning permission.

4.3.2(a)   Compulsory Purchase Code

The Law Commission has taken the first step towards a comprehensive compulsory purchase code by publishing a consultative report which addresses the need to simplify, consolidate and codify the law relating to the payment of compensation where land is compulsorily acquired by the state or by other statutory bodies.

The consultation period expired on 24 October 2002 and at the time of writing the Commission is preparing a final report to bring together the threads and narrow down some of the alternative solutions.

4.3.3   Rights of the utility companies
These involve both:

- rights over your property, e.g. for electricity cables, and
- rights under it, e.g. for sewers.

The services provided to you were once operated by public bodies. These are now privately-owned. They all have rights *(easements)* on your property which allow them to provide you with services.

4.4   Neighbours
It is difficult to establish in advance whether or not you will get on with your neighbours. The seller is obliged to answer questions on problems with neighbours on a property information form (see section 5.2 below; see as well the chapter on *Neighbours*).

Note of warning: just because the seller has got on with the neighbours does not necessarily mean that you will do so too; and contrariwise.

4.5   Boundaries
Problems with boundaries are discussed in the *Neighbours* chapter in section 3.

As a purchaser, you must establish that you have a clear understanding of what you are buying (on the seller's answers to the questionnaire on the position of the boundaries see section 5.2 below).

Do note: although plans are provided by the Land Registry, the Registry specifically states that the plan attached to the certificate of title does not guarantee the boundaries to the property involved. Except in the very few cases where the register of title states that boundaries have been fixed, the title plan only indicates general boundaries so that the exact line is left undetermined – for example, as to whether a boundary includes a hedge or wall, or runs along its centre etc.

4.5.1   Boundary problems in buying 'off the plan'
Older properties may have features, such as a line of trees, that can clearly indicate where the boundary runs. A buyer of a 'new build' home often only has plans on paper to assist.

In such cases, you would be well advised to ask the developer to erect the boundaries for you. If that is not possible, you can ask him to place site-marking pegs to delineate the boundary for you on the actual plot. If you are still uncertain, do consult a surveyor.

The Information Centre of the Royal Institution of Chartered Surveyors (tel. 0870 333 1600) will give you details of three chartered surveyors in your locality who practise the particular specialism of ascertaining boundaries.

Be warned: public funding [former legal aid] is not available for boundary disputes.

5   SELLING YOUR HOME
In many respects selling your home is the other side of the coin to buying your home.

So many of the steps, instructions to your conveyancer, etc. involve the same procedures. These have been dealt with above. However, there are certain particular aspects that apply to a sale, rather than to a purchase of a house, which will be dealt with briefly below. Some aspects have also been dealt with in other chapters.

5.1   Employing professional services

5.1.1   Estate agents
Estate agents act for the seller, who pays the agent according to the terms of the contract between them. Questions such as fees, written contract, and sole or multiple agencies are all dealt with in the chapter on *Goods and Services*, section 5.7. Generally, the seller pays the agent only after he or she introduces someone who completes the purchase of the property.

Estate agents also advise the seller on the likely price which he or she can expect on the sale of their house. If you want a valuation from a surveyor, that would have to be separately arranged.

Once you instruct an agent to act for you, you become responsible for supplying the estate agent with accurate information about your property (see also section 5.2 below). Estate agents rely on this information which the seller provides to them for making up their particulars of sale. They are not expected to establish the accuracy of the information which they receive from the seller, unless there is something which would put the agents on the alert and raise a query in their minds.

As we have seen (section 2.1.1(b) above), estate agents also usually print a disclaimer on the property's particulars which they distribute. The disclaimer could absolve the agent for misrepresentation but would not protect a seller who provided misleading information in the first instance.

5.1.2 Conveyancers

Your instructions will differ only in certain regards depending on whether you buy or sell. (Quite often, of course, people conclude both deals simultaneously by selling their own house and buying another.)

1) You must ensure that all the persons with an interest in the property are parties to a contract of sale, and inform your conveyancer of any such interest.

2) You will have to instruct your conveyancer whether you intend to pay the estate agent's commission from the sale proceeds or in some other way.

3) You must instruct your conveyancer to prepare a draft contract of sale once you have accepted an offer.

4) Your conveyancer will receive the 10 per cent deposit for you after exchange of contracts.

5) In general a seller is entitled to the deposit if a buyer fails to complete after contracts have been exchanged. There are also other legal remedies available to compensate for failure to complete in certain instances (see section 5.6 below).

6) In all cases, do try to establish, in advance, the costs involved in the conveyancing. These are generally slightly lower for selling a house than the fees involved in a house purchase.

7) You will have to make all proper arrangements in advance to pay off your existing mortgage on the property, if any. Your conveyancer will have to obtain the title deeds from the lender in order to have them re-registered in the name of the purchaser.

8) Although the buyer becomes liable for insuring the property once contracts have been exchanged, you are not advised to cancel your existing policy until completion has actually taken place. You should, however, inform your insurers of the current position. The Association of British Insurers issues helpful leaflets on all aspects of house insurance (see DIRECTORY on Property Law, page 215).

If you are unhappy with the service provided by your conveyancer (or solicitor if appropriate) and feel that they have not dealt satisfactorily with your complaint, you have a number of options:

- If you are complaining about a solicitor, contact the Office for the Supervision of Solicitors (OSS) (See *The Legal System* DIRECTORY for details). The OSS has power to order your solicitor to refund your fees or pay compensation.

- If you are not satisfied with the way the OSS dealt with your complaint, you can take the matter to the Office of the Legal Services Ombudsman (see DIRECTORY for details).

- If you are complaining about a conveyancer, you should contact the Council for Licensed Conveyancers (CLC) (see DIRECTORY for details).

5.1.3 Surfing the Web

A growing number of sellers is deciding to cut out the middleman and sell their property on the Internet. There are many and varied sites from which you can sell, buy or rent your home including, for example, *www.upmystreet.com*; *www.easier.co.uk* and many, many more.

Trying to sell without using an estate agent can have its pitfalls. As in any other area, the DIY approach will involve extra work and possibly a degree of risk. Prospective buyers will not have been vetted by an estate agent before you see them so be sure to take a telephone number and call them to confirm appointments.

Remember:

- when you arrange a viewing make sure there is someone else in the house with you

- ask whether the buyer is in a chain or has sold his/her property
- do not exaggerate or mislead when describing the property
- be realistic about the price you want
- retain a good solicitor.

5.1.4   E-Conveyancing

The much-promised home buying revolution (introduced by the Land Registration Act 2002) was boosted in May 2002 by the launch of the official consultation on an electronic conveyancing system and the Land Registry's 10-year strategic plan.

The online service promises to link conveyancers, lenders, the Land Registry and possibly other professionals such as surveyors and estate agents, in a single network enabling then to communicate online and allowing simultaneous completion and registration.

The Land Registry expects to roll out a fully electronic conveyancing system in 2006. More details on the proposals are at *www.e-conveyancing.gov.uk*.

5.2   Property questionnaire

The general rule is that it is for the buyers to satisfy themselves that the property is in order, that there are no structural faults, and no unresolved legal issues (such as problems of title) in connection with it. In other words, *caveat emptor* – let the buyer beware. (See, however, 5.7 below.)

As a seller, it is not your duty to inform a would-be purchaser that, for example, your house is rather too close for comfort to a local public house so there is noise from departing customers at night. It is for the buyer to ascertain the location and amenity of the house he or she intends to buy. You also do not need to report that – as another example – there has been a recent spate of burglaries in your neighbourhood.

You also do not have to volunteer the information that there are physical defects in the property, but if specifically asked you cannot give false information. (For possible future changes, see 5.7 below.)

However, you are required to inform a buyer of any easement of which you are aware.

Most probably you will be asked to fill in a standard-form questionnaire known as the property information form (PIF), which has been prepared by the Law Society. This should be done as soon as you decide to put your house on the market.

5.2.1   Misrepresentation

If you do not answer the questions truthfully on the PIF, you may be liable for misrepresentation. For example, if you state that you received planning permission for an extension that you have built, when that is not the case, you would become guilty of breach of contract and be liable to pay damages to your buyers if they had to demolish the extension.

5.2.2   Scope of the questionnaire

You must study the questionnaire carefully as some of the information required is very broadly framed – e.g. 'have you had any negotiations or discussion with any neighbour or any local or other authority which affect the property in any way?'

This might be wide enough to cover a public-spirited approach to a highway authority to install traffic calming measures!

In a recent case, the would-be sellers had been embroiled in a dispute with their neighbour who had harassed and abused them for a number of years. As a result, their house went on to the market at a figure which was considerably less than its true worth. Their recourse was to consider suing their neighbour for the diminution in value of their property (see chapter on *Neighbours*, section 4.1.1(a)).

5.2.3   Fixtures and fittings

You will also be called upon to fill in a form detailing the fixtures and fittings which you intend to sell with the house. Again this should be done as soon as possible to assist the estate agent in preparing the particulars.

'Fixtures and fittings' are usually attached to the premises so that their removal would cause visible damage; kitchen units are an example. 'Chattels' are removable items, such as curtains, which generally are not included in a sale. However, they can be included but must be specified.

Note: it is in your interests as well as in those of the buyer to sort out as many areas as possible of potential future dispute regarding the sale, at the very outset.

In one case a purchaser bought a property which included a garden area covered in old flagstones. Prior to exchange of contracts, the seller removed the flagstones and stacked them elsewhere on the property. On being queried, the seller both denied that she had hidden them and asserted that they were not included in the sale. The purchaser then claimed that he was entitled to the flagstones under the contract, that he was entitled to their return, and the cost of re-laying them. Alternatively the seller should pay the cost of purchasing and laying replacements.

The Court of Appeal held that the flags had been deliberately concealed. On a proper construction of the contract, the flagstones were part of the property and thus part of the original sale.

Another salutary tale is the case of sellers who removed stepping stones, the water pump which operated a garden water-feature, a bathroom mirror and towel rail, light bulbs and a variety of other items before the purchasers moved into the house. The sellers were ordered to pay over £1,000 in compensation.

In a separate judgment concerning the same purchase, the court ordered the estate agents who handled the sale to supply a garden statue to the value of £800 which they had offered in writing as a sweetener to close the deal but which the sellers had also removed.

5.3   Searches and surveys

Again, it is for the buyers – not the sellers – to make certain that the results of the searches are satisfactory. Similarly, they must establish that the property is sound, by employing their own surveyors. However, in some instances, particularly when sellers are in a hurry to conclude a deal, they will ensure that the documentation on local searches, draft contract of sale, answers to preliminary enquiries, and documents of title, are already available for a would-be purchaser.

Warning: if you are buying a property, you should check what the survey purports to cover in case you have any complaint later.

Getting your own house surveyed, before you put it on the market, has certain advantages. You can then handle negotiations from a position of greater certainty and are less likely to be ambushed by a buyer who produces a negative surveyor's report. These advantages have to be weighed against costs which would normally be borne by the buyer, particularly those of survey and searches. Such requirements for a survey will become mandatory when the concept of a 'seller's pack' comes to fruition (see 5.7 below).

The Government praised progressive local authorities who have signed up to the National Land Information Service (NLIS), enabling homebuyers in their areas to benefit from high speed, high technology property searches. The NLIS gives people a better and quicker service when buying properties as long as their local authority's land search department is participating electronically in the service. If their systems are electronic then they can successfully interface with NLIS and searches can be completed in hours rather than days or even weeks. The quickest recorded search to date was completed in just 13 minutes.

5.4   'Lock out' agreements

At the time of a property boom, buyers find themselves in the position where they spend money on having properties surveyed, and agree a purchase price, and then find that the sellers have accepted a higher price from someone else. This is known as 'gazumping'. Of course, in a weak market, gazumping is less of a problem; indeed the boot can be on the other foot, with buyers sometimes offering lower prices, at the last minute, before contracts are exchanged.

There is a way out of these nasty surprises for both buyer and seller, however: the 'lock out' agreement. Under this agreement, which is capable of forming a legally binding contract, a seller enters into a contract with a buyer not to negotiate with anyone else for a short period, usually about a fortnight. The field is then clear for the buyer to arrange his or her affairs, in order to conclude the deal within the time stipulated.

5.5   Completion and moving out

Your buyer should be entitled to reasonable access to the property between exchange and completion to allow for plans to be made and measurements to be taken.

Note of warning: do not allow the buyer to have a set of keys until completion has taken place.

You must be informed by your conveyancer that the money has actually been transferred to a designated account before releasing the keys. This can take time while the money is transferred from one account to another – even in these days of electronic banking.

If you have already vacated your property, leave a set of keys with your estate agent, with precise instructions on how and when to hand them over.

Completion can only take place on Mondays to Fridays inclusive, and not on bank holidays.

5.6   Failure to complete

1) Failure to complete the formal documentation does not necessarily invalidate the purchase.

☞ *Two students jointly purchased a property. When they separated the following year the man bought out the woman's share for £1,400. The transfer of the mortgage was never formalised and the woman subsequently refused to sign a draft conveyance. When the property was repossessed and sold some years later, the woman claimed a share of the proceeds of sale.*

The court held that failure to complete the formalities of the buyout did not negate the deal. It would be a miscarriage of justice if, as a result of the deal, the woman became entitled to a half share. She had disposed of her interest and the sale was enforceable.

2) If your buyer fails to complete on time, there is generally a clause in the contract of sale which entitles you to interest on the late payment.

3) If your buyer fails to complete at all, you are entitled to keep the deposit. There are also other legal remedies which might be available to compensate you for breach of contract depending on the contract's terms.

☞ *You have a house which has been on the market for some time. You have found a buyer who has exchanged contracts with you. On the strength of the intended completion in four weeks from the date of exchange, you have made plans to move out of the area. Now you are informed that the buyer cannot complete and your plans are in disarray.*

Depending on the contract, you might be able to get an order for specific performance [i.e. an order that the buyer must complete the transaction] if he is in a position to complete but has simply refused to do so. However, there would be no point in such an order if the buyer has not got the funds to complete the purchase.

You would have to try to sell your property at the highest possible price obtainable in a hurry. If you then had to drop your price, you might be able to sue the first buyer for damages for the difference between the price he promised you and the price you subsequently obtained. You could also obtain damages for distress and inconvenience because of the disruption to your plans, although these might be fairly nominal only.

Note: equally if the seller fails to complete, he or she becomes liable for breach of contract. The same remedies might then be available to the buyer against the seller: i.e. suing for damages and/or specific performance. The buyer would also be entitled to return of the deposit as a matter of course.

5.7   Proposed changes – extension of a seller's obligations

In 1998, the government announced new measures to speed up the process of homebuying. These include a 'seller's pack' which a seller will have to provide – at his or her own expense – to a would-be purchaser. The pack would include such matters as a survey, searches, a valuation, and details of fixtures and fittings, and would be prepared before the house is first advertised for sale. Trials have been carried out in Bristol and have proved to be successful in reducing the time it takes to sell a property – one house changed hands in four and a half weeks under the homesellers' information pack scheme. The average time is eight weeks.

However, the pilot scheme in Bristol in 2001 found that the packs were not popular with sellers, particularly those with cheaper properties who resented the extra cost involved. Buyers – who did not have to bear the cost –were more enthusiastic.

It was not until 2000 that seller's packs were included in the Homes Bill – which ran out of Parliamentary time before the General Election and so never entered the statute books. However the seller's pack was given the go-ahead on 13 November 2002 in the Queen's speech. It will be included in a Homes Bill expected to be introduced around February 2003.

It is currently proposed that the seller's pack will include the following:

* copies of draft consents and approvals relating to planning and listed building consents and building regulations
* copies of any current warranties and guarantees
* a specimen draft contract
* a home condition report; and
* a home energy report.

The main aim is to reduce the time it takes to get from the 'sale agreed' stage to exchange of contracts.

Note: although the idea is to speed up the selling process, sellers would not be placed under greater legal responsibility for the accuracy of the information provided than they are at present.

5.8 Effect of Land Registration Act 2002

One of the most far reaching measures affecting conveyancing is the introduction of the Land Registration Act 2002. The Act, which will not be in force until the end of 2003, provides a system of electronic conveyancing to replace the traditional paper-based system. More disposals, charges and interests will be included on the Land Register – even short leases – and in general property transactions will have no effect unless they are registered.

Signficantly, the Act introduces a new system of adverse possession for registered land on the basis that registration rather than possession should be the basis of title (see chapter on *Neighbours*, section 8.2).

Under the new rules, it will be possible for the first time to access the history of a registered title. At present leases or charges cannot be inspected for past transactions.

Note: leases of seven years or over will have to be registered, rather than leases of more than 21 years as at present. You will therefore have to pay stamp duty on such leases to effect registration and this will mean extra costs.

5.8.1 Adjudicator to Land Registry

A new judicial office of adjudicator to HM Land Registry is being created to provide an independent dispute resolution procedure for land registration matters. At present there are about 80-90 land registration cases each year that require adjudication. Typically they relate to boundary disputes; squatters' claims; claims to land ownership; and claims to rights over land. Appeals against a decision are very rare.

5.8.2 Concerns about e-conveyancing

Some concerns have been expressed about the security aspects of e-conveyancing. In a recent case land was purchased from the ostensible registered proprietor who, it turned out, had obtained a registered title by fraud. There are no guarantees that this could not happen under the new system.

DIRECTORY
PROPERTY LAW

Architecture and Surveying Institute
St Mary House
15 St Mary Street
Chippenham
Wilts SN15 3WD
Tel. 01249 444505
www.asi.org.uk

Association of British Insurers
51 Gresham Street
London EC2V 7HQ
Tel. 020 7600 3333
www.abi.org.uk

The Association of Building Engineers
Lutyens House
Billingbrook Road
Weston Favell
Northampton NN3 8NW
Tel. 01604 404121
www.abe.org.uk

The Banking Ombudsman
(see under Financial Ombudsman Service)

British Property Federation
7th Floor
1 Warwick Row
London SW1E 5ER
Tel. 020 7828 0111
www.bpf.org.uk

Building Societies Association
3 Savile Row
London W1X 1AF
Tel. 020 7437 0655
www.bsa.org.uk

Building Societies Ombudsman
(see under Financial Ombudsman Service)

College of Estate Management
Whiteknights
Reading
Berkshire RG6 6AW
Tel. 0118 986 1101
www.cem.aac.uk

Commonhold Team
Lord Chancellor's Department
Room 3N 5
3rd Floor Southside
105 Victoria Street
London SW1E 6QT
Tel. 020 7210 1986
www.lcd.gov.uk

Council for Licensed Conveyancers
16 Glebe Road
Chelmsford
Essex CM1 1QG
Tel. 01245 349599
www.conveyancers.org.uk

Council of Mortgage Lenders
3 Savile Row
London W1X 1AF
Tel. 020 7437 0075
www.cml.org.uk

Department for the Environment, Food and Rural Affairs (DEFRA)
17 Smith Square
London SW1P 3JP
Tel. 08459 335577
www.defra.gov.uk

Estate Agents Ombudsman
(see Ombudsman for Estate Agents below)

Estates Gazette
151 Wardour Street
London W1V 4BN
Tel. 020 7411 2511
www.egi.co.uk

Federation of Private Residents' Associations (FPRA)
Enterprise House
113–115 George Lane
South Woodford
London E18 1AB
Tel. 020 8530 8464
www.fpra.org.uk

Financial Ombudsman Service
South Quay Plaza
183 Marsh Wall
London E14 9SR
Tel. 08450 801 800
www.financial-ombudsman.org.uk

Independent Housing Ombudsman Service
Norman House
105 The Strand
London WC2R 0AA
Tel. 020 7836 3630
www.ihas.org.uk

The Land Registry
Lincolns Inn Fields
London WC2A 3PH
Tel. 020 7917 8888
www.landreg.gov.uk
(see local directory for your nearest one – this address is headquarters)

Lands Tribunal (England and Wales)
48–49 Chancery Lane
London WC2A 1JR
Tel. 020 7936 7200
www.courtservice.gov.uk/tribunals/lands_frm.htm

The Law Commission
Conquest House
37–38 John Street
Theobalds Road
London WC1N 2BQ
Tel. 020 7453 1220
www.lawcom.gov.uk

The Law Society
113 Chancery Lane
London WC1A 1PL
Tel. 020 7242 1222
www.lawsociety.org.uk

Leasehold Advisory Service (LEASE)
70–74 City Road
London EC1Y 2BJ
Tel. 020 7490 9580
www.lease-advice.org

Leasehold Reform Team
Office of the Deputy Prime Minister
HPS Division
2nd Floor, Eland House
Bressenden Place
London SW1E 5DU
Tel. 020 7944 3462
www.housing.odpm.gov.uk/information/
leaseholdreform/index.htm

Legal Services Commission
LeafletLine
Tel. 0845 300 0343
Email: LSCleafletline@direct.st.ives.co.uk

National Association of Estate Agents
Arbon House
21 Jury Street
Warwick CV34 4EH
Tel. 01926 496800
www.naea.co.uk

The National House Building Council
Buildmark House
Chilton Avenue
Amersham
Bucks HP6 5AP
Tel. 01494 434477
www.nhbc.co.uk

National Housing Federation
175 Gray's Inn Road
London WC1X 8UP
Tel. 020 7278 6571
www.housing.org.uk

National Land Information Service
Local Government Information House
Layden House
76–86 Turnmill Street
London EC1M 5LG
(Helpdesk) Tel. 020 7296 6568
Tel. 01279 451 625
www.nlis.org.uk
www.idea-infoage.gov.uk

National Landlords' Association
78 Tachbrook Street
London SW1V 2NA
Tel. 020 7828 2445
www.landlords.org.uk

Office of Fair Trading
Fleetbank House
2–6 Salisbury Square
London EC4Y 8JX
Tel. 020 7211 8900
www.oft.gov.uk

Office of the Legal Services Ombudsman
3rd Floor, Sunlight House
Quay Street
Manchester M3 3JZ
Tel. 08456 010 794
www.olso.org.uk

Ombudsman for Estate Agents
Beckett House, 4 Bridge Street
Salisbury
Wiltshire SP1 2LX
Tel. 01722 333306
www.oea.co.uk

Royal Institution of Chartered Surveyors
12 Great George Street
Parliament Square
London SW1P 3AD
Tel. 020 7222 7000
(Contact Centre) Tel. 0870 333 1600
www.rics.org.uk

Tenancy Information Centre Association
(TICA UK) Ltd (for checking on prospective tenants)
PO Box 64
Tiverton
Devon EX16 1XY
Tel. 01884 38731
www.ticagroup.com

Welsh Assembly Government
Housing Regulation Branch
Ground Floor
Cathays Park
Cardiff CF10 3NQ
Tel. 029 2082 3025
www.wales.gov.uk/subhousing/topics-e-htm

8 PROVIDING FOR YOUR RETIREMENT

INTRODUCTION

The good news is that increasing numbers of us are living longer but the downside is that rising longevity combined with a reduced birth rate poses important challenges for the affordability of the pension system. If we want to see continuing rising standards of living in retirement, we either have to save more or work longer, or a mixture of both.

The Government takes the view that the UK is in a stronger position to meet this demographic challenge and the projection is that public spending on pensions in the UK will remain stable over the next 50 years at about 5% of GDP.

The expectations of middle-income earners, perhaps as many as three million, who are currently not saving enough for their retirement, is one of the challenges facing society today. And others may not be saving enough to provide the pensions they want.

At the same time, occupational pension schemes are under increasing pressure from rising costs and ever-greater complexity. More and more employers are closing schemes or cutting the level of contributions. Moreover many people are leaving the workforce earlier.

Stock market falls and greater life expectancy have made final salary schemes, which guarantee to pay a retirement income based on your final salary and the number of years you have been a member of the scheme, increasingly expensive to run, which has led to many firms closing the schemes to new members. They are being replaced by less generous defined contribution schemes (see section 3.5). The timing of these changes is particularly unfortunate for part-time employees who have campaigned long and hard and have only recently been allowed to join their company pension schemes (see section 4.5 below).

More and more women are building up their own pension rights, either as single people or as part of a two-income household. As the pattern of a woman's working life may be different from a man's, pension provision must allow for particular working patterns and personal circumstances. For example, women often combine paid work with caring for children, or for disabled or elderly relatives. Thus they might end up with very low pensions of their own, or, if they are married, they might have to depend on their husband's pension rights (see section 4).

The Government has recognised that simplification has to be at the heart of any strategy to encourage greater pension provision. Nowhere is that truer than in taxation of pensions, which has grown so complex that it challenges even the experts.

An important weakness of the tax rules is that they have not kept pace with evolving social and economic patterns. It is proposed that in practice most people saving into pensions, including employers sponsoring pension schemes, will simply be able to save, with tax relief, whatever they can afford and whatever suits their circumstances. This method of dealing with pension-saving will be very different from the current rules (see section 7.2 below).

The current eight separate pension tax-regimes, each with over-complex rules limiting the amount an individual can contribute to a pension scheme and the benefits a scheme pays out, make pensions difficult to understand and impose unnecessary administrative burdens on employers, individuals and pension providers. Complexity is said to discourage people from saving and to restrict individual choice and flexibility.

In a bid to encourage people to save more the Government also proposes massively extending the coverage of combined State and occupational pension forecasts, showing people what retirement income they could expect (see section 1.4 below).

Meanwhile we all continue to wrestle with the baffling and complex maze that is the pensions system. In this chapter we aim to provide a broad overview, pointing out some of the legal pitfalls along the way.

Note of warning: the chapter is intended as a general guide only. You should seek independent professional advice before taking a decision which will affect your long term security.

This chapter looks at:

- the State sector
- the private sector
- legal pitfalls
- pensions and women
- pensions on divorce
- pensions if you live abroad
- pensions and tax
- shake-up proposals
- pension mis-selling
- the Financial Services Authority.

1   THE STATE SECTOR

1.1   State pensions

It is now generally recognised that you need to plan ahead for retirement. The basic State pension is now regarded as only the starting point towards a comfortable retirement. Anyone in paid work who earns more than a yearly limit (the primary threshold) (£4,615 for 2002–2003) has to pay national insurance contributions (NIC).

Your employer will deduct NIC from your pay but if you are self-employed you are obliged to make the payments yourself. Each year during which you pay NIC is known as a qualifying year and as a general rule, the more qualifying years you complete, the higher will be your basic State retirement pension when you become eligible to claim it. Once you start to receive your basic State retirement pension, it will normally be increased in April each year.

If you earn between £3,900 (the lower earnings limit (LEL)) and £4,165 a year in 2002–2003, you will be treated as paying NICs even though no contributions are taken out of your pay.

You do not pay NIC if you earn less than the lower earnings limit (£3,900 for 2002–2003). If you have not paid, or are not treated as having paid sufficient NIC, you will not be entitled to a basic State retirement pension. However anyone aged 80 or over is entitled to a 'non-contributory' pension (see chapter on *Growing Old*, section 3.1.2).

1.1.1   Pension age

You can start to collect your basic pension once you reach State pension age. At present this is 65 for men and 60 for women. However from 6 April 2020, the State pension age for both men and women will be 65. The change is to be phased in gradually for women over a 10-year period from 2010–2020. The Pension Service (part of the Department for Works and Pensions) has produced a calculator to enable women due to reach State pension retirement age during that period to work out exactly the age at which they will be eligible to claim their pension.

☞   *Eve will be turning 60 on 1 June 2003. She would like to know when she can expect to receive notification of the amount due to her. She does not intend to stop working and would like to defer her pension. She is concerned to know whether she can do so.*

Eve will be notified of her entitlement approximately four months before reaching turning 60, i.e. on or about 1 February. However it is not compulsory for her to claim a pension as soon as she becomes eligible. If Eve claims it later, her weekly amount will be higher but she cannot claim for the weeks which she has given up.

Warning note: very strict time limits apply for an appeal against the letter which informs you of the amount of pension which you are awarded [the 'decision letter']; see section 1.5 below.

1.1.2 Amount of pension

As stated above, the size of your pension will depend upon the number of qualifying years you have accumulated.

1) A man needs 44 qualifying years to claim the full State pension (£75.50 per week for a single person for 2002–2003).

2) A woman who will reach the age of 60 before 2010 needs 39 qualifying years to receive a full pension. This will increase to 44 years once the State pension age is 65 for both men and women.

3) Years in which a woman has chosen to pay the married woman's reduced rate of NIC do not count towards qualifying years for purposes of claiming her State pension. This is discussed further in section 4.3 below.

Note: not everyone receives the full pension. If you retire with less than 25 per cent of the required qualifying years, you will not receive any State pension. To make matters worse you will not be entitled to a refund for NIC which you have already paid, since the contributions cover other insurance as well as pensions (e.g. sickness and unemployment).

If you do not qualify for the full State pension but have built up more than 25 per cent of the necessary qualifying years you will be entitled to a pension of between £18.12 per week (for 2002–2003) and £75.50 per week (for 2002–2003).

1.2 State Second Pension (SSP)

If you decide that the basic State retirement pension will not be sufficient for your needs in retirement, you can build up a second State pension. Until 6 April 2002, this was known as the State Earnings-Related Pension Scheme (SERPS). It was based on your NIC record and your level of earnings as an employee.

From 6 April 2002, the additional State pension is known as the State Second Pension (SSP). It has replaced SERPS to provide a more generous additional State pension for low and moderate earners. For the first time it also benefits some carers and those with long-term illness or disability whose working lives have been interrupted or shortened. They are now able to build up an additional State pension for those periods in which they are unable to work.

☞ *You have heard about the new scheme but have already built up money under the previously-existing SERPS scheme. You are concerned to know what will become of this fund as you are due to retire shortly.*

Any SERPS entitlement already accumulated is protected both for retired people and those still below the State pension age.

1.2.1 How the State Second Pension works

Anyone who earns less than a minimum level (£10,800 for 2002–2003) but more than the NIC lower earnings limit (see section 1.1. above) will be treated as if they had earned £10,800. The rate at which the additional State pension will accumulate (the accrual rate) is greater than under SERPS.

☞ *Ann works part-time in a printers and earns £8,000 per year. She appreciates the importance of starting to save for her retirement but cannot afford to start a private pension.*

Under the SSP rules Ann will be treated as if she earned £10,800 a year (for 2002–2003) and her additional pension will accumulate to build up a pension. The result is that she will receive at least twice as much additional State pension under SSP as she would have received under SERPS.

1.3 Home Responsibilities Protection

As we have seen, the amount of basic State retirement pension you receive depends on the number of qualifying years you build up before you reach retirement age.

At present, women whose State pension age is 60 need 39 qualifying years for a full 100% basic State pension. But between 2010 and 2020 that number will increase in line with State pension age until in 2020 women will need 44 qualifying years in the same way as men do.

Although you may still be entitled to some basic pension if you fail to build up sufficient qualifying years for a full pension, if you have less than 25% of the necessary qualifying years, you will not be entitled to any basic pension at all.

If you give up work to look after children or someone with a long-term illness or a disability, or if you work part time or take low-paid work, you can still build up a pension, notwithstanding that you do not pay contributions throughout your working life. Special rules called Home Responsibilities Protection (HRP) help you to do so and apply mainly to women (although some men can also benefit). HRP can be useful as it helps to protect the basic State retirement pension position of carers (in practice mainly women).

Do remember: Home Responsibilities Protection is not a benefit. It helps you to build up additional State pension through a State second pension.

1.3.1 How to claim Home Responsibilities Protection

You can claim HRP if the person you are caring for receives attendance allowance, constant attendance allowance or the highest-rate or middle-rate care component of disability living allowance for at least 48 weeks in the tax year, and you are not in paid work or do not earn enough in a tax year for it to count towards the basic State retirement pension. Further, you must not already be receiving invalid care allowance, income support or national insurance credits.

If you need to apply for HRP you have to fill in the form *Home Responsibilities Protection* (CF411). You can get the form from your local social security office or contact the Inland Revenue on 0845 915 8224 or 0845 915 8225. The lines are open from 8.30 am to 5 pm, Monday to Thursday and from 8.30 am to 4.30 pm on Friday. Calls are charged at local rates. You can also write to the Inland Revenue, National Insurance Contributions Office, Caseworker DM Team, Newcastle upon Tyne NE98 1ZZ.

Home Responsibilities Protection can reduce the number of qualifying years you need to earn a full basic State retirement pension, but you should be aware that to get the full basic pension, you will need at least 20 qualifying years in addition to any years you were covered by the scheme.

1.3.2 When to claim Home Responsibilities Protection

From April 2002, you must claim Home Responsibilities Protection within three years of the end of any tax year you spend caring for someone with a long-term illness or disability. The time limit applies to caring during or after the tax year 2002–2003.

☞ *In June 2002 you gave up work to start caring for your disabled sister. You do not receive invalid care allowance and have no underlying entitlement to it, income support or national insurance credits.*

You must make a claim between 6 April 2003 and 5 April 2006. However you cannot claim before the end of the tax year 2002–2003.

If you wish to claim Home Responsibilities Protection for years spent caring for someone with a long-term illness or disability between April 1978 (when HRP was first introduced) and 5 April 2002, you can claim at any time up to State pension age. However it is obviously better to claim as soon as possible.

1.4 Forecasting

It is possible to get an estimate of how much your State pension will be when you retire by contacting the Retirement Pension Forecasting Team (RPFT) on 0845 3000 168 (textphone 0845 3000 169) who will fill in a forecast application form over the phone. You can also contact them in writing asking for a forecast form (BR 19) (see DIRECTORY). Further you can collect Form BR 19 from your local social security office or complete the form online; it can be downloaded at *www.dwp.gov.uk*.

It is useful to get a forecast to enable you to decide whether your current savings will be sufficient for your retirement needs and to take action now if they are not.

As the forecast is based on your current circumstances which might change, it is likely to be more accurate the nearer you are to your retirement age. On the other hand, the earlier you apply for a forecast, the more time you will have to make additional pension arrangements if necessary.

1.4.1 Combined pension forecasting

In these uncertain times most people are unsure as to whether they have in fact provided adequately for their retirement. The Government is aware of this and the Pension Service, which is part of the Department of Work and Pensions, has set up a service which allows pension scheme members to see forecasts of both their State pension and private pension together for the first time.

This means that you should get a much better idea of your possible retirement income as the forecast will give you clear information in a single statement about the income you may expect in retirement from both the State and your private scheme, and thus raise your awareness of the importance of having suitable pension arrangements. The way the scheme works is through your pension scheme provider who has to register with the Pension Service.

Note: You must be given the chance to say that you do not want your State pension information passed to your pension provider for a combined forecast. You should receive an opt-out form to let you do this but you only have to reply if you do not want a combined forecast.

1.5 Appeals

The Government has set up the Pension Service to improve the service you receive regarding your pension – whether you are already a pensioner or are planning for your retirement, no matter how far off it might be.

The plan is to give an improved local service nationwide, operating in the community and providing face-to-face contact. You should continue to use your local social security office for any queries or complaints until you are told that the new arrangements apply to you.

If you think you are not getting the right amount of money to which you are entitled, you must contact the pension service or social security office (whichever applies to you) asking them to explain the decision you wish to challenge within one month of the date of the letter giving you the decision. The appropriate office will be given on your decision letter.

Your complaint should be dealt with (or at least acknowledged) within seven working days of it being received.

If you are not satisfied with the explanation given, you can ask the relevant office to look at their decision again. You may also be able to appeal to an independent tribunal which has the power to review and amend the decision if the tribunal agrees that it is wrong. The letter telling you about the decision will tell you if you are entitled to appeal.

If you want to appeal, you must let the office know within one month of the date of the decision letter.

1.5.1 The Appeals Service

The Appeals Service will decide your appeal at a tribunal hearing. The tribunal has three members who are not from the Department of Work and Pensions or the Employment Service. Tribunal members will be experts on the issues involved in your appeal and one will be legally qualified to help apply the law to your appeal.

The tribunal can only look at the evidence, the law and the circumstances at the time the decision was made that you are appealing against. It cannot look at changes of circumstances that may have taken place after the decision was made.

Do not wait if a change of circumstances could affect your future payments, but report it straight away. Do not wait for any appeal hearing but contact the office shown on your decision letter.

1.5.2 Time limits

The time limits for challenging a decision are most important. The Appeals Service may not be able to accept your appeal if its is received more than one month after the date of the decision letter. They can only accept a late appeal if there are special circumstances that caused the delay such as a death, a serious illness, absence abroad, a postal strike or some other exceptional situation.

☞ *You missed the deadline for an appeal against the amount of your pension. At the time that the decision letter was posted to you, you had suffered a slight stroke while on holiday, and were hospitalised far from home. You are wondering what you can do.*

You must write to the Appeals Service, explaining why you could not appeal within one month. A legally-qualified tribunal member will look at the reasons you have given for not appealing in time and will decide if your appeal can be accepted.

In all cases they will look at:

- whether and what were the special circumstances for the delay
- the length of time since you received the decision
- whether it is in the interests of justice that your appeal is accepted; and
- whether your appeal is reasonably likely to succeed.

Note: a late appeal cannot be accepted if the only reason is that you misunderstood the law, or the interpretation of the law has changed since the decision was made. Under no circumstance can your appeal be accepted if it is lodged 13 months or more after the date on the decision letter.

Remember: if an appeal tribunal finds that you have been getting too much money, your payments will be reduced!

For further information see leaflet GL24: *If you think our decision is wrong.* You can get this by phoning The Pension Service, tel. 0113 232 4143 or by visiting your social security office.

2   THE PRIVATE SECTOR

You are not allowed to leave the basic State retirement pension, but in some circumstances you can choose to leave SERPS/SSP and join a private scheme instead. This is known as 'contracting out'.

You can join an occupational pension scheme if your employer provides one, or you can take out a personal pension policy (see section 2.2 below). Finally since April 2001, you can build up a pension fund through a stakeholder pension scheme (see section 2.3 below).

If you decide to join an occupational pension scheme, run by your employer, contracting out means that both you and your employer will pay lower national insurance contributions (NIC). When you retire, your second pension will come from your employer's scheme and not from the SSP.

Many employers provide an occupational pension scheme for their employees, sometimes known as a company or works pensions.

However your employer is not obliged to provide such a scheme. It is a voluntary arrangement by your employer to provide retirement and/or death benefits for you and your dependants.

2.1   Occupational pensions

There are several types of occupational pension scheme. The rules relating to these schemes are complicated and it is beyond the scope of this book to go into any one of them in detail. There are however some important general rules which apply to them all.

2.1.1   The general rules

1) An occupational pension scheme can be set up for a large number of employees or for just one.
2) It will usually be in the form of a trust with legally appointed trustees.
3) It should be completely separate from your employer's business.
4) It will have its own scheme rules and be subject to trust law.
5) The trustees may delegate the day-to-day management of the scheme to an administrator who should be named in the scheme documentation. The administrator can be either an employee or one of the scheme trustees.
6) When you join an occupational pension scheme, you should be told what benefits it provides for you.
7) You should also receive a membership booklet or an announcement letter which will explain the main features of the scheme.
8) The documentation should also tell you who to contact if you have any queries and where you can look up scheme rules in full.
9) The rules of a pension scheme will specify who may join but membership cannot be made compulsory.
10) You may opt out of a scheme at any time.

See also 2.1.3 below with regard to the rules applying to contributions to a scheme.

The maximum benefits permitted by the tax rules on retirement are the same whether your occupational pension scheme is a final salary scheme (where your benefits are expressed as a fraction of your salary when you retire) or a money purchase scheme (where your pension depends on how much you have paid into your scheme and how the invested funds have grown and where there is no guarantee of the level of benefits that you will receive at retirement).

Note: your employer is not obliged to pay benefits as high as those allowed under the tax rules, and very few schemes do.

Although occupational pension schemes are voluntary, the Government is keen to encourage employers to provide such schemes for their employees and offers incentives through tax reliefs. If your scheme is tax-approved, you will be entitled to relief from income tax on your contributions (if you pay any), but not relief from national insurance contributions; and part of your benefits may be paid as a tax-free cash lump sum on retirement or death. Your employer will be entitled to corporation tax relief on its contributions (and national insurance relief).

Although your employer's contribution is of benefit to you, you will not be charged tax on that benefit. There will also be exemption from income tax and capital gains tax on the income and growth of the scheme investments.

2.1.2 The types of scheme

There are several types of occupational pension scheme:
- contracted-out salary related (COSR) scheme
- contracted-out money purchase (COMP) scheme
- contracted-out mixed benefit (COMB) scheme.

The courts have decided that the term 'occupational pension scheme' should be given a wide – and not a narrow – interpretation.

☞ *You were the managing director of a company and your remuneration package included a pension on your retirement. Following your retirement, the company challenged your right to the pension on the ground that you did not belong to an occupational pension scheme. So what, in the circumstances, does an occupational pension scheme mean?*

An occupational pension scheme, according to a recent case, means a scheme or arrangement which applies to 'earners' with qualifying service in an employment, that is a person who earns remuneration from his or her employment. While 'qualifying service' has not been defined, it should also be viewed as having a very wide meaning, the court held.

2.1.3 Contributions

How much you are required to pay into your occupational pension scheme will depend on the particular scheme rules. It is usually a percentage of your earnings. However your contributions cannot exceed 15% of your annual earnings before deductions (tax and national insurance contributions).

If you earn £30,000 a year your contribution must not exceed £4,500 (£30,000 × 15%).

Tax relief is automatically given through the PAYE system. Your employer will deduct your contributions from your pay before income tax is calculated on the balance. A higher rate taxpayer will also get higher rate tax relief. For example, your gross pay is, say, £30,000. Your pension contributions are £1,500. Your net pay will be £28,500. Your income tax will be calculated on £28,500 (subject to any other allowances or relief).

2.1.4 Tax approved schemes

The administrator will arrange to get tax approval for your scheme from the Inland Revenue which will probably grant approval provided that the contributions paid into the scheme, the money held by the scheme and the benefits paid out of the scheme in the form of pension benefits etc. do not exceed specified limits. The Inland Revenue maximum limits ensure that the tax reliefs cost no more than Parliament intended.

Tax relief is automatically given through the PAYE system. Your employer will deduct your contributions from your pay before income tax is calculated on the balance. A higher-rate taxpayer will also get higher-rate tax relief.

However, tax relief will only be available on payments made to you out of funds held for the purposes of an occupational pensions scheme if they were authorised by the rules of the scheme.

☞ *At the age of 55 you retired from your position as executive director of your company at a time when you were suffering from high blood pressure and mild diabetes. However, you continued to work as a non-executive director. You were a member of the company's occupational pension scheme under which there was a discretion to award an immediate pension to an early leaver who retired 'in normal health at or after the age of 50'. You have received payments under the scheme but the Inland Revenue have informed you that they intend to tax you on these payments. You wish to challenge that view.*

In a recent case, the Court of Appeal held that:

a) a company included its directors in its employees and

b) retirement meant ceasing service altogether.

It did not mean or include a change in the nature of that service from executive to non-executive director. It followed that the payments were not authorised by the scheme rules because they were not made to a member who 'retired within the meaning of the trust deed'. Accordingly, the payments were taxable.

2.1.5   Minimum benefits

The most popular occupational scheme is the contracted-out salary-related scheme (COSR) which provides members with a pension related to their earnings. These are also known as final salary schemes. Both you and your employer can make contributions into this kind of scheme.

Note: Your employer must decide to contract out for the whole scheme. As a scheme member you have no choice and if you object to being contracted out, your only option would be to leave the scheme.

Up to April 1997, contracted-out salary-related schemes were obliged to pay members a guaranteed minimum pension (GMP) when they retired. Guaranteed minimum pension rights broadly equate to what your additional pension would have been you had not been in a contracted-out scheme.

Since 6 April 1997, a test of overall quality (the reference scheme test) was set out in the Pensions Act 1995 with regard to contracted-out salary-related schemes. This means that before it can contract out of the additional State pension, a scheme has to offer you benefits roughly the same as, or better than, the test standard. After that date, in order to continue to contract out, salary-related schemes have to meet the reference scheme test.

2.1.6   Maximum benefits

The benefits which can be paid out from a tax-approved occupational pension scheme are restricted to maximum limits. These are expressed as a fraction of your final salary for each year you worked for your employer. This applies both to pension and lump sum benefits. The fraction is expressed as:

Accrual rate × Service × Final remuneration

The *accrual rate:* this is the rate at which your pension builds up according to the rules of your pension scheme. The maximum pension which can be paid under the tax rules is two-thirds of final remuneration.

Service: as a general rule 'service' includes all the time you have worked for your employer but the term should be defined specifically in your scheme membership booklet. For instance, where you have contributions transferred from another scheme, those credits may be included.

Final remuneration: remuneration can include your salary, wages, overtime pay, bonuses, commission, benefits-in-kind etc. It will depend on the provisions of your scheme. Your membership booklet should set out which types of remuneration will be taken into account for pension purposes.

In a recent case the court held that in one particular scheme the 'total remuneration from the employer' did not include benefits in kind, which were not therefore to be taken into account in the computation of either benefits or contributions payable out of or into the scheme. In that case the terms of the trust deed governing the scheme variously referred to an employee's total 'pay', 'salary', 'earnings' and 'remuneration' and were concerned solely with cash payments. That conclusion was supported by the fact that there was no mechanism in the scheme for valuing and apportioning the relevant benefits.

Your final remuneration is the pay you received at or near retirement on which your pension benefits are calculated. An average over three years is taken of payments which vary, such as overtime and bonuses.

2.1.7 Additional payments

If you are an active member of an occupational pension scheme your employer must allow you to make additional voluntary contributions (AVCs) in order to improve your pension benefits. Your scheme will only accept additional voluntary contributions and regular contributions if the increased benefits they secure will remain within the maximum permitted limits.

2.2 Personal pensions

You can make regular savings for your retirement through a personal pension scheme (PPS). These are provided by financial service companies such as insurance companies, banks, investment companies and building societies. The money in your pension fund will be invested to provide you with regular income when you retire. Personal pension schemes are not run by the State but they are approved by the Inland Revenue and have tax advantages.

Note: you will normally get tax relief on your contributions but remember that you may have to pay charges to your pension scheme provider.

From 6 April 2001, you no longer have to be working to join or pay into a personal pension scheme.

Before your purchase a personal pension, you must seek independent financial advice. The adviser you chose should be authorised by the Financial Services Authority (FSA) (see section 9 below) which is the independent watchdog set up by the Government and is the sole body for regulating the UK financial services industry and protecting the rights of retail customers.

The Financial Services Authority also provides online comparative tables that compare different financial products, for example for their charges and flexibility. See *www.fsa.gov.uk/tables*.

2.2.1 Main features of personal pensions

Personal pensions can be attractive as they offer choice and flexibility. They are available through a wide range of organisations (see above). Your employers may contribute if they wish to do so.

You can start taking your benefits at any time between 50 and 75-years-old. You may contribute to a PPS even if you are not working so long as your contributions do not exceed certain limits (see below).

If you pay contributions based on the level of your earnings, you do not need to provide proof of earnings every year. Once you have provided evidence of your earnings, you can make payments based on those earnings for that year and the following 5 years.

2.2.2 Joining a personal pension scheme

From 6 April 2001 you are entitled to join a personal pension scheme if you are under 75-years-old and you have earnings chargeable to UK tax which are not covered by your employer's occupational pension scheme (OPS).

You may also join a personal pension scheme if you have no earnings at all but you are:

- resident and ordinarily resident in the UK; or
- a Crown servant serving overseas; or
- the spouse of a Crown servant serving overseas.

Most people who are members of their employers' occupational pension schemes may make personal pension contributions at the same time.

For further guidance see Inland Revenue Leaflet IR3 (*www.inlandrevenue.gov.uk*) and see DIRECTORY.

2.2.3 Contributing to a personal pension scheme

Contributions can be made to a personal pension scheme (PPS) by yourself (as the scheme member), by your employers (if they wish to make contributions) and by the Inland Revenue National Insurance Contributions Office (if the PPS has been used to contract out of the additional State pension).

Every person who is eligible to make contributions to a PPS can make payments up to the earnings threshold limit in each year. This is the case even if you have no earnings. The annual limit includes the total amounts paid by you and your employer.

2.2.4 Earnings threshold

The earnings threshold is £3,600 for the tax years 2001–2002 and 2002–2003. This figure includes tax relief at the basic rate. However you may be allowed to make contributions above the earnings threshold in certain circumstances.

Moreover, if you have left work but your income level means that you could pay contributions higher than the earnings threshold, special rules allow you to continue to pay the higher contributions even though you no longer have earnings.

☞ *You stopped work four years ago. You would like to continue to pay contributions in to your pension fund from interest on your savings. You have no earned income.*

You are allowed to make contributions for up to five years after the year in which you ceased employment.

2.2.5 Return of contributions

Personal pensions are provided to give you an income when you retire. The contributions you make and the fund investments both benefit from tax relief. The contributions and the fund investments cannot be refunded as they will be used to provide you with pension benefits on your retirement. However if you should pay an amount which does not qualify for tax relief, it will be returned to you.

2.2.6 Tax reliefs

From 6 April 2001, personal pension scheme contributions are treated as paid net of basic rate income tax (22% for 2002–2003). The pension scheme will then claim tax relief at the basic rate from the Inland Revenue on your behalf and add it to your fund.

If you pay tax at the higher rate (40% for 2002–2003) you can claim the balance of the tax relief due from the Inland Revenue. There is a section on your self-assessment return for this purpose. Alternatively, you can get form PP120 from your scheme administrator or your local tax office and return it to the tax office.

Further, your pension fund will be exempt from tax on any capital gains and most of the profits from investments made with your contributions. Some of the benefits paid under the scheme are also tax free (see section 2.5 below).

2.2.7 Retirement annuity contracts

Before personal pensions were introduced in June 1988, retirement annuity contracts existed. Individuals who were using a retirement annuity contract in 1988 can still make pension contributions to those schemes. Their rules are similar to those for personal pensions.

2.3 Stakeholder pensions

The stakeholder pension scheme has been available since 6 April 2001. It is a low-charge contracted-out scheme aimed at those individuals earning between £9,000 and £20,000 a year who currently have no pension provision. You use your own money to build up your pension fund. Your stakeholder pension scheme will put your contributions into investments such a stocks and shares for you and when you retire the fund will be used to purchase a pension for you.

Employers who have five or more employees are required by law to offer their employees access to a stakeholder pension scheme but they are not obliged to set up and run a scheme themselves – that is the job of pension providers who need to register as such. However, employers who offer access to a stakeholder pension must give you information about the scheme they choose and give you the option to have your own pension contributions deducted from your pay.

Employers with fewer than five employees are exempt, although they can voluntarily offer access to stakeholder schemes. Employers who offer an occupational pension scheme or a personal pension scheme may also be exempt as long as they contribute at least three per cent of earnings into that form of non-State pension and as long as the pension does not impose penalties for employees who leave the scheme.

2.3.1 Why choose a stakeholder pension?

Stakeholder pensions must by law meet a set of minimum standards to ensure that they offer value for money, flexibility and security. According to these standards:

- scheme providers can only charge you a maximum of one per cent of the value of your pension fund each year to manage you fund
- if you choose to transfer into or out of a stakeholder pension, or you stop paying your contributions for a time, the scheme provider cannot charge you extra
- all stakeholder schemes will accept contributions of as little as £20, which you can pay weekly, monthly or at less regular intervals
- each scheme must be run by trustees or an authorised stakeholder manager, who will be responsible for making sure that the scheme meets the various legal requirements.

Note: if you are paying your contributions through your employer, you may be able to change the amount you pay only every six months.

2.3.2 Contributing to a stakeholder scheme

You can invest up to £3,600 in your stakeholder pension each year no matter how much you earn. That limit includes the contributions you make, any contributions made by your employer and any tax relief from the Inland Revenue. However the limit does not include any NIC rebate paid if you have contracted out of the State earnings-related pension scheme (SERPS) or State second pension (SSP).

2.3.3 Employees

If you are a member of an occupational pension scheme, you may be able to add to your pension by starting a stakeholder pension as well. You will need to check with your scheme administrator as to whether this is permitted.

2.3.4 Pension benefits

When you start to receive your pension it will be paid through an annuity which you buy with the money invested in your stakeholder pension (see chapter on *Growing Old*). You do not have to purchase an annuity from the scheme provider with whom you had your stakeholder pension. It is worth shopping around to compare other options on offer. (See also section 2.5.2 below.)

2.4 Pensions for the self-employed

If you are self-employed, you can build up an entitlement to the basic State pension but you will not receive any additional State pension (SSP). Also, if you are self-employed you cannot join an occupational pension scheme (OPS). You may therefore wish to consider joining a stakeholder pension scheme and/or a personal pension scheme (see above, section 2.2) to provide you with extra income in retirement.

2.4.1 Contribution breaks

If you think you might wish to, or have to, take a break in the regular pension contributions you pay, it might be worth considering a stakeholder pension before starting a personal pension scheme (PPS), as a PPS may charge you if you stop making contributions. As a general rule it is better to start paying into the same scheme when you start to make contributions again as this is likely to be cheaper than starting another scheme.

2.4.2 Charges for advice

You may also pay for financial advice indirectly if you buy a personal pension scheme (PPS) from a financial adviser. They must tell you how much commission they will make from selling you a personal pension.

Note: the adviser's commission and charges will be deducted from your contributions, which will reduce the amount actually invested.

Before committing to a pension scheme be sure to check the following:

- any charges you might have to pay
- the level of investment risk; and
- exactly how much of your contributions will be invested in your pension scheme.

On the other hand, any advice regarding a stakeholder pension has to be optional if an extra charge is made for it. Any charge must be made separately and not deducted from your pension contributions.

2.5 What you can do with your pension

Personal pensions are designed to be flexible and benefits can be taken at any time between the ages of 50 and 75. Not all benefits have to be taken at the same time so long as they are all taken by the age of 75.

Special rules apply if you are under 50 and incapable of carrying on your normal occupation because of illness or injury. You may also be entitled to take benefits before the age of 50 if the Inland Revenue have agreed a lower pension age for your particular occupation.

Note: these rules will no longer apply under the new pension proposals (see section 7 below) from 2004.

2.5.1 Tax-free lump sums

You may elect to take up to 25% of your pension fund as a lump sum but you are also required to buy an annuity or take income withdrawals at the same time. It is not permitted to take the lump sum without touching the other 75%.

2.5.2 Annuities

An annuity is an investment product that you are required to purchase with your pension fund to provide you with a pension. It is a contract between you and an insurance company. The insurance company agrees to provide you with a guaranteed pension income for the rest of your life in return for the money in your pension fund.

The cost of an annuity will depend on the market annuity rates at the date when you purchase it. It will be based on factors such as your age and sex, the type of annuity you opt for and which provider you buy it from.

You can buy an annuity from your pension provider (if it is an insurance company) or from any other insurance company which offers annuities (the open-market option).

The purchase of an annuity means that you have to forgo the capital which you have accumulated in your fund (with the exception of the lump sum (see 2.5.1 immediately above).

2.5.2(a) What your annuity can provide

Your annuity may pay you one of the following:

- a level pension
- a pension which increases at a fixed rate each year
- a pension linked to the growth in the underlying assets; or
- an index-linked pension.

It is also possible to purchase an annuity guaranteed for up to ten years from the date of purchase or which guarantees to increase your pension at a fixed rate each year, but such annuities are more expensive.

The size of your pension will depend on a number of factors including how much you have paid in; how successfully the money has been invested; whether you are providing benefits for your spouse and/or dependants; whether you decide to take a tax-free lump sum; and the type of annuity you purchase.

☞ *Your pension scheme providers have announced that guaranteed annuity rates under the scheme will not apply to new members or other additional premiums payable on or after a specified date. They say that they are entitled to make these changes and have pointed out that the guaranteed rates will continue to apply for existing members in relation to premiums paid or contracted to be paid prior to the date of the change.*

Depending on the terms of your occupational pension scheme, the insurer may be entitled to make amendments to the guaranteed annuity rates for new entrants to the scheme or to subsequent increases in the premiums to be paid or benefits accrued. The High Court has held that so long as the changes do not affect any existing insurance, there is no more reason for precluding changes to the terms applicable to new insurances than for preventing an insurance company from increasing the rates charged to a householder on an annual renewal of his contents policy.

2.5.2(b) Annuities on death

If you are receiving pension income from an annuity when you die, your pensions scheme may provide for an annuity for your surviving spouse or dependants.

An annuity for your spouse must be payable for life unless it is designed to end if he or she remarries. An annuity for your child has to end at the age of 18 or when the child finishes full-time education, if later, unless the child continues to qualify as a dependant.

2.5.3 Income withdrawal

Income withdrawal allows you to put off purchasing an annuity and take benefits direct from your pension fund. If you choose this option, your fund will remain invested under the scheme rules. However, you must still purchase an annuity by your 75th birthday.

If you opt for income withdrawal, you must withdraw from your fund each year at least 35% and no more than 100% of the annuity which could have been purchased with your fund on the day you started taking your benefits. You can make withdrawals at regular intervals (e.g. monthly or quarterly) or annually, either in advance or in arrears.

The withdrawal limits will be calculated by your scheme administrator based on tables produced by the Government Actuary's Department. The limits will generally be reviewed every three years.

2.5.4 What happens when you die

If you die whilst drawing benefits by way of income withdrawal, the treatment of your fund will depend on the rules of your scheme, but you will normally have nominated a surviving spouse or dependant to receive benefits from the fund when you die. If so, he or she will be have several options. They can:

- purchase an annuity to provide immediate benefits
- postpone purchasing an annuity if he or she is under 60
- take pension payments by way of income withdrawal, although an annuity must be purchased by their 75th birthday
- take their share of the fund as a lump sum which will be taxed at 35% (protected rights must be used to provide a pension only).

Note: the initial amount of all survivor's pension benefits cannot be more than the highest annual amount of the annuity that your fund would have provided for you at the date of your death.

3 LEGAL PITFALLS

In this section, we cover some of the legal pitfalls of pension provision. Do note, however, that the issues discussed below are not exhaustive. Furthermore, each scheme depends on its own rules, and entitlements are governed not only by our personal circumstances (such as retirement age) but by circumstances beyond our control (such as market volatility).

For issues relating to pension mis-selling, see section 8; for the role of the Financial Services Authority, see section 9.

3.1 Fixed-term and temporary employees

From October 2002, regulations came into force designed to prevent discrimination against employees on fixed-term contracts.

If you are a fixed-term employee and feel you are receiving less favourable treatment than permanent employees as regards your pension, you will need to identify a full-time employee carrying out the same duties against whom you can compare your circumstances to show less favourable treatment. Your employer will then have to show that the difference in treatment is objectively justified.

☞ *You are on a fixed-term contract of 18 months. Your application to join an occupational pension scheme has been turned down. You have been told that there is a minimum two-year qualifying period.*

  It is not unusual for an occupational pension scheme to require a two-year service period before a member qualifies for retirement benefits. Following the new regulations, it is questionable whether a tribunal would accept that it is justifiable to exclude fixed-term employees with contracts of less than two years from pension scheme membership.

Temporary workers are often employed on fixed-term contracts, in which case the regulations will apply to them. For the position of part-time employees, see section 4.5 below.

3.2   Leaving a scheme

If you leave your pension scheme, your benefits have to be preserved to give you a pension at normal retirement age. If you retire before that, your benefits will be calculated according to the scheme rules. If you have been in the scheme for two years or more, it is a legal requirement that your pension rights are so protected.

If you have been in the scheme for less than two years, and the scheme rules permit it, you may claim a refund of the contributions already paid. However once you have received the refund, you will not be entitled to any benefits for the period to which the refund relates. If a refund is not allowed under the scheme rules, your pension rights must be preserved in any event.

Note: if you have transferred benefits from a previous scheme, you may not be entitled to a refund.

Warning: any refund of pension contributions within two years will be taxed at a special rate of 20%. The tax will be deducted by the scheme administrator and the balance paid to you. This applies even if you do not normally pay income tax, and it is not possible to reclaim the tax deducted.

3.3   Early retirement

If you retire early, the rules for occupational pension schemes are different from those which apply to personal or stakeholder schemes.

3.3.1   Occupational pensions

Each occupational scheme sets its own rules within the framework of what is permitted by the Inland Revenue. Early retirement is permitted by the Revenue any time after the age of 50 but the scheme can adopt any age it wishes provided it is not before the age of 50.

Before benefits can be paid early under an occupational pension scheme, you must actually leave the employment to which the scheme relates. There are usually other conditions you need to comply with under the scheme rules before you can claim early retirement benefits. The most common is that early retirement may be subject to the consent of the employer who in practice often refuses to grant it. If your employer refuses to allow you to take early retirement benefits, it is difficult to challenge that decision successfully.

Most schemes will reduce the pension earned to the date of early retirement to allow for the fact that it is going to be paid earlier and for a longer period. The rate of reduction may be laid down in the scheme rules but often it varies according to the recommendation of the scheme actuary.

The effect of reducing the pension entitlement to allow for early payment might result in the early-retirement pension being reduced to a level which is less than the guaranteed minimum pension (see 2.1.4 above). If that is the case, many schemes will not grant an early-retirement pension until the reduced pension is at least equal to the guaranteed minimum pension. Some schemes offer preferential terms if you retire directly from the company's employment rather than if you seek to retire some time after you have left the company's service.

Some schemes provide enhanced early-retirement terms in the case of redundancy. This can take the form of applying a lower rate of reduction or even no reduction at all. In some cases the company may go further and augment the pension earned at the date of redundancy.

3.3.2 Personal and stakeholder schemes

The rules governing personal and stakeholder schemes differ from those which apply to company schemes significantly in that you do not have to retire from your employment before you can draw on the benefits of your scheme.

You can draw benefits any time after the age of 50 but you have to start to draw benefits by the time you reach the age of 75.

Remember: the earlier you draw your pension, the lower the income provided will be.

3.3.3 Additional voluntary contributions

The Inland Revenue applies different rules to the extra contributions you pay into your occupational scheme through additional voluntary contributions (AVCs) even though they are treated as part of the same scheme.

Note: the different rules will only apply if the trustees of the scheme agree. There is no automatic right to apply them.

Under the rules, you are allowed to take your AVC pension any time after the age of 50 but before the age of 75 without having to retire from the relevant employment. This pension does not have to be taken at the same time as other benefits under the company scheme.

3.3.4 Illness

The issue of early retirement on grounds of ill-health has caused controversy down the years. Ill-health retirements are undoubtedly expensive and employers often complain that they can be abused. The rules of your particular pension scheme will dictate who decides whether you qualify for retirement on grounds of ill-health, and stringent medical tests are often imposed.

☞ *You have just passed your 50th birthday and have left your job as a secretary in a busy office citing stress-related ill-health as the reason. You claimed an immediate early pension from your employer. The rules of your pension scheme require the consent of your employers on the ground that the employer was to be the sole judge of ill-health. You were examined by a doctor who stated that while you are not capable of doing your former job, you could do part-time, less demanding work in the future. Your employer has therefore rejected your claim for an ill-health pension on the basis that the doctor did not say that you would not be able to work again prior to your normal retirement age of 62. Do you have any right of appeal?*

In a similar case, the court held that the pension rules did not require the employer to assess whether, as at the date of the proposed retirement, the member would or might have the potential to engage in any alternative income-earning activities. The only question was whether or not the ill-health from which the member was suffering was such that he could not continue performing his current job. If the answer was that he could not, and so would have to leave service, then he would in principle be entitled on retirement to the payment of an ill-health pension.

3.4 Transferring your fund

It is possible to transfer your pension fund provided that you are not already receiving benefits. Transfers can be made, inter alia, as follows:

- between personal pension schemes (PPSs)
- from retirement annuity contracts to PPSs
- from personal pension schemes to employers' occupational pension schemes (OPSs)
- from occupational pension scheme to personal pension schemes and vice versa
- from one occupational pension scheme to another.

Note: your personal pension scheme may impose a charge for arranging a transfer but your pension scheme administrator is not under any duty to advise you as to whether you have made the right decision to transfer.

☞ *You have just changed your job and considered transferring the accrued benefits from your old employer's scheme to the Local Government Superannuation Scheme (LGSS). You were unclear about the definition of 'qualifying' service in the scheme literature but have been unable to find a definition in the leaflet you have been given. You telephoned the pension fund to ask for clarification and were told that your service with your old employer would be added to your pensionable service in the LGSS to give you a pension based on 40/80ths of your final salary on retirement. You went ahead with the transfer on that basis. You have now discovered that the transfer in fact had the effect of substantially devaluing your rights under the old scheme. You want to know whether there is anyone you can complain to.*

In one reported case, an employee complained that his pension scheme administrators had not explained to him the difference between the types of service or explained on what disadvantageous terms the transfer would be made. The court held that the administrators were not under any duty to give the advice which would have prevented the employee from transferring his pension benefits. Moreover, there was no general duty on an employer to provide information and/or advice to an employee in order to prevent economic loss, or any such duty on trustees of a pension scheme.

3.5 Pension scheme changes

There has been a lot of publicity in the press in recent months about employers closing their pension schemes to new members, or winding up their pension schemes. Employers and scheme trustees are often given wide powers to amend the rules (usually subject to each other's consent).

Your pension scheme should make detailed provision for what would happen if it is wound up and the trustees have to distribute the assets in the scheme fund in accordance with the rules laid down.

☞ *You have been working in the same job for 19 years and have been a member of its contracted-out pension scheme throughout. The company has just given you notice of its intention to close down the existing scheme and launch a new one and you are not sure what your rights are.*

Your employer will normally have to get your consent if it wants you to transfer to the new scheme. It can only transfer you without your consent if both the old and new schemes are run by your employer or connected employers or if you and your colleagues are being transferred as part of a take-over or a sell-off. It must also be certified that your rights under the new scheme are no less favourable, broadly speaking, than those in your existing scheme. Any pension benefits must also be broadly the same.

It is not easy to get most actuaries to make such a certification so it is likely that you will be offered extra credits to induce you to transfer rather than leave your deferred pension on the old scheme.

The scheme trustees will distribute the assets in the fund either by transferring them into another scheme or by taking out insurance policies with immediate annuities for existing pensioners and deferred annuities for all other members. However you will not be entitled to a cash handout as the funds set aside for pensions are required to be placed into some other pension arrangement.

The trustees are under a duty to apply the pension fund in strict accordance with its rules.

☞ *Your company is winding up and distributing its occupational pension scheme. The scheme is in part a final-salary scheme and in part a money-purchase scheme. The trustees are concerned about the possibility of adverse claims being made against them after the final distribution when there will be no assets left to meet the expense of any litigation. They want to acquire an indemnity insurance policy but you do not think that would be a proper use of the pension moneys.*

In a case on similar facts, the court said that although it sympathised with the trustees' wish to acquire insurance cover, it could not be said that the cost of the premium was an expense of the administration of the scheme or its determination. They were simply costs which the trustees wished to expend for their own exclusive benefit.

3.6   Shortfalls

If your pension is in a money-purchase scheme, the amount available for transfer will depend on the value of your pension fund. However if your scheme is a final-salary or mixed scheme there may be a shortfall in the funds available. In this case, the statutory rules will apply which set out the order in which the funds are applied as follows:

1) costs and expenses
2) additional voluntary contribution (AVC) benefits
3) 'live' pensions already being paid out and future pensions for pensioners' spouses, but not pension increases in the future
4) contracted-out pension rights; and
5) remaining deferred pensions and current members' accrued pensions.

As a last resort, if there is a shortfall in the funds as a result of fraud or misappropriation, the Pensions Compensation Board has power to pay benefits to individuals until the scheme is unravelled, after which it can pay a lump sum to close the scheme.

If an occupational pension scheme has a shortfall in funding, it is open to the trustees to negotiate a compromise with the employer.

☞   *You are a member of a final salary pension scheme which is subject to the statutory minimum funding requirements (MFR) imposed by the Pensions Act 1995 which requires periodic actuarial valuations of the scheme. The funding requirements' valuation disclosed a serious under-provision but the contributions required from your employers to bring the fund up to the required provision will force your company into liquidation, in which case the trustees would only receive a small proportion of the deficit. The scheme trustees have taken independent professional advice and negotiated a compromise under which the scheme would receive significantly more than it would recover in a liquidation but considerably less than the full amount of the minimum funding requirement deficit. A question has arisen whether the trustees are entitled to compromise the shortfall.*

In a recent case, the court said that the Pensions Act characterised the shortfall as a debt and there was no reason why, as a matter of construction or public policy, a trustee should not be able to compromise such a debt in the exercise of its powers by means which it honestly and reasonably believed would secure the largest possible amount towards the shortfall. It was giving effect to the legislation in the best practical way.

3.7   Surplus

It is possible that there may be a surplus in your scheme fund, which means that there is more money available than is required to pay all the benefits due.

☞   *Your employer is closing its pension scheme and it appears that there will be a surplus which the company is claiming for itself. You and your fellow employees want the scheme trustees to use the surplus to increase your benefits up to the permitted limits before it goes back to your employer. Is there anything you can do?*

If you are lucky enough to be a member of a scheme which provides that any surplus must be used to increase members' benefits before it goes to the employer, the trustees must apply that rule.

Otherwise, before your employer can obtain the surplus, your scheme trustees must be satisfied that all liabilities under the scheme have been met. This includes making pension increases. The trustees should also exercise any discretion to make further increases or take a decision not to do so and indicate why.

Once the trustees decide to pay any remaining surplus over to the employer, they must inform all the scheme members of their intention and you must have at least two months within which to write to the Occupational Pensions Regulatory Authority (OPRA) if you wish to raise any objections. The trustees are required to check whether there have been any objections and give you three months' notice if they still intend to go ahead. OPRA also have detailed technical requirements and the scheme rules may need to be modified before the payment can go ahead. (See DIRECTORY for details of the Occupational Pensions Regulatory Authority (OPRA).)

Where an employer decides to close an existing pension scheme to new entrants, and creates a new scheme to coexist with the original scheme, it is entitled to fund its contributions in respect of the new scheme from the surplus in the fund which had accrued when only the original scheme was in operation.

☞ *Your employer has closed its final salary pension scheme to new entrants and established in its place a money-purchase scheme. The final salary scheme was substantially in surplus. As an existing employee you were free to transfer from the old to the new scheme if you wished. Your employer used the surplus to reduce to nil its contributions to both schemes. You believe that the use of the surplus to fund its contributions to the new scheme amounted to maladministration.*

In a case on similar facts, the court decided on the evidence that there were two separate schemes operating within a single trust fund. The employer had the right to use the surplus in the fund to finance its contributions to the new scheme. The court concluded that the introduction of the new scheme was not intended to cause the employer to lose that right in relation to either fund. In any event, the surplus did not belong to the pensioner or employees under the old scheme. It could not sensibly be argued that a member of a pension scheme had any 'right', much less an accrued right, to or in relation to a surplus.

3.8 Change of employer

If your company is taken over or sold off and its business transferred to a new owner, the transaction is subject to the Transfer of Undertakings (Protection of Employment) Regulations 1981 (TUPE). However, until recently, it was generally accepted that TUPE covered everything except occupational pension schemes and that liabilities relating to occupational pension scheme 'benefits for old age, invalidity or survivors' did not transfer.

This has now been thrown into doubt by a decision of the European Court of Justice which ruled that benefits payable by a pension scheme after the age of 50 on the redundancy of an employee were not 'old age benefits' so that the rights to those benefits did transfer.

The full implications of that decision are still to be worked out but it would appear that, where TUPE applies, redundancy benefits under a pension scheme will transfer with the business, as may other benefits such as early retirement. But it looks as though invalidity benefits and benefits for spouses and dependants still do not transfer.

If you may benefit from the changes as a result of the decision, you may be able to make a claim even if the TUPE transfer occurred long ago and even if you left your job in the last six years. If you feel you may have a claim, do seek legal advice on your particular circumstances.

3.9 Misrepresentation

If your employer is trying to persuade you and your fellow scheme members to accept a transfer of your employment contracts, they must take care not to misrepresent the effect of the transfer on your pension rights.

In a recent case, the court held that hundreds of employees were entitled to damages for loss sustained as the result of allegedly false and/or misleading promises and representations made to them by both their former employer and their new employer in order to persuade them to agree to the transfer of their contracts of employment. The former employer had represented to the employees that their pension rights under the new employer would be broadly similar to their former rights, whereas in fact some would have been as much as five per cent worse off.

The court was satisfied that, in the context of this case, 'broadly similar' would meant that the benefits under the new scheme would be within two per cent of those under the old scheme. Although no employee would have been able to prevent the transfer from going ahead by withholding consent individually, had they been advised properly as to the pensions position, the employees as a whole would not have agreed to some of their number being as much as five per cent worse off. This would have necessitated further negotiations between the two companies which would have achieved the level of comparability that the court considered appropriate. In the circumstances the employees were entitled to damages equal to the additional benefits that those negotiations would have achieved.

4 PENSIONS AND WOMEN

Women often have very different career patterns from men and so they need to give special consideration to their pension arrangements in the light of their personal circumstances. For instance, women often combine paid work with caring for children or disabled or elderly relatives, which can lead to them building up inadequate pensions. If they are married, they may be dependent on their husband's pension rights.

4.1 Eligibility for State pension

At present, women can get their State pension at the age of 60 and men at age 65. From 6 April 2020, the State pension age for both will be 65. The change is being introduced gradually over the 10-year period 2010–2020 for women (see also above section 1.1.1).

If you are a woman born before 6 April 1950, you will not be affected by the change. You can claim your State pension at 60.

If you were born between 6 April 1950 and 5 April 1955, your State pension age will be between 60 and 65. To find out your State pension age and the date on which you will reach it, see Leaflet PM6: *Pensions for Women – Your Guide*; *www.pensionguide.gov.uk*.

If you were born on or after 6 April 1955 you can claim your State pension at 65 years of age.

Note: the changes will not affect men.

4.2 Consequential changes

2010 is a very significant year in the development of pension rules. From 2010 the current arrangement allowing married women to get a pension based on their spouse's national insurance contributions (NICs) is to be extended to men. Thereafter, both men and women will be able to get a pension based on their spouse's NIC if that is better than a pension based on their own contribution record.

From 2010 if you choose to put off claiming the State pension on reaching pension age, you will gain at least 10% (currently 7.5%) for each year you delay drawing your pension. You can also put off claiming your State pension for as long as you wish; and the extra pension claimable for adult dependants will be the same for men and women.

Note: graduated retirement benefit after 6 April 2010 will be calculated for women on the same basis as men.

4.3 Married women's contributions

Before April 1977, married women could choose to pay a lower rate of national insurance contributions (NIC). If you made this choice and have not paid full-rate contributions, you have not built up any basic State pension of your own and have to rely on your husband's contribution record. This option ended in April 1977 but anyone already paying the lower rate could continue to do so.

☞ *You are a married woman aged 53 who works as a secretary in an insurance firm. After you married in 1975 you chose to pay the lower rate of NIC and continued to do so when the rules were changed in April 1977. Your sister has just told you that you will not be entitled to a basic State pension when you retire or get any benefit from credits or home responsibilities protection (HRP) while you are paying the lower rate. What can you do?*

It is true that you will not be earning a basic State pension or get any benefit from credits or HRP while you are paying the lower rate. On the other hand you will be able to get a pension based on your husband's contributions when you both reach pension age and make a claim. You could also improve your pension position by opting to pay the full rate NIC at any time before you reach State pension age. It is worth considering this course as you can build up entitlement to a State second pension with as little as one year's contributions at the full rate.

Warning: you will need at least ten years of contributions before you can receive any basic State pension at all based on your own record.

4.4   Pension based on husband's contributions

If you are a woman with no State pension of your own or have only built up a small pension, you can get a pension based on your husband's pension when you and your husband have both reached pension age (see section 4.3).

Such a pension will be, at most, 60% of the full rate of the basic State retirement pension but only so long as your husband has earned a full pension himself.

☞ *You are a 61-year-old woman and your husband has just retired at the age of 65. You have worked part-time during your marriage except when your children were small. When you did work you chose to pay the lower rate NIC until 1977 when the rules changed and you elected to pay the full rate. You have been told that you are entitled to a small pension but it is lower than the full basic-rate pension. You wonder whether you are entitled to a State pension based on your husband's contributions since he has earned a full pension himself.*

You should be entitled to up to 60% of the full basic State pension based on your husband's contributions. However you cannot claim a pension based on your husband's pension as well as your own State pension. If the pension you have earned on your own contributions is more than the amount that you would get based on your husband's contributions, you will be paid the higher amount but not both.

At present, a married man cannot claim a pension based on his wife's NIC record but this is to change from 2010 when the State pension age for women starts to change to bring it into line with that of men (see section 4.2).

4.5   Part-time employees

It is unlawful to exclude part-time employees from membership of a company's occupational pension scheme. It is still the case that most part-time employees are women so that if only full-time workers were allowed to join, it would amount to indirect discrimination against women.

Following a ruling in 2000 by the European Court to that effect, around 60,000 claims were made by former part-time employees, mostly teachers, nurses and health workers, local government employees and bank staff. The European Court ruled that Community law precluded the UK rule that compensation for such claims could cover only the two years prior to the date of claim. As a consequence, the two-year cap was abolished from 1 October 2002 to bring English law into line with EC law. However, claims are time-barred unless brought within six months of the date when you leave your employment.

In addition, since July 2000, regulations have been in force to ensure that part-time workers in the same category as full-time employees must also be able to join the pension scheme. The benefits from the pension have to be on a pro-rata basis, in line with those of full-time staff.

☞ *You have worked part-time in a supermarket for three years but you are not allowed to join the company pension scheme as you only work part-time. However all full-time employees can join the scheme. A colleague has told you that she read in the newspapers that you are now entitled to join the scheme but your employer still says you are not. Is this correct?*

Your colleague is right. You are entitled to join the company pension scheme retrospectively from the date you joined the company. However you will be required to pay any compulsory employee's contributions that would have been due during that period. You should approach your employer again who will hopefully be willing to reach an informal settlement. But if they refuse to allow you to join, you can apply to an Employment Tribunal claiming discrimination.

Further, women cannot be made to retire earlier than men in the same category of job, but the position is complicated by the fact that for schemes which provided for unequal retirement ages before 1990 (when the European Court of Justice ruled that men and women had to be treated equally) those ages can still be used to calculate the pension built up before that date.

5   PENSIONS ON DIVORCE

If you get divorced or have your marriage annulled, the courts must take into account the value of all your assets, including the value of your pension rights in order to decide how all your assets should be divided.

The first significant attempt to permit a former spouse to acquire statutory pension rights on retirement was the introduction of 'earmarking' in 1995.

It was soon realised that earmarking was not a satisfactory solution in every case, but it was not until 1 December 2000 that rules were introduced to allow couples whose marriage had ended in divorce or annulment to share the value of their pension rights by pension sharing. This is intended to provide greater flexibility and choice and a clean break.

Note: pension sharing does not apply if you separate but do not divorce.

Pension sharing is not compulsory. If you want a share of your spouse's pension, the court will only use its powers to grant an earmarking order or pension-sharing order against a scheme member if you cannot reach agreement with your former spouse.

5.1   Earmarking pensions

The concept of reserving pension for a former spouse was introduced by the Pensions Act 1995 and gives the court power to make an order to earmark pension benefits accrued by one spouse for the benefit of the other. This has to be done by the court issuing and serving an order on the trustees of the pension scheme. Therefore an order can only be made if negotiations for financial settlement have been unsuccessful and the matter goes to court.

☞ *You are divorcing your husband and as you have been a full-time home-maker and mother during your marriage you have not built up a pension for your retirement. As your husband has few assets apart from his pension, you would like to secure a part of his pension benefits on retirement for yourself. However you cannot get your husband to agree on an appropriate percentage. You want to ask the court to sort it out but what can it do?*

The court can order that part or all of the following be paid to a former spouse:

* the pension benefit at retirement
* a cash sum resulting from the conversion of the benefits, paid over at retirement
* any lump sum due together with part or all of a pension income; and
* any death in service benefits.

The order must specify the percentage of the pension member's rights to be earmarked, expressed as a percentage of the cash equivalent transfer value (CETV).

Earmarking future retirement benefits does not create a clean break, which is one of the main reasons why it is not regularly applied, whereas pension sharing creates two separate pension arrangements.

It does not apply to the basic State retirement pension since divorced people can already replace their own contribution record with their spouse's record for the time the marriage lasted; nor to couples who started divorce or annulment proceedings before 1 December 2000.

5.2   Advantages of earmarking

If an earmarking order is made and you have the smaller retirement provision you will have the benefit of some additional provisional for your retirement.

On the other hand, if you have built up a pension benefit up to the Inland Revenue maximum (e.g. in the case of an OPS, a pension of two-thirds of final salary), you are entitled to receive the additional earmarked benefits in addition to your own pension benefits. There is no restriction.

Note: this means that in practice you get a larger pension than you would usually be allowed to take. Furthermore, you will not have to pay income tax on the additional earmarked pension benefits.

5.3   Disadvantages of earmarking

The main problem with earmarking is that the spouse who is the pension-scheme member has full control over the pension. There is no guarantee of when the pension will be paid out as the pension scheme member will decide when to retire, and they could delay retirement until the age of 75. There is also no guarantee that the benefit will ever be paid. If poor investment decisions have been made, the pension fund can be severely reduced.

Neither your former husband or wife (the pension-scheme member) nor the pension-scheme trustees or managers are under any duty to keep you informed of the state of the pension fund or to notify you when the benefits are due to be paid. It is up to you to keep in touch with them.

If you have obtained an earmarking order and you remarry, you are likely to lose any right to a share of your former spouse's retirement benefit. As a general rule, you will not be entitled to the pension income benefits earmarked for you although orders in respect of lump sum benefits are more likely to be left in place even after you remarry.

If you are the one who has given up part of your pension to your former spouse, you will not be permitted to make up the loss by making additional pension investment beyond the allowable maximum. The maximum includes any amount given over to your former spouse. You will also have to pay income tax on all the pension income paid out (minus allowances) even though your former spouse will receive part of that income. This is because it is the member of the pension scheme itself who is liable to tax.

It is not possible to apply for an earmarking order if a pension scheme is already the subject of a pension-sharing order (see immediately below). They are mutually exclusive.

Be warned: if your former spouse, the member of the pension scheme, dies, the earmark order will cease. This is the case even if the death occurs after your spouse has retired and you are already receiving pension income. This could leave you with very reduced pension or none at all depending on what other provision you have made.

5.4   Pension-sharing orders

Since 1 December 2000, for the first time, a pension scheme member can transfer the value of his or her rights to his or her spouse. This means that your spouse will have an indefeasible pension in their own right. The new pension benefits are entirely independent so that he or she can choose when to retire without reference to you.

There has to be a court order before a pension share can be implemented. It is not enough to have an agreement or a deed of separation stating that it is going to happen. That is not enforceable and cannot be implemented. However it is possible to have a consent order where agreement is reached between between you and your spouse through your solicitors. In practice, this is what happens in the majority of cases.

Pension sharing is not retrospective and it is not possible to apply for a second pension-sharing order against the same scheme. But it is possible to have separate pension-sharing orders against separate schemes.

If your husband or wife has a series of pension plans, you may be able to apply for a pension-sharing order against one or more of those plans when you divorce. However, provided that you have an open-ended maintenance agreement, you could apply for a pension-sharing order against the other plans when you retire. It remains to be seen whether the court will consider this to be fair, depending on your particular circumstances.

☞ *You are a woman aged 52 who has made no pension provision as you looked after the home and children for most of your married life. You have been married for 25 years. You are in the middle of a divorce from your husband who is 60-years-old and has now retired. He has three occupational pensions and has been in his main scheme for the past 24 years. You are concerned about the treatment of your husband's pension rights. His various schemes have been valued at £175,000 and you have been offered a cash settlement of £35,000 in respect of his pension rights. You wonder whether this is a reasonable offer.*

Whether an offer is reasonable will depend on your particular circumstances. In your case points to be considered include the fact that a large portion of your husband's State pension was earned during your long marriage; the fact that as a consequence of the divorce you will only be entitled to a percentage of the full pension whereas your husband has access to the full State pension; the difference in your ages; and the fact that the basic State pension is index-linked. In a similar case, a wife eventually received a cash settlement of £70,000.

Remember: it is important to take into account the basic State pension. The general perception is that it is not worth much, but as the benefits are fully index-linked, it can add a substantial amount to the value of pension rights.

Note: if you divorce for a second or subsequent time it is possible to get a pension-sharing order against your pension in respect of which an order has already been made in a previous marriage.

5.5 Effect of pension-sharing order

A pension-sharing order can only take effect after the divorce decree has become absolute and only after seven days have elapsed following the end of the period allowed for filing a notice of appeal against the order. If you have obtained an order and your spouse appeals, the order cannot take effect until the appeal has been dealt with.

The order must state what percentage of the cash-equivalent transfer value (CETV) of the pension member's rights is to be transferred (in the same way as for earmarking orders, see 5.1 above).

The spouse transferring his or her pension will then be subject to a pension debit for the appropriate amount, while the transferee spouse will be entitled to a pension credit for the same amount.

☞ *You are a member of an occupational pension scheme and your fund has a cash-equivalent transfer value (CETV) of £250,000. Your wife obtains a pension-sharing order whereby you have been ordered to transfer 40% of your CETV to her.*

Your pension fund will be debited by £100,000 and your wife will receive a credit whereby she gains a pension fund of £100,000 in her own right.

5.6 Internal and external transfer

If you receive a pension credit, you can choose to become a member of the pension scheme of which it forms part (an internal transfer) or to have your credit transferred to a different scheme (an external transfer).

Which option you choose may depend on the rules of the scheme from which the credit is to be transferred. If it is an occupational pension scheme, it is more than likely that you will be offered only an external transfer. You can also ask for an external transfer where the order relates to a personal pension. By contrast, if the scheme in question is an unfunded public service scheme it may only be possible to call for an internal transfer so long as the scheme is not closed to new members.

6 PENSIONS IF YOU LIVE ABROAD

If you are planning to live abroad when you retire, any pension you receive from an occupational pension scheme will increase each year in line with the scheme rules and the current legislation.

However if you are going to live abroad permanently you will not be entitled to an annual increase in your State pension, which includes any additional State pension, unless you live in a country within the European Economic Area (EEA) or a country with which the UK has an agreement that permits these increases (called upratings).

The EEA is made up of all EC countries, Austria, Belgium, Denmark, Finland, France, Germany, Greece, Italy, Luxembourg, Netherlands, Portugal, Republic of Ireland, Spain, Sweden and the UK, together with Iceland, Lichtenstein and Norway.

The Department of Work and Pensions provides leaflets giving details of the position in particular countries (*www.dwp.gov.uk* and see DIRECTORY for the Overseas Benefits Directorate).

6.1 Length of time abroad

6.1.1 Three months or less

As regards your basic retirement pension, if you are planning to be abroad for three months or less, and your pension is paid into an account, this will continue as usual. If you have an order book, you will be able to cash the orders when you return to the UK.

6.1.2 Six months or less

If you will be abroad for six months or less, your benefit can continue to be paid into an account and you can arrange to transfer the money abroad from there.

If you have an order book, cash the orders up to the day you leave the UK and return the book to your social security office. You can request that the money be paid into an account or paid as a lump sum when you return to the UK.

6.1.3   Between six and twelve months

If your stay abroad will be for between six and twelve months, any payments into an account can continue and the money transferred abroad. However if you do not wish to continue, a sterling cheque can be sent to you at the end of every four or thirteen weeks. This can be sent straight to you, your overseas bank or someone else appointed by you. If you prefer, the benefit can be paid as a lump sum when you return to the UK.

6.1.4   More than twelve months or permanently

If you are going abroad for more than twelve months, or permanently, your benefit can be paid straight into your overseas account in some countries. If that is not possible, or if your prefer, your benefit can be paid into a UK account, a cheque can be sent to you every four or thirteen weeks or, if you are away for less than two years, it can be paid as a lump sum when you return to the UK.

6.2   Pension uprating

The fact that pensions are not always granted to expatriate UK pensioners has caused some controversy and in a recent case to test the rules, a UK pensioner living in South Africa applied for judicial review of the Government's refusal to uprate her pension. The judge said that it was wrong for people to think that their State pensions were funded by their own national insurance contributions. The scheme is financed on a 'pay as you go' basis. Current NICs fund current benefits. Thus a person's contributions fund not her own benefits but those of others.

The current contribution rates naturally do not include an allowance for uprating all retirement pensions paid to those who have chosen to reside abroad. Given the amount required to fund payment of pension uprating to those living in South Africa, New Zealand, Australia and Canada, it follows that if uprating were applicable to their pensions, either contributions would have to be increased or the additional cost financed out of other taxation.

The judge also pointed out that if you are a pensioner resident abroad you may be better off, in real terms, than a pensioner living in Great Britain, because of different local costs of living which are not fully reflected in exchange rates.

However no satisfactory reason was put forward as to why a pension should not be uprated when it would be increased automatically if the pensioner was resident in the UK. The difference in treatment does not appear to be entirely logical. The judge acknowledged the 'lack of consistency in State practice' and pointed out that the remedy for such pensioners was political and not judicial. The decision to pay uprated pensions has to be made to by Parliament. It remains to be seen whether there will be an appeal against the court's decision.

7   SHAKE-UP PROPOSALS

The Government published its long-awaited Pensions Green Paper on 17 December 2002. A raising of the State pension age from 65 was ruled out but it is intended to scrap compulsory retirement ages.

A 'radical simplification' of pension taxation rules was announced, sweeping away eight separate tax regimes and replacing them with a single lifetime limit. The case for compulsion in relation to pension provision had not yet been made but the setting up of an independent pensions commission was announced to examine the case for moving beyond a purely voluntary approach.

7.1   Summary of key proposals

Under the proposed changes there will be no link between the basic State pension and earnings, and targeted support for pensioners will continue but you will not be compelled to contribute to a pension.

Employers will be encouraged to make better pension provision for their employees and may have to make joining their pension scheme a condition of employment for new recruits.

If you are self-employed you will be offered the opportunity to opt into the State second pension (SSP).

A new pensions regulator is to be appointed to ensure a fairer sharing of assets when pension schemes close.

An end is proposed to the restrictions on how and at what age contracted-out benefits can be drawn, and new legislation against age discrimination would be introduced by 2006. This would be accompanied by an end to compulsory retirement ages.

Note: from 2006 the normal pension age for new entrants into public service would be raised from 60 to 65.

If you defer your pension, you may be offered a lump sum instead of an enhanced pension and the rules will be scrapped preventing OPS members from working after retirement and drawing their pensions.

But note: by 2010 the minimum age at which benefits can be drawn from a pension scheme will be increased from 50 to 55.

7.2 A simpler framework for taxing pensions

The Government has decided that the distortions caused by the tax treatment of pensions should now be removed. Proposals include introducing a single, lifetime limit on the amount of tax-privileged pension saving – with a lifetime ceiling of around £1.4 million (on the value of the total fund, rather than the amount of contributions) and an annual limit of £200,000 (on the value of contributions to the scheme including increases in value of the funds already invested). Under new rules over 99% of the population will be able to save more in a pension – with tax incentives. Many people will be able to build up a bigger tax-free lump sum. For the first time people will be able to decide how much they want to save and when. There will also be more scope to save in the form that best suits the individual. The overhaul is expected to sweep away most tax controls on pensions.

The Government intends further consultation in 2003. Legislation to implement the new scheme could then be included in the 2004 Finance Bill which would allow the date of implementation to be 6 April 2004.

8 PENSION MIS-SELLING

There have been many complaints in recent years from people asserting that they had been wrongly advised to leave or not to join their company pension scheme and take out a personal pension instead.

If you feel this applies to you, the first step is to get in touch with the insurance company or financial adviser who advised you, in order to check that they are reviewing your case and to find out when they will be offering you compensation.

In a test case, it was held that where negligent pensions advice led to a pension holder transferring from an occupational pension scheme to a less advantageous personal pension plan operated by a mutual society, the amount of the compensation to be paid to him was not to be reduced by the value of the shares and/or dividend received by him when the society was demutualised.

The court said that the question was whether the negligence that caused the pension holder's loss had also caused the profit from the sale of the shares and/or dividend in the sense that the profit was part of a continuous transaction triggered by the loss. In that case the demutualisation was not caused by the negligence of the adviser but arose from the Society's desire to have the corporate structure best suited to compete in the new financial services market. Therefore the value of the shares and any dividend was not to be taken into account in reducing the compensation otherwise payable.

Note: one of the things that has delayed a review in many cases is that the 'victim' has not answered letters trying to find out if they have lost money. If you receive any correspondence, reply to it immediately, even if you cannot provide all the information it requires.

If you are unable to get in touch with your adviser, as in the case where it has ceased trading, you can contact the Personal Investment Authority (Pensions Unit) to find out how your case is progressing. Tel. 020 7417 7001.

It is worth getting in touch with your company pension scheme to find out whether you would be allowed back in as if you had never left. Some schemes do not allow you to do this but others are willing.

8.1 Remedies

Once you establish that you were wrongly advised, the firm in question has three options:

1) to try and reinstate you back into the occupational pension scheme
2) to top up the personal pension so that you are no worse off than if you had been in an occupational scheme; or
3) to guarantee that you will not be any worse off in a personal pension when you retire than if you had been in an occupational scheme.

Note: option (3) is probably only practicable in the case of larger firms since it involves calculating what your fund should have built up by the time you retire and compensating you to that amount when you retire. It applies not only to pension income but also to benefits such as life insurance.

8.2 Rejoining occupational scheme

If you are still working for the same employer, you can choose to stop paying into your personal pension and rejoin your company pension scheme. You will not be compensated for past losses but you can start to build up benefits for the future.

If you do decide to rejoin your company scheme, a useful tip is to start paying additional voluntary contributions (AVCs) (see section 2.1.6). There are advantages in doing so in that you will get tax relief on the extra payments which will help to boost your retirement income from the company scheme.

8.3 Legal action

As a last resort, if your adviser refuses to cooperate, you can take legal action to force them to compensate you for your loss resulting from their mis-selling.

It is worth contacting your trade union for advice if you have one since the unions have been very active in trying to sort out cases of pension mis-selling.

9 THE FINANCIAL SERVICES AUTHORITY

By law, most financial services firms must be authorised by the Financial Services Authority (FSA) to do business in the UK. Once they are authorised, they must follow the FSA rules and the FSA must regulate the firms, i.e. they check that they are following the rules.

The institutions regulated by the FSA are banks, building societies, credit unions, insurance firms, friendly societies, independent financial advisers (IFAs), stockbrokers and fund managers.

The FSA does not cover credit, loans, debt, occupational pension schemes and their administration, general insurance advice (such as car, home, travel etc), or mortgage lending and advice (see DIRECTORY for organisations that can offer advice).

But note: from 2004 the FSA will regulate mortgage lenders and advisers and general insurance brokers.

9.1 Authorisation

Firms that need to be authorised must show they can meet set standards which require them to be competent and financially sound and to treat their customers fairly. When firms reach those standards they are then authorised and placed on the FSA register.

Warning: it is important for you to always check that the firm or person you are dealing with is authorised by the FSA. If they are not, the FSA asks you to let them know! To check, you can visit the FSA Firm Check Service on *www.fsa.gov.uk/consumer* or phone the Consumer Helpline on 0845 606 1234, available Monday to Friday 8.00 am to 8.00 pm.

9.2 Monitoring standards

Once a firm is authorised by the FSA, they monitor how it is being managed, what its financial resources are and whether its internal systems (such as information technology or accounting) are working correctly. They also look at the way it deals with consumers to ensure the information it gives is clear and not misleading.

9.3 Enforcement

Where necessary, the FSA will investigate, discipline or prosecute any firm or individual who breaks the rules while conducting financial business. This can mean anything from a fine to withdrawing authorisation or prosecution through the courts.

The FSA also have the power to publicly censure or impose an unlimited fine on anyone, whether they are authorised or not, who commits market abuse. Examples of this are buying shares in a company in advance with inside knowledge about, say, a forthcoming takeover; creating false or misleading impressions; or purposely talking up (or down) the price of shares to a distorted level.

9.4 Protecting consumers

The FSA say they work to secure an appropriate degree of protection for consumers, helping you to understand your rights and responsibilities and also the limitations of the FSA in its role as regulator.

Note: they do not deal with complaints against firms, although they set rules which firms should follow when dealing with complaints.

The Financial Ombudsman Service (tel. 0845 080 1800) is the independent body set up by law to investigate a complaint against a firm operating in the UK if you are not satisfied with the way the firm has handled it. The Financial Services Compensation Scheme (tel. 020 7892 7300) can usually pay you compensation if a UK authorised firm goes out of business.

9.5 Overseas firms

Firms established in another European Economic Area (EEA) country are authorised by that country, although the FSA may regulate some aspects of the way they do business with you.

Note: firms that provide e-commerce financial services do not need authorisation by the FSA to provide financial services in the UK.

DIRECTORY
PROVIDING FOR YOUR RETIREMENT

Citizens Advice Bureau
115–123 Pentonville Road
London BB1 9LZ
Tel. 020 7833 2181
www.nacab.org.uk

Financial Ombudsman Service
South Quay Plaza
183 Marsh Wall
London E14 9SR
Tel. 0845 080 1800
enquiries@financial-ombudsman.org.uk
www.financial-ombudsman.org.uk

Financial Services Authority
25 The North Colonnade
Canary Wharf
London E14 5HS
Tel. 020 7676 1000
Fax. 020 7676 1099
www.fsa.gov.uk/consumer/your_rights/pensions

General Insurance Standards Council *(GICS)*
110 Cannon Street
London EC4N 6EU
Tel. 020 7648 7800
www.giscco.uk

Inland Revenue Savings, Pensions and Share Schemes
St. John's House
Merton Road
Bootle
Merseyside L69 9BB
Tel. 0845 980 0645
www.inlandrevenue.gov.uk
or
Yorke House
PO Box 62
Castle Meadow Road
Nottingham NG2 1BG
Tel. 0115 974 0000
www.inlandrevenue.gov.uk

Legal Services Commission
Franchise Development Group
85 Grays Inn Road
London WC1X 8AA
Tel. 020 7759 0000

The Mortgage Code Compliance Board
MCCB Ltd
University Court
Stafford ST18 0GN
Tel. 01785 218 200
www.mortgagecode.org.uk

Occupational Pensions Regulatory Authority
Pension Schemes Regulator
Invicta House
Trafalgar Place
Brighton
East Sussex BN1 4DW
Tel. 01273 627 600
Fax. 01273 627 683
www.opra.gov.uk

Office of Fair Trading
Fleetbank House
2–6 Salisbury Square
London EC4Y 8JV
Tel. 020 7211 8000
www.oft.gov.uk

Pensions Advisory Service *(OPAS)*
11 Belgrave Road
London SW1V 1RB
Tel. 0845 601 2923
www.opas.org.uk

Pensions Compensation Board
11 Belgrave Road
London SW1V 1RB
Tel. 020 7828 9794
Fax: 020 7931 7239

Pensions Guide
Freepost
Bristol BS38 7WA
www.pensionguide.gov.uk

Pensions Overseas Benefits Directorate
Department for Work and Pensions
Tyneview Park
Benton
Newcastle-upon-Tyne NE98 1BA
Tel. 0191 218 2000
www.thepensionservice.gov.uk
www.dwp.gov.uk

Pension Schemes Registry
PO Box 1NN
Newcastle upon Tyne N199 1NN
Tel. 0191 225 6316
www.opra.gov.uk

Personal Investment Authority Ombudsman
Hertsmere House
Hertsmere Road
London E14 4AB
Tel. 020 7216 0016

Retirement Pension Forecasting Team
Room TB 001
Tyneview Park
Whitley Road
Benton
Newcastle upon Tyne NE98 1BA
Tel. 0870 010 1684
www.thepensionservice.gov.uk

War Pensions Helpline
Tel. 0800 169 22 77

Other useful websites

www.info4pensioners.gov.uk
www.inlandrevenue.gov.uk/pensionschemes/
 guidance.htm
www.thepensionservice.gov.uk

See also the Directories at the end of the chapters
Working for a Living (Part 2) and *Growing Old.*

9   GROWING OLD

Previous chapters have made it clear that we are living in a society in which dramatic and rapid changes are taking place in family life. One of the most striking features of these changes is in society's demographic composition. In this chapter, we discuss the issues which face – in many different ways – the growing numbers of people who are living well beyond the age of retirement.

To what do we owe this change? Our ever-increasing longevity can be explained by a number of factors, in particular the general improvement in the standard of living over the past century, and steady advances in medical knowledge, technology, and pharmacology.

The number of those in retirement has grown fourfold over the course of the 20th century (from 2.87 million in 1901 to 12.2 million in 2001). Moreover, this increase must be set against the fact that while the number of senior citizens in the general population is growing, the number of young people is diminishing because of a declining birth rate.

Forecasting is always fraught with uncertainty. Nevertheless, it has been predicted that by the mid-21st century, the number of people in retirement will increase to just under half of those of working age (at present they represent 16 per cent of the population). So not are we only living longer, but older people are comprising a larger and larger proportion of the population. At the same time, we may face a declining number of those who will be in work and able to support the elderly population of the future.

Talk of a 'demographic timebomb' is alarmist and unhelpful, particularly as many of the retired remain active and well, and continue to live in their own homes. However, these figures do give governments of the day cause for concern about future costs of social care services, welfare provision, retirement pensions, and additional calls on an already overstretched national health service. These concerns, in turn, have a direct impact on the law of the land – in particular, in questions of distribution of resources, development of services, and assurance of uniform and adequate standards of care.

These are the national issues. Looked at from the personal point of view, there is a natural tendency to avoid thinking about one's relentless progress towards old age. Only the prospect of not reaching it is less appealing than its achievement. However, it is worthwhile attempting to contemplate it coolly while you still have the mental capacity to do so as there are steps that can be taken to cushion yourself against its likely impact.

Old age is not a discrete legal topic and it may be a factor in considering any of the subjects dealt with in this book. However, in dealing with advancing age, we can treat it, for the purposes of this chapter, as having two main divisions.

The first is proactive – the making of dispositions to allow old age to be as comfortable as possible; and the second passive – dealing with things that may be done to you by others because you are old. The first is concerned mainly with retirement – the provision of adequate income, taking advantage of available state benefits, the provision of accommodation suited to need, arrangements for care if necessary and the protection of assets; the second with the protection of the person, assets, and human rights of the old who are mentally and physically handicapped. Both aspects are present in many of the topics dealt with here.

In this chapter, we look at:
- questions of definition
- personal relationships
- taking care of your finances
- taking care of your property

- living at home
- buying your home – sheltered accommodation
- leaving your home – residential care
- protecting people who cannot look after themselves
- seeking redress for complaints.

1   QUESTIONS OF DEFINITION

Generally speaking you become an adult when you are 18 for legal purposes (see chapter on *Children (Part 2)*, *The Legal Stages of Growing Up* on page 107). However, there is no comparable date for the arrival of old age. Nevertheless both men and women, if eligible, become entitled to the state retirement pension on attaining 'pensionable age'.

1.1   What is the 'pensionable age'?

Pensionable age is currently 65 for men and 60 for women though later ages are presently under discussion while the pensionable age for women is due to be raised to 65 from 2010, to be phased in over a 10-year period (see also chapter on *Providing for your Retirement*, section 1.1.1).

The provision of benefits is discusssed below (see section 3.3). In addition, at pensionable age, you can take advantage of a range of price concessions which are then on offer, which sugar the pill that you have to swallow by admitting that you are a 'senior citizen'. They include often significant reductions in theatre and cinema tickets, entry fees to National Trust sites and exhibitions and, in London and some other big cities, free travel on public transport after 9.30 am and at weekends.

Another statutory indicator of old age is the reference to 'normal retiring age' in the employment protection legislation. If there is no established age in a particular occupation it is 65 for both men and women.

Because of concerns about pension provision and inadequate savings against retirement, with a concomitant drain on the resources of the State, the government has recently suggested that the retiring age should be set at 70 years and not 65, but on a voluntary, and not on a compulsory, basis (see also introduction to the chapter on *Providing for your Retirement*).

1.1.1   Age discrimination

Age discrimination as such is not currently a ground for claims in either UK or EU law though it is possible to petition the European Parliament for compensation. However, discrimination on the grounds of disability is a ground for applying to an employment tribunal under the Disability Discrimination Act 1995, and an EU directive is expected to come into force in 2006 which will make age discrimination itself unlawful (see the introduction to the chapter on *Working for a Living (Part 1)*).

Many people now take early retirement or are forced to retire through redundancy long before they reach 65 or whatever is the 'normal retiring age' in their particular occupation. Before you reach that age you are entitled to the statutory protection against unfair dismissal and redundancy (see section 4.2 in the chapter on *Working for a Living (Part 2)*). After you reach that age you are not entitled to use the legislation but can still make a claim for wrongful dismissal under common law if the dismissal is in breach of the express or implied terms of your contract of employment. See, however, chapter *Working for a Living (Part 2)*, section 4.2.4.

☞   *A 66-year-old personal assistant and secretary to the head of a small firm has a contract of employment which entitles her to one month's notice and four weeks holiday. She is sacked without any notice because of alleged incompetence. There is no 'normal retiring age' in the firm. The real reason for her dismissal is that the head of the firm wants to replace her with his young girlfriend who says she will leave him if he does not get rid of his personal assistant whom she dislikes intensely.*

If she can prove these facts, the personal assistant can probably only claim in the County Court for one month's pay for the notice she should have received, and accrued holiday pay. If she had been 64 she could have made a claim to an employment tribunal for reinstatement and for the standard and compensatory awards, almost certainly several thousands of pounds.

1.2 Disability discrimination

Disability for the purposes of the Disability Discrimination Act is defined as 'physical or mental impairment which has a substantial and long-term adverse effect on the ability of a person to carry out normal day to day activities'.

Discrimination occurs if the disabled person is treated differently from other members of the public because of his or her disability; reasonable adjustments must be made to enable a disabled person to use the services available to persons not suffering from disability.

It is clear that the older one becomes, the more likely that there will be supervening disability and this fact has to be taken into account in making adjustments to premises and, in this particular context, to homes in which the elderly live (see below, section 5.2).

1.2.1 Establishing your entitlement – the Benefit Enquiry Line

If you wish to establish your likely entitlement to disability benefits or to find out about your present claim, you can consult the Benefit Enquiry Line for People with Disabilities. This service is confidential and provides advice and information by telephone for disabled people, their carers and representatives: tel. 0800 882200. You can also visit the Disability Unit in the Department for Work and Pensions at their website: (*www.disability.gov.uk*).

Do note: if it appears to the local authority that a person is disabled, then there is an automatic obligation to assess that person in order to ascertain the care services which may be required, for example a need for an adaptation to his or her home such as a chair lift (see section 5.2 below).

1.2.2 Disability and goods and services

If there is discrimination in the supply of goods and services because of disability, then the first port of call should be to the Disability Rights Commission (see also the chapter on *Goods and Services*, section 2.5.1). The Commission can and does consider valid claims, which it will support by legal action if need be. A Disability Conciliation Service which provides mediation to help resolve disputes between disabled people and service providers is run by Mediation UK.

1.2.3 Disability and transport

Strenuous efforts are being made to ensure that the disabled are able to use buses, coaches, trains, taxis etc. Concern is also focused on their needs as pedestrians.

In order to ensure that mobility needs are being met, the government has set up a Disabled Persons Transport Advisory Committee (DPTAC) under the Transport Act 1985. The Committee's brief is to ensure that disabled people can go where everyone else goes and to do so as easily as possible and without extra cost. For further information, you can view the website at: *www.dptac.gov.uk* or tel. 020 7944 8011.

1.2.4 The older driver

The requirements which affect drivers aged 70 and over are to be found in the chapter on *Motoring*, section 1.1.7.

2 PERSONAL RELATIONSHIPS

Of course, many of the topics mentioned throughout the book apply to older people in a way that does not distinguish them as a special category in law.

However, in two particular spheres the question of age affects personal relationships directly. The first is the question of the role of the family in caring for the elderly, and the second is the role of the elderly in caring for other members of the family, more precisely in their role as grandparents. We deal with both of these topics below.

2.1 Carers

It has been estimated that there are over six million people providing carer services on a voluntary basis for disabled – mainly elderly – people. These carers are typically daughters looking after disabled elderly parents, or spouses looking after disabled partners. They obviously have a crucial role in overall government policy of enabling disabled people to stay in their own homes as long as possible. Their position was formally recognised in the Carers (Recognition and Services) Act 1995 which gives them the right to request an assessment. This will normally consist of an interview with a social worker to whom they will explain their problems.

The Act does not provide for assistance to the carer directly but the important effect of the legislation is to ensure that information and assistance are given to the carer in obtaining all the services available and, in particular, adaptations to the home that may make their physical tasks easier (see section 5 below).

Respite care, day-centre attendance and home support services, such as visits by social workers and district nurses to the person cared for, will all be of great help to the carer.

Carers can request that the local authority carry out an assessment of the disabled person which may give access to a range of help and services. See section 5.2 below. The ability and/or willingness of the carer to continue to act in that role must be taken into account in the assessment.

2.1.1   Invalid care allowance

This is an allowance for carers who look after someone who is receiving:

* attendance allowance; or
* constant attendance allowance (at the full day rate); or
* disability living allowance (at the middle or highest rate for help with personal care).

In order to qualify, you must be aged 16 or over and look after a disabled person for at least 35 hours per week.

Do note however: invalid care allowance can affect other benefits (see below).

☞ *Your father fell and broke his hip. Unfortunately, his hip replacement operation was not successful and he is presently quite incapacitated. He has just been discharged after a lengthy hospital stay. You have had to give up your job in order to look after him. He has made application for disability living allowance and is waiting for his assessment. You want to know whether you can apply for invalid care allowance in the meantime, as you are in financial difficulties because you are no longer receiving your weekly pay packet.*

The answer is 'yes'. You can claim the allowance now even if the person you are caring for is waiting to hear about his benefit. However, the allowance which you receive can affect other benefits that you may be receiving, which may increase or decrease. It may also affect the benefits which your father receives.

For each week that you qualify for invalid care allowance, you will be treated as if you have paid your national insurance contribution. You should check whether you can protect your retirement pension, through Home Responsibilities Protection (HRP) (see chapter on *Providing for your Retirement*, section 1.3).

You must make enquiries from your Social Security Office and ask for leaflet SD4 (October 2002) or use the dedicated line at for the Invalid Care Allowance Unit: tel. 01253 85 61 23 or Customer Service Section: tel. 01772 89 94 88.

The Disability and Carers Service has issued a Customer Charter in a number of languages available from the Department for Work and Pensions, PO Box 56, Heywood, Lancashire, OL10 2GF.

More substantial legislation for the assistance of carers is in prospect.

2.1.2   State pension and carers

From 6 April 2002, for the first time, an additional state pension for certain carers and people with long-term illness or disability was introduced. Any SERPS entitlement (see chapter on *Providing for your Retirement*, section 1.2) already built up when the second state pension came into effect is protected, both for people who have already reached state pension age and for those who have not. Do phone the Benefit Enquiry Line for ill and disabled people and their carers on tel. 0800 88 22 00.

2.2 Grandparents

In these days of working mothers, grandparents are an increasingly important source of child care. The rights which grandparents have without court intervention are few. Parental responsibility – which means being able to exercise all rights and duties in relation to a child – is not automatically available to grandparents (see section 2.7 below). Anyone in charge of a child is entitled to do what is reasonable for the purposes of safeguarding or promoting the child's welfare, for example, authorising immediate treatment in the event of an accident, but grandparents are not generally entitled to make long-term decisions in the absence of specific authority to do so.

☞ *You are looking after your grandson while his parents are on holiday. He falls and cuts his leg badly. You take him to the nearest casualty department where the doctor on duty advises a couple of stitches.*

You are entitled to consent to essential medical treatment.

However in less urgent cases, although treatment may be required, you may find that the doctors will be less willing to accept a grandparent's consent. In one case the local education authority would not accept the grandmother's consent allowing her granddaughter go on a school trip, notwithstanding that the child had lived with her for years.

Grandparents may be able to get orders from the court giving them parental responsibility, ordering that the child should reside with them or that they should have contact with the child. They can also apply for adoption and guardianship. However, to obtain an order for parental responsibility, residence or contact, the grandparent must first apply to the court for permission ['leave'] to make the application and only if that leave is granted can the application actually be made. Leave is unlikely to be withheld but is nontheless a hurdle which grandparents must first cross. Thereafter the court must always have regard primarily to the welfare of the child.

☞ *Your son parted from his girlfriend in circumstances of great acrimony. Their child lives with the mother who has moved away and has refused to allow you contact with your granddaughter. You have always been close to her and wish to remain so.*

(For applying for a contact order, see section 2.2.2(c) below.) If the mother's hostility to your son and through him to you is so great that she is likely to upset the child, the court may well decide that you should not have access – however unfair it is to you – because it is more important to the child's welfare that her relationship with her mother should not be damaged.

The Grandparents' Association has been set up to provide practical assistance, advice or support to grandparents who wish to maintain contact with their grandchildren or have childcare responsibilities on a full or part time basis. The advice and information line is: tel. 01279 444964, and the website is at: *www.grandparents-federation.org.uk*.

Do note: grandparents very often live on a pension so the cost of bringing an action in court can be prohibitive.

However, community legal service funding [formerly legal aid] may be available to apply for orders under the Children Act if an applicant's capital and income fall below the legal limit. See also section 2.7 below, *Attitude of the courts*.

2.2.1 Orders under the Children Act

Grandparents may be able to obtain certain orders under the Children Act. The orders available under the Act, in this context, are:

- Parental responsibility order
- Residence order
- Contact order
- Care order.

In certain circumstances, grandparents can also apply for:

- Adoption
- Guardianship
- Wardship (see section 2.4 in the chapter *Children (Part 2)*)
- Fostering arrangements.

2.2.2(a) Grandparents and parental responsibility

As can be seen from the chapter on *Children (Part 1)* section 1, having parental responsibility means being able to exercise all rights and duties in relation to a child. To have parental responsibility for a child you must:

- be a married parent of the child; or
- be the mother of the child; or
- be the unmarried father who has acquired parental responsibility; or
- have adopted the child; or
- be the child's guardian; or
- have a residence order in your favour.

So grandparents looking after their grandchildren do not normally have parental responsibility unless they have a residence order (see immediately below).

2.2.2(b) Residence order

A residence order is an order of court that decides upon the person with whom the child is to live. If grandparents receive a residence order in their favour, it automatically confers parental responsibility on them.

The parents will also still retain parental responsibility.

2.2.2(c) Contact order

A grandparent can apply for a contact order which requires that the person with whom the child lives should allow either visits or other forms of contact e.g. telephone calls.

☞ *Your grandson lives with your former daughter-in-law. She blames you for the breakdown of the marriage. You have tried to keep in touch with the boy but even your birthday cards have been returned.*

You can apply to court for leave to bring an application for a contact order.

In a case where the mother opposed contact with the paternal grandparents, a court held that the grandparents' application had 'overwhelming merit' and that the child could actually be harmed if she lost contact with her grandparents. In another case, however, the Court of Appeal stated that the mother's implacable hostility to the grandchild having contact with her paternal grandmother had to be respected. So each case depends on the facts and the view the court takes of them.

2.2.3 Adoption by grandparents

A child must have lived with his or her grandparents for 13 weeks before they can make an adoption application.

At one stage it was felt that adoption by grandparents 'distorted' normal family relationships. However, the courts also recognise the importance to a child of a permanent arrangement rather than stopgap measures. The courts will make the order most suited to a child's welfare in the circumstances of the case before it.

☞ *You apply for adoption of your granddaughter as both parents have become apparent strangers to their child. The court, instead, makes a residence order for her so that you acquire parental responsibility but not the adoption order which you wanted.*

The court is entitled to make any order under the Children Act in a case before it.

2.3 Becoming a guardian to your grandchild

Guardians are appointed where:

- the child has no parent with parental responsibility for him or her; or
- a residence order was made for the child and the person responsible under that order has since died.

☞ *Your unmarried daughter had a baby girl. Sadly your daughter has become terminally ill. The child's father has played no part in her life and does not have parental responsibility for her. You would like to take care of the child.*

Your daughter can appoint you guardian of the child or, if it is too late for her to do so, you can apply to the court to appoint you as guardian.

2.4 Wardship

A grandparent could apply to court for wardship as an 'interested person' (see chapter on *Children (Part 2)*, section 2.4).

2.5 Grandparents and local authorities

The Children Act has encouraged, as far as possible, the view that a child is best left in the care of his or her genetic family, and specifies that it is the duty of a local authority to 'promote contact between the child and any relative' if a child is already in care.

When there is a proposal to take a child into care (see chapter on *Children (Part 2)*, section 1.4) because, for example, the parents are unable to care for their child, grandparents can apply to court for a care order.

They can also apply for a contact order if a grandchild has been placed in care.

Even if a care order is made in favour of the local authority, grandparents may still be able to look after the child. In fact a care order might be to their advantage as they will receive financial support if, for example, the child is disabled and has special needs.

Do remember: grandparents will still have to seek the court's permission to apply for a contact order or any of the other orders.

2.6 Fostering

Grandparents might consider looking after their grandchild as foster carers so that they can obtain the financial and professional support of the local authority's social services department.

2.7 Attitude of the courts

Note of warning: even if grandparents successfully obtain leave from the court, which may not be difficult to obtain, it by no means follows that the actual hearing will result in their favour. Indeed, in one judgment the court said that although there were 'cogent reasons why a natural parent should have contact, that approach did not apply towards any other member of the family: grandparent, aunt, uncle or anybody else'. It must always be the welfare of the child which is the paramount consideration.

2.8 Passing on your tenancy to your grandchild

In one case, the Court of Appeal allowed a 13-year-old grandchild to succeed to the secure tenancy of her grandmother with whom she had been living for two years before the grandmother's death (see chapter on *Landlords and their Tenants*, section 8.1.2).

3 TAKING CARE OF YOUR FINANCES

3.1 Pensions from the State

Do note: the subject matter of this section is covered in more detail in the chapter on *Providing for your Retirement*. However, the discussion there is from a different standpoint from the immediate concerns of the elderly.

3.1.1 Basic state retirement pension

If you are in paid work and earn more than £4,615 a year (2002/2003) you pay national insurance contributions. Your employer also pays a proportion of your contributions. Each year that you pay contributions is called 'a qualifying year'. There are certain provisions covering deemed contributions if you earn less than £4,615 a year.

Currently if you are a man you have to have 44 qualifying years to be entitled to the full basic rate of retirement pension, to which you become entitled at 65. If you are a woman you currently become entitled at 60 and only need 39 qualifying years. However, this limit is to be raised to 65 (to be phased in) and when this happens a woman too will need 44 qualifying years to get the full state pension.

The full pension is currently £75.50 per week for a single person. This amount will be reduced proportionately if you do not have the full number of qualifying years, and you will get nothing if you have less than 25% of those years.

3.1.2 Pensions for the over-80s

If you are over 80 and you are not getting any state retirement pension or receiving only a partial one, you can claim an over-80 pension – up to 60% of the full pension.

You can claim your pension by filling in a form, or by contacting the Retirement Pension Teleclaims which will fill in the form for you over the telephone: the number is 0845 300 1084.

3.1.3 Querying your pension amount

If you do not agree with the amount of your pension, you must get in touch with the appropriate office which will be given at the head of the letter telling you of the amount which you are awarded for your pension.

Alarm bells: you should act straight away, as there is a time limit of one month in which you can lodge an appeal (see chapter on *Providing for your Retirement*, section 1.5).

3.1.4 Requesting a forecast

If you want to know how much basic State Retirement Pension you can expect to get when you retire you can get the information from the Retirement Pension Forecasting Team (RPFT). You can write to them at the Pension Service, Time View Park, Whitley Road, Newcastle-upon-Tyne NE98 1BA and they will send you a forecast form, or you can get one from your Social Security Office. Alternatively, if you phone them on 0845 3000 168 they will fill in an application form for you over the phone.

3.1.5 State second pension

By paying appropriate contributions you can belong to the State Second Pension Scheme which until 2002 was known as the State Earnings Related Pension Scheme (SERPS). The scheme has been improved from 6 April 2002. It now covers certain carers and people suffering from longterm illness or disability which prevents them from working.

It is possible to contract out of the State scheme and join a private scheme. Careful financial advice should be taken before doing this. Many of the private schemes have proved disastrous because of the fall in stock-market values over the last few years, and the former scheme SERPS has performed better than most of them.

Do take heed: regulations and benefits constantly change and you should try to update the information you have concerning your pension at fairly frequent intervals, initially by contacting your local Social Security office.

The Department for Work and Pensions website has clearly laid out information at: *www.pensionguide.gov.uk.*

3.2 Private pension provision

It is clearly desirable within reason to make provision for old age while one is young by pensions savings and insurance, and the government provides some tax allowances to encourage pension and savings provision. However, care should be taken not to overspend unnecessarily.

3.2.1 The legal provisions

The law currently permits you to spend part of your income on private pension provision. The proportion depends on age. It starts at 17.5% and rises to 40% at 61 though the maximum allowable earnings from which the proportion can be taken is currently £97,200. The payment is deducted from your income so reducing your tax, which is particularly significant if you are a higher-rate taxpayer.

At the designated age when the pension becomes payable, it produces a lump sum. You may use the whole of this lump sum to buy an annuity, i.e. a regular annual payment which will last for the rest of your life. It may be index-linked and cover your spouse, in which case it will be more expensive and the amount you get will obviously be less.

Annuities are taxable and form part of your income. However, at present you can take up to one-third of the amount which becomes due when the policy becomes payable as a lump sum. That lump sum is currently not taxable (though it appears that the Government is considering doing away with this concession). If you have an outstanding mortgage, the lump sum so produced can be used to pay it off or reduce it.

3.3 State benefits

It is not possible in a book of this nature to deal in detail with the conditions which have to be complied with to secure entitlement to the plethora of state benefits available; moreover, the benefits themselves and the conditions for entitlement change, but it is hoped than an outline of the main benefits available will enable you to approach the relevant authorities to check the qualifying conditions. The first approach should be to your local Social Security Office, but help and advice can be obtained from major charities, such as Age Concern, Help the Aged, or the Alzheimer's Society.

Cause for concern: many benefits to which the elderly are entitled go unclaimed. The reasons generally put forward are that claimants are reluctant to be seen as the recipients of 'charity'. The bureaucracy and form-filling are also daunting. However, if you should be receiving certain benefits and are failing to do so, you must make sure that you are not losing out. Do approach your local Citizens Advice Bureau which can assist.

3.3.1 Minimum income support

If you are:

- over 60
- on a low income and
- not working or working less than 16 hours a week

you may be able to get extra income for yourself and your family.

3.3.2 Housing Benefit and Council Tax Benefit

If you live on a low income and are paying rent you can claim Housing Benefit and Council Tax Benefit from your local authority. This will mean that the whole or part of your rent is paid and all or part of your council tax remitted.

3.3.3 Help with health costs

Medical care is free at the point of delivery under NHS rules. If of pensionable age you should get free NHS prescriptions and free items like wigs and false teeth, supports for the lame, and special shoes (all of which may otherwise be chargeable). You should also receive help towards the purchase of glasses and contact lenses.

3.3.4 Attendance allowance

If you are 65 or over and need help with personal care because of an illness or disability, you could be entitled to Attendance Allowance. There are currently two rates of allowance, depending on the degree of help required. If you are in residential care you continue to be entitled and the payment can be used to reduce your contribution to the costs of your care in the house (if any). See also section 7.6 below.

3.3.5 Winter Fuel Payments

An annual payment (currently £100) is made automatically to persons of pensionable age, but additional payments may be available.

3.4 Life insurance

There are two principal types of life insurance.

3.4.1 Whole life policies

A whole life insurance policy provides that on your death, a lump sum will be paid either to your estate or to a nominee. The policy may be for a fixed term or go on for as long as you live. Normally you will have to pay a premium for the fixed term or, if the policy is to last for the whole of your life, for the whole of that period. A policy taken out for a fixed term is often used to protect a mortgage. For instance, if you take out a mortgage over a 25-year term a whole life policy covering that term can be taken out to produce enough to pay off the policy should you die before the end of the 25-year period. If you survive the 25 years you generally get nothing back though the policy will probably have a surrender value while it is still running after part of the period has elapsed.

If the proceeds of a whole life policy are to go to a nominee or a trust they will not form part of your estate and a trustee can, for instance, use the policy proceeds to pay off inheritance tax on your estate. This type of policy is useful for inheritance-tax saving purposes.

Note of warning: if there is no nominee or trustee, the proceeds will form part of your estate and will be liable to inheritance tax.

3.4.2   Endowment policies

Whereas with a whole life policy you get nothing back during your life time, with an endowment policy you take out the policy for a fixed period, normally as a way of paying your mortgage. The policy has two elements:

1) a life policy, which will produce a fixed sum (as with a whole life policy) if you die during the period of the policy; and
2) an investment element, which is supposed to produce a profit at the end of the term.

If you survive the whole period of the policy you will get the fixed sum plus a profit. These policies are normally used as part-security for mortgages. The life policy element is intended to produce enough to pay off the mortgage if the borrower dies before the end of the mortgage term. If he or she does not die before the end of the mortgage term, the intention of the insurers was that sufficient should be produced by the profits on the policy to pay off the mortgage when the term of the mortgage had expired.

The calculations of the main insurers were based on the premise that the stock market would maintain the steady rise which had continued for two decades. Over the last two years it has fallen dramatically, with the result that many unfortunate mortgagees have found that the policies they took out did not produce enough to pay off their mortgages at the end of the period of the loan. If this happens to you and you can prove a promise by the lending or selling source that the policy would definitely produce enough to pay off your mortgage, you may have a claim for the shortfall against the organisation responsible for giving the promise, and you should take legal advice.

3.4.3   Commissions

Brokers are paid commissions on both whole life and endowment policies. Because of their commissions brokers tend to sell life policies very hard. The premiums on whole life policies can be surprisingly cheap so they seem tempting.

Whole life policies are normally taken out to protect dependants (see chapter on *Goods and Services*, section 7.2.1, for an explanation of an 'insurable interest').

If you have no dependants to protect, whole life policies, no matter how cheap, are probably a waste of money.

Before taking out any form of life policy you should seek informed advice. Apart from the cost of the policy it is important to check on what surrender value, if any, it would have if you cease to pay the premiums.

3.4.4   Insurance for long-term care

Policies are available which can cover the cost (or part of the cost) of staying in a residential or nursing home. Premiums would depend on your age and state of health, as well as the level of care which your policy may cover.

The two types of policy available are:

• pre-paid
  and
• immediate need.

The Association of British Insurers (*www.abi.org.uk*) has extensive and useful leaflets on long-term care insurance which should be read carefully as they address many issues of which you should be aware. You will then be in a better position to ask the right questions in discussion with your professional advisors before you choose whether or not to proceed further.

3.4.5 Other types of policy

It is obviously sensible to consider policies which protect your income in the event of illness or accident, but again taking advice is an essential first step. For other forms of insurance, e.g. to protect your household possessions, see chapter on *Goods and Services*, section 7.2. For insurance in the event of an accident, see chapter on *Accidents*, section 1.1.2.

3.4.6 Savings

The government encourages savings by the creation of two forms of tax-free investment known as Individual Savings Accounts (ISAs). These replace a previous scheme permitting a form of investment called the Personal Equity Plan (PEP).

You can invest up to £3,000 a year in a cash ISA [called a mini-ISA] or up to £7,000 a year in a maxi-ISA which is an investment in some form of security, e.g. the stock market. ISAs are free of both income tax and capital gains tax.

3.4.7 Complaints procedure

The financial service industry as a whole, in all its various manifestations, has been heavily criticised of late for selling unsuitable products to clients who have not been properly informed of the schemes which they have entered into.

The Financial Ombudsman Service has been set up to investigate complaints about financial products and services. However, it can only act once the consumer has tried and failed to get redress from the particular insurer, bank, or finance house with which he or she has been dealing.

The Ombudsman's service is free to consumers. The decision is final and binding as far as the firm is concerned, but if a consumer is still dissatisfied he of she retains the right to go to court afterwards.

The Financial Services Authority, which is the regulatory body for the financial industry as a whole, also provides consumer help about making a complaint. The relevant leaflet can be ordered from their consumer helpline: 0845 806 1234. See also *www.fsa.gov.uk* also the chapter on *Goods and Services*, section 7.

4   PROPERTY

Property Law is dealt with in the chapters on *Landlords and their Tenants* and *Buying and Selling your Home*, and this section merely mentions matters which particularly relate to problems which are likely to arise as you get older and have either retired or become unwell.

4.1.1 Freeholds and long leases

For explanations of these terms you are referred to the chapter on *Landlords and their Tenants*, section 1.3. You may hope that by the time you reach old age, if you have been buying your freehold or a long-leasehold property with the help of a mortgage, the mortgage is either paid off or almost paid off.

If you have a mortgage and are unable to keep up payments because infirmity has cut off your income, you may be able to get assistance in making mortgage payments. Age Concern (see DIRECTORY) issues a Factsheet (No 25) on *Income Support (Minimum Income Guarantee and the Social Fund)*. You are strongly advised to seek advice as not everyone is eligible and the rules for lending are complicated.

4.1.2 Public and private tenancies

The distinction between public and private tenancies is dealt with in the chapter on *Landlords and their Tenants*, and you will note from section 8 of that chapter that both types of tenancy can be passed to a surviving spouse or to a member of your family who has been living with you at the date of your death.

Again the rules regarding the rights of succession are fraught with difficulty so do ensure that before you deal with your landlord, you seek advice.

4.1.3 Right to buy

Most public tenants and tenants of housing associations which are not charitable have the right to buy their properties at a substantial discount. If you happen to be a council or housing association tenant in a desirable location such as central London the discount can be worth an enormous sum.

1) You may want to realise the value which the discount gives you, either because you would like to sell your property and move somewhere different leaving yourself a considerable surplus to make your declining years more comfortable, or perhaps because you wish to leave money to your family.

2) You normally have to repay the discount in whole or in part if you dispose of the property within three years of its purchase. Disposal includes sale and certain mortgages, so that if you want to borrow to purchase the discounted interest in the property to which you are entitled it may be difficult for a lender to secure himself adequately.

3) If you wish to benefit your children, you may be able to borrow the money from them on the basis that you will leave the property to them in your will or pay them back if you sell it.

4) If you have no family whom you wish to benefit you may nevertheless be able to exploit the added value which the discount gives you. It therefore is certainly worthwhile seeing a solicitor to discuss the possibility of how best to use the discount.

Do note: the government is intending to issue new guidelines to tighten up the question of discounts in an endeavour to restrict the right to buy so as to preserve the housing stock.

4.2 Extension or conversion of long leases – buying the freehold

You can also use your ability to extend the long lease of which you are the tenant, or possibly convert it in to freehold property, in order to benefit your children or others whom you wish to benefit. This is known as buying your freehold or, in technical terms, as 'enfranchisement' (see chapter on *Landlords and their Tenants*, section 10).

In this case there is no reason why any money lent to you to enable you to enfranchise cannot immediately be protected for the benefit of the lending source. If this is done then you should take care that the arrangements between you and the lender enable you to sell the property and buy another, transferring the mortgage to the new property. Again you should see a solicitor to discuss the possible advantages of enfranchisment if it is available to you.

4.3 Equity release

4.3.1 Releasing equity in your home

Because of the recent extraordinary increase in property values, a large number of house owners own an asset which is extremely valuable – but it is a value which they cannot use and which they may have difficulty in passing on to their heirs because a significant part of the value of their asset will be taken by the State in the form of inheritance tax.

There are a number of schemes known as Equity Release Schemes under which financial institutions release capital sums or make income payments to property owners, either:

• in return for a share of the property's value on sale or death; or
• an arrangement for the payment of compound interest on a loan which is charged on the property and is repaid on death (though the schemes normally permit earlier repayment).

Usually the schemes will provide that if the property is to be sold and replaced by another one the charge can be transferred to the new property. Thus these schemes – to some extent – unlock the value of your property and enable you to enjoy it while you are alive, instead of leaving it all to your heirs to enjoy after you are dead.

The schemes have improved in recent years. They were generally heavily criticised in that they normally involved repayment of loans during your lifetime so that you had to borrow a capital sum and then buy an annuity from which interest was paid to the lending source and the balance only was left for you to enjoy.

4.3.2 Lending sources

The rate of interest charged by lenders is currently quite high but more lenders are coming into the market and the competition may force them down.

4.3.3 Note of warning

Over the last few years the increase in the value of properties for anyone taking advantage of the various equity release schemes will have largely covered the amount of compound interest accruing, but it is unlikely that this situation will be permanent.

However most of the schemes provide that if the sale proceeds of the property are insufficient to meet the amount of the loan plus the interest, the shortfall will be borne by the lender, not by the estate.

Certain schemes are considered particularly risky – to give just one example, plans where the mortgage rate can rise and your income can fall.

You must, therefore, take professional advice before going in for an Equity Release Scheme or a Home Reversion Scheme (see section 4.4 immediately below) and consider all the consequences very carefully.

Age Concern produces a very helpful Factsheet (no. 12): *Raising income or capital from your home.* See also *Unlocking the value of your home: A guide to equity release,* issued by the Council of Mortgage Lenders: tel: 020 7437 0075, as well as the website of the Financial Services Authority: *www.fsa.gov.uk/consumer/shop_around/products_services/mn_home_income_plan.*

There is also a leaflet issued by Help the Aged at: *www.helptheaged.org.uk.*

4.4 Home reversion schemes

This is another scheme for older people to realise some benefit from the capital value of their home. A reversion company will purchase your home, or an agreed share of your home in return for a lump sum or a monthly annuity. The company also gives an undertaking that you can remain in the house until your death, rent-free or for a peppercorn monthly rent. The property is then sold, and the proceeds of the sale, proportionate to its share, reverts to the company.

See also **Note of warning** (section 4.3.3 above).

4.5 Sharing with children

Quite frequently elderly parents with a house which is too big for them have children with young families who need better accommodation than they are able to afford. The parent then sells the house and the child buys a larger property with accommodation for the parents, with the capital contribution which the parents can provide from the sale proceeds of their house and to which the child can contribute by obtaining a mortgage using his or her earning capacity.

If this sort of arrangement is made, it is essential that the elderly parents protect their position, preferably by getting their names on the title to the property. If the parents' interest is not formally protected and they quarrel with their children, it is possible that they may be evicted in the absence of any legal protection.

This is because the courts are generally reluctant to assume [or 'infer'] that there is an 'intention to create legal relations' in private family arrangements.

☞ *An entrepreneurial son gets his parents to sell their house and give him the proceeds. With these he purchases a splendid house in his own name with a 'granny flat' in which his parents live in comfort and with assistance given by a maid employed by the son.*

The son borrows further money on the house to finance his business, which fails. The bank repossesses the house which on sale does not produce enough to pay off the son's debt in full.

The parents stand to lose their money and their accommodation.

There are also other dangers and – even if the courts do offer legal protection – it can prove inadequate as can be seen from the case below.

In this case a man provided money towards the purchase of a house for his son and daughter-in-law. They agreed that he would live there rent-free for the rest of his life. He was then accused of sexually molesting his grand-daughter, a charge which was withdrawn by the family as totally without foundation. Nonetheless, he felt he could no longer continue to live under the same roof and claimed the return of the money which he had put in towards the purchase price. The court ruled that he was only entitled to a return of a sum equivalent to the value of living in the house rent-free for the rest of his life. That was less than the capital sum which he had originally provided.

4.5.1   Duty of local authority to provide housing

If, through circumstances like those in the sad scenario described above or for other reasons, you become homeless in your old age, the local authority has a duty to house you.

4.6   Passing on property to heirs

Your estate on death is liable to inheritance tax. Nothing is payable if you leave all of your estate to your spouse, but on the second death part of the estate (currently £250,000 and generally increased annually) is free of tax and the rest bears tax at 40%. The prosperous will generally take financial advice to mitigate this tax as a matter of course but because of the huge increase in property values in recent years many people who would not have regarded themselves as wealthy will have suddenly found themselves in possession of assets worth much more than £250,000.

It is a natural desire to hand on as much of your property as possible to your children instead of to the State. Most schemes for the avoidance of inheritance tax involve giving part of your estate away by paying premiums to insurance companies or by straightforward gifts – for instance, capital released through an equity release scheme can be given away (see above). To achieve full relief you have to survive seven years from the date of the gift, but you get some relief after three years. You must not put your own standard of living in danger by giving away too much. You might brush up your Shakespeare by reminding yourself of the plot of *King Lear*.

There are steps which can be taken to mitigate the effect of inheritance tax by will, and it is sensible to see a solicitor if your assets significantly exceed £250,000 or whatever the inheritance tax threshold is at the time. See also chapter on *Death – Before and After*.

4.6.1   Other steps you can take

There are, however, two sensible steps which can be taken.

1) The first, if you have a partner but are not married, is to get married, thus acquiring the surviving-spouse exemption. Whether or not this price is regarded as worth paying is for you to decide.

2) The second step is to make sure that if you are husband and wife or partners, your property is vested in you as tenants-in-common (see chapter on *Buying and Selling your Home*, sections 4.1.1(a) and 4.1.1(b)). This means that each of you owns a specific proportion (probably a half) of your house. If, on the first death, that half is left to your children, half the value of the house would not form part of the joint estate on the second death. The effect is that the child or children to whom the half of the first-dying is left would be entitled to live in the house with the survivor and, moreover, if that child got into financial difficulty it would be possible for creditors to make a claim against the half given away. There is accordingly an element of risk in this strategy which should not be used if there is any possible doubt about the financial standing of the child or children concerned.

If you have to go into residential care, the value of your house may be used up in making contributions to the local authority (see immediately below), but it appears that local authorities are prepared to accept that your interest in your house as a tenant-in-common has no value. The local authority must ignore the value of your house if your spouse or partner or certain other relatives are living in it. The authority may possibly disregard the value of your share in your house if it is vested in you and your spouse or partner as tenants-in-common even if they are not living in it.

Do remember: if you give away your house to your children when you are comparatively young in case you should ever need to go into residential care, you may simply lose the house if the need for residential care never arises.

Remember also: if you continue to live in your house after you have given it away, without paying a proper rent, you will not escape inheritance tax on its value.

4.6.2 Your house and residential care

If you give your house away in order to avoid charges for residential care:

- after assessment
- while in care; or
- within six months of going into residential care

the person to whom you give the house will be liable to pay for any part of the cost of the care which is not covered by other income or assets.

5 STAYING IN YOUR HOME

5.1 Help from relations

It is natural for people to want to stay in their own home for as long as possible even if they suffer from disabilities which make it difficult for them to look after themselves entirely on their own. Their children may be prepared and able to help. In fact, the comforting figures are that many more people are cared for in their own homes than have to go into residential or nursing homes.

5.1.1 Care in the community

If your own resources and those of your relatives are insufficient to maintain you in your own home, significant state or local authority benefits are available. It is government policy that those who are disabled should, as far as is possible, be able to remain in their own homes and that they should be supported by a range of benefits which the local authority and the social services are obliged to provide.

The benefits available are contained in a mass of legislation dating from 1945. It is thought that there should be a single Act of Parliament amalgamating all the benefits within a single framework, but there is no current proposal that this should be done.

The legislation applies generally to those in need, but the circumstances giving rise to need are with the majority of us most likely to occur in old age.

5.2 Assessment

Assessment is the necessary preliminary before the storehouse of services for those in need of them can be accessed. It is the duty of the local authority to assess a person who is in need of the services which the local authority can provide.

The local authority must first decide whether a person seems to be in possible need of community care services. If it appears to the authority that the person is in need then that person must be assessed. If, during the assessment, it appears that the person is disabled then the authority must decide what services are required under the Chronically Sick and Disabled Persons Act 1970.

The application for an assessment may be made by the person in need himself or by a carer for that person. There is an initial screening process when the local authority will try to ascertain whether the person in question needs its services and at the same time seek to consider what services are required and their urgency.

If a person appears to the local authority to be disabled then there is an automatic obligation to assess. Once assessment has taken place the local authority should regularly review the assessment so that the plan for the care of the assessed person can be regularly updated.

☞ *You are suffering from incapacity as a result of rheumatoid arthritis. Your bathroom is upstairs and climbing the stairs several times a day presents enormous difficulties. You would like to have a downstairs lavatory installed but you hesitate to call in the social services as you are not registered disabled.*

There is no need to be registered disabled provided that you can prove disability, which is widely defined. The local authority has then a mandatory duty to assess your needs (see section 5.3 and 5.3.2 below).

During assessment the local authority has a duty to invite health and/or housing authorities to participate if it seems that medical help or help in relation to housing may be required. The Community Legal Service issues a leaflet (CLS Leaflet No. 19): *Community Care – Your rights to care services.* You can order it from their leaflet line: tel. 0845 3000 343.

5.2.1 Unsatisfactory assessment or refusal to assess

In certain instances the council may refuse to assess you or, if you have been assessed, you may feel that the service being offered to you is inadequate.

☞ *You live with your elderly uncle but he is becoming increasingly difficult to manage. He flies into sudden rages and is restless both day and night, frequently rushing into the street for no apparent reason. You have asked the council social services for an assessment but have been told, quite abruptly, that they have much more serious cases on their hands to deal with. You wonder if you can take the matter further as you feel that you are reaching the end of your tether.*

You should approach the complaints officer of your local social services on an informal basis. If you do not receive a more sympathetic response, you must address your complaint in writing and, if this also produces no results, you should ask for a panel to review your complaint. You are entitled to attend the meeting of the review panel and can be accompanied by someone to speak on your behalf if you so wish. If the problem is not resolved to your satisfaction, you can approach the Local Government Ombudsman (see section 9.2 below), or the Secretary of State for Health. See also section 8.3 on *Committal procedures.* Do consult, as well, Age Concern's Fact Sheet No. 32: *Disability and Ageing: your rights to social services* (see DIRECTORY).

5.3 Home adaptations

If the local authority in making its assessment thinks that there is a need for housing services, it must notify the local housing authority and invite it to assist in the assessment.

Housing adaptations are regarded as one of the means of achieving the prime objective of community care and support for the user in his or her own home.

5.3.1 Grants

Home adaptation work or grants are available to disabled people but disability is widely defined and includes impairment of sight, hearing or speech, mental disorder and physical disablement whether caused by illness, injury or impairment present since birth.

Adaptation may be carried out by the housing authority itself without cost to the disabled person, or by a grant under the provisions of the Housing Grants Construction and Regeneration Act 1996. Grants, which are means-tested, can currently be up to a maximum of £20,000 in England and £24,000 in Wales. The grants known as Disabled Facilities Grants must be granted to eligible persons for access to the property or rooms in it, making the building safe, facilitating cooking of food, improving heating systems and altering the position of switches. Discretionary grants for other purposes may be made.

The grants are available to owner-occupiers and private and council and housing-association tenants. The consent of landlords, which would include the local authority and the Housing Association, to the works is required. The grants can cover installation of stair lifts, showers and toilets in bathrooms, central heating, ramps, handrails, kitchen alterations and general adaptations in relation to wheelchair use.

Housing authorities can carry out adaptations of their own properties at no cost to the disabled person but payment is usually made through grants under the provisions of the 1996 Act.

5.3.2 Mandatory purposes

Grants for a list of purposes are mandatory, that is they must be made if the person applying for them is in need. Mandatory purposes include access facilitating the use of lavatories and baths and showers and the preparation and cooking of food. The council has grants for other purposes not specifically listed in the Act to help a disabled occupant. If the applicant or the applicant's partner has means then they may have to pay for or contribute towards the cost of the improvements. The contributions are means-tested.

5.4 Other care services

The National Assistance Act 1948 provides that in relation to persons ordinarily resident in the area of the local authority, the authority should make arrangements for promoting the welfare of those persons. The persons in question were disabled persons who were defined as people aged 18 or over who are blind, deaf or dumb or who suffer from mental disorders of any description, and other persons aged 18 or over who are substantially and permanently handicapped by illness, injury or congenital deformity or such other disabilities as may be prescribed.

The local authorities have a duty to inform people to whom the legislation relates about the services available, and they must provide the facilities for social, cultural and recreational activities. They can provide these facilities for disabled people who are not ordinarily resident within the Authority's area.

The duties cover the provision of holiday homes, provision of subsidised travel, and paying for wardens in warden-assisted housing. The general provisions of the National Assistance Act were defined in more detail in the Chronically Sick and Disabled Persons Act 1970 and provided that in order to meet the needs of persons under the Act the Authority should give practical assistance which includes the provision of wireless and television, lectures, games and outings, travel, holidays and the provision of meals.

5.5   Charges

Local authorities have power but not a duty to make charges for non-residential care services but they will normally do so to avoid an unfair burden on non-disabled community charge payers. The charges must be reasonable and contributions are means-tested.

The value of capital is taken into account and that includes the value of a disabled person's dwelling house but it may be disregarded (see *Passing on your property to your heirs*, section 4.6. above). There is no uniformity in the charging policies of local authorities.

6   BUYING YOUR HOME – SHELTERED ACCOMMODATION

Sheltered accommodation, often referred to as retirement housing, can be a preferred alternative to staying in your own home for a variety of reasons: an additional sense of security, the presence of a warden or manager, the company of other retired people.

There are a number of different schemes available and the services on offer can differ considerably. The Elderly Accommodation Counsel (see DIRECTORY or their website at *www.housingcare.org*) is a charity, completely independent of any provider, which can supply detailed information directly to the public from a nationwide database of the types of housing available including 'extra care' housing.

Decisions on matters such as size of the house or flat, location, and facilities available are highly personal and should all be thoroughly explored before you make any commitments.

If you do decide that you wish to purchase such accommodation, make sure that you obtain legal advice at all stages of the procedure.

Both the chapters on *Buying and Selling your Home*, and *Landlords and their Tenants* are useful starting points for a transaction which involves dealing with property. However, sheltered accommodation raises its own particular questions – such as what would happen if you wished to leave – which will need careful consideration. Very useful and detailed information on the factors to be taken in to account is contained in Age Concern Fact Sheet No. 2.

6.1   Leasehold or other purchase

Sheltered accommodation is usually built as a development and sold on a leasehold basis to be run by a management organisation. The functions of the management organisation are to collect the service charges, to ensure that the common parts are maintained, and to appoint a warden or house manager (if the scheme provides for one).

Some schemes allow you to part-exchange your home, while others may involve buying only part of the accommodation of your choice. For example, you might buy three-quarters of the flat or house in a sheltered housing development and pay rent on the remaining 25 per cent.

6.2   Service and other charges

Leaseholders will pay a service charge towards the cost of meeting the services provided. The amount of the charge will vary, depending on the services provided and the level of duties which the warden is expected to undertake.

6.3   Codes of practice

There are two codes of practice, one of which applies to the building industry and the other which applies to those who are charged with managing sheltered housing.

The National House Building Council (NHBC) Sheltered Housing Code of Practice can be obtained from the National House Building Council. The Association of Retirement Housing Managers (ARHM) Code of Practice can be purchased from the Association itself. The Advice Information and Mediation Service for Retirement Housing (AIMS) has a free booklet: *Leasehold retirement housing: your rights and remedies.* (See DIRECTORY for all these organisations.)

7   RESIDENTIAL CARE

If staying in your own home becomes impossible because of physical or mental impairment, it is the duty of local authorities to provide you with residential care. The duty is in no sense restricted to the elderly but they are likely to form a large proportion of those in need of residential accommodation particularly because of physical and mental disorder caused by Parkinson's or Alzheimer's Disease. Medical assessment will determine the degree of care which a disabled person needs.

7.1   Do you have a choice?

Subject to the level of care required, a person requiring it is to be given a choice as to where he or she wants to go. In practice it will not be easy for the person to choose accommodation outside the local authority in which he or she is normally resident, and local authorities will not fund you in a home which provides a greater level of care than that which the medical authorities have decided that you need.

7.2   Paying for residential care

The resident in principle has to pay for his own care until his or her capital drops below whatever limit is prescribed for the time being (see below). You can therefore choose a private home outside the area in which you are normally resident if you can afford to pay its fees. When you become unable to do so you are then likely to be ordinarily resident in the place you have chosen and at that stage you may well be able to stay in the home you have chosen. If that home has a level of service greater than that which the medical and social assessment decides that the person requires, the local authority would be likely to refuse to pay and the person would then have to move to another home.

7.3   Meeting regulations

Residential homes may be provided by the local authority itself or may be private homes for which the local authority provides finance. Private residential homes are heavily regulated and many are currently going out of business because they are unable to comply with the latest government regulations. For instance these intended to require that residents should not have to share rooms and that rooms should all have their own toilets.

Mentally confused old people do not always mind sharing rooms and may be unable to use normal toilets so regulations such as these are proving a blunt instrument and in some instances are causing harm. In the light of such criticism, the period of compliance has now been extended for some of the requirements to April 2007 (see also *Care Standards Commission*, section 7.7 below).

7.4   Remaining in the residential care home of your choice

It is apparently cheaper for local authorities to fund private homes rather than to maintain their own and many local authority homes have been closed. Before they are closed there has to be local consultation but clearly local council-tax payers may feel disinclined to favour a solution which increases their council-tax burden. The closure of a local authority home in which residents may have lived for many years can be an extremely disturbing event for people already frail, and in certain cases may be held to amount to a breach of the residents' human rights under the provisions of the Human Rights Act.

☞   *Mr Baskins, in his mid-seventies, had an illness which made him extremely physically infirm. He had a series of operations and after the last one found that it was impossible for him to look after himself in his own home. He was mentally perfectly well and on his discharge from hospital, with the help of his children – who lived in other parts of the country and were unable to care for him – he chose a local authority residential home after inspecting many residential homes. The home indicated that he would be able to live there for the rest of his life.*

Having assured himself that this was the case he sold his own house and over the next ten years the amount he got for it was paid to the local authority for his care. By the time he was 85 his resources were exhausted and the whole cost of his care was funded by the local authority. The local authority then received a very attractive offer from a local developer for the acquisition of the site of the home and decided to sell. There were a number of other people in the home in the same situation as Mr Baskins.

It is possible that in those circumstances a court might decide, depending on the view that it takes, that Mr Baskins' and the other residents' human rights were being breached and that the proposed sale should be stopped, whatever the result of the local consultation.

7.4.1 The 'nursing element'

The nursing element of care in a residential home is supposed to be funded by the NHS. This is care that has to be provided by a registered nurse, unlike routine personal care. Some residential homes have put up their charges to the amount of the NHS payment available. There are three levels of costs payable, depending on immediate needs, for which the NHS will pay after an assessment – made by a nurse trained for the task – to establish the degree and severity of the case and the nursing care needed to deal with it. The levels of costs payable are currently £35 per week, £70 per week, and £110 per week for the most severe cases. This funding is due to be raised from 1 April 2003.

7.4.2 Paying for care

The whole of the income of a resident in a care home will be taken if it does not exceed the cost of residential care, and any shortfall will be taken from capital. Currently however a resident is allowed to retain £11,750 of capital. If the capital of a resident of a nursing home is £19,000 or over, it will be used by the residential home to cover the care costs where the income falls short of the fees assessed at the 'standard rate'. Once that capital falls below £19,000 but is more than £11,750 then the income shortfall is met approximately half from capital and half by the local authority. Once a resident's capital is reduced to £11,750 the whole of the cost is borne by a combination of the residents's pension or pensions, any interest on the remaining capital, and the local authority.

A detailed explanation of charging procedures can be found in Age Concern's Factsheet (No. 10): *Local authority charging procedures for care homes (April 2002).*

7.5 Paying for care – Selling your own home

If you are the sole owner and sole occupant of your dwelling house its capital cost is taken into account in providing for your care, and when you run out of other capital it will have to be sold and the sale proceeds will be used to supplement your pension for payment of the residential care you require as detailed in section 7.4 immediately above (see also section 4.6 above on passing property to your heirs).

However, it appears that if the house is owned by you and your partner jointly as tenants-in-common (see section 4.6.1 above), its value may be assessed at nil by the local authority on the basis that your half-share is unmarketable.

7.6 Attendance allowance

Attendance allowance is payable in independent-sector homes, not local authority homes, so long as no financial report is received from the local authority and the resident is not entitled to Income Support or Housing Benefit.

7.7 Care Standards Commission

The Care Standards Act 2000 set up a regulatory body, the Care Standards Commission, to monitor standards in social care institutions, as well as in private and other voluntary health care services.

In April 2002, the National Care Standards Commission took on the registration, inspection and regulation of care and other institutions from local and health authorities in an endeavour to enforce uniform standards of care throughout the country. Its national headquarters is in Nottingham (see DIRECTORY) with 71 area offices. The equivalent body for Wales is the Care Standards Inspectorate.

With regard to those services relevant to this chapter, the Commission registers and inspects:

- care homes
- domiciliary care agencies
- acute hospitals
- mental health hospitals
- hospices
- nurses' agencies.

It is a non-governmental body whose performance is monitored by the Department of Health and it is required to make information about services available to members of the public generally.

7.8   Powers of the Commission

The Commission is empowered to take action against poor-quality, dangerous or unsafe services. It can:

- grant or refuse an application for registration (in effect a licence to operate)
- impose conditions and insist on improvements and/or
- in the last resort, prosecute providers of services for breaches of regulations.

It has laid down standards of care homes for older people; see the leaflet 'Frequently Asked Questions' at *www.carestandards.org.uk.*

8   PROTECTING PEOPLE WHO CANNOT LOOK AFTER THEMSELVES

The financial affairs of someone who has become incapable through age or illness can cause great anxiety to the relatives. They may see bills being left unpaid or valuable assets being disposed of for a fraction of their value.

If the sick or elderly relative agrees, and if it is a matter of increasing forgetfulness, using a form from the bank to add another signatory to their bank account may solve the problem and means bills can be paid.

Similarly, an additional person can be nominated to collect the pension or benefits of someone unable to do so. In such a case, contact your local benefits agency.

Age Concern produces a fact sheet on handling the affairs of those unable to act themselves (see DIRECTORY).

If the relative can be persuaded to give a power of attorney to someone to handle their affairs while, for example, they are ill or in hospital, problems can be dealt with by the appointed agent. Unfortunately, however, an ordinary power of attorney becomes ineffective if the donor loses mental capacity. The law has provided for this by introducing 'enduring powers of attorney' (see section 8.2.2 below).

If, as is often the case, the relative's increasing incapacity is accompanied by suspicion and paranoia, it may be difficult to persuade them to sign over any powers of authorisation to those who wish to protect them. In such a case it may be necessary to apply to the Court of Protection to act as their statutory guardian (see Public Guardianship Office in DIRECTORY).

An enduring power of attorney, if obtained in advance when mental capacity is still present, is intended to avoid these problems.

A leaflet advising the elderly on putting their affairs in order can be obtained from Age Concern (see DIRECTORY). Ask for the leaflet entitled *Instructions for my next of kin and executors upon my death.*

Where a decision has to be made to administer medical treatment to a patient who does not have the capacity to consent, the court will have to be consulted, and will take into account the patient's rights under the Human Rights Act (see section 9.1).

Consent by the patient to treatment may also not be required where it is administered under the Mental Health Act 1983 (see section 8.3.5 below).

8.1 Living wills

It is a general principle of law and medical practice that all adults have the right to consent to or to refuse medical treatment.

Thus an adult of full mental capacity may direct that particular medical procedures, including life-saving ones, should not be used on him at a time in the future, in a so-called 'living will' or 'advance statement'.

Such documents are currently being made available by certain organisations, including the Voluntary Euthanasia Society and the Terence Higgins Trust (see DIRECTORY). A patient's refusal to give consent to treatment may be effective, even if it was expressed at an earlier time, before he became unable to express that refusal. Such a document will have force, although there may be difficulties about proving that the document still represents the patient's wishes in the circumstances which have arisen. The document cannot, however, legally authorise active steps to terminate life.

English law is unclear about the validity of the prior appointment of a proxy decision-maker with power to refuse consent to treatment on a patient's behalf. An enduring power of attorney (see section 8.2.2 below) can only authorise dealing with the patient's property and other affairs, not his health. The government is proposing changes which would include health care and personal welfare matters in 'continuing powers of attorney' which would enable decisions to be made on health matters where specific authority has been given to do so. A general authority to make health care decisions will not, however, give authority for withdrawal of artificial nutrition, for example. Healthcare powers could not be used until the person becomes incapacitated and will never be used to consent to compulsory treatment under the Mental Health Act 1983.

It is also proposed that there will be a single court, based at the Court of Protection, which will deal with all areas of decision-making for adults without capacity, including the power to appoint a manager to make decisions on their behalf.

Do note, however: under these proposals serious health-care decisions (such as the withdrawal of life support) as well as questions of treatment where the patient has made an advance statement are to remain a matter for the court and cannot be delegated to a manager appointed by the Court of Protection.

Most US states accept and regulate advance directives, as do some jurisdictions in Australia and Canada. Problems have arisen about defining the 'trigger event' activating such an authorisation, and about ensuring that it can be revoked if the patient changes his mind.

The 'living will' (which allows a patient, knowing he or she may lose the capacity to consent to treatment, to provide for that consent in advance) cannot require a doctor to do anything unlawful, including taking steps purely to end the patient's life, or insist that a doctor provide treatment that he or she does not regard as in the patient's best interests. There are not any immediate plans to attempt to implement these proposals and they are strongly opposed by some as being likely to provide a backdoor for the introduction of euthanasia, which is – and is intended to remain – illegal.

The government has accepted that the law needs reform and clarification in relation to the difficult and uncertain field of decision-making and mental capacity. It has set out its proposals in a document entitled *Making Decisions*, but new legislation will take time, particularly in the light of the division of opinion which exists on such complex and sensitive issues.

A case which attracted a great deal of attention in 2002 concerned a professional woman who had made a living will stating that futile medical treatment was not to be prolonged if a medical catastrophe befell her and she remained beyond recovery. Such a catastrophe occurred and she became tetraplegic, requiring a ventilator to breathe. The hospital resisted her demand that the living will be given effect to and the ventilator switched off, which would lead to her certain death. Psychiatric assessment established she had mental capacity to make such a decision. On her application to court her wishes were upheld and the hospital was ordered to cease to treat her.

The court stressed that a mentally competent patient must consent if medical treatment is to be lawful; for patients to be treated against their wishes is unlawful. The doctors' view that continuing treatment would be in the patient's best interests was irrelevant.

8.2   Powers of attorney

As you age, you may be glad of someone – one of your children or perhaps a friend – to take over some of the administrative chores involved in running your life. This may be done informally, e.g. by authorising the person to sign cheques on your bank account so that he or she can pay your debts without bothering you. However a formal authority known as a power of attorney may be required.

☞ *You are going to Tenerife for three months during the winter and you want your daughter to have power to let your house and collect the rents.*

You, as 'donor', can give your daughter, 'the attorney', a document known as a Power of Attorney which can either be general – which will enable her to act on your behalf with all the commercial power which you have yourself – or limited simply to the function of letting your house and collecting the rents.

8.2.1   Enduring powers of attorney

In all events, an ordinary power of attorney is only effective while the donor is mentally capable.

Thus powers of attorney cease to have effect if you become incapable of managing your own affairs. Persons dealing with the attorney may be reluctant to rely on the Power without evidence that the person who gave the Power (the donor) is still mentally capable. All of us can become mentally incapable and are quite likely to do so as we become old. Legislation has therefore provided for the creation of a Power called an Enduring Power of Attorney (EPA) which is not revoked if you become mentally incapable.

An Enduring Power of Attorney is immediately effective as an ordinary Power and if it is produced to someone who is being asked to act on it it will be more useful than an ordinary Power because the person to whom it is produced will not need to make any enquiries as to the mental condition of the donor. However, the donor can limit the Power so that it only becomes effective if he becomes mentally incapable. In that event the Power has to be registered with the Public Guardianship Office before it becomes effective, and before registration Notice of Intention to Register must be given to at least three relatives in an order prescribed by the legislation creating the Power. Once registered it remains effective until the donor's death unless he revokes it when he has regained the ability to deal with his own affairs.

An Enduring Power of Attorney can be signed by someone who is not able to manage his own property or affairs as long as he understands the effect of what he is doing in giving the Power, although obviously in that event it would be sensible for the attorney to get independent evidence of the donor's ability to understand, e.g. by getting a medical practitioner to act as witness to the donor's signature.

An Enduring Power of Attorney gives immense power to the attorney, particularly if the donor's assets are substantial. The system has been abused and one way of protecting yourself is to have joint attorneys – which is permitted by the legislation – so that they can act as a check on each other.

An Enduring Power of Attorney must be in a prescribed form which can be purchased. It contains directions for its completion so legal advice is not essential though desirable in all the circumstances.

8.2.2   Other protection in law

Many of us will suffer a disastrous decline in our mental powers as we age and may make irrational decisions in dealing with our affairs. To some extent the law may be employed to reverse or cancel damaging transactions in to which we have entered.

☞ *Your elderly father has for many years collected military medals, and his collection is now valuable. He sells it for a fraction of its value to a conman he has met in a pub.*

If it can proved that he did not understand what he was doing, and that the person who bought the collection knew of his incapacity, it may be possible for the court to set the transaction aside. However, it is likely to be difficult to trace the conman and unless your father can get community legal service funding [formerly legal aid], the attempt to undo the damage may be prohibitively expensive.

8.2.3 Court of Protection

If you become so mentally impaired that you cannot deal with your own affairs a Receiver can be appointed by the Court of Protection.

The day-to-day administration of cases under the jurisdiction of the Court of Protection is carried out by the Public Guardianship Office. It charges an initial fee for investigating your means if you are mentally incapable, and for appointing the Receiver, and it oversees the carrying out of his function by the Receiver, charging an annual fee for doing so. These procedures can be slow, bureaucratic, and comparatively expensive, and if you have friends, relatives or professional advisers whom you trust, you can appoint them to look after your affairs instead, thus avoiding the need for an application to the Court of Protection. This is done by means of an enduring power of attorney (see section 8.2.1 above).

8.3 Psychiatric treatment and committal procedures – The Mental Health Act 1983

As longevity increases, health problems in the elderly become more prevalent. Older age groups have an increased risk of mental health problems such as depressive illness, suicide, and dementing disorders such as Alzheimer's disease, which may be compounded by other physical illness and disability. Sometimes legal measures are needed to safeguard the health of the patient. These measures are also relevant to the treatment of younger people.

8.3.1 What is 'mental disorder'?

Mental disorder is defined under the Mental Health Act 1983 as 'mental illness, arrested or incomplete development of mind, psychopathic disorder and any other disorder or disability of mind'. Guidance for professional staff is provided by a Code of Practice.

The government has proposed far-reaching changes to mental health law.

Most people who receive treatment for psychiatric illness do so on a voluntary ('informal') basis. Some patients, however, may require 'formal' admission to a psychiatric hospital unit against their will, under the powers given by one of the sections of the 1983 Act (often referred to as being 'sectioned'). Such compulsion is only permissible in the interests of the patient's health or safety, or for the protection of others. The other requirements of the Act must also be satisfied (see below, 8.3.2).

Important: if you are worried about the mental state of a spouse or relative, your first step should be to approach their general practitioner (GP) or local social services. Depending on the arrangements in your local area, and the urgency, they may call for an initial assessment to be arranged at home by members of the local area's Crisis Team or the Community Mental Health Team (which includes community nurses, social workers, medical and other staff). Options for further assessment and treatment will be explored: compulsory admission will only be sought as a last resort.

Usually there are separate community teams for adults and the elderly. Demarcating ages differ in different areas. Separate provisions will be made for child and adolescent patients.

8.3.2 Compulsory admission

The process of compulsory admission requires that an application is made, preferably by an Approved Social Worker (ASW), although the Act allows for the application to be made by the nearest relative. The ASW must interview the patient in order to be satisfied that the patient's civil rights are adequately protected, that compulsory admission is necessary to provide the assessment and treatment which the person requires, and that less restrictive alternatives have been properly explored. The application has to be supported in writing by the medical recommendations of two doctors who have assessed the person. One of the doctors (usually the GP) should know the patient personally, and the other must be approved (under Section 12 of the Act) as experienced in the diagnosis and treatment of mental disorder. It is recommended that two approved doctors should assess the patient if no doctor who knows the patient is available. The nearest relative should be consulted.

Usually the initial admission to hospital will be for assessment; section 2 of the Act, for example, allows for admission for assessment and treatment for up to 28 days, while section 3 allows for a longer period of detention for treatment, up to six months in the first instance. There are also other sections in the Act, which provide for urgent admission for assessment, where the procedures under sections 2 and 3 are not immediately feasible (see 8.3.3 immediately below).

8.3.3   Police warrant – 'place of safety'

A provision of the Mental Health Act 1983 authorises a magistrate to issue a warrant to a policeman to enter premises and remove someone to a 'place of safety' where that person is suffering (or is believed to be suffering) from a mental disorder and:

- has been, or is being, ill treated or neglected, or is not under proper control; or
- is unable to care for him- or herself and is living alone. (Section 135.)

A 'place of safety' includes a hospital, local authority accommodation, a police station, a mental nursing home or a residential home for mentally disordered persons. In practice, it will usually be a hospital.

The application must be made by a social worker who must provide information on oath that the person is mentally disordered and that the other conditions apply to his or her state. The policeman must be accompanied by a doctor and a social worker who can then decide whether the removal is appropriate.

☞   *You have seen your very elderly neighbour wandering round the garden in a distracted state. It is now winter, and she appears on the grass barefoot and in her nightgown. You are very worried about her well-being as you know that she has been living alone for some time and appears to have no visitors. You have always called her 'Emily' but are not sure of her surname. You would like to approach the local authority social services to discuss her plight but are concerned that you do not have enough information.*

The social worker will only have recourse to an application for a warrant for removal to a place of safety as a last resort. He or she may be able to persuade Emily to receive care from a GP, a visiting mental health team, or other health and social services. However, under section 135, a warrant does not have to name the person provided that it states the address of the premises.

Section 47 of the National Assistance Act 1948, which is seldom used, is another legal option which allows for a vulnerable person to be removed to a 'suitable hospital or other place' if they are living in excessively insanitary conditions and are unable to accept appropriate support. A diagnosis of mental disorder is not required. Application is made by the local council to a magistrates' court. Only one medical recommendation, by a community physician, is required; the rights to appeal are less than for patients 'sectioned' under the Mental Health Act, and relatives do not have the power of veto.

8.3.4   Guardianship

The Mental Health Act also permits a form of guardianship where a person is suffering from mental disorder to a degree which merits such a step (see section 8.2.4 above). The purpose is to ensure that patients receive community care with a minimum of constraint.

Application can be made by the person's nearest relative or by a social worker. The usefulness of this provision is limited because it requires a considerable degree of co-operation from the patient.

8.3.5   Treatment

The general rule is that any patient – no matter how elderly or infirm – can consent, or withhold their consent, to treatment. Where consent is given, it must be 'informed consent', i.e. the patient must be given a proper explanation of the treatment and the risks which may be involved in the proposed treatment. Exceptions to this rule do exist, however: for example, if you are knocked unconscious on the road by a truck, and an operation is necessary to save your life, informed consent is not required, on the basis that the accident victim would have consented had he or she been able to do so.

Another exception exists under the Mental Health Act where some treatments for mental disorder can, in some circumstances and for a limited time, be given to detained patients without consent, if the responsible medical officer decides that the patient, because of their disorder, does not have the mental capacity to understand and make an informed choice. However, electro-convulsive treatment (ECT) cannot be given against a patient's wishes unless the need to proceed without consent is supported by a second medical opinion given by a doctor appointed by the Mental Health Act Commission (see below 8.3.8) on behalf of the Secretary of State. The extremely rare procedure of psycho-surgery requires both consent and a second opinion.

8.3.6   Rights of Appeal

Patients detained under the Mental Health Act have the right to appeal against their detention. The hospital management must inform them of their rights, and, if they appeal, arrange for a hearing to be conducted by a Mental Health Review Tribunal. The Tribunal will be composed of three people who are wholly independent of the detaining hospital; one will be a doctor, who will make an independent assessment of the patient, and the others will be a legally qualified president of the Tribunal and a lay person with appropriate experience. Evidence will be heard from the patient (assisted by an appointed representative, normally a solicitor invited by the patient or by the hospital managers) and from professional staff caring for the patient. The patient may also, at the Tribunal's discretion, invite other people, such as a relative or friend, to attend.

Mental Health Review Tribunals have the right to discharge patients from the 'section' order and can make other recommendations.

In certain circumstances the nearest relative has a right to discharge a patient from the 'section'. If the hospital managers oppose this, they are allowed a 72-hour period in which to organise an urgent Tribunal to review the case.

Helpful information on mental disorder and patients' rights can be obtained from MIND (National Association for Mental Health) – see DIRECTORY.

8.3.7   Care Plans

An important provision for patients discharged from hospital or for those treated in the community by a Mental Health Team is a written Care Plan, which sets out the role of each professional involved in the care of the patient. A copy should be made available to patients and (with the patient's consent) to the nearest relative, and both should be invited to participate in regularly-scheduled Care Plan Meetings which require that the professional staff review the patient's needs and record how they are to be met.

8.3.8   Mental Health Act Commission

The Mental Health Act Commission's role is to oversee the operation of the Mental Health Act on behalf of the Secretary of State. Commissioners make regular visits to psychiatric units where patients receive treatment under the powers of the Act, interview detained patients, investigate complaints and provide reports to the managers and staff on any deviations from good practice. Their interest includes the welfare of patients who are not detained.

You can ask to see a member of the Commission in private or contact its office on 0115 943 7100. However, the Commission has no powers to discharge you from hospital, or transfer you to another one. Members of the Commission are not authorised to offer individual medical or legal advice. Further details can be obtained from its website: *www.mhac.trent.nhs.uk.*

9   WHERE TO TURN TO FOR REDRESS

The Chapter on *The Legal System* explains where you can turn to for help when faced with a legal problem. An approach to these agencies does not necessarily mean legal fees, and those of limited resources, living on a pension, can always turn to the voluntary sector first. The directories at the end of the chapters of this book also provide a host of organisations which may be able to assist you with a particular problem – whether you need advice on a consumer dispute, a health matter, or are facing difficulties in your personal relationships. So what follows below should be read in conjunction with the material to be found elsewhere in these pages.

9.1   The Human Rights Act

The Human Rights Act 1998 incorporated into English Law the basic protection of human rights which was part of EU Law. The Act became effective in 2000. Whereas before the Act came into force, if you believed your human rights had been infringed your only remedy was an application to the European Court of Human Rights in Strasbourg, you can now apply for relief or compensation in the English Courts.

The Human Rights Act is general in its application and its specific effect on every aspect of English law is being worked out by the courts. The particular effects of the Act on the problems of old age are as yet unclear.

However in one case a resident of an old people's home run by a local authority, who had reason to believe he could stay there for life, successfully claimed that his proposed transfer to another home was a breach of his human rights (see section 7.4 above). Certainly the possibility of using the Act should be considered in any circumstances in which you believe you have been badly or unfairly treated whether by the State or by a public authority which acts on behalf of the State, such as the NHS or local government bodies.

9.2   Local Government Ombudsman

The Local Government Ombudsmen investigate complaints of maladministration by local authorities including housing, care, and other social services. They publish an annual digest of cases which they have investigated.

There are three Ombudsmen in England to cover different parts of the country.

If you have a complaint and appear to have suffered an injustice as a result, you must first approach the council and use their own complaints procedure. Only if you are dissatisfied can you approach the Local Government Ombudsman. Your complaint must be in writing. Generally there is a 12-month time limit within which you must lodge your complaint to the Ombudsman.

9.3   The Commissions

In the course of this chapter, we have made reference to the Mental Health Act Commission, as well as to the Care Standards Commission. In addition, there are other bodies such as the Disability Rights Commission, the Commission for Health Improvement, and the Social Services Inspectorate. All these bodies have regulatory powers and if you feel that standards have been breached, or your rights have been infringed in a manner which relates to the work of one of these Commissions, do make your complaint known to them.

9.4   The Tribunals

There is a plethora of tribunals for appeals on such matters as social security, pensions, housing benefit, mental health, and care standards. From these tribunals there may be further appeals – for example to the Social Security Commissioners on a point of law.

It is beyond the scope of this book to detail the procedures, the cases which are appealable and those which are not, and the time limits involved. If you wish to appeal against a decision which you feel affects you adversely, e.g. on a benefit received, then you are strenuously advised to seek legal assistance from the voluntary or private sector.

You may make initial enquiries on the internet from:

www.appeals-service.gov.uk/about_us/who_and_what.htm.

9.5   Judicial review

A procedure for applying to the Court to deal with abuses of power by public bodies or associations may also be available to a person who claims to have been improperly or unfairly treated by them. The process is known as judicial review. See the chapter on *The Legal System*, section 7.7.4.

DIRECTORY
GROWING OLD

Able Community Care
The Old Parish Rooms
Whitlingham Lane
Trowse
Norfolk NR14 8TZ
Tel. 01603 764567
www.uk-care.com

Age Concern England
(National Council on Ageing)
Astral House
1268 London Road
London SW16 4ER
(Freephone) Tel. 0808 808 6060 *(verbal advice)*
(Freephone) Tel. 08000 009966 *(for factsheeets)*
www.ageconcern.org.uk

Age Concern Cymru
4th Floor,
1 Cathedral Road
Cardiff CF1 9SD
Tel. 02920 371 566
www.accymru.org.uk

Aid for the Aged in Distress
54 London Road
Morden
Surrey SM4 5BE
Tel. 020 8640 5523
www.agedisstress.org.uk

**Advice Information and Mediation Service for
Retirement Housing** *(AIMS)*
Age Concern England
Astral House
1268 London Road
London SW16 4ER
(Advice Line) Tel. 0845 600 2001
www.ageconcern.org.uk/aims

Alzheimer's Society
Gordon House
10 Greencoat Place
London SW1P 1PH
(Helpline) Tel. 0845 300 0336
www.alzheimers.org.uk

Arthritic Association *(offers natural treatment)*
1 Upperton Gardens
Eastbourne BN21 2AA
Tel. 020 7491 0233
www.arthriticassociation.org.uk

Arthritis Care
18 Stephenson Way
London NW1 2HD
(Helpline) Tel. 0808 800 4050
www.arthritiscare.org.uk

Association of Retirement Housing Managers
3rd Floor
89 Albert Embankment
London SE1 7TP
Tel. 020 7820 1839

Benefits EnquiryLine *(DSS)*
(Freephone) Tel. 0800 882200

British Red Cross Society
9 Grosvenor Crescent
London SW1X 7EJ
Tel. 020 7235 5454
www.redcross.org.uk

Care and Repair Cymru
Norbury House
Norbury Road
Fairwater
Cardiff CF5 3AS
Tel. 02920 576 286
www.enquiries.careandrepair.org.uk

Careaware *(deals with long-term care issues)*
PO Box 8
Manchester M30 9NY
(Helpline) Tel. 08705 134 925
www.careaware.co.uk

Carers UK *(offers advice on benefits and services
available to carers)*
20-25 Glasshouse Yard
London EC1A 4JT
(Carers Line) Tel. 0808 808 7777
www.carersonline.org.uk

Caring Matters
132 Gloucester Place
London NW1 6DT
Tel. 020 7402 2702
www.caring-matters.org.uk

The Cinnamon Trust *(provides register of
accommodation which accepts pets)*
Foundry House
Foundry Square
Hayle
Cornwall TR27 4HE
www.cinnamon.org.uk

Citizens' Advice Bureau
115-123 Pentonville Road
London BB1 9LZ
Tel. 020 7833 2181
www.nacab.org.uk

Continence Foundation
2 Doughty Street
London WC12PH
(Helpline) Tel. 020 7831 9831
www.continence-foundation.org.uk

Counsel and Care *(provides advice on
accommodation and funding for residential care)*
Twyman House
16 Bonny Street
London NW1 9PG
(Advice Line) Tel. 0845 300 7585

Crossroads – Caring for Carers
(supports needs of carers)
10 Regents Place
Rugby
Warks CV21 2PN
(Advice Line) Tel. 01788 573 653
www.crossroads.org.uk

Cruse Bereavement Care
Cruse House
126 Sheen Road
Richmond
Surrey TW9 1UR
(Helpline) Tel. 0870 167 1677
www.crusebereavementcare.org.uk

Diabetes UK
10 Parkway
London NW1 7AA
(Helpline) Tel. 020 7424 1030
www.diabetes.org.uk

Dial UK *(disability information advice line)*
St. Catherines
Tickhill Road
Doncaster DN4 8N
Tel. 01302 310 123
www.dialuk.org.uk

Disability Alliance
(produces publications about social security benefits)
88-94 Wentworth Street
London E1 7SA
(Helpline) Tel. 020 7247 8763
www.disabilityalliance.org

Disabled Living Centres Council
Redbank House
4 St. Chads Street
Manchester M8 8QA
Tel. 0161 834 1044
www.dlcc.org.uk

Disabled Living Foundation
380–364 Harrow Road
London W9 2HU
Tel. 0870 603 9177
www.dlf.org.uk

Elderly Accommodation Counsel
Third Floor
89 Albert Embankment
London SE1 7TP
Tel. 020 7820 1343
www.housingcare.org

Financial Ombudsman Service
South Quay Plaza
183 Marsh Wall
London E14 9SR
Tel. 0845 080 1800
www.financial-ombudsman.org.uk

Financial Services Authority
25 The North Colonnade
Canary Wharf
London E14 5HS
Tel. 020 7676 1000
www.fsa.gov.uk/consumer/your_rights/pensions

Foundations *(national co-ordinating body for
Home Improvement Agencies)*
Bleaklow House
Howard Town Mills
Glossop
Derbyshire SK13 8HT
Tel. 01457 891 909
www.cl.co.uk/foundations

General Insurance Standards Council
110 Cannon Street
London EC4N 6EU
Tel. 020 7648 7800
www.gisc.co.uk

Help the Aged
207-221 Pentonville Road,
London N1 9UZ
(Seniorline) Tel. 0808 800 6565
www.helptheaged.org.uk

Home Improvement Trust
7 Mansfield Road
Nottingham NG1 3FB
Tel. 0115 934 9511
www.hitrust.org

Hospice Information Service
St. Christopher's Hospice
51–59 Lawrie Park Road
Sydenham
London SE26 6DZ
Tel. 020 8778 9252
www.hospiceinformation.info

Huntington's Disease Association
108 Battersea High Street
London SW11 3HP
Tel. 020 7223 7000
www.had.org.uk

Independent Financial Advisers Promotion Ltd
17–19 Emery Road
Brislington
Bristol BS4 5PF
Tel. 0117 971 1177
www.unbiased.co.uk

Independent Healthcare Association
Westminster Tower
3 Albert Embankment
London SE1 7SP
Tel. 020 7793 4620
www.iha.org.uk

Inland Revenue Savings
Pensions and Share Schemes
St John's House
Merton Road
Bootle
Merseyside L69 9BB
Tel. 0845 980 0645
www.inlandrevenue.gov.uk
or
Yorke House
PO Box 62
Castle Meadow Road
Nottingham NG2 1BG
Tel. 0115 974 0000
www.inlandrevenue.gov.uk

Law Centres Federation
Duchess House
18–19 Warren Street
London W1P 5DB
(Helpline) Tel. 0845 608 1122
www.lawcentres.org.uk

Local Government Ombudsman (England)
21 Queen Anne's Gate
London SW1H 9BU
Tel. 020 7915 3210
(This tel. no. covers London, Kent, Surrey,
E. and W. Sussex – *see The Countryside* DIRECTORY
on page 441 for other regions)
www.lgo.org.uk

Macmillan Cancer Relief
89 Albert Embankment
London SE1 7UQ
Tel. 0845 601 6161
www.macmillan.org.uk

MIND
Granta House
15–19 Broadway
London E15 4BQ
Information lines
(London) Tel. 020 8522 1728
(Non-London) Tel. 08457 660 163
www.mind.org.uk

The Mortgage Code Compliance Board
MCCB Ltd.
University Court
Stafford ST18 0GN
Tel. 01785 218 200
www.mortgagecode.org.uk

Multiple Sclerosis Society
372 Edgware Road
London NW2 6ND
(Helpline) Tel. 0808 800 8000
www.mssociety.org.uk

The National Association of Almshouses
Billingbear Lodge
Carters Hill
Wokingham
Berks RG40 5RU
Tel. 01344 452 922
www.almshouses.org

National Benevolent Fund for the Aged
(helps with pain relief and provides alarm phones
for people on low income)
1 Leslie Grove Place
Croydon, Surrey CR0 6TJ
Tel. 020 8688 6655
www.nbfa.org.uk

The National Care Standards Commission
St. Nicholas Building
St. Nicholas Street
Newcastle upon Tyne NE1 1NB
(Helpline) Tel. 0191 233 3556
www.carestandards.org.uk

The National House Building Council
Buildmark House
Chiltern Avenue
Amersham
Bucks HP6 5AP
Tel. 01494 434 477
www.nhbc.co.uk

Occupational Pensions Regulatory Authority
Pensions Schemes Regulator
Invicta house
Trafalgar Place
Brighton
East Sussex BN14DW
Tel. 01273 627 600
www.opra.gov.uk

Parkinson's Disease Society
215 Vauxhall Bridge Road
London SW1V 1EJ
(Helpline) Tel. 0808 800 0303
www.parkinsons.org.uk

Patients Association
PO Box 935
Harrow
Middlesex HA1 3YJ
(Helpline) Tel. 020 8423 8999
www.patients-association.com

Pensions Advisory Service
11 Belgrave Road
London SW1V 1RB
Tel. 0845 601 2923
www.opas.org.uk

Pensions Compensation Board
11 Belgrave Road
London SW1V 1RB
Tel. 020 7828 9794

Pensions Guide
Freepost
Bristol BS38 7WA
www.pensionguide.gov.uk

Pensions Overseas Benefit Directorate
Department for Work and Pensions
Tyneview Park
Whitley Road
Benton
Newcastle upon Tyne NE98 1BA
Tel. 0191 218 2000
www.thepensionservice.gov.uk
www.dwp.gov.uk

Pension Schemes Registry
PO Box 1NN
Newcastle upon Tyne NE99 1NN
Tel. 0191 225 6316
www.opra.gov.uk

Pre-Retirement Association
9 Chesham Road
Guildford
Surrey GU1 3LS
www.pra.uk.com

The Princess Royal Trust for Carers
142 Minories
London EC3N 1LB
Tel. 020 7480 7788
www.carers.org

Public Guardianship Office
*(provide information about Court of Protection
and Powers of Attorney)*
Archway Tower
2 Junction Road
London N19 5SZ
Tel. 0845 330 2900
www.guardianship.gov.uk

Registered Nursing Home Association
15 Highfield Road
Edgbaston
Birmingham B15 3DU
Tel. 0121 454 2511
www.rnha.co.uk

Retirement Pension Forecasting Team
Room TB 001
Tyneview Park
Whitley Road
Benton
Newcastle upon Tyne NE98 1BA
Tel. 0870 010 1684
www.thepensionservice.gov.uk

Royal Association for Disability and Rehabilitation *(RADAR)*
12 City Forum
250 City Road
London EC1V 8AS
Tel. 020 7250 3222
www.radar.org.uk

Royal National Institute of the Blind *(RNIB)*
105 Judd Street
London WC1H 9NE
(Helpline) Tel. 08457 669 999
www.rnib.org.uk

Royal National Institute for Deaf People *(RNID)*
19–23 Featherstone Street
London EC1Y 8SL
(Information Line) Tel. 0808 808 0123
www.rnid.org.uk

The Samaritans
10 The Grove
Slough SL1 1QP
Tel. 08457 909090
www.samaritans.org.uk

Seniorline *(run by Help the Aged)*
Tel. 0808 800 6565

Terence Higgins Trust
52-54 Grays Inn Road
London WC1X 8JU
Tel. 020 7831 0330
(Helpline) Tel. 0845 1221 200
www.tht.org.uk

The Stroke Association
Stroke House
240 City Road
London EC1V 2PR
(Infoline) Tel. 0845 303 3100
www.stroke.org.uk

Third Age Employment Network
207-221 Pentonville Road
London N1 9UZ
Tel. 020 7843 1590
www.taen.org.uk

Tripscope
(provides advice and information about travel)
Vasall Centre
Gill Avenue
Fishponds
Bristol BS16 2QQ
Tel. 08457 585 641
www.tripscope.org.uk

Voluntary Euthanasia Society
13 Prince of Wales Terrace
London W8 5PG
Tel. 020 7937 7770
www.ves.org.uk

Women's Royal Voluntary Service
Milton Hill House
Milton Hill
Oxon OX13 6AD
Tel. 01235 442 900
www.wrvs.org.uk

War Pensions
(Helpline) Tel. 0800 169 2277

Other useful websites
www.info4pensioners.gov.uk
www.inlandrevenue.gov.uk/pensionschemes/
   guidance.htm

10 GOODS AND SERVICES

In a modern industrialised society, we are constantly acquiring, producing or selling products or services, weaving a web about us of legal rights and obligations. Each time you hop on a bus, buy a pint of milk or leave your suit at the cleaners, you are entering into contractual relationships which have legally enforceable consequences.

The law used to stand back as far as possible from contracts of all kinds, taking the view that it was up to each individual to negotiate terms and conditions in order to protect his or her position. In a mass age, this was increasingly seen as unfair, if not unworkable. The result is that today the law regulates the content of most types of contract, which have particular legal results whether the parties know of this or not at the time. At the same time, the need to prevent individuals being taken advantage of by those with greater muscle, or from being cheated by the dishonest, has created an ever-strengthening legal shield to protect the consumer from dangerous products, from being misled by false claims, from being taken advantage of financially, and from being trapped by unintelligible or unreasonable 'fine print' clauses.

Even where this protective legislation exists, it is still up to individuals actively to protect themselves by taking precautions, reading the small print, shopping around where possible. This chapter is designed to help you to take such precautions; but, of course, also to tell you about your remedies if things go wrong. In most cases, tradesmen and retailers are honest and doing their best; if things go wrong, they will often respond to a complaint, in order to keep a customer happy, without the letter of the law having to be invoked.

Unfortunately, of course, things do not always run smoothly. When this is the case, complain first, clearly and promptly. If this is unsuccessful, in the last resort you can sue the supplier; if you use the small claims procedure this will not be very expensive, but it is often less trouble and quicker to complain to the trading standards department of your local authority. They also produce a wide range of very helpful leaflets on a variety of consumer topics. See *www.tradingstandards.gov.uk*. Sometimes, you may be able to seek recourse through the trade association, if there is one, which if it cannot mediate the dispute may run an arbitration scheme. With some disputes, e.g. with an insurance company, there may be an Ombudsman to investigate your complaint. The Director-General of the Office of Fair Trading can regulate unfair terms in contracts.

Suing will always be a last resort – but getting legal advice should not be. It can be obtained from a solicitor, a Citizen's Advice Bureau or law centre. See the chapter on *The Legal System*.

In this chapter we look at some of the ways of acquiring goods or commissioning services which arise most frequently in our lives:

- entering into contracts
- consumer protection
- purchase and sale of goods – foodstuffs, clothing, cars, etc.
- other ways of acquiring goods – mail order, the Internet, HP etc.
- services, from plumbers to estate agents
- dangerous products
- dealing with your bank and your insurance company; credit and debt
- eating out
- going on holiday.

1 A MATTER OF CONTRACT

Whenever you enter into an arrangement to obtain goods or services you are entering into a contract.

No writing may exist, indeed words may not even be exchanged, as when you get on a bus and tender the correct fare. But it is a contract which you have entered into nevertheless and if something goes wrong – such as an accident – your rights and obligations can be legally enforced.

What distinguishes a contract from other situations with legal consequences is that in a contract there are mutual, reciprocal rights and obligations. Both parties give something and receive something.

1.1 Written contracts

If there is a written contract, it may define your legal position whether you read it or not. Terms and conditions, a ticket or receipt can be part of the contract and define your position under it, even if you have not signed it. On the other hand, changes in the law do mean that businesses may no longer be able to hide behind small print in their contracts if they contain unreasonable or unfair terms (see section 2.4 below on 'small print' regulations).

1.1.1 Signing a contract

If you are asked to sign something, read it first or ask to take it away to study. Once it bears your signature you may be bound by its terms whether or not you knew of them. Never sign a blank or partially completed form. Only if someone is unable to read or understand a document, and is misled about its nature, may he or she be able to escape the consequences of signing.

Contracts for large items such as computer systems or cars often contain an 'entire contract' clause which states that the documents contain the entire agreement between the parties or a clause stating that the supplier is not liable for any misrepresentation made orally to the consumer. If you agree to this clause you may lose your right to complain of any misrepresentation that was made to you before you signed. However, the clause might be regarded as unfair and therefore unenforceable.

☞ *The owner of a stationery shop leases a photocopy machine which the salesman tells him will have particular copying features. The lease agreement excludes liability for misrepresentation. The machine supplied does not in fact have the promised features.*

In a similar case the court held that the exclusion clause was unreasonable and unfair and the company was therefore liable for breach of contract.

1.2 Unwritten contracts

There is no legal requirement that contracts should be in writing: contracts are equally enforceable in law whether written or oral. Most of our day-to-day contracts are oral – as when you buy goods in a shop. In fact, it is not even necessary that words should be exchanged at all, as when you buy a ticket from an automatic vending machine at a car park or Underground station. Contracts can also be partly oral and partly in writing.

1.2.1 Being bound by terms

Few of us read printed clauses on the back of a ticket, or a reference to terms and conditions in a timetable or insurance policy (often available in a separate document). However, these terms may still bind us in the event of a mishap, although the court may regard them as unfair and unenforceable if you had no real opportunity of becoming acquainted with the term.

Sometimes there are no written terms and the absence of writing may mean difficulties in proof.

1.3 Who has rights under contract?

Do note: normally, only persons who are actually parties to the contract can rely on its terms even as modified by the law. If you buy a food processor which does not work, you have contractual rights against the shop. If you give the item to your niece as a wedding present, until recently she would have had no rights at all under the contract because she was not one of the parties to the sale. In other words, the only two parties to the contract were the purchaser and the shopkeeper.

This rule has now been changed. Someone else, in this case your niece [in legal terms the 'third party'], can now enforce rights under a contract either:

• where the contract says so in so many words, or

- where she is identified in a contract which is designed to benefit her. A clear case of this would be where you bought the food processor from the 'Wedding List' department of the store and asked for it to be delivered direct to your niece. If, however, the contract does not make it clear that the machine was intended for a third party, and it doesn't work, your niece will either have to ask you to enforce the shop's obligation under the contract, or find out whether the shop will ignore the legal position and deal direct with her in the interests of goodwill. (The change in the law does not apply to employment contracts.)

If however, the food processor is actually dangerous, she can complain to the shop under the Consumer Protection Act – whether or not she was a party to the contract. She can also complain to her local trading standards officer. If she is injured by the dangerous defect she could sue the manufacturer for damages (see also section 6 below).

1.4   Non-contractual arrangements

Not all transactions are contractual, of course.

☞ *A friend asks you to drive him to the airport to catch a flight to New York. You oversleep and turn up late so that he misses his plane.*

Because you were doing him a favour and not receiving payment, there are no legal consequences, although he could have sued a taxi firm in similar circumstances.

A minor does not incur contractual obligations except in limited circumstances. For the purposes of the law of contract, a minor is anyone aged under 18.

☞ *A 17-year-old neighbour, a trainee hairdresser, offers to do your hair for a fee, with disastrous results.*

You cannot sue her for breach of contract, although you might have been able to sue an adult in the same circumstances. Probably you could sue for negligence (see the *Accidents* chapter), if you could prove negligence on her part. On the other hand, you may have voluntarily assumed the risk by going to her in the first instance.

2   CONSUMER PROTECTION

In theory, there is 'freedom of contract' in English law. This means that, generally speaking, people can put any terms they like into their contracts which the other side is then free either to accept or to reject.

In reality, of course, consumers are often faced with a choice of accepting fixed terms which a business may offer, or going without. You cannot usually negotiate all the terms of your car insurance, but are offered a printed policy, take it or leave it; and if you leave it you will probably find other companies' policies are very similar (but see section 2.4 below where the law has endeavoured to constrain the use of unfair terms in small print). The law has intervened to correct the balance in favour of consumers in certain other significant ways.

First, where it considers conduct sufficiently grave it has made wrongful trading a crime. So it imposes *criminal* penalties if a trader attempts to mislead potential customers. The system of prosecuting businesses for false trade descriptions (see section 2.2 below) is an example. Other examples would be traders who serve short weights or measures, or dealers trying to pass themselves off as private sellers.

It is the responsibility of Trading Standards Officers, who are employees of local councils, to enforce these laws and prosecute traders committing offences. All breaches of trading standards should be reported to them (see their website, *www.tradingstandards.gov.uk* or your telephone book for your local trading standards office – sometimes called the Consumer Protection Department – of your local authority). Should you have to report an offence against the food safety provisions, you should contact your local authority Environmental Health Officer.

Second, the law writes certain terms into contracts for the sale of goods whether or not the parties to the contract have included them. In other words, the law intervenes directly in the contractual process. See section 2.1 below. The law may also strike out certain terms (section 2.4 below).

2.1 Implied terms

The law defines the content of the parties' respective rights and obligations, by providing that all contracts of a particular type automatically *include* certain terms – such as that all goods sold should be fit for their purpose and of merchantable quality (see section 3.1.1 below). Or, in a sale of goods contract, the law will always imply a term that the goods which are sold will match a sample provided by the seller.

It also decrees that certain terms are automatically *excluded* from all contracts ('excluded terms') – for example, under the Unfair Contract Terms Act, a business is not allowed, by law, to exclude its liability for causing death or personal injury.

These implied terms are generally not enforced by criminal sanctions. A consumer can bring a legal action in the civil courts for damages where a trader has breached a term – for instance, where a shopkeeper has sold a faulty product.

English law has reacted in a piecemeal way to consumer problems so that the law on the subject is intricate.

2.2 Criminal sanctions

In the interests of protecting consumers against unfair trading practices, there are many regulations in effect prescribing codes of conduct for business. Breaches give rise to criminal liability rather than to compensation claims, but the possibility of being reported to trading standards officers may lead a trader to mend his ways and offer an informal settlement (see further, section 6.4 below).

2.3 European law – additional protection

EU law has already had an impact on consumer law in this country, e.g. in imposing uniform liability for dangerous products (see section 6) and in the interests of protecting the consumer in a disadvantageous bargaining position (see section 2.4. immediately below).

A new European Directive which it is hoped will soon be implemented by all the EU States gives better rights to consumers shopping throughout the EU. If goods are found to be faulty or do not conform to the contract, the buyer can ask for a repair or replacement. If this cannot be done, they will be entitled to a full or partial refund. Further, if a defect appears within the first six months after purchase, it will be presumed that the defect was present at the time of sale.

These rights are in addition to the rights which already benefit UK consumers under the Sale of Goods Act 1979.

2.4 Unfair terms – the 'small print' regulations

European law has also resulted in regulations which mean that businesses can no longer rely on unfair terms in their contracts with consumers. The regulations only apply to terms in standard form contracts, such as a pre-printed hire contract, which a business uses for all its customers on a 'take it or leave it' basis.

The regulations require that all terms must be written in plain and intelligible language. But on the whole, their intention is to tackle the clauses printed in fine print ('ancillary terms') which the consumer does not usually bother to read, or if he or she does read them, cannot understand them.

The regulations describe an 'unfair term' as any term 'contrary to the requirement of good faith which causes a significant imbalance in the parties' rights ... to the detriment of the consumer'. In assessing good faith, particular regard will be had to the bargaining strength between the parties.

The Director-General of Fair Trading can take action to prevent businesses putting terms which are unfair to customers in their standard contracts. Under the regulations, he is obliged to consider serious complaints from the public about any contract terms (see DIRECTORY under Office of Fair Trading).

The OFT has been using the regulations to deal with a large number of complaints from individual consumers, trading standards officers and consumer organisations. It normally acts by 'persuading' individual firms to give undertakings that they will not enforce objectionable terms in existing contracts, and will delete or alter them in future contracts. A very substantial proportion of complaints dealt with by the OFT concerned mobile phone contracts. Home improvements and letting agencies' terms of agreement also feature significantly in the volume of complaints received by the Office of Fair Trading (see also chapter on *Landlords and their Tenants*).

☞ *You enter into a contract with a mobile phone service provider, Ring Ltd. After signing the contract you notice that it entitles Ring to charge you a flat disconnection fee of £50 plus VAT even if the phone is disconnected because of a technical failure of the system. Another clause states that if you wish to cancel the contract, you must give three months' notice, which can only be given after the minimum period of 12 months has expired. As you are very dissatisfied with Ring's service, you are reluctant to pay for the extra 3 months.*

In a similar case, under pressure from the OFT the company agreed to delete the first clause and to shorten the notice period to only one month.

The Office of Fair Trading publishes detailed bulletins which contain examples of the kind of term where such action has been taken. These include terms in contracts used by (among others) dating agencies, care homes, and wedding-reception companies. (See DIRECTORY at the end of this chapter.)

Other areas where action has been taken are terms restricting airlines' liability for goods damaged in transit or which allow them to re-schedule flights without compensation; mortgage contracts which give lenders unrestricted powers to vary interest rates or require tie-ins with compulsory insurance; banks and building societies raising interest rates at will and without notice, and loss of interest on withdrawal of savings or enforcing mortgage redemption penalties (see also the chapter on *Buying and Selling your Home*, section 3.2).

It was due to action by the Office of Fair Trading that scheduled airlines had to alter unfair conditions that prevented passengers from seeking compensation if they had to miss a flight due to unavoidable circumstances. Airlines have also been told that non-refundable and non-transferable tickets are unenforceable. See *www.oft.gov.uk*.

The Consumers Association, the Financial Services Authority, local authority Trading Standards Officers, statutory industry regulators for gas, electricity, water, rail and telecommunications, and the Information Commissioner (formerly the Data Protection Registrar) are among those empowered to take action against those who use terms in their standard contracts which mislead or confuse customers.

Do note:
a) The regulations do not apply to individually negotiated terms.
b) If a term is found to be unfair, that term alone may be struck out and the rest of the contract may continue in force.
c) Not all contracts are covered by the regulations, which are intended to cover contracts between consumers and traders. Thus, for example, contracts of employment are specifically excluded, as are contracts entered into before the regulations came into force (i.e. July 1995).

Apart from the requirement for 'plain and intelligible' language (see above), the regulations do not otherwise affect the main terms of the contract, known as 'core terms' – for example, the price – provided these are clear and understandable.

While an individual consumer can complain to the OFT about unfair terms in a standard form contract, the OFT cannot take up an individual dispute; it will only negotiate with the company to change the terms for future contracts, and probably also obtain a general undertaking not to rely on the objectionable term in current contracts. This may or may not help the individual complainer who can still go to court to solve the dispute if need be.

There may be a term in a contract that arbitration is final and binding on the parties and such a term may be considered fair under the regulations, depending on all the surrounding facts, e.g. that an independent arbitrator is used. However, a legal challenge could still be mounted if it could be shown that the arbitrator reached a decision that no reasonable person in that position could have reached, or that bias was shown.

Do note: community legal funding [formerly legal aid] may not be made available – even if you are otherwise eligible for it – if, in the opinion of the Legal Services Commission, there are alternative ways of resolving your dispute, e.g. by using the services of an Ombudsman.

For the 'small print' regulations and insurance contracts, see section 7.2.3 below.

2.4.1 'Stop Now' orders

Under the 'Stop Now' regulations made under the Supply of Goods and Services Act, the Office of Fair Trading can apply for a court injunction against a trader who breaches or threatens to breach a number of laws so harming the collective interest of consumers. It can also seek written assurances from traders that they stop their harmful practices. Breach of the undertaking or of the assurances can lead to court action.

The regulations cover doorstep selling, timeshare, unfair contract terms, consumer credit, distance selling, package travel, misleading and comparative advertising, sale of goods rights, TV and broadcasting activities and the advertising of medicinal products for human use. Enforcement bodies in other European Union countries can also act.

'Stop Now' orders have been obtained against suppliers of shoddy kitchens or those who fail to deliver ordered goods. They were also used to change the advertising of credit deals so that they reveal the overall – and not just the introductory – cost of credit.

The 2002 Enterprise Act enlarges the areas in which 'Stop Now' orders can be obtained. These extensions are still to be specified by the Secretary of State at the time of writing, but the main extension is expected to apply to services. (See section 5 below.) Service providers who fail to act with reasonable care and skill will become liable to 'Stop Now' procedures. The legal mechanisms are expected to come into force by June 2003 and the brunt of enforcement action will be via local authority trading standards departments, so complain to them if you want action taken.

2.5 Discrimination

It is unlawful for a supplier of goods or services to discriminate against a prospective customer on the grounds of race, sex, marital status or disability, e.g. for a restaurant to refuse entry to a blind person because she is accompanied by a guide dog.

This applies across a whole range of areas – accommodation, access to public places, banking, insurance and loan/credit facilities, refreshment, entertainment, transport etc. The person who unlawfully discriminates can be sued in the ordinary courts for damages (including compensation for injured feelings). If the discrimination takes place in the sphere of employment, the remedy must be sought from an employment tribunal (see the chapter on *Working for a Living (Part 2)*, sections 2 and 3). For racial or sexual discrimination, action can also be taken by the Commission for Racial Equality or the Equal Opportunities Commission respectively.

2.5.1 Disability Discrimination Act

Since October 1999, service providers have had to make reasonable adjustments to enable disabled persons to access their services.

The Act affects anyone who provides goods, facilities or services to members of the public. It does not matter whether the service is one which is paid for or is free of charge, such as use of your local library facilities.

The Act is being implemented in three stages:

1) Since December 1996, disabled people cannot be treated less favourably than others for a reason related to their disability, e.g. a disabled driver should not be made to pay more for insuring his or her car simply because of the disability. It would be different if a health or safety factor was involved so that insurance was either refused or offered on different terms.
2) Since October 1999, service providers have had to make reasonable adjustments for disabled customers. This can entail taking reasonable steps to change practices, policies or procedures, or providing a reasonable alternative method of making your services available.

An ancillary aid, such as an induction loop to facilitate effective communication with customers with impaired hearing, would be an example of such a reasonable adjustment, and the cost of installing it cannot be passed on only to the disabled customer.

In considering the question of reasonable adjustments, factors such as the type of services, the size and resources of your business, the disruption and cost etc. are all taken into account.

3) The final stage of the goods, facilities and services part of the Act will come into force on 1 October 2004, to cover the providers of services where physical features prevent or hinder disabled people from having access to their services. The Code of Practice governing this is published by the Disability Rights Commission at *www.drc-gb.org/drc/InformationandLegislation/PAGE331a.asp.*

The Disability Rights Commission (DRC), which opened its doors to the public in April 2000, supervises the workings of the Act (see also the chapters on *The Legal System* and on *Working for a Living*). Its Chairman has stated that the DRC will not hesitate to sue any company that denied equal treatment to the disabled, e.g. a hotelier who refused a booking from someone with a disability because they feared that it might inconvenience other guests.

The DRC have set up an independent service for goods and service providers and disabled customers, the Disability Conciliation Service. This is run by Mediation UK (see DIRECTORY). Often service providers find this a more convenient way of admitting to mistakes and making amends. However, if mediation fails, the disabled client can still go to court.

Thus although the DRC tries to settle cases through mediation, as well as provide information and advice on how service providers can meet their obligations under the Act, it also is empowered to bring test cases to court and build up a body of case law.

3   SALE OF GOODS

The first principle is that whenever and wherever one buys goods, there is a contract with the seller. This is so whether one signs a long document or signs nothing. There is a contract even when the transaction is conducted without words – as when you choose goods off a shelf and pay for them at a supermarket till.

Under a contract of sale both buyer and seller have defined rights and obligations, which are set out in the Sale of Goods Act. The Act does not, however, apply to sales from a private seller (someone who is not a shop or business), or to sales of a house or flat. When buying from a private seller the buyer is on his own, although the seller still must not misrepresent the goods or features of the goods, e.g. by turning back the odometer on a car.

3.1   Obligations of seller

The seller's obligations are more complex than the buyer's, because the law implies (see section 2.1 above) certain terms in every contract of sale.

3.1.1   Satisfactory quality and fitness for purpose

Every seller is responsible for the quality of the goods which he or she sells. In the words of the law, goods must be of 'satisfactory quality'. The goods must also be fit for their normal purpose.

Of course, these two conditions can overlap: for example, a hair dryer with a faulty thermostat which overheats is not of satisfactory quality and is not fit for its purpose. Sometimes, however, these two conditions can be distinguished: if you ask a dealer for a microwave oven with a browning function and he sells you a basic model microwave without that feature, the microwave may be of satisfactory quality but is not fit for your purposes.

On the other hand, inadequate instructions can make a product unsatisfactory, as in the case of a lawn weedkiller with instructions which do not make it clear that it will scorch the grass if applied in hot weather.

Even if a purchase is in good working order, it will not be of satisfactory quality if it is bought new but its appearance is impaired, e.g. it is dented or scratched, *unless* it is sold as 'shopsoiled' or 'imperfect'.

The condition of 'satisfactory quality' is met if a reasonable person would regard the goods as satisfactory, taking into account appearance and finish, safety, price, durability and the absence of minor defects, as well as fitness for the usual purpose for which the goods are being bought.

Although a buyer of a secondhand car cannot complain that it is not of satisfactory quality just because it needs certain repairs as long as it is not actually unsafe, it is a criminal offence to sell a car in an unroadworthy condition.

☞ *You bought a car which had done only 5,000 miles from a dealer, and you had to replace a hub cap. You are now very upset to discover that the brakes are defective.*

With regard to the brakes, the dealer is in breach of his contractual duty to provide you with a car of 'satisfactory quality'. He has also committed a criminal offence. However, with regard to a replacement hub cap, it is not unreasonable for the purchaser to have to make some replacements in a secondhand car – even a 'nearly new' one. See also the chapter on *Motoring*.

A shop cannot get out of its legal obligations by putting an exemption clause in the contract. Equally, displaying notices such as 'No refunds or returns' will not exempt a shop if it sells goods of unsatisfactory quality.

☞ *You bought an electric toaster at a sale at a reduced price. Sale goods were advertised as being on a 'no returns' basis. The toaster simply does not work and you ask the shop to take it back.*

The fact that the goods were bought for a reduced price or during a sale is irrelevant. You are entitled to your money back, or a working replacement if you would prefer it. However, you could not complain if the goods were sold as 'seconds' so that their defects were drawn to your attention at the time of the sale.

If you tell the seller you are buying goods for a specific purpose, they must be fit for that purpose. Thus a computer shop is in breach of this obligation if it sells you software which is incompatible with your hardware when you had asked for advice, or which cannot produce spreadsheets if this is what you said you needed.

Do note: goods must be fit for their purpose provided that they are subjected to normal use.

☞ *You buy a kitchen knife, which has a laser-edge guaranteed for five years. You use it as a screwdriver and the point breaks off.*

It is doubtful whether using a kitchen knife as a screwdriver would be classed as normal use.

Goods are considered fit for their purpose if most consumers would be satisfied with the product. If you have a particular problem which you have not made clear at the time of purchase, you cannot claim that a product is not fit for its purpose when you find it unsatisfactory.

☞ *You suffer from an allergy to a particular chemical used in fabric conditioners. You use some conditioner in your washing machine and get dermatitis as a result.*

If you failed to establish the ingredients at the time when you bought the conditioner, and if most consumers would not suffer from the same problem, you probably would not be able to ask the shop to take the package back or to refund you.

3.1.2 Extended warranty

Producers of household appliances such as washing machines often offer an extended warranty or service contract for an additional fee. Typically, such a warranty can add 50% to the cost of an electrical item. Before paying extra for this, remember that you automatically have rights against the seller if the machine proves to have been defective at the time of sale. If a defect becomes apparent later, you are entitled to compensation for up to six years after the purchase but you must show that the defect existed when you bought the goods and it was reasonable for goods to last that long. Compare also the possible cost of repairing the appliance against the overall cost of the extended warranty before deciding that it is worth paying extra for the latter. At the time of writing, the Office of Fair Trading is investigating the cost of extended warranties as it appears that consumers are not adequately informed or protected.

3.1.3 Goods must meet description

There is another obligation on the seller: the goods must also be *as described*.

☞ *You buy a scarf from your local boutique after having been told by the sales assistant that it is cashmere. Afterwards, you see the same scarf on display in a big department store as 'angora and wool mix'.*

You are entitled to take the scarf back and ask for a refund. You would also be entitled to complain to the local trading officer of your local authority for breach of trading standards.

Goods are too often misdescribed; for example, a label on a packet may describe its contents as 'pure' fruit juice whereas they are actually water in which fruit pulp has been soaked.

Food manufacturers have been prosecuted under the Trade Descriptions Act for describing a product as 'tender chopped chicken breasts' and 'pure ground beef burgers' when they were composed of re-formed meat and soya.

New regulations came into force in 2002 to implement a further European Union directive on the sale of consumer goods. The seller is liable where lack of conformity with the contract description becomes apparent within two years of the buyer receiving the goods. The consumer will be entitled to free repair or replacement of the goods where practicable, or if it is not, to a price reduction.

3.1.4   Seller must give title to goods

There is an implied term that the seller has the right to sell the goods. If you buy golf clubs at a car-boot sale, which subsequently turn out to be stolen and which are reclaimed by their owner, you are entitled to a full refund of the price from the seller – if you can trace him! (See also *Stolen goods*, below, section 4.7.)

3.1.5   Seller must deliver in time

If you are not taking the goods with you at the time you buy, because they are to be delivered later, the seller is under a duty to deliver within a reasonable time. Otherwise he will be in breach of contract. If you want the goods by a particular date make sure you specify this at the time – preferably in writing. Unless agreed, the seller is not normally entitled to deliver by instalments – if you buy a dining-room suite he is in breach of contract if he delivers the table and then makes you wait several weeks for the chairs.

3.1.6   Seller must display the price

The Price Marking Order 1999 requires that retail prices must be visible to consumers so that they can see the price of products without having to ask. A unit price as well as a sales price must be shown for pre-packaged products where the quantity of the contents is not visible, for example on a carton of fruit juice. Consumers should then be in a position to compare prices of similar products which are packed in different-sized containers.

Do note: exemptions apply to small shops.

3.1.7   Guarantees

There is no obligation on the seller or manufacturer to offer guarantees, but if they are offered at no extra cost to the buyer, they are legally binding. The guarantee must be written in plain English with clear details on how to make a claim.

3.2   Obligations of the buyer

A buyer is obliged to pay the agreed price and to take the goods. So once you have agreed to buy, you cannot change your mind because you've spent more than you should have or seen something you like better in another shop. Even if you only paid a deposit and then try to get out of the contract, the seller may still be entitled to keep the deposit and possibly to claim the balance of the price as well.

If you are selling goods such as a car, it is risky to let the buyer take it away before paying you. You may have no remedy if he gives a false address and his cheque then bounces. Insist on receiving payment first, in cash, by bank draft, or a *printed* (not hand-written) building society cheque. A Buyer's Guide is available from the Office of Fair Trading Mailing House, PO Box 366, Hayes, Middlesex UB3 1XB. A public enquiry line is available: tel. 0345 224499, and online at *www.oft@eclogistics.co.uk*. See also the chapter on *Motoring*.

3.2.1   What if the price changes after the contract?

☞   *You order a three-piece suite from a furniture shop, to be covered in the fabric you choose from a catalogue in the shop. You are told the price is £2,500 and that delivery will take six to eight weeks. You pay the £2,500, but after a month the shop informs you that the factory has put its prices up and asks for an extra £400.*

Unless you were told at the time of contracting that the price could be varied, you can insist that the shop bears the excess, or you can cancel the contract and claim compensation e.g. for the extra inconvenience you will suffer in not having the suite if you have to place a new order elsewhere. A right to vary the price of a product may fall within the scope of 'unfair terms'. See section 2.4. above.

Do note: shops are entitled to charge more if you do not pay cash (e.g. by negotiating credit). However, shops must give clear notification of the fact by notices displayed at the entrance and at each till or checkout point. See below, section 7.3.1.

3.2.2   Paying in advance by credit card

If you have paid in advance but the goods are not received you would be protected if you paid by credit card – and could claim a refund from the credit card company. This only applies if the price was between £100 and £30,000; otherwise, if the seller goes bust after you have paid in advance, you may have only a claim in the liquidation. For example, a customer pays £600 by cheque for a pine bed; the shop then closes down. She cannot get a refund or the bed because the liquidator, who has to wind up the business, has to sell it to share the proceeds out among all the creditors, of which the unhappy customer is only one. It would not matter if the customer paid by cheque or in cash. However, paying by credit card protects you against such an event. If not paying by credit card, take the goods with you or have them delivered as soon as possible – the same day if you can.

3.3   Buyer's remedies

Quite often when you complain to a shopkeeper about faulty merchandise, he or she may tell you to write to the manufacturer. However, remember that your contract is with the shopkeeper. It is for the shop to enforce its own rights against its supplier or manufacturer.

3.3.1   Getting a refund

If the goods are totally unusable or unsatisfactory from the start, a customer is entitled to a full refund.

☞   *You bought a clockwork train set for your grandchild's birthday. When the present was opened, it was immediately apparent that one carriage only had three wheels, and that the engine could not be wound up because the key did not fit. When you complain to the shopkeeper she tells you to write to the manufacturer.*

Do not let the shopkeeper try and shelter behind the manufacturer. Your contract is with the shopkeeper, and not the manufacturer. You are entitled to pursue any claim against the shop itself. You are not obliged to accept a credit note for the broken toy nor are you obliged to accept a replacement or a repair, although this may be the most convenient course.

If you do take a replacement, in its turn the new model train set must satisfy all the requirements as to quality explained above.

3.3.2   Rejecting the goods

In certain circumstances, you may be said to have 'accepted' faulty goods, and you will then lose the right to a full refund. However, you will not be regarded as having accepted the goods until you have had a reasonable opportunity of examining them – what is reasonable will depend on the type of goods and other circumstances. If you keep the goods for a considerable length of time, you will be taken to have accepted them.

Prior to 1995, if you allowed the seller to repair faulty goods, you could not subsequently reject them. This has now changed, so if you are still not satisfied with the goods after repairs, you can now claim your money back in full.

If you do reject the goods and tell the seller so immediately (confirm this in writing), you are not bound to return them – it is the seller's responsibility to repossess. Often, though, customers are quite willing to return portable goods to the shops from which they were bought. In any event, do not use them while you are waiting for them to be collected or are intending to return them.

3.3.3   Manufacturer's guarantee

If there is a guarantee from the factory, it may give you additional rights against the manufacturer, but these will not necessarily be worth pursuing e.g. if you have to pay the costs of packaging the goods and returning them. Unless the goods are actually dangerous, you may have difficulty in legally enforcing the terms of a guarantee, if the manufacturer's response is unsatisfactory.

Remember: the existence of such a guarantee in no way reduces the scope of your rights against the shop with whom you actually dealt.

4   OTHER WAYS OF ACQUIRING GOODS

4.1   Mail order

You have the same rights as any buyer when you order goods by post, but it may be harder to enforce those rights. Keep a copy of all relevant data – the ad, the journal and the date on which it appeared, all correspondence, and the counterfoil of your cheque or postal order as proof of payment. It is always safer not to pay money in advance if possible.

The Mail Order Traders Association deals with complaints about goods sold through catalogues (tel. 01704 563 787). The National Newspaper Mail Order Protection Scheme deals with complaints when goods are bought by mail order through a newspaper advertisement: 16 Tooks Court, London EC4A 1LB, tel. 0171 269 0520.

If you wish to remove your name from direct mailing lists to cut down on junk mail, contact the Mailing Preference Service, Freepost 22, London W1E 7EZ.

4.2   Shopping on the Internet

More and more people are using the Internet to purchase goods online, and at the same time Internet fraud is increasing exponentially, with sellers sometimes sending shoddy or counterfeit goods or failing to deliver at all. Before dealing online, and certainly before giving your credit card details, follow the basic safety precautions outlined on the Office of Fair Trading's website (*www.oft.gov.uk*). In particular, make sure you have the name and geographical address of the seller and that he has an encryption facility which will scramble card details.

Online sellers are obliged by law to give an electronic acknowledgement of a consumer's order, so that both sides can check the details before the transaction is completed. It also gives the seller the time to make sure that the goods ordered are in stock at the price quoted on the website.

Airline tickets bought online are one of the most frequent Internet purchases.

☞   *You bought a ticket for a flight to Singapore, booked online from a site offering cheap flights. It looked a very good deal and you gave your card details as requested. You then discovered that you had been billed for a much larger amount than that originally displayed. When you remonstrated with the company, you were told that prices change from hour to hour, that the cheap deals 'had gone', and that you had to be charged accordingly.*

   If you book this way, it is a good idea to print off the page before the final 'confirm', as well as printing off the confirmation. That way you have proof if the confirmation details are not as you expected – there are, increasingly, reported instances of the final confirmation of prices differing substantially from the sum originally displayed.

If you have used a credit card to pay for items worth between £100 and £30,000, the credit card company is liable for any loss arising, e.g. non-delivery. However, note that this does NOT apply if you used a debit card! (For the difference between credit and debit cards, see below section 7.3.6.) And if you purchased from an overseas seller, even using a credit card, the company may contend it is not liable. However, the OFT takes the view that a customer is protected where the seller is abroad. Three credit-card companies, in September 2002, agreed with the OFT that they would honour valid claims and would not differentiate between claims that are based on where a purchase is made. Discussions are proceeding with other credit-card companies in the hope that they will fall into line.

From 31 October 2000, the Distance Selling Regulations gave new protection to those who buy online, by mail order, through digital TV or by telephone selling. These regulations require full information about such matters as the name and address of the seller where payment is made in advance of delivery, delivery charges etc. Failure to give such information makes the contract unenforceable against the buyer. The consumer also has a 7-day cooling-off period within which he can withdraw from the contract in writing without penalty. (These rights do not apply to online ticket sales for particular events, to bespoke goods supplied to the customer's specification, or to audio/video recordings or computer software that is unsealed by the consumer.) If the goods ordered do not arrive within 30 days the seller must refund any money paid.

Unsolicited goods and services are also covered by the regulations. A recipient who did not contract for goods or services is not obliged either to pay for them or to keep the goods safe for collection by the seller.

For buying at online auctions, see section 4.5.6 below.

4.3 Hire purchase and hire

It is important that you check precisely who the seller is. When you buy goods on HP or under a conditional sale agreement, the supplier of the goods is not, technically, the seller; the finance company is, and it is primarily against them that your rights will have to be enforced. You may also have rights against the dealer if you relied on assurances by his staff about the quality or fitness for purpose of the goods. In practice the finance company and the supplier may have arranged that the latter will deal with your complaints, but in law your rights are against the finance company.

In the case of major consumer items such as a car, the manufacturer may also agree to bear some of the responsibility although he may not necessarily be legally liable to do so. If the supplier has gone bust, the finance company can still be held liable under any guarantee which came with the goods (see also section 7.3.5 below on consumer protection).

When you hire goods (e.g. a digger to excavate a garden pond) or buy them on HP, you have similar rights in respect of the goods hired as a buyer has, as far as quality is concerned. The goods must be as described and fit for their purpose (see section 3.1 above). If you hire a TV set you do not lose your right to reject the set and end the contract, even if you let the hire company have a go at repairing it.

4.4 Part exchange

You have the same rights as any buyer paying in full in money when the deal includes a trade-in, e.g. when your old cooker or car is taken in part exchange.

4.5 Auction sales

Land and many types of goods are bought at auctions, and on the whole the law is the same for all, from the valuable fine art auction houses to sales of livestock in the country.

4.5.1 Making the contract

Once the bid has been accepted by the auctioneer and his hammer falls, a contract is formed. The seller of the 'lot' is legally obliged to give it to the successful bidder, who is legally obliged to pay the price to the auctioneer. Even in the case of land no formal written contract is necessary but there must be a written memorandum of the sale after the auction (and the auctioneer can sign this on behalf of both parties!).

Note: you will usually be charged a 'buyer's premium', which is an additional sum of 5–10% of the bid price. VAT is not charged on items sold at auction by private buyers.

4.5.2 Misdescriptions

A potential buyer should always take the opportunity to inspect the property or the 'lot' in which he is interested, before the auction takes place. In the case of buildings, have a survey carried out and make mortgage arrangements *before* the auction. You are nevertheless entitled to expect an accurate description of property or goods in the auctioneer's catalogue. The conditions of sale usually exclude liability for terms imposed by law in other sales, e.g. that the goods are of 'merchantable quality' or fit for their purpose, but they can only do so if this is reasonable (see the 'small print regulations' section 2.4 above). If there is a misdescription of the goods, however, even if it is an oral statement made by the auctioneer during the sale, the buyer should act promptly to reject the goods and claim back the price. See section 3.3.2 above.

The buyer may claim damages from the auctioneer for a misdescription by him, even if the owner of the goods was not at fault.

4.5.3 Reserve price

The conditions of sale should also make it clear whether the seller has fixed a minimum price, and whether the seller can bid against potential purchasers as a way of encouraging higher offers.

☞ *You make a bid for a Persian carpet at a local auction house. You understand that there is no reserve price. However, your bid is not accepted and the carpet is withdrawn from sale.*

If there was no reserve price, the auctioneer will be in breach of contract to the highest bidder if he withdraws the lot from sale: the highest bid cannot be rejected simply because it was not high enough.

4.5.4 The buyer and the auctioneer

The auctioneer is the agent of the seller, and receives a commission on the sale. The price must be paid to the auctioneer (who can sue for it), but apart from this the contract is made between the seller of the goods and the successful bidder, and it is between them that any disputes about the property should be settled in the civil courts. But the auctioneer can be liable for selling goods which the seller had no right to dispose of, so if you bid for an antique table which turns out to have been stolen and it is subsequently reclaimed by its true owner, you can get damages from the auctioneer.

4.5.5 Valuations

If an auctioneer is asked to value an item, he must exercise skill and care in doing so. The amount of skill expected will vary according to the circumstances, so that more expertise would be expected from one of the large London auction houses than from a small provincial auctioneer, although the latter might be expected to discharge his duty of care by obtaining expert advice in a field in which he is inexperienced.

4.5.6 Buying at auction online

If you buy at auction online, you do not have the opportunity to inspect the goods on offer although the seller may supply a photograph to accompany his description.

As we can see above, auctioneers do not have to accept responsibility for the quality of the goods which they sell at auction – in other words unlike other sellers, they can exclude certain terms implied by law, provided that it is reasonable to do so. Therefore, auctioneers would still be liable if the standard terms of their contract are unfair under the tests stipulated in section 2.4 above.

Buyers beware: even these tests are excluded if the person who sells online at an auction is a private seller. It would appear that many online auctions offer goods for sale by private individuals so you would have little or no protection in such a case.

4.5.7 Criminal offences

Criminal legislation outlaws dealers' bidding rings (where dealers agree not to bid against each other, thus keeping bids low) but this is very difficult to prove. It is also an offence for anyone to conduct a mock auction.

4.6 Private sellers

Unlike commercial traders, a private seller can exclude liability for defects in quality, but is still required to ensure that goods satisfy their description. If your neighbour sells you a 'leather suitcase' you can complain if it isn't leather, but not if the lock is defective.

Note: that traders who pretend to be private sellers are committing a criminal offence.

4.7 Stolen goods

A particular danger with private sellers is that the goods may not be theirs to sell. If the car you bought privately turns out to be stolen and is reclaimed by the true owner, you can claim the full price from the seller, if you can find him.

4.7.1　Cars under HP agreements

In the case of cars – not other goods – which are wrongly sold by someone who had possession under an HP agreement, an innocent purchaser will not have to hand the car back to the HP seller, if unaware of this fact. See the chapter on *Motoring*.

4.7.2　Stolen goods in open market

In 1993 two valuable paintings were stolen from Lincoln's Inn. A purchaser bought them for £145 at Bermondsey Market; he took them to Sotheby's who valued them at £65,000. The purchaser acquired ownership of the paintings because of an old rule, which provided that if goods were bought in good faith at a public, legally constituted market, the purchaser acquired good title and the original owner could not claim back the goods. The rule was much criticised as protecting the disposal of stolen goods, and has now been abolished. This means that wherever the goods are bought, the original owner will be able to reclaim them from the purchaser.

5　SERVICES

In the ordinary course of life you enter into many contracts for services throughout the day – when you leave your suit at the dry-cleaners, take a cab, visit the hairdresser, hire an electrician or a music teacher, or leave your car at the garage to be serviced. In all such cases you are entering into a contract governed by the Supply of Goods and Services Act, even if the transaction is entirely oral and nothing is signed.

Where you have a complaint about services and cannot get satisfaction from the supplier, you can, in some cases, apply to an ombudsman (see below, section 7.1.7 regarding banks, and section 7.2.11 regarding insurance companies and see also DIRECTORY at the end of this chapter), set up either by the industry itself or by law – NHS complaints, for example, go to the Health Service Ombudsman. For the formerly nationalised industries of gas, water, electricity and telecommunications, there are Regulators who fulfil a similar function. See also the Community Legal Services leaflet No. 13 *Problems with Goods and Services*, available from LSC leaflet line on 0845 3000 343.

The Lord Chancellor's Department has issued a booklet, *Resolving Disputes*, which contains details of all the schemes, with their advantages and disadvantages.

For enhanced powers to issue 'Stop Now' orders where service providers fail to meet standards of reasonable care and skill, see section 2.4.1 above.

5.1　Obligations of supplier

The supplier of services is obliged to perform precisely the obligations he has undertaken. A builder who has agreed to paint your house white is in breach of contract if he paints it cream.

In one case a homeowner instructed a builder to construct a 7′6″-deep swimming pool in his garden. The builder constructed a 6′-deep pool, which was safe for diving. The homeowner was awarded £2,000 compensation – even though the shortfall did not decrease the value of the pool – because he had not received what he had wanted and had paid for.

Under the Act, certain terms are implied into a contract for services, in the same way that, as we have seen, certain terms are implied into a contract of sale for goods. See sections 2.1 and 3 above.

5.1.1　Reasonable competence

Where a contract has been entered into, the provider of the services is under a duty to carry out the services with reasonable care and skill. His or her lack of formal qualifications or experience is no excuse. However, a specialist must show a higher standard than a non-specialist.

☞　*You call in your builder/oddjob man to give you a hand with painting the kitchen walls. A kitchen tap springs a leak and he offers to repair it with disastrous results. Your kitchen is flooded.*

　　In similar circumstances, you could certainly have sued a firm of plumbers called in to repair the leak. However your rights against a decorator, who did not hold himself out as a specialist, are probably minimal.

☞ *You visit the hairdresser and ask her to apply a colouring tint to your hair. The hairdresser carelessly allows it to drip so that it stains your clothes.*

You can claim for cleaning, or if this is not possible, replacement (second-hand value) of the clothing.

Note: the legal requirements of reasonable care and skill only apply when the provider of the services is acting under a contract.

If your aunt offers out of affection for you to make up curtains from new fabric which you have purchased, you cannot sue her if the curtains are a failure. If you agreed to pay her for her services, however, you could claim compensation (if you are hard-hearted!) even though she is not in business as a curtain-maker.

If a hairdresser does the job so badly that your hair or skin are damaged, compensation must be paid. There are cases where customers have ended up with severe injuries. In one case, when a woman had a perm the solution soaked into the cottonwool in her ears and round her face, causing burns to the ear, scalp and eye. But you would have no claim just because you do not like the style or colour as long as it was competently done.

5.1.2   Reasonable charges

If a price for the services is not agreed at the time of entering into the contract, the customer is under a duty to pay no more than a reasonable charge. It is always sensible to ask for a fixed price in advance, especially for emergency or out-of-hours services. If you are asked to pay an exorbitant price you can make payment under protest and then reclaim the excess. What is a reasonable charge depends on the circumstances. Where the payment was by credit card, you could ask the credit card company to suspend the payment.

If the work is so inadequately done that you derive no benefit from it, you can refuse to pay at all.

Sometimes you will be asked to pay part of the charge in advance – as a decorator, for example, may need to lay out money buying lining paper and paint before he can start the job. Only pay enough to cover the cost of the materials. If you pay in full in advance you have no bargaining counter left if things do not go according to plan.

You may be asked to sign a form by e.g. a washing-machine repairman, stating that the work has been carried out to your complete satisfaction. If you cannot check the work there and then, cross this sentence out and write 'unexamined' when you sign, otherwise you may be signing away your right to complain about the job later when inadequacies emerge.

5.1.3   Reasonable time for providing services

The provider of services is also under a duty to carry out the services within a reasonable time. A simple or routine job will naturally take less time than a specialised or complicated one; but it is wise to agree the date by which you expect the job to be done.

☞ *After a heavy storm, you ask a roofing firm to replace some loose tiles on your roof. After stripping off the loose tiles they cover the hole in the roof with polythene sheeting and then, despite repeated telephone calls, do not reappear to complete the job for ten days. During this time there are heavy rainfalls and rain gets in under the polythene. The walls below are stained and furniture and carpets damaged.*

You are entitled to compensation for the damage. You should call in another firm to complete the repairs so as to prevent further damage.

You will also be entitled to compensation if the provider of the service fails to turn up at all; for example if a wedding photographer failed to attend the wedding.

5.2   Excluding liability

You may be asked to sign a form which contains a clause limiting or excluding a firm's liability, or there may be a notice on their premises to the same effect, e.g. 'Cars Parked at Owners' Risk' in a parking garage; or in a drycleaners', 'No liability is accepted for belts, buckles or trimmings'. Such clauses are valid if they are fair and reasonable in the circumstances.

☞ *You take an entire film of photographs at your daughter's graduation. The photographic shop accepts the film on the basis that their liability is limited to the cost of a replacement film. They lose the film.*

You are entitled to say the exclusion clause is unreasonable and therefore ineffective. If however they had made it clear when accepting the film that when a higher charge is paid they accept full responsibility, the exemption on the normal charge contract would be reasonable as you would then have had a choice.

If the firm or its employees are grossly negligent it is unlikely an exemption clause will enable them to avoid liability.

☞ *You take a two-piece suit to the cleaners for the removal of a stain. The manager points out that they cannot guarantee that the stain will be completely removed, which you accept. There is also a notice in the shop stating 'While all care will be taken we cannot be held liable for loss or damage'. When you return to collect the suit you find that they have lost the jacket.*

The shop probably has a responsibility to pay for a replacement suit, despite the oral disclaimer and the notice.

Any notice or term in a contract which exempts or limits liability for death or personal injury resulting from negligence is totally ineffective in law.

☞ *You take your young son to a local fairground and give him a ride on a helterskelter. Due to its negligent maintenance or operation you are both flung out of the seats and are injured.*

Despite any exempting notices you can both sue for full compensation (see the *Accidents* chapter).

A fitness centre included a term in its standard contract with members saying: 'All members and guests use the facilities and equipment provided by the club at their own risk and the club does not accept responsibility for any harm or injury to a member or guest however caused.' The terms also provided that items left in lockers overnight would be removed and disposed of. Both terms would now be disallowed as unfair – see section 2.4.

5.2.1 Consumer protection

Note: many suppliers of services belong to trade associations which issue codes of practice. These lay down certain standards to which their members are expected to adhere. On the one hand, the extent to which an individual member abides by these standards is a voluntary matter and a dissatisfied customer would certainly not be able to enforce them by law. On the other hand, customers do have some recourse to a trade association where a member has provided a below-standard service. Certain trade associations also provide arbitration and complaint procedures.

It is a criminal offence to make in the course of trade or business, false statements about the nature or provision of services, such as if an unqualified masseur claims to be a fully trained physiotherapist. Inform the local trading standards officer, who may prosecute.

Under the Enterprise Act 2002, from mid-2003 the Office of Fair Trading will have the power to monitor trade association codes of practice and their workings, although the only enforcement sanction is withdrawal of the OFT's approval where the codes are not working properly.

5.3 Supply of goods plus services

In many situations, a contract requires the provider of services to supply goods as well as do work, for example a central heating engineer may also supply the boiler which he is to install.

In these situations the law implies certain requirements into the contract (unless expressly excluded by agreement between the client and supplier). The main requirement is that the materials or goods supplied will be fit for their purpose and of satisfactory quality. In the case of building services to a house, a builder may be responsible even to subsequent owners for faulty workmanship or materials.

If the goods supplied are unsuitable or defective, you should act as soon as possible to make it clear that you are rejecting them and that you expect them to be replaced or repaired as appropriate.

In providing goods or material it is no defence for the provider of services to say that reasonable care and skill were used in selecting the goods (unless there is a reasonable exemption clause in the contract).

Of course, the goods may be of adequate quality and the reason for the failure lies elsewhere. For example, if a vet treats your dog's fractured leg using the wrong-sized compression plate, it is the vet who is at fault, and not the plate, if the fracture does not knit.

5.4 Sub-contractors

Sometimes your arrangement for services does not necessarily contemplate the supplier doing all the work himself. For example, a small jobbing builder doing a house conversion will subcontract out part of the work to plasterers, electricians, etc. Similarly most opticians do not make spectacle lenses personally but order them to be made by specialist firms. If the work is badly done or not in accordance with what you specified, the builder or optician cannot shelter behind the subcontractor with whom you never dealt. As far as you are concerned you dealt only with the builder or optician. Whether he does the work himself or through someone else is beside the point. He is liable to you whether or not he can claim reimbursement from the subcontractor.

5.5 Customer's duty to pay

The customer must pay the fee he agreed to pay, within a reasonable time. If no fee was agreed, he is obliged to pay a reasonable charge (see section 5.1.2 above). Providers of services, such as hoteliers or repairers, are usually entitled to keep any of your property in their possession until their charges are met. Even solicitors and accountants will have a right to keep your papers and can refuse to return them until paid.

If you pay in advance it is safest to do so by credit card. Then if the services are not provided (because, for example, the firm goes bust) you can still recover the money from the credit card company (provided the payment is between £100 and £30,000). This does not apply to other kinds of card such as debit cards (see also section 7.3.6 below).

If you do not return within a reasonable time the firm may need to dispose of the goods to recoup their losses. Frequently there will be a notice to this effect on the premises, e.g. in shoe repairers' or electrical goods shops. If there is no such notice, the goods can only be sold if the contractor takes reasonable steps to trace the tardy customer to tell him of the impending sale in writing, giving enough time for the customer to turn up, pay the fee and collect his property. As to payment by credit card, see section 3.2.2 above.

The courts have held that a clause in the contract that you must pay the full price in spite of any set-off, is invalid because it is unreasonable. So if you feel you have a claim that the services are not satisfactory, you could deduct the shortfall from the due price.

If you are disputing the amount you need to pay, and decide to send a cheque with an accompanying letter stating that it is being sent 'in full and final settlement', the fact that the dealer or trader then cashes the cheque does not necessarily mean he is accepting it on those terms, particularly if he rejects the terms within a few days.

5.6 Professional services

You only have a legitimate complaint about providers of professional services on the basis of the quality of their services, not on the basis of the results. Doctors do not guarantee a cure, nor do solicitors guarantee a successful outcome to litigation. As long as they have acted with the degree of care and skill reasonably to be expected from their profession, you cannot complain.

Where the profession itself embraces more than one tenable view of acceptable practice, competence is not measured by a single standard. Where there is more than one acceptable standard, the law judges competence by the lowest acceptable standard. On the other hand, there are cases of professional negligence where you have a good claim for compensation.

☞ *You buy a property to which access can only be obtained via a narrow lane. The solicitor acting for you in the purchase fails to discover that the lane actually forms part of the property of a neighbouring landowner, who begins to build on it, effectively blocking access.*

The solicitor is responsible for your damages.

An architect who designed a house extension failed to warn the client that the extension would block the neighbours' right to light. When the extension was built the client had to pay compensation to the neighbours but could sue his architect for reimbursement as the litigation was foreseeable. See also the chapters on *Neighbours* and *Accidents*.

Solicitors, doctors, accountants and other professionals will be insured against liability. Make a complaint as soon as possible after the event. If you get no satisfactory response you can complain to the appropriate supervising professional body (see DIRECTORY, and also see *Accidents* chapter, section 9).

☞ *Thomas employed a surveyor to investigate whether a house he proposed purchasing was affected by aircraft noise, because he did not want to live under a flight path. The surveyor reported that such noise was unlikely, and Thomas went ahead with the purchase. When he moved in he discovered that aircraft frequently flew over the house. He sued the surveyor for negligence.*

The court awarded him £10,000 damages to compensate for the discomfort and inconvenience of living with the aircraft noise.

In the case of surveyors, case law has established that they can in some circumstances be held liable to pay compensation not only to their own clients but also to some third parties.

☞ *You buy a house without instructing your own surveyor, but relying on a valuation report carried out by the surveyors instructed by the building society giving the mortgage (for which you have been charged by the building society). You subsequently discover that the surveyor negligently failed to notice that when the chimney breasts had been removed the chimneys remained inadequately supported, with consequent damage to the roof.*

You may be able to recover damages from the surveyor in negligence although you had no contract with him (see also chapter on *Buying and Selling your Home*, section 2.2.1(a)).

Note that the provider of services is only liable if he does negligently what he is instructed to do. A solicitor instructed to assist with the renewal of a lease is under no duty to advise on matters outside the scope of the instructions – he cannot be made a general insurer of the client's legal problems.

☞ *Peter asks his private dentist to treat a tooth. On looking into Peter's mouth the dentist notices that an adjacent tooth is also in need of treatment.*

The dentist would be under an obligation to inform Peter of this, but is not required to do extra work outside the instructions, for which Peter has not agreed to pay.

5.7 Estate agents

The vast majority of people selling or renting property use an estate agent, although you can do so privately or through a property shop. If you do decide to use an estate agent, you will be entering into a contract for his or her services. As with any other contract for services, the estate agent must show reasonable care and skill in carrying out the duties contracted for.

☞ *Mr. Smith, who owns a house, asks estate agents to find him a company tenant for the house while he is working abroad. They put in as tenant Mr. Jones, who claims to be a senior employee of a cricket club, but who is in fact only a part-time barman at the club.*

If the estate agents had checked with the club they would have discovered the true position, but they failed to make such checks. When Mr Jones falls into arrears with the rent, Mr Smith can sue the estate agent for compensation.

5.7.1 Regulation by law

Although they deal with the largest and most important transaction in people's lives – the purchase and sale of property – estate agents are not required to have undergone any professional training, nor do they require a licence. Many do in fact have a surveyor's or auctioneer's qualification.

However, estate agents are subject to increasing regulation by law. The Director General of Fair Trading can act to prohibit an individual from continuing to act as an estate agent if the legal requirements are not observed. In particular, these require estate agents:

a) to keep any of the customer's money which they receive in a separate deposit account, and to keep it insured

b) to inform a potential customer (seller) of their itemised charges before any commitment is entered into; and

c) to disclose to both potential buyers and sellers whether they have any financial interest in the property.

An individual can also be declared unfit to be an estate agent if he fails to inform the seller in writing about all offers from potential purchasers (e.g. because they did not agree to accept mortgage or insurance services from him), or if he misrepresents offers received.

An estate agency sent a letter to Peter, claiming that it had several people on its books specifically looking for a property in Peter's street. When challenged by the Office of Fair Trading following a complaint to it by Peter, the estate agency could not produce details of such prospective buyers, and was obliged by the OFT to give undertakings not to send out further misleading mailshots (see also the chapter on *Buying and Selling your Home*, section 2.1.5).

Note: the Estate Agents Act does not apply to an estate agent who is acting as a letting agent.

5.7.2   Regulation by Association

The National Association of Estate Agents is open to persons practising as estate agents. It lays down rules of conduct and has a guarantee bonding scheme to protect clients' deposits. It also offers correspondence courses which lead to certificates at senior and junior levels (see DIRECTORY).

The Estate Agents Act 1979 empowers the government to make regulations prescribing minimum standards of competence for estate agents. No such regulations have yet been issued.

Where possible, choose an estate agent who has signed up to the Ombudsman for Estate Agents' Code of Practice, which will at least provide access to an ombudsman if problems arise. (See DIRECTORY.) If as a buyer or seller you believe the estate agent has not met its obligations, you can also complain to the trading standards department of your local authority.

In 2001 the Ombudsman received over five and a half thousand complaints from consumers, an increase of 25% on the previous year. In addition, about five thousand complaints were made to trading standards offices, mostly related to selling techniques.

The Office of Fair Trading can issue warnings and banning orders if the law has been breached, and can question whether an estate agent should continue to hold a consumer credit licence. Misrepresentation, holding back offers, and discrimination against those who do not use the estate agent's financial services, e.g for insurance or mortgages, are all undesirable practices in law, which can be the basis for the Director General of Fair Trading to ban the estate agent from practising as such.

5.7.3   Commission

5.7.3(a)   Effective cause

If property is put up for sale through an estate agency, the agents are entitled to commission (usually 1–2% of the price) from the seller if they are the effective cause of the property being sold.

☞   *Mr Brown, a prospective purchaser, is introduced to Mr Green, the seller, by an estate agent, ABC, but Mr Green rejects his offer as insufficient. Mr Brown then receives details of the same property from another estate agent, DEF, and due to the efforts of DEF his subsequent offer is accepted by Mr Green.*

Depending on Mr Green's agreement with ABC, it would seem that only DEF is entitled to commission from Mr Green, as DEF was really the effective cause of the sale.

The estate agent must act with due care and skill, which includes telling the seller if another purchaser materialises who offers a higher price. If he or she fails to do so, no commission is payable.

The terms on which the estate agent will be appointed must be communicated to potential sellers in writing before they commit themselves to a particular firm. Scrutinise the terms carefully, and make sure that you do NOT agree to pay the estate agent commission:

a) if the property is sold through the efforts of another agent

b) if the property is sold entirely through your own independent initiative

c) if the sale falls through for whatever reason.

Avoid agreeing to pay commission merely on the 'introduction' of 'a ready, willing and able purchaser'. You should ensure that you only agree to pay commission if the estate agent introduces a purchaser who completes the deal – and not one who merely exchanges contracts.

It is advisable to check also whether the agent's expenses, e.g. for advertising the property, are included in the commission, or whether they are payable in addition. Note that VAT will be payable on the commission. If the agent gets a discount from a newspaper for advertising he must pass this on to you. Estate agents must also tell you what services they will offer to potential purchasers of the property, and whether they themselves have any financial interest in it.

5.7.3(b) Sole agency

If you have given a 'sole agency', put a time limit on it so that if the property is not sold within, say, six or eight weeks, you can go to another firm. Before the time limit expires do not deal with another estate agent, or you could end up being liable to pay commission to both.

☞ *Ellen enters into a sole selling agreement for the sale of her bungalow with estate agents JKL. Without any involvement on their part she then sells the bungalow to her cousin Jack. Does she need to pay commission to the agency?*

Ellen may not have to pay JKL commission on the price received from Jack, as he was not introduced by them. But conversely, JKL may be able to claim damages from Ellen for breach of contract because she negotiated privately during the period of the sole agency.

The estate agent is obliged to explain (in terms laid down by Parliament) precisely what is meant by the phrases 'sole selling rights', 'sole agency', and 'ready, willing and able purchaser'.

5.7.4 Sign boards

You are entitled, as part of the contract with the estate agents, to stipulate that no 'For Sale' or 'Sold' boards should be erected on the property, although you might only get nominal damages if the agent puts up a board. If more than one board is put up, however, an estate agent may be committing a criminal offence.

5.7.5 Misdescriptions

The estate agent is the agent of the seller, and it is the seller who will suffer if the estate agent has misdescribed the property.

Ask to see a draft of any advertisements before he publishes them or circulates details about your property. If you subsequently become aware of errors in those details, you must tell your conveyancer and ask him to inform the purchaser before the transaction is completed. The 1991 Property Misdescriptions Act extends criminal liability for misdescriptions to builders and property developers as well as to estate agents. It applies to both commercial and residential property. A misdescription can be made orally or by pictures. The misdescription need not be dishonestly given. A private seller incurs no criminal liability under the Act for misdescriptions, although like all sellers he can of course be held liable for misdescription in the civil courts.

☞ *A firm of auctioneers and estate agents described a property in the auction particulars as 'a wine bar by day, cocktail lounge by night', with accompanying photograph. Graham successfully bids for the property, which he is buying as an investment, but then discovers that the local justices have revoked the liquor licence for the wine bar and the cocktail lounge.*

Graham can withdraw from the contract with the seller and claim damages from him and/or from the auctioneer, as the particulars given had wrongly induced him to believe the wine bar was a going concern bringing in a regular rent. The seller may be able to claim a contribution from the estate agents if they were in breach of their contract with him; and they will also be criminally liable under the Property Misdescriptions Act.

However, the estate agents are not obliged to check everything they are told by the seller, unless they suspect it may be inaccurate.

☞ *Harriet instructs ABC Estate Agents to sell a property. She tells them, and believes, that there is planning permission to develop part of the garden, but is mistaken in this belief. When the buyer discovers the error he pulls out of the sale, and asks the local authority to prosecute ABC under the Act.*

ABC will not be held criminally liable – they do not have to check up on every item of information given to them by their client.

However, if they (or the vendor) reply to specific questions such as whether there are rights or easements affecting the property, by saying 'not as far as we are aware', this implies that they have checked the records. If you genuinely do not know or have not checked, it is safer to say just that!

An estate agent and the seller may not be liable for misdescription if the sales particulars have specifically disclaimed any such responsibility.

5.7.6   Buying or renting through an estate agent

It is a criminal offence for an estate agent to apply a false description to goods or services he offers.

An estate agent is the agent of the seller, not of the buyer (he is paid by the seller). Agents usually try to disclaim liability for misdescriptions, so if you are a purchaser you should take steps to check all the particulars yourself; ideally, get your own survey done.

Gazumping is a common complaint made by the buyers of properties. It is, however, not illegal. In fact, the estate agent has a duty (to the seller) to pass on to the seller all offers being made for the property by other potential purchasers. In law, the seller is free to accept a higher offer at any time until contracts have been exchanged, however distressing this is for the first-offering buyer.

If you pay a deposit to the estate agent, to show that your offer to buy is serious, the estate agent is under a legal duty to keep it in a separate 'client account'. You will not normally get interest on it even if the transaction is prolonged, so keep the sum as small as possible. You can try and specify when making the payment that it is paid on condition that you will be entitled to interest.

Payment of such a deposit does not mean the sale is legally binding; until the contract is signed on both sides the seller can still accept a higher offer or withdraw the property from sale, and equally the buyer can change his mind and back out. You can enter into a 'lock-out' agreement with the seller, however. This means that the seller agrees not to enter into any other negotiations for a limited period. Because the estate agent is acting in the seller's interests, he must tell him of higher offers made by other potential purchasers. It is only when property is bought at auction that the sale is binding without a written contract, simply on the fall of the auctioneer's hammer.

If the seller has authorised the estate agent to receive the deposit on his behalf, the seller will be obliged to refund the deposit to the buyer if the estate agent becomes insolvent or misappropriates the money.

It is unlawful for a letting agency to charge potential tenants for providing them with lists of accommodation available for renting, but when the tenant enters into an agreement to rent particular premises, a fee can be charged. See also section 2.4 on unfair terms, above.

6   DANGEROUS PRODUCTS

When we shop, we anticipate with pleasure using the goods which we purchase. We seldom think that the goods we are buying may cause us grief! But misfortunes do occur, even with the best-run of shops and the most careful of customers. This is not necessarily because of a defect in the product, it may be due to faulty design.

If damage or injury does result, it is not only the person who contracted to acquire it who may suffer. Anyone who is hurt or whose property is damaged may be able to claim compensation from the manufacturer or supplier. Liability does not depend on the existence of a contractual relationship.

We could get sick or hurt when we buy something because:

a) it is inherently dangerous (e.g. contaminated food, or fireworks)

b) it is wrongly used (e.g. a drug which is safe in a limited dosage but dangerous if an overdose is taken)

c) it is badly marketed (e.g. it is misleadingly labelled, is supplied with inadequate instructions, or is in an unsafe container).

From these examples, we can see that sometimes blame for the accident can be laid at the door of the shop or manufacturer. Of course, sometimes our own lack of care can be blamed – for example, if we hurt ourselves on a new pair of scissors.

6.1   Having to prove negligence

Where a manufacturer or retailer could have foreseen that there was a chance that a consumer might get hurt, then those responsible for the article, its condition, or its supply will be classified as negligent. If this can be proved, they will be liable to compensate the victims of the accident under common law.

The product must have been used for its intended purpose and not for some other purpose – for example, using inside a kitchen a drain cleaner product which is only meant to be used out of doors would disqualify the user from compensation.

A manufacturer of an article will also be liable for faulty components, even if these were manufactured by someone else, or for faulty packaging if it is this which caused the damage (e.g. an ill-fitting stopper on a container of dangerous chemicals).

Where the product is safe if used correctly, a manufacturer or supplier is responsible for providing adequate instructions or appropriate warnings.

☞ *You purchase hair dye and apply it to your hair in accordance with the printed instructions. You suffer a bout of dermatitis.*

> The manufacturers of the hair dye are liable in negligence for failing to include a warning that before use the product should first be tested on a small area of skin.

However, a victim of such an accident has to overcome the real difficulty of proving that it was the hair dye which was the cause of the dermatitis.

6.2   Difficulties in proving negligence

What has to be proved is that danger should have been known and guarded against. In some cases, it is perfectly obvious that there must have been a faulty manufacturing process, as when the blade of a Stanley knife was found embedded in a chocolate-covered 'nut crunch', which cut the mouth of the unsuspecting consumer! In other cases fault may be much harder to prove. Difficulties in proving negligence have led to changes in the law in the interests of consumer safety, imposing liability without proof of fault – see section 6.3 below.

6.2.1   Who can be found liable?

It is not only manufacturers who can be held liable for negligence. Decided cases have fixed liability on negligent assemblers, distributors, installers, repairers and builders. Accordingly, a garage mechanic is liable to those injured if an accident results from his negligent repair of a car's brakes, and those who install a lift negligently are responsible for a resulting accident to a passenger in the lift. In all such cases liability is based on fault and this will have to be proved, although in some cases it is obvious. It is no defence for the manufacturer to prove that the product was as safe as those of its competitors, because the common practice of the industry may itself be unsafe or negligent.

The courts have said that a manufacturer who discovers a danger in a product is negligent if he fails to recall the product from buyers, by appropriate action. We have all seen advertisements in the newspapers where manufacturers call for the return of certain products – even cars.

6.2.2   No liability for misuse

As we have seen, a manufacturer or supplier is not liable, of course, if an accident resulted from the product being wrongly used. If a doctor negligently prescribes an excessive dose of an otherwise safe drug, the manufacturers of the drug are not at fault. Similarly, while a hammer has the inherent potential to crush a thumb, it is not defective merely because it has done so. Misuse will reduce or even prevent damages for compensation.

In order to claim for negligence, then, fault must be established. A retailer or other seller is not negligent just because he or she sold the product.

Do take heed: research on the patterns of home accidents showed that by far the majority of them happen because of our behaviour rather than because of faulty products.

6.2.3 Position of the seller

Against the seller, the remedies lie in the law of contract. A customer can sue the seller for breach of the obligation implied by law that goods shall be:

a) of satisfactory quality
b) reasonably fit for their purpose, and
c) in compliance with their description (see section 3 above).

It is not necessary that there should have been a written contract – a verbal sale over the counter will also be treated as containing these terms. The seller's liability under these implied obligations does not depend on his being at fault, and he cannot escape these obligations by putting up notices that no responsibility is accepted for the goods' condition, safety, etc. But because this liability arises out of contract, it can be relied on by the buyer, and no one else.

☞ *You buy an electric lawnmower from Bloggs Ltd. Your son-in-law borrows the mower and receives an electric shock due to an electrical fault while it is being used, causing burns.*

He has no claim against Bloggs Ltd in contract, as he was not the purchaser of the article.

Bloggs Ltd may however, be liable in negligence, if they should have known the mower was defective; or under safety legislation (see section 6.3 immediately below).

6.3 Consumer protection legislation

Since March 1988, the limitations of both proof of negligence or proof of a contract have been made largely irrelevant by an Act of Parliament embodying a consumer protection Directive from the European Community. In 1994, further duties were imposed on producers of consumer goods by the General Product Safety Regulations, and in 1999 came a further European Directive on certain aspects of the sale of consumer goods and associated guarantees.

6.3.1 Who is liable under the legislation?

Strict liability without proof of fault now rests on:

• the manufacturer of a product (including the manufacturer of a component part)
• firms which market goods under their own label (whether or not they are the manufacturer); and
• the firm or person who first imported the goods into the European Union.

Under the directive, the National Blood Authority has been held liable to patients who received blood infected with hepatitis C, even though at the time of the blood transfusions no test to screen blood for the virus existed.

However, women who were taking the 'third generation' of contraceptive pills sued the manufacturers, but failed in their lawsuit because the scientific evidence did not prove that the pills materially increased the risk of cardiovascular disease (it is significant that it was already assumed that any contraceptive pill can cause such a condition).

6.3.2 When is a product unsafe?

Consumers are given the right to claim compensation for injury or loss caused by defective products. It applies to products which must be found to be defective in the sense that their safety is not such as persons generally are entitled to expect.

Liability arises where the defect causes death, ill health or other personal injury, or property damage exceeding £275 in value.

Note: the Act does not apply to building construction and does not cover unprocessed food such as fruit, meat or fish. However, processed food ranks as a product.

The Act does not apply where the goods are simply shoddy or malfunctioning, such as an iron which fails to heat up, or where the only damage is done to the product itself, for example where the iron's temperature control fails so that the heating element in the iron melts. If the fault in the iron causes a fire which damages the kitchen, however, the consumer can rely on the Act.

The dangerous defect can be in the packaging or in the instructions for use which accompany the product.

An injured consumer must establish that the injury was caused by a defect in the product. It was this hurdle that prevented compensation from the courts for children who alleged that they suffered brain damage as a result of receiving the pertussis (whooping cough) vaccine.

☞ *Mrs B was fitting an infant's sleeping bag to her baby's pushchair when one of the elasticated straps on the product slipped her grasp and flew back, so that the buckle on the strap injured her eye.*

Despite the fact that there had been not a single previous case of such damage resulting from use of the product, the distributor was held liable to compensate Mrs B for the injury, as the defect was easily discoverable had the safety of the elastic fasteners been tested.

If a fault appears in a product during the first six months after purchase, there is a presumption that the fault was in existence at the time of sale, which makes it easier to hold the supplier liable.

If it can be proved that the product had a safety defect, and that it caused the damage, it is not necessary to prove negligence or other faults in the design, product or quality control procedures.

However, it seems that manufacturers will not be liable for a latent danger which could not have been known at the time they supplied the product. It is not clear how much research they should have done before they can escape liability under this heading.

6.3.3   Exclusion clauses

The manufacturers, suppliers or own-branders whom the Act makes responsible to compensate consumers cannot escape from their liabilities by exclusion clauses in any notice or contract, or in any 'guarantee' given to the consumer. In fact, the legal effect of such a guarantee is not entirely clear in law.

Even if the guarantee does create a contract, it does not necessarily cover all the manufacturer's possible liability – for example it may guarantee free replacement parts but not free labour or refund of postage. If the damage caused by the defect is substantial, the victim is probably on more reliable ground if he insists on his rights under the Consumer Protection Act rather than confining himself to the 'guarantee'.

6.3.4   Liability of retailer

It will be noticed that the Consumer Protection Act does not impose a primary liability on the retailer who sold or hired out the defective product. The Act does oblige him to inform a consumer of the name of the manufacturer or importer, and he can be held liable himself if he does not.

Any claim under the Act must be made within three years from the time that the claimant knew of the damage or injury, the defect in the product and the identity of the producer, subject to a cut-off point of ten years from the date of the product's first being put into circulation. Where the consumer's own lack of care contributed to his loss or to his injuries, his damages will be reduced to reflect this.

6.4   Criminal liability

It should be noted that the law also imposes criminal penalties on those who manufacture or supply unsafe products, or whose products do not comply with the safety standards laid down by various sets of regulations. It is of great assistance to a claimant if a criminal prosecution is brought, because the court can award compensation when convicting and this is likely to be much speedier than bringing a civil case. It will also be of help in establishing the claim if civil compensation has to be sought.

Criminal penalties extend also to the suppliers of second-hand consumer products (except antiques or goods expressly stated to have been repaired before sale).

If an accident is due to defective products installed in a building, such as faulty electrical plugs, the builder is liable just as he is if the work is done negligently.

Note: when purchasing, always remember to pay heed to the safety marks on products (for example, the *kitemark*). This means that the product has passed the British standards safety tests.

6.5 Defective equipment at work

An employee who is injured by defective equipment provided by his employer can claim damages from the employer under the Employers Liability (Defective Equipment) Act 1969. This right does not depend on the employer being at fault in choosing equipment or his knowledge of the defect.

The employer will be able to claim reimbursement from the manufacturer of the equipment.

7 FINANCIAL INSTITUTIONS

In almost all cases when you are contracting with financial institutions, you will be using their standard forms. Although you can shop around, there will not be major differences between the terms institutions use, which put consumers in a disadvantageous 'take it or leave it' situation. If the standard terms do not suit, negotiate if you can.

Attempts to deal with consumer complaints about the financial institutions led to various industry regulators and ombudsmen being set up. These have now been amalgamated into the Financial Ombudsman Service (see DIRECTORY), which has taken over the functioning of eight previous complaints bodies such as the Insurance Ombudsman and the Banking Ombudsman, even though the previous bodies may still be shown in the firm's literature.

The Service will investigate complaints about financial products and services only after the consumer has first tried to get the firm to deal with the problem. The role of the Ombudsman is to try and mediate to settle the dispute, not to fine or otherwise punish the firm – that may be a matter for the Financial Services Authority, the regulatory body.

The Ombudsman's service is free to consumers. The decision is final and binding as far as the firm is concerned, but if a consumer is still dissatisfied (s)he retains the right to go to court afterwards.

The Financial Services Authority also provides consumer help about making a complaint. The relevant leaflet can be ordered from their consumer helpline: 0845 806 1234. See also *www.fsa.gov.uk*.

In one case of pension mis-selling, Gregory wanted a pension that would create a benefit for his dependants if he died before them. An insurance company sold him a pension which did not provide this, whereas they should have advised him instead to remain in his employer's pension scheme. Gregory sued the company, and they were held liable to compensate him, as they were under a duty not to give negligent advice to customers which caused them loss.

7.1 You and your bank

When you open a bank account, you enter into a contract with the bank. Under this contract, the bank undertakes to honour cheques up to the amount deposited into an account or up to an agreed overdraft limit. A 'cash card' is an entitlement to draw cash from automatic vending machines also up to an agreed limit.

It is a simple fact that if we draw out more money than we are entitled to, and an account is overdrawn, we are in debt to the bank. Banks can charge compound interest on the debt. The bank can 'dishonour' (i.e. refuse to pay) your cheque if there are insufficient funds to meet it, or if the overdraft limit has been exceeded. A bank can also refuse to honour a cheque for any one of the following reasons:

- the cheque is incorrectly written, e.g. the words and figures differ, or it is undated
- the bank is notified of the death of the account-holder (which freezes the bank account until an executor takes control of it – see chapter on *Death – Before and After*)
- the cheque is 'stale', i.e. more than six months old, although technically a cheque is valid for six years.

Note: to give someone a cheque knowing it will bounce because of insufficient funds is a criminal offence under the Theft Act.

You have a contractual duty to your bank to refrain from drawing cheques in such a way as to facilitate forgery or fraud, e.g. by leaving gaps in writing out the amount. You must also inform the bank of any forged payment if you know of the forgery.

Where a cheque has been materially altered by someone else after it left your hands, for instance, the name of the payee is altered, your bank cannot debit your account. (The reverse is true for a banker's draft, which is debited to your account as soon as it is issued to you.)

The Banking Code is a voluntary code followed by banks and building societies in their dealings with personal customers. It sets out such matters as the banks' obligations to require customers' consent to the practice of banks providing each other with credit references on the state of their customers' accounts [see paragraph 4.5 of the Code]. To get a copy of the Banking Code, go to *www.bankingcode.org.uk.*

The British Bankers' Association puts out helpful information on its website about your bank's obligations in operating your account. See *www.bba.org.uk.*

7.1.1 Stopping a cheque

You have a right to stop any cheque by instructing your bank not to pay. You can phone your bank and explain that as a matter of urgency it should take your verbal instructions and that you will send in written confirmation later. Banks charge for putting a stop on a cheque.

☞ *You gave a plumber who did some emergency repairs a cheque for £45. You want to stop the cheque as you now discover he failed to fix the leak.*

If he asked for your banker's card to guarantee the cheque for the amount, you will not be able to stop it.

☞ *You gave your brother-in-law a cheque, which he cashed immediately, just before the bank's closing time. You told your bank to stop the cheque first thing next morning.*

As the cheque had already been paid out, the bank is entitled to debit your account with the amount of the cheque.

Do take heed: even if you have stopped a cheque you may still be liable on the underlying transaction. For example, you may owe the unpaid price for goods you have bought. So if you give a cheque in payment for a word processor you bought from a shop, but overnight realised that you could have bought it more cheaply from another dealer, you will still owe the shop the amount of the price, even though the bank will follow your instructions to stop the cheque. So do remember that stopping the cheque is only a stage which strengthens your hand in negotiating with the supplier. If he sued you for payment, the court could disagree with you and therefore order you to pay the price.

If you lift a stop on a cheque but the bank in error fails to pay it, the bank is in breach of contract.

7.1.2 Crossed cheques

A person to whom a cheque is made out (the payee) can exchange the cheque for cash at the issuing bank. Crossing the cheque means it can only be paid through a bank account, which provides some safeguard against its falling into anyone else's hands. The best way to ensure that only the payee gets the money is to add the word 'only' after the payee's name, cross the cheque, and write the words 'not negotiable, a/c payee only' in the crossing. This is often printed on the cheque by the bank.

7.1.3 Lost or stolen cheques

If a cheque is lost or stolen, the bank should be informed immediately so that the account-holder is not responsible for cheques written out by anyone else. If the bank then happens to pay out on such a cheque it cannot debit the account. It also cannot debit your account if it pays out on altered or forged cheques, provided you did not draw the cheque in such a way as to facilitate forgery, e.g. by leaving large spaces between words when writing the amount.

Banks are liable to meet cheques presented by retailers even with forged signatures, where they have been supported by a cheque guarantee card.

The banks are presently trying out various methods to try to obviate fraud by giving customers 'smart' cheque cards.

7.1.4 Credit cards, cash cards and cheque guarantee cards

Cards should only be issued to customers who request them, or to replace or renew those previously issued. If you do not wish to use those functions on a card operated by a personal identification number (PIN) you can request that no such number be issued to you. If you have a PIN make sure you do not write it on the card or keep a note of it with the card, or you may have to bear the losses if the card is misused by some unauthorised person. Under the Consumer Credit Act you, the customer, are liable only up to £50, provided you were given details of a telephone number and an address to contact to report the loss or theft of a card. (If you were not given such contact details you are not liable at all.)

You are also not liable at all if a fraudster, having obtained details of your card and PIN, manufactures a false duplicate to make unauthorised withdrawals from your account. But if you have been grossly negligent, by for example leaving the card and PIN in an unlocked car, the bank can debit your account in full for a thief's withdrawals.

7.1.5 Bank's errors

Where the bank by mistake credits your account with more money than you have paid in (e.g. by confusing your account with that of another customer with the same name) you may be able to refuse to pay the money back if you did not know of the mistake and you acted to your detriment e.g. you spent the money without being aware of the bank's error. It thus needs two elements:

a) that you are unaware of the mistake; and
b) that you have acted on the mistake to your detriment.

You can thus argue that the bank negligently misrepresented to you the true position of your account. But if you did know of the mistake you have to pay it back. Do seek legal advice.

What if the bank dishonours a cheque which it should have paid? This can cause great embarrassment and inconvenience, because, for example, a creditor may insist on being paid in cash in future. Technically, it could be libel on the bank's part. A customer could also find his name has been added to a credit register (see section 7.3.8 below) which would make it difficult for him to get credit or obtain a mortgage in the future. Accordingly, the bank can be held liable to pay substantial damages for such an error.

If you feel that your bank's wrongful refusal to honour a cheque may lead to a run on your credit, do take legal advice.

See also *Bank charges*, section 7.1.9 below.

7.1.6 Confidentiality

The bank is under a duty to keep confidential any information about your account.

> ☞ *You have an overdraft. An employee of your bank tries to telephone you at your place of work, and in the course of conversation with your boss, the bank clerk mentions that you have not paid instalments due to the bank, and that you may be betting on the horses. As a result of this conversation, you lose your job.*
>
> The bank is liable to you in damages for breach of its contractual duty of confidentiality.

There are certain exceptional circumstances where a bank may be obliged by law to disclose details of the account to the police or the Serious Frauds Office, for the purposes of their investigations into certain criminal offences such as major frauds, tax offences, insider dealing, proceeds of drug trafficking, or terrorist links. The bank is under no obligation to inform you about any such investigation.

The bank should not disclose information about you or your account, even to other companies in the same banking group, except with consent, but there is evidence that some banks may not always observe this – as the receipt of marketing material about other financial services shows.

7.1.7 The Banking Ombudsman

If you are unhappy about a bank's services (including the way your mortgage account is being handled), and get no satisfaction from the manager of the branch or from the head office, you can complain to the Financial Ombudsman Service, who has taken over the functions of the Banking Ombudsman (for a form, telephone 0845 080 1800 or turn to the website: *www.Financial-ombudsman.org.uk* also see DIRECTORY).

The purpose of the service is to make good losses and the Ombudsman can order the bank or other firm to compensate for loss up to a total of £100,000 (as long as the aggrieved account-holder is an individual or small company). On the other hand, you may be told that you have been treated correctly or that the compensation offered is fair. The bank will be bound by the Ombudsman's decision, but a customer who remains dissatisfied still has the option of taking legal action against his or her bank.

Deadline: generally, the complaint form must be submitted within six months of the date of the final letter from the bank. However, other time limits may apply if you have delayed complaining after you know that there is a problem.

7.1.8 Traveller's cheques

Usually there are terms in the purchase conditions which exempt the bank issuing the traveller's cheques from liability to give a refund for stolen or lost cheques unless the purchaser had properly safeguarded the cheques. Where there is such a condition, purchasers can only obtain a refund if the loss occurred without their carelessness – which they would have to prove. Some institutions' traveller's cheques may not contain such a condition, in which case the purchaser's claim to a refund may be valid even if he or she was seriously at fault.

Some terms go further – for example, traveller's cheques can be issued with the condition that a refund will not be due if the purchaser gives the cheques to another person or company to keep. If you cautiously deposit your unused traveller's cheques in the hotel safe you would be in breach of such a condition!

Not all banks operate a bring-back service to redeem unused traveller's cheques. It makes financial sense to buy from a bank which does.

If you lose your traveller's cheques while abroad, report the loss promptly to the local police. You will need their report when you contact the number given on the sales advice document about replacement.

7.1.9 Bank charges

The Code of Banking Practice states that banks will notify customers of any changes in the terms and conditions, with reasonable notice of variations before such variations are applied. Failure to do so could mean the new terms are unenforceable under the unfair terms regulations (see section 2.4 above).

It is up to each bank to take commercial decisions on the rates they charge or pay, as long as customers are given proper notice of this and changes are not made without due warning. You cannot complain to the Ombudsman if you were notified of the charges or rates; your only sanction is to move the account to another institution.

The Banking Code of Practice which, for example, requires banks to publicise their charges, also limits loss to £50 if a cash withdrawal card is used by someone else without the customer's negligence. However, some banks have rejected the Code as a basis for doing business.

Always check your bank statements. There are a growing number of complaints about errors, such as that banks mistakenly charge a higher rate of interest on overdrafts than agreed; they may debit payments twice due to computer error; may not show credits; or may delay direct debits.

7.1.10 Moving your bank account

This can be a simple procedure. The bank to which you are transferring your account may deal with all the administration required. If it does not, check the advice on the British Bankers' Association website at *www.bba.org.uk*.

7.2 You and your insurance company

An insurance policy is a contract between a policyholder and an insurance company under which, in return for a stipulated fee (a 'premium'), the company will pay a sum of money on the occurrence of a specified event, such as death, fire, burglary etc. Certain insurance policies are compulsory – for example, third party cover for car owners.

Take note: insurance contracts have several special features which do not occur in other types of contract.

7.2.1 What you can insure

You can only take out valid insurance to cover an eventuality where you stand to lose financially, technically called your 'insurable interest'. For example you cannot insure property unless you stand to lose if it is damaged or destroyed.

☞ *You run a successful desktop publishing business from a suite of offices which you rent. You have now formed your business into a limited liability company. However, you continue to insure the premises and assets of the business in your own personal name.*

    The insurance policy will be void, as you no longer have an insurable interest in the premises and assets. You must take out a new policy and name the company as the policyholder.

Life insurance: the law assumes you have an insurable interest in your own life and that of your spouse, but you cannot insure the lives of others you care for – a favourite pop star, say, or even your own child. However, if your children are giving you financial support which will cease on their death, you will have an insurable interest in their lives, and can take out such insurance on their lives.

7.2.2 Telling the company everything

Generally, persons entering into contracts with others have no obligation to volunteer information about themselves or the subject matter of the contract to those others, although of course they must not actually misrepresent the facts. But insurance contracts are different. Every insurance contract carries with it the duty to make disclosure of all relevant facts. This means that not only must you give accurate and truthful answers to all questions in the proposal form, but you must in addition *volunteer* information which could be relevant. If you do not, the insurance company can treat the policy as void. In fact, if the proposal form states, as they usually do, that the answers form the basis of the contract, *all* information – even if not particularly relevant to the risk insured against – must be correct and honestly given.

☞ *When filling in a proposal form to insure your car, you inadvertently give an incorrect address for where the car will be garaged, and also fail to volunteer information about a previous minor motor accident in which you have been involved.*

    The insurance company can avoid liability on the grounds of either the inaccuracy or the non-disclosure.

The consequences of non-disclosure can be very serious. In one case a husband and wife who had both suffered from cystic fibrosis since birth took out a joint life policy without telling the insurance company of their illness. When the husband died, the wife could not recover anything under the policy. The insurance company were entitled to treat the whole insurance as void.

Very important: if the insurance contract is renewable, for example annually, each renewal is treated as making a fresh contract and the duty to disclose arises again – so if the facts have changed make sure you tell the company.

A broker or agent may fill in the proposal form for you. If they do, you should read it carefully – never sign it without checking it first. Even though they get their commission from the company and not from you, as far as filling in the form is concerned they are your agents and if information is not correctly recorded you lose your insurance cover. If, however, they fail to obtain the cover you requested or if on renewal a new exclusion clause is put into the policy without your knowledge, you could sue the broker for professional negligence. A broker cannot withhold information from an insurance company, so do not ask him to do so.

7.2.3 Unfair terms

The Unfair Contract Terms Act, which prevents businesses from putting terms in their contracts that limit their liability, does not apply to insurance contracts, but the 'small print' regulations do (see section 2.4 above). These regulations invalidate the common clause giving an insurer a unilateral right to choose the level of deductions made to cover their administration charges in e.g. life and pensions policies.

☞ *You ask your holiday insurers to cover you for a bungee jumping expedition. They point to a clause in their standard term contract which excludes such risks. You want to know whether this type of exclusion is allowed under the small print regulations.*

The Office of Fair Trading cannot test for fairness for any risk which the insurer is not prepared to undertake (see section 7.2.6 below). This is known as a 'core' term. However, it can test for:

- time limits (see below, section 7.2.9)
- provisions relating to cancellation of policies
- unduly harsh or unreasonable duties to disclose
- insistence on arbitration to the exclusion of other legal rights
- whether any clause, even one covering a core term, is written in plain and intelligible language (otherwise it will be deemed unfair).

Further, if a clause is ambiguous, the interpretation most favourable to the consumer prevails.

7.2.4 Sticking to the letter of the contract

Insurance policies always contain terms about what the policyholder must or must not do, and if these are not strictly abided by, the insurance company may refuse to pay out. For instance, a home contents' policy may require you to install and use a properly functioning burglar alarm.

☞ *Philip's car was stolen from outside his house. He admitted that due to a fault in the ignition barrel he had for two years left the key in the ignition and taken no steps to have the car repaired.*

His insurance company was entitled to refuse to pay out on the policy because he had not taken reasonable precautions, as the policy required, to prevent loss.

☞ *Steve drove his Porsche, which was fitted with a remote-controlled immobiliser, to a petrol station to fill up. He left the key in the ignition, because he had complete faith in the immobiliser. While he was paying for the petrol a thief entered the car, locked the doors and using a code grabbing or scanning device, overcame the immobiliser and drove the car away. Steve claimed on his insurance policy, which contained the usual clause requiring him to take all reasonable steps to safeguard the car.*

The insurance company's refusal to pay out, because he had left the keys in the car, was upheld by the court.

☞ *Caroline's house contents insurance required her to have and use locks on doors and ground floor windows. One evening she went out having failed to set the locks. While she was out, thieves broke through a window and stole several items.*

The insurance company refused to pay because Caroline had not kept to the terms of the policy. But the police, the glazier and the loss adjuster all agreed that even if the window had been locked, the thieves would not have been significantly hampered. She complained to the Insurance Ombudsman, who ordered the company to pay out.

However, it is always safer to stick to the terms of your policy and err on the side of being too careful, rather than relying on the insurers' goodwill in paying out to you in the event of a mishap.

7.2.5 Being under-insured

Am I under-insured with regard to my home contents policy?

Review the amount you have insured for, periodically, to take account of new acquisitions, increases in value, etc. If you overvalue the insured property this may invalidate the policy, but if you undervalue it you may not get even the amount at which you valued it.

☞ *You take out £5,000 fire insurance for property worth £10,000.*

When half of it is destroyed by fire, you get only £2,500.

You can limit your cover by insuring for a specific amount. In turn, the insurance company will limit its liability by imposing an 'excess', so that claims below a certain level will not be paid out.

If your holiday insurance specifies an excess of £200, and your pocket is picked and £200 or less is taken, the loss will be treated as not covered by the insurance.

Some policies also exclude items exceeding a particular amount in value, so particularly valuable items have to be separately insured.

If you have to get a valuation of lost or stolen goods to make the claim, include the cost of obtaining the valuation in your total claim on the policy.

If you claim more than you are entitled to this is, legally, fraud, and the insurance company may refuse to pay out even the lesser amount you would have received for a proper claim.

☞ *Stanley insured a racehorse for £200,000. When the horse died after foaling, it was found to have been worth only £20,000. As the discrepancy was so large, the court took the view that Stanley must have known the claim was fraudulent, and so he did not receive even the £20,000 the horse had been worth.*

☞ *In another case, Sam was the victim of a burglary. He claimed under his household insurance for the loss, but unwisely exaggerated the genuine claim to include the loss of a non-existent personal computer 'worth' £2,000. This fraudulent claim, though small in relation to the total, contaminated the whole and meant that Sam's entire claim failed.*

If following a burglary you claim for the loss of cutlery, but subsequently discover the cutlery was not stolen because the thieves dropped it in some bushes in your garden on making their escape, you must withdraw that aspect of the claim or it will be treated as fraudulent.

If the dishonesty is minor, the Financial Services Ombudsman might regard an insurance company's refusal to pay out anything at all as being unfair.

The insurance company may also insist on replacing damaged or stolen items rather than giving you cash compensation. Your premiums should reflect this, as insurance companies get discounts from suppliers.

7.2.6   Excluded risks

Policies generally contain a list of 'excepted perils' namely, the risks which are not covered by the policy; for example, damage caused by 'war, riot or civil commotion' or by 'contamination from nuclear fuel or nuclear waste'. The terms of the policy can also cut down the scope of protection in ways you may not expect, for example home contents policies may exclude cash, cheques and documents, which may have to be insured separately. The Insurance Ombudsman has ruled that all exclusions must be set out fairly and must satisfy the test of reasonableness. You should ask about particular items and risks you want covered – it may be necessary to shop around to obtain cover. You may have a claim against your broker if he or she did not obtain cover which you specified was needed. Homeowners may find that their household contents insurance excludes plants, fences, garden ornaments and pets. Note that you will not be covered for loss or damage occurring before the start of the insurance period.

7.2.7   No-claims bonus

Insurers limit their liability by trying to reduce the number of claims made, by giving policyholders an inducement not to claim – in the form of a discount or no-claims bonus. If the amount of the claim is less than that of the no-claims bonus, it will not be worth claiming, but it is probably sensible – in the light of your duty of disclosure – to tell the insurers of the loss anyway, making it clear that this is for information only.

7.2.8   Police notification

In the event of theft, always inform the police promptly, as your insurers will insist on a report from the police as a precondition of paying out.

7.2.9   Time limits

Policies usually fix time limits for the notification of a claim, as a condition of the company's liability. It is always prudent to inform the insurers as soon as possible that a claim is to be made, even if you do not yet have full details of the value of the loss.

7.2.10   Insurance losses

The insurance industry has had to pay out a record amount through claims for a series of unprecedented natural disasters in recent years. There have also been large, recession-related claims such as mortgage indemnity cover, as well as massive payouts on losses from theft.

In addition, insurers feel that they have become the victims of all sorts of fraudulent claims or scams from members of the public, such as when someone holidays abroad, spends all his money, and then, on returning to England, claims for a 'theft' of traveller's cheques which never took place. It is not surprising, therefore, that insurers would want to sift through claims very carefully in order to trap those that may not be above board. However, if you have had your money stolen on holiday and your claim is genuine, you may be upset and resent any delay on your insurer's part. Remember, though, that the cost of fraud will be recouped by the insurers in increased premiums, so reduction of fraud is in your own interest.

Note: for certain claims, your insurance company may employ the services of a loss adjuster to assess the potential loss. The loss adjuster's report may then be used by your insurers as the basis on which to pay out your claim.

7.2.11   Uncooperative insurers

If you have a dispute with your insurers, persist in your claim by, if necessary, going up through managers and directors to the very top. If you still can't get satisfaction, within six months you can complain to the Financial Ombudsman Service (see DIRECTORY). He has the power to award compensation of up to £100,000 against an insurance company, and getting his award does not prevent you taking subsequent legal action if still unhappy. (Not all insurance companies are members of the Ombudsman Service.)

Alternatively, you can have your claim arbitrated through the Personal Insurance Arbitration Scheme (PIAS), run by the Chartered Institute of Arbitrators (see DIRECTORY).

Note: that both these schemes are voluntary, so that not all insurance companies participate in them.

7.3   You and your debts

The law is concerned to oversee the business of lending money. It tries to ensure – within the limits of usual business practice – that the innocent are not taken advantage of and that persons who lend money are properly licensed (see *Consumer protection*, section 7.3.5 below). A helpful leaflet is CLS Leaflet No. 1, obtainable from the Community Legal Services (see DIRECTORY).

7.3.1   Getting different types of credit

A new European Union consumer credit directive to harmonise the rules relating to consumer credit throughout Europe has been proposed, but its implementation is some way in the future.

It is usually cheaper to buy for cash than on credit, as the price will have added on to it the amount of interest and additional charges. Some forms of credit will be cheaper than others, so just as you would do for anything else, it is sensible to shop around to find the best source. Sometimes goods are advertised at 0 per cent interest, but then there may be some other hidden cost – for example, loss of a discount on a new car. In recessionary times, of course, when consumers hold back from spending in the High Street, ever-increasingly attractive offers are put out by shops and other businesses to tempt reluctant customers. Interest-free credit does not mean that regular repayments do not still have to be made. Credit card borrowing may be more expensive than borrowing elsewhere, if you do not repay the credit card bill in full each month.

Remember: as always, take time to consider before you sign anything, and keep a copy of the credit agreement.

7.3.2   Standard credit agreements

There are various forms of standard credit agreements but the main forms of credit for retail sales are:

- hire purchase agreements
- conditional sale agreements
- credit sale agreements.

7.3.2(a)   Hire purchase agreements

A standard HP agreement reflects a situation where a customer wants to buy goods from a shop on credit. He or she makes the purchase and the shop then sells the goods to the finance house which, in law, becomes the seller. The finance house makes finance available to the customer who has to repay it in instalments. The customer 'hires' the goods, which do not actually become his property until the last instalment is paid. Technically, he has the option to become the owner at this point. In some cases, the dealer or retailer may himself provide the finance in which case he is both seller and lender, but this is not as common as finance house agreements.

7.3.2(b) Conditional sale agreements

In a conditional sale, which is more unusual than HP, a customer 'buys' the goods on instalment from the finance house. Again, the goods belong to the finance house and not to the customer until the last instalment is paid. Unlike an HP agreement, the customer is under a legal obligation to buy the goods at the end of the instalment period.

7.3.2(c) Credit sale agreements

In a credit sale agreement, too, the customer buys goods which he or she pays for by instalments. However, the goods actually belong to the customer from the outset of the contract – unlike a conditional sale agreement.

7.3.3 Legal controls on lenders and other creditors

All these agreements are governed by statute. The law lays down who can finance them; how they are to be financed; what documentation should be used; and how the customer should be protected.

Persons who offer finance must be licensed to do so by the Office of Fair Trading. It keeps a register which is open to members of the public who can inspect the register for a fee.

It is important that you check precisely who the seller is. When you buy goods on HP or under a conditional sale agreement, the supplier of the goods is not the retailer, as we have seen. It is the finance company which in law 'sells' the goods and it is primarily against them that consumer rights will have to be enforced. There may also be rights against the dealer if you relied on assurances by his staff about the quality of the goods. In practice the finance company and the supplier may have arranged that the latter will deal with complaints, but in law rights are against the finance company.

By law all advertisements for, and offers of, loans and credit must specify the APR. This stands for Annual Percentage Rate, and is meant to enable you to compare overall the cost of borrowing from different outlets. In practice, the APR has come in for criticism as being deliberately confusing to the customer.

The Office of Fair Trading takes the view that advertisements for 'interest free credit' or '0% APR' mislead the public and are unlawful because they imply that the consumer can get credit without paying interest, whereas in fact he would still be liable for consumer charges. Several major retailers have agreed to stop putting out such advertisements in the light of the OFT's powers to issue 'Stop Now' orders (see section 2.4.1 above).

7.3.4 Giving security

If you can give security you may get a cheaper loan. However, be on guard against lenders who want you to put up your home as security; by law, their advertisements must make it clear that this is the security they require. If you cannot keep up the instalments you may end up with no roof over your head.

Also be wary of acting as guarantor for someone else's debt – if they default you will have to pay the creditor. Always check the details of the debtor's agreement with the creditor before you sign any guarantee to make sure you could afford to pay if you have to. The creditor is obliged to tell you the terms of his contract with the debtor if they are in any way out of the ordinary.

So it is wise to get independent legal advice before you sign a transaction where its purpose is to benefit someone else (i.e. where you are acting as guarantor for someone else's loan) or where you may lose your home.

It is also illegal for anyone to ask for your social security benefit books as security for a loan. You must report any such request from a creditor to the local Trading Standards Officer.

7.3.5 Consumer protection

The safest procedure when asking for a loan or credit is to ask for a written quotation and take it home to study. If you look at the agreement you will see whether it contains, as the law requires, a clear notification to you about your right to cancel. *Never* sign an agreement in blank or without all the details being filled in. If you agreed to the loan or credit arrangement over the telephone, even from your home, you will not have the right to cancel.

Always fill in an application for credit yourself or check it carefully before signing it. If the details are inaccurate, you may be committing a criminal offence.

If you exercise your right to cancel, you will be entitled to the return of any deposit paid and goods given in part exchange. At the same time you will have to return the money borrowed or the goods you received.

Once you have signed the agreement you must be sent another copy through the post. Keep it in a safe place, together with a record of each payment you make and any correspondence you have with the lender. If these get mislaid, on payment of 50p to the creditor you are entitled to receive a copy of the agreement and a statement of instalments paid and balance owing.

☞ *You agree to buy a moped on HP from a dealer and ask to take the documentation home to study the terms of the agreement. Subsequently you are asked to come in person to the offices of the finance house to sign the forms so that the deal can be finalised. You wonder why the dealer has made this stipulation.*

 Do take care as you may be deprived of your consumer protection rights.

 If you sign an agreement on the business premises of the dealer or the finance house, you will be bound by it, whereas if you sign at home you may have a 'cooling-off' period during which you are entitled to cancel the agreement if you have second thoughts.

7.3.6 Credit cards

If you have used a credit card such as Access or Visa (as distinct from a charge card or debit card, e.g. American Express or Diner's Club) to buy goods or services worth more than £100, you can hold the credit card company liable, together with the defaulting trader, if you do not get what you paid for. This does not apply to hire purchase transactions (and see also *Tour operators*, section 9.2 below).

The companies often ask you to approach the supplier first, but you are not legally obliged to do so.

7.3.7 Defaulting on a debt

If you buy goods on hire purchase and then find you cannot keep up the payments, do not be tempted to sell the goods to raise funds. You have no right to dispose of them until all the instalments have been paid, and you may be committing a criminal offence if you do. Further, if you offer to return the goods to the seller, be warned that your liability to keep up instalments does not automatically terminate – ask them to agree to this in writing when you relinquish the goods.

☞ *You bought an expensive hatchback car on HP at a time when you were earning considerable sums as a broker in the City. You have since been made redundant and cannot afford the payments on the car. You have seen an advertisement in a local paper from what seems to be a reputable firm offering to take over your car and to make the payments on your behalf.*

 Do not be tempted. You may find that although you part with your car and log book, so losing your vehicle for good, the payments may not be made on your behalf so that you are still liable to the finance house for a car you no longer have. It would be better by far to approach the finance house and ask for advice on how best to get out of your present plight (see *Ending the agreement*, below, section 7.3.10).

Failure to pay means that the goods can be repossessed, but a court order is necessary to enter your home without your permission. If you have paid more than one-third of the instalments, there cannot be a repossession at all without a court order. If a creditor takes you to court and gets a judgement against you, it may not be the end of the matter. You may end up on a register of debtors which could seriously affect your chances of getting credit again. County Court judgements are passed to the Registry Trust, which is consulted by credit rating agencies and mortgage institutions, so it makes sense to have your name removed while you can. If you pay the debt within one month of the judgement, the judgement is removed and an entry in the credit reference agencies' files will be cancelled in its entirety. If you pay the debt after one month, you can obtain a 'certificate of satisfaction' from the court and this will be recorded on the files although your name generally remains on file for six years nonetheless. (The Registry Trust Limited can be contacted at 173–175 Cleveland Street, London W1P 5PE.)

Do not pay anyone to 'repair' your credit rating. The Office of Fair Trading publishes a number of free booklets dealing with credit and debt (see DIRECTORY), as does the Community Legal Services' leaflet No.1 (see DIRECTORY). Be very wary of advertised offers of help with debts from debt management and credit repair companies. There have been many cases where such companies have let their customers down badly. The OFT is, at the time of writing, investigating debt management companies to ensure they are dealing fairly and openly with consumers.

7.3.8   Credit reference agencies

If you find yourself unable to obtain credit or a loan from a particular firm, it may be because your name appears on a credit reference agency's records, because, for example, a judgment for debt has been obtained against you. If you think this may be the case, and the amount involved is under £15,000, you are entitled on request to be told the name of the agency used, so that you can ask them for a copy of the record affecting you. The credit reference agency is obliged to send you a copy of the record for a fee (at present £1). If the records are inaccurate you can have them amended. The booklet *Your Rights – No Credit* sets out the procedures which you must take. It is important to note carefully the time limits which are laid down in the booklet for these procedures. It is obtainable from the office of the Information Commissioner (see next paragraph, or the DIRECTORY). It is also available online at *www.dataprotection.gov.uk/dpr.*

Information about organisations that hold personal information about individuals on computer file can be obtained free from the office of the Information Commissioner, Wycliffe House, Water Lane, Wilmslow, Cheshire SK9 5AF, tel. 01625 545 745. All the provisions of the Data Protection Act 1998 were in force by December 2000. A free introduction to the Act can also be obtained from the Office of the Information Commissioner (*www.dataprotection.gov.uk*).

7.3.9   Extortionate interest

If you think you are paying interest at extortionate rates, you may be able to have the agreement set aside by the courts. Take legal advice before you stop payments, however, as it is extremely rare for this to be allowed. The courts will not regard a high rate as extortionate if the creditor has run an extra risk in giving you the credit.

7.3.10   Ending the agreement

If after embarking on a hire-purchase agreement you wish to terminate it, you can pay off all the instalments ahead of time. If you want to do this, write to the creditor and ask him about the rebate to which you are entitled because of the early payment. Companies often penalise consumers who want to settle loans early, perhaps in order to switch to a better deal. The government is currently investigating this practice with a view to make the calculations fairer.

On the other hand, if you want to terminate the agreement and give back the goods, you will have to pay up to half the price for the privilege of doing so. If you default on the instalments and the hire-purchase company wish to enforce the agreement, they must send you a default notice. If you cannot pay off the arrears when you get this, take legal advice immediately – you may be able to ask the court for a 'time order' giving you extra breathing space.

If you get into difficulty with debt, write and tell the creditor about the problem. Most creditors would prefer not to go to court and would rather make arrangements for the repayments, if feasible. Where you owe money to more than one creditor, inform all of them about your difficulties rather than skimping on one creditor's repayments in order to satisfy another's. Dickensian debtors' prisons are a thing of the past, and it is a criminal offence for a creditor to harass a debtor. If you do get sued, get legal advice from a solicitor or consumer adviser. Always try to put before the court realistic proposals about the amounts you can afford to repay regularly.

8   EATING AND DRINKING OUT

Earlier surveys showed that one in ten of catering premises had poor hygiene with consequent high risks to health. Rigorous regulations for food safety are now in force, and premises can be closed down or their owners prosecuted in the criminal courts for failing to comply with safety and hygiene standards. See also section 8.2.2 below.

8.1   Pubs

For many years, pub hours were strictly controlled. The licensing laws regulating pub hours were introduced during the First World War and it is only recently that these regulations have been relaxed. Pubs can now remain open throughout the day. However, publicans still often maintain a routine for their opening hours, particularly on Sunday afternoons, and it is advisable to check. Licensed restaurants are allowed to serve alcohol in certain circumstances, for example, with 'substantial food'.

8.1.1   Who can be served?

Until now the law has endeavoured to keep children out of pubs. It is a very familiar and very English scene to see, on summer days, parents bringing out lemonade and packets of crisps to their bored children waiting about in pub doorways and parking grounds. Proposals are progressively being put forward to allow children more readily into pubs.

Regulations governing the offences of serving alcohol to minors fall heavily on the publicans themselves. They are forbidden to sell alcohol to anyone under 18 – whether they know their age or not. In fact, even serving a drink to an adult who intends it to be consumed by a minor is a criminal offence. Children over 14 are allowed into a bar as long as they do not drink. Children's certificates may be granted to licensees allowing under 14-year-olds to be in a bar until 9 pm or later, provided that it is a 'suitable environment', that the minor is accompanied by an adult, and that one of them is eating a meal. 16 to 18-year-olds are allowed to have beer or cider with a meal in a pub – provided that it is not taken at the bar but in an area usually set aside for the provision of meals.

A publican must also refuse to serve someone who is already drunk – of whatever age. Moreover, he or she is under a legal duty to tell a drunk or violent person to leave the premises. Such a person commits an offence if he does not then depart.

8.1.2   Publican's duty

On the other hand, it is clear that a publican will be committing an offence if a refusal to serve someone is based on that person's race, sex or ethnic origins, or disability.

8.1.3   Credit

It is illegal for a landlord to sell drinks on credit. However, it is perfectly legal to pay by credit card for a meal at a pub provided the drinks are paid for separately.

8.1.4   Weights and Measures Act

The Weights and Measures Act 1985 and the secondary legislation made under it does a number of things including defining in law the units of measurement used for trade, setting out the requirements that apply to weighing machines and measuring equipment, the regulation of transactions in goods (including goods sold loose from bulk by weight), and quantity control of packaged goods.

Do note: it is a criminal offence to serve short measure. Enforcement of this legislation is a matter for local authority trading standards departments, and consumers should contact their trading standards department if they believe a short weight offence or other similar offence has been committed.

The law itself is complex and difficult to follow as it is often product-specific. Legislation is expected to simplify and streamline the law, taking into account new technology for packaging, marking and processing goods, as well as developments in other EU Member States.

Consultation will take place on new proposals which are likely to be issued in 2003.

8.1.5 Displaying prices

Prices of drinks and foods must be displayed on notices which are visible where they are served.

8.2 Restaurants

Certain problems crop up again and again with restaurants. What should be a pleasant evening out can be marred by off-hand service, poor food, over-expensive menus, and imbroglios over lost property. Not all these problems can be solved by legal redress – often one simply decides to grin and bear it – but it is as well to know what are one's rights in law.

8.2.1 Food description

The food served must be fit for its purpose, comply with its description and be of a quality reasonably to be expected in an establishment of its kind. If you are dissatisfied with the food on tasting or inspecting it, complain at once. You can deduct an equivalent amount from the bill for the inedible course, or pay under protest, recording this at the time or as soon as possible.

Beware: if you take more than a few mouthfuls you will be regarded as having 'accepted' the food and will have to pay for it.

If the food is not as described (e.g. a 'mixed seafood platter' which contains only one kind of fish; or 'scampi' which is really reshaped minced fish), tell the local trading standards officer. Restaurants can be fined for such misdescription even if the actual food is not sub-standard otherwise.

By law, food providers must indicate which goods contain genetically modified ingredients. If you are concerned about this, and there are no statements either way on the menu, ask the staff to check the packaging for you.

However dissatisfied you are, do not just walk out without paying! You could be committing an offence under the Theft Act. At the very least, give your name and address to the manager before you leave.

New regulations, to meet EU requirements, are in force to provide consumers with information on the contents of bottled waters. Strict safety requirements apply to natural mineral water, spring water, and other bottled drinking waters. The levels of all minerals in 'natural mineral water' must be labelled, while labelling requirements will also apply to spring water which must be bottled at source.

8.2.2 Food Safety

The Food Safety Act 1990 makes it a criminal offence to sell food which is injurious to health, or is not of the nature, substance or quality demanded, or does not comply with the food safety requirements. If you are served food which makes you ill, report the restaurant to the local environmental health officer.

☞ *You book several tables at a restaurant to celebrate your silver wedding with a dinner among 30 friends. Everyone at the party gets food poisoning after the meal.*

> The restaurant will be liable to pay damages to everyone who suffered, to compensate them for the illness, and will be liable to criminal penalties under the 1990 Act (which could result in them being closed down temporarily if not permanently).

Note: doctors are under a statutory duty to inform the authorities about any patient suffering from food poisoning.

After considerable consumer alarm concerning the safety of food across the whole food-chain, the Foods Standards Agency was set up in April 2000 to rebuild public confidence by overseeing safety standards in the interests of the consumer and of public health. The Agency works through Environmental Health Officers and Trading Standards Officers, but also produces a range of leaflets on foods, their storage and cooking, catering precautions, allergies and diet (see DIRECTORY at the end of this chapter).

8.2.3 Displaying prices

A restaurant menu with VAT-inclusive prices must be displayed at the entrance, or in the case of a self-service cafeteria, at the point where the food is selected. If service charges are automatically included, this must appear on the exhibited menu; so must any cover charge (which is for what is put on the table – such as bread or olives).

8.2.4 Service charges

If the service is unreasonably bad you are entitled to refuse to pay a service charge. There is no requirement by law that you have to tip – unlike, for example, the legal requirement that menus must state prices inclusive of VAT. So even though a menu may state '10 per cent added for service', you can withhold it if the circumstances warrant it.

8.2.5 No-shows

Do remember: when you make an advance reservation at a restaurant, you are entering into a contract. If you fail to turn up and the restaurant cannot fill the table with other guests in your place, you could be held liable to pay damages.

Conversely, if after you booked you turn up at the restaurant to find no table has been kept for you, you could claim compensation from them, for, say, the costs of the wasted journey.

8.2.6 Belongings

If a careless waiter spills soup on your suit, compensation (for example, the cost of cleaning) is due from the restaurant, because they are responsible for the negligence of their staff.

☞ *You are sitting at a table in a restaurant. As you lift your glass of red wine, another customer pushes past your table jogging your arm, so that the wine spills on your dress.*

> The proprietor is not responsible for the cleaning or replacement of the dress (unless you could prove that the placing of the tables was such as to make such an accident reasonably foreseeable).

On the same principle, if your coat is stolen from coathooks placed in the restaurant for the convenience of customers, the restaurateur is not responsible. However, if you hand your coat over to a waiter who then disappears with it, and the coat is stolen, the restaurant would be responsible for its loss.

☞ *As you enter a restaurant, a waiter approaches you and gestures towards the cloakroom where there is an attendant. After pausing for a moment, you decide to hand over your briefcase together with your coat. When you return, the briefcase is missing. The manager points to a sign above the attendant's desk which says that property is left at the customer's own risk.*

> It would seem that the disclaimer would be effective if the sign is sufficiently prominent for you to have noticed it when you handed over your belongings.

A disclaimer would not be effective, however, if the attendant had been negligent – if, for example, during a slack moment she had wandered over to chat to the barman.

Different considerations would apply where you are told to leave your belongings at a cloakroom and you have no choice in the matter. For example, for security reasons one cannot take umbrellas or briefcases into an art gallery. It would seem that under these circumstances, the management takes complete responsibility for them and owners are not leaving the goods at their own risk.

9 GOING AWAY ON HOLIDAY

9.1 Hotels

Given the nature of the trade, it is not surprising to learn that an hotelier is under a legal duty to take all comers if there are rooms available.

A distinction is drawn between hotels on the one hand, and boarding houses, residential hotels and bed-and-breakfast establishments on the other hand, which are not expected by law to take in all would-be guests.

It is of course an offence to refuse to serve someone solely on account of race, sex, ethnic origins or disability – whatever the nature of the establishment.

9.1.1 Displaying charges

An hotel must display its charges and specify which meals – if any – are included in the price. This information must be clearly available at reception – it is insufficient to put a notice on the back of a bedroom door.

9.1.2 Cancellations

As with booking a restaurant table, a contract is made with an hotel on booking a room. In the event of a failure to take up a booking, the hotel is entitled to charge a reasonable amount for lost profits if it cannot re-let the room.

☞ *You have booked an hotel room and given your credit card number to the receptionist to make sure of your reservation. You cannot keep the booking and you telephone the hotel to cancel it. You are dismayed to see that you have been charged the full amount for you and your wife on your credit card statement which you receive a month later.*

If you book a room in an hotel but cancel your stay, you are still liable to pay something to the hotel. However, you are not liable in law for the full cost of the room, as the hotel has saved on providing food, laundry, etc. Hotels are supposed to charge a reasonable amount only on lost profits but of course, these can form a considerable proportion of the amount charged for an overnight stay.

If you can persuade your credit card company that the hotel charges are exorbitant, it may take action on your behalf.

If you had paid a deposit instead of giving your credit card number, the hotelier would be entitled to keep it – again within a reasonable amount.

In recessionary times, hoteliers and restaurateurs are not always able to fill rooms and tables which have been booked. Their proprietors are therefore much more likely to take a tough stance against 'no-shows' than at other times.

9.1.3 Overbookings

Conversely, if you book a room but when you arrive find the hotel is full, the hotelier is liable to you for any extra costs involved in staying somewhere else (which could include your travel costs to the alternative place).

9.1.4 Specific requests

If particular requirements, such as a sea view, are specified at the time of booking, an hotel is in breach of contract if the room does not meet the specification.

☞ *You have a mobility problem and find stairs difficult. You ask for a ground floor room when you book at an hotel in the Lake District. When you get there you find that the hotel's only ground floor room is occupied by another guest and you have to climb a flight of stairs to get to your room.*

In such a case, you are entitled to a deduction, and even to cancel. You may also wish to contact the Disability Rights Commission (see DIRECTORY).

☞ *The brochure of the Hotel Comfortable stated that it had suitable facilities for the disabled (defined in the brochure as those with walking difficulties or needing a wheelchair). In fact, when you arrived there, accompanied by your wheelchair-bound mother, you found that it was not suitable for a wheelchair user.*

In a similar case the hotel in question was successfully prosecuted for an offence under the Package Travel regulations.

For the implementation of the Disability Discrimination Act 1995, see above, section 2.5.1.

9.1.5 Guests' property

Once you are a guest in an hotel, it is responsible for the safety of your property (though not for your car or items left in it unless the hotel's employees are negligent). You can claim compensation for the loss or theft of your belongings on hotel premises.

In most cases, the hotel will have limited its liability, as it is entitled to do by putting up a notice in the reception area or in the entrance, making clear that it will only be liable for up to £50 per item or £100 per guest. The figures for compensation for loss were laid down in the 1950s and are clearly quite out of date.

A notice limiting liability must be in the front of the hotel and a notice which is only put up in a bedroom has no legal effect.

The hotel is then only liable to pay more than these statutory amounts if its employees are grossly negligent or if the property is deposited for safe custody with the management.

☞   *You book into an hotel for a weekend. There is no notice in the reception area, but after you have signed the register and are shown to your room, you see a notice limiting the hotel's liability prominently displayed in the room. Your jewellery case is stolen from the room while you are out.*

   The hotel must pay you the full value of the jewellery as the notice in the bedroom is insufficient in law to limit its liability.

(For the liability of the hotel for accidental injuries, see *Accidents* chapter, section 6.5. For package holidays, see *Tour operators* below, section 9.2.)

9.1.6   Driving while on holiday

Make sure you have full insurance cover, whether you are taking your own car abroad or hiring a car at your destination.

In some countries, such as the USA, you may find that the insurance cover on a hire car is only the legal minimum, which could leave you liable to pay personally the huge damages bill if you happen to cause an accident. Top-up insurance cover is available – make sure you are covered because few insurance policies taken out in the UK cover you when driving abroad.

The 'Green Card' is a card recognised only in countries which are members of the Green Card System (not all countries are members). It does not give insurance cover in itself, but is merely convenient evidence that minimum legal insurance requirements are covered by your motor insurance policy. Information sheets on this are available from the Association of British Insurers, 51 Gresham Street, London EC2V 7HR.

9.2   Tour operators

So many things can go wrong with a holiday – from the bankruptcy of a travel organiser to an hotel being unsuitable or overbooked – that it is essential to take out travel insurance to cover against as many eventualities as possible. Make sure in particular that the policy:

a) gives cover for cancelling at short notice
b) gives adequate cover for medical expenses abroad (skiers, and tourists to the United States, be warned!)
c) covers the full replacement value of possessions which might get lost or stolen.

Do check, however, that you are not paying twice for insurance. Some private medical insurance covers you for treatment abroad, and your luggage may be protected under your household contents policy.

It is now illegal for travel agents and tour operators to require customers booking foreign package holidays to have discounts tied to the customer's buying travel insurance from a particular company; it may be cheaper to shop around for the best deal.

A package holiday is just what its name would imply. It is an all-inclusive deal which covers travel and hotel. Package holidays are booked by coach, train or plane, and are arranged for travel both in Britain and abroad. A package holiday is also one of the few items you buy where you cannot know the final cost when you enter into the contract, i.e. at the time of booking (see section 9.2.1 below).

By law, the travel organiser must – before you book – give you information about visa and health requirements, and details about the security of any money you pay over, e.g. as a deposit. The protection of deposits is not necessarily guaranteed, however.

In determining whether a tour operator is liable in negligence to a British holidaymaker, the appropriate safety standards to apply are the local ones, not the equivalent UK standards. Where a toddler was injured by a hotel lift in Spain, it was Spanish safety standards which the court ruled were relevant in deciding whether the tour company was negligent, even though these standards were less rigorous than those in the UK.

9.2.1   Surcharges

Surcharges to cover variations in transport costs, taxes and exchange rates are commonly payable under the booking conditions – if they are not expressly mentioned you cannot be invoiced for them. After you have booked it is only in limited circumstances, which must be clearly set out in the brochure, that the organiser can change the price of the holiday. No one can be asked to pay a surcharge within 30 days of the commencement of the holiday. If the price of the holiday has been increased significantly you may be entitled to cancel the holiday without penalty and claim reimbursement. If the travel agent or tour operator is affiliated to ABTA (the Association of British Travel Agents), the ABTA Code protects against alterations being made less than two weeks before the start of the holiday. High penalties for cancellation by the customer or for last-minute alterations by the tour companies could be hit by the unfair contract terms regulations (see section 2.4 above).

9.2.2   Compliance with brochures

Don't forget: the brochure's glossy pictures and enticing descriptions form part of your contract with the tour operator. This applies to all package holidays, whether you book for an hotel or choose self-catering accommodation through a tour operator.

The operator must therefore provide exactly the holiday described, with the accommodation and facilities as promised.

If the company has to alter anything major – like switching you to another hotel or resort – it must tell you in advance and give you the choice of cancelling and taking a refund if the changes do not appeal. It is also responsible for getting you home safely: even if the company goes bust it should have made adequate financial arrangements in advance under EU rules.

Of course, booking conditions also form part of the contract but the tour operators cannot rely on these conditions unless they have been properly communicated to you. The question is what recourse a holidaymaker has where there are clauses which limit or exclude liability – if, for example, a promised swimming pool is unexpectedly closed.

9.2.3   Whose fault is it anyway?

If the accommodation and facilities fall short of your expectations, the tour operator might claim to be relieved of any liability by the inclusion of clauses in the booking conditions limiting or excluding its liability. Under the Unfair Contract Terms Act such clauses are invalid unless they are reasonable, and cannot in any event exclude or limit the extent of liability for negligence resulting in death or personal injury.

The trouble, legally speaking, with package holidays is that when something goes wrong with transport or accommodation, tour operators have often claimed that they cannot be held responsible for the running of airlines and hotels over which they have no control.

EU regulations require airlines which have overbooked passengers to pay compensation of up to £210. Passengers also have the option of being rerouted or taking a refund. Under new regulations brought in as a result of an EU Directive on package travel, the organiser can now be held responsible for the failure of others, such as airlines or hotels, to carry out the obligations paid for by the customer – unless the failure was unforeseeable or unavoidable.

Take heart: no exemption clause in the booking conditions will protect the tour operator if it fails to provide what was substantially the holiday you bought, even if there is a term allowing the substitution of hotels or resort.

☞   *You book a holiday in a 3-star hotel. When you arrive you are told the main building is full and you are offered a dirty room in a dilapidated annexe infested with beetles.*

You are not obliged to accept this substandard accommodation, and the tour operator is responsible for finding you an appropriate alternative and for paying compensation.

Equally, you are not obliged to accept a room in a large hotel in a noisy city resort, when you were buying a holiday described in the brochure as being in a small family hotel in a quiet resort village.

If the brochure describes the hotel as having such facilities as an English-speaking management, a paddling pool for toddlers, a beauty salon, a discotheque, or house-party atmosphere, then when any of these are absent or inadequate you can claim substantial compensation from the tour operator.

☞ *Mr Jackson paid £1,200 and bought his family of four a holiday at an hotel described in the brochure as luxurious with many specified facilities. The hotel turned out to be dirty and badly run, and most of the promised facilities did not exist or were unusable; halfway through the holiday they were moved to a better but only partly-built hotel.*

He sued the tour operator and was awarded £1,100 (including damages for the disappointment of the whole family).

Note: you do not have to accept an alternative if one is offered, although you may prefer to do this rather than lose the holiday altogether. In any event, complain to the local representative immediately, and keep a written record of your complaints and their response. Take photographs if appropriate (of, for example, locked fire escapes, unhygienic eating areas, dangerously low balconies) and try and get the names and addresses of other holiday-makers who can support your allegations if they are contested.

You are entitled to copies of complaints from other travellers if you take the tour company to court.

Note also: if the situation is not rectified, you can book yourself into another hotel (keep the receipts) and claim reimbursement when you get home, as long as the alternative accommodation is not extravagant by comparison with what you were promised.

The tour company may be liable to compensate customers for more serious problems than poor accommodation. If a war situation or extended rioting breaks out at your destination and the travel company, knowing of this, does not warn customers and perhaps offer an alternative holiday somewhere safer, the customers would get compensation. This is what happened to those unfortunate people flown into Kuwait as the Iraqis invaded, or those who had booked a West Coast holiday starting in Los Angeles in 1992 in the middle of the worst race riots in American history.

Before departure, travellers must be given information about passport, visa and health requirements for their destination. They must also be told about arrangements to safeguard the money they have paid for their trip, as well as repatriation arrangements if the tour operators become insolvent.

9.2.4   Paying by credit card

If you pay by credit card for a holiday costing more than £100, the credit card company can also be held liable. This may not apply if you paid the travel agent and not the tour operator direct.

If you have paid by credit card direct to an airline which has gone out of business, you can expect a refund from your credit card company. If you had paid a travel agent by credit card for the same air ticket, you would not be refunded. Credit card companies argue that the contract is not between the cardholder and the credit card company, the contract is with the travel agent, who should reimburse the customer.

9.2.5   Complaints

If the tour operator does not accept your legitimate complaint, and it is a member of ABTA, try the Personal Insurers Arbitration Scheme (PIAS) run by the Chartered Institute of Arbitrators (see DIRECTORY).

You can also complain to your local trading standards officer about misdescriptions in the brochure. If he or she successfully prosecutes the tour operator the court may make a compensation order in your favour. This will not be for as much as you might get through litigation, but it costs you nothing.

9.2.6   Accident abroad

If the holiday was a package holiday sold in the UK, then the holidaymaker can sue the tour operator in the UK even though the injury was suffered abroad. If it was not a package holiday the injured holiday maker will have to sue in the country where the injury occurred, unless the person causing the injury was also from the UK, e.g. if you are run over in France by a car driven by another British tourist driving on the wrong side of the road, you can sue him in this country; but if the car was being driven by a French driver you would have to claim compensation through the French legal system. See chapter on *The Legal System*, section 3.6.4.

The Foreign and Commonwealth Office has produced a leaflet on travelling and living in the European Union, which deals with rights and benefits when travelling in Europe, e.g. advice on your entitlement to free emergency health care anywhere in the EU and compensation if flights are overbooked. Telephone 020 7270 1500 for a copy.

9.2.7 Compensation

A honeymoon couple who contracted severe gastro-enteritis due to poor food hygiene at their hotel received substantial compensation from the tour operator, in the region of four times the price they had paid. But if it had been an ordinary family holiday rather than the special and one-off occasion of a honeymoon, the compensation would have been on a lesser scale.

Note also: even if you are entitled to compensation because the hotel or tour operator is at fault, you will not necessarily be able to reclaim the full cost of the holiday. For example, the cost of air travel to the resort may not be refunded if your complaint is about substandard accommodation.

9.2.8 When the tour company goes bust

If a holiday firm goes under and it is a member of ABTA, holidaymakers who have paid in advance can expect to receive their money back. Moreover, they will not be stranded away from home if they are already on holiday when their firm collapses. Under the EU Directive and new regulations, all tour organisers must now provide security against their going insolvent, so the problem of stranded holidaymakers should, it is hoped, be a thing of the past.

9.2.9 Money abroad

See *Traveller's cheques*, section 7.1.8 above. The Foreign and Commonwealth Office has produced a leaflet on Euro notes and coins, available free from banks, libraries and by telephoning 020 7270 1500.

9.3 Activity holidays

Following upon the death of four teenagers on a canoeing course in Dorset in 1993, legislation came into force in 1996 under which organisers of adventure activities for children are required to be licensed and to comply with certain safety regulations. The regulations are designed to tighten up standards considerably; however, they do not apply to such courses or facilities which are run for adults. Of course, the governing bodies of some sports, e.g. rock climbing, do lay down strong guidelines, though not all activities have a ruling body.

Before going on such a course or allowing your children to do so, make enquiries about the instructors' qualifications, the safety standards and the insurance cover of the organisers, and obtain full insurance cover yourself.

9.4 Timeshares

A large number of people every year buy timeshares, and the high-pressure (and often dubious) selling methods of the companies involved led to the passing of the Timeshare Act 1992.

9.4.1 Details of the Timeshare Act

This requires a timeshare company which offers you a contract to inform you in writing that:

a) You have the right to change your mind and withdraw from the contract.
b) You must receive a blank cancellation form.
c) You will be entitled to the return of your deposit.
d) You have 14 days from the date of the contract to exercise this right, so do not give in to pressure to confirm the agreement sooner.
e) If you do cancel, you can cancel any financing arrangements.

You must then repay the whole of any credit given to you within one month but you will not have to pay interest.

If you received no notification of your right to cancel, you can cancel the agreement at any time.

Failure on the companies' part to comply with the provisions of this Act will be an offence.

9.4.2 Limitations of Act

Beware: the provisions of this Act only apply to timeshare agreements entered into under British law, or where one of the parties signs the agreement on British soil; but in these circumstances it does apply even if the accommodation is abroad.

If you buy a timeshare abroad, you are bound by the laws of the country in which you have bought.

The text of a European Directive was adopted in October 1994 which gives buyers a cooling-off period of 10 days. No advance payments may be made within that period and buyers can withdraw without giving reasons. Spain, where most UK-owned timeshares are located, has implemented the Directive, as have all the other EU countries. Portugal's timeshare law pre-dates the Directive. Anyone thinking of buying a timeshare should first read the DTI guidance booklet *The Timeshare Guide*, available from the DTI's leaflet request line: tel. 020 7215 0344.

The Department of Trade and Industry has issued proposals to improve timeshare law to give consumers more protection and provide them with a clearer understanding of their rights.

In particular, there is concern over pressure-selling techniques and certain cases of the misuse of 'presentations' offering free gifts or holidays to the unwary. High-pressure sales teams can use these presentations to get round some of the current safeguards on timeshare purchase, e.g. an automatic right to cancel.

Misdescription applies to timeshare properties as much as to any other contract for sale.

☞ *You bought a timeshare property from a firm in England. The property, in Tenerife, was described as a 'luxury development' with sensational views. When you arrive, you find that the building is on a bare hillside overlooking a building site and the builders' ablution block.*

You should report the matter to your local trading standards department for a criminal prosecution for making false statements, as well as suing the firm itself for damages. A successful prosecution always assists in a civil case for damages.

In a similar case, the disappointed customer was awarded by the court one-third of the price he had paid plus £1,050 for the distress and disappointment of a ruined holiday.

DIRECTORY
GOODS AND SERVICES

Advertising Standards Authority
Brook House
2–16 Torrington Place
London WC1E 7HW
Tel. 020 7580 5555
www.asa.org.uk

Air Transport Users' Council *(AUC)*
CAA House
45–59 Kingsway
London WC2B 6TE
Tel. 020 7240 6061
www.auc.org.uk

Association of British Credit Unions Limited
Holyoake House
Hanover Street
Manchester M60 0AS
Tel. 0161 832 3694
www.abcul.org

Association of British Insurers *(ABI)*
51 Gresham Street
London EC2V 7HQ
Tel. 020 7600 3333
www.abi.org.uk

Association of British Travel Agents *(ABTA)*
68–71 Newman Street
London W1T 3AH
Tel. 020 7637 2444
www.abta.com

BBC Radio Consumer Programmes:
Radio 4 *Action Line*
Tel. 08700 100 444

BBC Television Consumer Programmes:
Watchdog Information Line
Tel. 08700 107 070

British Bankers' Association
Pinners Hall
105–108 Old Broad Street
London EC2N 1EX
Tel. 020 7216 8800
www.bba.org.uk

British Holiday and Home Parks Association Ltd
Chichester House
6 Pullman Court
Great Western Road
Gloucester GL1 3ND
Tel. 01452 526911
www.ukparks.com

British Insurance Brokers' Association *(BIBA)*
BIBA House
14 Bevis Marks
London EC3A 7NT
Tel. 020 7623 9043
www.biba.org.uk

British Standards Institution
Information Services
389 Chiswick High Road
London W4 4AL
Tel. 020 8996 9000
www.bsi-global.com

Building Societies' Ombudsman
– *see* Financial Ombudsman Service

The Chartered Institute of Arbitrators
12 Bloomsbury Square
London WC1A 2LP
Tel. 020 7421 7444
www.arbitrators.org

Commission for Local Administration in England
21 Queen Anne's Gate
London SW1H 9BU
Tel. 020 7915 3210
www.lgo.org.uk

Commission for Local Administration in Wales
Derwent House
Court Road
Bridgend CF31 1BN
Tel. 01656 661325
www.ombudsman-wales.org

Community Legal Services
(Directory Line) Tel. 0845 608 1122

Consumers' Association
2 Marylebone Road
London NW1 4DF
Tel. 020 7486 5544
www.which.net

Consumer Credit Association (UK) *(CCA)*
Queens House
Queens Road
Chester CH1 3BQ
Tel. 01244 312044
www.ccauk.org

Consumer Credit Trade Association
Suite 8
The Wool Exchange
10 Hustlergate
Bradford
West Yorkshire BD1 1AE
Tel. 01274 390 380
www.ccta.co.uk

**Department of the Environment,
Food and Rural Affairs** *(DEFRA)*
17 Smith Square
London SW1P 3JR
Tel. 020 7270 8080
www.defra.gov.uk

**Department of Trade & Industry
Consumer and Competition Policy**
1 Victoria Street
London SW1H 0ET
Tel. 020 7215 5000
www.dti.gov.uk

Direct Marketing Association (UK) Ltd
DMA House
70 Margaret Street
London W1W 8SS
Tel. 020 7291 3300
www.dma.org.uk

Direct Selling Association
29 Floral Street
London WC2E 9DP
Tel. 020 7497 1234
www.dsa.org.uk

Disability Rights Commission
DRC Helpline
Freepost MID 02164
Stratford-upon-Avon CV37 9HY
Tel. 0845 622 533
www.drc-gb.org

Experian Limited
Consumer Operations
PO Box 8000
Nottingham NG1 5GX
Tel. 01159 410 888
www.experian.com

Federation of Information and Advice Centres
12th Floor
New London Bridge House
25 London Bridge Street
London SE1 9ST
Tel. 020 7407 4070
www.fiac.org.uk

Federation of Small Businesses
2 Catherine Place
London SW1 6HR
Tel. 020 7592 8100
www.fsb.org.uk

Financial Ombudsman Service
South Quay Plaza
183 Marsh Wall
London E14 9SR
Tel. 0845 080 1800
www.financial-ombudsman.org.uk

Food Standards Agency
Aviation House
125 Kingsway
London WC2B 6NH
Tel. 020 7276 6000
www.food.gov.uk

General Medical Council
178 Great Portland Street
London WIN 6JE
Tel. 020 7580 7642
www.gmc-uk.org

Health Service Ombudsman for England
11/13th Floor
Millbank Tower
Millbank
London SW1P 4QP
Tel. 020 7217 4051
www.ombudsman.uk

Independent Television Commission
33 Foley Street
London W1W 7TL
Tel. 020 7255 3000
www.itc.org.uk

Information Commissioner
(formerly Office of the Data Protection Registrar)
Wycliffe House
Water Lane
Wilmslow
Cheshire SK9 5AF
Tel. 01625 545700
www.dataprotection.gov.uk

Law Centres Federation *(offices nationwide)*
Duchess House
18–19 Warren Street
London W1P 5LR
Tel. 020 7380 0133
www.lawcentres.org.uk

Local Authorities Coordinators of Regulatory Services
10 Albert Embankment
London SE1 7SP
Tel. 020 7840 7200
www.lacors.ov.uk

London Transport Users' Committee
6 Middle Street
London EC1A 7JA
Tel. 020 7505 9000
www.ltuc.org.uk

Mailing Preference Service
DMA House
70 Margaret Street
London W1W 8SS
Tel. 020 7291 3300
www.mpsonline.org.uk

Mediation UK
Alexander House
Telephone Avenue
Bristol BS1 4BS
Tel. 0117 904 6661
www.mediationuk.org.uk

National Association of Estate Agents
Arbon House
21 Jury Street
Warwick CV34 4EH
Tel. 01926 496800
www.naea.co.uk

National Consumer Council
20 Grosvenor Gardens
London SW1W ODH
Tel. 020 7730 3469
www.ncc.org.uk

National Consumer Credit Federation
98–100 Holme Lane
Sheffield S6 4JW
Tel. 01142 348101

Office for the Supervision of Solicitors
Victoria Court
8 Dormer Place
Leamington Spa
Warwickshire CV32 5AE
Tel. 01926 820 082
www.oss.lawsociety.org.uk

Office of Fair Trading
Fleetbank House
2–6 Salisbury Square
London EC4Y 8JY
Tel. 020 7211 8000
www.oft.gov.uk
Free leaflets available

OFTEL
50 Ludgate Hill
London EC4M 7JJ
Tel. 0845 714 5000
www.oftel.gov.uk

Ombudsman for Estate Agents
Beckett House
4 Bridge Street
Salisbury
Wiltshire SP1 2LX
Tel. 01722 333306
www.oea.co.uk

Personal Insurance Arbitration Service –
see Financial Ombudsman Service

Registry Trust Limited
173–175 Cleveland Street
London W1T 6QR
Tel. 020 7380 0133

Retail Motor Industry Federation
201 Great Portland Street
London WIW 5AB
Tel. 020 7580 9122
www.rmif.co.uk

Royal Institution of Chartered Surveyors
12 Great George Street
London SW1P 3AD
Tel. 020 7222 7000
(Contact Centre) Tel. 0870 333 1600
www.rics.org.uk

Trading Standards Institute
3/5 Hadleigh Business Centre
351 London Road
Hadleigh
Essex SS7 2BT
Tel. 01702 559922
www.tradingstandards.gov.uk

11 WORKING FOR A LIVING (Part 1)

The laws which govern relations between employers and employees clearly reflect the social, political and economic attitudes of our times. They also reflect the changing perspective and policy views of the government of the day. Since the 1970s, major Acts of Parliament on employment law have been passed. Among the many matters which this enormous mass of legislation deals with, trade union law, discrimination in the workplace, and unfair dismissal have all been addressed.

In December 2000, the Government published a Green Paper: *Work & Parents: Competitiveness and Choice*, which emphasised the need for a flexible labour market and the desirability of bringing more working parents into the labour force. There has been much discussion about the difficulties experienced by parents in trying to juggle work with bringing up children, and the Employment Act 2002 has introduced changes intended to make life easier for working parents and lead to changes in the workplace culture. Most of the new rights are actually in force since April 2003 and together they represent the most far-reaching changes ever made to employment rules in relation to the family.

The impact of European law on our domestic labour-relations law also cannot be over-emphasised. The introduction of the Working Time Regulations 1998 gave rise to great debate amongst employers as to the effect these regulations would have, particularly on small businesses. The Working Time (Amendment) Regulations 2001 which came into force in 2001 tightened up the rules even further, granting employees the right to paid annual leave from the first day of employment. This will have a big impact on employers who employ casual/temporary employees and will impact on all employers who use a probationary period.

Important Acts of Parliament have been passed as a direct consequence of the UK's need to conform to its EC Treaty obligations. The Government has been grappling with the need to implement the EU Anti-Discrimination Directive. The aim is to protect against discrimination on grounds of age, race, disability, sexual orientation, religion and belief. The main provisions of the Race Relations Act 1976 and the Disability Discrimination Act 1995 already comply but the main features of the proposed UK legislation include a shift in the burden of proof, the prohibition of victimisation, and single definitions of indirect discrimination and harassment. The changes must be implemented by 19 July 2003 and 2 December 2006 respectively.

One of the most controversial debates is regarding age discrimination. By 2 December 2006 legislation will be in place preventing mandatory retirement and introducing a 'justification' defence. This will supplement the existing Code of Practice on Age Diversity in Employment.

In this chapter we look at:
- whether you are an employee or a self-employed person
- employment tribunals
- employment agencies
- starting work – written terms
- an employer's duties
- an employee's duties
- continuous service
- privacy in the workplace.

1 EMPLOYMENT OR SELF-EMPLOYMENT?

Before you are subject to the rights and liabilities of the employer–employee relationship, you must show that you are an actual employee. If you are an employee, you may, for example, be able to claim unfair dismissal, or receive redundancy payments. A lump sum paid on termination of employment could be tax free, which would not be the case if the payment was merely an incident of self-employment. There may also be VAT consequences as the services of an employee as such are outside its scope. Employers are also likely to suffer the consequences of getting it wrong, since they are liable to account for PAYE and national insurance contributions from their employees.

Employment status is not a matter of choice. Parties cannot simply decide to treat working arrangements as either self-employment or employment. The circumstances of the agreement determine how it is to be treated. People are self-employed if they are in business on their own account and have responsibility for its success or failure. There are a number of indicators as to whether or not this is the case.

1.1   Indicators of self-employment

- you supply the materials, plant or heavy equipment needed to do the job
- you bid for the job and will bear any additional cost if your bid is too low or something goes wrong
- you have a right to hire other people who answer to you and are paid by you to do the job
- you may be paid an agreed amount for the job regardless of how long it takes, or be paid according to some formula other than a salary, such as per hour; or, for example, as a freelance journalist you may be paid per 1,000 words
- within an overall deadline you have a right to decide how and when the work will be done
- you agree that if you are unable to do the work personally, someone else can do it in your stead.

1.2   Indicators of employment

- you have to carry out the work personally
- you work wholly or mainly for one business and work is carried out at the premises of the business
- you do not risk your own money and there is no possibility that you will suffer a financial loss
- you have no business organisation – for example, yard, stock, materials or employees
- you work a set number of hours in a given period and are paid by the hour, day, week or month
- someone else has the right to control what you have to do – where, when and how it is to be done – even if such control is rarely practised
- payment for overtime, and over holidays or during sickness.

The Revenue look with concern on those who claim to be 'self-employed' but do all their work for one company. Generally its enquiries are targeted against contract workers, e.g. in the media or computer fields, who have left their present employment, call themselves 'consultants' and then set up a 'service company', essentially working for the same firm as before and receiving the same remuneration but using the company to receive their fees as a means of mitigating their tax burden.

☞ *You are an IT contractor working through your own service company for a large retail company client. You work as part of the customer support team and your team leader tells you what duties to carry out each day at any particular time.*

    The extensive control that the client has over you is a strong pointer to employment. A significant factor is the client's right to move you from task to task and to specify how the work should be done. Moreover the client can control when and where the work is carried out.

☞ *You work through your own company as a contract engineer. The company is in business and has many similar arrangements with different clients. If you are unable to attend on a particular day, you are entitled to provide a substitute engineer in your place. You are generally employed to provide an expert service to clients with little engineering expertise.*

    The company has a business organisation and has many different clients and you control who will attend each day and can provide a substitute as a matter of course. These are strong pointers to self-employment.

You can ask the Inland Revenue to look at your contract and to advise you. Requests can be made by post to IR35, Penhaligon House, Trinity Street, St Austell, Cornwall, PL25 5BA. The Inland Revenue also issue leaflets such as *Employed or Self-employed?* (IR56) available free from local offices.

1.3 Home working

There is a growing trend towards home working which prompts the question whether home workers are employed or self-employed. It does not mean that you are self-employed just because you work from home. As in any other circumstances, it will depend on the specific conditions of your employment. The words 'self-employed' or 'employee' are not defined by statute but have emerged through cases coming before the courts. In deciding the precise nature of a particular working relationship, all the relevant facts must be considered in detail. It is then a question of standing back and taking a view of the circumstances as a whole.

☞ *You have been working for your employer for three years when you are asked to work from home. Your employer carries out a risk-assessment exercise at your home and instals all the equipment necessary for you to carry out your duties as before. You are also supplied with a computer and the company pays for a business telephone line.*

You will still be regarded as an employee protected by the employment legislation intended to safeguard your rights, and are entitled to sick pay, holiday pay, overtime or unemployment benefit as required.

☞ *You have been working in an office-based job but do not wish to continue commuting fifty miles to work each day. You would also like to take on a wider variety of projects with other organisations. You tender your resignation but your employers ask you to continue working for them on a freelance basis. You agree to work three days a week from home but indicate that you will also be taking on work from other organisations as well. You set up an office in your spare room at home and supply your own equipment. You organise your workload to suit yourself so long as you meet agreed deadlines. You are paid an agreed fee for each job you undertake. You acquire a number of different contracts and take on an assistant to help you. You pay the assistant and direct his workload each day.*

In these circumstances you will probably be regarded as self-employed. You are working for several clients and have ultimate control over your operation. You supply your own equipment and are entitled to any profits as well as bearing any losses. Also if anything goes wrong you have to correct it at your own expense.

2 EMPLOYMENT TRIBUNALS

Tribunals were set up with the precise aim of providing employees with a ready recourse to law to settle their disputes. Industrial tribunals were renamed 'employment tribunals' by the Employment Rights (Dispute Resolution) Act 1998. Thus, once you have established that you are an employee (see section 1.2 above), should you have a legally-recognised grievance with your employer you are entitled to apply to a tribunal.

However, the 1998 Act also introduced internal procedures and binding arbitration as a means of resolving employment disputes. These developments complement the attitude of unions and employers to employee relations in a modern environment where it is generally thought to be preferable to have the assistance of a third party in resolving problems rather than using an adversarial process where there are seen to be winners and losers. The Government is encouraging the use of alternative dispute resolution to ease the burden on employment tribunals.

2.1 Jurisdiction

Employment tribunals are creatures of statute. They are made up of a legally qualified chairman and two lay members who are encouraged to make use of their knowledge of industry, and their practical experience, in reaching their decisions. Each member's vote carries equal weight and most decisions are unanimous. They can only deal with claims up to £25,000 arising from breaches of contract. If your claim is for more than this, you will have to go to the County Court or the High Court.

There has been growing concern about the number of applications to employment tribunals which have increased threefold since 1990, and reforms are to be introduced in 2003 to reduce the number of applications (see section 2.5 below).

2.2 Time Limits

As a general rule the time limits within which claims can be brought are strictly enforced. These are generally three months from the date of termination of employment, or three months from the date of the act complained of. For example, if you feel your employer has discriminated against you on racial grounds but you do not wish to leave your job as you live in an area of high unemployment, you will have three months in which to lodge a complaint, from the date of the discriminatory act.

However in some exceptional circumstances there is provision for the possible extension of time limits where it was not reasonably practicable to comply with the time limit or where it is just and equitable to hear the claim outside the normal limit.

☞ *Within a fortnight of leaving employment, you suffer a nervous breakdown. You are unable to give instructions to lodge a complaint to an employment tribunal.*

It is in such a situation that a tribunal may decide to exercise its discretion to grant an extension of time. It may do so at a preliminary hearing to consider why your application was late.

Different time limits, generally six months, apply to redundancy payments. Special rules also apply when there is dismissal for union and other work-related activities.

Warning note: always seek advice on time limits (see DIRECTORY at the end of the next chapter for HelpLine telephone numbers).

2.3 Costs

You may be able to get some immediate legal help in making your application to a tribunal under the Community Legal Services Funding [formerly legal aid]. You would not get funding for a lawyer to represent you at the hearing unless he or she took on the case on a *pro bono* basis (see the chapter on *The Legal System*) or under a conditional fee agreement.

Even where an employer is represented by a lawyer, you would not be expected to pay the other side's costs if you lost your case.

The Employment Tribunals Field Support Unit issues a helpful booklet: *How to apply to an Employment Tribunal* (see DIRECTORY at the end of the next chapter), which also contains an application form. The booklet is usually available at Jobcentres or Citizens' Advice Bureaux or you can phone the Employment Tribunal Enquiry Line: 0845 795 9775.

You could enter into a conditional fee agreement if your solicitor is prepared to conduct your case before a tribunal on this basis (see chapter on *The Legal System*, section 3.4).

2.4 Tribunal workload on unfair dismissal claims

Over forty per cent of the current annual employment tribunal case-load of 130,000 concerns unfair dismissal.

The law endeavours to strike a balance between the needs of the workforce to be protected against arbitrary and unfair dismissal and the needs of management to run their businesses efficiently (see also the chapter *Working for a Living (Part 2)*, section 4.2).

An ACAS arbitration scheme was launched in May 2001 to offer a voluntary alternative to the employment tribunal procedure. It applies only to cases of alleged unfair dismissal and should help to ease the workload of employment tribunals (see the chapter on *The Legal System*).

The Government set up a taskforce to consider ways to make employment tribunals more efficient and reduce the case overload which threatens to bring the system to a halt. The task force has produced a report which recommends a greater use of alternative dispute resolution, with cases only coming into the tribunal system as a last resort. In particular, voluntary mediation and arbitration could be more widely used in discrimination cases, which are often difficult to settle in tribunal. This would enable tribunals to concentrate on cases where they can make a difference. The Government is still considering the report.

2.5 Changes to Tribunal System

Meanwhile, the Employment Act 2002 introduced a package of changes intended to reduce the number of cases going to the employment tribunals. Consultation is still taking place about the changes to be published as regulations in 2003.

To discourage frivolous cases, under the regulations employment tribunals will be authorised to

- take account of a party's ability to pay when deciding whether to award costs against him or her;
- order a party's representative to meet the costs as a result of his/her conduct of the case;
- order one party to pay the costs of the other party for time spent preparing its case.

A fixed period of conciliation is being introduced, during which no hearing date before the tribunal can be fixed and after which ACAS will have the power to conciliate (though not a duty). Some cases will be determinable without a hearing. Weak cases might be struck out at a pre-hearing review.

3 ON ENTERING EMPLOYMENT – EMPLOYMENT AGENCIES

Many people approach an employment agency when they first look for a job. The law has laid down a legal framework which governs employment agencies. Updated regulations have been proposed governing the conduct of employment agencies which should come into effect in 2003, subject to Parliamentary approval. The overhaul of the existing legislative framework is designed to provide simpler, clearer regulations which are relevant to the labour market of today and the future.

3.1 The legal framework

Until 1995 employment agencies had to register and obtain a licence from the Department of Employment. This is no longer required. However regulations still lay down minimum standards of conduct, enforced by the possibility of criminal fines. In the last resort, employment tribunals have power to make prohibition orders on application by the Secretary of State if an employment agency fails to maintain proper standards.

The DTI has a dedicated website which explains the rules relating to employment agencies: *www.dti.gov.uk/er/agency/regs-pl971.htm.*

An explanatory booklet which sets out the standards of conduct expected of Employment Agencies is available from Jobcentres or from the DTI Employment Agency Standards Office. The DTI Inspectorate has a public helpline number with calls charged at local rates: 0645 555 105.

3.1.1 Acting for the employer

The agency acts for the employer in finding suitable applicants and is entitled to commission:

- only from the employer, and
- only where it has introduced the successful candidate.

3.1.2 Must an employee pay commission too?

A job applicant cannot be asked to pay an employment agency for finding a post: to demand any such fee is a criminal offence.

☞ *You approach an employment agency looking for a job. You are asked to complete an appraisal form and to pay a fee to the agency as part of the exercise of assessing your suitability for work and their subsequent invitation to register with them. Is the agency entitled to charge the fee?*

Such a fee is unlawful as the assessment is part of the process of seeking employment for which the agency must not charge a fee.

The exceptions to this rule are:

a) in the fields of entertainment and modelling, where a fee can be charged to the client, but cannot then also be charged to the employer (this is to be extended in 2003 to include stunt arrangers, stage managers, producers, choreographers and theatre designers); and
b) where *au pair* work abroad is sought, when an applicant can be charged once a job has been arranged.

In all other cases the agency must look exclusively to the employer for payment.

Note: the agency can however charge for any other services it provides to candidates, such as job counselling, or refresher courses.

☞ *Your daughter is looking for a secretarial post. She registered with an employment agency. She has been told that she will need to get her typing up to speed and that she cannot be put forward for a job until she has completed one of the agency's WP courses.*

The agency is entitled to charge her if she takes on their course. However, an applicant cannot be required to take up one of these paid services before the agency will look for a job for her.

Under the new rules, provision is made for agencies to charge applicants a fee in some circumstances such as where the agency is connected with the potential employer, so long as it informs the applicant of the relationship before providing work-finding services.

3.1.3   Agency worker

In the area of agency workers, as well as of 'temping', an employment agency itself can employ the temp, paying wages, holiday and sickness pay. The fee charged by the agency to the businesses using the temp will then reflect an amount covering the wages and the administration costs of the agency. In each case, it is a question of fact and the degree of control whether a person is employed by the agency or the employer.

☞ *You found a part-time job as a telephonist through an employment agency. The agency arranged for payment by the hour. After you had been working for two years, the company asked the agency to terminate the engagement. You want to make a complaint of unfair dismissal against the company. You are told that you are not the company's 'employee'.*

In a similar case the Court of Appeal held that – looking at the situation as a whole – the work relationship, in reality, existed between the employee and the company and not with the agency.

3.1.4   Details of work

An applicant should not rely on an employment agency to provide all relevant information about the job and the remuneration before committing him or herself to the employer, but should obtain such details from the employer direct (see section 4 immediately below).

Do remember: an employer would not be bound by inaccurate information about a job furnished by an agency.

Under the new rules, before introducing or supplying a suitable applicant the agency/employment business should obtain, where applicable, sufficient information concerning the potential employer's business.

Warning: under the proposed amended regulations, an agency is under a duty to act where it receives information concerning the unsuitability of the applicant to carry out the job once he/she is in post.

4   STARTING WORK – WRITTEN TERMS

It is clearly in the interests of both employer and employee to understand at the outset of their relationship, the terms and conditions of employment.

The legal relationship between employer and employee is one of contract. Both parties are bound by the agreed terms. A contract of employment need not be in writing, although contracts of apprenticeship must be. However, employees are entitled by law to have their terms of employment set down in a written statement. The statement is not a contract in itself but it may be used to establish what has been agreed in the contract of employment (see booklet: *Contracts of Employment* (PL810 (Rev6)) available free from the DTI or online *www.dti.gov.uk*).

The House of Lords has held that an implied legal obligation to promote 'trust and confidence' between employer and employee must be written into every employment contract. Lord Nicholls said that an employer was under a general obligation not to act in a way likely to undermine the trust and confidence required if the employment relationship is to continue as envisaged in the contract.

Do note: all employees are entitled to a written statement regardless of hours worked provided that they are employed for more than one month. Contracts must be issued within two months of the employee's start date.

4.1 Principal statement

These terms must state, in a single document:

a) the parties to the contract of employment
b) the date of commencement
c) continuity of service, i.e. whether employment with a previous employer is to count as part of the employee's continuous service and the date on which such a continuous period started (see also section 7 below)
d) job title
e) place of work
f) rate and frequency of pay
g) hours of work
h) holiday entitlement and holiday pay.

4.2 Other written terms

a) sick pay
b) pension rights
c) notice period
d) disciplinary and grievance procedures
e) details of any collective agreements
f) where employment is temporary, the date it is to end.

If an employee is based overseas for longer than one month, the employer must also include:

a) the duration of employment overseas
b) details of transport provision to and from Britain
c) the currency in which the salary is being paid
d) details of any relocation allowance.

Note: these details can be given in instalments. An employer who, together with any associated employers, has fewer than 20 employees is not required to give employees a full note on disciplinary procedure. However they must give the name of the person to whom the employee should go with any grievance.

4.3 Time limits

The legislation sets down the time in which:

• a statement must be served
• a statement's terms can be altered.

4.3.1 Serving a statement

The statement of terms and conditions must be furnished to employees within two months of starting work.

4.3.2 Changing the terms

Employees must be notified of any change in the terms not later than one month after the change is made.

4.4 Failure to provide a statement

If an employee is not supplied with a statement, or is given an incomplete statement, or disputes the accuracy of the statement, he or she can go to an employment tribunal which can determine what particulars should have been provided.

Do beware: there are time limits. If the employment has terminated, a reference to the tribunal must be made within three months from the end of the employment.

4.5   References to other documents

There can be a reference to a collective agreement or to a statute for notice periods, details of sick pay and disciplinary procedures, but such documents must be made reasonably accessible to the employees.

Do remember: if you are employed for less than one month, none of these provisions apply.

4.5.1   Fixed Term Contracts

In 1999 the EU adopted the Fixed Term Work Directive to improve the lot of fixed-term workers by applying the principle of non-discrimination to fixed-term contracts and preventing abuse through the use of successive fixed-term contracts.

4.6   Non-Discrimination

The Directive was incorporated into UK law from 1 October 2002 after which fixed-term employees have the right not to be treated less favourably than comparable permanent employees. The rules apply specifically to employees as defined in the Employment Rights Act 1996 rather than to the wider class of 'workers'. Agency workers and apprentices are also excluded. The position of these workers is currently being reviewed and the rights may be extended to include them in the future.

Less favourable treatment can be in connection with levels of pay, bonuses, holidays, pensions, qualifying periods for benefits and access to permanent employment.

You can no longer be asked to waive your right to a statutory redundancy payment. Any such waiver in your contract will be invalid if it was renewed on or after 1 October 2002.

An employer can justify less favourable treatment if the terms of the employment contract, taken as a whole, are at least as favourable as the terms of a comparable permanent employee contract (the 'package approach').

If you feel you have been treated less favourably than a comparable permanent employee, you can ask your employer for a written statement of reasons, which they must provide within 21 days. If you still feel you have been treated less favourably you can go through any internal grievance procedures. You can also make a complaint to an employment tribunal but you must do so within three months of finding a discrepancy in your terms of employment.

Note: if you are a fixed-term employee you have the right to be informed of any vacancies in your company and must have a reasonable opportunity to see details of the job, e.g. through an advertisement on a notice board or the intranet.

4.7   Anti-abuse

Under the new anti-abuse rule, if you have a fixed-term contract renewed, or you are re-engaged on a new fixed-term contract after you have already been employed for at least four years, the new contract will take effect as a permanent contract of employment.

If you consider that you should be regarded as a permanent employee under this rule, you have the right to ask your employer for a written statement confirming your status. A response is required within 21 days and should include any reasons for refusing to give the confirmation sought. If you are dissatisfied by the response, you may apply to an employment tribunal for a declaration that you are a permanent employee.

Note: if you think you may be dismissed because you are about to qualify for rights under the anti-abuse rules or because you are trying to exercise such rights, any such dismissal will automatically be regarded as unfair (see *Working for a Living (Part 2)*, section 4).

5   AN EMPLOYER'S DUTIES

There are certain general duties which an employer owes to all employees. These need not be written into the contract but are implied by law. They include the following:

* the obligation to pay an employee for work done
* the obligation to treat the employee fairly
* the obligation to take reasonable care for employees' health and safety (see chapter on *Accidents*, section 7)

- the obligation to provide equal treatment for men and women in an 'equality clause' (see the chapter *Working for a Living (Part 2)*, section 1.1.1(a)).

5.1 Implied duty to pay

An employer is clearly obliged to pay an employee for work done. The amount must be specified in an itemised pay statement which must be provided to an employee by law. The statement must show gross pay and take-home pay, with amounts and reasons for all variable deductions. Fixed deductions must also be shown with detailed amounts and reasons.

5.1.1 The minimum wage

A national minimum wage of £3.70 per hour (before deductions) was laid down for employees over 21 with a lower rate of £3.20 for 18 to 21-year-olds with effect from 1 October 2000. From 1 October 2002 the main rate for workers aged 22 and over was increased to £4.20 per hour. The development rate for 18 to 21-year-olds inclusive was increased to £3.60 per hour.

The Government asked the Low Pay Commission to continue to monitor and evaluate the impact of the minimum wage and to make recommendations, if appropriate, for changes to the rates, by the end of February 2003. It was asked to have regard to the wider economic and social implications; the likely effect on employment and inflation; the impact on costs and competitiveness of business; and the potential costs to industry and the Exchequer.

To check how the national minimum wage applies to you, use the TIGER interactive website at *www.dti.gov.uk/er/nmw*. For further information, or if you think you are being underpaid, telephone the National Minimum Wage helpline on 0845 6000 678.

In a recent case, the European Court of Human Rights ruled that a restaurant owner was entitled to count credit-card tips towards payment of a minimum wage to its waiters. The court ruled that waiters had no legal right to tips even if customers wished to give them the money in recognition of good service.

This ruling has been widely criticised and highlights the need for reform in this area as it does not reflect the reality of the situation in which customers presume that the waiter will get the tips intended for them in addition to their pay.

5.1.2 Sick pay

An employee has no statutory right to insist on being paid by his/her employer during absence on sick leave (apart from any rights to statutory sick pay).

☞ *You work for a national call service. It entails working at night so that your sleep patterns are disturbed and, during the day, you look after your infant. You become so run down that you go to see your doctor who says that you are suffering from anaemia and ought to take a couple of weeks off to recover. You wonder whether you are entitled to sick pay from your employer.*

While there is no right in law to insist on being paid, many employment contracts entitle the employee to full pay during at least a certain amount of time off for illness. If there is no express contractual term dealing with sick pay, there may be an implied term, depending on the relevant facts including the customs of the particular trade and the normal practice of the employer.

5.2 Implied duty to provide work?

There is no obligation on an employer to provide work for an employee so long as he or she is still being paid. However, a contract of employment can make provision for lay-off and short time working.

5.2.1 Lay-off

This can arise when an employee's pay depends on being provided with work and he or she is not entitled to be paid under the contract when no work is provided.

The question then arises of whether a lay-off is a temporary suspension from work or a dismissal with a prospect of re-engagement. If it lasts for more than four consecutive weeks, or more than six weeks in any thirteen weeks, an employee can give notice that he or she intends to claim redundancy.

5.2.2   Short-time working

This can arise when the amount of work required of an employee is reduced. However, short-time working only applies if less than half the normal week's wages is being earned. An employee can claim redundancy if four consecutive weeks of short-time working have elapsed or short-time working has been applied for six out of thirteen weeks.

Guarantee payments are available to compensate employees in the event of short-time working. Guarantee payments must be made to employees with at least one month's service, when they can normally expect work but no work is available.

An employee laid off in this way is entitled to receive a maximum of £17 per day (from 1 February 2002) for up to five working days in any period of three months. This figure is reviewed annually.

A fast-food chain paid out compensation to 900 of its employees who were told to take unpaid breaks when there were too few customers.

Do note: your employer does not have to make guarantee payments if:

- you have not worked for your employer for at least one month
- you unreasonably refuse to do suitable alternative work
- you fail to comply with your employers' reasonable request to make yourself available for work
- the lack of work is the result of a strike, lock-out, or other industrial action in which you or your fellow employees are involved.

5.2.3   Contractual rights are paramount

To sum up, the contract itself must allow for lay-offs or short-term working before an employer can resort to them.

☞   *You work for an advertising agency but business has fallen off badly in the recession. You go to your office every day but find yourself doing crossword puzzles for most of the day. Your employer says that he will be withholding some of your salary pending an upturn in business. He says that he is entitled to lay off staff or to insist on short-time working in view of the exigencies of his situation. You wonder what your position is.*

Even if no work is provided, your employer is under a general duty to pay you once you are willing and able to work. He has no automatic right to lay off staff or put them on short-time working and must have a contractual right to do so either by an express or implied term in the contract of employment. However, in recessionary times, staff will often accommodate their employers rather than see them go under!

5.2.4   No work

If an employer becomes insolvent the employment contract comes to an end. Employees should be entitled to wages owing to them and to redundancy pay (see the chapter *Working for a Living (Part 2)*, section 5 on *Redundancy*). If administrators carry on the business in order to realise its assets, they 'adopt' the contracts of employment. Employees' wages then take priority over the administrator's expenses.

If you are dismissed by your employer when the business becomes formally insolvent as defined by the legislation, you can get payments from the National Insurance Fund within limits. The amounts covered include:

- arrears of pay for a period of at least one week but not exceeding eight weeks in all
- holiday pay for a period of up to six weeks
- compensation for the employer's failure to give proper notice based on your statutory entitlement to notice
- any basic award of compensation for unfair dismissal.

Full details are contained in the DTI booklet *Your Rights if your Employer is Insolvent* (PL718 [Rev7]).

5.2.5   Transfer of business

If an undertaking (business) is transferred to a new employer, the employees who were employed by the old employer at the time of the transfer automatically become employees of the new employer as if their contracts of employment were originally made with the new employer. Employees are entitled to object to their contracts being transferred to the new employer.

Do note: if you do object you will usually lose the right to claim that you were dismissed unless you can show that the transfer would have involved a substantial and detrimental change in your working conditions.

☞ *Your company has been taken over and your employment contract was transferred to the new company. Your new employer is putting you under pressure to change your working hours but you want to continue as before. Can your employer insist that you comply with their demands?*

Under the Transfer of Undertakings and Protection of Employment (TUPE) Rules your contract still has basically all its terms and conditions as with your old employer. Your new employer cannot force you to change your terms and conditions. If they try to do so you may be entitled to claim breach of contract and constructive dismissal.

Your new employer could try to terminate your contract and offer you a position on new terms. Your employer must give you notice of such a decision and if they do not, you may claim breach of contract. If you had completed more than a year's service when the current contract ended, you might also be entitled to claim unfair dismissal. You will usually only be successful if you can show that the business transfer was the reason for the issue of a new contract.

If the change of working hours would put you at a disadvantage because of your sex, race or disability, you might also have grounds to claim discrimination.

5.2.6   Right to work in the UK

If an employer hires someone who has no legal right to work in the UK, they will be breaking the Asylum and Immigration Act 1996. You may have to show that you have the right to work in the UK by producing a national insurance number; a P45; a work permit; or the right stamp on your passport.

If you do not have the legal right to work in the UK, but an employer wants to hire you, they will usually have to apply for a work permit for you from Work Permits UK at the Immigration and Nationality Directorate of the Home Office.

5.3   Implied duty to treat employees properly

An employer is expected to treat his staff properly. This duty is implied in every contract of employment. The cases speak of a relationship of trust, confidence and respect. For example, an employer has failed to treat his or her employees properly when:

* in a big business with many employees, he or she has refused to allow an employee to leave the premises to deal with an emergency at home
* s/he has refused to give one employee an increase in salary awarded to all other members of staff.

☞ *Your boss has been humiliating you in front of your work colleagues. You feel quite persecuted and wish to resign. There is nothing in your contract of employment which specifies that you are to be treated with respect.*

The law will imply such a term in your contract on your behalf. Employers are not allowed to behave in an arbitrary or malicious manner towards employees.

To amount to a breach of the implied trust and confidence term in a contract, the employer's misconduct has to amount to constructive dismissal so that the employee is entitled to leave immediately, without any notice, on discovering it. The test is whether the employer's conduct was such that the employee could not reasonably be expected to tolerate it a moment longer once it was discovered.

For details of the Working Time Directive, see the chapter *Working for a Living (Part 2)*, section 6.4.

Do take heed: a code of practice has been introduced by the Data Protection Commissioner to stop employers intercepting e-mails and using CCTV cameras to keep watch on their workforce. New technology is viewed seriously as a threat to employees' personal privacy. See section 8.

5.3.1 Part-time workers

Part-time workers must not be treated less favourably than full-time employees. They are entitled to the same hourly rate of pay, access to company pension schemes, annual leave, maternity/parental leave (on a *pro rata* basis), contractual sick pay and access to training.

5.3.2 Young workers

The Government announced a consultation in June 2002 on proposals to introduce greater protection for young people in the workplace. The proposals under the Young Workers Directive relate to the working hours for those between minimum school-leaving age and their eighteenth birthday. Under the proposals the working time would be further limited to 40 hours a week, 8 hours in any one day; and night working prohibited between 10 pm–6 am or 11 pm–7 am.

5.4 Duty to ensure health and safety

An employer is under a duty in law to provide:

- competent staff
- a safe system of working
- proper, safe equipment and plant.

Details are discussed in the chapter on *Accidents* (see section 7).

Note: employers with five or more employees must issue a safety policy.

There are criminal sanctions for failure to provide a healthy and safe working environment.

☞ *You are 17-years-old and have just started working on a building site. Your supervisor asks you to move some bricks from one area of the site to another. You have been issued with a hard hat but you are only wearing trainers and no gloves. You are keen to please your boss but are worried about suffering injury as you are not properly dressed and are not sure how best to tackle the job.*

If you are 16 or 17, your employer must take account of your lack of experience, lack of awareness of the risks and lack of maturity. You cannot be asked to do work which is beyond your physical or psychological capacity or which could cause accidents due to your employer's insufficient attention to safety, or to your lack of experience or lack of training.

☞ *You have just started a new job in a fast-food restaurant and one night a fight starts between two men waiting to be served. The manager tells you to break up the fight and throw them out of the shop. They appear to be drunk and are very violent and you are concerned that if you intervene you will be injured. Your employer says it is part of the job and that if you do not do it you will be fired.*

Under the Employment Rights Act 1996 you have a legal right to refuse to do anything you believe will put you in serious and imminent danger, so long as you have a genuine reason for thinking it would harm you.

If you are asked to do something unsafe, say why you are refusing to do it. If your employer takes action against you, you can ask to see a senior manager and, if necessary, go through your employer's grievance procedure if it has one. As a last resort you can go to an employment tribunal. A tribunal cannot force your employer to give you your job back. It can order it to pay you compensation up to £50,000, although the average payment is around £3,000 (see also section 5.4.3 below).

5.4.1 Stress at work

As employees work longer and longer hours to meet the demands of their employers, work-related stress levels are rising and it is estimated by the Department of Health that working days lost to workplace stress cost British business over £5 million a year. More and more employees are suing their employers for illness caused by stress at work.

In a leading case a social worker with a heavy caseload suffered a nervous breakdown and was off work for several months. On his return his employer promised to provide him with assistance but it was never given and his workload increased. When he suffered a second breakdown he sued his employer. The court found that the employer was responsible for the second breakdown since it should have foreseen it as the consequence of failing to provide assistance and reduce his workload after the first breakdown. The case was eventually settled with the employer agreeing to pay £175,000 to the employee.

Note: most of the cases which come before the courts are union-backed. It is important for employers to be alert to stress in the workplace and to be aware of the size of settlements currently being awarded.

An employee who walks out of his or her job claiming that the pressure was unreasonable might have a claim for constructive dismissal against the employer. Also the operation of the Working Time Directive (see the chapter *Working for a Living (Part 2)*, section 6.4) and the Disability Discrimination Act (see *Working for a Living (Part 2)*, section 3) indicate how protection for employees is being strengthened.

In a variety of cases heard together, the Court of Appeal held that the ordinary principles of employer's liability applied to claims for psychiatric or physical injury or illness due to stress at work. The test is whether the harm to the particular employee was reasonably foreseeable. An employer is usually entitled to assume that the employee can withstand the normal pressures of the job. A claimant has to show that the employer's breach of duty caused the harm. Occupational stress is not enough.

5.4.2 Bullying

The issue of bullying, which used to be thought of as confined to the school playground, is now a common problem in the workplace. Although it is sometimes physical, bullying in the workplace is more often verbal or psychological, and can be very costly for employers through lost working time and absenteeism due to stress and ill health. In extreme cases bullying can lead to thoughts of suicide. Furthermore, bullying can lead to legal action against the employer.

It is not always easy to spot a bully at work but bullying can take a variety of forms; it spans a range of behaviour from talking about someone behind their back, taking advantage of positions of power by indulging in constant criticism, ignoring someone and not responding to their memos or returning their phone calls. On a more vocal level, it can descend to trading insults and shouting at the staff. A bully can also act to block a staff member's promotion. Forms of sexual or racial harassment are dealt with separately in the chapter *Working for a Living (Part 2)* sections 1.2.4 and 2.

Employers have a statutory duty to ensure the health, safety and welfare of employees and should have an anti-bullying policy which must be properly implemented. The policy should state that:

1) Bullying of any kind will not be tolerated.
2) Disciplinary action will follow on legitimate complaints.

Examples of unacceptable behaviour and how and where bullying might occur, e.g. through e-mail or memos etc., should be drawn to the attention of staff.

☞ *You are secretary in a large office and for some time your supervisor has been criticising your work for no apparent reason, shouting at you and making sarcastic comments in front of your colleagues. You have just found out that she has also been talking about you behind your back which has reduced your chances of the promotion you applied for. You enjoy your job and do not want to leave but have been feeling very ill due to the stress and pressure at work.*

Don't suffer in silence! You have the right to respect as an employee and should not accept this treatment as just part of your job. Keep a written record of times and places when you are bullied or feel harassed with details of what happened. Try to find someone who you can talk to about it within the firm and report the incidents to your supervisor. If it is your supervisor who is bullying you, approach the next level of management.

If you have to make a formal complaint and go through the grievance procedures, never go to any meetings without a friend or union representative as a witness. Bullying is very serious and your employer and/or the bully may be liable to a fine, to pay compensation or even be liable, in substantive cases, to a prison sentence – so it is in everyone's interests to put a stop to unacceptable behaviour.

5.4.3   Violence at work

One in five workers are subject to a violent attack or abuse at work every year just for doing their job. According to a TUC Report, nurses are most at risk with one in three attacked; second most at risk are those working in the security industry, followed by care workers and education and welfare workers. No one knows the real cost of violence at work but more than three million working days are lost due to violent incidents at work every year.

If there is a violent incident involving the workforce, employers need to respond quickly to avoid any long-term distress to employees, and they should plan how employees are to be provided with support, before any incidents occur.

Employers should conduct a risk assessment in order to protect their staff against violence or potentially violent incidents.

Employers should also consider:

- debriefing to allow victims to talk through their experience as soon as possible after the event
- time off work to enable victims to recover from their experience and, if needed, organise specialist counselling
- providing legal help in serious cases
- supporting other employees who may need guidance and reassurance to enable them to respond appropriately to the incident.

The Health and Safety Executive have published a guide: *Violence at Work – a Guide for Employers*, to assist employers (see DIRECTORY at end of next chapter). See also chapter on *Accidents*, section 7.

5.5   Providing references – is it a duty?

An employer is not under a duty to provide a reference for employees.

☞   *You have always worked conscientiously. You now wish to apply for a job with another company. You have asked several times for a reference but your employer has not written one out for you.*

    There is nothing you can do to insist upon being given a reference.

5.5.1   Reference must not be malicious

However, if an employer does provide a reference, he or she is then under a duty to ensure that the reference is not malicious. If it is malicious then the ordinary laws of defamation will apply.

☞   *An employee whom you disliked has left you and has applied for another post. You are asked to supply a reference.*

    As we have seen, an employer is not obliged to supply a reference. However, if you do write one, you are under an obligation to ensure that your personal dislike does not lead you into writing a reference which is actuated by malice. See also section 5.5.4 below.

5.5.2   Is an employer under a duty of care for inaccuracies?

If a statement in a reference is inaccurate because of a negligent mistake, then an employer is liable to his former employee if he fails to get a job because of the negligent misstatement.

Thus an employer owes an employee a duty to make sure that the reference contains only accurate statements.

5.5.3   Telephone references

Employers seeking a telephone reference should send the referee the following:

a) a copy of the personnel specification (describing the attributes required for the job); and
b) a job description (describing the nature of the job itself).

5.5.4   Giving a reference

Care should be taken in giving work references, especially for a less than satisfactory employee. Particular care needs to be taken about saying negative things which may be considered to border on defamation. It may be possible to turn a negative point into a positive. For example, if a former employee was not reliable when working independently it might be appropriate to say: 'works well under close supervision'. But still great care must be taken.

Note: refusal to give a reference for a specific employee when it is your practice to give references for other employees can be a cause for complaint.

Some basic facts are fairly safe to state:

• date and length of employment
• whether the employment was full-time or part-time
• a description of the employee's job
• the salary range.

Some basic steps for an employer to take, to avoid the pitfalls of reference-giving, are to:

• ask the leaving employee for written permission to respond to a reference check
• ensure that only authorised people provide employee references
• ask for reference check requests to be supplied in writing, and respond in writing
• keep a record of job related comments.

5.5.5   Employers' liability insurance

Hundreds of people suffering from occupational diseases and injuries are reportedly being denied compensation from employers because they cannot trace their employers' insurers despite a Government Code designed to tackle the problem.

In 1999-2000, out of 1,062 inquiries made by claimants to the Association of British Insurers (ABI), liability policies were traced in only a quarter of cases. Failure to track down the correct employer insurance policy at the time the disease is contracted or the injury incurred means that claimants are unable to claim compensation.

The voluntary Code of Practice, drawn up by the Government, the ABI and the non-marine associations at Lloyd's, requests insurers to keep employers' liability policy records, to search the policies and ensure all searches of future policies are made as easy as possible.

Note: it appears that even many lawyers are unaware of the Code. Be sure to submit further inquires if you are unsuccessful on the first attempt. See also chapter on *Accidents*, section 7.2.2.

6   EMPLOYEE'S DUTIES

Employees have a general duty to:

• carry out their tasks, and
• conduct themselves in such a way as to serve their employer's interests.

They are also under a duty to keep secret their employers' confidential information irrespective of whether there is an express contractual term (see section 6.3 below). However the most reliable means of protecting confidentiality is by virtue of an express confidentiality clause in the standard employment contract.

6.1   Obeying orders

All lawful and reasonable orders should be carried out with reasonable skill and care.

6.1.1   Illegal orders

An employee is not under a duty to obey a plainly illegal order – such as falsifying the accounts or driving a vehicle with faulty brakes. (See also the chapter *Working for a Living (Part 2)*, section 2.6, where an employee received instructions that were in breach of the race discrimination legislation.)

6.1.2   Unreasonable orders

An employee is under a duty to obey reasonable orders. What is an unreasonable order? This is much harder to ascertain than establishing an illegal order. What is reasonable to one person may appear quite unreasonable to another.

6.2   Part performance

If an employee refuses to carry out contractual duties, an employer can withhold payment as long as it had been made clear that a partial performance would be unacceptable.

☞ *You have informed your employer that you are no longer prepared to work on Saturday mornings although your contract specifies that you have to work one Saturday morning in four. You come to work on Mondays to Fridays as usual. Your month's pay in its entirety has been withheld.*

Your position will depend on whether you knew in advance that a refusal to work on Saturday mornings would be regarded as a non-performance of your contractual duties.

6.3 Confidentiality

6.3.1 Present employees

Employees are under a general duty not to disclose confidential information relating to their employers' affairs which they might obtain in the course of their work. (For the definition of 'confidential information' see section 6.3.3 below.)

They are also under a duty not to assist a competitor of their employer. This is the employees' side of the duty to ensure that the relationship between employees and employers is one of trust.

6.3.2 Ex-employees

The question is what happens when an employee leaves his or her employer? How much of the employer's confidentiality should s/he still observe?

The answer is that confidential information is not to be disclosed but that employees can use general information they have acquired during their employment.

6.3.3 Confidential information

Whether a particular piece of information comes within this duty of confidence depends on the following factors.

6.3.3(a) Nature of job

Certain jobs where confidential information is dealt with on a regular basis would indicate a high obligation of confidentiality. This might even be written into the employment contract.

6.3.3(b) Nature of information

Not all information obtained in the course of employment is of equal weight. Distinctions can and must be drawn between trade secrets and other information.

Trade secret
The information must be a trade secret, or material so highly confidential that it requires the same protection as a trade secret. How is a trade secret determined?

Two factors are likely to be taken into consideration:
a) the employer's attitude
b) the separability of the information.

If the employer stresses the confidential nature of the information it might show that s/he regards it as a trade secret.

If a particular piece of information cannot be separated from a package of information, which is generally not confidential, it might throw doubt on its designation as a trade secret.

6.3.4 Patent or invention

Any patent or invention an employee has made – provided it was in the course of normal duties and s/he has a special obligation to an employer because of those duties – belongs to the employer. However, an employee may still be entitled to be compensated for any 'outstanding benefit' an employer receives as a result of the patent.

6.3.5 Preventing wrongful use of information

An ex-employee is not at liberty to use information regarded as confidential to set up a rival business or to help a competitor. An ex-employer can ask the court for an injunction to prevent such misuse. If the court thinks an employer has made out a case, an injunction can be granted, whether there is an express covenant not to disclose confidential information, or a covenant which the court implies.

6.3.5(a) Express covenants

In general, express restrictive covenants are there to protect confidential information which an ex-employee has acquired – for example, from an employer's mailing lists. To protect their business, employers also often insist in their contracts of employment that their employees sign a covenant not to compete with them if they leave – 'restrictive covenants' (or 'covenants in restraint of trade' as they are also called); see below, section 6.4.

6.3.5(b) Implied covenants

Even if an employee has not entered into an express covenant with an employer, s/he may be restrained from using confidential information acquired during the course of employment. This is because every contract of employment contains an implied term not to use or disclose such information.

However, in such a case, an ex-employee is entitled to approach customers, suppliers or contacts of a former employer although s/he must not make any list or memorise the names of customers etc. before s/he leaves. That would be in breach of the implied duty of fidelity during the subsistence of the contract of employment.

6.4 Restrictive covenants

The law realises that employers want to protect their business against competition. At the same time, there is a strong perception that ex-employees are entitled to make a living as best they can. Their chances of doing so should not be unfairly curtailed by their relationship with an ex-employer, so a restrictive covenant will only be enforceable if it can be shown that it is reasonable and that it is in the public interest.

Restrictions are more likely to be regarded as unenforceable if their terms are very wide.

6.4.1 The restriction must be reasonable

As a general rule, the parties themselves are regarded as the best judges of what is reasonable between them. Two key factors in assessing reasonableness are time and distance.

6.4.1(a) Time

A contract term for a year would be regarded as reasonable whereas a 7-year restraint would be regarded as unreasonable – depending on the type of contract.

☞ *You were a director of a mail-order firm in charge of preparing a catalogue. You left and went to work for a rival. Your former employers have applied to the court for an injunction to prevent you working for their competitors on the ground that you signed an agreement that you would not join any rival firm for 12 months.*

In this case, the restriction could be regarded as reasonable for a person of your seniority.

6.4.1(b) Distance

☞ *You are a solicitor and have a contract with your firm, which is in the City, not to practise within a 10-mile radius of the City of London for five years if you leave. You are now offered a job with another firm of solicitors situated in the West End of London.*

It is likely that the court would consider the density of the population as a factor in deciding whether the restraint is reasonable. A 10-mile radius restriction might be a more reasonable term in a contract between solicitors in a small country town than in one between London solicitors.

6.4.2 The restriction must be in the public interest

In deciding what is in the public interest, the courts will always favour the right of someone to find work. They will protect an employer's legitimate interest – but only insofar as that is necessary and specific.

6.4.3   The restriction must be enforced in ordinary courts of law

The rights and duties of an employer and employee in relation to restrictive covenants are only enforceable by bringing proceedings in the ordinary courts. They do not involve employment tribunal hearings.

7   CONTINUOUS SERVICE

7.1   Rights dependent on continuous service

As we have seen, many of an employee's rights depend on the need to show that he or she has worked for the appropriate period. This is known as *continuous service*. Generally, the stipulated periods are:

- one year's full time (for more than sixteen hours per week), or
- five years' part-time (for between eight and sixteen hours per week).

(See DTI Booklet PL711: *Rules Governing Continuous Employment.*)

Any week during the whole or part of which your relationship with your employer is governed by a contract of employment counts in calculating your period of employment.

7.1.1   One year's continuous service (full-time)

Employees must show that they have worked for their employers for one year continuously at the effective date of dismissal. The statutory qualifying period was two years prior to 1 June 1999.

The reduction in the qualifying period is intended to ensure that employees now have greater protection from being arbitrarily dismissed.

However, an employee dismissed in connection with a business transfer does not need to satisfy the length of service qualification in order to bring a claim for unfair dismissal, and is free to pursue such a claim irrespective of his or her length of service.

7.1.2   Continuous service (part-time)

Part-time workers have the right not to be treated in a less favourable manner than comparable full-time workers just because they work part time. Legislation was introduced in July 2000 which gives part-time workers equal rights in the areas of pay rates, sick pay, maternity benefits, overtime, access to training and redundancy.

Do take heed: those working less than eight hours per week are not protected.

7.1.3   When continuity begins and ends

Continuous service starts on the day the employee begins work. Periods such as overtime are not included in the computation.

Where an employee has worked under multiple contracts with the same employer, he or she may not be entitled to aggregate the hours of work where the contracts are separate and distinct.

There is a cessation of work when the employer has no work available for the employee to do. Whether or not the absence is temporary is a question of fact to be determined by an employment tribunal (see also above, *Employer's duty to pay*, section 5.1).

If you leave or are dismissed, and are then reinstated or re-engaged in your old job, your period of continuous service runs from the date your contract of employment is treated as starting.

7.1.4   Must be with one employer

An employment must usually be with one employer only, in order to be treated as continuous. However there are exceptions where:

a) a trade, business or undertaking is transferred
b) an employer dies
c) there is a change of partners, personal representatives or trustees
d) an employee works for an associated employer.

There must be a transfer of a business as a going concern and the new business must be the same as the old.

Two employers are treated as associated if one is a company of which the other directly or indirectly has control, or if both are companies of which a third person has control.

7.1.5   Interruptions

If the continuity is broken, an employee has to start all over again in accumulating the legally required period of continuous service.

7.1.6   Interruptions which do not count

Continuous service is not interrupted if:

a) there is a break in service for no more than 26 weeks because of sickness or injury; it still counts as normal employment

b) an employee is loaned to another employer for a period of time

c) absence from work is due wholly or partly to pregnancy and the other conditions of maternity leave apply. A woman must have returned to work when her maternity leave comes to an end (see *Gender issues* in the chapter *Working for a Living (Part 2)*, section 1)

d) absence from work for the whole or part of a week is due to a 'temporary cessation' of work

e) an employee takes part in a strike. The period during which s/he stops work will not be counted as a break in his or her continuity of employment. Its effect is to postpone the date on which the employee started work by the number of days on which s/he was on strike

f) interruptions are relatively short in relation to the period worked.

7.1.7   Exclusions

Protection from dismissal for some specified reasons has no qualifying period. This includes dismissal on the grounds of discrimination (race, sex and disability); for some trade union or health and safety related reasons; on grounds of pregnancy; for asserting a statutory employment right; in connection with Sunday working for betting or shop workers; and for carrying out duties as a pension trustee. The National Minimum Wage and Public Interest Disclosure Acts contain unqualified protection against dismissal.

8   PRIVACY

8.1   The Data Protection Act

The Data Protection Act came into force on 1 March 2000 and gives you the right to have access to personal information held about you and to have that information corrected or deleted where appropriate. This applies in the workplace as well as elsewhere. If your employer refuses access to your files, you can enforce this right by complaining to the Information Commissioner, who has the power to prosecute or to serve an enforcement notice on your employer. The entire Act must be in force by October 2007.

8.2   Data Protection Code

The Information Commissioner has issued a Data Protection Code of Practice for employers:

Part 1:   Recruitment and Selection: An Employer's Guide (March 2002)

Part 2:   Employment Records (August 2002)

Part 3:   Monitoring of Staff at Work (not yet available)

Part 4:   Medical Information (including drug testing) (not yet available)

The Code applies to employers in businesses of all sizes and a fine of up to £5,000 can be imposed if an employer fails to comply with it.

A 'data protection toolkit' is available from a commercial website: *www.data-protection-act.co.uk*.

Details of the rules and how they apply are on the website of the Information Commissioner: *www.dataprotection.gov.uk*. ACAS also produces a booklet on the practical aspects of Personnel Data and Record Keeping.

8.3   Monitoring employee communications

The DTI has adopted regulations which authorise businesses to monitor or record employees' communications, including e-mails, for specific purposes:

- to establish the existence of facts relevant to the business
- to ascertain compliance with regulatory or self-regulatory practices or procedures
- to ascertain or demonstrate standards which are or ought to be achieved by employees
- to prevent or detect crime
- to investigate or detect the unauthorised use of the businesses' systems, and
- to ensure the effective operation of those systems.

The regulations also authorise businesses to monitor (but not to record) employees' communications to determine whether such communications are relevant to business.

☞ *You are aware that your employers have certain powers to monitor your incoming and outgoing e-mails. On the other hand, you think that they are doing so covertly. You wonder whether you have any rights, at all, to confront them in the matter.*

Before your employers monitor your communications – provided that such monitoring is bona fide for the above purposes – they must make all reasonable efforts to inform you that your communications may be being intercepted, and to give you the reason why, and the extent.

12 WORKING FOR A LIVING (Part 2)

It is not easy to find a parallel to the sheer volume of statutes which deal with work-related issues. Employment law also reflects the priorities of the governments of the day, on which there can be diametrically opposed views, which nonetheless appear in successive Acts of Parliament. Yet all current statutes have to be applied and enforced, on a daily basis, in factories, organisations, and businesses, both large and small, up and down the country.

Among the many matters which this enormous mass of legislation deals with, discrimination in the workplace, unfair dismissal and redundancy, as well as trade union law, have all been addressed. These topics are dealt with below.

On the whole, however, Acts of Parliament are only a means to foster good working relations. We can only legislate up to a point for the fair treatment of women, minorities, or the disabled. It is what happens in shops, offices and factories which truly determines these and other issues. We cannot pass laws which make people good or kind to one another, but the law can assist in remedying injustice. To this end, too, an additional and significant factor which will increasingly impinge on employment issues – as in so many other spheres – is that the rights of the individual have to be taken into account by the judges in deciding the cases before them, following the enactment of the Human Rights Act 1998 (see also the chapter on *The Legal System*).

Further, and apart from those who may be pursuing a purely political agenda, the effectiveness of employment law in general depends on the health of our economy. It stands to reason that if jobs are scarce, employees are not in a strong position to assert their rights. Moreover, employers in recessionary times may find that economic exigencies can and do force them into making difficult decisions to keep their businesses afloat – such as making staff redundant.

In order to deal with the ever-growing volume of employment law, industrial (now employment) tribunals were set up in the 1970s. They were intended to settle industrial relations disputes effectively, speedily, and cheaply. They were also intended to be more informal than the ordinary courts, allowing unrepresented employees to bring their own actions. The work of the tribunals is dealt with in *Working for a Living (Part 1)*, section 2.

At the moment, tribunals, more than 40 per cent of whose annual case load of 130,000 concern unfair dismissal, have a very heavy workload, which entails long waits for hearings. The hearings themselves are becoming more technical under the pressure of difficult legislation. The scope of work covered by them has been extended and, in addition, litigation between employers and employees is spiralling beyond expectation as workers become more aware than ever of their rights and entitlements at work. The Government set up a task force to consider ways to improve the employment tribunal system and is considering its recommendations.

To address these problems, the Employment Act 2002 introduced new dispute resolution procedures and reforms to employment tribunals. The changes were prompted by a Government consulation paper published in July 2001, *Routes to Resolution*, which set out reforms to reduce the number of tribunal applications in order to encourage settlement of disputes in the workplace itself. The changes will be introduced through regulations to be introduced in 2003.

According to recent figures, the number of applications to employment tribunals has trebled in a decade (in 2000, there were 130,000 applications compared with 44,000 in 1990). The number of cases continued to rise with the introduction of the Employment Relations Act 1999, which increased the number of unfair dismissal claims alone by between 10,000 and 14,000 to more than 52,000 a year. Under the Act, the qualifying period for employment protection was reduced from two years to one, and the ceiling on maximum compensation payments was increased from

£12,000 to £50,000. The ceiling is now increased annually in line with inflation (it is currently £61,100). Employers' liability insurers have warned that workplace compensation is 'buckling under the strain' of expectations of awards (see also the chapter on *Accidents*, section 7).

In this chapter we look at:

- gender issues
- race discrimination
- discrimination against the disabled
- dismissal
- redundancy
- trade union activities.

1 GENDER ISSUES

1.1 Equal pay

The cases show that the law is particularly dynamic in the sphere of discrimination on grounds of sex or race. The law has to address difficult and touchy issues, as well as having to adapt to changing social modes and work patterns. European law has a continuing impact in the sphere of sex discrimination provisions. Again and again our national law has been obliged to alter in order to accommodate European judgments and directives.

1.1.1 A right by law

In 1970, the Equal Pay Act was passed in order to lay down the principle of equality between the sexes in employees' terms and conditions. Under the Act, a woman can claim equal pay with a man if she is employed in 'like work' or 'equivalent work' or where her work is of 'equal value' to that of a man in terms of the demands made on her.

Take note: a man is just as entitled to receive equal pay under these provisions as is a woman. However, in discussion, we will refer to women – who are usually found to be most in need of the protection afforded by the terms of the Equal Pay Act – rather than to men.

1.1.1(a) Equality clause

Every contract of employment includes an equality clause either express or implied. If a term in a woman's contract is, or becomes, less favourable than a term in a man's contract, that term will be modified to make it as favourable as the corresponding term in the man's contract.

The only time when an equality clause will not operate is where an employer can prove that the variation is genuinely due to a material factor other than that of sex (see *Material factors*, section 1.1.1(e) below).

1.1.1(b) Same employment

A man is in the *same employment* as a woman if he is employed by the same or an associated employer at the same establishment or at establishments in Great Britain which include that one. There must be common terms and conditions of employment either generally or for employees of the relevant class.

1.1.1(c) Like work

A woman is to be regarded as engaged in *like work* with a man if her work and his are of the same or broadly similar nature and the differences, if any, between the things they do are not of practical importance in relation to the terms and conditions of employment.

1.1.1(d) Equivalent work

A woman is employed on work *equivalent* to that of a man if their work has been given an equal value in terms of the demands made on the employee under various headings.

This requires the carrying out of a job evaluation scheme (JES). Jobs are evaluated in terms of the demands made on a worker under headings such as skill, effort and decision-making. Once a JES has been carried out and the woman's job is found to be of equal value with that of a man, the woman may claim equal pay.

1.1.1(e) Material factors

An employer may defeat a woman's claim for equal pay if it can be shown that the pay differential is due to some objectively justifiable reason other than sex ('material factors').

To show that discrimination is objectively justified, an employer must show that s/he is:

* taking measures which correspond to a real need of the business
* that the measures are appropriate in the circumstances
* and that they are necessary to meet the need.

For example, a health authority decided to attract qualified and experienced persons from the private sector to get a particular service started by offering them a higher salary. A woman who qualified and came directly into the service – but did not come from the private sector – wanted to be paid at the higher rate. It was held that there had been a material factor, namely the need to attract private-sector personnel, to justify the higher pay rate. That had nothing to do with the sex of the individual.

If it is shown that there is a significant imbalance between the wages of a man and a woman, the burden is on the employer to justify that imbalance.

For a defence of material factor to succeed, an employer must show that any difference is material and it must be objectively justifiable between the man's and the woman's case.

For example, a male canteen worker was paid more than a woman for doing like work. The employers claimed that special arrangements had been made in the man's case because of the difficulties in recruiting night-shift workers and that was not a difference related to sex. The court held that the employers had not shown that there was a material difference between the man's case and that of the woman to which the difference was genuinely due. The man was being paid at a higher rate in order to secure his services and that was not a material factor between the case of the man and that of the woman.

Factors such as additional obligations and amount of responsibility attached to the job, experience and length of service, and the job's location may all be regarded as material factors.

1.1.1(f) Impact of Community law

Article 119 of the EC Treaty provides that member states should ensure and maintain the application of the principle that men and women should receive equal pay for equal work. The Equal Pay Directive (75/117) and Equal Treatment Directive (76/207) deal with the general implementation of the equal pay and equal treatment principles. Those provisions are now being relied on by employees in this country who feel that UK law is not providing the same comprehensive rights as are available in Community law.

On the other hand in one case the European Court of Justice took the view that although the Community rules on equal treatment of men and women in general applied to public service, including the armed forces, the Royal Marines were entitled to refuse to engage a woman as a chef on the grounds that her presence was incompatible with the requirement of 'interoperability': the need for every Marine irrespective of his specialisation to be capable of fighting in a commando unit.

There are proposals to amend the 1976 Equal Treatment Directive, probably to be implemented with effect from April 2005. Sexual harassment is not currently specifically dealt with under either UK or EU law. However a new draft directive has been proposed that will require Member States to outlaw sexual harassment specifically, and inserts a specific definition of sexual harassment into the Equal Treatment Directive.

Meanwhile sexual harassment will count as 'discrimination' for the purposes of sex discrimination if an employee is treated less favourably than others on grounds of sex.

If you are sexually harassed by a fellow employee, it counts as an act of misconduct which may justify dismissal of the offending employee, subject to the normal rules relating to dismissal.

1.1.1(g) Equal-pay questionnaires

Questionnaires similar to those currently used in sex, race and disability discrimination cases are to be introduced in equal-pay cases. Their use is intended to make you consider carefully whether to start an action at all and, if you decide to go ahead, to help you to prepare and present your case most effectively. The details are still being ironed out and the regulations are expected in early 2003.

1.2   Sex Discrimination Act

This Act was passed in 1975. It makes it unlawful to discriminate against men or women on the grounds of their sex, or against married persons. It must be stressed that the Act is applicable to both sexes. In fact the Equal Opportunities Commission (see DIRECTORY and chapter on *The Legal System*) has found that 40 per cent of complaints to it about sex discrimination in recruitment are from men. The Sex Discrimination (Gender Reassignment) Regulations 1999 extended the protection of the legislation relating to sex discrimination to employees who have undergone, are undergoing or are about to undergo gender reassignment.

Do note: positive discrimination in employment is unlawful under EU law because it breaches the Equal Treatment Directive.

The Court of Appeal held that a male nurse who retired at the age of 55 with pension benefits less favourable than those of a female nurse could not claim unlawful sex discrimination as the differences in benefit due to age differentials applied prior to 17 May 1970 and were allowed at the time under EU law.

1.2.1   Direct discrimination

Direct discrimination occurs when, on the basis of sex, a man or a woman receives less favourable treatment than his or her female or male counterpart.

A well-intentioned motive is not a defence.

☞ *You and a colleague are the only two men in an otherwise all-female team. Your male colleague leaves his employment and you are withdrawn from the team and placed in another department. Your employers state that the reason for your withdrawal is that, in the past, a sole male found it difficult to work in an all-female team.*

This is an instance of direct discrimination, the good intentions of your employers notwithstanding.

Employers are entitled to insist that members of staff dress conventionally if that is a factor in attracting customers. It has been thought that there could be different requirements for the appearance of men and women provided that such requirements were equally rigorously enforced. However cases involving employers' objections to the wearing of trousers by women in the workplace have opened up the debate as to just what is acceptable in this regard. The employment tribunal took the view that insisting that women wear skirts in the office was unacceptable as being discriminatory.

☞ *Your boyfriend has been employed as a delicatessen counterhand at a large supermarket. He has grown a ponytail and has been told to have his hair cut. He protests that women counter staff have long hair and that he is being discriminated against.*

In a similar case, the appeal court ruled that a code of appearance was not discriminatory if it insisted on a conventional appearance for both men and women. Although what was conventional in each case could differ, the requirement to abide by the appearance code should apply to both sexes equally.

In a different context, the lack of any formal basis for distributing bonuses in some City institutions leaves the institutions open to attack for sex discrimination if one employee receives less than others of a different gender or race.

In one case a woman was awarded £1.4 million for sex discrimination when she was given a discretionary bonus of only £25,000 (increased to £50,000) while two male colleagues received bonuses of £440,000 and £650,000 respectively. The Tribunal said that because there were no written records of the reasons for the bonuses, it was difficult for the employer to counter the woman's argument that her bonus was much lower simply because of her sex.

In another case a 32-year-old biochemist in a highly paid job in banking complained that that her immediate superior continually made sexist jokes in the office. These were about women in general but specifically included what he said was a joke about her sleeping with a client. She complained to the management but was not taken seriously. She claimed over £400,000 in compensation for sex discrimination, breach of contract and constructive dismissal. She won her claim and settled the question of damages which were expected to be in the region of £500,000.

However, instances of direct discrimination – for good or bad motives – are usually hard to prove. For that reason, the Sex Discrimination Act includes the concept of indirect discrimination.

1.2.2   Indirect discrimination

Indirect discrimination occurs when an employer imposes a term or condition which is such that the proportion of persons of one sex who can comply is considerably smaller than that of the other sex, and:

- the term cannot be justified without regard to the sex of the person to whom it is applied, and
- it is to that person's detriment that he or she cannot comply with it.

As we will see below, a term or condition may be justified where there is a genuine occupational qualification (see section 1.2.5 below).

Two changes have been made to the Sex Discrimination Act with an amendment to the definition of indirect sex discrimination and a shift in the burden of proof to employers. Before the change you had to show that your employer applied a 'requirement or condition' to you which was such that the proportion of women who could comply with it was considerably smaller than the proportion of men (or vice versa), and that it was to your detriment as you could not comply with it.

In the new definition 'requirement or condition' has been replaced with 'provision, criterion or practice'. This means that you can challenge work policies, e.g. long-hours culture.

There is also no requirement that you cannot comply with the provision etc. so that you can now challenge your employer's policies in general if they are discriminatory.

You must also establish less favourable treatment than someone of the opposite sex. But your employer must show that the reason for the treatment was not discriminatory. If your employer fails to give a satisfactory explanation, a tribunal must draw the inference of less favourable treatment on grounds of sex.

1.2.3   Other discriminatory acts

The Act also stipulates that there must be no discrimination in:

- the arrangements made for the purpose of deciding who to employ
- terms on which employment is offered
- refusing or deliberately omitting to offer employment because of a person's sex
- the way access to promotion, training etc. is offered
- dismissing a person or subjecting him or her to detrimental treatment.

As we can see the terms are very wide.

The House of Lords held that a local council's action in reducing the pay of female catering assistants in order to compete with commercial organisations was discriminatory against women.

1.2.4   Sexual harassment

As we have seen, employment law must keep pace with changing social attitudes. Behaviour in the workplace which once might have been tolerantly viewed (by the perpetrator!) as an acceptable form of sexual encounter, is now seen as a form of discrimination.

When women or men are subject to physical or verbal abuse or other hostile behaviour because of their sex, they are entitled to make a claim to an employment tribunal under the Sex Discrimination Act 1975.

☞   *You worked for a large corporation. Your line manager insisted on caressing you despite your clear objections to his behaviour. You were offered another job and you accepted the offer. However, you are still incensed by the behaviour which you had to endure – often in front of other colleagues. You wonder whether you can make a claim to an employment tribunal in the circumstances.*

If it can be shown that an employer permitted such harassment to take place, a tribunal might award compensation even though you have suffered no financial loss.

Further if your employer failed to prevent such harassment in circumstances which it should be able to control, the employer is likely to be held liable for the acts of its employees.

The courts have held that harassment of an employee undergoing gender assignment or for being a transsexual amounts to sex discrimination.

1.2.5 Genuine occupational qualification

There is no discrimination if it is specified that it should be a man or a woman who is employed in a job where their sex is a genuine occupational qualification. The following are some examples of where this would be the case:

- where physical characteristics are needed for authenticity (e.g. a male actor is employed to play a male role)
- where decency or privacy might otherwise be infringed (e.g. the attendant in a women's changing room is female)
- the post involves a single-sex institution (e.g. the matron in a girls' boarding school is female).

If you are an employer wishing to employ someone in your own home, you are entitled to specify the sex of that person. However, there cannot be an official policy determining a particular sex – e.g. that an *au pair* should always be female.

1.3 Maternity rights

There are many detailed and complex rules on the subject of the rights of pregnant employees. It is important that employers should spell them out to their employees and explain them as fully as possible. It is unfortunate for both employers and employees that this particularly sensitive area of employment law should be as complicated as it is.

A maternity leave period is available to all employees regardless of length of service or hours worked. It lasts for 18 weeks. Six months' employment is required to qualify for statutory maternity pay (SMP), however.

Employees should seek advice from their trade union representatives or from other organisations (see DIRECTORY).

There are certain basic statutory rights applicable at the time of writing but maternity rights are being extended from April 2003 to encourage mothers back to work.

1.3.1 The right not to be unfairly dismissed on grounds of pregnancy

The dismissal of a woman because she is pregnant or for any reason connected with pregnancy ('inadmissible reasons') is automatically unfair under the Sex Discrimination Act. Remedy is via an employment tribunal. A woman dismissed in this way can make a complaint of unfair dismissal, regardless of how long she has worked for her employer.

Take note: the dismissal will not be automatically unfair if her pregnancy makes it impossible for a woman to do the job properly and there is no suitable alternative work she can do.

In this case, the ordinary redundancy rules apply (see section 5 below).

1.3.2 General rights

The Employment Protection Act gives pregnant employees other rights, in addition to protection against unfair dismissal. These rights are:

- the right to time off work for ante-natal care (this can include relaxation classes)
- the right to maternity leave
- the right to return to work after maternity leave
- the right to statutory maternity pay.

1.3.3 Ante-natal care

An employee is entitled to be paid the appropriate hourly rate for any periods of absence to receive ante-natal care.

There is no minimum qualifying period of employment before this right is acquired.

☞ *Your secretary, who has been working for you for under a year, says that she is pregnant and will need to see a doctor during working hours. You ask whether she has already made an appointment and whether she can re-arrange her working hours so that she can see a doctor in her own time.*

Your secretary is under no duty to rearrange her working hours or to make up lost time. Her right is to time off during working hours. The fact that she has not worked for you for a qualifying period does not affect her minimum right to time off work to receive appropriate ante-natal care. It will, however, affect her entitlement to the level of maternity pay that she will receive, and to maternity leave (see immediately below).

The appointment to receive ante-natal care must have been made on the advice of a doctor, midwife or health visitor and you are entitled to see her doctor's certificate and appointment card after her first visit.

1.3.4   Maternity leave

Employers are required to take account of health and safety risks to a new or expectant mother when assessing risks in her work. Employers must not allow a woman to return to work within 2 weeks of having her baby. If they do, they can be fined up to £500.

1.3.4(a)   Length of maternity leave

At present pregnant employees are entitled to 18 weeks' ordinary maternity leave regardless of length of service. This rises to 26 weeks from 6 April 2003. Women who have completed one year's service with their employer are able to take additional maternity leave which starts at the end of ordinary maternity leave and finishes 29 weeks after the birth (counting from the Sunday at the beginning of the week in which the baby was born).

There has been confusion caused by the variation in reference points which currently determine the start and end of additional maternity leave. To avoid confusion in the future, from April 2003 the start of additional maternity leave will be at the end of ordinary maternity leave as at present and will just continue for 26 weeks thereafter. This could mean that many women may take up to a year off work compared with the current limit of around 40 weeks.

Additional maternity leave is also being made available to more mothers as the period of continuous employment to qualify for additional leave is to be reduced to 26 weeks, the same period required to qualify for statutory maternity pay (see section 1.3.4(b)).

1.3.4(b)   Contractual benefits

Women are entitled to the benefit of their normal terms and conditions of employment, except for terms relating to remuneration (the money element of normal wages or salary), throughout the 18-week ordinary maternity leave period. Remuneration will not be due but most women will be entitled to statutory maternity pay or maternity allowance for this period. During additional maternity leave, the employment contract continues and some contractual benefits and obligations remain in force, such as contractual redundancy rights and notice. The entitlement to paid holiday under the working time regulations is not affected by maternity leave.

1.3.4(c)   Starting maternity leave

Women can start maternity leave any time from the eleventh week before the baby is due, provided that before they want to start their maternity leave, they give the employer at least 21 days' notice of the expected week of childbirth and of the start date of maternity leave. The expected week of childbirth and the start date of maternity leave must be given in writing if requested by the employer. A woman no longer has to state that she is exercising her right to return to work.

From April 2003 new notification requirements are being introduced. The employer is under a new obligation to respond in writing to the employee within 29 days of her giving notification. The response must specify the woman's expected date of return, assuming she intends to take the maximum leave available. Draft model documents are being provided to help employers to comply with these obligations.

1.3.4(d) Returning to work

A woman has the right to return to work provided she has worked for the same employer for one year full time. If a woman wants to return to work before the end of maternity leave she must give her employer 21 days' notice (increased to 28 days from 6 April 2003). No further notification is required for employees intending to return to work at the end of ordinary maternity leave. Where a woman qualifies for additional maternity leave, she should let her employer know when the baby is born so that she and her employer can plan for her return 29 weeks later (up to one year from 6 April 2003).

1.3.4(e) Postponement of return to work

Return to work may be postponed by the employer or the employee.

An employer may postpone a woman's return to work provided that s/he notifies the woman when she can return within a four-week period of notification and gives reasons for the postponement.

An employee may postpone her return for up to four weeks provided that she furnishes a doctor's certificate to the effect that she is not able to return to work.

1.3.4(f) Returning to the same work

Provided all the proper conditions are met, a woman can return to the job in which she was employed under her original contract of employment and on terms and conditions which are not less favourable than those which would have been applicable to her if she had not been absent because of her pregnancy.

1.3.4(g) Failure to return to work

If a woman fails to return to work after the end of her maternity leave without proper notice of her intention to postpone her return, she will lose her statutory rights.

1.3.4(h) Protection of health and safety

Employers must take account of the health and safety of expectant and new mothers and their babies. When assessing risks in the workplace they must take all reasonably practicable preventative steps to remove or control hazards. If a risk remains, the employer must offer the woman any suitable alternative work that is available, under no less favourable treatment and conditions. If no such work is available, the employer must suspend the employee on full pay for as long as necessary to protect her health and safety.

1.3.4(i) Parental leave

In order to comply with the Community Parental Leave Directive, both parents of children born or adopted on or after 15 December 1999 are entitled to take up to 13 weeks' unpaid leave to be taken before the child's fifth birthday so long as they have one year's continuous service with their employer (to be reduced to 26 weeks in April 2003 ending with the 15th week before the expected week of confinement or the week in which notification of a match for adoption is given, whichever is applicable.). If the child is disabled the leave can be taken any time before their 18th birthday. It is intended to extend the period to 18 weeks and to apply to all parents of children under the age of five.

You must give at least four weeks' notice of your intention to take leave, the actual notice period being double that of the time you intend to take off. For example, if you intend to take four weeks' leave you must give eight weeks' notice.

Do note: your employer can require you to postpone the leave for up to six months if the needs of the business make it necessary to do so. However, if you intend to take leave immediately after the birth or adoption you must give at least three months' notice and your employer cannot require you to postpone it for any reason.

At the end of parental leave your right to return to the same job as before or, if that is not practicable, to a similar job, is guaranteed. If the leave was taken for four weeks or less, you are entitled to go back to the same job.

Where possible employers and employees should make their own arrangements about how parental leave will work in a particular workplace. In small firms especially, where employers and employees work closely together, the needs of each can be agreed on an individual basis.

The take-up of paternity leave has so far been poor as it is unpaid leave, but from April 2003 fathers and adoptive parents will be entitled to two weeks' paid paternity leave to co-exist with the existing right to unpaid leave. It will be paid at the same rate as the lower rate of statutory maternity may.

Paid leave must be taken within eight weeks after the birth or placement for adoption and may only be taken in a single two-week block or two one-week blocks. The leave cannot be deferred.

1.3.4(j)   Adoption leave

At present, although 2,000 children are adopted each year and 70% of adoptive parents work full time, there is no automatic right to take leave from work. If an employer refuses to grant leave, the employee tends to resign and so is lost to the workforce. To remedy this, the Government is proposing to introduce adoption rights from April 2003. Either adoptive parent will be able to take 26 weeks' ordinary adoption leave followed by 26 weeks additional adoption leave. The other parent will be entitled to take 'paternity' leave.

The rules for adoption leave were intended to be the same as maternity leave but there are two important differences:

• you must have at least 26 weeks' continuous employment ending in the week in which notification of being matched for adoption is given
• there is only one rate of pay, equal to the lower rate of statutory maternity pay.

1.3.4(k)   Time off for needs of dependants

You are entitled to unpaid leave to deal with a family emergency:

• if a dependant of yours falls ill, or is injured or assaulted; there is also entitlement where the victim is hurt or distressed rather than injured physically
• when your partner is having a baby
• to make longer-term care arrangements for a dependant who is ill or injured
• to deal with the death of a dependant, e.g. to make funeral arrangements or to attend a funeral
• to deal with an unexpected disruption or breakdown in care arrangements for a dependant, e.g. when the childminder or nurse fails to turn up
• if your child is involved in a serious incident at school or during school hours.

The right does not include a statutory right to pay, so whether or not you will be paid is left to your employer's discretion or depends on the terms of your contract. The amount of leave will usually be one or two days at most but will depend on individual circumstances. For example, if your child falls ill the time off should be enough to help you cope with the crisis – deal with immediate care of the child, visit the doctor and make longer-term arrangements.

A dependant includes your partner, child or parent or someone who lives with you as part of your family.

Note: in the past, employers had a discretion whether to grant such leave but it is now an employee's right in appropriate circumstances. You cannot be disciplined or subjected to any detrimental treatment for exercising your statutory right.

☞ *You took time off work when your young teenage son was starting to play truant. You felt it was important that he was properly supervised during a stressful time for the whole family. You kept your employers informed of your domestic situation. However, since your return to work, you feel that your boss, who is clearly annoyed, is also treating you unfairly in the assignment of tasks.*

If you think your employer has unreasonably refused you time off, or you have been victimised for taking it, you may make a complaint to an employment tribunal against your employer.

1.3.4(l)   Flexible working

The most radical change introduced by the Employment Act 2002 in this area is the right of either parent to request a change in their employment contracts to look after a young child (generally up to 6-years-old). The regulations are still being discussed, but broadly, from April 2003, employees who have at least 26 weeks' continuous employment will be entitled to apply to vary the number of hours they work, and when and where they work, to enable them to care for a child.

You may apply for flexible working at any time up to 14 days before the child's sixth birthday (or the 18th birthday for a disabled child). You will have to show that you are eligible to apply.

It is up to you to put in writing what changes you would like together with the proposed starting date. You must also explain what effect the change will have on your employer (if any) and how this could be dealt with.

Your employer has 28 days to fix a meeting to discuss the proposed changes and has to give its decision within 14 days of that meeting.

Your employer can refuse to agree to flexible working if he or she can show that there is a clear business reason such as:

- additional costs
- a detriment to work performance or quality
- a detrimental effect on customers.

Note: if your employer refuses to comply with your request you have a right of reply but you can only make one application in any 12-month period, so if your appeal is unsuccessful you will have to wait a year before you can reapply. It is important, therefore, to make your application for flexible working as detailed as possible, dealing with all potential objections and obstacles you can think of.

Warning: once the changes have been agreed you have no right to revert to your old working pattern when your child is older.

☞ *Your employer agreed to your working a three-day week to look after your baby. The child is now starting school and you would like to work a five-day week but leave work early each day to collect him from school.*

  At present, there is no provision in the Employment Act or the draft regulations to demand this change if your employer does not agree.

1.3.5 Where an employer cannot offer the old job back

1.3.5(a) Redundancy situation

Where a redundancy situation arises while a woman is on maternity leave, it may not be possible for her to return to her old job. However, if there is a suitable vacancy, the employer must offer her alternative employment and the terms of her new employment must not be substantially less favourable than her old contract. The job must also be suitable and appropriate for her to do.

Where there is no suitable vacancy, the woman will be entitled to claim a redundancy payment.

When deciding which of several employees to make redundant, an employer must disregard the inconvenience arising from the fact that one is pregnant and will be taking maternity leave. If the employer does not do so and makes absence on maternity leave the factor determining the pregnant woman's dismissal, then it will be unfair. See section 4.

1.3.5(b) Small firms

If the number of employees working for the employer before the start of a woman's maternity leave was five or less, the employer's refusal to allow her to return may not amount to a dismissal if it was not reasonably practicable for her to return or for the employer to offer her suitable alternative employment.

1.3.6 Statutory maternity pay (SMP)

Note: there is no payment made to men who might take time off to help at home except for a fortnight's paid paternity leave from April 2003. See section 1.3.4(i) above. Thus SMP is only paid to females – and only when they actually stop work. It is only payable to women between the ages of 16 and 60.

1.3.6(a) Obligation to pay SMP

An employer is obliged to pay SMP for 18 weeks (increased to 26 weeks from April 2003).

Take note: this obligation applies whether or not an employee intends to return to work provided that continuity-of-service requirements are met.

1.3.6(b) Two rates of pay

There are two rates of SMP:

a) 6 weeks payable at the higher rate (90% of average earnings); and

b) 12 weeks at the lower rate (currently £75 per week – the amount changes annually in April). To reflect the eight-week increase in ordinary maternity leave the lower rate period is extended to 20 weeks from 6 April 2003. The lower rate is increased to £100 per week (or 90% of average weekly earnings) whichever is lower.

1.3.6(c) Calculating earnings

Earnings include bonuses, overtime, statutory sick pay, and arrears. However, redundancy payments, reimbursement of business expenses, benefits in kind and pension payments are excluded.

1.3.6(d) Other allowances

To be entitled to the higher-rate SMP, a woman must have been continuously employed for 26 weeks up to and including the qualifying weeks (QW), i.e. 15 weeks before the expected week of confinement (EWC). No distinction is made between full-time and part-time employees.

To be entitled to the lower-rate SMP, a woman must have 26 weeks' continuous employment. There is no minimum working hours' requirement but her average weekly earnings must be at or above the lower earnings limit (LEL) of £75 (increased annually on 1 February).

To qualify for SMP, a woman must also still be pregnant during the 11th week before the EWC. She must produce satisfactory medical evidence of the date the baby is due at least 21 days before going on maternity leave.

The actual maternity pay period is flexible and need not be restricted to the 11th week before the anticipated confinement date.

☞ *You are in your sixth month of pregnancy, in full-time employment, and would like to work up until the sixth week before the baby is due. You are concerned as to whether you will jeopardise your rights to SMP.*

You can choose to work up until the sixth week before the expected week of confinement and still retain your right to the full 18 weeks' SMP.

(See also *A Guide to Maternity Benefits* (NI 1 7A) published by the Benefits Agency.)

☞ *You have only been in your present position as legal researcher for two months when you discover that you are pregnant. You know that you do not qualify for SMP as you lack sufficient continuity of service, but would like to know what other benefits you may receive.*

Any woman who is not eligible for SMP at the higher or lower rate may be entitled to claim maternity allowance direct from the DSS. Entitlement depends on the employee's NIC record rather than continuity of employment with one particular employer.

Do remember: SMP is subject to PAYE income tax.

1.3.6(e) Appeal against refusal to pay

If an employer refuses to pay a woman SMP, she is entitled to ask an adjudication officer of the DSS for a formal decision. Both the employer and the employee must send written submissions to the adjudication officer stating their positions although they need not attend in person.

1.3.7 Women company directors

Company directors are treated differently from other employees if pregnant. Their income – for contributions and benefits purposes – is calculated using annual earnings.

1.4 Dismissal

A woman will automatically be deemed to be unfairly dismissed if the principal reason for dismissal is that she is pregnant or for any other reason connected with pregnancy (e.g. morning sickness).

She is also entitled to written reasons for dismissal, if she is dismissed at any time during pregnancy or maternity leave. There is no minimum service requirement and she should not have to request the reasons – they should be given as a matter of course.

1.5   Compensation for discrimination

The European Court ruled in August 1993 that the purpose behind the sex-discrimination provisions was to guarantee real protection for employees and to act as a real deterrent to discrimination by employers. Therefore it was unlawful for a State to set a fixed amount so as to limit the compensation which a victim of sex discrimination could receive from the national courts. Every case depended on its particular circumstances. A fixed award of damages might not be an accurate reflection of the actual loss suffered.

2   RACE DISCRIMINATION

It is unlawful to discriminate against a person on grounds of colour, race, nationality and ethnic or national origins (see the Race Relations Act 1976). The Act applies not only to a person who is an employee but also to any person who is engaged under a 'contract personally to execute any work or labour' or who is a job applicant. It also applies to contract workers and to partnership arrangements in larger partnerships with at least six partners.

The Commission for Racial Equality keeps the 1976 Race Discrimination Act under review and may advise, assist or give legal help to individuals (see DIRECTORY). It also issues a Code of Practice in order to assist employers to establish procedures and records for monitoring the ethnic composition of their workforce.

The Department of Trade and Industry began a consultation in May 2002 on a new race equality scheme covering policy, services and employment of staff pursuant to the implementation of the Race Relations (Amendment) Act 2000. The Act places a general duty on public authorities to promote race equality and equality of opportunity and good relations between persons of different racial groups. A final version of the Scheme had been expected in December 2002.

2.1   Defining ethnic origins

The term 'ethnic origins' embraces more groups than the term 'race'. In law a person's ethnic origins are determined by his ethnic group. An ethnic group is a distinct community on account of:

- its long shared history, and
- its cultural traditions, including family and social customs.

These two characteristics are regarded as essential.

In addition, the following characteristics are considered relevant:

- common geographical origins or common ancestry
- common language and literature
- common religion
- being a minority group, or
- being part of a minority or an oppressed majority (for example, a conquered people) within a larger community.

2.1.1   Selecting for employment

An employer must not discriminate against a person as regards:

- making arrangements for job offers
- terms on which jobs are offered
- recruitment or selection for employment.

A teacher won a race-discrimination case against a local authority which had rejected her application for a job because she was white. A tribunal ruled that she had been unfairly turned down for the job of teaching mathematics to a class of ethnic-minority students.

2.1.2   Prospects in employment

Once a person is employed he or she must not be discriminated against on grounds of race:

- in the terms of employment – in opportunities for training and promotion etc.
- with regard to other benefits

as reason for dismissal.

2.2   Direct discrimination

There is direct discrimination where one person treats another less favourably on grounds of race, colour, nationality or ethnic origins.

Segregation constitutes less-favourable treatment, but voluntary consegregation (living as a separate community) is lawful.

The motive for discrimination is irrelevant. A worthy motive may still be unlawful discrimination. For example, an employer might refuse to take on a Jewish applicant simply in order to shield him from anti-Semitic remarks from other members of staff. The employer would nevertheless still be guilty of racial discrimination.

2.2.1   Difficulties in proving direct discrimination

Generally speaking, it is not easy to prove that an employer has discriminated against an employee on the grounds of race, so if the facts of the case indicate discrimination and no other reasonable explanation is forthcoming, then the court may assume that discrimination occurred.

2.3   Indirect discrimination

There is indirect discrimination where an employer:

a) applies a requirement or condition to a job
b) the proportion of persons from one racial group who can comply with it is smaller than the proportion of persons from other racial groups
c) the requirement or condition is not justified on other grounds, and
d) it is to the person's detriment that he or she is unable to comply with the requirement or condition.

2.3.1   When a condition does not amount to indirect discrimination

a) An employer may be able to justify a condition which would otherwise amount to indirect discrimination, provided it is not imposed for discriminatory reasons.

For example, a food company imposed a rule prohibiting the employment of persons with beards or long hair. A Sikh applied for a job and when he was turned down, he claimed indirect discrimination on grounds of race. The Court of Appeal dismissed his claim. The court held that although the requirement did indirectly discriminate against Sikhs, it could be justified on grounds of health and hygiene.

b) An employer may be able to justify a condition where it is just one of a number of factors which are taken into account in assessing a candidate's suitability for a job. In other words, it is not a condition with which it is essential for an employee to comply.

For example, an inner London borough advertised for a head of its legal department. One of the criteria was that the candidate should have experience in the borough. A candidate felt that this constituted indirect discrimination because the number of persons from his racial group who could comply with that condition was smaller than from other racial groups. However the Court of Appeal found that the condition was not a 'must' – it was just one of a number of factors for drawing up a shortlist.

2.4   Reverse discrimination

Discrimination in favour of an ethnic minority can also breach the provisions of the Act.

☞   *A local authority advertised for a manager in its housing department but insisted upon someone from the ethnic minorities in order to deal with housing problems in a racially mixed area. You are not from an ethnic minority but feel that your qualifications entitle you to apply for the job.*

If your application is turned down out of hand because you do not qualify on the grounds of race, you can make a legitimate claim of discrimination to a tribunal.

Note: in certain welfare tasks (as opposed to managerial jobs), requirements as to race do not constitute discrimination (see section 2.10 below).

2.5   Victimisation

A person is victimised if he is treated less favourably because he has:

- brought proceedings claiming discrimination on grounds of race
- given evidence or provided information in connection with such proceedings; or
- made allegations of an unlawful act of discrimination.

However a person is not victimised if he is less favourably treated because his allegations were untrue and not made in good faith.

In one case the courts took the view that an applicant had been victimised when he was not selected for promotion because the interviewers were 'consciously or sub-consciously' influenced by the fact that he had previously brought race-discrimination proceedings against the company.

Under the Race Relations Act compensation is available for injury to feelings and for psychiatric illness resulting from racial discrimination, and employment tribunals have jurisdiction to award compensation for personal injury under that head. The court has held that where an applicant signed a compromise agreement 'in full and final settlement of a claim' that included any claim for personal injury caused by the discrimination.

☞   *You complain to your employers that you have been victimised at work but your bosses close ranks and no action is taken. Your application for voluntary redundancy is accepted but you would still like to claim compensation for the alleged victimisation.*

The Race Relations Act, the Sex Discrimination Act and the Disability Discrimination Act all give specific protection from victimisation. You must make a formal complaint within three months of the alleged act of victimisation but the tribunal has power to extend the time limit if it is 'just and equitable'.

If your complaint is a more general one of mistreatment or harassment, the act(s) complained of might amount to a breach of trust and confidence. This might give rise to a claim for breach of contract in the county court but you will have to show that the breach has resulted in loss or personal injury. Such a claim must be made within six years of the date of the breach but you need to act quickly or you may be seen to have waived your right to compensation by leaving your job for a reason unconnected with the claim.

2.6   Putting pressure on employees to discriminate

It is unlawful to engage in discriminatory practices, to publish discriminatory advertisements, to give instructions to other persons to discriminate or to put pressure on a person to discriminate.

☞   *You are offered a job in a pub but the landlord tells you to take as long as possible before you serve a black or Asian customer. You do not intend to carry out his instructions. You also would like to report it to someone in authority.*

An unlawful act of discrimination such as this should be brought to the attention of the Commission for Racial Equality (see DIRECTORY).

In one case, a woman was taken on as a receptionist for a car and van rental company. She was told that when she received telephone enquiries, she was to tell 'any coloureds or Asians' that there were no vehicles available. Unable to work under those conditions, she resigned. Thereafter she wrote to her employers giving her reason for resignation. She applied to a tribunal complaining of constructive dismissal on the grounds that she had been required to carry out unlawful instructions and race discrimination.

The Court of Appeal held that if an employee was requested to carry out a racially discriminatory trading policy, as in these circumstances, there was:

a) constructive dismissal and
b) a breach of the Race Relations Act 1976 notwithstanding that the company policy was related not to the race of the complainant but to that of her prospective customers.

2.7   Individual's remedies

A person who feels that he or she has been discriminated against may complain directly to an employment tribunal. If the tribunal finds the complaint is well-founded, it can make a declaration of rights, award compensation, or recommend that the employer should take steps to remove the effects of the discrimination.

2.8   Proving your case

It is notoriously hard to prove that a particular act has been motivated by race discrimination. Even an employer who decides not to employ someone from an ethnic minority may not admit to himself or herself – let alone to others – the real reason for refusal. Even a professed desire to employ someone 'who will fit in' can disguise discriminatory intent.

☞   *You have been thwarted in gaining promotion in your firm. You suspect it is because you are from an ethnic minority. It is of course very difficult to prove your case and you want a tribunal to draw the inference that you are the victim of racial discrimination. You would also like information from your employers concerning the ethnic composition of their workforce in order to show that they generally operate discriminatory practices.*

The courts are well aware of the difficulties of proving racial discrimination in the workplace. Usually an employee can only point to certain facts which are consistent with having been treated less favourably on the grounds of race. It is then up to the employer to furnish a convincing alternative explanation – for example, that there were other good reasons for taking that particular action. If no good explanation is put forward, then a tribunal could well infer discrimination.

The courts will order an employer to provide information on the ethnic composition of the workforce in a race discrimination case, provided it is reasonable to impose such an order. For example, if the data already exists, then it is not asking too much from an employer to provide it. However, where the information is not available and it would take great expense and trouble to assemble it, then an order is unlikely to be made.

However, this may change when, from 19 July 2003, there is a shift in the burden of proof and the onus is on employers to ensure that employment practices and procedures do not disadvantage employees on grounds of their race.

2.9   Exceptions to the rule – where there is no discrimination

a) Discrimination on grounds of birth, nationality, descent or residence is permitted in the civil service.

b) Employment in private households is not covered by the Race Relations Act.

c) If particular occupational qualifications are required, discrimination is permitted. Thus an employer may discriminate against a person on grounds of race in very particular circumstances – where race is a 'genuine occupational qualification' for the post (see section 2.10 immediately below).

2.10   In what circumstances might belonging to a particular racial group be a 'genuine occupational qualification'?

a) Where an employee will be required to participate in a dramatic performance or other entertainment and someone from a particular racial group is needed for purposes of authenticity.

b) Where an employee will have to act as an artist's or photographic model and authenticity is needed.

c) Where an employee will be working in a place where food or drink is served to members of the public in a particular setting and a person of a particular racial group is needed for purposes of authenticity (such as a Thai waitress in a Thai restaurant).

d) Where an employee will be providing welfare services to a particular racial group, which could most effectively be provided by a member of that group. The question of what are welfare services has been considered by the courts. The term is given a wide interpretation. However it will not apply where, for example, the services – even in a welfare department – are of an administrative nature which could be performed by someone from any racial group.

Note: The Race Relations (Amendment) Act 2001 came into force in April 2001. It imposes a new duty on public authorities to eliminate racial discrimination.

3   DISCRIMINATION AGAINST DISABLED PEOPLE

The Disability Discrimination Act 1995 is particularly relevant in the employment context as the Act's main goal is to enable people with disabilities to lead independent lives and be allowed to enjoy equal opportunities. If you have a disability, it is illegal for an employer to discriminate against you. The Act is linked to Codes of Practice which set out the things that employers should do to make life easier for you. By 2004, organisations may have to make alterations to their buildings to make sure that they can be easily accessed by people with disabilities.

3.1   What is a disability?

A person is defined by the Act as disabled if he or she has a physical or mental impairment which has, in the words of the Act, a 'substantial long-term effect' on his or her ability to carry out 'normal day-to-day activities.'

'Long-term' means that the impairment lasts at least 12 months. The impairment may affect the following:

- mobility
- manual dexterity
- physical co-ordination
- speech, hearing or eyesight
- memory or ability to concentrate, learn or understand
- perception of the risk of physical danger
- ability to lift or carry everyday objects.

Progressive conditions are dealt with, as are conditions where there has been remission but the impairment is likely to recur.

The question whether a particular impairment is 'substantial' is to be decided by an employment tribunal, not by a doctor. The tribunal must take account of medical evidence but it may reject it for good reason. It is likely to be a question of fact and so will not normally be open to appeal.

There are currently proposals before Parliament to ensure that HIV and cancer are treated as disabilities from an early stage.

Booklet DL60: *Definition of Disability* gives general help (available free from Disability on the Agenda from the Department for Work and Pensions (see DIRECTORY)).

3.1.1   Mental Impairment Guidelines

The Employment Appeal Tribunal has laid down guidelines on claims for disability discrimination relating to mental impairment.

If you wish to complain that your employer has discriminated against you because of your mental illness, it is up to you to prove your illness on the balance of probabilities. You will need to identify clearly and in good time what illness you are alleging so that your employer can indicate whether that illness is in issue and, if so, why.

A loose description such as 'anxiety', 'stress' or 'depression' of itself will not suffice unless there is credible and informed evidence that in your particular case that description identifies a clinically well-recognised illness.

If your employer disputes your illness on technical medical grounds, you will need to get medical evidence not just of the mental illness but also when, over what periods, and how it can be expected to have shown itself, either generally or to the employer in the course of your employment.

Note: if your case goes before a tribunal, it must not form a view of your 'mental impairment' based only on the way you give evidence on the day of the hearing.

3.2   What does discrimination entail?

The Act states that it is unlawful for an employer to discriminate against a disabled person who applies for a job, with regard to:

- the offer of employment
- the employment terms

- job opportunities that may arise in the future; and
- the kind of training given.

Please note: this list is not exhaustive.

As with race and sex discrimination, a disabled person is discriminated against if he or she is treated less favourably than other employees and the employer cannot show that the treatment is justified.

3.3 Duties of an employer

If a disabled person is placed at a substantial disadvantage in the workplace, an employer will have to take reasonable steps to make other arrangements. These can include the following:

- making adjustments to the premises
- reallocation of duties
- alteration of work hours
- acquiring or modifying equipment, instructions, or reference manuals
- providing supervision.

However, in deciding what is 'reasonable' for an employer to have to do in meeting these requirements under the new law, regard must be paid to the practicality of taking a particular step, its cost, and the disruption involved etc.

A new campaign has been launched to persuade the government to give tax relief to employers who make their workplaces more accessible for disabled workers. The Disabled Rights Commission and the Confederation of British Industry are pushing for tax relief for employers to reduce the cost of improving access to premises for disabled staff. They say that access will be improved for disabled people faster if fiscal incentives are offered to businesses to do so.

The Disability Discrimination Act requires businesses to make their services acccessible to disabled people by 2004. Many businesses will need to make alterations to their buildings so that they can be accessed by the disabled. A time-limited tax allowance would be helpful to small firms that might otherwise be unable to afford the necessary physical adjustments.

Do note: the Act extends to employers employing 15 or more people. However the small employers' exemption is to be removed in October 2004.

Remember: in general the current exemption for prison officers, firemen, educational establishments etc will not apply from 1 October 2004.

3.4 Can discrimination be justified?

If an employer can show that:

- the disabled person is unsuitable for employment
- the nature of the disability would significantly impede the work the disabled employee would be called upon to do
- training, in the circumstances, would be of little value, or
- employment would endanger the health and safety of any person on the premises including that of the disabled person

then there may be legal justification for what would otherwise be a discriminatory act.

3.5 How do the anti-discrimination provisions work?

A Disability Right Commission (DRC) began work in April 2000 to oversee the implementation of the Act. The DRC:

- works towards eliminating discrimination against disabled people
- promotes equal opportunities for them
- provides information and advice to the disabled, employers and service providers
- prepares codes of practice
- keeps the working of the Act under review
- arranges for a conciliation service in disputes in regard to access to goods and services.

It also has considerable power to take those in breach of the Disability Discrimination Act (DDA) to court. It has investigative powers and will use them to ensure that the anti-discrimination provisions are complied with.

The DRC can help to enforce the DDA in the following ways:

a) It can provide or arrange for legal advice or other representation in relation to proceedings brought by individuals under parts II and III of the DDA if one or more of the following conditions are met:

- the case raises a matter of principle
- it is unreasonable to expect the applicant to take the case unaided
- there is some other special consideration.

☞ *You feel you have been discriminated against in not being offered promotion by your employer because you suffer from a mild form of epilepsy. You are not in a position to challenge your employer, which is a large multi-national corporation. You are also not union-represented and you wonder whether an approach to the DRC must be through a trade union or some other referral agency.*

Individuals can approach the Commission. Referral from any other agency is not necessary.

b) It can undertake formal investigations. If in the course of a formal investigation the Commission is satisfied that a person has committed or is committing an act which is unlawful for the purposes of the DDA, it can issue a non-discrimination notice requiring the person concerned to stop committing the act. A non-discrimination notice remains in force for a period of five years after it becomes final. If it appears to the Commission during that time that the person concerned has failed to comply with any of the terms of a non-discrimination notice, it can apply to a county court for an order requiring it to do so.

c) If during the life of a non-discrimination notice the Commission has reason to believe that the person concerned is likely to commit one or more unlawful acts, it can apply to a county court for an injunction requiring them to stop doing so.

3.6 Ambit of the Act

Small businesses, i.e. those with fewer than 15 employees, are exempt from the employment provisions of the Act. However the small employers' exemption is to be removed in October 2004.

3.7 The Act in operation

The Disability Discrimination Act 1995 came into force in December 1996.

The working of the Act has been monitored and the findings show that there have been more cases taken under its employment provisions at its inception than there were under those of the Sex Discrimination or Race Relations Acts in their first years.

In most cases the claim was identified and initiated by an adviser (e.g. a trade union or citizen's advice bureau) rather than by the applicant.

ACAS played an important role in resolving cases, having settled 41 per cent of claims brought. It appeared that employers were concerned over the extent of their duty to establish the medical condition of potential employees, while workers were uncertain about the extent to which they would have to discuss their condition when applying for a post.

Most of the cases concerned unfair dismissal and most claimants were men. The commonest disabilities concerned conditions relating to the back or neck; depression or anxiety; and problems with arms or hands. The Disability Rights Commission Helpline is 0845 7622 633.

☞ *You have been dismissed from your job as a sales co-ordinator. Your employer said that it was because of gross misconduct in that you had exploited a company scheme to get free weekend breaks. However you believe that the real reason was because you have agoraphobia which makes you afraid of travelling by train or alone by car.*

In a similar case an employment tribunal found that the real reason for an employee's dismissal was because of her agoraphobia and awarded her over £7,000 in compensation.

☞ *You are a part-time school teacher employed on a one-year fixed-term contract. Soon after starting your job, you were diagnosed as having breast cancer. You arranged to have treatment on your days off but had to go for surgery in December, followed by scans and radiotherapy. Your contract was not renewed and you complained that the school has used your temporary contract as an excuse to dismiss you because of your cancer.*

In a similar case, an employment tribunal awarded an employee over £9,000 compensation for unfair dismissal and disability discrimination, which included over £7,000 for injury to feelings.

3.8   Exceptions to the Act

At present the DDA does not apply to prison officers, firefighters, the police, the armed forces, educational establishments, jobs on board ships, aircraft or hovercraft, and jobs where you would have to work outside Great Britain most of the time. However, the new laws will prevent discrimination against people with disabilities working in most of these areas (see also section 3.3 above).

3.9   Anti-Discrimination Directive

The EU Anti-Discrimination Directive protects against discrimination on grounds of age, race, disability, sexual orientation, religion and belief.

3.9.1   Race discrimination

The main provisions of the Race Relations Act already comply with the EU Directive. However the Directive shifts the burden of proof to employers to provide that their employment practices and procedures do not disadvantage employees on grounds of their race. There is also a specific prohibition on harassment on grounds of race. This must be implemented by 19 July 2003.

3.9.2   Age discrimination

There are currently no laws to stop people or organisations from discriminating against you because of your age. However, from 2 December 2006 rules will be introduced to prevent mandatory retirement at a certain age. Under the new rules, which apply from 2 December 2006, your employers must ensure that their practices and procedures, e.g. recruitment, training, promotion and redundancy policies are not discriminatory on grounds of age.

However, if you think you have been fired or made redundant unfairly because of your age, you can still take a case to an employment tribunal or the court under the Employment Rights Act.

3.9.3   Discrimination on grounds of religion, belief or sexual orientation

From 2 December 2003, a prohibition is to be imposed on discrimination, victimisation and harassment on grounds of religion, belief or sexual orientation in employment and training. There is no definition as yet of 'religion', 'belief' or 'sexual orientation'. Your employers must ensure that their employment practices and procedures do not disadvantage employees on grounds of their religion.

People who have had 'gender reassignment' (a sex change) do have some legal protection against discrimination in employment and work training. The Sex Discrimination Act affords protection to anyone who is about to go through, or has gone through, gender reassignment. Apart from avoiding discrimination in recruitment, dismissal etc., your employer should allow you time off work for necessary medical treatment as they would for other kinds of necessary medical treatment.

4   DISMISSAL

4.1   Notice requirements

Both employer and employee are normally entitled to a minimum period of notice of termination of employment. After one month's employment, an employee must give at least one week's notice. An employer must give an employee at least one week's notice after one month's employment, two weeks after two years, three weeks after three years and so on up to 12 weeks after 12 years or more. A longer period of notice may be provided in the contract of employment.

4.2   Actionable dismissal

There are two types of actionable dismissal: *wrongful dismissal* and *unfair dismissal*.

The common law allows an employee to bring a claim for *wrongful dismissal* in the ordinary courts. At common law an employer could end an employee's contract of employment by giving proper notice or payment in lieu. A failure to give proper notice was treated as a breach of contract and an employee could sue for damages for wrongful dismissal. This right still exists.

Statute law allows an employee to bring a claim for *unfair dismissal* in an employment tribunal. Changes have been introduced so that employment tribunals are now able to hear *wrongful dismissal* cases as well (see immediately below).

If you are in any doubt as to what action best suits your particular situation, you must seek legal advice.

4.2.1   Wrongful dismissal

4.2.1(a)   Conditions of wrongful dismissal outlined

a) An action for wrongful dismissal only arises where there has been breach of contract.

b) There is no maximum award in damages for wrongful dismissal in the ordinary courts (£25,000 limit in tribunals).

c) A claim for wrongful dismissal does not involve a continuous service requirement (see section 4.2.5 below).

d) The court will not normally order that an employee be reinstated in an action for wrongful dismissal.

e) There is no age barrier to a claim for wrongful dismissal, whereas under statute, an employee past the normal retiring age cannot claim for unfair dismissal.

f) A claim for damages may be brought within six years from the date of the alleged breach of contract, whereas under statute an employee must generally bring an action within three months.

g) There is no ceiling on damages in a wrongful dismissal case. A highly paid employee with a long notice provision may be entitled to sue for considerable sums of money. In one case an employee entitled to 30 months' notice was awarded over £70,000 damages.

4.2.2   Unfair dismissal

The provisions relating to unfair dismissal are now contained in the Employment Rights Act 1996 and the Employment Relations Act 1999.

a) There may be a case of unfair dismissal even where there has been no breach of contract.

b) The maximum award of compensation for unfair dismissal is currently £52,600 (linked to the rate of inflation from 1 February 2002).

c) Employees generally require one year's continuous service before they can bring a claim for unfair dismissal.

d) An employment tribunal may order reinstatement or re-engagement of an employee.

e) An employee who is over normal retiring age is not entitled to bring a claim for unfair dismissal.

f) There is a time limit of three months for bringing a claim for unfair dismissal.

g) Only employees can claim unfair dismissal, but workers who are not employees, i.e. contract workers (see also section on the self-employed, section 1 above) can claim that they have suffered a detriment if their contracts are terminated for seeking to enforce a right to the national minimum wage, exercising a right under the Working Time Directive, or making a protected disclosure under the Public Interest Disclosure Act 1998 (the 'whistle-blowing' provisions). See section 4.6 below.

Note of warning: once again employees are warned to pay particular heed to the three-month time limit.

Additional note of warning: not all types of employment are covered.

4.2.3   Exceptions

A claim for unfair dismissal is not allowed in the following employment situations:

- in the armed forces
- in the civil service if national security is involved
- where you are employed by close relatives
- where diplomatic immunity applies
- where a dismissal procedures agreement is in force
- where the employee is not within the definition in the Employment Rights Act 1996

- at the expiry of a fixed-term contract
- where there is immunity of international organisations
- in the police service
- in the case of profit-sharing fishermen
- where the qualifying period of service has not been completed
- where the contract involves the evasion of tax and should not be enforced as illegal
- where you are the temporary replacement for a woman on maternity leave
- where the work is ordinarily carried out outside Great Britain.

So in certain circumstances, a claim for wrongful dismissal may still be more to an employee's advantage than pursuing a claim for unfair dismissal under statute. Also, a claim for wrongful dismissal may be the only avenue open to an employee – for example, when s/he has not worked the continuous period necessary to qualify for his or her statutory rights.

4.2.4   Employee's rights against unfair dismissal

By law, an employee has the right not to be unfairly dismissed by his or her employer.

The above statement is subject to certain reservations:

a) While a dismissal in certain instances may appear to be unfair, an employer can put forward reasons to show why the dismissal was fair in the particular circumstances of the case (see section 4.2.6 below).
b) In general an employee must have worked for a qualifying period (see *Continuous service*, section 4.2.5 below). However in certain instances, there is no need for a qualifying period (see section 4.2.5(a) below).
c) In certain capacities employees have no protection – for example, members of the armed forces or the police.

The right to claim unfair dismissal or redundancy is governed by the Employment Rights Act which prevents an employee from bringing a claim if he or she is over the company retirement age or, if it does not have one, the state retirement age of 65.

However, in a recent case, two employees claimed unfair dismissal and redundancy after they were dismissed, and won, even though they were aged 67 and 71 respectively. They had argued that the rules which stopped them making a claim amounted to indirect sex discrimination because more men than women continued in work after the age of 65. The tribunal considered the case in detail and agreed with that argument. It was not satisfied that the rules could be justified as they were contrary to the equal pay principle under European law.

Following this decision – but subject to appeal – it looks as though any employee who does not want to retire may claim unfair dismissal whatever his or her age.

4.2.5   Continuous service

To bring a claim for unfair dismissal, an employee must show that he or she has worked for the appropriate period. This is known as continuous service (see *Working for a Living (Part 1)*, section 7).

4.2.5(a)   Where there is unfair dismissal and no requirement of continuous employment

If a dismissal is based on:

- sex discrimination
- race discrimination
- trade union activities or membership
- non-membership of a trade union

there is no requirement of continuous employment before a claim can be made.

(See DTI Booklet: *Rules governing continuous employment*, PL711.)

4.2.5(b)   Lockouts

When an employer closes the place of employment or refuses to continue employing staff, then there is a lock-out.

An employment tribunal can only determine whether there has been an unfair dismissal where

i. other employees were not dismissed; and

ii. if they were dismissed, they were re-engaged within three months.

This is the 'no picking and choosing' rule.

4.2.5(c) Strikes

An employment tribunal has no jurisdiction to determine whether a dismissal was unfair where, at the time of the dismissal, the employer was conducting a lock-out or the employee was taking part in a strike or other industrial action.

However the employer has no right to pick and choose whom he dismisses in such circumstances. He must dismiss all those who are on strike at the time of the dismissal and must not re-engage them for three months. If the employer dismisses or re-engages only some, those persons who were not re-engaged, or were dismissed, may bring a claim of unfair dismissal before an employment tribunal.

Employees who, at the time of dismissal, are taking part in unofficial action are excluded from the right to bring a claim of unfair dismissal.

4.2.6 When an employer claims a dismissal was fair

An employer may defend a claim of unfair dismissal by establishing a potentially fair reason for the dismissal. Among these reasons are:

a) the capability or qualifications of the employee; poor performance; or ill health;

b) the conduct of the employee;

c) redundancy (see *Redundancy*, section 5 below);

d) illegality (it would be potentially fair for an employer to dismiss an employee if he would be breaking the law if he continued to work; for example, it would be fair to dismiss a driver who had lost his licence);

e) some other substantial reason (see ACAS advisory booklet: *Discipline at Work*); this may include such things as unacceptable absence levels, criminal convictions, etc.

Even if an employer has dismissed an employee fairly, the employee is still entitled to a period of notice.

4.2.7 Dismissal which is automatically unfair

There are some dismissals which are automatically unfair. Unfair circumstances of dismissal include:

- where an employee is a member of a trade union
- where an employee is involved in union activities
- where an employee refuses to join a trade union
- closed shop dismissals
- where an employee is pregnant and the principal reason for dismissal is her pregnancy
- where an employee has been selected unfairly for redundancy
- where there has been a transfer of the employer's undertaking
- where the dismissal is on grounds of sex
- where the dismissal is on grounds of race.

4.2.7(a) Failure to follow procedures

Under the provisions of the Employment Act 2002, if an employer fails to follow any step of the statutory dismissal procedure (see section 4.7 below) it will render the dismissal automatically unfair. However the employee must still have one year's continuous service before he or she can bring an unfair dismissal claim. If a tribunal orders reinstatement the employee will usually be awarded four weeks' pay as well, subject to a cap of £250 per week.

4.2.8 Reasons to be in writing

An employee may request a written statement of the reasons for dismissal (fair or unfair). To be entitled to such a statement, an employee must have completed one year's continuous employment with an employer at the effective date of dismissal.

The statement should be provided within 14 days of requesting it. An employer cannot unreasonably refuse to provide a statement.

An employee who is dismissed during her pregnancy or maternity leave is entitled to a written statement of the reasons regardless of her length of service and whether or not she has requested it.

4.2.9 Time limit for claims

A claim for unfair dismissal must be presented within three months from the effective date of termination unless the tribunal considers that this was not reasonably practicable.

Note: an employee who was dismissed but offered re-employment within the statutory time limit for bringing a claim for unfair dismissal, which was later withdrawn, was not entitled to bring a claim outside the time limit.

4.2.10 Compensation for injury to feelings

At present damages for unfair dismissal can only be awarded in respect of the period of notice in question, but the courts have indicated that future claims for unfair dismissal may include an element for injury to feelings, subject to statutory limits in the same way as in discrimination cases.

☞ *A worker was summarily dismissed for gross misconduct. No specific allegations were put to him during the employer's disciplinary meeting and he was given no opportunity to appeal. The worker later proved that his dismissal was in breach of his employer's own disciplinary procedures. He brought an action claiming breach of contract in the county court two years later, complaining that the manner of his dismissal had caused him to suffer a mental breakdown which had prevented him from working since.*

The Appeal Court held that damages could not be awarded for the manner of dismissal, injury to feelings or losses directly accruing from the dismissal. The House of Lords confirmed that the statutory right to claim unfair dismissal could not be supplemented by a common law remedy in respect of the manner of dismissal but it was suggested that damages might be payable in future for distress, humiliation and loss of reputation in appropriate cases.

4.2.11 Compensation adjusted

If a tribunal finds that the employer failed to comply with the statutory dismissal procedure, it will usually be required to increase any award of compensation by between 10% and 50%. On the other hand, if the employee fails to comply with the statutory procedures, any compensation awarded will be reduced by the same percentage.

4.3 Summary dismissal

In certain exceptional circumstances, an employee can be dismissed without notice. The dismissal takes effect immediately. The courts require 'gross misconduct'.

Summary dismissal has been justified where:

- an employee has acted dishonestly
- an employee has gained unauthorised access to computer records
- an employee has knowingly breached an express contractual term (e.g. where a coach firm expressly forbids drinking on or off duty and one of its long-distance drivers reports for work over the limit).

Employers must make sure that they carry out sufficient investigations into alleged employee-misconduct or dishonesty before taking the decision to dismiss.

A worker was dismissed for making personal phone calls at work but the dismissal was later found to be unfair because the employers had made insufficient investigations into the circumstances to find out the purpose of the calls and whether there were any personal problems which had prompted the calls.

Even if dishonesty had been proved, dismissal was not inevitable under the employer's disciplinary procedures.

Employers must act reasonably and in a considered fashion. They should give the employee an opportunity to:

- state his or her case under the rules of natural justice
- be accompanied to any formal hearing where dismissal might be the outcome
- have the assistance of an experienced trade-union official or an 'inexperienced' friend (i.e. attending in a personal capacity for moral support) at the hearing
- appeal against the outcome of the hearing.

4.4   Constructive dismissal

In certain cases, an employer will try to engineer a situation where an employee resigns so that it does not look like a case of unfair dismissal. However, if the circumstances are such that no reasonable employee could be expected to remain in employment, the law regards this as 'constructive dismissal'. The employee is thus still entitled to complain to an employment tribunal. Generally, an employer is in breach of contract as well when, for example, he changes a contract term, such as holiday entitlement. This need not always be the case, though: a situation can simply be made untenable for the employee by, for example, subtle forms of bullying or unreasonable demands being made, without an actual breach of contract.

4.5   Sunday working and betting

Retail workers have the right not to be dismissed, selected for redundancy (when others are not selected), or subjected to other detrimental action for refusing to work on Sundays. Similar rights apply to betting workers including all employees at licensed betting offices, and those employed at a horse-race course or licensed track whose work involves dealing with betting transactions.

4.6   Whistleblowers

The Public Interest Disclosure Act 1998 provides protection for workers who are dismissed or victimised as a result of making a disclosure that qualifies under the Act ('whistleblowers'). It applies to employees whose dismissal is held to be unfair if it is wholly or mainly for making a disclosure within the meaning of the Act; and to workers who are not employees, who can complain to an employment tribunal that they have suffered a detriment if their contracts are terminated for making such disclosure. Compensation is awarded on the same basis as for unfair dismissal.

However, a 59-year-old accountant was dismissed by his employer for blowing the whistle against the managing director and awarded £293,441 by the Employment Tribunal, which is almost six times the maximum the tribunal would have been permitted to award if the claim had been brought under the normal unfair-dismissal provisions.

4.6.1   Victimisation

Both employees and those workers who are not employees are protected from detrimental action, i.e. victimisation, or from deliberate inaction by their employer that falls short of dismissal or termination of contract.

4.7   The new dismissal, disciplinary and grievance procedures

The Employment Act 2002 has overhauled the rules on dismissals, disciplinary matters and grievances although the new rules do not come into force until later. If an employer fails to follow the statutory procedures they will be considered to be in breach of the employment contract. At present, employers with 20 or fewer employees do not need to have any procedures in place but the new rules will apply to all employers.

4.7.1   Major changes

Under the revised rules, a meeting with the employee must be arranged within a reasonable time in respect of every dismissal and not just those concerning disciplinary matters. This will include dismissals in connection with redundancy, poor work performance and long-term illness.

4.7.2   Appeals

At present appeals are in general limited to disciplinary cases. Under the changes, any employee who is dismissed has the right to appeal. This extends the right of appeal to cases of redundancy where appeals are currently rare. In future, appeals will involve face-to-face meetings with the employer to give the employee an opportunity to explain his or her case in person.

4.7.3 Written grievances

If a dispute cannot be resolved in the workplace and an employee goes to an employment tribunal, he or she may not raise any new grievances which could have been raised with the employer. The tribunal will refuse to consider any new grievances. However, an aggrieved employee could still walk out of his or her job and claim constructive dismissal as there is no provision for ex-employees to raise grievances with their former employer.

5 REDUNDANCY

Redundancy is firmly back in the limelight. Between December 2001 and February 2002, the Office of National Statistics reported that 214,000 people were made redundant in the UK, compared with 168,000 the previous year.

Your employer can make you redundant for a number of reasons such as falling profits, cost cutting, relocation or closing down. The traditional approach of last in, first out is increasingly being replaced by skills, experience and performance as the criteria for deciding who should stay and who should go.

Employees are entitled to payment of compensation if made redundant. This means that employment has been terminated because an employer:

- ceases altogether to carry on business
- ceases to carry on business in the same place
- ceases to need some employees.

5.1 When redundancy occurs

Redundancy occurs:

- if an employer ceases or intends to cease carrying on the business for the purposes of which the employee was employed
- if an employer ceased or intends to cease carrying on the business in the place where the employee was employed; or
- the needs of the business for an employee to carry out work of a particular kind, or to do so in the place where he worked, have ceased, or diminished, or were expected to do so.

5.2 When an employee can claim

To claim a redundancy payment an employee:

- must be aged between 18 and 65
- must have been employed for at least two years continuously (see *Working for a Living (Part 1)*, section 7 for computing 'continuous service') and
- must work for 16 hours or more each week.

A worker was held not to be an employee where his contract specified that if he was unable or unwilling to perform the services personally, he could arrange for another suitably qualified person to do so. Therefore he had no right to a redundancy payment when his contract was terminated.

However an employment tribunal has held that the application of the upper age-limit was unjustified as being indirect sex-discrimination under EU law. This suggests that, subject to an appeal, the imposition of the upper age-limit may be unlawful.

5.2.1 When part-time workers can claim

Part-time workers have the same rights to redundancy payments as full-time workers.

5.2.2 Presumption

There is a presumption that an employee who is dismissed has been dismissed for reasons of redundancy and is entitled to a redundancy payment.

5.3 Employer's defence to claim – reasonable alternative

An employer can prove that an offer of suitable alternative employment was made and the employee refused it unreasonably.

5.3.1 When an employee's refusal of alternative employment is justified

Employees can refuse alternative employment if it is unsuitable. An unsuitable offer entails:

- a significant loss of pay, including the opportunity to earn overtime and bonuses; or
- radical changes in hours of work.

☞ *You have been a long-serving headmaster. Your local education authority has now proposed to offer you a job as a supply teacher as an alternative to redundancy. You have refused, and claim redundancy payment.*

Your refusal would probably be considered reasonable as the council has made an unsuitable offer of alternative employment.

5.4 Redundancy procedure: fair dismissal procedures

An employer must follow certain steps in order to carry out a fair dismissal on grounds of redundancy. There must be:

a) Consultation with trade union representatives or elected employee representatives within 30 or 90 days as appropriate, on the steps to be taken (e.g. selection criteria, alternatives to dismissal etc.). The 90-day period applies where 100 or more employees are to be dismissed in any one establishment. The 30-day period applies where ten or more employees are to be dismissed.

b) Consultation with non-union staff individually or collectively. Employee representatives must be elected. An employer cannot appoint a person to act as employee representative and then claim to have complied with the law.

c) Determination of the number of redundancies necessary.

d) A call for volunteers.

e) Consideration of the possibility of re-deployment within the organisation or an associated company, with the possibility of retraining.

f) Selection of employees to be dismissed made according to agreed procedure or custom and practice.

g) Notification of dismissal to those concerned as soon as possible.

h) Reasonable paid time off during working hours to seek alternative employment.

i) Notification to the DTI of impending redundancies within a 30-day or 90-day period as appropriate (see also section 6.3.5 below).

j) Issue of notices of dismissal.

k) Calculation of redundancy payments and issue of statement of calculations to each employee to be dismissed.

Note: if there are fewer than 10 employees to be made redundant, there is no statutory minimum consultation period. However, the court has held that 'two or three' days for consultation is totally inadequate.

Additional note: new consultation and information rights for employees of all employers with 50+ staff are to be introduced by March 2008.

5.4.1 Importance of correct procedures

Prior consultation and warnings of impending redundancies are most important.

An employer will not normally be considered as acting reasonably unless he warns and consults any employees affected, or their representatives; adopts a fair basis on which to select for redundancy and takes such steps as are reasonable to avoid or minimise redundancy by redeployment within his own organisation.

Advice and guidance are available from regional branches of ACAS, the Employment Tribunals Services helpline – 0845 7959775 – or on the Department of Trade and Industry website: *www.dti.gov.uk.*

5.4.2   Time off when facing redundancy

An employee who is being made redundant and has been continuously employed by his or her employer for at least two years is entitled, whilst under notice, to take reasonable time off with pay in working hours to look for another job or to arrange training for future employment.

5.4.3   Redundancy and unfair dismissal

Acceptance of redundancy pay does not preclude the possibility of an employee later claiming that his or her dismissal was an unfair dismissal. Redundancy pay received will normally be set off against any unfair dismissal compensation if it later transpires that the dismissal was unfair and an award is ordered. If redundancy was not the real reason for the dismissal any purported redundancy paid by the employer cannot be set off against or cancel out the basic award if the dismissal was unfair. It could, however, be set off against any compensatory award.

5.4.4   Statutory redundancy payments

If your contract does not contain a redundancy package, you are entitled to the minimum statutory redundancy if you have been with your employer for at least two years.

Statutory redundancy pay is as follows:

- age 18 to 21: half a week's pay for every year you have worked
- age 22 to 40: a week's pay for every year worked
- age 41 to 65: a week-and-a-half per year worked (based on a maximum of 20 years service and a weekly wage ceiling of £250)
- after the age of 64, the overall payout is reduced by one twelfth for every complete month worked after that birthday.

If the company is insolvent, the Government Redundancy Office will make the statutory payments.

6   TRADE UNION ACTIVITIES

6.1   Time off for trade union duties

Any employee who is a union official has the right to have paid time off during working hours to carry out certain union duties and to train for those duties. This right also applies to part-time employees. The employer is not obliged to pay the employee for time off for other trade union activities.

6.1.1   What are trade union duties?

For the rule to apply, the duties must concern the following matters:

- terms and conditions of employment or working conditions
- engagement, termination or suspension of employment
- allocation of work
- disciplinary matters
- trade union membership
- provision of facilities for trade union officials
- negotiation or consultation machinery.

These duties are likely to be defined in a clear-cut way.

☞ *You are a teacher and a member of a teachers' union. You object strongly to a Bill currently before Parliament which is intended to introduce a new curriculum. You wish to lobby Parliament during the debate. That would entail leaving school during working hours. You argue that you are entitled to the time off with pay as it involves a question of working conditions and allocation of work.*

It is unlikely that a tribunal will decide that lobbying Parliament falls within 'trade union duties'. It is more likely to be seen as generalised political activity.

6.1.2   What is trade union training?

For an employee to qualify for time off for training, certain conditions are also laid down:

- it must be relevant to his particular trade union duties, and
- it must be approved by either the TUC or the official's own union.

6.1.3   Union Learning Representatives

There are around 3,000 Union Learning Representatives (ULRs) in the UK who advise union members on their training, education and development needs. At present ULRs have no clear statutory right to reasonable paid time off to carry out their duties and attend training courses etc., neither are employees entitled to take unpaid time off to take advantage of the services of a ULR. This is set to change in 2003 although details are not available at the time of writing.

6.2   Dismissal connected to unions

6.2.1   When dismissals are automatically unfair

From April 2000 onwards, an employee who takes 'protected' industrial action and is dismissed for this reason, can claim that the dismissal was unfair. The claim can be made to an employment tribunal regardless of length of service or age of the applicant.

'Protected industrial action' applies where it is union-backed and the union itself has complied with all the legal stipulations before embarking on the action.

A claim for unfair dismissal can also be made where an employer chooses to dismiss some of the workers taking part in industrial action but not others, or offers reinstatement to some within three months of dismissal but not to all those involved.

If a tribunal concludes that an employee has been unfairly dismissed, it can award compensation which can be in three parts:

a) a basic award which will be calculated on the employee's age, length of service and weekly pay
b) a compensatory award which is to compensate for the employee for loss up to a limit of £52,600 from 1 February 2002 (subject to annual revision in line with the retail price index)
c) an additional award where the employer fails to reinstate the employee when the tribunal has ordered that he do so.

Do note: such claims do not apply where the industrial action has lasted for more than eight weeks and the employer has taken 'responsible procedural steps' to settle the dispute.

6.3   Redundancy: need to consult unions

An employer who intends to make employees redundant must consult with the trade union of which the employees are members, if any, and not with employee representatives. Consultation must take place at the earliest opportunity. Union representatives of all affected employees must be consulted, not just employees who will be made redundant.

6.3.1   Information must be in writing

Certain information must be disclosed in writing to the union for the purposes of consultation (see also section 6.3.4(a) below):

• the reason for the redundancies
• the number and categories of employees to be affected
• the total number of employees in the categories to be affected
• the selection criteria to be applied
• the method of carrying out the redundancies to be used, having regard to any agreed procedures.

6.3.2   Consideration of union views

The employer must consider any representations made by the union and state the reasons for rejecting them. An employer need only comply with those requirements in so far as it is reasonably practicable.

6.3.3   Special circumstances

If there are special circumstances which make it not reasonably practicable for an employer to comply with the statutory provisions, he must take all steps which are reasonably practicable.

The following may be examples of special circumstances:

- the failure to renew trade with an important customer
- the sudden withdrawal of credit facilities.

Insolvency will only be regarded as a special circumstance if it results from some unusual or unexpected event.

6.3.4   Failure to comply with statutory requirements

If an employer fails to comply with the statutory requirements of consultation and consideration of representations, the union may appeal to an employment tribunal for a declaration that the employer has not complied with the statutory requirements and for a protective award.

6.3.4(a)   Consultation

The employer should consult with the union at the earliest opportunity. Where between 10 and 99 employees are to be made redundant, consultations must take place at least 30 days before the first dismissal takes effect. If 100 or more employees are to be made redundant, 90 days for consultation must be allowed before the first dismissal takes effect.

6.3.4(b)   Protective awards

The award is remuneration for a protected period for the employees who have been dismissed. That period is:

- 90 days where 100 or more employees are affected
- 30 days where 10 or more employees are affected
- 28 days where fewer than 10 employees are affected.

If the employer does not comply with the protective award order the employee himself can apply to the tribunal for an order.

6.3.5   Fine for failure to provide information

The DTI issues Form HR1 for notification. It can be obtained from any Redundancy Payments Office, Jobcentre or Unemployment Benefits Office. A copy of this must go to a trade union recognised by the employer. It is an offence not to provide the requisite information, involving a potential fine of up to £5,000 on a summary conviction.

A Guide to the statutory provisions can be found in the DTI Booklet PL 833: *Redundancy, Consultation and Notification*.

6.4   Working time regulations

In October 1998, regulations were introduced to implement the EU Working Time Directive. This applies to workers over the minimum school-leaving age with a contract of employment, and to agency workers and freelances who undertake contract work. The regulations were amended in 2001.

Under the regulations:

- an average weekly limit of 48 working hours is set, obtained over 17 weeks. Under certain circumstances the average can be extended over 26 weeks and even up to 12 months if agreed between employer and employee
- an average of 8 hours in each 24-hour period is set for night workers, obtained over 4 months
- night workers are entitled to a health assessment before being required to undertake night work (with periodic assessments thereafter)
- employees have a right to 11 hours' rest a day
- employees are entitled to a day off each week
- employees have a right to an in-work rest break if the working day is longer than 6 hours
- employees have a right to 4 weeks' paid leave per year.

Note: from 25 October 2001 you have a right to paid annual leave from the first day of your employment.

Warning: holiday cannot be carried forward from one year to the next.

A free *Guide to Working Time Regulations* is published by the Department of Trade and Industry and can be obtained by calling 0845 6000 925.

In the first action of its kind against a British firm, a shop manager who worked up to 97 hours a week successfully sued her employer for breaching the Working Time Directive. The 51-year-old was contracted to work a 39-hour week in a newsagents but suffered stress and anxiety after working long hours serving customers and stocking shelves. When she complained to her local council it launched a prosecution on her behalf. The manager frequently had to work up to 12 hours without a meal break. During five months in 2000, she had repeatedly raised her concerns with her manager but nothing was done to cut her hours. The employer admitted failing to protect her health and safety under the 1998 Working Time Regulations Act and was fined £5,000. It was also ordered to pay the manager £1,200 in compensation.

Do note: certain categories of worker are exempted, such as junior doctors.

6.4.1   Calculating leave

Before October 2001 you could apply to take all of your four weeks' leave after a 13-week qualifying period. After October 2001 you can only take the amount of accrued holiday during the first year of employment. Annual leave entitlement builds up monthly in advance and accrues at a rate of 1/12 of annual entitlement per month.

☞   *You are a full-time employee in your third month of employment. How much leave are you entitled to?*

You will be entitled to five days' leave (i.e. 20 days x 3/12).

6.4.2   Payment in lieu of holiday

You have the right to payment in lieu of outstanding holiday on termination of your employment. This applies even if you are dismissed for gross misconduct. However this right can be limited in the terms of the contract of employment.

An employee was summarily dismissed for gross misconduct. His contract provided that he would not receive accrued holiday pay if he was dismissed for gross misconduct. His employer argued that the provision in the contract was a relevant agreement as provided for in the regulations so that the payment the employee was entitled to receive was £0.

The employment Appeal Tribunal held that the clause in the employee's contract could be a relevant agreement but that the particular clause was ineffective as the regulations did not allow the agreed payment to be £0 as this was an attempt to exclude or limit the regulations.

However it looks as though an employer could use a clause in its employment contracts to set out the total payment that would be paid upon termination, which could be very little. This is yet to be tested.

6.5   National Works Councils

A draft EU Directive on National Works Councils has been issued. It will require all employers with 50 or more employees to inform or consult employee representatives on a wide range of business issues affecting employees, such as business development plans, the financial situation of the company and any substantial organisational changes. It is expected to be implemented by early 2005 but the UK will be given additional time to implement the directive for employers with fewer than 150 employees.

DIRECTORY
WORKING FOR A LIVING

Advisory, Conciliation & Arbitration Service
(ACAS)
Brandon House
180 Borough Street
London SE1 1LW
Tel. 020 7210 3613
(See listing under ACAS in local phone directories)
www.acas.org.uk

The Andrea Adams Trust
(dedicated to workplace bullying)
Hova House
1 Hova Villas
Hove
E. Sussex BN3 3DH
Tel. 01273 704 900
www.andreaadamstrust.org

Central Arbitration Committee
Third Floor
Discovery house
28–42 Banner Street
London EC1Y 8QE
Tel. 020 7251 0747
www.cac.gov.uk

Certification Office for Trade Unions and Employers' Associations
Brandon House
180 Borough Street
London SE1 1LW
Tel. 020 7210 3734
www.certoffice.org

Commission for Racial Equality
St. Dunstans House
201–211 Borough High Street
London SE1 1GZ
Tel. 020 7828 7022

Department for Education and Skills
Sanctuary Buildings
Great Smith Street
London SW1P 3BT
Tel. 020 7925 5555
www.dfes.gov.uk

Department for Work and Pensions
Correspondence Unit
Room 540
The Adelphi
1–11 John Adam Street
London WC2N 6HY
Tel. 020 7712 2171
www.dwp.gov.org

Department of Trade and Industry
Redundancy Payment Service
Hagley House
83–85 Hagley Road
Birmingham B16 8QG
(Helpline) Tel. 06451 450 004
www.dti.gov.uk

Disability Law Service
39–45 Cavell Street
London E1 2BP
Tel. 020 7791 9800

Disability Rights Commission
7th Floor
222 Grays Inn Road
London WC1X 8HL
Tel. 020 7211 4110
www.drc-gb.org

Employment Appeal Tribunal
Audit House
58 Victoria Embankment
London EC4Y 0DS
Tel. 020 7273 1041
www.employmentappeals.gov.uk

Employment Rights Advice Service
See Low Pay Unit *below*
Tel. 020 7387 2522
www.lowpayunit.org.uk

Employment Tribunals Field Support Unit
100 Southgate Street
Bury St. Edmunds
Suffolk IP33 2AQ
(Employment Tribunal Enquiry Line)
Tel. 0845 795 9775
www.employmenttribunals.gov.uk

Equal Opportunities Commission
Arndale House
Arndale Centre
Manchester M4 3EQ
Tel. 08456 015 901
www.eoc.org.uk

The Gender Trust
PO Box 3192
Brighton BN1 3WR
Tel. 07000 790347
www.gendertrust.org.uk

Health and Safety Executive
Daniel House
Trinity Road
Bootle
Merseyside L20 3TW
(Infoline) Tel. 08701 545 500
www.hse.gov.uk

Industrial Relations Services *(Lexis Nexis IRS)*
18–20 Highbury Place
London N5 1QP
Tel. 020 7354 5858
www.irseclipse.co.uk

Lesbian and Gay Employment Rights
Unit 1G
Leroy House
436 Essex Road
London N1 3QP
Tel. 020 7704 8066 *(lesbians)*
Tel. 020 7704 6066 *(gay men)*
www.lager.dircon.co.uk

London Hazards Centre
Hampstead Town Hall Centre
213 Haverstock Hill
London NW3 4QP
Tel. 020 7267 3387
www.lhc.org.uk

Low Pay Unit
10 Dukes Road
London WC1H 9AD
Tel. 020 7387 2910
(Advice Lines)
London Tel. 020 7387 2522 (2–5 pm)
Greater Manchester Tel. 0161 953 4024
West Midlands Tel. 0800 220 823
Yorkshire & Humberside Tel. 01924 439 381
www.lowpayunit.org.uk

Maternity Alliance
45 Beech Street
London EC2P 2LX
Tel. 020 7588 8582
www.maternityalliance.org.uk

National Association of Victim Support Schemes
see Victim Support *below*

National Minimum Wage Information Service
Freepost PHQ1
Newcastle-upon-Tyne NE98 1ZH
(Helpline) Tel. 0845 8450 360
www.tiger.gov.uk

Parliamentary Commissioner for Administration
Millbank Tower
21–24 Millbank
London SW1P 4QU
Tel. 0845 015 4033
www.ombudsman.org.uk

Public Concern at Work
Suite 306
16 Baldwins Gardens
London EC1N 7RJ
Tel. 020 7404 6609
www.pcaw.co.uk

Suzy Lamplugh Trust
(Personal safety for those at risk)
14 East Sheen Avenue
London SW14 8AS
Tel. 020 8392 1839
www.suzylamplugh.org

Third Age Employment Network
207–221 Pentonville Road
London N1 9UZ
Tel. 020 7843 1590
www.taen.org.uk

Trades Union Congress *(TUC)*
Congress House
Great Russell Street
London WC1B 3LS
Tel. 020 7636 403
(Helpline) Tel. 0870 600 4882
www.tuc.org.uk

Victim Support
Crammer House
39 Brixton Road
London SW9 6DZ
Tel. 020 7735 9166
www.victimsupport.org

Victim Support Scotland
15–23 Hardwell Close
Edinburgh EH8 9RY
Tel. 0131 668 4486
www.vssdirectory.org.uk

13   NEIGHBOURS

Most people live amicably enough with their neighbours, helping and supporting each other in a myriad different ways. In such cases, we do not think in terms of legal relationships. The questions of how the law governs our immediate environment or how it endeavours to resolve disputes between neighbours simply do not arise. Nevertheless, our patterns of living have changed to such an extent that a recent survey suggested that 30 per cent of people never talk to their neighbours and many others do not know who they are. This increasing isolation has been attributed in part to such technological 'necessities' as the motor car and the PC. As a result the social network we build up in our immediate environment is being depleted all the time.

With regard to issues which do arise between neighbours, the law tries to strike a balance. On the one hand, householders should be free to use their property and to behave as they like with the minimum interference from others. On the other hand, we have to use our property and behave in such a way that we do not interfere with the way our neighbours choose to enjoy their home environment. So the law strives to apply the maxim of 'give and take' – in the hope (sometimes a vain hope) of reducing the scope for quarrels between neighbours.

To those not involved, quarrels between neighbours may seem trivial indeed. Why should one litigate over a few inches of brick wall? What purpose can such litigation possibly serve? Can a few inches of wall, land or overhanging shrub ever justify the costs and the heartache? But we should never underestimate the anger and bitterness of those involved in such disputes. Television programmes such as 'Neighbours from Hell' provide graphic depiction of the depth of feeling which these quarrels engender.

As far as some house owners are concerned, particularly those in the country or in the suburbs, a great source of tension between neighbours is that of high hedges. There is no law on how high any hedge can grow and, indeed, in 2001 a Bill was introduced to limit height but did not complete the legislative process. Hedgeline (*hedgeline.org*), a large lobby and support group, pointed out that August 2002 marked the second anniversary of the Government's promise to legislate against problem high hedges and that still they continue to grow. Since then the government has reiterated that it remains committed to legislation.

In urban areas, the sources of complaint generally concern noise, litter, pollution, and other forms of anti-social behaviour. All these topics are addressed in the course of this chapter.

There are organisations which endeavour to take this particular aspect of social relations outside the sphere of the law courts altogether. Their view is that a court case is not the best way to solve problems between people who have to live in close proximity to each other for years. Mediation on a voluntary basis may be the best solution by far (see below, section 2.2.5, and the DIRECTORY at the end of this chapter). The Lord Chancellor's Department has issued a booklet on *Resolving Disputes Without Going to Court*. It has a special section on disputes between neighbours.

At the same time, the law has also been strengthened to combat growing problems in neighbourhood disputes. 'Antisocial behaviour orders' have been made part of the criminal law to deal, in particular, with the few who can make life a misery for the many, while the Housing Act 1996 has given public landlords increased powers of possession in cases of antisocial behaviour. Local authorities and housing trusts give 'introductory tenancies' so that new tenants can be 'on probation' for a year. The scope for eviction for bad behaviour has also been widened and now covers a tenant who causes disturbance to those in the vicinity or has visitors who do so. See the chapter on *Landlords and their Tenants*, section 4.3.1.

Alas, arguments between neighbours have led to more than bad feelings and ensuing litigation: over the years, several people have died as a result of such disputes.

Note of warning: the seller of a property has to inform a buyer of any problem which has arisen with a neighbour which could be categorised as a dispute, in the 'seller's pack'. So if you want to complain to a local authority, your landlord or a solicitor about your neighbour, do consider the issues very carefully in relation to a possible detriment to the value of your home.

Do always consider mediation as an option (see section 2.2.5 below).

In this chapter, we look at:

- the 'neighbour' principle
- problems with peace and quiet
- problems with boundaries and fences
- problems with nuisance
- problems with smoke and fumes
- problems with gardens
- problems with rights and properties
- trespass on neighbouring land
- problems with litter.

1 THE NEIGHBOUR PRINCIPLE

1.1 We have many neighbours in law

The line of the song runs 'Next door is just a footstep away'. However, the law takes a much wider view of the people we can and must call our 'neighbours'. In the legal sense, our 'neighbour' is any person whom we should reasonably have in mind if we were to act so carelessly as to cause him or her harm.

1.1.2 Reasonableness

Who are these people we should have in mind? Among other elements, the law defines the duty of care we owe to them on the basis of 'reasonableness'.

Of course, stating the principle on paper is easy, implementing it in practice is more difficult. Fine lines have sometimes to be drawn. Actual situations, as we all know, are infinitely variable.

☞ *In order to deter birds from eating the ripening cherries in your garden, you fire blanks into the air. Your garden is close to a road. A passing motorist is so frightened by the sound of the shots that he loses control of his vehicle and careers into a passing cyclist. What is your responsibility for the accident?*

In law, both the car driver and the cyclist would be considered your 'neighbours'. You should have realised that the sudden sound of gunshot near a well-used road might cause a panic reaction.

However, if you live in a very isolated spot and choose to frighten birds from your garden with blank shots (as you regularly have done in the past), you would probably not be responsible if a cyclist a couple of miles away fell off his bicycle from fright. He is not your 'neighbour' in the legal sense. It would not be 'reasonable' to expect you to have considered the possible harm to him in these circumstances.

Thus the emphasis is on the word 'reasonableness'. You do not owe a duty to take care of someone else's welfare if their presence is so remote that you couldn't be expected to be conscious of their well-being. In other words, you don't owe a duty of care to everyone in the world; you owe a duty to take care only to those who are reasonably likely to be affected by your careless actions.

In general, of course, the people who do become involved in neighbourhood disputes are indeed those who live close at hand. They are 'neighbours' in the most accepted sense of the word. But it is important to know that the legal definition of a 'neighbour' can take us well beyond those who live in our immediate vicinity.

2 PROBLEMS WITH PEACE AND QUIET

2.1 Noise as a form of pollution

Of all the complaints which neighbours make against each other, the commonest concern noise. It can come from loud music, crying children, barking dogs or DIY equipment; in summer, when one should most enjoy being out of doors, neighbourhood noise can become even more disturbing – whether it be the sound of lawnmowers and hedgetrimmers or of music through open windows.

Noise, quite rightly, is considered in law to be a form of pollution under the law of nuisance (see section 4, as well as section 2.3 below).

2.1(a) Modern society

Changing social and domestic patterns have also added to the problem: large houses which were built for one family are often subdivided into several flats with inadequate sound insulation; unemployment often means that the elderly and the relatively young find themselves sharing the same space during the day; the young may be inconsiderate and play music loudly; the elderly may be deaf and they too may turn up the volume.

Finally, hi-tech also works against those who like peace and quiet: stereo equipment is getting more and more sophisticated – as well as portable – so an escape from unwanted sound becomes increasingly difficult.

Motor traffic and aircraft pose problems of their own. Their volume grows all the time with their concomitant effects on the environment. However, the laws governing noise from traffic and overflying aircraft are largely outside the scope of this chapter.

2.1(b) Criminal Sanctions

In an endeavour to deal with the phenomenon of mass trespass and rave parties, criminal sanctions are now in force; see chapter on *The Countryside*, sections 6.3 and 6.4.

2.2 Interpersonal attempts to combat noise

In all disputes with neighbours, resort to the law should be your last course of action. There are many other routes to explore first.

☞ *You have put up with the fact that your neighbours lock their dog in their house when they are out so that it howls. You have put up with the fact that they play their radio loudly when they are home. But lately, they have been giving all-night parties with what sounds like professional disco equipment. What do you do?*

The answer involves several factors. To take the social aspects first:

It is always best to try to settle problems amicably, particularly with people you may have to co-exist with for years to come. But in view of the fact that you have already put up with a reasonable amount of disturbance, from their radio and dog, you are entitled to feel that the noise from disco parties is unreasonable. 'Reasonableness' is the key aspect of the case.

2.2.1 Talking to your neighbours

The first thing is to approach your neighbours and speak to them about the noise: try to establish whether there was a run of recent celebrations that has now come to an end. If not, ask them whether they would agree to break up their social gatherings at a reasonable hour so that others may sleep.

2.2.2 Contacting other neighbours

If, despite your request, they refuse to be more considerate, speak to your other neighbours to find out whether

a) they are affected by the noise and
b) whether a concerted approach with them may help.

2.2.3 Keeping written records

It would be advisable at this stage to put your complaints in writing to your noisy neighbours – very politely – and keep copies of your letters as well as any reply. Also keep a log of the noise, of all kinds, that you suffer from. Take note of when the parties begin and when they end. (See section 2.3.2 below.)

2.2.4 Contacting the landlords

In a block of flats, approach the Residents' Association if there is one, the managing agents, or the landlords. The noisy neighbours are probably in breach of the terms of their lease.

Where there is a speculative conversion of a house into a couple of flats you may find out that the 'landlord' is a shell company and that there is little help to be had from that quarter.

In public sector housing, contact the Housing Officer.

Unfortunately, for certain kinds of noise, an action against the landlord may not be of assistance.

☞ *You have recently bought a flat but are upset to find, once you moved in, that you are disturbed by your neighbours' everyday activities. The other tenants now tell you that they suffer from the same problem; they too can hear the neighbours' televisions, their babies crying, their cooking and cleaning, even the switching on and off of electric lights. The lack of privacy is causing tension and distress. It is apparent that the building, which is a pre-war block, was built with inadequate sound insulation. You and two other tenants decide to bring an action that your landlord is breaching the covenant of quiet enjoyment (see the chapter on Landlords and their Tenants, section 2.1.1) and for nuisance.*

In a similar case, the House of Lords held that the tenants' complaint was not that their landlord was actively interfering with their quiet enjoyment but was due solely to a lack of soundproofing. That was an inherent structural defect for which the landlord had not assumed responsibility. Further, the normal use of a residential flat, e.g. cooking in the kitchen, or cleaning rooms, could not possibly be a nuisance; nuisance had to be an unreasonable interference with adjoining land or property (see section 4 below).

In another case, where a tenant complained about traffic noise, the landlords again were held not liable. The problem, the court said, arose because of reasons external to the block of flats.

2.2.5 Seeking mediation

Try to establish whether there is a voluntary mediation service which could act so as to resolve the problem between yourself and your neighbours. If you contact Mediation UK (tel. 0117 904 6661) you will receive information on the nearest available service in your area (see also DIRECTORY). Most of the services are staffed by trained volunteers and are free to the user. The Royal Institution of Chartered Surveyors also runs a dispute resolution service: the Helpline number is 020 7334 3806.

2.3 Legal attempts to combat noise

If all else fails, you have to consider your legal position.

Remember the note of warning in the Introduction – a dispute can hinder you from trying to sell your property (see below, section 4.1.1.(a)).

2.3.1 The police

You could telephone the police and no doubt they get many such calls in the middle of the night. But the police are only likely to intervene if there is, or is likely to be, a criminal offence (see, however, section 2.7 below).

Do remember: in your dealings with your neighbours, you should call the police if they use intimidation or threats of violence.

In other cases, however, the law supplies alternative remedies.

2.3.2 Local authorities

You can complain to the Environmental Health Department of your local authority. Someone will come round to investigate – usually in office hours – so that is why if you are complaining of all-night parties you will need evidence to back up your complaint.

Note: some local authorities run call-out squads who do operate at night, so check the position in each case.

Local authorities are getting so many complaints of noise, some 70,000 per year, that they have great difficulty in dealing with them all on their available resources. In order to streamline procedures, certain local authorities have devised standard forms for the complainant to fill in so that the authorities can make their own assessment of the seriousness of the complaint. They may then get an officer to make a follow-up visit. It is the intermittent nature of noise – as well as the fact that it often takes place at night – which makes this aspect of the environmental health officer's job so difficult.

If he or she is satisfied that the complaint is genuine, the EHO might write an informal letter to the noisy neighbour. In the majority of cases, that might suffice. However, if the problem persists, the local authority can serve a notice under Section 80 of the Environmental Protection Act 1990 that the noise levels are to be reduced or curtailed. Your neighbour ignores the notice at his peril. If he fails to observe it, the authority can prosecute.

Remember: by contacting the local authority, you might prevent the dispute ever reaching the courts. If nevertheless it has to be litigated, the local authority does so on your behalf. For an increase in local authority powers, see section 2.3.5 below.

2.3.3 Going to magistrates

You can yourself go to a magistrates' court under Section 82 of the Environmental Protection Act 1990. Before you do so you have to give your neighbour formal written notice of your intention of taking out proceedings – and that may even be sufficient to stop the noise. Otherwise you will have to make an appointment with the court and produce your evidence to them.

The court will need to be satisfied that you have genuine cause for complaint, so you must specify time, date, duration of the noise, the nature of the noise and why you think it is a genuine nuisance. (For the definition of nuisance, see section 4 below.) In effect, you are launching a private prosecution. If satisfied by the presentation of your grievance, the court will issue a summons against your neighbour.

2.3.4 Going to the county court

Going to the county court is another route you could follow. You could begin a civil action in a county court for an injunction to stop the noise. (An injunction is a remedy which the law provides – in this case, telling the other party to refrain from acting in a particular way.)

You could also sue for damages. However, you would have to establish that you have suffered damage to your health or depreciation in the value of your property.

In one case, the seller of her house failed to inform the buyers that she had suffered from noisy neighbours and had made complaints about them to her local authority. As a result she had to pay the buyers £15,000 in damages, which represented their loss on the house when they tried to sell it some years later. See also the chapter on *Buying and Selling your Home*, section 5.2.

Do take heed: the outcome of litigation is always uncertain and it will depend on the view that the judge takes of the evidence which you present to the court.

In one case concerning noise from an upper flat to the flat below, the tenant of the lower flat applied to the court for an injunction that the owners of the flat above install appropriate floor coverings with acoustic barriers. Previously the tenants of the upper flat had carried out alterations that involved changing the use of certain rooms, and removing carpets, rugs etc which were then replaced with marble and ceramic tiled floors. This resulted in a substantial increase in the amount of noise penetrating to the flat below. In the opinion of a jointly-appointed expert, the noise clearly exceeded the appropriate limits under Building Regulations. The court granted the injunction. By any objective standard of reasonableness, the court held, the noise from the upper flat was unreasonable, unacceptable and constituted an actionable nuisance. The standard of comfort enjoyed prior to the nuisance and the standards envisaged by the lease were significant and important factors in deciding what was reasonable.

2.3.5 Increased powers to combat noise

The Noise Act 1996 was passed in response to an ever-growing number of complaints. It created an offence – the 'night noise offence' – which is intended to complement the existing statutory law of nuisance. The Act sets a 'permitted level' of noise during night hours (defined as being between 11 pm and 7 am).

Under the Act, local authorities which opt to do so are able to use an objective standard for measuring noise, thus reducing uncertainty. Most complaints of night noise concern amplified music and parties. Extra powers are available to local authorities: if the noise is not reduced within a time specified in a warning notice, the hi-fi equipment can be confiscated and a fixed penalty fine imposed.

The Government plans to improve soundproofing in new or recently converted flats in an endeavour to minimise the problem of noise in future. Amendments to the established tests for sound insulation between new homes are being published, under which the sound insulation in a sample of new homes will have to be tested.

2.4 Checklist

Do's

- Do examine your own feelings to see that you are not being hypersensitive and that your reactions are reasonable.
- Do satisfy yourself that an attempt to solve the problem by legal action would be worth the increase in neighbourly ill-will.
- Do check whether you can bring in the services of a mediator.
- Do keep careful records.
- Do get statements and/or co-operation from other neighbours when making your complaint.

Don'ts

- Don't put up with the noise until you reach bursting point. You also weaken your case if you do not take some measured steps to indicate your displeasure.
- However, do not assume that going to law will bring speedy relief – it is generally slow and expensive. There is also no guarantee of success.
- Don't ignore the various kinds of conciliation procedure.
- Don't, on the other hand, be too faint-hearted in pursuing your rights.

In all cases you should seek advice before resorting to legal action. In the chapter on *The Legal System* there is information about advisers who may be in a position to help you. See also the DIRECTORY at the end of this chapter.

2.5 Building standards

The discussion above concerns problems faced by one particular person who has to deal with a noisy neighbour. However, all the neighbours – for example in a block of flats or in a terrace – may share the common problem of inadequate sound insulation in the building.

The Office of the Deputy Prime Minister (created in May 2002 to take responsibility for the policy areas previously covered by the old Department of Transport, Local Government and the Regions) issues guidelines concerning requirements on soundproofing and also density requirements for party walls, stairs etc. However, these requirements are not mandatory.

The Building Research Establishment tests soundproofing to establish whether the level of noise penetration is reasonable.

2.6 Other sources of noise

2.6.1 Noise in the streets

A recurring problem is noise from faulty alarms, both car alarms and house alarms, which can ring and ring while the owners are away. In one case, a car alarm went off every night for several months, apparently set off by the wind! A maddened householder eventually tried to get into the car and was arrested for criminal damage. He was not charged but was bound over to keep the peace.

2.6.2 Statutory powers to deal with street noise

In order to combat these problems, the Noise and Statutory Nuisance Act 1993 extended the scope of the Environmental Protection Act 1990 so that street noise is also classified as a statutory nuisance (see below, section 4.3).

2.6.2(a) What is included

The Noise and Statutory Nuisance Act 1993 covers nuisance from vehicles, machinery or equipment in the street. It deals in particular with car alarms and burglar alarms (see sections 2.6.2(c) and (d) below).

'Street' not only covers a highway or road, but extends to a footway, square or court open to the public 'for the time being'. It would therefore cover a situation where a car with a faulty alarm is parked in a residential square – the parking being limited to residents only.

'Equipment' includes musical equipment – so that it would appear to cover the faulty, or even the persistent, bell of an ice cream van. Whether or not it could apply to busking remains to be seen.

2.6.2(b) What is excluded

The Act does not apply to traffic noise, political demonstrations or noise made by 'any naval, military or air force'.

2.6.2(c) Car alarms

(This is also dealt with in the Chapter on *Motoring*, see section 2.2.)

The person 'responsible' for a car with a faulty alarm is:

- the person whose name is registered as owner with the DVLA, or
- any other person who 'for the time being' is the driver of the vehicle.

An environmental health officer (EHO) can serve an abatement notice on that person to remedy the fault. If the vehicle is unattended the EHO can put a notice on the vehicle and if, after an hour, nothing further has been done or the person responsible has not been found, the EHO can:

- immobilise the alarm, or
- remove the vehicle.

The EHO can open and enter the car provided there is 'no more damage than is necessary'. The car must also be secured against theft 'as effectually' as when it was found!

2.6.2(d) House alarms

Householders have to inform their local authorities of alarms which they install. The alarm must meet prescribed requirements and the police must be notified of the names, addresses and telephone numbers of current key-holders.

If any alarm operates for more than an hour after it has been activated so as to annoy people nearby, an officer of the local authority can turn off the alarm by entering the premises provided he has authority to do so. He can obtain a warrant from a justice of peace to enter the premises – if need be by force – provided stringent stipulations are met. No more damage is to be caused than is necessary, the alarm should be re-set if reasonably practicable, and he must leave the premises – also so far as is reasonably practicable – as effectually secured against trespassers as when entered.

The owner can be called upon to reimburse the local authority for expenses incurred.

2.6.3 Noise from children

There is not much a neighbour can do if there are rowdy children in the house next door, the street, or the block. Speaking to their parents may only antagonise them, and the parents themselves may be powerless to stop the noise. However, under the Crime and Disorder Act 1998, power is given to local authorities to operate a local curfew on children under 10 years of age to prevent them being in a public place during specified hours unless in the charge of an adult. The power proved to be ineffective because it was not used. Despite this the power has now been extended to include 15-year-olds from 1 August 2001 and the Home Office has produced a *Guide to implementation of curfews* (*www.homeoffice.gov.uk*).

A town in Northamptonshire was reportedly gearing up to become the first in the country to use child curfew orders to tackle juvenile nuisance. The general feeling among children's groups and penal reformers appears to be that the curfew powers are popular with no one and would be virtually impossible to enforce.

The Act also empowers police forces, local authorities or crime and disorder partnerships to apply to magistrates courts for an 'antisocial behaviour order' (ASBO) for children aged 10 or over, as well as adults, who are causing harassment, alarm or distress outside their home.

ASBOs have been implemented haphazardly across England and Wales. According to a Home Office report in April 2002, just 466 orders had been imposed since they were introduced, costing an average of £5,360. It takes an average of 66 working days to get an order granted and nearly 6 out of 10 cases required three or more court hearings.

There are widespread variations in the way different areas use the powers. Cheshire, Essex, Wiltshire and Dyfed Powys have imposed no ASBOs, Gwent, North Wales and Lincolnshire one each, Cumbria, Bedfordshire and South Wales two each; whereas the West Midlands handed out 65 and West Mercia 47.

If children are playing truant, or appear to be playing truant, they should be reported to the education officer of your local authority. Similarly, if there is anxiety that a child's persistent crying could be the result of cruelty or neglect, the matter should be reported to the social services office of your local authority or to the NSPCC (this matter is dealt with more fully in the chapter on *Children (Part 2)*, section 1.6.3).

2.7 The Noise Act 1996

This Act provides machinery for the prosecution of night noise offences, covering principally amplified music or prolonged and noisy DIY activity. A local authority officer can leave a warning notice for the 'person responsible for the noise' and stipulate the time by which the noise is to cease. If, after measuring the volume, the officer is satisfied that an offence has been committed, the local authority can decide whether to prosecute or to serve notice of a fixed penalty (generally £100). A person guilty of a persistent night noise offence can be prosecuted and could be fined up to £1,000.

3 PROBLEMS WITH BOUNDARIES AND FENCES

3.1 Establishing boundaries

There is no rule of law that requires you to mark the boundary of your property or to enclose it with a fence. If there are stipulations about these matters, they will be as a result of an agreement with your neighbour or an obligation in your conveyance or lease.

But even if there are no such legal rules or no particular stipulation in your conveyance, it is always advisable to reach agreement with your neighbour about the boundaries between your properties.

3.1.1 Note of warning

The courts resound to quarrels between neighbours over the position of the fine line which divides their properties. Litigation reaches the highest courts over a matter of inches.

These cases can lead to the recovery of a disputed piece of land or the demolition of an offending fence for the winning party, who may also win damages. In fighting a hopeless cause, however, the other side can end up much worse off than before – indeed their entire property may have to be sold in order to pay a huge bill for costs on both sides – in addition to the damages which they may have to pay. Even those on the winning side can find themselves out of pocket in a lawsuit (see the chapter on *The Legal System*).

In a dispute over a boundary between Grade II listed properties, a defendant successfully challenged a county court decision that he pay his neighbour £2,904 damages for an encroachment on a 2.5 inch strip of land between their garages. The Court of Appeal reduced the amount of damages to £906.75, which comprised an unchallenged award of £904.75 plus £2 by way of nominal damages. In reducing the award of £2,000 for general damages, the court said that the figure was not based upon any evidence. It was plucked from the air as an attempt to compensate the neighbour for the loss of his land, as an injunction had been refused.

And do take heed: community legal funding [formerly legal aid] is not available to fund boundary disputes.

What is striking – and disheartening – is how fiercely both sides feel and how absolutely convinced they are that the other side is in the wrong.

The battle is over the boundary, the battlefield is the court. The judge endeavours to resolve the issue on legal grounds. Nonetheless it is often a profound clash of personality which is the significant factor in the litigants' presence in court at all.

One dispute between neighbours over a small strip of land worth £200 ended with a couple facing the prospect of selling their Cotswolds retirement home to pay a huge legal bill. The ruinous row over where the boundary lay lasted 18 years.

3.1.2   Prevention is always better than cure

If you are buying a property, always try to establish in advance where the boundaries to the property lie. Ascertain the rights of way and parking rights, if any. It is much better to sort out all these matters in advance than to try to assert your rights once you move in. See also the chapter on *Buying and Selling your Home*, section 4.5.

Be particularly wary of buying a property where the plan does not tally with what you actually see on the ground (see immediately below). If in doubt, contact the Boundary and Party Walls Working Group of the Royal Institution of Chartered Surveyors (see DIRECTORY).

3.1.3   When there is a plan

In general, in any conveyance there should be a plan, annexed to the register of title or the title deeds, which is supposed to show where the boundaries to a property lie. But a plan can be misleading, inaccurate or out of date.

The use of maps or plans such as the Ordinance Survey, prepared to a high standard of accuracy, is now widespread.

Warning note: no map or plan can reproduce to anything like the same scale every feature or detail which is found on the ground. Furthermore the Ordnance Survey's purpose is topographical and not to fix private boundaries.

In one case, the House of Lords stated that 'no workable system of conveyancing can be expected to eliminate entirely the opportunity for disputes about boundaries.' In most cases neighbours are content to accept that absolute precision is unattainable and a certain amount of latitude has to be given to whatever method was used to fix the boundaries of their land.

If you have not established the boundaries before you moved in, or you are unexpectedly under challenge from a neighbour, what do you do then?

3.1.4   The objective test

In general, the court takes an objective view of a factual situation. It asks itself the question 'What would a reasonable person think that he or she was buying at the time and in the circumstances of the case?'

☞ *You bought a bungalow which was built by the seller on part of his land. The seller still lives in the house next door. At the time of the purchase, you explained to him that you were thinking of building an extra room because you and your wife were expecting another child. The plan which the seller attached to the title deeds was not up to date. As far as you were concerned you assumed you were buying an extra ten feet of land next to the garage, on which you intended to build. The seller now says that that strip of land belongs to him. What can you do?*

The court will look, in such a case, not just at the plan in isolation but at all the surrounding circumstances, the negotiations leading up to the sale, and at the other documentation, such as the seller's answers to your solicitors' enquiries.

Then the court will ask itself the question: 'What would the reasonable person think he or she was buying?' The answer to that question may not necessarily be the answer that you would wish to hear – the court may decide that you simply acted on the assumption that the land would be yours but failed to ascertain your position properly.

3.1.5   When there is no plan

We have looked at the situation in which a plan can be misleading. There are also situations where there is no plan attached to the title deeds.

Where there is no plan of your property at all, or the plan is of no practical assistance, certain legal presumptions come in to play, i.e. the law makes certain generalisations about boundaries.

3.1.5(a) Ditches

If there is a man-made ditch at the 'end' of your garden which is not marked on any map or plan, then the law assumes that the boundary runs up to the near side of the ditch.

3.1.5(b) Hedges

If there is a hedge at the 'end' of your garden, your boundary will incorporate as much of the hedge as you trim; if you trim the whole of the hedge, then you may be able to claim that it is all yours. Otherwise the boundary is assumed to be the middle of the hedge.

3.1.5(c) Hedge and ditch

If there is a ditch and then a hedge, you are presumed to own the land as far as the near edge of the ditch. It would not be neighbourly practice, in the eyes of the law, to dig a ditch on someone else's land. If there is a hedge and then a ditch, you are presumed to own the land up to the further edge of the ditch. It is assumed that the ditch digger has thrown the soil onto his own land when digging the ditch, and has then planted the hedge on the bank of soil.

This presumption was recently confirmed when one landowner grubbed up the hedge along his section of the boundary and erected a fence along the far side of the ditch. His neighbour objected, asserting that the true boundary ran along the middle of the ditch. Proceedings were brought in the county court, the Court of Appeal, and the House of Lords over this 'tiny strip of garden'. Nonetheless, a point of general importance about farm boundaries had been raised and, on the facts of the case, the hedge and ditch presumption was found to be the 'best guide to the boundary line'.

3.1.5(d) Right of way

Where there is a right of way, a boundary is assumed to run in the middle of the right of way. In the same way, a boundary is said to run in the middle of a natural stream or river.

Note: these presumptions (or generalisations) are not binding rules. They can be displaced if you have other cogent evidence to the contrary. But they do serve a useful purpose in specifying certain guidelines in determining this kind of dispute.

3.1.6 The court's attitude

The court may also decide to leave the situation as it is even if it involves a permanent loss of property rights. In that case, the claimant will only receive damages rather than an order to have his or her property, access, or rights of way restored. The general rule is that a property owner should be entitled to have his rights permanently protected; however, the courts will order damages if:

a) the infringement is trivial
b) a small money payment could equally make up for the loss
c) it would be very hard on the defendant to remedy the wrong in any other way. For example, your neighbour has built a garage which impinges on your side of the boundary by a matter of inches. The court will weigh up the alternatives of ordering him to demolish the garage or ordering him to pay you for the token loss of your land. It may well decide that the latter is the fairest course, even though technically you are in the right in demanding your land back.

In a recent case, where a neighbour trespassed on his next-door wall by placing six flowerpots and an oil tank on the old stone boundary wall, which was not a party wall, the judge held that the acts amounted to a trespass. The fact that the owners of the wall objected after considerable delay did not prevent them from asserting their right to ask for removal of the tank and flowerpots. There was no difficulty or detriment in having them taken down.

3.2 Fences

Even where there is no demarcation dispute over a boundary to a property, a frequent source of ill-feeling between neighbours arises from the fence between them. Who owns the fence? Who should keep it in repair? Must it be kept in repair?

The answers to these questions ought to be amicably sorted out with goodwill on both sides. Too often, however, angry litigants ask the courts to supply the answers; this means there has to be a winner and a loser with regard both to the issue at stake and to the costs which litigation inevitably entails.

3.2.1   General rules regarding ownership

Again there are certain presumptions regarding fences. Do be warned that these presumptions can be displaced by other evidence.

(a) Plan with 'T' marks

The general rule is that where the title deeds have a plan, the usual practice is for there to be a 'T' mark on one side of the fence. If the 'T' mark falls on your side of the fence, then you are the owner.

(b) No 'T' marks or no plan at all

If there is no 'T' mark, or no plan to the deeds, then there is a general presumption that you own the fence if the supporting posts are on your land.

(c) Party fences

You can decide to have a party fence with both sides owning the fence and both sides contributing to its cost of repair.

Note: all rules regarding fences, boundaries and party walls are in general terms, so do not assume that you are in the right in a dispute with your neighbour!

3.2.2   Mending fences

In general, if a fence belongs to your neighbour and it falls into disrepair, he or she is not under an obligation to repair it unless there is some obligation which has been written into the conveyance (in new housing estates, for example, there are often obligations of this kind imposed). You can only insist on repair if it is more than an eyesore and presents an actual danger to you on your side of the property.

If you need to repair the fence at your own expense because it constitutes a danger, you might have to give notice to your neighbour to go on to his land. Otherwise you could apply to court for leave to go on to his land (see *Access to neighbouring land*, section 8.1 below).

The Party Wall Act 1996 provisions apply to a 'party fence wall', i.e. a wall such as a brick-built garden wall that is astride the boundary between the lands of different owners and separates their properties.

Note: the Act does not apply to wooden fences or similar structures.

If the fence constitutes an immediate danger to anyone on your property, you are entitled to take remedial action. For example, a brick wall belonging to your neighbour separates his garden from yours. The wall is bulging out so badly that it is likely to fall down at any moment and hurt you or your children. You may be entitled to pull down the wall and ask your neighbour to foot the bill. However, in such a case the court will only allow resort to self-help where there is an immediate danger to life or limb.

3.3   Party walls

A wall is a 'party wall' if:

1) It forms part of a building and stands astride the boundary of land belonging to two (or more) different owners; or
2) It separates buildings, and it either:
   - stands astride the boundary of land belonging to two or more different owners; or
   - stands wholly on one owner's land, but is used by two or more owners to separate their buildings. Where one person has built the wall in the first place, and another has butted their building up against it without constructing their own wall, only the part of the wall that does the separating is 'party'.

In theory, the neighbour on each side of a party wall owns half the wall (whether the division is made vertically or horizontally).

Moreover, where two buildings have been standing for 20 years or more, each neighbour acquires a right, called an easement, against the neighbour on the other side for the right of support to their property. (See *Right to support*, section 7.2.5 below.)

Rights, as well as ownership, generally entail duties too, and party walls are no exception.

3.3.1 Party Wall Act 1996

It is reasonable for the law to impose a duty to take care on the owner of a party wall, so that whether he uses it, removes it, builds on it or repairs it, he must minimise the possibility of damage or inconvenience to neighbouring property.

In effect, each side of a party wall owns the wall in common with his neighbour on the other side. Each side therefore has the right to carry out work on his or her side of the wall. However, this right is subject to protection for the owner on the other side.

The Party Wall Act was passed in 1996, re-enacting the legislation which had applied to London, so as to make it countrywide. It is intended to prevent or resolve disputes with regard to party walls, boundary walls, and excavations near neighbouring buildings. Its main feature is that notice must be given if 'work' (as described in the Act) is to be carried out – even if the work is only to be done up to the centre of the party wall.

The Act covers work on:

- an existing party wall
- new building at or astride the boundary line between the properties; and
- excavation within 3 or 6 metres of a neighbouring building (depending on the depth of the hole).

☞ *You intend to insert a damp proof course all the way through the party wall. You want to know what your duties are to your next-door neighbour.*

- At least two months before the planned work, you must serve notice on any adjoining owner. If for example, the next-door house is divided into two flats, you will have to serve notice on both tenants and the landlord as well.
- The notice must give your name and address, state that it is issued under the Party Walls Act, and give details and plans, and when you intend starting the work.

☞ *What can your neighbour do?*

- He can serve a counter-notice setting out how he would like the work done or he can simply give his consent.
- In either event, he must communicate his views within 14 days.
- Your neighbour is not entitled in law to prevent you doing the work but, if you cannot reach agreement, a surveyor, whom you both agree upon, can be appointed to settle the differences. Alternatively, you can each appoint your own surveyor to reach an agreement between them.

Do remember: you must not cause unnecessary inconvenience; you are liable to pay compensation for any damage; and you may have to offer security against the possibility that work on the party wall will be left incomplete.

3.3.1(a) Nuisance

Allowing a party wall to fall into disrepair can cause a nuisance. An adjoining owner could then sue for damages. For example, if your neighbour allows dry rot on her side of the wall to spread to your side, she would be liable for damages if she knew that it could happen but failed to take any steps to deal with the dry rot and to halt its spread.

3.3.1(b) Liability of owners for third party contractors

☞ *Your home is one of a Victorian terrace of houses. Your roof has been leaking and you decide that it would be best to replace the tiles. You engage a builder, who has been highly recommended to you, and the job seems well done. You are now approached by your immediate neighbour who says that the wall and ceiling of an attic room in his house are showing signs of damp. You endeavour to locate the builder as you understand that, as an independent contractor, he is liable for any damage. You discover that he has gone out of business. Your neighbour commences litigation for the cost of the repairs to his house. He says that it is no concern of his that your builder was at fault and is no longer available. What is your position?*

Where there is damage to an adjoining building as a result of negligent work to a party wall, roof, or basement, the owner may have to bear the responsibility if the builder disappears.

As far as London was concerned, there has always been specific legislation which dealt with party walls (the London Building Acts).

☞ *You live in a two-storey terraced house in inner London. Your next-door neighbours have decided to convert their ground floor into an open-plan living area. They have begun work which involves redistribution of the loading on the party wall. This has only just come to your attention and you are told by a friend, who is a surveyor, that there is a strong risk of possible damage to your own home. What can you do?*

You must inform the local authority immediately and ask for a Stop notice. Your neighbour is under a legal obligation to you under the Party Wall Act 1996 to give you two months' notice before he does any work which could affect a party wall.

4   PROBLEMS WITH NUISANCE

There are three categories of 'nuisance' in law:

- private nuisance
- public nuisance
- statutory nuisance.

4.1   Private nuisance

A private nuisance has been defined as something that occurs on someone else's property which detrimentally affects your property or your enjoyment of your own property.

☞ *Your next-door neighbour is a car enthusiast. He spends hours in the back garden stripping down cars and souping up their engines. You are assailed by the noise of revving engines and the smell of chemicals from bodywork repairs.*

You could complain that your neighbour was using his property in such a way as detrimentally to affect the peaceful enjoyment of your own amenities.

Of course, it is always a matter of degree but there is no doubt that these activities can constitute nuisance.

Equally, something which occurs on your property can be a source of nuisance to your neighbours and interfere with the enjoyment to which they also are entitled.

4.1.1   Scope of private nuisance

The examples given so far all concern nuisance emanating from neighbouring properties. There is a query whether someone can cause nuisance (in the legal sense) from or on your own property, such as if your ex-partner tries to deprive you of the use of your telephone by interfering with your telephone line.

The Protection against Harassment Act 1997 (the so-called anti-stalking Act) might be of assistance in such a case, as 'harassment' is not defined but covers a course of conduct which causes alarm or distress. A victim of harassment can sue for damages or for an injunction to make the person refrain from his activities. It can also be a criminal offence if a victim is put in fear, on at least two occasions, that violence may be used.

In one case it was held that the ringing of bells in a parish church which might constitute a private nuisance was not actionable against the bishop of the diocese in which the church was situated. A resident was seeking damages for nuisance caused by the ringing of bells at high levels in the local church. The defendants to the action were the vicar, two churchwardens and the parish council but the bishop was also included. The High Court struck out the claim against the bishop as he did not authorise the ringing of the bells and had no power to make the vicar stop since the ringing of bells was specifically within the remit of the parish priest.

☞ *You are a tenant farmer of land situated either side of a main road. A couple of years ago, travellers moved onto a large strip of land owned by the council on one edge of the road. They have just been evicted but while they occupied the land they frequently trespassed onto your land, obstructed your access, left rubbish and excrement on it, and tethered their own horses. They also stole fences and damaged a stone wall as well as letting their dogs chase your sheep. You want to sue the council for nuisance as owners of the land which the travellers occupied but the council denies liability. What can you do?*

In a similar case the Court of Appeal held that a council which was owner-occupier of land could be liable in nuisance for the unlawful activities of licensees or persons based on its land and which took place on the victims' land (in other words off the council's land). In this particular case, the nuisance consisted of repeated acts committed on the victim's land, to the council's knowledge, and which interfered with the victim's use and enjoyment of his land.

4.1.1(a)   The cost of a quarrel

The press constantly reports stories of neighbours who sometimes – and for no apparent reason – decide to make life a misery for those who have the misfortune to live near them.

One couple endured a torrent of abuse from their neighbour for six years which resulted in court action against him. They eventually wished to sell their home which would normally have been valued at around £250,000. However they were required to inform potential purchasers that their neighbour had two convictions for harassment and they had also obtained an indefinite restraining order against him. As a result their property was reduced to an estimated value to £190,000. Thus, it would appear that their neighbour's mere presence had knocked £60,000 off its value. The couple are reportedly planning to sue their neighbour under the 1997 Protection from Harassment Act which permits homeowners to claim damages for financial loss caused by nuisance neighbours. If they had tried to sell their house without disclosing the proceedings, they could have been be sued in turn by their potential purchasers (see chapter on *Buying and Selling your Home*, section 5.2.1).

4.1.2   The need for some continuity

In general, nuisance denotes some notion of continuity – particularly in establishing nuisance against a neighbour. However, a one-off event could also be a nuisance; for example, a sudden and unexpected inflow of chemicals from neighbouring land that pollutes your stream.

4.1.3   The need for a measured response

A problem with nuisance is that you do not want to over-react and to antagonise your neighbours. On the other hand, the longer the delay, the more difficult it becomes to prove a case of nuisance. In other words, some form of measured response should be made promptly.

The law will only allow you to take personal steps to remedy a nuisance in two cases:

a) where it poses an immediate physical danger to you or anyone else on your property (see section 3.2.2 above); or

b) where it is so trivial that it would not justify taking legal action.

An example of a trivial case would be the lopping-off of a branch of your neighbour's tree that overhung your garden (see section 6.1.1 below).

4.2   Public nuisance

A public nuisance is something that, as the name suggests, detrimentally affects a large group of people and not only an individual. It often concerns obstructions on the highway.

Note: neighbours can band together in residents' committees to act as a pressure group against certain kinds of nuisance. For example, they might try to prevent heavy traffic using certain roads by lobbying for the installation of 'sleeping policemen'.

4.3   Statutory nuisance

Certain kinds of nuisance are covered by legislation. In particular the Environmental Protection Act 1990 has laid down various matters associated with property, that qualify as statutory nuisances. As the name of the Act would suggest, the law is primarily concerned with those who use (or neglect) their property in such a way as to cause a potential health hazard. The Act refers to the state of premises, the state of an animal kept on premises, smoke, fumes, dust, and any 'accumulation or deposit' of substances that could be prejudicial to health or could cause a nuisance.

It is the well-being of the population as a whole that the Act is concerned to protect. However, you can use its provisions for the protection of your own wellbeing by notifying apparent breaches to your local authority which has a duty, under the Act, to ensure that the Act's provisions are observed.

The local authority has to inspect its area from time to time and to detect any statutory nuisances:

- if a complaint is made, it has to take such steps as are reasonably practicable to investigate the complaint
- if it is satisfied that a statutory nuisance exists, or is likely to occur or recur, it must serve an abatement notice (i.e. a notice on the person causing the nuisance to take steps to end it)
- it may take proceedings to abate the nuisance and 'do whatever may be necessary' to execute the notice.

☞ *The house next door was sold to a buyer who has been living abroad. Twelve months have elapsed and he still has not taken up occupation. During the year, his garden has grown ever more unkempt and has become an eyesore. Animal feed has apparently been left in the garden shed. When you last looked out of your window and glanced towards the next-door house, you were appalled to see a large rat scurry towards the back fence. What can you do about it?*

You must complain to your local authority environmental health officer (the details can be looked up in your telephone book). Under the Act it is up to the environmental health officer (EHO) to take action on your behalf. In general, the council is under a duty to investigate your complaint. The EHO will try to get the owner of the premises to take action to remove or abate the nuisance. But in a case such as this, where the owner might not be traced, the council itself can take steps under the Act to remove the foodstuff and make the premises vermin-free. If the premises next door are in themselves a hazard to health by, for example, containing something that gives off a noxious smell, quite apart from the presence of vermin, they could certainly constitute a nuisance under the Act.

For problems with litter, see section 9 below.

4.4   Planning permission and nuisance

The mere fact that your neighbour has received planning permission from a local authority may not take away your right to protect yourself against nuisance. In one case, a farmer received planning permission to put up sheds for his pigs, the smell from which affected the neighbouring property. The next-door neighbours succeeded in their court action and the sheds had to be moved.

4.5   Appealing against an abatement notice

The person on whom an abatement notice is served is entitled to appeal against the notice. There are several grounds for appeal, among them

- that the wrong person has been served (for example, the notice has been served on a tenant while the only person who can deal effectively with the problem is the landlord)
- that all reasonable steps have already been taken to deal with the nuisance.

5   PROBLEMS WITH SMOKE AND FUMES

There are many forms of pollution which can affect our immediate environment: dust, noise, chemical or noxious fumes, pollutants in water, blocked drains. One of the commonest that leads to disputes between neighbours is smoke. Smoke can come from a bonfire in someone else's garden or from a barbecue party next door. Again it becomes a question of degree. When does one person's pleasure become a pain to others?

5.1 Reasonable use

In general, the law looks to property owners to make reasonable use of their premises. If a person wishes to complain about how a neighbour uses his premises, he or she must show unreasonable use, that is, must show some sort of harm such as damage to health or to enjoyment of property. In other words it must constitute a legally defined wrong. It must be a nuisance, a trespass of some sort, or a hazard. These are quite high thresholds to cross.

Furthermore, we must take our neighbourhoods into account. If we buy a house in a semi-industrial area, we may have to put up with a greater degree of pollution in the form of noise or chemicals than we would in a residential area. If we buy our house in a semi-rural area, we may not be able to complain about noise from a nearby farmyard. If we buy a flat in a high street, we may have to put up with the smells from take-away food shops.

5.1.1 Smoke

As we have seen, smoke, fumes or dust can be a nuisance under the Environmental Protection Act 1990. The question – as always – is what point must be reached in order to transform an everyday nuisance into a 'nuisance' in law.

☞ *Your neighbour is a most enthusiastic gardener so she has lots of garden clippings to burn. You find that quite often the smoke from her bonfires spoils what would otherwise be a couple of pleasant hours in your own garden. It soils your washing if there is any on the line. Even more problematic and unpleasant, however, is the fact that her children sometimes throw household rubbish on to the fire and the dense fumes from this burning rubbish irritate your chest. What should you do?*

The first thing is to establish whether you really have grounds to complain of a nuisance. Keep a diary and take a note of how often the bonfires next door affect you, how long they usually burn for, whether a fire is lit irrespective of the time of day or the weather (for example, on a windy day the effects from smoke will be worse), what sort of rubbish is being burnt and causing dense smoke. Then speak to your neighbour to try to establish some sort of amicable arrangement. For example, perhaps she will agree to light bonfires only on the days when you are out. You might persuade her that her children should not amuse themselves at the fire – for their own good as much as for yours.

If all this is to no avail, and you feel a cause for complaint to the local authority is justified under the Environmental Protection Act 1990, you can call in the environmental health officer. The local authority will then decide whether or not to take action under the Act. It can issue a notice to the person to put an end to the nuisance (an abatement notice) if:

a) it is satisfied that a nuisance exists, and

b) the nuisance is likely to recur.

5.1.2 Barbecues

Alas, barbecues have become a very frequent source of dispute since so many more people today own them.

A barbecue party can lead to a combination of factors which can annoy one's next-door neighbours; there is the smoke, the smell, and probably noise too. There are not even walls to absorb some of the sound from an outdoors party!

In one tragic case, a neighbour in an upstairs flat doused the barbecue on the patio of the people living downstairs by throwing two buckets of water on to the flames from his upstairs balcony. A quarrel ensued in which a person died.

5.1.3 Insecticides and pesticides

The use of insecticides or pesticides can be a statutory nuisance under the Environmental Protection Act 1990 if their use is prejudicial to health or a nuisance. Their use can also cause damage under the common law rule of negligence.

☞ *Your neighbour knows that you keep bees. Nonetheless she goes ahead and uses insecticide on her rose bushes and the breeze wafts the substance on to your land. As a result, your bees are killed. What can you do?*

As in all instances, one wants to try the 'softly-softly' approach with neighbours – you should ask that it should not happen again in the future and perhaps ask for compensation for the loss of your bees. However, if your neighbour refuses to co-operate, you might have a case to sue for damages – possibly in the small claims court (see the chapter on *The Legal System*, section 4). You could also ask a county court for an injunction to stop her using harmful substances.

6 PROBLEMS WITH GARDENS

6.1 Intrusions from next door

Trespass and/or nuisance are the most common aspects in which the law is invoked in connection with gardens and neighbours' disputes.

Trespass, as we all know, usually involves people or animals (see the chapters on *Accidents*, section 4.3.2, and *The Countryside*, section 5 and *Pets*, see section 6 on straying animals). It may come as a surprise therefore to discover that trespass can also be committed by plants or trees. These can either overgrow your property or – more insidiously – grow beneath it.

6.1.1 Overhanging plants and trees

The general rule is that you are entitled to your own 'space' – in, under, and, to some extent, above your own property. So branches from neighbouring trees or shrubs which overhang your garden are intrusions into your space, therefore they can be regarded as trespass and a nuisance.

☞ *Your neighbour has a very fine apple tree. Several branches, laden with fruit, overhang your garden where you have planted a delicate clematis against the fence. You have asked him several times to do something about the branches but he has taken no action. What can you do?*

You are entitled to lop off those branches which actually intrude over your side of the fence. You must take great care that only those branches, and no others, are pruned. You are supposed to return the branches to your neighbour and are certainly not entitled to any of the apples!

However, to take unilateral action against a neighbour's tree, even if you are entitled to do so in the strict legal sense, may not be the best policy when you have to live next door to him. It might be better to ask his permission to prune beforehand, or even to consider simply planting a more robust shrub against your fence.

Note: under the Access to Neighbouring Land Act 1992, you can apply to court for an access order to deal with trees or shrubs on someone else's property in certain circumstances. (See section 8.1 below.)

6.1.2 Roots growing underground

Trespass and nuisance can be caused by roots that grow underground and into and under neighbouring property just as much as by branches that overhang property from next door.

☞ *Your neighbour has written to you stating that the roots of one of your birch trees is in danger of causing settlement to her house. She is threatening you with an injunction to restrain you from continuing to permit the intrusion. Can she ask the courts for such a drastic remedy?*

The answer is 'yes'. Where roots cause material damage to adjacent property, the householder can sue for damages and ask for an injunction. The two remedies can be sought at the same time and are not mutually exclusive.

She is also entitled to cut back the roots from the point where they intrude on to her land (as in the case of an overhanging branch).

See also *Access to neighbouring land*, section 8 below.

6.1.3 If your neighbour fails to take action

If there is a shrub, climber or tree in your garden which poses a danger to a neighbouring property, your neighbour is not under a legal duty to take action.

☞ *You have planted a Virginia creeper against your back wall. You notice that it is now beginning to extend to your neighbours' tiled roof. You point this out to them and ask them to ensure that the tendrils do not damage their tiles. They do nothing about it. Thereafter, in the winter they complain to you about a leak from their roof.*

It is your responsibility to have ensured that no damage was done to their roof from your climber. Moreover, you are liable for the cost of repair, although the court may reduce the compensation you will have to pay, if your neighbour fails to mitigate the damage.

6.1.4 Interference with sunlight

With regard to gardens, you are not entitled to ask your neighbour to cut or prune branches of trees to ensure that you have uninterrupted sunlight. You are only entitled to reasonable airspace above your own property – you cannot impose airspace on neighbouring property.

You also cannot insist that your neighbour prunes his hedge to a certain height even if it is a party hedge. You are only entitled to prune your half to the height that you prefer – unless a maximum height has been stipulated in the conveyance. (See section 7.2.2 below with regard to the 'Right to light' for your premises.)

You may try to reach an agreement with your neighbour in the form of an easement (see section 7.2.1 below) for an agreed height of trees or hedges. In one case, the court stated that a neighbour was in the right when he trimmed a 25-foot high cypress *leylandii* hedge which cast a shadow over the whole of his garden. A voluntary Code of Conduct with regard to the height of *leylandii* hedges is available from the Office of the Deputy Prime Minister in an endeavour to address nuisance hedges, which cause many neighbourhood disputes.

The potential problems caused by high hedges cannot be overstated. Some house owners have reported problems with property insurance. It can be difficult to change insurers, and premiums can be much higher because of a neighbour's hedge. Some insurers refuse to provide cover at all. In one case a householder faced a £2,500 policy excess due to the close proximity of a 30-ft high hedge.

A leaflet, *The right hedge for you*, is available from the Office of the Deputy Prime Minister, and comes with a 'hedge selector table'. It lists the factors to be considered in selecting any hedge and suggests that you also check with your local council for planning conditions which might apply to your garden.

You can also contact HEDGELINE at 0870 2400627; *hedgeline.org*.

6.2 Dangerous trees

Your local authority is under a statutory duty to ensure that trees do not pose a danger to other persons or to their property.

Any person who thinks that a tree is in a dangerous condition (whether in a public place such as a street or on private property such as a neighbouring garden) has the right to notify the local authority. The authority is then empowered by law to establish whether there is indeed a real risk posed, and if so, to take action by tracing the owner of the land. It can then give notice of a 21-day period in which he or she must ensure that the tree is made safe. If there is no action and the owner does not appeal against the notice, the local authority can take the necessary action to make the tree safe.

In 2001 a company purchased the freehold of a block of flats after structural damage had been identified as a result of the encroachment of the roots of an 80-year-old plane tree. The company wished to sue the council which was responsible for the tree. The council had refused to fell the tree and so the company had to incur costs of over £500,000 to carry out underpinning work. The judge had initially held that the company was not entitled to sue the council as it had insufficient interest in the property when the damage occurred.

The House of Lords held that there was a continuing nuisance at least until the underpinning was completed. It did not matter that further cracking of the superstructure might not have occurred after the company took possession of the flats. The encroachment of the roots was causing continuing damage to the land by dehydrating the soil and inhibiting rehydration. The impairment of the load-bearing qualities of residential land was itself a nuisance, and cracking in the building was consequential.

A real risk of damage to the land and the foundations was foreseeable on the part of the Council because of the proximity of the plane tree to the flats. If the tree had been removed, the need to underpin would have been avoided. However, once the Council declined to remove the tree, the underpinning costs were reasonably incurred. The Council had had ample notice and time before the underpinning was carried out and so it was liable.

(See also *Access to neighbouring land*, section 8 below.)

6.3   Protecting trees

It is a welcome feature of our law that specified trees are given special statutory protection under the town and country planning regulations. The latest regulations came into force in August 1999 and these lay down the procedure relating to the making of an order and an appeal against it.

☞ *You have recently sold your large Victorian house to a couple who intend to turn it into a residential home for the elderly. There are some very fine and unusual trees in the garden which you feel add much to the amenity of the area. If the couple build on to the house, as they intend to do, the trees may be felled. What can you do?*

If you think that there are trees which should be protected, you can write to your local planning authority under the Town and Country Planning Act 1990. If you offer convincing reasons, the planning authority will order its own inquiry and then may impose a tree preservation order (TPO) on the trees to protect them from harm. These must be indicated on a map annexed to the order.

The couple to whom you have sold your house would be entitled to object to the TPO as the local authority is obliged by law to serve them with a copy of the order and a notice, also in a prescribed form, stating the reasons for the order. They are then entitled to make their objections and representations in writing within the time limit specified (at least 28 days from the date of the notice). An order cannot be confirmed until the local authority have first considered their views.

The local authority could also use its powers to protect the trees by attaching conditions to the planning permission for their proposed extension to the building.

Do note: other rules apply to trees in conservation areas.

7   PROBLEMS WITH RIGHTS AND PROPERTIES

7.1   Restrictive covenants

In order to protect the amenities of an area, particularly a residential neighbourhood, property owners have frequently resorted to imposing restrictions on the way that neighbouring property owners may use their land.

There is a real problem, however. Property changes hands all the time. You may agree with someone that land, or the buildings on it, should only be used in a certain way (for example, that the land should not be built on, or the house should never be converted into flats). But can that agreement be enforced if the property is sold to someone else?

In order to enforce such agreements, property owners impose restrictive covenants on the property. These covenants are then registered with the Land Registry and will pass with each conveyance. As a result no purchaser can come forward and claim that he did not know of the covenant's existence. Restrictive covenants are usually imposed when a property is being developed or sold (see however, section 7.1.1(c) below that a covenant must directly affect the land).

☞ *You have a house with large grounds. There is an old boiler house at the bottom of the garden. You obtain planning permission from the local council to allow a 'back garden' development to convert the boiler house into a studio flat. You intend to sell the flat once it is built. However, you would like to restrict the use that any potential buyer might wish to make of the studio. For example, you might want it to be for residential purposes only or you might want to make sure that a would-be purchaser does not build any extension on to the studio. What can you do to ensure these conditions?*

In the deed of sale you stipulate that these conditions of sale are restrictive covenants which your solicitor must then register as land charges. These are registered as an interest affecting the property.

7.1.1 Rules on restrictive covenants

7.1.1(a) Two properties are necessary

Restrictive covenants always need two properties: the *dominant* property for the benefit of which the covenant is made in the first place; and the *servient* property, i.e. the property on which the covenant is imposed. In the example above, the dominant property is the main house because the main house has the benefit of the ban on any further building. The studio is the servient property which has the detriment of a restrictive covenant against building imposed on it.

7.1.1(b) Must be negative covenants

Restrictive covenants are negative in nature. You cannot use a restrictive covenant to insist that the purchaser of your studio paints the outside of the building at regular intervals.

You cannot even disguise a positive obligation under a negative cloak – for example, to stipulate that 'the purchaser shall not let the studio go unpainted'. Its effect, even though expressed negatively, is to impose a positive obligation to paint the studio.

Do note: the Commonhold and Leasehold Reform Act 2002 was passed to get around the problem of negative/positive covenants. It is a new form of tenure intended to provide a better system for future ownership of interdependent premises with shared services and common parts. Commonhold could apply to flats, houses or shops, or even light industrial units, and it might be in a development containing more than one unit type, e.g. shops with flat above. However, there must be common parts in the development; this might be no more than a staircase and entrance hall or might extend to an estate with roads, swimming pool, landscaped gardens and car park.

The new form of landholding is intended – in the main – for new developments once all the provisions of the Act are brought in to force. Existing leaseholders who have already brought their freehold will also be able to convert to commonhold, provided that there is 100-per-cent agreement of the unit-holders. Each unit-holder will own his or her flat in perpetuity and will be given membership of the Commonhold Association which will own the land, the structure of the buildings, and common parts. All unit-owners will have a vote in the operation of the Commonhold Association and thereby in the management and maintenance of their properties (see also chapter on *Landlord and their Tenants*, section 10.5.4).

7.1.1(c) Enforcing covenants that 'run' with the land

Even if you sell your house, the new owner should be able to enforce the restrictive covenant provided it 'touches and concerns the land' or 'runs' with the land – as the lawyers say. This means that not all restrictive covenants can be enforced against new ownership. It only applies to covenants that directly affect the land itself – for example a covenant not to build.

Thus the owner of the studio could not wait for the sale of the main house and then carry out plans to build an extension. The covenant becomes attached to the properties, irrespective of who owns them. In such a case the restrictive covenant will continue to 'run with the land' unless other steps are taken to remove it (see below, section 7.1.2).

7.1.1(d) Indemnity covenants

In order to make certain that a covenant will be respected, sellers sometimes insist that an indemnity covenant be entered into by the purchaser.

Under an indemnity covenant, the buyer agrees to indemnify the seller if any of the restrictive covenants in the title deeds are broken. Subsequent purchasers generally then enter into the same indemnity covenant so that the original purchaser is protected against any breaches by them. Indemnity covenants have the effect of a guarantee. The chain of indemnities protects the original buyer who could otherwise be sued by the seller long after he has left the property.

7.1.2 Removing covenants

7.1.2(a) Application to a Lands Tribunal

Application can be made to a Lands Tribunal to have a restrictive covenant removed or modified.

☞ *You have bought a Victorian house in the high street of a busy market town. The house has a restrictive covenant on it that it must be used for residential purposes only. However, you would like to convert the ground floor into an office suite for your own use and use the upper storeys for a maisonette in which you would live. All the rest of the street now comprises offices and shops and the restrictive covenant appears wholly out of date.*

You would seem to have a good case in seeking the discharge of the restrictive covenant as an unreasonable restriction on the use of your property. The fact that the other properties are non-residential means that you are not likely to be challenged by neighbours who are entitled in law to raise an objection to the removal or modification of a restrictive covenant. Always take proper advice on these issues first, though. You would also have to check on the 'change of use' provisions of the planning legislation. (See section 7.3.)

Where a restrictive covenant binds several plots of land or a housing estate, the courts will pay heed to the importance of maintaining the scheme as a whole. For example, a restrictive covenant stipulated that there should be no subdivision of six plots of land in a residential suburb. Each plot was large and there was one house on each of the plots. A modification of the covenant was sought that each plot should be subdivided into two lots for residential purposes only. The modification was rejected as the 'thin edge of the wedge' which could ruin the scheme as a whole.

7.1.2(b) By agreement

Another way of getting round a restrictive covenant is to persuade the other owner(s) of the property who benefit from it to forgo their rights. In this case, you may have to pay them compensation if they are likely to suffer a loss or disadvantage once the covenant is lifted.

7.1.3 Leasehold property

One of the features of leasehold property is that positive obligations can be imposed on tenants under the terms of their lease. The circumscribed nature of restrictive covenants does not apply in a lease – for example tenants can be required to paint the outside of the building every five years (see chapter on *Landlords and their Tenants*). For that reason, too, certain residential estates, concerned about upkeep, will sell houses on their estate on long leasehold, such as 999-year leases. See also the chapter on *Buying and Selling your Home*, section 1.5.

7.2 Easements

7.2.1 Rules on easements

Restrictive covenants must be negative, as we have seen above. There are however, certain positive rights which properties can and do acquire against neighbouring properties. Such rights are called easements. Common examples of easements are rights to light, and rights of way over someone else's land.

7.2.1(a) Easement entails two properties

Like a restrictive covenant, an easement also involves two properties: a dominant one and a servient one. The dominant property has the benefit of the easement while the servient property has the burden, i.e. the easement, imposed on it.

If we take the example above of the studio flat built in someone else's grounds, we can now see that the roles can be reversed from those in the situation under the restrictive covenant against building. For example, if the owner of the main house agrees that the buyers of the studio can use his main driveway for parking their car, the studio will benefit from the right of way and so it becomes the 'dominant' property, while the main house and grounds, on which the right of way has been imposed, will now be the 'servient' property.

7.2.1(b)   An easement can be positive

Unlike a restrictive covenant, which must always be negative, (e.g. an agreement not to build), easements can be positive in nature. Thus an easement can impose on land a positive duty, such as the duty to permit someone else to lay services over or under your land, to walk across it, or to support an adjoining building.

7.2.1(c)   An agreement 'runs' with the land

Both the benefit and the burden of easements run with the land, irrespective of the owners. Thus anyone who buys the dominant property will enjoy an easement, such as a right of way; the owner of the servient property, on the other hand, has to put up with having someone else use his property by walking across it, driving his car on it, or driving animals along it – depending on the nature of the easement.

Even if he sells his property, such rights of way or other easements can be enforced against any new owner.

7.2.1(d)   Enforcing easements

It is important to realise that an easement is an interest in land. It is not a mere agreement to use land in a particular way, which is called a licence. A licence is an agreement which can be revoked at any time. Easements on the other hand, are rights that are registered to ensure that they are enforced in all subsequent conveyances.

7.2.1(e)   Limiting factors

Because of the nature of an easement – i.e. that it is a right enforceable, theoretically, in perpetuity – for the benefit either of, or against, someone else's land, the law circumscribes the operation of easements. For example, no one can acquire an easement to a fine view. The law regards such a right as too vague to bind someone else's property. If you wish to have a fine view, you must be in a position to impose a restrictive covenant on adjacent land that it should not be built on. Planning law may also come to your assistance in such a case.

You also cannot expect your television reception to be uninterrupted by tall buildings.

7.2.1(f)   Scope for dispute

Neighbours can find cause for quarrels over easements. For example, you can have a right of way which is a registered easement and not a licence. Nonetheless there can be a dispute over its nature. Is it meant for cars? Or lorries? Can you drive sheep along it?

Many easements date back for a century or more so their present scope has to be determined against today's very different environment from that prevailing at the time of the original deeds

See also above, section 7.1.1.

7.2.2   Right to light

A striking example of an easement is the right to light. It is also a frequent source of vexation – not to speak of litigation – between neighbours.

The problem usually arises when one of the neighbours builds an extension to his house. Can you do more than say 'I don't like your extension – it makes my house darker'?

The law on the subject is very complicated and you would always be well advised to consult a solicitor or chartered surveyor who has experience in property law. The position depends in part on an Act, called the Prescription Act, which was passed in 1832. It is still binding law on the issue of the right to light.

In principle, your only right is that your neighbour should not 'unreasonably' obstruct light from your windows, since your property has benefited from that light from your neighbour's property for 20 years without interruption.

In fact neighbours can reach an agreement which would preserve the existing light; such an agreement might be by means of a restrictive covenant against building on neighbouring land or by some other form of registered charge.

However:

a) there has to be existing light to a window of your house;
b) the light must have been uninterrupted for 20 years.

Note: acquiring a right to light applies to buildings only. It does not apply to open land, such as a garden. In view of the current enthusiasm for conservatories, it would be interesting to know whether one can acquire a prescriptive right to light for them. It would appear to apply to a greenhouse.

7.2.3 Obstructions to light – when you can act

If there is an obstruction to light, caused, for example, by proposed additional building at the next-door house, you can only take action if the obstruction to that light would be 'unreasonable'. In other words, the question now is whether you have sufficient light left at your window, not how much light has been taken away.

Do take heed: you must object effectively to the changes. If you are aware of plans to build and you take no action by making your objections plain, the law may regard you as having 'acquiesced' to the loss of light.

☞ *You have recently bought an old cottage. You use one of the upstairs bedrooms as a studio where you pursue your hobby of engraving. You have chosen this room because of the amount of light it receives throughout the day. Your neighbour had spoken to you several times concerning his plans for a garage but you were unaware that he intended to build a floor above the garage comprising a bedroom and ensuite bathroom. The building has since gone up and your bedroom is now very dark. You have protested to your neighbour about it, as well as to your local planning authority. The planning authority insists that the former owner was sent written notice of the planning application which was also advertised in the local press. You put the matter in the hands of your solicitors but have not heard from them for some while. What is your position?*

The test is concerned with how much light has remained rather than how much has been taken away. In this case, there clearly has been such a loss of light that your room can no longer be used for its former purpose. You may therefore, on the face of it, have a good case against your neighbour.

However, the court may decide that you only need enough light 'for ordinary purposes' and to use a bedroom as a studio is to use it for other than ordinary purposes. The question is one of fact and degree – how much light is left? Would it be dark even for an ordinary bedroom? In a recent case, the judge stated that 'in a room that is already ill-lit every bit of light is precious' so each case is judged on its merits.

The fact that you have recently acquired the property does not affect your right to object to the extension provided there has been 20 years' uninterrupted light to your property – no matter who owned it before you. Also the fact that your neighbour was granted planning permission by the local authority does not affect your private right to light provided you can prove your case.

As nothing has happened for a while since you handed the matter over to your solicitors, this could be seriously damaging to your legal position. If one year elapses and you would appear not to have taken really effective action, the law may hold that you have 'acquiesced' in the obstruction to your light.

Do note: in general, if more than 50 per cent of the rooms affected remain well-lit, this is usually considered sufficient for ordinary purposes but the test is not merely a statistical one.

7.2.4 Preventing a right to light arising in the first place

You can also stop your neighbour from acquiring a right to light!

Action can be taken under the Rights to Lights Act 1959 by registering a notice with your local authority. The notice is called a 'local land charge'. It has the effect of preventing the 20-year period from running in favour of a neighbouring house and has the same effect as if you built an obstruction which barred the light to your neighbour's windows.

Conveyances of property can also state that the building for sale cannot acquire a right to light against neighbouring property.

7.2.5 Right to support

In general, there is a natural right to support for your land. In other words, your neighbour cannot start excavating on his side of the fence in order to build a swimming pool which will cause the land on your side of the fence to subside.

The Party Wall Act 1996 (see also section 3.3.1 above) deals with excavations within three or six metres of neighbouring buildings, according to the depth of the proposed digging, so as to protect them.

Buildings can, however, acquire their own easement of support from adjoining buildings provided they have been standing together for 20 years or more. So, if you carry out major works to your property which cause damage to the next-door property through removal of support, you will be liable for the cost of repairing the damage.

The owner of a terraced house who demolished his property but failed to provide adequate support to, or weatherproofing of, the common wall between his property and that of his neighbour was liable for the damage done to the adjoining property by the instability caused by the lack of support, including damage as a result of wind suction. Furthermore, the Appeal Court said that the owner owed his neighbour a duty of care and was liable in damages for the consequences of failing to take reasonable steps to protect and weatherproof the exposed wall.

Of course, these problems are usually minimised if people take care and sensible precautions. Surveyors and architects are at hand to give advice and to ensure – as far as possible – that no damage should occur to adjoining property from major works to one's own land or buildings.

Where a neighbour does nothing to create a danger to your land, but a danger arises through natural causes, e.g. a landslip, there is a 'measured duty to take reasonable steps' which depend on:

* the ease and expense of those steps
* whether the neighbour could indeed take steps to remedy the situation, and
* whether (s)he could foresee possible damage to your land and/or its extent.

Your neighbour may not be under a duty to undertake expensive remedial work to prevent possible damage although there is certainly a duty to warn you of any known risk and to share information.

7.2.6 Questions of privacy?

A property owner has no inherent right to privacy, neither can a householder claim the right to a view, as we have seen.

In general, therefore, you cannot stop someone building next door even if it means that your neighbours will then be able to overlook your grounds or look through your windows.

You can only prevent them where you can show that:

* there is a restrictive covenant against building which you can enforce against your neighbours (see above) or
* a right to light and the building would unreasonably interfere with that right or
* planning permission has taken into account the need to ensure privacy for neighbouring property.

Take note: indeed planning controls can be a more effective way of ensuring privacy, a right to light, or protecting an uninterrupted view.

7.2.7 Planning laws and privacy

Planning laws may be able to assist you in an endeavour to ensure privacy. Such control may be even more effective if your neighbours plan to build in a conservation area, a green-belt area, or an area designated as one of natural beauty (see *Planning controls* immediately below).

☞ *Your neighbour has applied for planning permission to knock down his house and build a block of flats on his property which immediately adjoins your house. At the moment you are not overlooked but you fear that one of the flats, on the top floor, will overlook your garden thus interfering with the privacy which you now enjoy. You wonder what you can do.*

You can endeavour to ensure that the planning permission contains a condition that no windows should be put into that part of the wall of the flat which will overlook your garden.

For example, in one case, privacy was protected in this way. Indeed the block of flats was put up with an unauthorised dormer window which overlooked a neighbour's garden. An enforcement notice was issued against the man who bought the flat that the dormer window should be removed. He appealed to the High Court and the Court of Appeal, to no avail. The court held that the house next door should not suffer from 'an impression of overlooking'.

7.3   Planning controls

In this section, we have seen that the rights of ownership of property are hedged about with qualifications. It becomes most apparent, however, that 'an Englishman's home is *not* his castle' in the sphere of planning legislation. Controls govern what you can and cannot do with your property if you want to build on to it, make fundamental alterations to it, or change the way you intend to use it.

Many planning applications involve a public inquiry which is when neighbours can most forcefully put their objections to the proposed change to their neighbourhood or neighbouring property. They may form themselves into groups – some such groups are long-standing organisations dedicated to preserving their neighbourhood; other groups may be formed *ad hoc* to prevent or oppose a particular development in their immediate vicinity.

Note: many developers have the resources to fight a sustained legal action against such groups. In general voluntary bodies – by their very nature – cannot fund such disputes.

7.3.1   Development and presumption against development

The local authorities draw up plans for controlling development in their area. Any development must take place within these guidelines.

There is a presumption against development in certain areas – in particular, within green-belt and conservation areas. That does not mean that all development is automatically barred; it does mean, though, that anyone who wants to build or change the use of an existing building in say, a conservation area, has a much harder job in persuading the local authorities that they ought to give the go-ahead.

Decisions are not always reached on purely planning grounds, however. As in so many other aspects of law, the policy of the day can dictate not only the scale of development but where it should take place. If new homes are needed in areas of high employment, for example, then planning concerns over the undesirability of 'greenfield development' may take second place to economic considerations.

7.3.1(a)   Change of use

Under the Town and Country Planning Act 1990, you must apply for planning permission where you intend 'developing' your property or where you intend to change the use of your property in a material way. An example would be change of use of purely residential property into part business use (such as for a dental surgery) which could generate disturbance and parking problems for the neighbours.

7.3.1(b)   Changes without planning consent

A local authority cannot serve an enforcement notice requiring the removal or regularisation of work carried out without consent after 4 years of the substantial completion of the work, unless the work carried out without planning permission involved an unauthorised change of use.

The courts have decided that the 4-year rule extends to cover change of use of a building divided into flats to a single family house, and the subdivision of a single dwelling into two separate dwellings.

In other cases where there have been changes of use without consent, the local authority has 10 years within which it can serve an enforcement notice. When that period expires, the change of use will be treated as lawful.

7.3.2   When there is no development

In fact, the law does not specify the meaning of a 'development' and it does not define a material change of use. However, it does state that there is no development, if:

- you carry out repairs to the interior of a building
- the building works would not materially affect the outside appearance of your house
- the building is within the grounds of your existing house and is intended to be used for its benefit; the new building might, for example, be a garage. In the words of the statute, the building must be 'ancillary' to the main dwelling house.

Even if there is no development so that you do not require planning permission, you still need to conform to local authority building regulations. A booklet is issued by the Office of the Deputy Prime Minister which provides an introduction to building regulations. It also issues a planning guide for householders, available from the Planning Inspectorate (see DIRECTORY).

Warning notice: planning permission does not take away your neighbour's private rights. So even if you need, and then obtain, planning permission, your neighbour can still object if the change of use causes a nuisance (e.g. leads to an unpleasant smell, see section 4.4 above) or infringes on your neighbour's right to light (see section 7.2.2 above).

8   TRESPASS ON OR ACCESS TO NEIGHBOURING LAND

8.1   Access to neighbouring land

The laws of trespass apply to people, animals and things, such as an overhanging eave or a bulging fence. It also applies, as we have seen, to plants and trees (see above, section 6).

The chapter on *Accidents* deals with trespass in relation to occupier's liability (see section 4.3.2) and the chapter on *The Countryside* considers trespass and straying animals (see section 6.)

In this section, we deal with the question of trespass on, and access to, neighbouring land. These disputes can quickly get out of control.

One man faced criminal damage charges after a row about access to garages. A dispute began when he saw his neighbour's car parked near a garage. The neighbour claimed to have undisputed right of way over the vehicular access behind the man's property. While the neighbour was trying to drive up this shared access, the man kicked the car.

8.1.1   Unlawful access

In general, unless you are invited on to land, or are there on business (for example to lay gas pipes), you are a trespasser. (For rights acquired through persistent trespass, see section 8.2 below.)

☞   *In order to repair your roof, you place a section of your ladder in your neighbour's garden without permission. You then go indoors to fetch your tools. Your irate neighbour shouts across the fence that your actions amount to 'trespass'. Is he correct?*

The answer is 'yes'. You are committing a continuing trespass by leaving the ladder in his garden just as much as you have committed trespass by walking on to your neighbour's land with your ladder in the first place. It is not a defence for you to tell your neighbour that your roof is in urgent need of repairs.

(However, see immediately below.)

8.1.2   Lawful access

An Act was introduced into Parliament to get round this problem of a householder/'trespasser' who has to go on to adjacent property in order to carry out repairs to his own property. It is called the Access to Neighbouring Land Act 1992, and gives a temporary right of access, by court order, on to neighbouring property to carry out reasonably necessary operations which must be 'basic preservation works'.

Thus the Act does not cover alterations or improvements for their own sake but covers maintenance, repair and renewal. It would allow for an inspection visit. You must also show that you could not carry out the works without access to neighbouring land. See also section 3.3.1 above.

8.1.2(a)   Can your neighbour object?

☞ *The person living next door to you wants to do some major remedial work to his roof and, as you live in a terrace, he requires that some of the scaffolding is placed against your wall. You feel that it will be a major inconvenience and have strongly objected. He has now applied to court for an access order on to your land. You wonder what you can do.*

First, your neighbour must show the court that the works to his roof are 'basic preservation works'. Second, he must show the court that he would not be able to carry out those works without coming on to your property. If he satisfies those terms, you cannot object, strictly speaking. However, you can insist on certain protection for yourself. The access order must be drafted in very specific terms and you can ask for conditions to be attached which would protect – insofar as possible – your privacy, and would minimise inconvenience. You could also insist on knowing who will be coming on to your land and when.

Note: you cannot ask for payment in a case where there are two residential properties involved.

8.1.2(b)   Trees

An access order can be made where 'basic preservation works' are necessary to deal with trees or shrubs which are in danger of becoming 'damaged, diseased, dangerous, insecurely rooted or dead'. (See also *Problems with gardens* above, section 6.)

8.2   Acquiring title to someone else's land – adverse possession

Can the law give you rights of ownership over someone else's land or property? If so, when?

The acquisition of rights over someone else's land in certain clearly defined circumstances is known as 'adverse possession'. Previously, if you used someone else's land for 12 years without interruption and without permission from the owner, who failed to assert his rights to the property in that period, you could become the owner of it. However the Land Registration Act 2002 (which is expected to come into force on 13 October 2003) will abandon the 12-year-possession concept and a squatter will be able to apply to become registered as owner after 10 years' adverse possession.

However, the Act gives greater protection against adverse possession to owners of registered land by providing that a registered proprietor's title is not lost merely through a lapse of time. The onus will be on the squatter to take the initiative if he wants to acquire title to the registered land. Actual registration will confer title, instead of the act of possession.

Under the Act, if you are the registered proprietor of land, the Land Registry will have to notify you of a squatter's application to be registered as owner. As a general rule you will be able to object by counter-notice. If you object the application will be rejected. You must then take steps to evict the squatter but if he is still in adverse possession after 2 years, he will be entitled to be registered as proprietor without any objection from you.

☞ *For years you have been parking your car on a piece of wasteland next to your country cottage. You do not know who owns the land. One day you find a fence around the land. Have you any rights?*

The fence around the land is definitely an assertion of ownership on the part of someone else.

If you want to challenge that assertion, you must show that:

a) you have used the land as though you owned it
b) that use has been uninterrupted for 12 years (10 years from October 2003)
c) there has been no challenge to that use from the owner of the land.

If you can prove these three essential characteristics of adverse possession, you may have acquired title to it. You should apply to the Land Registry to have title registered, so that the true position can be established.

Recent cases have highlighted the question of adverse possession where squatters obtained two free homes worth a total of £300,000 from a local authority in London after the council lost its attempt in court to reclaim both properties. The High Court held that the council had failed to exercise its ownership rights over 16 years and that the squatters had treated the properties as their own.

In a dispute over farm land, the House of Lords held in 2002 that a paper owner of land was 'dispossessed' by a squatter where the latter had simply taken possession without the consent of the owner. Possession of the necessary intention was, in the normal case, to be inferred where the squatter had occupied the land and made full use of it in the way an owner would.

There does not have to be an intention to own the land, nor is the requisite intention displaced where the squatter is willing, if asked, to pay for his occupation.

Note: you are well advised to seek advice if you are in dispute over restrictive covenants, easements or other property matters. Land law is very technical and full of pitfalls for the unwary.

8.3 Vacant premises

Two problems can arise when you live next to vacant or repossessed premises. The first concerns dereliction through lack of habitation; the second concerns squatters.

8.3.1 Repossessed homes

It is self-evident that if a next-door property is empty, it can cause problems to your own home, such as damp or dry rot. It can be difficult to establish who owns the property and how to take remedial action. As we have seen too (*Access to neighbouring land*, section 8.1 above) sometimes you can only take remedial action for basic preservation works by access on to the land next door.

In such a situation, you should try to establish the identity of the owner. Quite often it will be a bank or a building society that has repossessed the property. Where the problem is causing a statutory nuisance (see section 4.3 above), you can ask the local authority to invoke its powers under the Environmental Protection Act 1990.

8.3.2 Squatters

People squat in properties ranging from mansions to empty shop premises, although about 90 per cent of squatters are found in council premises. They may be assisted by squatters' organisations.

As a neighbour, there is nothing you can do about squatters next door unless they cause problems to you of the kind already dealt with – for example, nuisance. Under the Criminal Justice Act 1994 squatters can be guilty of a criminal offence if they fail to leave residential premises after the owner has asked them to do so.

9 PROBLEMS WITH LIT'TER

There is no precise definition of litter but we can all recognise it when we see it, whether it be discarded sweet wrappers, bags of half-eaten takeaway food, empty beer cans, or scattered advertising leaflets.

9.1 Litter and the law

The Environmental Protection Act 1990 (EPA) makes so-called 'duty bodies' responsible for keeping their land clear of litter and refuse. It also gives both local authorities and citizens the right to take legal action to get areas cleared up.

Duty bodies are organisations with a legal responsibility for keeping specific public places clear of litter and refuse (a 'cleansing duty'). They are mainly local authorities and utility companies (e.g. water boards), but may also be e.g. schools, colleges and universities.

9.1.1 What does the cleansing duty involve?

These bodies must make sure that public land and highways under their control are kept free from litter and refuse as far as is practicably possible and within reason. Details of how they must comply are contained in the Government Code of Practice on Litter and Refuse which accompanies the EPA.

Based on land use and time, the Code sets out reasonable and acceptable standards of cleanliness which duty bodies can be expected to meet.

Compliance with the Code is measured in two ways:

a) cleanliness grades which set out how clean an area should be; and
b) cleanliness standards which indicate response times for cleaning up.

All areas have to be 'zoned'. Each zone has a timescale within which the duty body should return it to a litter-free standard. Zoning maps produced by local authorities are public information and must be made available to you on request, usually at council offices or the public library.

9.1.2   What can you do if litter is not cleared?

The EPA gives all citizens the right to take legal action to get litter removed if an area falls below the standard for longer that is allowed.

☞ *You are unhappy with the state of your street where rubbish has been piling up for some weeks and is being spread across a wide area. There are unconfirmed reports of rats being seen around the rubbish but the council does not seem to be doing anything. What can you do?*

> Before exercising your right under the EPA, you should give the council a chance to clean up the mess. Make a formal complaint by telephone or in writing and take care to specify accurately the location, type and amount of litter. Some local authorities have litter 'hotlines' and respond quickly to complaints. If you don't have a special number to ring, try the Cleansing, Environmental Health or Technical Services Department of your local authority.

> If the council fails to take action even though the area falls below the required standard, you can take legal action to get a Litter Abatement Order to force the council to clean up the area.

> You need to make an application through the magistrates' court and there is a charge (currently £3.50) to apply for a Litter Abatement Order. For details on how to do this you can contact the Tidy Britain Group (see DIRECTORY).

As with any legal action, the process is time-consuming and complicated but it is considered to be an important power as it allows the public to have a say in cleaning up their community.

9.1.3   Local authority powers – litter as a criminal offence

Local authorities have powers to take action against individuals and businesses who create litter. Dropping or depositing litter is a criminal offence, subject to a maximum fine (currently £2,500, although the average fine is around £90, plus court costs).

Either the police or a local authority can prosecute litterers. Local authorities can also appoint litter wardens who can issue on-the-spot fines which have recently doubled from £25 to £50. Local authorities are allowed to keep the money raised to give them more incentive to tackle litter. However, latest Government figures show that only 422 people a year throughout the UK were fined for dropping litter.

Warning: throwing litter from vehicles onto public land is also an offence. Vehicle registration details can be taken and the authorities can trace the owner through the DVLA. A £25 fixed penalty can be imposed.

9.2   Business litter

Where the source of litter can be traced to a particular business, such as a takeaway-food restaurant, the local authority can issue a Street Litter Control Notice to make the owner responsible for keeping the front of its premises, plus a reasonable distance either side, clear of litter.

'Fly tipping' (i.e. the deliberate dumping of rubbish in an unauthorised place), which is potentially more serious and hazardous than litter, is a separate offence under the waste legislation. Its gravity is reflected in the penalty imposed which on conviction can be a fine of up to £20,000 or six months imprisonment, or both.

9.3   Litter control

Where certain kinds of private land to which the public has access, such as supermarket car parks, are badly littered, the local authority can declare a Litter Control Area. The owner or occupier of the land is then under a duty to clear the land and keep it free of litter.

Anyone under a duty to keep land free of litter and refuse can be served with a litter abatement notice by the local authority. Once served with a notice, the owner or occupier must clean up the area within a given time. Failure to do so will result in a fine plus a daily penalty if the offence continues. However, rather than use this power, some authorities have developed partnerships with local businesses to encourage them to adopt a responsible attitude to the problem.

Premises covered include those used for the sale of food and drink; petrol stations; betting shops; premises selling lottery tickets; places of entertainment and those with automatic teller machines (ATMs) on outside walls.

Local authorities have power to collect abandoned shopping- or luggage-trolleys in their area and charge the owners for their return.

9.4 Particular litter areas

9.4.1 Schools

There is often a litter problem around schools. While litter created by school pupils is not necessarily a direct result of the activities on the school site, councils can seek to address this issue in conjunction with the schools through initiatives such as litter awareness campaigns.

9.4.2 Markets, car boot sales etc

Events which are held periodically can cause litter problems. Different rules apply for markets, car boot sales etc., which generate litter on public highways and roads, or for those on private land.

Where the market is on a public highway maintainable at the public expense and where the council is the operator, the council can reflect the cost of street cleaning in the rents it charges to stall holders.

Where the market is on private land, it may be possible to designate a Litter Control Area (see section 9.2.2 above).

However, where a market takes place once a week or less frequently, the landowner is under a duty to clear up within a certain time after the event. A similar approach is taken where land is used only occasionally for fairs and circuses.

9.4.3 Leaflet distribution

Distributors of free leaflets, free newspapers and other similar activities can cause significant litter problems.

The London Local Authorities Act 1994 gives authorities in London discretion to designate certain places (e.g. off-street car parks, recreation grounds, open spaces under council control etc.) where free literature (anything which advertises for commercial gain) may not be distributed without the council's consent. Consent may be subject to conditions or withheld or revoked. Distribution without consent can attract can attract a fine of (currently) £500.

The Government is evaluating the experiences in London before deciding whether to extend the system across the country.

9.5 Business rubbish

Businesses and local authorities are under a duty to control business refuse and litter. It is outside the scope of this book to cover the details of the regulations. However, do note that anyone who produces, keeps or disposes of 'controlled waste' has a duty to prevent its escape from his control. Controlled waste includes domestic (except your own household rubbish), commercial and industrial waste.

Warning: it is unlawful to put trade or commercial waste in litter bins. They are strictly for general litter and refuse.

DIRECTORY
NEIGHBOURS

Association of Noise Consultants
6 Trap Road
Guilden Morden
Nr Royston
Herts SG8 OJE
Tel. 01763 852958
www.association-of-noise-consultants.co.uk

Boundary and Party Walls Working Group
Royal Institution of Chartered Surveyors
12 Great George Street
Parliament Square
London SW1P 3AD
Tel. 020 7222 7000

Centre for Dispute Resolution *(CEDR)*
Exchange Tower
1 Harbour Exchange Square
London E14 9GB
Tel. 020 7536 6000
www.cedr.co.uk

Cleanair
33 Stillness Road
London SE23 1NG
Tel. 020 8690 4649
www.ezme.com/cleanair/

**Department of the Environment,
Food and Rural Affairs** *(DEFRA)*
Nobel House
17 Smith Square
London SW1P 3JR
Tel. 08459 33 55 77
www.defra.gov.uk

Environmental & Consumer Services
(Contact your local council)

Environmental Services Association
154 Buckingham Palace Road
London SW1W 9TR
Tel. 020 7824 8882
www.esauk.org

Hedgeline
Tel: 0870 240 0627
www.hedgeline.org.uk

Institute of Waste Management
9 Saxon Court
St. Peter's Gardens
Northampton NN1 1SX
Tel. 01604 620 246
www.ciwm.co.uk

Lord Chancellor's Department
Selborne House
54–60 Victoria Street
London SW1E 6QW
Tel. 020 7210 8500
www.lcd.gov.uk

Mediation UK
Alexander House
Telephone Avenue
Bristol BS1 4BS
Tel. 0117 904 6661
www.mediationuk.org.uk

**National Association of Councils for
Voluntary Service** *(NACVS)*
3rd Floor
Arundel Court
177 Arundel Street
Sheffield S1 2NU
Tel. 01142 786636
www.nacvs.org.uk

Noise Network
PO Box 327
Chatham
Kent ME5 8AW
Tel. 07887 940 004
www.superscript.co.uk/tnn

Office of the Deputy Prime Minister
(for Planning)
Eland House
Bressenden Place
London SW1E 5DU
Tel. 020 7944 4400
www.odpm.gov.uk

Planning Inspectorate
Temple Quay House
2 The Square
Temple Quay
Bristol BS1 6PN
Tel. 0117 372 6372
www.planning-inspectorate.gov.uk

Pyramus & Thisbe Club
Florence House
53 Acton Lane
London NW10 8UX
Tel. 020 8961 3311
www.partywalls.org.uk

Royal Institute of British Architects
Client Services
66 Portland Place
London W1B 1AD
Tel. 020 7580 5533
www.architecture.com

Royal Institution of Chartered Surveyors
12 Great George Street
London SW1P 3AD
Tel. 020 7222 7000
(Contact Centre) Tel. 0870 333 1600
www.rics.org.uk

Tidy Britain Group
Elizabeth House
The Pier
Wigan WN3 4EX
Tel. 01942 824 620
www.tidybritain.org.uk

Waste Watch *(for information on recycling)*
(Wasteline) Tel. 0870 230 136

See also organisations listed in *The Countryside* chapter.

14 THE COUNTRYSIDE

For those who live in cities and towns, a trip to the countryside provides a means of escape from urban living – from buildings, traffic, noise, pollution and the pressure of people. Estimates are that about 10 million people from the towns visit the countryside every day during the summer months.

Of course, this poses an immediate problem: is it possible to prevent the inundation of our open spaces by the very things from which many citydwellers seek to escape – cars, noise, pollution, and overcrowding?

The law, as we shall see, tries to strike a balance between preservation and necessary development; between conservation of our natural environment and opportunities to enjoy it; between the needs of citydwellers and those of landowners; between those who work on the land and those who want to use it for fun.

At present, as never before, there is a particular focus on, and anxiety about, protecting our environment. This is just as much a local and national issue as it is a global one. Indeed, the intensity of the debate on environmental issues has made us all very aware of just how important it is to strike the right balance between competing needs for our available natural resources.

Many of us think of 'the countryside' in terms of our recreation and enjoyment; indeed it is this aspect on which this chapter concentrates. However, above all, the countryside is a working, living environment and the source of our food. In the most literal sense, we all live off the land.

Much attention is given to the deep-seated and often bitter conflicts of interest between landowner or farmer and visitors on their land. But there are common interests as well. Not all visitors are necessarily unwelcome! Because of overproduction, farmers today are being urged to diversify. Tourists, far from being viewed as undesirable interlopers, may often help to sustain a dwindling income from farming. Summer visitors, too, can help to sustain the economy of many of the fishing villages along our coasts.

As much as possible, therefore, the laws governing access to the countryside must be devised in such a way as to serve the interests of us all, while protecting those aspects which we most seek from our rural environment.

Traditionally, the authorities involved in 'managing' the countryside span central government, specialised governmental agencies, local authorities, private authorities, voluntary bodies; and, increasingly, EU bodies. Since 1996, overall control of conservation of nature and the heritage has been vested in the Environment Agency which took over the functions of HM Inspectorate of Pollution, the National Rivers Authority and local authority waste regulation authorities. In building an integrated approach to environmental protection and enhancement, the Agency liaises closely with public authorities, local authorities and other representatives of local communities and regulated organisations.

The number of pressure groups involved in countryside activities is striking. Many are active in trying to preserve rural tranquillity; others are concerned with the protection of our flora and fauna; others with sporting activities and others again wish to assert the right of greater access to what they feel is our national heritage (see end of chapter for a DIRECTORY of organisations involved in countryside matters).

The passing of the Countryside and Rights of Way Act in November 2000, when it comes in to force (expected in 2005) will radically alter the entitlement of the general public to access large areas of land, under the so-called 'right to roam' legislation. The Act grants a general right of public access to 'open countryside' of more than four million acres of mountain, moor, heath, downland and registered common land in England and Wales (see section 3 below).

Intense controversy both within and outside of Parliament has been generated by countryside concerns, such as the hunting with dogs, questions of greater public access, of industrial farming, the rural economy, and the introduction of genetically modified crops on an experimental basis. These issues have exacerbated the divisions and polarity of views between town and country. It is not our purpose to enter into current argument; rather, it is hoped that by reading through this chapter, a greater understanding of the complexity of the issues in debate will emerge.

In this chapter we look at:

- rights of way
- open spaces
- the right to roam
- encounters with animals
- sporting rights
- trespass
- protection of flora and fauna.

1 RIGHTS OF WAY

The basis of the law concerning access to the countryside in England and Wales is that all land is under ownership. There simply is no land available to belong to the public at large. For every tract of land there is a landowner – whether that landowner is a private individual, a private body (such as the National Trust), a public body (such as the Ministry of Defence), or the Crown. Therefore we have to establish a right to go on to that land – either a right of way or a right to roam. Rights to roam were until recently severely circumscribed, so generally we could only go on to land with permission. In other words, we had to have a right of way. Rights of way give the public the right to cross land via a defined route. The Countryside and Rights of Way Act 2000 (CROW) has introduced, in addition, rights of access, which gives the public the right to wander more freely over some land. This is dealt with in section 3 below.

Accordingly, the first aspect which we shall consider is the question of rights of way. How do we get to, or through, the countryside?

1.1 Public rights of way

A right of way is a peculiar legal hybrid. It is tangible: i.e. it is the actual path that you tread on; it is also intangible, i.e. it is a 'right' in law which you can acquire and which, once acquired, you or someone else on your behalf can enforce.

1.1.2 How do we acquire a public right of way?

As all land is under ownership, we need to have a 'right' to go on to land. How is such a right acquired?

It is acquired either:

- by dedication and acceptance
  or
- by statute – in particular the Highways Act.

Under the Countryside and Rights of Way Act 2000, the Countryside Agency is able to apply for the creation of a new public path to provide a route of access to land which is open country or registered common land, or which has been dedicated as access land by the owner.

1.1.2(a) By dedication and acceptance

The legal concept called 'dedication and acceptance' stems from the fact that all land in this country is owned.

Where there is a right of way for the general public, that right is regarded as having been 'dedicated' to the public for public use by the landowner. The public, in turn, by using the right of way has, in the eyes of the law, 'accepted' that dedication. The right of way must have been in use for 20 years for the right to be established, unless the landowner has entered into an agreement by deed with the local authority.

1.1.2(b) Under the Highways Act

The Highways Act 1980 has taken over the common law concept of dedication and acceptance and states that

> 'Where a way over land ... has been actually enjoyed by the public as of right and without interruption for a full period of 20 years, the way is ... deemed to have been dedicated as a highway ...'.

Once a right of way has actually been used by the public 'as of right and without interruption' for the 20-year period, it is then 'deemed' dedicated [i.e. taken to have been dedicated] as a right of way unless there is sufficient evidence of a contrary intention.

1.1.2(c) Must be uninterrupted use

Thus continuous use for 20 years is conclusive evidence of existence of a public highway or footpath unless there is evidence to the contrary, i.e. evidence that there was no intention on the landowner's part during that period to dedicate it. See section 1.3.2(a) below for ways in which a landowner can show that he has not intended to dedicate a right of way and has, for example, interrupted its use by closing it for one day per year.

To sum up:

Public rights of way come into existence in two ways:

- through continuous use, and dedication under the common law
- through legislation.

1.1.3 What does a right of way give the public?

As we have seen, a right of way is a hybrid: both a tangible route and an intangible right. In particular we are given the right to use it.

1.1.3(a) The right to pass and repass

The public are allowed to come and go [in legal terms 'to pass and repass'] along a highway for their lawful business without permission from anyone – in other words, members of the public use a highway 'as of right'.

However, although we use the highway as of right, not all highways can be used in the same way. In fact, as we shall see, highways are defined according to their use (see below, section 1.1.5).

1.1.4 For how long does a public right of way last?

The phrase is 'once a highway, always a highway'. This means that it should be there for the public use forever. However, loss does occur – particularly of footpaths – and roads can be stopped up under the Highways Act.

1.1.5 What is the distinction between a public and a private right of way?

Private rights of way exist for private use and for limited classes of people – a private access road for individual owners to a common car park is an example. Private rights of way are known as 'easements'. (See also section 1.3.1 below.)

1.1.6 Maintenance and upkeep

Once there is an established right of way through dedication, then if a footpath or bridleway was legally in existence on 1 January 1960, the responsibility for its maintenance and upkeep is placed on the local highway authority or, in the case of major roads, the Highways Agency, i.e. these rights of way are publicly maintainable.

Since that date, the position is as follows:

1) If a path or way is constructed by a highway authority or by a council acting as a housing authority, or is created by a public path creation or diversion order under the highways or planning legislation, it is maintainable at the public's expense.

2) The cost of maintaining any other new path will depend on whether or not the highway authority has accepted responsibility for it. For example, a developer may construct a new road into a housing estate but it will not be publicly maintainable unless accepted by the authority as such.

Do Note: The Countryside and Rights of Way Act (see section 3 below) contains provisions for the maintenance at the public expense of paths which are to be treated as restricted byways (see section 1.1.8(b) below)).

1.1.7 What limits are there on the right to pass and repass?

Obviously, not all rights of way can be used in the same way. A footpath through a field may be unsuitable for wheeled traffic, while pedestrians would be most unwelcome on a motorway.

Public rights of way are classified into:

- footpaths
- bridleways
- carriageways
- byways open to all traffic (BOATs)
- roads used as public paths (RUPPs).

1.1.7(a) Footpaths

You can only use a footpath on foot. You can push a pram along it and you can be accompanied by a dog, which does not have to be on a lead but must be kept under control.

☞ *You are seeking out a picnic spot and see a track marked 'footpath'. It looks wide enough to take your car so you drive down the footpath for about 100 yards and then park. An irate passer-by approaches you and says you have committed a criminal offence; you reply, that at the most, you might have trespassed by driving your car down the footpath. Which of you is correct?*

You are a trespasser because it is trespass to bring a wheeled vehicle – even a bicycle – on to a footpath. You have also committed an offence.

It is a criminal offence to drive a car down a footpath under the Road Traffic Act 1972 unless you have 'lawful' authority, i.e. you are allowed to use the footpath for your car by consent of the owner of the land, or some other authority has given you leave to do so. For example, if you are a disabled driver, you might be given leave by a landowner to use a footpath to drive to a scenic spot.

In theory once a footpath has been established, it belongs to the public for its use forever.

☞ *Your local footpath has not been used for years; in fact it has become quite overgrown. When you tried to go along it recently, the landowner said that as the footpath was no longer in use, its use had lapsed. Can he be correct?*

A right of way, once established, remains such even if not used for any length of time.

In practice, footpaths can become unusable or lead to nowhere through neglect, desuetude or wilful obstruction (see section 1.2.1(b) below).

1.1.7(b) Bridleways

In the case of bridleways, you can go:

- by foot
- on horseback
- by bicycle – mountain bikes included (but cyclists must give priority to walkers and riders).

1.1.7(c) Carriageways

These are in fact roads which can be used for all purposes and are intended for motor traffic.

1.1.8 Other rights of way

There are two other forms of highway which constitute rights of way.

1.1.8(a) Byways open to all traffic (BOATs)

Although use is allowed for motor traffic, in fact these are used mainly on foot or by those on horseback. To fulfil the definition of a byway open to all traffic, there has to be evidence of use by those on foot or on horseback. It need not be proved that the byway is being currently used by vehicles, however, because it may be that the way has fallen into a state of disrepair which makes it more suitable for pedestrian or equestrian access.

1.1.8(b) Roads used as public paths (RUPPs)

Under the Act of 2000 these are to be reclassified as a new category and will be known as *Restricted Byways* (which are intended to stretch for 4,000 miles), giving a public right of way for all traffic except motor vehicles, i.e. on foot, horseback or cycle, and for horse-drawn vehicles. It will be an offence to drive a motor vehicle on a restricted byway without having lawful authority, e.g. permission from the owner of the land over which the way runs.

1.1.8(c) Long-distance trails

National trails have been created by the joining together of footpaths, bridleways and byways for long distances.

Since 1980, rights of way can be compulsorily imposed by law under the Highways Act 1980. In fact, this power has been very sparingly used for making new rights of way. The purpose of this provision has rather been served by linking existing rights of way into long-distance trails over several counties – the Pennine Way is an example.

1.1.8(d) Cycle paths

County councils can designate particular paths and bridleways as cycle tracks. These are generally marked (check with your local authority and refer to a definitive map). See section 1.2.2(a) below.

Cyclists take note: there is no right to cycle on a footpath. There is a code of conduct for mountain-bike riding and off-road cycling available from the Countryside Agency and cycling organisations (see the DIRECTORY at the end of this chapter). You can cycle on a bridleway provided you give way to those on foot and on horseback. It is an offence to use a mechanically propelled vehicle on a footpath, bridleway or restricted byway. (For the definition of a 'mechanically propelled vehicle', see chapter on *Motoring*, section 10.2.)

1.2 Problems with rights of way

1.2.1 Rights of way can be lost

Although rights of way, once they have been used for 20 years without interruption, are taken to be dedicated to the public forever, in fact they are quite often lost to the public for its use.

In general it is an offence for a landowner to disturb the surface of any footpath, bridleway or unsurfaced carriageway so as to interfere with a right of way or make it inconvenient to use.

Rights of way can however be lost through:

- ploughing and cropping
- physical obstructions
- diversion or extinction.

Under the Countryside and Rights of Way Act, owners and occupiers of land will be able to apply for public paths to be diverted or extinguished where the land is used for agriculture, forestry or the keeping of horses. Highway authorities will also be able to divert or extinguish highways in the interests of crime-prevention or school security.

Temporary diversions of a footpath or bridleway can be made by the occupier of land where certain works are required which could be a danger to the public. The path cannot be closed for this reason for more than 14 days in one calendar year. The diversion provided must be reasonably convenient for the public, and it must be indicated by signposts, etc. on the ground so that it is apparent to members of the public who wish to use it.

Notification of such temporary diversions must be given to the highway authority, but their prior authorisation is not required.

Highway authorities can order temporary diversion of a footpath or bridleway for up to three months where it runs over agricultural land and the occupier needs to carry out engineering operations or excavations for farming purposes.

(The procedures under which rights of way can be diverted or extinguished under the Highways Act 1980 and the Town and Country Planning Act 1990 are outside the scope of this chapter.)

1.2.1(a) **By ploughing and cropping**

The difficulties of securing acceptance of a voluntary code of practice by farmers who plough their fields over rights of way led to the passing of the Rights of Way Act 1990.

Remember: there is no right to plough a path which runs along the edge of a field.

After ploughing over a right of way which runs across a field, the footpath must be made apparent again and kept visible despite the growing crops. The surface must be restored within two weeks after ploughing.

Note: 'crops' do not include grass grown for pasture.

1.2.1(b) **By obstructions**

The law in relation to obstructions on footpaths and bridleways has been considerably tightened up by new legislation (in particular regarding the problems which have arisen because of ploughing of fields over which public paths run – see section 1.2.1(a) above).

☞ *You have been enjoying a walk along a certain footpath for years. You have been told that the land adjoining it has recently changed hands. The last time you tried to walk along the path your way was barred by the new owner who was threatening and abusive. The dog which was with him looked particularly fierce too. What can you do?*

Do not attempt to take the law into your hands in such a situation – no matter what the provocation. Instead, inform the Rights of Way Officer of your local highway authority which is under a duty to ensure that public rights of way are kept open and free of obstruction. He will then write to the new landowner, probably informally at first, explaining the position and asking him to desist from harassing people who use a public footpath as of right. If he is uncooperative, the highway authority can prosecute. Moreover, private individuals can also prosecute landowners who bar their rights of way. (See also section 1.2.4 below, on *Law enforcement.*)

1.2.1(c) **Physical obstructions**

☞ *You find your local footpath is blocked by a fallen tree. What can you do?*

Reasonably enough, the law suggests that you always try to walk round an obstruction. If that is not possible, you are entitled to try to remove it. You can also inform your local highway authority which is under a duty to maintain the footpath, including the removal of any obstruction. Moreover, where an authority has tried unsuccessfully to get the landowner to remove an obstruction, it can enter on his or her land and remove the obstruction itself. Costs can be reclaimed from the landowner.

An obstruction can be illegal even if it does not completely block the highway. Encroachment on the verges, e.g. by extending the boundaries of a garden, also constitutes obstruction.

☞ *You have been horse-riding regularly on a local bridleway for a number of years. Over the last while, however, you find that the trees on either side have become so overgrown that they brush your face. While the route is not totally obstructed and you can still make your way, you fear that you may be knocked off balance by a projecting branch.*

Where overhanging vegetation from adjoining land obstructs or endangers the passage of vehicles or pedestrians or those on horseback, the occupier of the land can be ordered by the highway authority to cut it back; if he fails to do so within the notified time, the authority can do the work itself but then recover the costs of doing so from the occupier.

You can serve a notice of the obstruction on the highway authority requesting them to have the obstruction removed. If they do not respond satisfactorily, the next step would be to apply to the magistrate's court for a court order. Do take legal advice before acting.

1.2.1(d) **By non-physical obstructions**

Footpaths can be obstructed in a number of ways. Not all of them may be something as clear to establish as a log of wood blocking your way.

☞ *A public footpath runs through a field which its new landowner uses for practising his golf shots. You were narrowly missed by a golf ball while crossing the field on the path.*

A landowner might seek to discourage the public from using the right of way by, for example, false or misleading notices, or by keeping an intimidating dog on the land. In such cases he is committing a criminal offence. The highway authority is under duty to take appropriate action to protect the public's rights.

The procedures for complaint are:

a) to approach the landowner personally; or if this is to no avail,
b) to follow up with a complaint to the highway authority.

Under the Countryside and Rights of Way Act the magistrates' courts have the power to require a person who wilfully obstructs a highway to remove the obstruction. Failure to abide by such an order would be contempt of court, a criminal offence.

1.2.1(e) The disabled

When local authorities consider applications to erect gates or stiles across footpaths or bridleways, they are obliged to take into account the needs of those with disability problems.

1.2.2 What can be done to stop paths disappearing?

In order to preserve rights of way, certain duties have been imposed on local authorities. These include the duties to:

* produce definitive maps
* signpost rights of way
* maintain rights of way
* enforce the public's rights against offenders.

1.2.2(a) Definitive maps

To safeguard against the number of usable footpaths diminishing because they were not being used or were obstructed, overgrown or forgotten, local authorities are under a duty to survey their areas and to produce definitive maps and written statements of all footpaths and bridleways in their area.

These maps are strong evidence that a public right of way exists. Ordnance Survey maps show rights of way which have been recorded on these definitive maps. Very cogent evidence is necessary to remove a public right of way from a definitive map, i.e. to prove it was marked on the map in error.

However, even when a public right of way has been recorded in a definitive map, its status is not defined forever.

☞ *A public right of way through your land was marked on the definitive map as a footpath. The local council made an order to change it to that of a bridleway. You objected and a public enquiry was held. You maintain that once a path has been designated, its designation remains fixed for all time. Evidence was brought to show at the enquiry that there had been longstanding use of the path for riding on horseback.*

An entry on a definitive map is not conclusive evidence forever. A path's status is liable to change so that rights of passage could be enlarged. For example, a footpath could become a bridleway in the light of fresh evidence.

If a change is to be made, it must be done according to a statutory procedure which involves a modification order. Such an order can be challenged in court.

☞ *Your local county council has recently included in a modification order a footpath over your land on the grounds that it was omitted from the definitive map in error. You wish to challenge the modification order. What steps can you take?*

The county council is under a duty to publish the order. You have six weeks from the date of receiving notice of the order in which to object to the council.

The matter will then be referred to the Secretary of State for the Environment, Food and Rural Affairs (DEFRA), who can hold a local inquiry. If s/he decides to confirm the order you can apply to the High Court to appeal against that decision again within six weeks of the confirmation.

When the relevant provisions of the Countryside and Rights of Way Act are brought into force, additions to the definitive map to show more BOATs (see section 1.1.8(a)) after 1 January 2026 will no longer be possible. The Act also requires local highway authorities to carry out a review and publish their plans for improving rights of way in their areas, taking into account the needs of the public, including those of people with mobility problems.

1.2.2(b) Signposting

Signposting or waymarking is often undertaken by groups of local volunteers. The colours are:

- blue for bridleways
- red for byways
- yellow for footpaths.

A highway authority is under a duty to signpost all:

- footpaths
- bridleways and
- byways

where they leave a metalled road.

Note: the landowner's consent is necessary if signs are erected along a route on stiles or gateposts.

1.2.3 Maintaining footpath widths

The widths to be kept clear across fields are:

- one metre for footpaths
- two metres for bridleways
- three metres for carriageways.

The widths to be kept clear around the edge of a field are:

- one and a half metres for footpaths
- three metres for both bridleways and carriageways.

1.2.4 Law enforcement

Under the Highways Act 1980 it is an offence for someone who – without lawful authority or excuse – in any way wilfully obstructs free passage along a highway. If found guilty he or she can be fined.

A direct approach to the landowner concerned would always be the best tactic. If that fails, or if it is difficult to establish who owns the land, you can report an obstruction to your local highway authority. You must back up your report with evidence – such as a map, a description of the nature of the obstruction, and the date on which you encountered it. Proceedings are heard in a magistrates' court.

If you, as an individual or an organisation, decide to take legal action, always seek professional advice.

If you wish to complain about an obstruction, significant new ways of obliging the relevant highway authority to act are set out in the Countryside and Rights of Way Act 2000. You can give notice to the highway authority of the obstruction and request it to secure its removal. The highway authority must within one month notify those responsible of the complaint and the action it proposes to take. Where the response is unsatisfactory within two months, notice of application to the magistrate's court can be given to the highway authority. The person responsible for the obstruction can appear at the magistrate's court hearing. The court can order steps to be taken by the authority for the removal of the obstruction within a reasonable period as fixed by the court. Failure to comply with a court order is a criminal offence.

1.2.5 Maintenance

A highway authority is under a duty to maintain a footpath so that it is fit for ordinary passage, because the surface of a footpath or other right of way that is publicly maintained is owned by the local highway authority. However, as landowners still retain ownership of gates and stiles, they remain responsible for the maintenance of these.

1.2.6   Improving rights of way

Highway authorities have the power to effect improvements to rights of way, for instance by signposting, by erecting barriers to prevent unlawful use by vehicles or by putting up handrails at steep or dangerous places along the path. The need for safe access for the disabled must be borne in mind. If the landowner's rights are seriously affected by such improvements he may be entitled to compensation.

To improve access for those of limited mobility, under the Countryside and Rights of Way Act highway authorities can enter into agreements with the owners or occupiers of land to modify or replace stiles or gates. The authority has the power to fund such improvements wholly or in part. The Act also requires an authority to assess the local rights of way and publish a plan setting out its proposals for their management and improvement.

1.2.7   Rights of way on navigable rivers?

The question of whether a public right of way could be established on navigable rivers was decided by the House of Lords.

A dispute had arisen between Malton town council and four nearby landowners whose land adjoined the river Derwent. The town council wished to protect the public rights of navigation of the Derwent for recreational purposes while the owners said that that would damage plant and river life.

The Law Lords emphatically stated that a right of navigation was not a right of way. It was wrong in law to regard a right of way over water as similar to a right of way over land. The physical feature of a path or road was the land over which it ran. On the other hand, in the case of a river its physical feature was the flowing water which made navigation possible.

No one could 'own' flowing water so it could not be 'dedicated' to the public for its use so as to establish a right of way.

1.3   Other rights on land

Apart from public rights of way, other rights can exist on someone else's land. These are generally known as easements (see also the chapter on *Neighbours*). In this section we deal with private rights of way.

1.3.1   Private rights of way

A distinction must be drawn between public rights of way, which are dedicated to the public at large, and private rights of way. These are only intended for a limited number of people.

☞ *For many years your neighbour has been allowing his own children, together with their school friends, to cut a path through his land on their way to school. Recently some farmers have attempted to use the path to get to their neighbouring fields, claiming that the path is now a public right of way. Your neighbour has objected strongly. What is his position?*

If use of a path has been restricted to a limited group of people with whom your neighbour has connections, and he has made clear that he has not intended to create a right of way, it cannot be acquired by dedication. To avoid such future claims, a landowner should lodge a map with his local authority (see below, section 1.3.2 (a)).

1.3.2   Landowners and rights of way

Not every landowner intends to allow the public – or even private groups of people – to acquire a footpath across his land by dedication and acceptance. He can show that he has no such intention even if people cross his land on a regular basis.

1.3.2(a) Rights of landowner in preventing formation of public and private rights of way

We have seen that uninterrupted use by the public for 20 years can lead to the deemed dedication and acceptance of a footpath – unless a landowner shows an intention to the contrary. How would a landowner show a contrary intention?

- By allowing the public, or only certain members of the public, to use the path only with the landowner's express permission
- by interrupting the public's use of the path by, for example, closing the path on one day per year
- by putting up a notice giving the public access only by leave of the landowner
- by informing the local county council that the path has not been dedicated as a public right of way.

Appropriate maps should be submitted. (For rights of a landowner to prevent trespass, see section 6 below.)

Do note: the situation as outlined above could change if a parcel of land is declared 'open country and registered common land' under CROW, and then mapped as such (see section 3 below).

2   OPEN SPACES

2.1   Laws governing open spaces

What is the position if you wish to roam freely in open land?

A right of way gives access to open space only along a defined route, as we have seen. If one deviates from the route, one commits a trespass.

These restrictions were felt to be too great. In 1949, a change was introduced to allow greater access to areas of natural beauty in this country. Certain land is covered by access agreements and is designated as open country (see section 2.1.2 below). The public can also enter private land if the landowner allows them to.

Despite these measures, it was still felt that the public was denied access to some 500,000 hectares of open countryside or, where they did have access to a further 600,000 hectares, it was on an informal basis. To this end access is enhanced in the Countryside and Rights of Way Act 2000 (see section 3 below). It is estimated that about one-ninth of the land area of England and Wales will be opened up to the public as of right for the first time.

Take heed: this right of access is not unrestricted, and measures are being put in place to take account of conservation interests, land management, and safety.

2.1.1   Permission of landowner

Landowners can expressly allow free access on their land. They can lay down certain conditions: e.g. that the public cannot enter the land during the breeding season for animals or wild birds.

Under the new Act, landowners will be able to dedicate land for permanent access (see section 3 below).

2.1.2   Designating open spaces

Under the National Parks and Access to the Countryside Act 1949, local planning authorities could conclude agreements with landowners so that 'open country' should be open to access by the public. (See section 2.3 below.) In the Act 'open country' is defined as meaning mountain, moor, heath, down, cliff or foreshore.

Again such access is subject to certain conditions. The most common are not lighting fires, not damaging trees or paths, and keeping a dog under proper control.

2.1.3   Designation against landowner's wishes

If a landowner does not wish an access agreement to be made over his land, the local planning authority can make an access order. The landowner must then appeal to the Secretary of State for the Environment who can order a public enquiry to be held before reaching a final decision.

A landowner against whom an access order is made is entitled to compensation.

(See also section 3 below for changes expected to the laws governing access to open country and registered common land expected to be implemented in 2005.)

2.2   Guarding open spaces

If we intend to preserve what we have got in the way of open spaces, historic buildings and beautiful landscapes, we must consider planning controls. For protection of natural habitats see section 7.

2.2.1   Town and country planning

Planning legislation was introduced on a comprehensive basis in 1947 at a time when much other sweeping legislation, which affected the nation as a whole, was passed.

Since the Town and Country Planning Act 1947, there have been many further Acts dealing specifically with planning: particularly one in 1971 and, since then, a codifying Act, the Town and Country Planning Act 1990, to which this chapter refers.

2.2.2   Structure plans

A structure plan is an overall plan for an area, set out by the county council. It encompasses a council's planning objectives for its administrative area – much in line with government circulars which offer generalised planning direction. Structure plans, therefore, will cover factors such as housing, roads, industrial development and recreational needs.

2.2.3   Local plans

At a local level, local plans are drawn up by the local authorities to flesh out the structure plan. This does not mean that all development outside these plans is forbidden. However, an applicant for planning permission who wants to persuade a local planning authority to deviate from its plans might have a more difficult task in justifying his proposals. (For the definition of what constitutes 'development' see section 2.2.5 below.)

2.2.4   Unitary development plans

A unitary plan is a combination of structure plan and local plan. It should include the authority's general policies in respect of the conservation of the natural beauty and amenity of the land, the improvement of the physical environment, and the management of traffic. Any objections are to be considered by an inquiry. Such plans were first introduced for Greater London and the six metropolitan areas of England on the abolition of metropolitan county governments, and have now been extended to Wales and a large number of areas of non-metropolitan England.

2.2.5   Planning controls

In addition there are strict planning controls in areas which have been specially designated as areas of outstanding natural beauty or as conservation areas. Again, permission for development will only be granted if it meets very specific needs and criteria.

Broadly speaking, no one can 'develop' land or property without first obtaining planning permission. The critical factor, therefore, is what constitutes 'development'.

2.2.6   Definition of 'development'

Development is defined as:

- building, engineering, mining and other operations, or
- a material change of use of property (land or buildings) from one purpose to another.

Note: a building operation can be widely defined and includes demolition.

☞ *You have a house on a plot of land which you would like to demolish. You are told that this would constitute a 'building operation' under the planning laws. You want to know if this is correct.*

The answer is 'yes'.

2.2.7   Material change of use

Change of use can involve:

- a totally different type of use, e.g. from residential property to commercial use
- intensification of existing use (e.g. from the stationing of one caravan to the stationing of several caravans); or
- from agricultural use to other use; e.g. conversion of a farm barn into a separate dwelling house.

Do note: planning law is complicated. In addition, the present legislation is to be superseded; the government has signalled its intention that planning law is to undergo 'a comprehensive programme of change' with the intention of delivering government objectives more effectively – particularly with regard to major projects and infrastructure. There is also to be a single tier of local development frameworks (LDFs) in place to the unitary, structure, and local plans (see sections 2.2.2–2.2.4 above). Thus apart from the broad-brush outline above, a discussion of planning issues is beyond the scope of this book. Do seek professional advice if faced with a planning problem.

2.3 Types of open spaces

As we have seen in *Designating open spaces* (section 2.1.2 above), certain areas of the country were felt to be of such intrinsic interest and beauty that they were designated as open spaces. These will be examined in more detail below.

2.3.1 National Parks

Approximately 10 per cent of the land area of England and Wales forms our National Parks. These were set up by the National Parks and Access to the Countryside Act, which was passed in 1949 at a time of major postwar reconstruction in all areas of national life.

The idea of National Parks was first mooted in the 1930s. The impetus behind the idea was that all citizens were not only entitled to, but should be able freely to enjoy some of the most beautiful expanses of landscape of their country. Certain areas of the country were seen as so special that they ought to be made part of the national heritage and that Parliament itself should give them status to that effect.

Do take note: 'National' does not mean that the parks are publicly owned.

Much of the land is still in private hands, as it always was before the designation of National Parks. About 250,000 people live in these areas, many of which are still being farmed.

2.3.1(a) Land designated for National Parks

The Countryside Agency describes these areas as 'the most beautiful, spectacular and dramatic expanses of country in England and Wales'.

2.3.1(b) National Parks objectives

These objectives are:

- the conservation and enhancement of the natural beauty, wildlife, and cultural heritage of the landscape
- the promotion of opportunities for the understanding and enjoyment by the public of the special qualities of the designated areas.

The balance between these two objectives is sometimes difficult to sustain. For example, some people would like to ban waterskiing and powerboating on some of our lakes in the interests of the natural habitat. Bird lovers complain that the bird population has declined as a direct result of the noise and intrusion of powerboats. Water sports enthusiasts, on the other hand, maintain that they bring jobs, money and tourists.

In response to a long-running conflict over fast vessels and waterskiing on Windermere, a bylaw was passed on 29 March 2000 to impose a speed limit of 10 mph in respect of the whole of the lake (except for a relatively small area where a 6 mph speed limit already applies). The limit itself will come into effect in March 2005.

2.3.1(c) Changing patterns

The fact is that the Parks may be in danger of being loved to death. In 1949, when they were inaugurated, few families owned a car. Now car ownership is so widespread that great and ever-increasing numbers of people make excursions and visits to the Parks.

2.3.1(d) List of National Parks

The list of National Parks in England and Wales gives an idea of their varied landscape including coast, moorland, fells, and precipitous mountainside:

- Lake District
- Snowdonia
- Pembrokeshire Coast
- Brecon Beacons

- Northumberland
- Dartmoor
- Exmoor
- North York Moors
- Yorkshire Dales
- Peak District
- South Downs (The Designation Order was published in 2002; it was made available in January 2003 for consultation, with a view to holding a public enquiry).

The designation of the New Forest as a National Park is under way – the whole process takes 2–3 years.

2.3.1(e) The Norfolk Broads

The Norfolk Broads were given a status akin to that of a National Park in 1988. A Broads Authority, set up by Act of Parliament, took charge of the Broads area from April 1989 with the tasks of acting as sole planning authority, being in charge of conserving and enhancing the natural beauty of the Broads and protecting landscape and navigation over the network of waterways.

2.3.1(f) Countryside Agency

The National Parks Commission was set up in 1949. It was later renamed as the Countryside Commission and then, in 1999, it merged with the Rural Development Commission as the Countryside Agency. The Agency has responsibility for advising government and taking action on issues relating to the environmental, economic and social well-being of the English countryside.

2.3.1(g) Planning controls

Planning controls for the Parks are the responsibility of the county councils of the areas in which the Parks lie. It was increasingly felt that more autonomy was needed to protect the Parks properly from depredation of all kinds but in particular from major industry.

2.3.1(h) National Park authorities

National Park Authorities (NPAs) were established under the Environment Act 1995 to foster the economic and social well-being of local communities within National Parks. The NPAs function as a single-purpose local authority to conserve and enhance the natural beauty and wildlife of the parks for the enjoyment of the public.

2.3.2 Areas of outstanding natural beauty (AONBs)

An area which is not in a National Park can be designated as one of outstanding natural beauty. The 37 areas of outstanding natural beauty cover approximately 15% of England. They are designated in order to conserve their landscape qualities. The Countryside Agency has the power to propose a designation after it has consulted with the local authorities and advertised its intention in the local press. The Secretary of State for the Environment then confirms the designation after public enquiry if need be.

☞ *You have read in the local paper that the Countryside Agency intends to designate an area of land which encompasses your own farm as an area of outstanding natural beauty. You feel aggrieved that you were not notified individually of the intention to designate.*

   a) There is no requirement to notify individual landowners of an intention to designate provided that the proposal is advertised in the London Gazette and local newspapers. Copies of the Secretary of State's order should be available from the Countryside Council and the relevant local authority.
   b) You are able to make objections against the proposal to your local authority if you wish; these objections will then be taken into account by the Secretary of State.
   c) A public enquiry may be instituted as a result.
   d) However, if after a public enquiry, it is decided to designate the area as one of outstanding natural beauty, the Secretary of State will confirm the designation order.

The local planning authority can take steps to conserve and enhance the area of natural beauty, as can a Conservation Board if one has been set up for the AONB – even if this limits the public's enjoyment of the area.

2.3.3 Conservation areas

These are areas of special architectural or historic interest, the character or appearance of which should be preserved or enhanced. Conservation areas are usually designated where there is a group or cluster of buildings which together make it an area desirable to preserve (whereas listed buildings are listed individually). Although often conservation areas are designated in towns and cities, they are designated in country areas too.

☞ *You own a field which adjoins a village which is a designated conservation area. You would like to develop the field for a housing project. Planning permission is refused and you argue that the field has no building on it so that it cannot be of architectural interest; the field has no historical associations so that there is nothing there to preserve or enhance either. Therefore it is only the village itself which could be called a conservation area.*

Interesting landscape features, together with their setting, can be regarded as an 'area' for conservation purposes. In cases of old villages, their settings would include greens and paddocks, trees and fields coming close to the houses. An area should be looked at as an entity giving rise to special historic or architectural interest and not every part of an area need have on it something of interest.

2.3.4 Country parks

These were set up following on from the Countryside Act 1968 and are run by the local authorities. A few are privately owned. Country parks use historical and natural features to enhance their appeal and sometimes include sports areas.

Entrance is free but a charge can be made for other facilities such as water sports or car parking.

2.3.5 Nature reserves

These are primarily designated for the protection of flora and fauna, and public access might be restricted in the interests of protecting natural habitats.

Nature reserves can be set up by:

- statutory powers under the 1949 Act; or
- private bodies such as the Royal Society for the Protection of Birds.

2.3.6 Sites of Special Scientific Interest (SSSIs)

These are sites which are designated as being of particular scientific interest. Sites may be designated not only for wild plant and animal life but also for geophysical and other landscape features of importance.

Wetland areas designated under the Convention on Wetlands of International Importance especially as Wildfowl Habitats, are also SSSIs. Special areas of conservation which will form part of the *European 2000* network are also in the process of designation.

It has long been argued that the level of protection given to SSSIs is inadequate and toothless. In addition, only 7% of the land area of England and Wales is so designated; this has the effect of fragmenting habitats, which is damaging to wildlife.

Under the Countryside and Rights of Way Act 2000, biodiversity considerations must be taken into consideration by Ministers, government departments and the National Assembly of Wales, in accordance with the UK's obligations under treaties agreed at the 1992 Rio Earth Summit.

Highway authorities now have the power, under the 2000 Act, to divert a highway in order the protect a SSSI. Only English Nature and, in Wales, the Countryside Council, have the power to apply for this to be done. New paths may be created to effect the diversion. Notice must be given to the owner, lessee or occupier of the land where these steps are to be taken.

2.3.6(a) Designation of SSSIs

Designation is made under the Wildlife and Countryside Act 1981 (as amended in 1985).

An owner or occupier is notified by English Nature (formerly the Nature Conservancy Council) of:

- the reasons for the site's designation
- operations likely to damage those features (for example drainage of land, which would damage the habitat of wild duck; or quarrying, which would affect geological sites).

The owner has three months in which to register any objections.

If the designation is confirmed, the owner cannot carry out the operations specified unless:

- consent has been given
- the work is carried out in accordance with a management agreement
- the owner has given four months' notice to English Nature, which has raised no objection.

Note: notice must also be given to the local planning authority. In fact there has been criticism that local planning authorities have given planning permission for development of SSSIs which is detrimental to their protection, and that between 200 and 300 sites are lost or damaged each year.

Under the Countryside and Rights of Way Act, conservation agencies have been given new strengthened powers:

- to refuse consent for damaging activities or impose conditions
- to introduce notices to combat neglect and to enter land; and
- to give conservation agencies a compulsory purchase power where they cannot secure an agreement for the management of an SSSI or where the terms of such an agreement have been breached.

Appeals may be made to the Environment Secretary.

Deliberate damage to SSSIs (except in emergencies) can incur fines of up to £20,000 in the magistrates' courts and unlimited fines in the Crown Courts. There will be power to order the restoration of the damaged special interest where practicable.

2.3.7   Environmentally Sensitive Areas (ESAs)

These are set up by the relevant government department to accord with EU law. Funds are available from the Community if an area is environmentally sensitive (a term which includes flora, fauna or features of natural beauty or of geological, archaeological or historical interest). Farmers are then paid to farm in a way which would enhance environmental protection (for example, by using organic farming methods rather than pesticides).

There are 43 ESAs in the United Kingdom, 22 of which are in England.

2.3.7(a)   Sites of Importance for Nature Conservation (SINCs)

Local authorities are entitled – but not obliged – to designate sites in their area for nature conservation.

2.3.7(b)   Special Areas of Conservation (SACs)

A number of wildlife sites are designated as special areas of conservation under the European Habitats Directive. Any plan or project which would affect the integrity of such a site can only be approved, in the absence of alternatives, on grounds of overriding public interest (see also section 2.3.11 below).

2.3.7(c)   Special Protection Areas (SPAs)

Following the European Birds Directive, certain areas have been designated as special protection areas in order to conserve the habitats of certain rare and endangered species of wild birds, such as the Sandwich tern, the gannet and the puffin. No site is classified under the European Birds Directive unless it has first been notified as a Site of Special Scientific Interest (SSSI) under the Wildlife and Countryside Act 1981. Such notification protects the site by law from activities likely to damage its nature-conservation interest. Development proposals that would be detrimental to the nature-conservation interest will be permitted only in very exceptional circumstances.

2.3.8   Common land

Rights to use common land stem from medieval times when tenants of a particular manor were entitled to certain rights on 'waste land' of the manor – generally the land unsuitable for cultivation. These rights were common to them – hence the terms 'common land' and 'commoners'. Such rights included, for example, the right to take peat for fuel or to graze animals.

2.3.8(a) Keeping common land open

By the mid-19th century, most of this land had been enclosed (appropriated by local landowners). However, a reaction set in against the systematic enclosure of common land and much more strenuous attempts were made to keep it open.

About one-fifth of common land is open to the public, who may roam freely. Access to other common land is restricted to rights of way. Other rights, such as to graze cattle or take peat, are restricted to certain 'commoners' in each case.

Note: keeping common land as 'open land' does not mean that it is public land.

Only a small percentage of common land in England and Wales had a statutory right of public access to take air and exercise, but registered common land is to be opened up to the public and become access land under CROW 2000.

2.3.8(b) Metropolitan areas

Common land can be found in metropolitan areas – Hampstead Heath in North London is an example. Generally speaking there is a right of access to all common land in towns and cities.

2.3.8(c) Rural areas

Common land in rural areas is still often subject to rights of common, such as grazing rights, but this does not mean that there is any general right of access. (For proposed changes under CROW, see section 3 below.)

2.3.8(d) Registration

Under the Commons Registration Act 1965, county councils have to keep a register of common land in their areas.

Since then another Act has been passed, the Common Land (Rectification of Registers) Act 1989 which allows a landowner to challenge an incorrect entry into the register of common land.

> *You own a large house with a garden and extensive grounds. Some of the grounds have been left uncultivated. You discover that one of your neighbours has registered part of your uncultivated ground as 'common land' and you apply to have the register rectified. A Commons Commissioner has visited the site and stated in his decision that the land is not really part of the gardens of your house. You want to know what you can do next.*
>
> You can appeal to the High Court. It has ruled that to succeed in an application for rectification, land has to be a 'garden' and ancillary to a house. However, a 'garden' does not have to be cultivated for flowers, fruit and vegetables. Frequently parts of a large garden are left wild and uncultivated but are still ancillary to a house and are part of its garden.

Despite the Act and its amendment, defects still allow for land to be mistakenly registered, while some common land has been forgotten and, in some instances, grazing rights have been over-quantified so that over-grazing has taken place. A consultation process is underway on the greater protection and better management of common land (also see section 3 below).

2.3.8(e) New town or village greens

Where an open area of land has been used predominantly by the inhabitants of a defined locality for sporting and recreational purposes, it may have become a town or village green and can possibly be registered as such under the 1965 Act. Residents have used this right to try and block developments which they consider unwelcome.

In one case the owner of a parcel of land of about 10 acres wished to build some houses on it. The land had been used for over 20 years by the local people for dog-walking, kite-flying, playing family and children's games, picking blackberries and tobogganing. The parish council applied to the county council to have the land registered as a town or village green, and succeeded – which therefore meant the landowner could not fence off the land or continue with the planned development.

In another case, the court ruled that the defendant's right to graze two horses on a village green did not entitle her to erect a temporary electric fence on the green within which the horses could graze, because no enclosure of any common land is permissible.

2.3.9 Beaches, rivers and waterways

The area of the foreshore between the low and high tide line belongs to the Crown. Although in theory there may be no public right of access, there is no likelihood of access being barred to the general public. Indeed, the foreshore is often leased or sold by the Crown to local authorities to develop beaches for popular enjoyment.

Land above the high water mark is usually under local authority control and bylaws often govern the area in the interests of public safety. Similarly 1,000 metres of water beyond the low water mark is also usually governed by local authorities which often impose bylaws to protect swimmers.

There is no general right of access over land adjacent to the beach or foreshore at present.

☞ *You park your car above a headland below which there is a very attractive cove. You start clambering down towards the beach when a man approaches and says that he owns the land and that there is no right of way for you.*

Owners of land abutting the coast line can exclude members of the public from using their land for access to beaches unless a public right of way exists. However, under CROW such land may in future be designated as public access land (see section 3.3. below).

There is an absolute right of navigation in tidal waters. 'Navigation' includes water sports such as water skiing, jetskiing ('wet bikes') and speedboats.

☞ *You and your children are wading in the sea at a resort on the South Coast when a wetbiker speeds past your little girl. She is not hit but she falls over in the wake. You write to the local council and ask why such activity is allowed near swimmers, particularly near small children.*

As a result of accidents involving personal watercraft like jet skis, a code of safe practice has been introduced. This strengthens bylaw powers, including the power to create exclusive bathing areas where craft are not allowed.

Note: there is no public right of way along the foreshore. A right of way has to have a delineated route but this is impossible in an area of land washed by daily tides.

2.3.9(a) Pollution

Standards of cleanliness of beaches and seawater have been laid down by the EU. A blue flag system is in operation for clean beaches.

Unfortunately, some beaches fail to reach these standards and there are complaints of pollution from sewage, oil slicks and dumping of chemical waste at sea. Discharge from ships at sea causes a great deal of coastal pollution even where the discharge takes place outside territorial waters: sooner or later, their discharge is washed up on beaches. Pesticides and other chemicals which flow into rivers from factories and farms also reach the sea at some stage and in some form.

Standards are being monitored all the time by local authorities in an endeavour to ensure that beaches are safe for swimming. The Environment Agency has an overall responsibility to regulate, prevent, remedy or mitigate the effects of pollution of water in rivers, estuaries and coastal waters and to promote their conservation, enhancement and use for recreation.

2.3.10 Heritage coasts

Certain areas of coastline have been designated as 'heritage' coast. These coastline areas are not nationally owned but are in private hands or owned by the National Trust or local authorities. Many of the heritage coasts are within the National Parks while others are in areas of outstanding natural beauty.

The purpose of the designation is both conservation, so that unspoilt coast should be protected by planning controls, and 'positive management' to:

- protect natural habitats
- repair footpaths, and
- try to mitigate the effects of pollution.

2.3.11 Marine nature reserves

These are areas of land covered by tidal water, or sea beds within the UK territorial waters, which have been designated for the protection of marine and bird life by the government.

In addition, a project is currently under way to establish management schemes on selected UK marine Special Areas of Conservation (SACs). The schemes will contain measures necessary to safeguard important marine features in line with the Habitats Directive to set up protected areas in the marine environment for wildlife conservation.

2.3.12 Canals and towpaths

There are about 2,000 miles of inland waterways which are run by British Waterways for commercial and recreational purposes. The canals are artificial waterways created at the time of the Industrial Revolution, and although there is no automatic public right of navigation through the canals, this is generally permitted subject to bylaw.

The towpaths of canals can be dedicated as rights of way and are very popular with walkers – subject to the overriding rights of those who use towpaths for navigational purposes. Even where a towpath is not dedicated as a right of way, the public is generally allowed to use it. However, if in doubt, the definitive map of your area should have the information you need.

3 THE 'RIGHT TO ROAM'

3.1 Permission of landowners

A landowner can choose to give permission for persons to have access to any part of his land, but equally can refuse or withdraw such permission at any time or impose conditions e.g. that such access should only be at specified times. Those ignoring such conditions or the withdrawal of the concession would therefore be trespassers. See section 6.

3.2 New rights of access

Where a landowner has not given permission to the public, the Countryside and Rights of Way Act 2000 introduces new ways of allowing the public to have access to land. The Act may not be fully in force until 2005. It is being brought into operation in stages. At the time of writing the right to roam has not yet come into operation because the mapping process (see section 3.4.1) must first be completed.

Note: the access provisions do not confer an unfettered right to roam. They are restricted to mountain, moor, heath and down, and to common land, and they only apply to persons on foot.

Landowners retain the right to farm, fence, improve or develop their land, and have no general obligation to improve or facilitate public access. As no compensation is payable to landowners under the Act for what they see as a curtailment of their property rights, issues under the human rights legislation may have to be considered in the courts.

Among other matters, the Act covers:

- access to the countryside
- public rights of way and road traffic
- nature conservation and wildlife protection.

3.3 Access

The Act sets out the categories of land to which the public are to acquire a right of access. It is defined as 'access for open-air recreation' where it is wholly or predominantly mountain, moor, heath or down. Land over 600 metres above sea level immediately qualifies as access land, as does registered common land (see section 2.3.8 above). Access land will also include land which is dedicated by the owner to permanent public access. Land that is already open to the public e.g. under an access agreement, will endure as such. It is expected that this will give people a right of entry to some additional four million acres of land in England and Wales as a result. Woodland, rivers and canals and their banks are not included. There is provision for the foreshore to be included in the future.

'Excepted land' excludes certain parts of open country from being access land. These include gardens, parklands, land covered by buildings, quarries, golf courses, racecourses, cultivated land, or land within 20 metres of livestock housing. The public therefore has no right of access over ploughed fields even if they happen to lie within an area of open land.

3.3.1 Restrictions

However, certain restrictions on access will apply and behaviour and activities which are not compatible with the quiet exercise of the right of access will be prohibited. In particular, the use of bicycles and craft, as well as horse-riding, will be excluded and restrictions will apply to dogs – e.g. they will have to be kept on leads. Persons who break these restrictions by, for example, damaging hedges, fences, gates or stiles, will lose their right of access for 24 hours and may be treated as trespassers by the landowner.

A person exercising a right of access does not have the right to do anything he chooses on the land. He loses any entitlement to be there if he engages in any of a long list of prohibited activities, such as:

- using a vehicle (other than a wheelchair)
- lighting or tending a fire
- injuring or killing any animal, bird or fish
- damaging or taking birds' nests or eggs
- using a metal detector
- interfering with any part of a plant, shrub or tree
- interfering with any fence or barrier
- putting up any advertisement or notice
- engaging in camping or in organised games
- bringing any animal on to the land, other than a dog which is on a short lead.

Note: that landowners can restrict the right to bring a dog on the grouse moors or land used for lambing.

In addition restrictions may be permitted to either exclude or limit access in the interests of land management or where there is a particular risk of fire, or a risk to members of the public. Similar restrictions will apply in the interests of wildlife and habitat conservation or to protect sites of historic or archaeological importance.

Landowners will be allowed to close land for up to 28 days each year without permission. Closure is not permitted on bank holidays, and there are restrictions on dates of closure over weekends and during the high summer. Other closures will be allowed so as to take account of conservation needs, safety etc. while certain land will be excepted altogether, such as that owned by the Ministry of Defence.

3.3.2 Notices

After consulting the owner or occupier of the land, the highway authority may erect and maintain notices informing the public about the boundaries of access land and excepted land, and about the restriction on the public's activities.

3.3.3 Public consultation

The Countryside Agency in England is responsible for deciding the extent of the land to be made accessible, and must produce draft maps for the whole of England on a rolling programme. Public consultations must be held on all draft maps. Any member of the public can submit his or her comment on the draft maps within a three-month consultation process. For more on the mapping process see section 3.4.1 below.

3.3.4 Liabilities of owners and occupiers

The liability of an owner or occupier to those who come on to the land for recreational purposes is restricted, to protect occupiers of land against having to take out expensive insurance against the eventuality of a claim by members of the public exercising their rights of access.

It is intended that no liability will be owed in respect of 'natural features of the landscape' and vegetation, or by ditches, ponds and streams even if they are not natural features. So this would cover an obvious natural feature such as a swiftly running stream which a landowner would not and could not fence in, or an artificially constructed pond. But there are other features, such as a path that has potholes caused, for example, by the passage of heavy farm machinery, which could pose a risk to the public, and it is difficult to know how such risks will be regarded. In the usual cases of occupier's liability a greater duty is owed to children and the elderly who trespass on land. There is also an additional duty of care to trespassers where there is a 'dangerous attraction' on the land.

However, the Act does not state how those who exercise their right to roam are to be regarded in law except that that they are not 'invitees' of the landowner. Thus until the issue is before the courts, it is difficult to gauge the extent, if any, of the duty of care of a landowner under the new legislation.

Further, where experience shows that warning notices are being disregarded, more may need to be done, thus imposing extra burdens on the occupier – for example, in having to fence off a known danger.

See also the chapter on *Accidents*, section 4.3.2.

3.3.5 Means of access

These include openings in a fence, wall, hedge or gate on the land, or the construction of a stile or bridge. Either a new means of access can be opened up or existing ones improved or repaired. A highway authority can agree to carry out the works itself or to pay for the owner to do so.

3.4 Public rights of way

The Act is intended to reform the rights of way system and requires local highway authorities to carry out a review and publish their plans for improving rights of way in their areas, taking into account the needs of the public, including those of people with mobility problems.

3.4.1 Statutory maps

Local authorities are to be encouraged to complete their historic record of rights of way on their definitive maps, while procedures for recording changes will be simplified. Existing maps made for different parts of a local authority area and statements inherited from other surveying authorities are to be consolidated. A cut-off date (1 January 2006) applies to the recording of footpaths and bridleways created before 1949.

3.4.1(a) Access mapping under CROW

The Countryside Agency in England, and the Countryside Council for Wales, are under a duty to undertake a rolling programme of drawing up maps showing open country and common land. To make the task easier, England has been divided into eight mapping areas.

3.4.1(b) A three-stage process

The programme has three stages:

1) *draft:* any person from the public can comment on the draft maps with regard to whether open country and registered common land has been correctly included (see section 2.3.8(d) above)
2) *provisional:* having considered the public's comments, a provisional map for an area will be then be issued; however, only those with a legal interest in a parcel of land can appeal (see below)
3) *conclusive:* when the provisional maps have been amended a conclusive map will be issued.

Thereafter, once all the conclusive maps have been produced the Secretary of State will be expected to bring the new access rights into force (projected for 2005).

3.4.1(c) How to view the maps

At the time of writing some provisional maps have already been published after a consultation period, and these can be viewed on the Countryside Agency's website: *www.ca-mapping.co.uk/mapping*. The provisional maps are also being promised to local authorities and parish councils. For where to view the maps (other than online) telephone the Countryside Agency at 0845 100 3298.

Do take heed: there is no requirement that a landowner should be directly informed that his land has been included in a map.

Extra heed: you have only three months in which to appeal if you feel that your land has been wrongly included in a provisional map (see section 3.4.1(f) below).

3.4.1(d)   The complaints

After the first two draft maps were drawn up, a very large number of complaints were received, mainly from those pointing out that land such as agricultural land, gardens and paddocks had been erroneously included.

3.4.1(e)   Who has a legal interest?

It is important to note that only persons with a legal interest in the land can appeal, once the public's comments are taken into account and a provisional map is issued (or reissued).

Those with a legal interest are:

- landowners
- tenants
- holders of common rights
- holders of sporting rights, or
- those who have any other interest in the land, such as a grazing right or a private right of way.

3.4.1(f)   How and when to appeal

You have only three months from the date of publication to appeal to the Planning Inspectorate if you have a legal interest and you think that land shown as registered common land or open country has been wrongly identified on the provisional map.

The appeal must be made on a particular appeal form, which can be downloaded from *www.planning-inspectorate.gov.uk/access/* or it can be obtained from the Planning Inspectorate, Regus House, 1 Friary Temple Quay, Bristol BS1 6EA.

3.4.1(g)   Failure to appeal

If no appeal is lodged, conclusive maps are expected to be issued 6–12 months after the provisional maps were issued. Reviews of the maps are to be undertaken every ten years.

4   ENCOUNTERS WITH ANIMALS

4.1   Liability: who is responsible?

Incidents involving animals, such as someone being bitten by a dog, can occur anywhere. However, it is in the countryside that we are most likely to encounter animals and where our own animals can do harm.

If an animal causes damage or injury, its 'keeper' i.e. its possessor or owner, is generally responsible. See the chapter on *Pets*.

☞   *Julian is thrown by the horse he was riding and is injured. The owner of the horse knew it had a propensity to be frightened by farm machinery, which was the cause of its reaction.*

   Julian can hold the owner responsible for his injuries (under the Animals Act.) See also *Pets* chapter, section 2.1.

Take note: under the Animals Act 1971, if an animal is owned or possessed by a child under 16, its keeper for legal purposes is the head of the household to which the child belongs.

4.1.1   Domestic and other animals

The law draws a clear distinction between the keeping of domestic animals and of other animals which are considered 'wild' by nature. It imposes far greater liability on the owner of the latter (see *Pets* chapter, section 1.3).

For the everyday responsibilities of a dog-owner, see the chapter on *Pets*.

4.1.1(a)   Dogs and livestock

Liability has always been imposed on the keeper of a dog which 'worries' livestock. Indeed, until the passing of the Dangerous Dogs Act 1991, it could reasonably have been argued that livestock were better protected by the law on dogs than were people.

Under the Animals Act 1971, livestock is widely defined to include cattle, sheep, pigs, goats, poultry, pheasants etc.

☞ *You are walking along a footpath across a field accompanied by your dog. It is always docile and well behaved and is not on a lead. All of a sudden, it spies some sheep in a corner of the field and starts to chase one of the lambs. In terror a lamb hurls itself against a fence, and injures itself. You are accosted by the farmer who says you are liable to compensate him. You explain that your dog has never done anything like chasing sheep before and in any event there was no negligence on your part.*

As owner, you are liable even if you had no previous knowledge of your dog's propensity to worry livestock, nor need negligence be proved. Dogs are to be kept under 'proper control' on footpaths – thus while they do not necessarily have to be on a lead, close control is required.

Beware: the owner of livestock is even entitled to kill a dog that has been worrying livestock if it is still on his or her premises and not under anyone's control (in such a case the police must be notified within 48 hours).

Finally, there are criminal penalties for keeping a guard dog unless:

- a competent handler is present and
- a warning notice is displayed at the entrance to the premises.

4.1.1(b) Bulls and cows

Under the Wildlife and Countryside Act 1981, a bull is not allowed to be at large in a field that has a public right of way crossing it, if it is over 10 months old and of a recognised breed. If it is not of a recognised breed, it may be at large in a field but it must be accompanied by cows or heifers.

The recognised breeds are Ayrshire, British Friesian, British Holstein, Dairy Shorthorn, Guernsey, Jersey, and Kerry.

Thus, for those who cannot readily assess the age of a bull, or its breed, the law does not make things too easy, but in any event there is liability if a bull's keeper knew or ought to have known that it posed a danger to passers by.

There have also been a number of incidents reported where people have been injured or killed by cows. Such attacks have, in general, happened on public footpaths through fields and have involved cows with their calves, and people walking with dogs. It is recommended that if you are accompanied by a dog and see cows with calves in a field, you either avoid taking that route or take extra precautions against separating cow from calf.

4.1.1(c) Straying animals

If a trespassing dog damages your garden plants, or a neighbour's cat kills your poultry, their owners are not normally liable to compensate you for the damage. But the owner of a dog runs the risk of the animal being lawfully killed if it goes on to someone else's land and worries livestock (see section 4.1.1(a) above).

Apart from this, there is no other right to destroy animals which stray on to your property.

If straying livestock cause damage to your own animals, crops or other property, their owners will be liable to pay compensation. Moreover, they cannot insist that you should have your land fenced from their animals unless you are under a duty to fence your land (such a duty would be stipulated in, for example, leases or title deeds).

☞ *Some sheep from the nearby farm stray off the land, wander into your orchard, and destroy some very expensive young trees which you have planted there. You ask to be compensated and the farmer replies that you should have fenced in your land.*

It is not a defence for him to say that the damage could have been prevented if your land were fenced. He must compensate you for the damage his sheep have caused.

Of course, if damage of this kind were to occur regularly, it would always be better to fence to protect one's property than stand on one's legal rights!

Surprisingly enough, the owner of the land on to which the animals have strayed, far from venting spleen on them, is under a legal duty to feed and water them adequately. He or she must also give notice within 48 hours to the police and their owner (if known). If within 14 days their owner fails to reclaim them or offer compensation for the damage caused, the victim is entitled to sell them at auction to recoup his losses.

See also the chapter on *Pets*, section 6.

Note: the owner of straying livestock is entitled to go on to someone else's land in order to recapture his animals. This is not trespass.

4.2   Private land

If you go on to private land without permission, you become a trespasser. A landowner has a duty to persons who come on to his land (see below section 6, and chapter on *Accidents*). This is known as *occupier's liability*. This duty diminishes according to who comes on to the land, but there is still a duty towards a trespasser, and a landowner cannot allow a dangerous dog to roam freely without a warning sign. However, if you are bitten by a dog when you have no business on the land in the first place and there is a warning sign which you ignored, the landowner may have a defence to your claim. (See also chapter on *Pets*, section 3.6, and chapter on *Accidents*, section 4.3.2).

4.3   Cruelty to animals

Animals must not be mistreated and it is generally a criminal offence to do so. This area of the law is dealt with in section 7 below.

5   SPORTING RIGHTS

Sporting rights are a form of property rights.

5.1   Exercising your rights

Landowners own very valuable rights to hunt, shoot or fish on their land.

5.1.1   Similarity with other forms of property rights

Like other property rights, landowners can keep these rights for their own use and enjoyment. Alternatively, sporting rights can be leased, sold, or licensed to other people, or to groups of people, e.g. sporting clubs. So, like other property rights, sporting rights can generate considerable income to those who own them. In addition, owners of sporting rights will be entitled to appeal if the land over which they have rights is classed as access land in provisional maps under CROW (see section 3.4.1(d) above).

Points to note:

a) like all other forms of property, sporting rights are protected by law – in particular by the Game Acts, the Poaching Acts and the civil law of trespass;

b) and also like other forms of property, sporting rights are subject to controls – even for those who own them. For example, it is generally no excuse for a landowner who kills or injures a protected species of animal to say that he did so on his own land.

5.1.2   Laws governing sporting rights

Many of the laws governing hunting, shooting and fishing date from the early 19th century. There is overlap and confusion between the provisions of the various Game Acts. Certainly the language in which they are couched and some of their prohibitions appear archaic. For example, it is an offence to kill certain game on a Sunday or on Christmas Day.

Under the Criminal Justice Act 1994, an offence of aggravated trespass has been created. It applies where a trespasser intends to disrupt a lawful activity such as hunting, or to intimidate the participants.

5.2   Hunting

5.2.1   The certification of shotguns and firearms

You cannot possess shotguns or firearms without a certificate.

You cannot hire a gun except under certain strictly defined circumstances.

Guns cannot be hired out except to someone who has a valid certificate. However, you can borrow a gun from the occupier of private land and use it on that land in the occupier's actual presence. Otherwise you will need a certificate.

In general, to possess a shotgun you need a shotgun certificate, and for a rifle you need a firearms certificate. Forms for these certificates are available from police stations. An application for a shotgun certificate must be countersigned by a reputable person.

Applications for a firearms certificate must be accompanied by references from two referees. You will have to satisfy the police, who may visit you in your home, that:

- you are of good character
- you have good reason to apply for a certificate
- you will not be a danger to the public safety or to the peace
- you have secure storage for the firearm.

No certificate is required to possess an air rifle (although this may change).

Note: following a number of tragic incidents in the UK involving the dangerous misuse of pistols, the Firearms Act 1997 was passed. This creates a general prohibition on small firearms so as to prohibit handguns including small-calibre pistols.

5.2.2   What happens if you are refused a certificate or your certificate is revoked?

☞ *You have a certificate to own a firearm. An altercation took place in your farmhouse between your sister and your brother-in-law and you called the police. You have since been informed that your certificate has been revoked. You feel that this is most unfair as the quarrel had nothing to do with you apart from the fact that it took place on your premises. You wonder what you can do?*

An appeal can be made to a Crown Court against either:

a) the police's refusal to issue a certificate or
b) a decision by the police to revoke an existing certificate.

The appeal must be made within 21 days. When considering the appeal, the court will now have to take into account your rights under the Human Rights Act of 1998.

5.2.3   Game licence

A game licence is needed in order to take certain game. 'Game' is defined as including hares, deer, pheasants, partridges and grouse, as well as woodcock and snipe.

Licences are available from main post offices. The fee varies according to the length of the authorisation:

- £6 per annum expiring on 31 July (red licence)
- £4 for 3 month (blue) licence or (green) 9-month licence
- £2 for an occasional (black) licence to kill game, valid for 14 days from the date of issue.

It is a criminal offence to take game without a valid game licence. The law also requires you to have a licence if you act as a gamekeeper or as a game dealer (£4 for one year).

Never forget: a game licence does not give you a right to hunt on someone else's land. The landowner's permission to hunt on his land is also always required. A game licence is not required to take wildfowl, rabbits, pigeons or other 'pest' species.

Note: there is no need for a game licence if you are:

- hunting deer with hounds (again with permission of the landowner!)
- a beater and are not carrying a gun
- an owner or occupier killing rabbits or deer on your own enclosed land
- acting under the orders of the Ministry of Agriculture.

You must show your licence, if you are on land with a gun or dog, if asked to by:

- a landowner
- the police

- someone else with a licence
- a gamekeeper.

☞ *You have a valid game licence, as well as permission of the landowner to hunt on his land. You are challenged by his gamekeeper when you are out on a shooting expedition with a dog and gun. You discover that you have not remembered to bring the licence with you.*

You can explain the position to the gamekeeper and give him your name and address. If he asks you to leave the land, however, you must do so.

5.2.4 Poaching
The laws against poaching date mainly from the 19th century. Poaching is banned by day or night (the latter is the more serious offence); and it is a separate offence to be on land (whether open or enclosed) with a gun or any other instrument for taking game.

5.2.5 Close season
(See also section 7 below.)

There are four close seasons for deer depending on sex and species. The Deer Act 1991 lays down the minimum calibre of weapons to be used against deer as well as outlawing other means to kill them (for example, traps or snares).

5.2.6 Lead shot
Regulations have been issued which prohibit the use of lead shot for shooting with a shotgun on the foreshore, on 190 wetland Sites of Special Scientific Interest that support significant numbers of waterfowl, and in respect of some wild birds. The regulations came into force in England on 1 September 2002. These prohibitions are in line with international agreements to phase out the use of lead shot for hunting in wetlands. The regulations can be viewed at *www.gov.uk/wildlife-countryside/ewd/rrrpac/shot/pdf/listofsites.pdf.* The restrictions are to protect wild birds from poisoning by lead shot, and refer to species which are particularly susceptible.

See also section 7.1.2(a) below.

5.2.7 Hunting with dogs
In November 1999, the Government announced the setting up of a Committee to inquire into hunting with dogs. The Committee examined the practical aspects of different types of hunting with dogs and its impact on the following:

- the rural economy
- agriculture and pest control
- the social and cultural life of the countryside
- the management and conservation of wildlife; and
- animal welfare in particular areas of England and Wales.

The Committee's findings related to the consequences that any ban might have upon these matters, and also how a ban might be implemented. The Committee reported to the Home Secretary in early June 2000. The focus was on the hunting with dogs of deer, foxes, hares and mink. The Committee was not asked to consider whether hunting with dogs should be banned, and nor was it asked to consider ethical issues.

At the time of writing, various legislative options to deal with this controversial matter are still under consideration.

5.3 Fishing

5.3.1 Rights on rivers
The owner of land adjoining one side of a natural river or stream owns the exclusive fishing rights on his or her side of the bank. These rights extend up to the middle of the water and can be sold or leased as separate and valuable property rights – quite apart from ownership of the land itself. These are known as 'riparian rights'.

An owner whose land adjoins a pond or lake has similar rights which extend only as far as the middle of the water unless his land encircles the pond or lake.

Although he or she owns the fishing rights, a riparian owner is still subject to the general laws protecting close seasons for fish. These are laid down in the Salmon and Freshwater Fisheries Act 1975.

☞ *You own land on both banks of the river and you use a speedboat to make your crossings from one side to the other. You do this throughout the year. You are charged with an offence of wilfully disturbing spawning fish during the close season. You protest that as owner you cannot be charged.*

It is no defence to the charge to say that you are the riparian owner.

5.3.2 Licensing

If you wish to fish with rod and line in rivers or estuaries, you will need a rod-fishing licence. These are available from some 17,000 post offices in England and Wales and also from bankside and Environment Agency regional offices. (Angling clubs may arrange the bulk purchase of licences for their members at local post offices.) The cost of a standard licence for non-migratory trout and coarse fish is £21 per annum, and £60 per annum to include fishing for salmon and sea trout. The cost is £5 for persons aged between 12 and 16. (Children under 12 years of age do not require a licence.) Eight-day (£6.50 and £16.50) and one-day (£2.50 and £5.50) licences are also available.

Concessionary licences for certain categories of the disabled and for those over 65 are half the cost of the full licence.

Subject to local bylaws, two rods may be used for coarse fishing and more than two rods may be used provided you hold an additional licence.

5.3.3 Permission from the owner of the fishing rights

While the National Rod Licence gives you a licence to fish anywhere in England and Wales, you will still need permission from a riparian owner where necessary to fish from his or her stretch of the river bank.

☞ *You park your car by a gentle stream and take out your fishing rods. You are asked by another angler to explain your presence. After a bit of discussion, it transpires that the person who is challenging you is a member of an angling club out for the day fishing there under licence. You tell him that as a member of a club, he is not the owner of the fishing rights and so is in no position to mount a challenge to your presence there.*

You are in the wrong. Whenever fishing rights have been leased or licensed to others, they exercise those rights on behalf of the owner and are entitled to ask trespassers to leave.

5.3.4 Enforcement

You must produce your licence if asked to do so by an Environment Agency bailiff or other authorised person. Failure to do so could result in a prosecution and a maximum fine of £2,550.

Remember to do the following:

- carry your licence at all times when fishing
- replace your licence if you lose it. There is a tear-off slip attached to the licence, which you should keep separately
- check and follow local bylaws
- (where appropriate) submit a catch return of salmon and sea trout to the Environment Agency by 1 January.

Note: salmon anglers will be required by law to release salmon they catch up to 16 June on certain rivers in order to preserve fish stocks.

5.3.5 Fishing rights at sea

Members of the public have a right to fish in the sea up to the highwater mark of ordinary tides. In general the public also has a right to fish in the tidal waters of all rivers and estuaries up to – but not beyond – the highwater mark.

Note: fishing – even at sea – is subject to controls over the manner in which fish can be caught, the minimum size of the fish, and the size of the mesh in nets. These controls are to protect against indiscriminate catches. In addition, EU quotas are applicable to commercial fishing.

There are annual close seasons for fish to spawn in as well as weekly close times in certain cases.

5.3.6   Poaching

Poachers can be fined up to £1,000, face imprisonment and have their boats, rods or nets forfeited. The Court of Appeal stated that it was 'easy to suggest that a bit of salmon poaching was not a matter of great consequence. Easy but entirely wrong. Such illicit activity had a real and damaging effect on the community at large'.

5.4   Metal-detecting: finding treasure

Anyone using a metal detector on land is subject to the Treasure Act 1996. Certain objects are defined as 'treasure' under the Act. These include coins over 300-years-old (but not a single coin), other objects over 300-years-old containing at least 10% gold or silver, and things found in the same place together with objects that are treasure.

If you find an object falling within these categories you must report the find to the coroner. It is an offence not to report a find. Once reported, the items can be bought by museums for public display.

If a museum wishes to acquire the find, you will be entitled to be compensated in full. Its value will be determined by independent experts. If you did not have the landowner's permission to use the metal detector on his land, the compensation will be paid to him. If you did have his permission, the compensation will usually be shared out between you.

The Department for Culture, Media and Sport (tel: 020 7211 6200) produces a useful leaflet which can be obtained free of charge. The Department is considering extending the Act to apply also to prehistoric base-metal objects. It is thought there may be up to 50 such finds a year.

As from April 2003, a scheme will commence to record all archaeological objects found by the public, on a voluntary basis. For more details see *www.finds.org.uk*.

6   TRESPASS

6.1   Nature of trespass

At common law, all landowners are entitled to enjoy their land free from the intrusion of others.

Remember: they are not entitled to use unreasonable force to protect that right – see section 6.8 below.

Indeed, if you do go on to the land of another without the permission of the landowner, you become a trespasser in the eyes of the law. Certain people (such as postmen) are on land by licence and so are not trespassers even though they may not have the landowner's express permission to be there.

Note: trespass is not normally a crime. However, under the Criminal Justice Act 1994, collective trespass, committed by two or more people or involving more than five vehicles, can be a crime, as is disruptive trespass, i.e. trespass committed with an intention to disrupt a lawful activity or intimidate persons taking part in lawful activities such as hunting.

Take heed: even if when you go along a public right of way you wander off it, you can commit a trespass. Similarly, you commit trespass if you use the highway in a way for which it was not intended – for example, by cycling on a footpath (see *Rights of way* in section 1 above).

☞ *You are a journalist working for a magazine devoted to field sports. You leave the road and walk up and down a field alongside the road, noting the horses that are practising there. One of the stewards tells you that you are a trespasser. You deny that you are a trespasser or had any wrongful intention.*

The steward is right in this instance; you are a trespasser because you left the highway and came on to private ground. But even if you had used only the highway for making notes of the horses, you would have been a trespasser. You are only allowed to use a highway for 'passing and repassing'.

Remember: there is no need to have wrongful intent to order to trespass; you can do so quite unwittingly.

6.2 How to stop trespass

Landowners were increasingly angered by what they saw as the law's inability to protect their land from trespassers. In particular, the phenomenon of New Age travellers in the countryside led to increasing calls for reform, now enacted in the Criminal Justice Act 1994.

6.3 Powers of enforcement

6.3.1 Travellers in convoys

The laws of access and trespass were not intended to manage large, well-organised groups of people, numbering up to tens of thousands, who travel together at certain times and then gather in pre-selected areas of the countryside for several days at a time – for example, for pop festivals.

6.3.2 Trespassers on private land

Under the Criminal Justice and Public Order Act 1994, power is given to the police to direct trespassers to leave private land and to remove their vehicles. This power is exercisable where a senior police officer, present at the scene, reasonably believes that:

a) two or more persons are trespassing on land
b) they are present there with a common purpose of residing there for any period
c) reasonable steps have been taken on behalf of the occupier to ask them to leave; and either
d) any of those persons has damaged the land or used threatening, abusive or insulting words or behaviour towards the occupier or his family etc., or
e) they have between them more than five vehicles on the land.

Failure to leave the land as soon as reasonably practicable is a criminal offence punishable on summary conviction by imprisonment or a fine, or both. Seizure of any vehicle is possible where there has been a failure to remove any vehicle without reasonable excuse.

6.3.3 Restrictions on eviction powers

It has been held that the power of local authorities to remove travellers or gypsies from their land is effectively circumscribed by guidance given by the Department of the Environment requiring such authorities to have regard to the personal circumstances of the occupiers before deciding to remove them.

6.3.4 Gypsies

Former provisions of the Caravan Sites Act 1968 imposed a statutory duty on local authorities to provide accommodation on caravan sites for gypsies, as opposed to New Age travellers. Although that statutory requirement has been removed, the Department of the Environment's guidelines provide that local planning authorities should still make adequate gypsy site provision in their development plans, and require local authorities to take careful account of their obligations under the Children Act, the Housing Acts and the Education Acts. They should not evict gypsies needlessly but should use their powers compassionately and primarily to reduce nuisance and to afford protection to private owners of land.

At present, several appeals are pending before the House of Lords regarding breaches of the planning laws by gypsies. The issues concern the local authority's need to safeguard the environment in relation to the protection of the gypsies' private and family life under the Human Rights Act.

6.4 Persons attending or preparing to attend raves

The police have powers to remove persons (whether or not trespassers) attending or intending to attend a gathering on land in the open air of 100 or more persons at which amplified music is played during the night, and which is likely to cause distress to the local inhabitants. Persons believed to be on their way to such gatherings may be stopped from going to the proposed site when they are within five miles of the site boundary.

A removal direction covering individuals, their vehicles and other equipment may be made by a senior police officer who has reason to believe that:

a) two or more persons are preparing for such a gathering
b) ten or more persons are waiting for such a gathering to begin; or
c) ten or more persons are attending such a gathering.

A criminal offence, punishable by imprisonment, a fine, or both, is committed by any person who fails to comply with a removal direction as soon as reasonably practicable.

These provisions do not apply to gatherings covered by an entertainment licence granted by a local authority.

6.5 Crop sabotage

Activists in the environmental movement have gone on to land to destroy genetically modified crops, and pranksters have damaged crops to create corn circles. Those responsible for such acts can be held liable for criminal damage under the Criminal Damage Act 1971, but the Act permits a defence of 'lawful excuse' which may arouse the sympathy of some juries. That defence was unsuccessfully raised by anti-nuclear protesters who were charged after cutting through the fencing at a US naval base, but in 1999 when 28 people (including Lord Melchett) were charged with theft and criminal damage after cutting down a farmer's genetically modified crops, the jury acquitted them all after they pleaded they were defending themselves against the threat which the crop represented.

Note: that it is theft – and therefore a crime – to dishonestly take possession of anything forming part of the land by detaching it. Even if it is left on the site it may have been rendered worthless. Anti-vivisectionists releasing animals from a research centre could be 'dishonest' in law even though they do not intend to keep the animals themselves. Again, if the jury takes the view that the defendants' actions were justified – the so-called 'Robin Hood defence' – they might decide to acquit.

If these offences are tried in the Crown Court, the maximum sentences on conviction are seven years in the case of theft, ten years for criminal damage.

6.6 Access by neighbours

If Andrew needs to go on to neighbouring land belonging to Basil in order to carry out necessary works on his own land, he must obtain permission from Basil. If Basil refuses, Andrew can apply to court to override this under the Access to Neighbouring Land Act 1992. See also chapter on *Neighbours*, section 8.

6.7 Aggravated trespass and trespassory assemblies

An offence is created under the Criminal Justice and Public Order Act where, in relation to any lawful activities in the open air (for example, fox hunting), a trespass is committed with the intention of intimidating the persons involved or of obstructing or disrupting that activity.

The police may also obtain a council order to prevent the holding of any assembly on land to which the public has either no right of access or a limited right of access, and which takes place without the permission of the occupier of the land. This applies where the assembly is likely to cause serious disruption to the life of the community or might result in significant damage to land, or to a building or monument, of historical, architectural, archaeological or scientific importance. For example, such assemblies have been prohibited in the environs of Stonehenge.

6.8 Occupier's liability to trespassers

An occupier of premises is entitled to use reasonable force against a trespasser but may be liable for damages, or even a criminal conviction, where excessive or unreasonable force is used. Thus, for example, a man who fired a shotgun at a person who was attempting to break into his garden shed was liable to pay damages as his action was excessive.

An occupier may not be liable to a trespasser injured by a guard dog on his property if a clear warning notice is displayed. However, he might be liable depending on the view that the judge takes of the facts. For more details see chapter on *Accidents*, section 4.3.2.

Note: the owner of straying livestock is entitled to go on to someone else's land in order to recapture his animals (see 4.1.1(c)). He is not a trespasser in that case (for trespass by animals generally, see section 4 above).

7   PROTECTION OF FLORA AND FAUNA

7.1   How protection works

Criminal sanctions have been imposed in order to protect certain species of wild birds, animals, reptiles, amphibians and insects. Certain plants are also protected.

Note of warning: the Countryside and Rights of Way Act (section 7.1.2 below) introduces stiffer provisions in order to police and enforce legislation which protects and conserves wildlife species in England and Wales.

7.1.1   Protected species

The present law is based on the National Parks and Access to the Countryside Act 1949, much amended, and the Wildlife and Countryside Act 1981. Their focus was on protecting rare species. Since then, there has been increasing emphasis on biodiversity and the need to protect other forms of wildlife, including common species of plant, animal and insect life. Common habitats such as hedgerows and meadows are also in need of protection.

Under the Hedgerows Regulations 1997, it is against the law to remove most countryside hedges without first getting the permission of your local council. The Department of the Environment, Food and Rural Affairs (see DIRECTORY) also administers two agri-environment schemes – intended to tackle the serious problems of hedgerow loss through neglect – by promoting the conservation and restoration of hedgerows in England. The Environmentally Sensitive Areas scheme (ESAs) provides incentives to farmers to protect the landscape, wildlife and historic interest of 22 areas of the country considered to be of national environmental significance (see section 2.3.7 above); and the Countryside Stewardship scheme similarly provides incentives to protect, enhance, restore and recreate priority landscapes, their wildlife habitats and historical features in areas of England outside ESAs.

Farmers receive payments for entering into 10-year management agreements. Incentives are also available for the restoration of other traditional forms of field boundary, such as dry-stone walls. However, they do not have statutory protection as hedgerows do.

Also, the schedule of protected animals, insects and plants is revised every five years and updated to some extent to include new species. The latest list of changes to the schedule was in 1998. In addition, Britain is a signatory to an international treaty on maintaining biodiversity.

7.1.2   Wildlife protection enforcement

Measures in the Countryside and Rights of Way Act 2000 substantially increase the enforcement powers and the range of sentencing options available to the courts by bringing in tough new measures.

For example, it was already an offence to intentionally disturb a place of rest or shelter of a protected bird and animal, but a new, and less exacting, offence has been created of 'reckless disturbance' which, it is hoped, will be easier to prove. And for the first time, instead of just fines, which have also been made heavier, wildlife offences can involve custodial sentences of up to six months.

In addition to the setting up of a new national wildlife crime unit, police officers and wildlife inspectors have the authority to order DNA tests to detect the parentage of birds and allow for tissue samples from other wildlife species. Police officers' powers are enlarged with new arrest and search warrant provisions. A multi-agency body acting in support of the enforcement of wildlife legislation, the Partnership for Action Against Wildlife Crime (PAW), has also been set up.

These and other measures are intended to close the loopholes in existing legislation and so, it is hoped, allow more offenders to be brought to justice. A team of around 100 wildlife inspectors are given an enhanced role in preventing – and in some cases detecting – crime in the environment which not only diminishes our protected species but, as an end result, reduces the quality of life for us all.

7.1.2(a)   Wild birds

Under the Wildlife and Countryside Act 1981, it is a criminal offence intentionally:

- to kill, injure or take any wild bird
- to take, damage or destroy the nest of any wild bird while that nest is in use or is being built
- to take or destroy an egg of any wild bird.

Note: to 'destroy' means to do anything calculated to prevent an egg from hatching.

A 'wild bird' is 'any bird of a kind which is ordinarily resident in or is a visitor to Great Britain in a wild state'.

So wild birds are those that:

- have not been bred in captivity
- are not included as 'poultry'
- are not generally included as 'game birds'.

These criminal offences are committed where the nest is disturbed either intentionally or recklessly.

7.1.2(b)   Special protection

With regard to certain species, it is an offence intentionally:

- to disturb any wild bird while it is building a nest or is in, on, or near a nest containing eggs or young; or
- to disturb dependent young of such a bird.

This special protection exists throughout the year.

7.1.2(c)   Close season

Certain birds are protected during their close season only. The dates of close seasons vary but in general they last from early February to the middle or end of August, i.e. the breeding season.

Note: the government can make orders altering the close season dates for any species, or adding the names of additional species to the lists.

7.1.2(d)   Game birds

It is not an offence to kill or take a game bird, or injure it in the course of killing and taking it, or destroying or damaging its nest or eggs, provided this is done outside the close season (subject to sporting rights – see section 5 above).

7.1.3   Protected areas for birds

The Secretary of State for the Environment can designate certain areas as areas of special protection for birds. This would apply where, for example, a rare species has built a nest in an unusual location and it is thought best that people in general should be kept away. The landowner and those who come on to the land with his permission are exempt.

A list of bird sanctuaries is available from the Royal Society for the Protection of Birds (see DIRECTORY).

7.1.4   Prohibited ways of killing or taking wild birds

The Wildlife and Countryside Act 1981 also prohibits certain ways of killing or taking wild birds. These prohibited means are:

- snares
- traps
- poisoned baits.

A live mammal or bird cannot be used as a decoy for the purpose of killing or taking any animal.

Self-locking snares which are 'calculated to cause bodily injury to any wild animal' coming into contact with them are forbidden.

The Act also protects certain species from sound decoys, sighting devices for night-shooting, automatic or semi-automatic weapons and dazzling lights.

These measures are obviously intended to minimise pain and suffering, as well as to prevent indiscriminate killing.

See also section 5.2.6 above on the use of lead shot on wetlands.

7.2 When you are allowed to kill protected species (outside close season)

Rules are in force which allow for the killing of protected species in particular circumstances. The rules relate to matters such as pests, public health and the pain and suffering of an animal. (See section 7.3 on the protection of wild animals.)

7.2.1 Pests

Certain birds are generally regarded as pests. These birds can be killed at any time of the year but only by authorised persons.

'Authorised persons' are:

- the owner; or
- the occupier of land; or
- persons acting with their authority; or
- persons authorised in writing by the county or district council for the area; or
- persons authorised in writing by English Nature or a water authority.

These persons will not be criminally guilty of killing or injuring such birds, or destroying their nests or eggs.

So even birds commonly regarded, and indeed, legally categorised as pests still have certain protection in that they can only be dealt with by a clearly defined group of people.

7.2.2 Public health

Killing or taking birds is not an offence if it is done in the interests of public health or to prevent plant or animal disease.

7.2.3 Pain and suffering

Birds which have been injured can be killed to be put out of their misery, or tended if recovery is likely.

☞ *You take into your care a wild eaglet which has fallen out of its nest. The bird is injured and you tend it carefully. It thrives under your care and you now want to return it to the wild.*

You obviously have not committed a criminal offence in 'taking' the bird from its natural habitat. You would be advised to contact the Royal Society for the Protection of Birds regarding its return to its own habitat (see DIRECTORY).

7.2.4 Works on the land

The killing of birds or disturbing of a nest may be lawful if it is the incidental result of a lawful operation.

☞ *You have a diseased elm at the far end of your extensive garden. You have to fell the tree for fear it may fall and damage the adjacent highway. You know that there is a family of owls which has set up home in the tree.*

In this case, the operation is not only lawful but necessary under the Highways Act.

Where someone is charged with any of the offences of killing, injuring or disturbing protected birds, they will not be convicted if it can be proved that it happened as an 'incidental result of a lawful operation and could not reasonably have been avoided'. This is a defence of very wide scope. Most people carry out lawful operations on their own land, the 'incidental result' of which could be harmful to wild life. Examples of lawful operations include activities such as ploughing or draining land.

In addition, authorised persons can show that their actions were necessary for public health, or to prevent serious damage to livestock, foodstuffs for livestock, crops, vegetables, fruit, growing timber or fisheries.

7.3   Protection of wild animals

Criminal sanctions have been imposed to protect certain wild animals.

7.3.1   Offences

The offences are:

a) Intentionally to kill, injure or take any wild animal; and to have in one's possession any live or dead wild animal under protection as specified in the Wildlife and Countryside Act.

b) To damage or destroy, or obstruct access to, any structure or place which any wild animal uses for shelter or protection. See above, section 7.2, for when it is not a crime to kill a protected animal.

Additional provisions to protect wild mammals against violence such as stabbing, burning, kicking, stoning, drowning and mutilation became law in April 1996, under the Wild Mammals (Protection) Act. Prohibited acts of violence constitute criminal offences punishable by imprisonment. The activities of fox hunting, stalking, coursing, shooting, fishing and falconry are not included within the Act, and it has no effect on farming or pest control.

The killing of a fatally disabled animal is also excluded as being an act of mercy.

7.3.2   The Protection of Badgers Act 1992

Under this Act, there are many offences laid down which involve the killing or taking or ill-treating of badgers, attempting to do so, or disturbing their setts. It is also an offence to sell or offer a live badger for sale.

Exceptions to the Act allow for mercy killing, or for injuring one as an accidental result of some other action which is lawful in itself. While driving a car, for example, you might accidentally run over a badger but, depending on the circumstances, you might not be liable under the Act.

Entrance to a sett for the purpose of fox hunting is exempted from the Act provided that this is done in accordance with the statutory provisions.

7.3.3   Cruelty to domestic animals by their owners or keepers

See the chapter on *Pets*, section 5.

7.4   Protection of wild plants

7.4.1   Offences

It is an offence intentionally to pick, uproot or destroy any protected wild plant. The term 'pick' is defined to include the gathering or plucking of any part of a plant without uprooting it, so it includes the collecting of seeds.

7.4.2   Exemption

Acts which are 'an incidental result of a lawful operation and could not reasonably have been avoided' are exempt. This, of course, covers farming operations.

Concern is mounting for the loss of distinctive wild flowers through agriculture, for example by use of certain fertilisers.

7.5   Licences

For scientific or educational purposes, for protecting a collection of wild birds or animals, or for conservation purposes, a licence can be issued for ringing or marking or for other appropriate measures to be taken. The licence might be general or specific or granted to a class of persons – say, those at an agricultural college.

DIRECTORY
THE COUNTRYSIDE

Aviation Environment Federation
Sir John Lyon House
5 High Timber Street
London EC4V 3NS
Tel. 020 7248 2223
www.aef.org.uk

The Bicycle Association of Great Britain
Starley House
Eaton Road
Coventry
West Midlands CV1 2FH
Tel. 02476 553838

British Association for Shooting & Conservation
Marford Mill
Rossett
Wrexham LL12 0HL
Tel. 01244 573 000
www.basc.org.uk

British Cycling Federation
National Cycling Centre
Stuart Street
Manchester M11 4DQ
Tel. 08708 712 000
www.britishcycling.org.uk

The British Horse Society
Stoneleigh Deer Park
Kenilworth
Warwickshire CV8 2XZ
Tel. 01926 707 700
www.bhs.org.uk

British Mountaineering Council
177–179 Burton Road
West Didsbury
Manchester M20 2BB
Tel. 0870 010 4878
www.thebmc.co.uk

British Orienteering Federation
Riversdale
Dale Road North
Darley Dale
Matlock
Derbyshire DE4 2HX
Tel. 01629 734042
www.britishorienteering.org.uk

British Trust for Conservation Volunteers *(BTCV)*
36 St Mary's Street
Wallingford
Oxfordshire OX10 0EU
Tel. 01491 839766
www.btcv.org.uk

British Trust for Ornithology
The Nunnery
Thetford
Norfolk IP24 2PU
Tel. 01842 750050
www.bto.org

British Waterways
Willow Grange
Church Road
Watford
Herts WD17 3QA
Tel. 01923 226422
www.britishwaterways.co.uk

Butterfly Conservation
Manor Yard
East Lulworth
Wareham
Dorset BH20 5QP
Tel. 01929 400 209
www.butterfly-conservation.org

Cadw – Welsh Historic Monuments
Crown Building
Cathays Park
Cardiff CF10 3NQ
Tel. 029 2050 0200
www.cadw.wales.gov.uk

Campaign for the Protection of Rural Wales
31 High Street
Welshpool
Powys SY21 7YD
Tel. 01938 552525
www.cprw.org.uk

The Camping and Caravanning Club
Greenfields House
Westwood Way
Coventry CV4 8JH
Tel. 02476 694995
www.campingandcaravanningclub.co.uk

Care for the Wild International
1 Ashfolds
Horsham Road
Rusper
West Sussex RH12 4QX
Tel. 01293 871596
www.careforthewild.com

Centre for Accessible Environments
Nutmeg House
60 Gainsford Street
London SE1 2NY
Tel. 020 7357 8182
www.cae.org.uk

Cleanair
33 Stillness Road
London SE23 1NG
Tel. 020 8690 4649
www.ezme.com/cleanair/

Council for British Archaeology
Bowes Murrell House
111 Walmgate
York YO1 9WA
Tel. 01904 671417
www.britarch.ac.uk

Council for National Parks
246 Lavender Hill
London SW11 1LJ
Tel. 020 7924 4077
www.cnp.org.uk

Council for the Protection of Rural England
128 Southwark Street
London SE1 0SW
Tel. 020 7981 2800
www.cpre.org.uk

Country Landowners Association
16 Belgrave Square
London SW1X 8PQ
Tel. 020 7235 0511
www.cla.org.uk

Countryside Agency
John Dower House
Crescent Place
Cheltenham
Gloucestershire GL50 3RA
Tel. 01242 521381
www.countryside.gov.uk

Countryside Alliance
The Old Town Hall
367 Kennington Road
London SE11 4PT
Tel. 020 7582 5432
www.countryside-alliance.org

Countryside Council for Wales
Plas Penrhos
Fford Penrhos
Bangor
Gwynedd LL57 2LQ
Tel. 01248 385 500
www.ccw.gov.uk

Cyclists Touring Club
Cotterell House
69 Meadrow
Godalming
Surrey GU7 3HS
Tel. 0870 873 0060
www.ctc.org.uk

Department for Transport
Eland House
Bressenden Place
London SW1E 5DU
Tel. 020 7994 8300
www.dft.gov.uk

**Department of the Environment,
Food and Rural Affairs** *(DEFRA)*
Nobel House
17 Smith Square
London SW1P 3JR
Tel. 08459 33 55 77
www.defra.gov.uk

Dry Stone Walling Association of Great Britain
PO Box 8615
Sutton Coldfield B75 7HQ
Tel. 01213 780493
www.dswa.org.uk

Encams *(incorporates former Going for Green
and Tidy Britain Group)*
Elizabeth House
The Pier
Wigan WN3 4EX
Tel. 01942 824620
www.encams.org

English Heritage
23 Savile Row
London W1S 2ET
Tel. 020 7973 3000
www.english-heritage.org.uk

English Nature
Northminster House
Northminster
Peterborough PE1 1UA
Tel. 01733 455 000
www.english-nature.org.uk

The Environment Agency
Rio House
Waterside Drive
Aztec West
Almondsbury
Bristol BS32 4UD
Tel. 01454 624400
www.environment-agency.gov.uk

Environmental Law Foundation
Suite 309
16 Baldwin Gardens
London EC1N 7RJ
Tel. 020 7404 1030
www.elflaw.org

The Forestry Commission – England
Great Eastern House
Cambridge CB1 2DU
Tel. 01223 314546
www.forestry.gov.uk

The Forestry Commission – Wales
Victoria Terrace
Aberystwyth
Ceredigion SY23 2DQ
Tel. 01970 625 866
www.forestry.gov.uk

Friends of the Earth
26 Underwood Street
London N1 7JQ
Tel. 020 7490 1555
www.foe.co.uk

The Game Conservancy Trust
Fordingbridge
Hampshire SP6 1EF
Tel. 01425 652381
www.gct.org.uk

Greenpeace UK
Canonbury Villas
London N1 2PN
Tel. 020 7865 8100
www.greenpeace.org.uk

Health and Safety Executive
Daniel House
Trinity Road
Bootle
Merseyside L20 3TW
(Infoline) Tel. 08701 545 500
www.hse.gov.uk

Health and Safety Executive (Wales)
Information Services
Caerphilly Business Park
Caerphilly CF83 3GG
Tel. 08701 545 500
www.hse.gov.uk

Institute for Outdoor Learning
Plumpton Old Hall
Plumpton
Penrith CA11 9NP
Tel. 01768 891 065
www.outdoor-learning.org

International Tree Foundation
Sandy Lane
Crawley Down
West Sussex RH10 4HS
Tel. 01342 712 536
www.tree-foundation.org.uk

The Landscape Institute
6/8 Barnard Mews
London SW11 1QU
Tel. 020 7350 5200
www.l-i.org.uk

The League Against Cruel Sports
Sparling House
83–87 Union Street
London SE1 1SG
Tel. 020 7403 6155
www.league.uk.com

Living Streets
(formerly The Pedestrians Association)
31–33 Bondway
London SW8 1SJ
Tel. 020 7820 1010
www.livingstreets.org.uk

Local Government Association
Local Government House
Smith Square
London SW1P 3HZ
Tel. 020 7664 3000
www.lga.gov.uk

Local Government Ombudsman (England)
(London, Kent, Surrey, E and W Sussex)
21 Queen Anne's Gate
London SW1H 9BU
Tel. 020 7915 3210
www.lgo.org.uk

(E Midlands, N England)
Beverley House
15 Shipton Road
York YO30 5FZ
Tel. 01904 663200

(E Anglia, S, SW, W and Central England)
2 The Oaks
Westwood Way
Westwood Business Park
Coventry CV4 8JB
Tel. 024 7669 5999

Local Government Ombudsman (Wales)
Derwent House
Court Road
Bridgend CF31 1BN
Tel. 01656 661325
www.ombudsman-wales.org

Long Distance Walkers' Association
Bank House
High Street
Wrotham
Kent TN15 7AE
Tel. 01732 883705
www.ldwa.org.uk

National Association for Bikers with a Disability
39 Low North Road
Wythenshaw
Manchester M22 6JU
Tel. 0161 233 0122
www.nabd.org.uk

National Council for Metal Detecting
51 Hilltop Gardens
Denaby
Doncaster DN12 4SA
Tel. 01709 868521
www.ncmd.co.uk

National Monuments Record
English Heritage
55 Blandford Street
London W1U 7HN
Tel. 020 7208 8200
www.english-heritage.org.uk

The National Trust
36 Queen Anne's Gate
London SW1H 9AS
Tel. 020 7222 9251
www.nationaltrust.org.uk

Nature Conservancy Council *(for England)*
(*See* English Nature)

Office of the Deputy Prime Minister
(for Planning)
Eland House
Bressenden Place
London SW1E 5DU
Tel. 020 7944 4400
www.odpm.gov.uk

The Open Spaces Society
25a Bell Street
Henley-on-Thames
Oxon RG9 2BA
Tel. 01491573535
www.oss.org.uk

Ordnance Survey
Romsey Road
Maybush
Southampton SO16 4GU
Tel. 01703 792000
www.ordnancesurvey.co.uk

Ramblers' Association
2nd Floor Camelford House
87–90 Albert Embankment
London SE1 7TW
Tel. 020 7339 8500
www.ramblers.org.uk

The Royal Commission on Ancient and Historic Monuments in Wales
Crown Buildings
Plas Crug
Aberystwyth
Ceredigion SY23 1NJ
Tel. 01970 621 200
www.rcahmw.org

The Royal Forestry Society of England, Wales and Northern Ireland
102 High Street
Tring
Herts HP23 4AF
Tel. 01442 822028
www.rfs.org.uk

**Royal Society for the Prevention of Cruelty
to Animals** *(RSPCA)*
Wilberforce Way
Southwater
Horsham
West Sussex RH13 9RS
Tel. 0870 333 5999
www.rspca.org.uk

Royal Society for the Protection of Birds *(RSPB)*
The Lodge
Sandy
Bedfordshire SG19 2DL
Tel. 01767 680551
www.rspb.org.uk

Sport England
16 Upper Woburn Place
London WC1H 0QP
Tel. 020 7273 1500
www.sportengland.gov.uk

Sports Council for Wales
Sophia Gardens
Cardiff CF11 9SW
Tel. 02920 300 500
www.sports-council-wales.co.uk

The Woodland Trust
Autumn Park
Dysart Road
Grantham
Lincolnshire NG31 6LL
Tel. 01476 581 111
www.woodland-trust.org.uk

WWF–UK
(formerly World Wide Fund for Nature)
Panda House
Weyside Park
Godalming
Surrey GU7 1XR
Tel. 01483 426444
www.wwf.org.uk

Youth Hostels Association
Trevelyan House
Dimple Road
Matlock
Derbyshire DE4 3YH
Tel. 01629 592 600
www.yha.org.uk

15 PETS

It has been estimated that over 23 million households in Britain own a pet animal of some sort. Less readily estimated is the number of such households that have considered their responsibilities in relation to their pets and in relation to the rest of the community. In this chapter we will consider the legal implications of keeping an animal.

Before you decide to buy an animal or bird you should consider your responsibilities towards this living creature. You should ensure that you can provide it with suitable living conditions, and that you know how to keep it healthy – which may include arranging for vaccination against various diseases. For organisations that can help with information on the needs and health care of particular species, as well as what to look for – or avoid – when buying, see the DIRECTORY at the end of the chapter. Your local veterinary practice may give advice, too.

You should also, of course, think carefully about the financial costs involved in keeping an animal: vets' bills, food and living quarters, health insurance, holiday care, etc. (In the case of a kitten or puppy, for example, these costs are likely to continue for up to 15 years.)

If you live in accommodation which you rent or lease, there may be a covenant in your lease or agreement which prohibits the keeping of pets – depending on the type of accommodation and whether they may cause a nuisance to neighbours (see the chapter on *Landlords and their Tenants*, section 4.3.1).

In addition, you need to be aware of your responsibilities as a pet-keeper towards the general public. For example, you could be guilty of causing a 'nuisance' if you allow your dog to bark in particular circumstances; you may have a duty to clear up after it in public places; with certain breeds you must take precautions to ensure that the public are not endangered. If you own a horse you may not allow it to stray on to the road, and there are rules as to where you may or may not ride it. Certain dangerous species of animal may only be kept if you have a licence to do so.

In order to prevent the spread of rabies, a very dangerous disease that may be transmitted from animals to human beings, you are only allowed to bring an animal into Britain from another country under very stringent conditions. Until recently, every animal coming into the country from abroad had to undergo quarantine for six months, but a 'Passports for Pets' scheme has been introduced for cats and dogs, which allows individual animals to enter Britain in very strictly controlled circumstances. You will find the regulations governing this scheme in section 7.

Note: although you are not obliged by law to have an animal vaccinated against the various diseases to which the particular species is vulnerable, you are well advised to do so, both for the health of your own animal and out of responsibility towards the owners of other dogs, cats or horses to whom your animal might transmit the disease. Your local veterinary practice will provide information.

Animal welfare legislation is a sensitive area. There are several Acts of Parliament which govern the welfare of pets but most of them are outdated and inadequate to meet today's concerns on how best to enhance the welfare of animals and protect them against abuse.

To this end, the government is proposing to introduce an Animal Welfare Bill to consolidate and bring up to date the present legislation which will apply to animals kept by us for our enjoyment, sport, companionship, or for agricultural purposes.

In this chapter we look at:
- buying an animal
- damage caused by animals

- your dog and the law
- horses and the law
- cruelty to animals
- strays
- passports for pets
- quarantine
- kennels and catteries
- veterinary surgeons and their responsibilities
- insuring your pet.

Do note: cats are probably the most popular domestic pets – it is said that they number in excess of 7.2 million – as they are more self-reliant than many other pets and fit well into a household. However, as cats are not put to economic use – apart from vermin-catching – nor do they cause significant damage to humans or to economically important animals, they are not under the law's particular focus. This chapter is concerned, in the main, therefore, with the law in its application to dogs and horses, as for historical and other reasons (e.g. agriculture, transport, country pursuits etc.), a large body of case law and legislation has built up over the centuries in relation to them.

1   BUYING A PET

When purchasing a household pet, the general law regarding the sale of goods is applicable so it is advisable to have the animal checked carefully before entering into any contract to buy it (see the chapter on *Goods and Services*). There are factsheets to assist you in what you should look for in choosing a particular pet; the RSPCA, for example, issues such leaflets (see DIRECTORY).

Under the Breeding and Sale of Dogs (Welfare) Act 1999 (see section 3.7 below), licensed pet-shop owners must ensure that a dog supplied from a breeding establishment wears an identification tag which clearly displays where the dog was bred, its date of birth, and an identifying number, if any, allocated to the dog by the establishment.

If you desire a pedigree cat, you may often see these advertised in your local press. If you lack personal, specialised knowledge you should obtain preliminary information and advice from the Governing Council of the Cat Fancy (GCCF), 46 Penel Orlieu, Bridgewater, Somerset. This is the feline equivalent of the Kennel Club.

Generally speaking if you buy from a pet shop or a recognised breeder, you have some protection in law which implies terms such as 'merchantable quality' and 'fitness for their purpose' into all contracts of sale for goods and chattels made in the course of a trade or business (see *Goods and Services* chapter, section 2). For example, if you buy a pony and you make it clear that you want it for a particular purpose, stressing that it needs to be suitable for a young, nervous child, and you are assured that the animal is 'very quiet and gentle' but the pony is neither quiet nor gentle, you should be able to return it or sue for damages. (In all such cases, of course, it is a matter of fact and degree and you also need to show evidence of the assurance which you received from the owner of the business.) Buying from a pet shop or breeder also ensures that a degree of care for the animal has been taken before it is sold (see section 1.2.2 below).

If you buy privately, on the other hand, e.g. from a private person who advertises in a local paper, you have no rights against the seller unless there was an actual misrepresentation, e.g. you are wrongly informed by the seller that the animal is of a particular breed. Again, you would have to prove that the misrepresentation was part of the contract of sale.

It must be borne in mind, however, that it is particularly difficult in the case of a pet to guard against a problem that may arise after purchase even if it existed at the time of sale, e.g. if a particular animal has been bred in such a way as to make it prone to disease later in its life, or is likely to develop a limp because of a congenital defect (see also Note immediately below). There may be redress if you can obtain a vet's certificate that an illness must have begun before the pet was sold.

Note: do try to obtain as much documentation as possible on the animal's breeding and provenance, e.g. pedigree and registration papers and, where possible, hereditary-disease screening certificates.

1.1   Age restrictions on buying a pet

☞ *Your daughter, who is ten, wants to buy a pet with the pocket money she has earned. She sees a rabbit in the window of a local pet shop. She is very anxious to 'own' the animal. You want to know the legal position.*

In general, 'minors' [i.e. under-18-year-olds] cannot enter into binding contracts under the law of contract.

It is an offence for a person to sell a pet animal to a child under 12 years of age.

Many local authorities also stipulate that no pet is to be sold to a child under the age of 16 without evidence of the consent of that child's parent or legal guardian. The government is considering introducing on a national basis a minimum age limit of 16.

Take note: if an animal is owned or possessed by a child under 16, its keeper for legal purposes is the head of the household to which the child belongs (Animals Act 1971).

1.2   Where to purchase

To safeguard the wellbeing of animals, legislation exists to protect where they can be sold for commercial purposes and to control the premises in which they are sold.

1.2.1   Streets or public places?

You have seen a caged hamster for sale at a stall at your local street market.

In order to ensure as far as possible the welfare of animals, pets may not be sold in streets or public places. They may also not be sold at a stall or barrow in a market.

1.2.2   Pet shops

You may wish to purchase your pet from a pet shop. There are strict regulations governing the sale of animals in shops, and the conditions in which these animals are kept. In no circumstances may a person keep a pet shop without a licence granted by the local authority. In determining whether to grant such a licence, the authority will have regard to the need for securing that:

- animals will at all times be kept in accommodation suitable with regard to size, temperature, lighting, ventilation and cleanliness
- animals will be adequately supplied with suitable food and drink and (so far as necessary) visited at suitable intervals
- mammals will not be sold at too early an age
- all reasonable precautions will be taken to prevent the spread among animals of infectious diseases
- appropriate steps will be taken in case of fire or other emergency.

The pet shop should provide you with written advice regarding the care and treatment appropriate to the animal you purchase. Likewise the shop should give you proper advice as to the maintenance and use of accessories you purchase for your pet.

If the animal you wish to buy is classified as a dangerous wild animal (see immediately below), the pet shop owner must inspect your licence to keep such an animal and will inform the issuing authority of the details once you have made the purchase.

1.3   What is a pet? – dangerous species

The law distinguishes between animals that are wild by nature, and other animals. There are far greater liabilities on owners of wild animals for any damage they may cause (see section below).

Animals which are considered wild by nature are those which are not usually domesticated in this country even though they may be domesticated abroad – e.g. a camel – or are of a size which would cause severe damage if unrestrained, e.g. an elephant. If you wish to keep such an animals you require a special licence.

Indeed, the acquisition of exotic pets has become increasingly fashionable over the last decades. Although they were often from the more dangerous species, including for example, from the 'big cats', there were no restrictions or controls imposed on either the buying or the keeping of such animals until 1976. In response to public concern, however, the Dangerous Wild Animals Act 1976 was passed which imposes much stricter control on the ownership of such species. It covers, among other animals, many primates, carnivores, bears, larger reptiles, poisonous snakes and scorpions.

A keeper of a dangerous animal is obliged to have a local authority licence authorising him or her to keep the animal and specifies the conditions under which it is to be kept (see section 1.3.1 below).

Take heed: liability insurance cover is a condition of all such licences (see also below).

1.3.1   Reptiles

These have been increasingly popular as pets and include terrapins, iguanas, and snakes. According to government figures there has been a huge increase in the number of exotic animals sold in Britain over the past ten years and thousands of reptiles are now kept as pets in private homes.

☞ *Your next-door neighbour has blithely informed you that he intends buying a viper as a pet which he will keep in his semi-detached house. You have young children and are understandably anxious. You want to know what legal safeguards are in place.*

Certain reptiles, including most snakes known as vipers and adders, and the rattlesnake, bushmaster, fer-de-lance, water moccasin and copperhead, may not be kept without a licence granted by your local authority. Your neighbour's application for such a licence must specify:

- the species (whether one or more) of animal, and the number of animals of each species, he proposes to keep
- the premises where the animal will normally be held.

Such an application must:

- be made to the local authority in whose area those premises are situated
- be made by a person who is neither under 18 years of age nor disqualified from keeping any dangerous wild animal; and
- be accompanied by the relevant fee stipulated by the local authority.

Before granting any such licence, the local authority will have to be satisfied that, among other things, the applicant for a licence is suitable, and that any animal concerned will be held in secure and suitable accommodation (see also section 2.2.1 below). A veterinary surgeon must inspect the proposed premises on behalf of the local authority.

If these conditions are breached or someone keeps a wild animal without a licence, a local authority has the power to seize the animal, and keep, destroy, or dispose of it.

As stated above, insurance cover must also be in place.

Health warning: the Department of Health has issued a warning to owners of snakes, lizards, terrapins and other reptiles, about the danger of increased risk of salmonella infection from pet reptiles. The warning comes in response to an increase in the number of salmonella cases, associated with exotic pets – in particular young children and infants are vulnerable. Further steps on control of these pets may need to be taken in light of current research into health hazards.

2   DAMAGE CAUSED BY ANIMALS

2.1   Liabilities of owners

Whatever species of animal you may own, you could fall foul of the laws on negligence, and become liable for failing to take reasonable care to prevent your animal(s) causing damage to others.

In one case a horse kept in a fenced field escaped, strayed into a road and crashed into a car, causing the driver to be seriously injured. The owner of the horse argued that the animal had been panicked into escaping from the field by some unknown cause. The court accepted that the owner had not been negligent, but he still had to pay damages to the injured victim, because under the Animals Act 1971 the owner of an animal is liable for damage caused by the animal behaving in a way which is normal for its kind when panicked – even though the behaviour might be unusual for that individual animal normally.

☞ *Julian is thrown by the horse he was riding and is injured. The owner of the horse knew it had a propensity to be frightened by farm machinery, which was the cause of its reaction.*

Julian can hold the owner responsible for his injuries [under the Animals Act].

2.1.1   Dangerous animals

If you are a licensed keeper of a non-domesticated animal (see section 1.3 above), you will be liable if it causes damage even if it is only to other animals and even if your animal is usually docile. So you would be liable if, for example, your tamed and tethered chimpanzee bites a visitor's puppy which wanders near it out of curiosity.

Thus where injury or damage is caused by an animal belonging to a dangerous species that you hold in captivity, such as a bird of prey, or a poisonous snake or spider, you will be held responsible without anything else having to be proved – precautions or lack of them make no difference.

You may also be able to claim if a neighbour keeps animals which escape on to your property, e.g. if he has unreasonable numbers of bees which swarm into your garden and sting you. What would be considered 'unreasonable numbers' would depend on the circumstances of the case.

By the same token, if you know that your neighbour keeps bees, and you spray your own field, knowing that his bees would be present in large numbers during the flowering season, and you do not take steps to minimise the danger to your neighbour's bees, you could be liable for damages.

2.1.2   When there is non-liability for damage

Neighbours are not liable, however, if the animals coming on to your land are 'naturally' there on their land.

☞   *Your family's pet rabbit is killed by foxes living on a neighbour's land.*

The neighbour has no responsibility for preventing the foxes making such forays.

2.1.3   Domesticated animals

If the owner of an animal purposely causes you harm by, for example, setting his dog to attack you, you could bring an action for trespass to the person. If he sets his large dog to attack your smaller one, the action will be for trespass to goods. It is also an offence under the Criminal Damage Act 1971 for a person who has 'anything' under his or her control to allow it to destroy or damage the property of another. This would cover an animal under your control, unless you had a lawful excuse for your action, such as if your dog tore the trousers of someone trying to snatch your handbag.

2.2   Can a pet owner set up a defence to a claim?

As with all potential civil wrongs, the keeper of an animal can set up certain defences to a claim for injury caused by his or her animal.

2.2.1   Contributory negligence

An animal's keeper can claim that injury or damage was partly the result of the victim's own lack of care. For example, if you, as an inexperienced rider, ask to ride a particular horse even though you suspect that it tends to be unruly, you are partly responsible for the injury it causes. As with all cases of contributory negligence, it is a matter of fact and degree. Another example would be if you exaggerated your riding skills so that you were given a horse which was beyond your capacity to keep under control (see below, section 4.4).

Liability for damages can be avoided altogether if the victim consented to run the risk of injury knowing of the dangers – for example by intervening in a fight between fierce dogs.

Note well: under the Animals Act 1971, however, the mere fact that a person took up employment with an animal owner does not mean that he or she consented to run any risk of injury, so that a stable girl who is kicked by a horse is not prevented from claiming compensation for the injury (assuming, or course that she had not herself provoked the horse by teasing it).

3   YOUR DOG AND THE LAW

Dogs, like other animals, are also items of property, and if they are hurt or otherwise damaged by another's fault compensation will be payable.

In one case a family's pet dog strayed on to a landowner's farm during a pheasant shoot, and the irate landowner shot and killed it. The landowner was fined by the criminal courts for causing criminal damage, and was also ordered to pay compensation to the dog's owners.

If you are a dog owner, it may surprise you that the law makes more provision in relation to the activities of dogs than it does with regard to other domestic pets. However, the intervention of the law in this area is perhaps explicable when you consider the harm certain dogs could do to other people's animals or indeed to members of the public, whereas a bad-tempered cat or rabbit or a noisy parrot is unlikely to cause serious disturbance or injury outside the home. The relevant legal requirements and restrictions are set out below.

3.1   Identity tags

While it is no longer necessary for an annual registration fee to be paid in respect of your dog, it is still a requirement (under the Control of Dogs Order 1992) that all dogs whilst on the highway or in public places wear a collar with their owner's name and address attached to it. Nowadays, of course, a telephone number is accepted as being an 'address'. Actually, this requirement is one with which all responsible dog owners happily comply, since it means that a lost dog can be more readily returned, rather than being impounded and even being destroyed as a stray! However, an owner who does not comply with the order is guilty of an offence.

The Order contains a list of exemptions, e.g. dogs while being used for driving or tending sheep, or guide dogs registered with the Guide Dogs for the Blind Association.

☞   *You lost your pet dog, which was wearing a collar with your name and address. You suspect that the dog was stolen and that the thief removed its identification. You have bought a new puppy but do not want the same thing to happen again.*

As dog collars and other tags can get lost, removed or defaced, a better solution is for your new puppy to have a microchip inserted under its skin. The procedure is painless. The microchip cannot be seen but can be read on a scanner. The unique code number can then be entered on to a database for life and if you change your address, new details can be entered. You can speak to your vet or RSPCA local branch for advice as there are various schemes available which may also accept details of animals with collar tags (see below also *Stray animals*, section 6, and *Reuniting owner with pet*, section 6.4).

3.2   Barking dogs

Legal action may be taken against the owner of a noisy dog under the Environmental Protection Act 1990. Noise nuisance is dealt with in the chapter on *Neighbours* (section 2). With all forms of statutory nuisance, court proceedings can follow if an owner does nothing to stop it. Many complaints are made to local authority environmental health officers because neighbours are disturbed by dogs which are locked up all day and bark or whine, or by a number of dogs kept together.

The Department of the Environment, Food and Rural Affairs (DEFRA) issues a booklet entitled *Constant barking can be avoided*. It offers reasons why your dog may bark and gives a number of tips for when a dog has to be left on its own for long periods. It also suggests that you should not place a kennel near your neighbour's fence. You can approach your local council's dog warden or your vet on ways to improve your dog's behaviour. You can obtain a copy of this leaflet by contacting DEFRA – Free Literature, PO Box No236, Wetherby, LS23 7NB: tel. 08459 556 000.

However, do not worry unnecessarily if you receive a notice saying that a complaint has been made, if you know that there may have been an isolated occasion on which your dog was barking excessively, such as a rare night when it was left alone, or during a thunderstorm. The environmental health officer will check personally whether any noise nuisance is being caused.

Where there are complaints, the local authority will serve a notice requiring the dogs' owner to 'abate the nuisance'. Getting rid of the dog or dogs would be one way – although extreme – to comply with the notice. Other methods might include insulating part of the house, or sending the dogs to an animal training centre to cure the problem. However, the council's notice will not normally need to specify the steps to be taken, but will leave it up to the owner to reduce the level of barking noise in any way which is the least expensive and most acceptable to him.

3.3   Dog fouling

Over recent years, health and safety concerns have arisen in relation to fouling by dogs in public places. Of particular concern has been the danger to small children who may pick up various infections from coming into contact with excrement from dogs. The Dog (Fouling of Land) Act 1996 has therefore been introduced, under which a dog owner who does not clean up after his or her animal in a public place may be issued with a penalty notice involving an on-the-spot fine, or be prosecuted. These rules are vigorously enforced throughout much of England and Wales.

3.3.1   What constitutes a public place?

Under the Act, a local authority has power to designate land in its area as a 'public place'.

In general, this means land to which the public has access within built-up areas, including:

- roads with a speed limit of 40 mph or less and any adjoining footpaths and verges
- any other footpath, footway, alley, passage, square or court (including any footbridge or pedestrian subway or underpass and irrespective of whether they are thoroughfares), and any adjoining verges
- parks, playing fields, playgrounds, open spaces, village greens, car parks, and land enclosed around village halls
- burial grounds, including churchyards, cemeteries or other grounds for interment
- the grounds of any school.

The rules may also apply to various specified country parks and sports fields.

Note: the Act does not apply to agricultural land, moor or heath or common land.

Any publicly owned property can be a 'public place' for the purposes of the Act, even if the wider public does not in general use it. In one case, a dog owner kept his dogs in a fenced and locked grassy area adjacent to a block of flats owned by the local council. He was held to have contravened the Act after a child entered the grassy area and was bitten by the dogs.

3.3.2   Fines

If your dog fouls in a public place and you do not clear the mess up immediately you may be issued a penalty notice by a dog warden or other person authorised by the local authority to enforce the law. The fine is usually set at £25. You may even be prosecuted (which could lead to a fine of up to £1,000).

☞ *You have received a penalty notice to the effect that your dog fouled designated land and that the mess was not cleared up. At the time, your 14-year-old son was walking his dog across a playing field. There was no notice stating that the land has been designated as such. You wonder what the position is in law.*

The Act states that 'a person who habitually has a dog in his possession shall be taken to be in charge of the dog at any time' unless at that time there was some other person in charge. As your son is under the age of 16, you are regarded in law as the dog's registered keeper (see also 'Do remember' below).

The position might have been different if your neighbour walked your dog on a regular basis, particularly for a fee, as he or she might have been considered as having been in charge at the time.

Moreover, councils are not obliged to place signs where the law applies. You should bear in mind that the rules generally apply to all 'built-up' areas.

Do remember: the head of the household is an animal's keeper for legal purposes where a pet is owned or possessed by a child under 16.

3.3.3   Reporting of breaches

If, as a responsible dog owner – or simply as a member of the general public – you see an offence being committed, most local authorities will welcome your reporting of the incident. (Your local authority probably advertises appropriate contact numbers for this purpose.) If you do wish to report such an incident it is helpful if you can provide, so far as possible, the following information:

- the exact location
- the type of dog involved
- a description of the person in charge of the dog
- vehicle registration and details where relevant
- the address of the person in charge of the dog, where known.

3.4 Accidents caused by dogs

If your dog causes an accident or injures someone, you may be liable to pay compensation. For this reason it is recommended that you obtain third party insurance for your dog(s) (see section 11 below).

☞ *You own four Jack Russell terriers which escaped from your land. They attacked a neighbour's child in his garden. Your dogs have not attacked people before.*

The owner of the dogs is liable to compensate an injured child on the basis of evidence that Jack Russell terriers are dangerous when left free to run in a pack.

You may also have committed an offence under the Dangerous Dogs Act 1991 (see below section 3.5).

Pay heed: it can be seen from this that an owner need not have had detailed evidence of a dangerous characteristic of his or her dog to have 'knowledge' in the legal sense. The popular saying that 'a dog is allowed his first bite' is therefore inaccurate. A dog may be considered 'dangerous' even if the only danger it presented was to another dog.

3.4.1 A dog must be controlled in a public place

It is also an offence under the Dangerous Dogs Act 1991 to allow any breed of dog to be dangerously out of control in a public place.

☞ *You let your Labrador off its lead in your local public park. A child was playing with a Frisbee. Your dog leapt up to seize hold of it and the child screamed in terror. He fell over and grazed his knee. His mother approached you and said that she would be reporting the incident to the police. No real harm was done to the child and you remonstrate with her that she is being unreasonable.*

An offence can be committed under the Act if there is 'reasonable apprehension' that an animal which is out of control in a public place might cause injury – even if it does not actually do so.

Note: the dog owner can be guilty of an offence even if he does not realise that his dog is liable to behave in a way which will cause injury to anyone, until, for example, a child pokes at the dog with a stick and the dog reacts.

The courts have power to order that a dog that has actually injured someone should be put down, and can disqualify its owner from keeping other dogs.

Your dog can also cause an accident if it runs into the street and a passing car swerves to avoid it, hitting another car or a child.

Under the Highway Code, a dog owner should not let it out on the road on its own. It should also be kept on a short lead when being walked on the pavement, road or path shared with cyclists. It is also very important to ensure that you restrain your dog or other animals in the car when you are driving, to avoid being distracted by them or injuring you if you brake suddenly.

If you injure a cat while driving a car, you are not under any duty to report it as an accident; see the chapter on *Motoring*, section 7.

Take heed: there is an obligation to report an accident if you injure some other farm or domestic animal.

3.5 Dangerous dogs

Even if your dog is not of a breed that would be considered to be inherently dangerous to people, you may be liable to pay compensation if you knew (or ought reasonably to have known) that your particular dog was likely to be dangerous or that it could be dangerous at a particular time, e.g. when guarding a litter of puppies.

☞ *Kenneth owns two rottweilers that run free on his land, which is fenced along an adjoining public path. The dogs jump up to the wire fence and bark furiously at passers-by, and occasionally the dogs' jowls even protrude over the fence, all of which frightens people using the path.*

In a similar case the dog owner, who was charged with obstructing the use of the path, was acquitted. The court stressed, however, that it would depend on the facts in each cases whether dog-keeping in such circumstances would amount to an unlawful obstruction.

It is the responsibility of the person in charge of a dog to ensure that it does not disturb livestock. See *The Countryside* chapter, section 4.1.1(a). However, magistrates have held that a dog which kills a cat should not be considered 'dangerous', as in such a case a dog is doing no more than what is natural.

The police have the power to prosecute the owner of a dangerous dog and may obtain an order for the dog to be kept under control or destroyed. 'Dangerous' does not only mean dangerous to humans. If the dog chased and injured cattle or poultry, that fact is sufficient to prove dangerousness.

3.5.1 Attacks on pet animals by dogs

Unfortunately there are occasions when your pet may be attacked and even injured by another animal. We have dealt with the situation where an owner deliberately sets his dog on to yours (see section 2.1.3 above) or the dog is out of control in a public place (see section 3.4.1 above).

Clearly, you have no means of redress where the offending animal was wild rather than domesticated; e.g. if your cat were to run up against an urban fox. Similarly, you may have no redress when the animals in question are natural enemies, such as dogs and cats (see immediately above), unless you can prove that the offending animal had a history of violence and was, nevertheless, not kept under control. If you are a pet owner and your pet is attacked rather than having engaged in a mere 'dog-fight', the evidence that you can provide has an important bearing if you wish to sue for compensation.

The law is clear that a single incident may 'reveal a dangerous disposition', and that the danger need not be confined to attacks on people or livestock but can include an attack on another dog. It will depend on the circumstances of the case. A dog-fight can be a direct danger to the public. It could cause a traffic accident, or injury either to someone trying to separate the animals or to a passer-by. In other cases, evidence of a single incident may be insufficient to show that a dog was necessarily aggressive and out of control.

So remember: if you intend to make a claim in court for damages for your animal's injuries, you must keep copies of the evidence of the attack, such as photographs, veterinary reports and bills, and correspondence.

If your pet is bitten by a dog classified as 'dangerous' under the Dangerous Dogs Act 1991, you should inform the police (see immediately below, section 3.5.2).

Note: appeal may be made to a county court against an order for a dog to be destroyed but not against an order to keep the dog under control.

3.5.2 The Dangerous Dogs Act 1991

3.5.2(a) Fighting dogs

In response to some attacks on people by imported species of fighting dogs, the Dangerous Dogs Act 1991 was introduced. Under the Act, the owner of such a dog was required to notify the police, take out third party insurance, and have the dog neutered and permanently marked by a tattoo or implant to prove ownership. These requirements had to be met by November 1991, otherwise the dog became 'illegal'. The breeds of dog to which the Act relates are 'types' known as the pit bull terrier, the Japanese Tosa, the Dogo Argentino and the Fila Brazilero. The Home Secretary may, by order, also designate other types of dogs which appear to him to be bred for fighting or to have the characteristics of a type bred for that purpose.

NB: the ban not only covers these breeds, but also includes cross-breeds of these types of dog, although problems of identification remain. Liability insurance is compulsory.

The Act states that you must not:

a) breed, or breed from, any such dog
b) sell or exchange such a dog, advertise or offer such a dog for sale or exchange
c) make, or offer to make, a gift of such a dog, or advertise it as a gift
d) allow such a dog to be in a public place without a muzzle and without being kept on a lead; or
e) abandon such a dog, or allow it to stray.

Any person who commits an offence under (a) to (e) above is liable on summary conviction to imprisonment for up to six months or a fine of up to £5,000, or both. The court can order the dog to be put down.

Certain amendments to the Act were introduced in 1997 which allowed an owner to register the dog provided:

• it does not constitute a general danger; and
• there was a good reason for failure to register it before November 1991.

3.5.2(b) Other breeds covered by the Dangerous Dogs Act

As we have seen, it is also an offence under the Act to allow any breed of dog to be dangerously out of control in a public place. The same applies if there is 'reasonable apprehension' that an animal out of control in a public place might cause injury – even if it does not actually do so (see above, section 3.4.1).

The Act goes further, however. If the owner or person in charge of a dog allows it to enter a place which is not a 'public place' but where it is not permitted, for example, a neighbour's garden, and while it is there

a) it injures any person; or
b) there are grounds to fear that it will do so,

the dog's owner is responsible for failing to keep his dog under proper control. An actual injury is considered 'an aggravated offence'.

The courts have power to order that a dog that has injured someone should be put down, if the circumstances warrant it, and can disqualify its owner from keeping other dogs.

3.6 Guard dogs

Under the Guard Dogs Act 1975, criminal penalties may be imposed for keeping a guard dog unless a competent handler is present and a sufficient warning notice is displayed at the entrance to the premises. See also the chapter on *Accidents*, section 4.3.2.

3.7 Dog breeding

The majority of dog breeders act responsibly and operate in a manner which takes into account the welfare of the breeding dogs and their offspring. However, in the latter part of the 1990s, concerns were raised about low standards of care in some dog-breeding businesses or 'puppy farms' where some breeders appeared to put profit before animal welfare. Rules to clamp down on such activities were introduced in the Breeding and Sale of Dogs (Welfare) Act 1999.

3.7.1 Puppy farm measures

The 1999 Act requires that:

• there should be local authority inspections of breeding establishments
• bitches should not be mated until they are at least one year old
• bitches should give birth to no more than six litters in a lifetime
• accurate breeding records be maintained by the establishment
• there should be tighter controls on the sale of dogs by dealers and pet shops
• traded dogs should be identified as such.

The Act imposes stiff penalties for offenders, including imprisonment.

☞ *You have good reason to suspect that a nearby breeding establishment is failing to maintain proper standards.*

> If you suspect that an establishment is flouting the provisions of the Act, the best course of action is to report your suspicions to the local authority or to the local RSPCA. It is not recommended that you take the matter up directly with the owners.

The government is considering requiring those who make a business of dogwalking and 'pet sitting' to be licensed.

4   HORSES AND THE LAW

4.1   May I keep a horse in my field?

Before acquiring a horse or pony you must first consider its maintenance, i.e. whether you can provide proper stabling and grazing. Even if you already own a suitable field, it is important to check whether there are any restrictive covenants on the property or covenants concerning rights of way or drainage (see the chapter on *Neighbours*). You must also consider the question of fencing so you must check your title deeds and liaise with your neighbours if necessary. You will also need to bear these matters in mind if you are considering the lease or loan of a horse – see below, section 4.3. Do consult your legal advisor with regard to these and any other possible restrictions.

4.2   Buying a horse or pony

Once you have established where you can stable and graze a horse or pony, you must then consider the costs entailed.

Keeping a horse is an expensive pursuit. Apart from accommodation, other costs include:

- feeding
- maintenance
- insurance
- grazing (if you have to lease a field)
- tack
- grooming
- veterinary fees
- training etc.

(this list is not exhaustive).

Welfare leaflets on caring for a horse or pony are available from the British Horse Society (see DIRECTORY).

4.2.1   Making the purchase

Generally, horses are bought and sold by way of private sale or by auction. Enter into any purchase with care, with due regard to your own rights under a contract of sale, as well as the obligations of the seller (see above, section 1 on *Buying a pet* and the chapter on *Goods and Services*, sections 3.1.1 and 3.1.3). You should also endeavour to have the animal checked by a vet.

4.2.2   Buying at auction

All the cautionary rules which relate to buying at auction sales apply particularly to buying horses at auction so do take great care to read all the conditions of sale (see chapter on *Goods and Services*, section 4.5.2). Before bidding, examine the horse carefully or, if you do not feel expert enough to rely on your own examination, have the animal checked on your behalf.

4.2.3   Horse passports

Because of a decision of the European Commission, all horses and ponies are required to have a unique registration number and 'passport' by 31 December 2003. The underlying reason is to prevent horses entering the human food chain if they have received certain veterinary medicines, but the legal rule applies even if the animal is not ultimately intended for human consumption. The equine industry believes that this will also help to improve the quality of the British herd by preventing overbreeding, and lessening the incentive to keep poor quality horses in poor condition. Local authority trading standards departments will be responsible for enforcing the legislation.

You can obtain a passport by applying to one of the private-sector organisations authorised by the Department of the Environment, Food and Rural Affairs (DEFRA). The full list is obtainable from the Department (see DIRECTORY) or online at *www.defra.gov.uk/animalsh/tracing/equine_societies.pdf*. Some of the organisations deal only with particular breeds, others will issue passports for all. The cost of the passport is on average between £20 and £30.

If the owner of the horse declares in the passport that the horse is not intended for human consumption, there will be no requirement to record the date of administration of certain veterinary medicines to the horse.

4.3   Leasing or loaning a horse or pony

In order to reduce costs, horse owners frequently enter into formal or informal arrangements to lease or loan horses and ponies. There are various types of loan agreements but in all cases, it is important that the rights and obligations of owner and borrower are clearly understood.

There are numbers of problems that may arise. For example, a horse may have an accident, get injured, and have to be put down. It may involve someone else in an accident, e.g. the driver of a car on the road, or a stable girl who is grooming it. It may be prone to illness. Certain horses may have a 'vice', such as shying at passing cars.

If the agreement does not specify responsibilities in such cases, it is easy to foresee that a dispute may arise – even between friends who have entered into an amicable, informal arrangement. It is also clear that the welfare of the animal involved may suffer as a result of a disagreement.

☞   *Mary has passed her A-levels and intends doing a course in environmental studies. The nearest college is 100 miles from Mary's home so she will only be returning on vacations. She has kept a horse since the age of 14 in a field which her parents lease for that purpose. Mary's friend, Ann, has offered to look after the horse in her absence provided that she can ride it.*

4.3.1   The borrower's position

As far as Ann is concerned, on the one hand she does not have to make the capital outlay involved in buying a horse for herself, or bear all the costs involved in leasing accommodation for it. On the other hand, however, she must consider all the other expenses involved, see section 4.2 above.

She must also be sure that the horse is a suitable one for her ride, e.g. it is not unruly or beyond her capacity to control. She must remember that she will be responsible for the animal's well-being and will have to know what to look for to prevent problems which may arise. She must also make sure that the horse is covered by insurance and, in case of an accident involving someone else, that there is also third-party liability in place. It is important to note whether it is Ann or Mary who is expected to pay the premiums on these policies. In addition Ann should take out personal insurance against an accident – horse-riding is a sport which involves serious, indeed sometimes fatal, risks even to very experienced riders.

There is also the question of veterinary expenses (see sections 10 and 11 below).

4.3.2   The lender's position

Mary will be able to leave home for long periods without having to sell her horse or to worry that it is not being properly looked after or exercised. However, she needs to ensure that Ann is sufficiently responsible to take care of her horse and is aware of her duties towards it.

It is also very much in her own interests to ensure that the points listed above in relation to expenses, insurance etc. are properly understood. In addition she should ensure that her vet is informed of the new arrangement and it is made clear who will be paying his or her fees.

Mary should also specify that Ann will be the only rider. The question of a contribution towards the cost of the lease of the field will also have to be sorted out both with her parents and her friend.

Take heed: from the outline above, it is clear that an agreement between them should be made in writing and signed by both Mary and Ann. If either is in doubt as to their rights and responsibilities, they should consult a legal advisor.

For a sample loan agreement, contact the British Horse Society (see DIRECTORY or online at *www.bhs.org.uk*).

4.4   Taking a horse on to the road

Horse riding is allowed along carriageways and bridleways but not along footpaths except with permission of the owner of the land (see the chapter on *The Countryside*, section 1.1.7). A person taking a horse along a footpath, without express permission to do so, therefore commits trespass and must get off the land if ordered to do so.

Roads used as public paths (RUPPs) are to be reclassified as a new category and will be known as Restricted Byways having a public right of way for all traffic except motor vehicles, i.e. those on foot, horseback or cycle, and for horse-drawn vehicles (see chapter on *The Countryside* section 1.1.8(b)).

4.4.1   Safety

The current Highway Code gives instructions to horseriders as to how to take care of themselves and their horses on the road (see rules 34–41). It is estimated that there are several accidents each day involving riders and horses and that the numbers of such accidents are increasing all the time. So indeed are the numbers of people who ride horses for sport – there are estimated to be about three million people who ride regularly.

Riding helmets should conform to BSI kitemark safety standards and be well-fitting and in good condition. Children under the age of 14 are required to wear a helmet by law which must be securely strapped on. If you ride at night make sure that you are wearing reflective clothing and that your horse has reflective bands above the fetlock joints. As with motoring, failure to obey the Highway Code is not in itself a crime, but can be used as evidence in proceedings, (e.g. for personal injury to a passing pedestrian) in order to establish negligence on the part of the rider.

Again, as with dogs, so with horses: a keeper is liable if he or she knew or ought to have known of a horse's propensity to kick or bolt or otherwise be unruly, with resulting injury to persons or to livestock.

4.5   Horse thefts

Unfortunately, horses have become the target of both thieves and animal sadists. As a horse owner you will wish to take all necessary steps to prevent loss or injury to your horse or pony. Do consult your local crime prevention officer for advice on how to ensure the safety of your animal.

4.6   Riding establishments

The Riding Establishments Act 1970 provides that a person can only keep a riding establishment if a licence has been granted by a local authority. Generally the business involves the hiring out of horses for riding, or the provision of riding instruction, or both. Premises where horses are merely stabled do not need a licence.

The Act specifies that in deciding whether or not to grant a licence the local authority must consider whether the applicant is suitable and qualified in managing horses, or employs someone to manage the establishment who is suitably qualified.

Consideration must also be given to the condition of the horses and to whether the animals are suitable for providing riding instruction. Specifications are also laid down as to accommodation and hygiene. The Royal College of Veterinary Surgeons and the British Veterinary Association keep a list of vets who are responsible for inspecting these establishments for the local authorities.

By statute the licence holder must hold a current insurance policy against liability for any injury sustained by those who:

- are hiring a horse in return for payment, or
- are receiving riding instruction.

The insurance must also cover injury to any third party.

☞   *Your daughter wants to learn to ride. You are concerned to know what you need to ascertain in order to ensure that she will be well taught and safe.*

In addition to the above, the Act states that an instructor will be expected to show the skills appropriate for his or her level of qualification. The horse must also be fit and sound, as well as being suitable for the pupil's standard of experience. You are also entitled to expect that the horse's tack is in a good and safe condition. Ask to see the insurance policy. The Act also specifies that no horse shall be provided for riding instruction without supervision by a responsible person over 16 years of age.

The Safety Department of the British Horse Society has a riding and road safety training programme as well as running a riding and road safety test to educate riders and reduce danger on our roads: tel. 01926 707 803.

In general, it is important that, in asking for teaching or for a straight hiring, you do not exaggerate your experience. If you do so and are given a horse that you are unable to control, it may be that you and not the establishment was negligent. See the chapter on *Accidents*, section 3.2. You may also find yourself liable for any resultant damage to the horse!

☞ *You have recently joined a riding school and have been taken out on a ride with a group of others along a bridleway. Your horse tends to hang back from the others to crop grass and you have not got the expertise to keep it firmly under your control. From a nearby road there is a sudden sound of a car backfiring and your horse turns, injuring a passerby.*

If you had been an experienced rider, you might have been liable in negligence for failing to control your horse. However, in this case, the school itself will probably be found negligent as it should not have handed that particular horse to a novice rider and then failed to ensure proper supervision.

4.7 Vaccination of horses

Your local veterinary practice will be able to advise you on the vaccinations your horse or pony needs. Note that many stud owners will require proof of vaccination before they allow a mare on to the premises.

4.8 Weeds poisonous to horses

Under the Weeds Act 1959, the Department for the Environment, Food and Rural Affairs can take action where injurious weeds are threatening to spread from neighbouring land to farms where horses are kept or used. Of the weeds covered by the Act, ragwort in particular is poisonous for horses, ponies, donkeys and other animals – if they eat ragwort it can lead to untreatable liver damage and death.

DEFRA has produced booklets on the control of harmful weeds.

See *www.defra.gov.uk/environ/weedsact/default.htm* or telephone 088459 335577.

5 CRUELTY TO ANIMALS

Criminal sanctions exist against owners and others who have charge of a domestic animal and who cause it suffering. A prosecution can be brought against anyone who is cruel to an animal under the Protection of Animals Act 1911. In addition, a person who abandons an animal whether permanently or temporarily in circumstances likely to cause the animal suffering is guilty of an offence of cruelty under the Abandonment of Animals Act 1960. However, it is not merely a question of how long an animal has been left unattended: it has to be proved that the person charged had totally disregarded his or her duty to care for the animal. There are a number of other animal welfare statutes in force. These are currently being reviewed and new extensive animal welfare legislation is being planned.

For example, if you leave a dog in a locked car, on a hot day, it may not be a question only of how long you have left the animal unattended. Even a short period may cause the dog unnecessary suffering in high summer through heat stress. It could even prove fatal.

Conveying or carrying any animal in such a manner as to cause it unnecessary suffering is also an offence. Other acts of cruelty include not only physical abuse, such as beating or ill-treating an animal, but also causing it terror or teasing it to the point which infuriates it.

In some breeds, puppies' tails are often docked for cosmetic reasons or to make grooming easier. As the law stands, docking a dog's tail is illegal if carried out by a lay person; it should only be carried out by a vet and only for therapeutic or prophylactic reasons (otherwise it amounts to professional misconduct). The practice is soon to be made illegal.

Statistics show that most cruelty convictions involve dogs as victims.

For the protection of wild mammals and other laws regarding the ill-treatment of animals, see also the chapter on *The Countryside*, section 7.3.

(Laws governing experiments involving animals are outside the scope of this book.)

5.1   Reporting possible offences

Do note: organisations such as the RSPCA rely on the public to keep them informed. They cannot insist that you give your name and address when reporting an incident of alleged cruelty, but would prefer if you do so. You can be reassured, however, that all such information is kept totally confidential. Note the RSPCA Cruelty helpline: 0870 55 55 999

So if you know of an animal that is being ill-treated or neglected, your first step is to report it to the RSPCA or Blue Cross or one of the other suitable organisations listed in the DIRECTORY at the end of this chapter. Give as many details as you can: e.g. of the owner (if known). Also give the animal's location and what the problem is, if you can.

Do remember: welfare organisations must follow certain procedures and always act within the law.

Even if you think that nothing is being done, do not take the law into your own hands and try to rescue a neglected animal as you may be breaking the law yourself. There is no automatic power to seize an animal.

If you have genuine grounds for belief that an animal is being cruelly mistreated, you can complain to your local police station. The police investigate formal complaints and may request the intervention of a vet or local RSPCA officer. Only when an animal is in such poor condition that it is actually 'suffering', as defined by statute, can it be taken away from its owner without permission.

6   STRAYS

The owner of an animal, whether dangerous or not, is under a duty to prevent it straying on to the highway (except in areas where land is customarily unfenced as in the North of England, or on village greens). If an accident results from a driver attempting to avoid an animal which has strayed on to the road, therefore, its owner will be liable, at least if he or she knows of its habit of wandering.

Under the Animals Act 1971, the keeper of an animal of a non-dangerous species is liable for damage caused by the animal if there is a likelihood of damage being caused because the particular animal has unusual characteristics, or because such animals have particular tendencies in certain circumstances.

6.1   Stray horses

☞ *Your horses cause injury to a motorist when galloping down a highway at night, having been released from their field by a malicious neighbour. The driver claims damages on the grounds that horses in the dark tend to panic and gallop aimlessly in any direction.*

The real cause of the accident was your neighbour's action. You are, therefore, not liable, although you would have been liable for your animals straying on to the highway had the horses escaped through your own negligence.

Horses and ponies are occasionally found wandering loose. If you find a stray horse, you must report it to the police, the local council, or a rescue organisation. Check also if there is a local pound where the horse will be kept safe.

☞ *You have found a stray pony wandering on the road. It was clearly in danger and you took it to a field which belongs to you for safekeeping. You have informed the police who impounded it but now think that the pony has been abandoned as they have been unable to trace the owner. You wonder if you would be allowed to keep the horse.*

Do consult a legal advisor. In some cases, the rule of 'finders keepers' may apply but you must first ascertain whether you would need to advertise it or what other steps you ought to take to ensure that the horse has indeed been abandoned.

Note: there are certain areas of the country, such as Dartmoor and the New Forest, where roads are unfenced and the native ponies (which do nonetheless have owners) wander at large.

6.2   Stray dogs

Under the Environmental Protection Act 1990, local authorities appoint dog wardens who are responsible for dealing with stray dogs on highways and public places. A stray dog may also be handed over to the police. Dogs unclaimed after seven days can be put down, given away, or sold.

Similar rules apply to dogs found worrying livestock on land; they may be seized and detained (see section 4.1.1.(a) in the chapter on *The Countryside*).

A register must keep particulars of seized dogs including a brief description, breed (if known) and any distinctive physical characteristics; any information on a tag or collar; the date, time and place of the seizure etc. If a dog is put down, the date of disposal must be recorded; and if the dog is sold or given away, the name and address of the person, and the price (if any).

The register is open for public inspection.

If the owner claims the animal, he or she is liable to pay for the costs of its detention.

☞ *You have found a stray dog. You would like to keep it. You approach your local dog warden and ask if you can become the dog's owner.*

The dog warden must enter a record of the dog (see above). He will also record the date and place where you found it, as well as your name and address. If the dog's owner can be found, he or she will be contacted and asked to collect it. Otherwise if you can offer assurances that you are able to take proper care of the dog, you may be able to keep it.

6.3   Stray cats

If a stray cat is found which appears to be sick or injured, you can telephone the Cruelty helpline: tel. 0870 55 55 999, or one of the other charitable organisations.

6.4   Reuniting owner and pet

Apart from the PetLog database which keeps details of animals that have had identification microchips inserted beneath the skin (tel. 0870 606 6751), the RSPCA has a register of lost and found animals, as do the organisations Petsearch (tel: 0121 743 4133) and Pet Match (tel: 0870 1600 999). Other organisations are listed in the DIRECTORY. Among other advice, the RSPCA also recommends that if you lose your pet, you contact your local authority, your vet, animal shelters and the police.

7   PASSPORTS FOR PETS – THE PET TRAVEL SCHEME

When we think of bringing animals into this country from abroad, our immediate anxiety is to keep the country rabies-free. Indeed, a great deal of the legislation, including the 'Passports for Pets' scheme, and the various quarantine requirements are directed – in the main – at the prevention and control of rabies. Animals which are rabies-susceptible include dogs, cats, rabbits, mice, rats, gerbils, and jerboas.

However, there are further controls in place to prevent animals which are not necessarily rabies-prone from posing health risks to other animals and to humans. Thus import licences are still required. People who own cage birds, such as budgies and canaries, can bring them into this country with an import certificate provided their pet is from an EU Member State. General import licences are also required for horses, and a specific import licence may be needed, if, for example, you wished to bring a pet lamb into this country. However, one would have to check, as well, that your pet has not been in contact with an animal such as a dog, which is subject to the rabies-related quarantine regulations. You will also need a licence if you decide to import an exotic reptile (see also section 1.3.1 above). In addition, import licences are required in order to conserve certain species and to protect against illegal smuggling.

With regard to this section, which deals specifically with 'Passport for Pets', the Government has introduced a scheme under which cats and dogs are able to travel between Britain and specified territories without having to spend six months in quarantine. The procedure is set out in fact sheets available online at *www.defra.gov.uk/animalh/quarantine/factsheet/sheet4.shtml* or by telephoning the DEFRA helpline at 08459 335577. Please do check these sources, as the procedures, countries included and permissible routes may change from time to time, and the information given below is for general guidance only.

7.1   Qualifying under the scheme

The Pet Travel Scheme (PETS) as at present set up:

- only applies to pet cats and dogs
- is limited to animals coming from the countries and territories listed at section 7.5 below
- operates only on certain sea, air and rail routes to England (see section 7.6 below).

Do note: other animals are expected to be allowed to join the Passport for Pets scheme: the government has announced that it is working on a new list of species for inclusion in the scheme, such as rabbits, hamsters, guinea-pigs, gerbils and mice. It is also hoped to extend the scheme to other countries; some long-haul countries have already been added to the list.

7.2   Eligibility

To be eligible to qualify for exemption from quarantine, your pet cat or dog will have to meet the following conditions:

a) it must have had an electronic microchip inserted beneath the skin (see also above, section 3.1)
b) after the microchip has been inserted, the animal must be vaccinated against rabies using an inactivated vaccine (it will also have to have regular booster vaccinations)
c) after it has been vaccinated, a blood test must be carried out at a laboratory that has been recognised by the Department of the Environment, Food and Rural Affairs (DEFRA)
d) it must be accompanied by a health certificate certifying that the above requirements have been met. This certificate must be signed by a veterinary surgeon, who may be a private vet but must be Government-approved by the country concerned for the issuing and signing of the appropriate documentation.

NB: do check the dates of validity on the certificate. It expires on the date that your pet requires its booster vaccination.

e) it must be treated against tapeworm and ticks.

☞ *You have been informed that blood sampling must be carried out at least six months before you travel to the UK with your pet. You wonder why it all takes so much time.*

The blood test result must show that the vaccine has given your pet sufficient protection against rabies. For this reason, six months must elapse before entry into the UK.

The certificate will be valid for a specified period of time, expiring on the date the pet's booster vaccination is required.

7.3   Other necessary treatment

Not less than 24 hours and not more than 48 hours before embarkation for the UK, your pet must have been treated against certain parasites and infections which may be acquired by cats and dogs outside the UK. This will also have to be recorded on a health certificate, called a 'certificate of treatment' signed by a Government-recognised vet.

☞ *Your pet was treated against parasites but more than 48 hours have elapsed and you have not yet set out on your journey.*

Your journey will have to be postponed, and you will have to get your pet treated again in the correct period. You will then be issued with another certificate of treatment.

7.3.1   Prevention better than cure

If you take your pet abroad from the UK, it may fall victim to tickborne infections which do not occur in the UK. It is expected that as animals travel more internationally – as with humans –

certain diseases will become more widespread. You are therefore advised to consult your vet before you leave about the preventative measures which you can take against ticks and fleas. Recently one of the first dogs to leave these shores under the PETS scheme died from a tick-bite which it received across the Channel.

7.4   Operation of the PETS scheme

Before you enter the UK on one of the scheme routes, the transport company will check your animal's microchip and health certificates. If all is well, your pet will be allowed to enter the UK. If not, your pet will have to go into quarantine on return to the UK, or, in the case of pets from outside the UK, return to the country it has come from. (See section 8 below.)

Take due care: you must make sure that you check that all is in order before you attempt to travel, to avoid possible disappointments.

7.5   Qualifying countries

Pet cats and dogs resident in the UK may visit one or more of the countries below and return to the UK under the scheme without the need for quarantine. Cats and dogs that come from one of these countries and have been resident there for six months may also enter the UK without need for quarantine.

Andorra, Austria, Bahrain, Belgium, Canada, Denmark, Finland, Germany, Greece, Gibraltar, Finland, Iceland, Italy, Liechtenstein, Luxembourg, Monaco, the Netherlands, Norway, Portugal, San Marino, Switzerland, Spain, Sweden, the Vatican and specific rabies-free islands, including Australia, Cyprus, Japan, Malta, New Zealand, Singapore and the USA.

('France' excludes French Overseas Departments and Territories; 'Norway' excludes Svalbarl; 'Portugal' includes the Azores and Madeira, and 'Spain' includes the Canary Islands but excludes Ceuta and Melilla.)

Note: that the order of the required procedures may differ from those described in this chapter if your pet has been resident in Denmark or France. There are also special requirements for pets travelling from Cyprus. For long-haul countries the procedures are also slightly different.

You will need to sign a declaration that you have not taken your pet outside the permitted countries.

If your pet has travelled outside the qualifying countries in the last six months, it will not be allowed to enter the UK under the PETS scheme and you will have to place it in quarantine on your arrival here (see below, section 8).

Cats and dogs resident in the Channel Islands, the Isle of Man and the Republic of Ireland may also be able to enter the UK under the PETS Scheme from these countries, provided the official certification is in place.

Pet animals resident anywhere within the UK continue to be able to travel freely around the UK without the need for quarantine. Such pets are not subject to quarantine, nor to the Pet Travel Scheme – in spite of devolution!

7.6   Applicable routes

Among others the routes include the Calais to Dover sea crossings, Eurotunnel Shuttle Services, certain sea routes into Portsmouth from France, and certain air routes into London Heathrow from Europe. You should check your proposed route with the operator, or call the PETS helpline: 0870 241 1710.

Note: transport companies may make a charge to transport your animal under the Scheme.

7.7   Guide dogs and hearing dogs

☞ *You are registered blind. You would like to visit your daughter who lives in Gibraltar. You would have to travel with your dog and would like to know if this is feasible under the PETS scheme.*

Dogs providing assistance to the disabled, including guide dogs and hearing dogs, are eligible for the scheme like any other dogs.

7.8 Steps to be taken

The procedures involved are lengthy and there can be no last-minute decisions if you wish to take advantage of the Scheme.

☞ *You have to return to London from Paris as the bank for which you work is moving you to its new branch in the City. You wish to take your two dogs with you and avoid placing them in quarantine. You want advice on how to prepare your animals to qualify for the Scheme.*

First and foremost: prepare well before the time you intend to travel, by:

a) getting your pet microchipped by your vet (see section 7.9)
b) getting your pet vaccinated by your vet (see section 7.10)
c) getting your pet blood-tested (see section 7.11).

Additional warning: because blood-testing capacity is very limited at laboratories, you may find you cannot use the scheme because your animal cannot be blood-tested in time.

7.8.1 Costs

You will have to pay for the insertion of a microchip, and for vaccination and blood testing.

For UK residents, it has been estimated that microchipping will cost in the region of £30, initial vaccination around £50 and a blood test about £70. Annual vaccination boosters are likely to be around £30. Veterinary Inspectors may also charge for issuing the official PETS certificate.

7.9 Microchip identification

A permanent number radio-frequency identification device (RFID), in the form of a microchip, must be inserted under the skin of the animal to identify it. The Government has not specified a particular type or brand of microchip to be used, but strongly recommends that it conform to ISO (International Standards Organisation) standard 11784 or the Annex A to ISO standard 11785.

1) You should check with your vet to ensure that the microchip meets an ISO specification.
2) The animal must be microchipped before it is vaccinated against rabies.
3) Your vet will implant the microchip according to the manufacturer's instructions. Ask your vet to check the number of the microchip once it has been fitted.

☞ *Your pet could not be identified properly.*

If the checking staff cannot read your pet's microchip, because for example it does not conform to the usual standards, you may have to provide your own microchip reader. If, on the other hand, the microchip cannot be found, it means that your pet either will have to go into quarantine (see section 8 below) or will have to be refitted.

7.10 Vaccination against rabies

The vaccine to be used must be a rabies vaccine authorised for use in the UK, or by the Government of the qualifying country in which you are resident. If in doubt, consult your vet. In the UK, rabies vaccinations are being made freely available to veterinary surgeons.

7.10.1 Timing of vaccinations

Your animal must be at least three months old before it is vaccinated.

Vaccinations can take place at any time after the pet has been fitted with a microchip, once your vet has confirmed that the animal is identifiable by a permanent number microchip implant. The vaccination record card will include details such as:

• the animal's age or date of birth
• microchip number, and (if known) the date of insertion
• date of vaccination
• due date of next vaccination (or booster).

☞ *Your pet has already been vaccinated against rabies when you lived abroad. You are told that it must be re-vaccinated after having a microchip fitted.*

Take heed: even if a pet has a record of previous vaccination against rabies without prior microchip identification, it has to be vaccinated again after insertion of the chip.

7.10.2   Re-vaccination (or boosters)

After an animal has been vaccinated against rabies, it must be given booster vaccinations. This must be done at the intervals specified by the vaccine manufacturers. Your vet will be able to give you details.

7.11   Blood testing

The vet who vaccinated your pet can arrange the necessary blood test for you. You must take the animal's vaccination card with you when the blood sample is taken.

The blood test must be performed at a laboratory recognised by DEFRA. You should leave it to your vet to contact the Veterinary Laboratories Agency (VLA) in Weybridge or another accepted laboratory about blood testing. At present, ten European laboratories are recognised but others in Europe are likely to be added as the scheme develops.

Should your pet fail its blood test it will have to be re-vaccinated and blood-tested again.

Note: blood tests performed by laboratories before they were recognised by DEFRA are not acceptable. This is because DEFRA can only be certain through the recognition procedure that the laboratory meets the necessary quality standards.

Blood-testing capacity may be limited. Accordingly, you should have your vet check on how long the wait for the test is likely to be before having your animal vaccinated. You may decide to delay vaccination if the wait is too long.

7.11.1   Action after the blood test

You will have to wait six months after your pet's blood was submitted for sampling to a recognised laboratory before the animal may enter the UK. However, there is an exception for cats and dogs resident in the British Isles (including the Republic of Ireland) that were microchipped, vaccinated and blood-sampled prior to the date of the scheme coming into operation. Such animals do not have to wait six months from the date a blood sample was taken before coming back to the UK after a trip abroad.

Note: no certificate will be issued to allow your pet to enter the UK unless the blood test shows that the animal is now immune from rabies.

Only certain blood testing laboratories are DEFRA-recognised.

7.12   Relevant documentation

To allow a pet animal to return to the UK after having left for one of the qualifying countries, a pet health certificate will have to have been issued by a local Veterinary Inspector. For pets resident in a qualifying country and coming to the UK, a pet animal health certificate is to be issued by the country concerned.

Your pet may also need a separate certificate to show that it meets the health requirements of the country (or countries) that you are visiting or travelling through.

Take heed: these certificates may be different from those under the Pet Travel Scheme. UK pet owners wishing to travel abroad with an animal should contact their local DEFRA Animal Health Office for advice.

8   QUARANTINE RULES

If you are bringing a pet animal into the UK and are unable or unwilling to utilise the PETS scheme outlined in section 7 above, the quarantine rules must be complied with. The Rabies (Importation of Dogs, Cats and other Mammals) Order 1974 provides for an animal landed without a licence to be directed into quarantine, re-exported or destroyed and its owner prosecuted. Serious offences may be tried on indictment at a Crown Court where offenders are liable to penalties of up to a year's imprisonment, an unlimited fine, or both. It is important therefore to ensure that all the licensing requirements are met. As well as cats and dogs, there are other rabies-susceptible species which are controlled by the Order. (A copy of the Order can be obtained from the Stationery Office, P.O. Box 276, London SW8 5DT, Tel. 020 7187 39090.)

When any of these animals are brought into the UK, they have to go into quarantine for six months.

Chinchillas, ferrets, gerbils, guinea pigs, hamsters, mice, rabbits and rats are all covered by the order.

Details of other mammals controlled by the Order may be obtained by contacting the relevant Agricultural Department.

The procedures are set out at *www.defra.gov.uk/animalh/quarantine/qindex.shtml*. An information pack is also available from the DEFRA helpline: 08459 335577. Please check these sources, as the procedures may change from time to time.

8.1   Completing your application form

If you are bringing an animal into quarantine in the UK, you must be issued with an import licence. There is an application form for this licence. This can be filled in by the quarantine premises on your behalf.

If you want to complete the application form yourself, you should do so only when you have received confirmation of your arrangements from both the quarantine premises and the carrying agent. You should then send the form to DEFRA. Then:

- a licence will be sent to your chosen carrying agent
- a 'boarding document' will be sent to you or to your named representative. This is the written evidence which a shipper or airline will need to see before allowing your animal to be carried into the UK
- you will also receive a red label (see 8.2 below).

8.2   Transporting your animal

You may bring your pet into the UK under a quarantine licence, either by air or by sea. In either case, DEFRA will send you (or your representative) a red label which must be completed and attached to your pet's crate. This label is issued only once you have an import licence for your pet and will be sent to you along with the boarding documents (see immediately above). The label must be completed and attached to the crate before your pet begins its journey. It is there to identify the crate as one that is carrying an animal subject to quarantine. You have to fill in the following information on the label:

- owner's name and address
- name and address of quarantine premises
- name of carrying agent.

8.2.1   Animals travelling by air

The International Air Transport Association (IATA) lays down standards for crates but the pet-owner has the primary responsibility to make sure his or her pet is properly confined for transport.

☞ *You have a large dog and are about to undertake a long flight from the Far East to the UK. You are concerned that the crate may be too confined for your pet's comfort. You also would like to know whether you can handle the animal during a stopover in Hong Kong.*

Under the Welfare of Animals (Transport) Order 1997, 'No person shall transport any animals in a way which causes or is likely to cause injury or unnecessary suffering.'

The airline will advise you on the correct size of crate. The IATA standards require that a crate must be sufficiently roomy to allow an animal to stand, sit, and lie down in a natural position. It must also be able to turn around easily. Your pet must travel in the freight compartment as 'manifest cargo' and not as excess or passenger baggage. Condition 2 of the import licence gives specifications of all containers to be used for transporting dogs and cats, e.g. that they must be completely nose- and paw-proof.

Your dog cannot travel in the cabin compartment or as accompanied passenger baggage. Further, it must not be handed over in transit to the owner.

For guidance on purchasing a crate for your pet, contact:

- a local veterinary surgeon
- the airline; or
- the quarantine premises.

Thorough advice on preparing your pet for a journey is found on the official DEFRA website. Their fact sheets are particularly helpful: *www.defra.gov.uk/animalh/quarantine/qindex.shtml*.

8.2.2 Animals travelling by sea

Your pet must be crated before it is allowed to leave the vessel, and the red label must be attached. At most ports, the carrying agent will board the vessel to collect your pet.

8.3 Quarantine requirements outside the UK

The various requirements of overseas countries in relation to other countries are beyond the scope of this book. If you intend to move to another country outside the UK and wish to take your pet with you, you should contact the immigration authority of that country to ascertain what, if any, restrictions and requirements there may be.

8.4 Your animal has landed – quarantine requirements

☞ *You would like some advice on choosing a suitable kennel for your dog as you feel that the six-month separation is going to be difficult.*

Kennels and catteries are privately owned so that the government takes responsibility only for ensuring that they meet its health requirements, e.g. proper isolation conditions.

However, the Department of the Environment, Food and Rural Affairs (DEFRA) issues a voluntary Code of Practice for the welfare of dogs and cats in quarantine premises. A copy of the Code can be obtained from the Ministry: Tel. 08459 556000.

You can also search on-line for sites which give details of catteries and kennels and the facilities which they offer, e.g. the DEFRA website has a map of the UK listing details of kennels and catteries which are audited for quarantine purposes. Those which abide by its Code of Practice are marked with an asterisk.

Owners of quarantine premises which abide by the Code are inspected by staff from the State's veterinary service.

Do note: under the Animal Health (Amendment) Act 1998, for the first time, DEFRA is empowered to set statutory welfare standards in place. These are in the process of being drawn up and a public consultation exercise is underway.

In choosing suitable kennels, you will consider:

- the level of comfort and care for your pet; and
- travelling distance from your home.

After you have chosen suitable kennels, you will need to reserve accommodation for your pet. It is advisable to book well in advance, particularly in the holiday months. It is recommended that you agree a contract with the owner of the premises. If so wished, a maximum of three pets of the same species belonging to the same owner may share accommodation; the owner or the veterinary superintendent at the quarantine premises may arrange this for you. The financial arrangements arrived at for quarantine are entirely a matter between you and the owner. See also section 8.4.2 below.

8.4.1 Authorised carrying agent

It will also be necessary to reserve the services of an authorised carrying agent. That agent will meet your pet at the port or airport of disembarkation and will be responsible for the animal's security whilst in transit to the quarantine premises. The quarantine premises may be able to provide this service for you.

Finally, check which port or airport in the UK your pet will be arriving at as animals going into quarantine can only be landed at certain ports and airports.

Most quarantine premises will deal with all the paperwork on your behalf, including submitting your application form for an import licence to the UK Government, arranging for your pet to be collected at the port or airport of landing, and clearance through customs.

8.4.2 Cost of quarantine

You will be responsible for all costs associated with the landing, transit and quarantine of your pet. Quarantine and transport charges vary considerably. Details of charges can be obtained direct from quarantine premises and carrying agents.

In considering the costs of quarantine, you should also note that the period of detention may, in exceptional circumstances, be extended beyond the normal six calendar months if:

- an outbreak of rabies occurring at the quarantine premises; or
- your animal shares accommodation with one that dies.

You would then have to meet the cost of any extended period of quarantine.

8.4.3 Arranging contracts with the kennel owners

When agreeing a contract, you are advised to ensure that the following points are covered:

Moving your pet to different premises or re-exporting it – what would be the period of notice?

Death in quarantine – you should agree what you will have to pay if your animal dies in quarantine.

Deposit and other money paid in advance – would there be refunds, and if so under what circumstances?

Postponements – will you have to pay a penalty if you postpone or cancel the arrival of your pet?

Other matters to consider in your agreement are:

Heating – method of heating and details of charges.

Special diets – is there an extra charge for special diets and would there be any reduction of boarding fees if you supply the food?

Coat care – what are the costs of grooming etc?

Any other additional charges – have these been described in full and agreed?

NB: if you are uncertain of any of the terms of your contract with the quarantine premises, you should make enquiries from a legal advisor who has experience in these matters, or contact one of the organisations listed in the DIRECTORY at the end of this chapter, which may be in a position to offer guidance.

☞ *You have arranged for kennelling near your home so that you can visit your pet. You are now told by the kennel owner that visits may not be allowed.*

Visiting is permitted at the kennel owner's discretion and may also require the agreement of a veterinary superintendent.

8.4.4 Additional charges

Are you sure of the total cost to you of placing your pet in quarantine? For example, have you reckoned on the following?

Airport charges – check on airline airport handling and customs clearance charges that you will be required to pay. Note that, if you are bringing an animal into the UK from outside the European Union, HM Customs and Excise may charge duty on the value of your animal and, under certain circumstances, the cost of the freight. You may also, under certain circumstances, have to pay the costs of holding your animal at the port or airport.

Veterinary fees – you must be given full details of the veterinary charges and how these are passed on to you during the quarantine period. Also consider whether a surcharge will be levied for additional supervision, attendance and nursing.

Insurance – you must establish what insurance is available, together with any associated charges.

8.4.5 Visits from the veterinary superintendent

At each quarantine premises a veterinary superintendent employed by the premises' owner is responsible for the veterinary care of your pet. If you have any questions relating to the health or welfare of your pet, you should bring it to their attention. The quarantine premises will give you the name of the veterinary superintendent.

The superintendent will vaccinate all animals against rabies within 48 hours of their arrival in quarantine. However, this may not be necessary in the case of animals that have been placed in quarantine temporarily as a result of their failing a check under the Pet Travel Scheme arrangements because, for example, you have fulfilled all the relevant legal and medical requirements, but have lost your certificate. Your pet is placed in quarantine temporarily while the carrying agent arranges for a replacement certificate.

8.4.6 Complaints about quarantine conditions

If you have any cause for complaint, you should first discuss it with the owner of the quarantine premises. If you are not satisfied with the responses in relation to:

a) *security or disease* – contact DEFRA.
b) *the welfare of your animal* – contact the veterinary superintendent at the quarantine premises; if you are still not satisfied, having discussed the matter with him/her, you should put your concerns in writing to DEFRA.
c) *the contract or brochure* – contact the Local Trading Standards department.

9 CATTERIES AND KENNELS – HOLIDAY CARE ARRANGEMENTS

If you wish to board your cat or dog while you are on holiday, irrespective of any quarantine requirements, you must enquire about boarding establishments available near your home. Reputable establishments are governed by statute (see 9.1.1 below) and licensed by your local authority or by a veterinary surgeon whom the local authority appoints to issue licences on its behalf. These are issued on an annual basis. You can contact your local authority or your vet who may also be able to provide you with details of suitable kennels and catteries.

9.1.1 Statutory requirements

The Animals Boarding Establishments Act 1963 lists a number of requirements which have to be met in order for a licence to be granted. Among them are:

- animal accommodation, e.g. size of quarters, number of occupants, exercise facilities, ventilation and cleanliness etc.
- supply of food, drink and bedding as well as adequate exercise
- suitable visits of inspection
- control of disease and the need for isolation facilities
- protection of animals in case of fire or other emergency
- register of animals received into the kennel, date of arrival and departure, owner's details – this register to be open for inspection by the local authority.

Furthermore, on producing proper authority, a local authority officer or veterinary surgeon can enter the premises at all reasonable times to inspect them and the animals which are kept there.

Do note: the Act only applies to the 'keeping' of dogs or cats as a main business activity.

☞ *You have been asked by your friend to take care of his dog, together with her litter of puppies, while he is working abroad for three months. He will be paying you for their keep. You wonder if you need any particular permission as you already have three dogs of your own.*

Under the Act, a person is not considered to be keeping a 'boarding establishment for animals' if he provides accommodation for other people's pets, on condition that such accommodation is not his main business activity. There are other matters to consider however, even in an informal arrangement, e.g. whether your friend has insurance to cover fees in case you need to consult a vet about his animal. Also consider whether the number of dogs will not cause a nuisance to your neighbours.

9.1.2 Pet-sitters

There is an increasing trend for pet owners to hire a pet-sitter so that their pets can be cared for at home when they are away, rather than sending the pet to a cattery or kennel. The government is currently investigating whether such pet-sitters should be licensed, although this would not apply to informal arrangements like the one mentioned in 9.1.1 above. The National Association of Registered Pet Sitters is a trade association with a code of practice, whose members are required to be registered and insured (see DIRECTORY).

Inspection and licensing of animal sanctuaries are also to be included in the proposed legislation.

9.2 Code of Conduct

Certain quarantine premises which abide by the voluntary Code of Conduct issued by DEFRA (see section 8.4 above), also provide accommodation for animals while you are on holiday. You can check by contacting the establishments directly.

10 VETERINARY SURGEONS AND THEIR RESPONSIBILITIES

As a pet owner you rely on the professionalism of your vet, just as you do on that of your general practitioner in relation to your personal health. In common with the majority of GPs, the majority of vets will meet their responsibilities. The Royal College of Veterinary Surgeons (RCVS) has issued a Guide to Professional Conduct of Veterinary Surgeons which is available to the general public on its website: *www.rcvs.org.uk*. Alternatively you can order it (cost £10) from the RCVS: tel. 020 7222 2001.

Only vets registered with the Royal College of Veterinary Surgeons (MRCVS) are allowed to practice veterinary surgery in the UK. There are some exemptions (e.g. farmers are permitted to carry out some surgical procedures such as tail docking on lambs, though the practice is now being reviewed by the government). Veterinary nurses are permitted to administer medical treatment or carry out minor surgery on animals not involving entry into a pet's body cavity, at the discretion of their employer. There are proposals to expand the range of permitted procedures which veterinary nurses can legally perform.

10.1 Legal responsibilities

Veterinary surgeons are required to comply with relevant legislation including:

a) the Veterinary Surgeons Act 1986 and associated regulations;
b) the Medicines Act 1968 and associated legislation concerning the use, prescription, sales and supply of veterinary, medicinal and related products;
c) the Health and Safety at Work, Radiation Protection, and other similar legislation applicable to veterinary practice;
d) the Data Protection Acts 1984 and 1999.

There are also a number of other laws, rules and regulations which relate to animal health and welfare, control of disease, breeding, and public health.

Veterinary practices must carry third-party insurance for the protection of the public, and all practising veterinary surgeons are advised to carry professional indemnity insurance.

Veterinary surgeons may also be called upon to act as witnesses or to provide expert evidence in civil or criminal proceedings, for example where a dog is attacked and severely mauled by another one and the owner wishes to sue for compensation. Evidence can provide records of the injuries to the animal, the course of treatment and the costs involved (see above, section 3.5.1). See also the chapter on *The Legal System*, sections 5.10.4 and 5.10.5.

10.2 The caring practitioner

A vet is expected to:

- treat all animals with primary concern for their welfare
- make adequate arrangements for 24-hour emergency cover
- take account the animal's age, the extent of any injuries or disease and its quality of life. An animal's condition may dictate that euthanasia would be a kinder option than treatment
- if a pet owner cannot afford private treatment and is not insured (see below, section 11), a vet may refer them to a charity hospital and provide records if possible.

Hygiene standards in practice premises and equipment, as well as in in-patient care and supervision, where appropriate, are important factors in choosing the right practice for your pet.

The British Small Animals Veterinary Association operates a Practice Standards Scheme which requires their listed vets to meet certain criteria which include premises, equipment facilities, staff qualifications and continuing education, dispensing of medicines etc. A detailed questionnaire must be filled in and the practice is then audited by an independent veterinary surgeon before being approved. Their factsheet, *Find a Vet*, is available online from *www.bsava.ac.uk/petzone.findavet/choose.htm*.

A veterinary surgeon must not cause any animal to suffer:

- by carrying out any unnecessary mutilation
- by excessive restraint or discipline
- by failing to maintain adequate pain control and relief of suffering
- by neglect.

10.3 Responsibilities to clients

The provision of veterinary services creates a contractual relationship with the owner of the animal, under which veterinary surgeons should:

- ensure that clear information is provided about practice arrangements and out-of-hours attention
- take all reasonable care in using his or her professional skills
- keep up to date with current advances
- restrict themselves to areas of their competence (e.g. a vet may know more about horses than about hamsters), except where they have to provide emergency first aid
- keep proper case records and other documentation
- ensure that a range of reasonable treatment options are offered and explained, including prognoses and possible side effects
- give realistic fee estimates based on treatment options
- keep the client informed of progress, and of any escalation in costs once treatment has started
- obtain the client's informed consent to treatment unless delay would adversely affect the animal's welfare
- ensure that all staff are properly trained and supervised where appropriate
- ensure that the client is made aware of any procedures to be performed by support staff who are not veterinary surgeons
- recognise that the client has freedom of choice.

A vet is also expected to:

- maintain client confidentiality
- avoid conflicts of interest
- give due consideration to the client's concerns and wishes where these do not conflict with the animal's welfare.

A vet is legally entitled to refuse to treat a pet if its owner is a persistently slow payer or bad debtor. He can also refuse to return the pet to the owner until his fees are paid, but this is only likely to happen in extreme circumstances.

10.4 Responsibilities when things go wrong

The profession is self-regulating. From the above, it is clear that in proper compliance with his or her responsibilities, a vet should not be negligent in the treatment of your pet. However, errors or malpractice may occasionally occur.

Note: a vet is not necessarily at fault just because the outcome of treatment is unsuccessful. Like all professionals, vets cannot guarantee success. Furthermore, where there is a body of professional opinion which would support the particular vet's chosen method of treatment, he will not be regarded as negligent even if there is another school of thought in the profession about the appropriate treatment. See also the *Goods and Services* chapter, especially section 5.

As a vet is a supplier of both goods and services, it will be helpful to see the chapter on *Goods and Services*, in particular section 5.3. At the time of writing, the Competition Commission is investigating whether there are monopoly issues in the supply and dispensing of veterinary medicines. One question is whether vets should be obliged to provide prescriptions which the animal's owner can choose to have filled by a pharmacist, rather than the drugs always being supplied by the veterinary practice directly.

If you have any problem with your vet, or with the treatment which has been carried out, speak to someone senior at the practice in the first instance.

Note: an expression of sympathy made by a vet does not in itself amount to an admission of liability.

If you do not feel your complaint has been dealt with adequately, under the Veterinary Surgeons Act 1966 it can be considered by a preliminary investigation committee. Where there is a serious allegation which might justify removal or suspension from the Register, the complaint would be referred to the Disciplinary Committee of the RCVS.

A veterinary surgeon's name may be removed from the register if among other matters:

- he or she has been convicted of a crime which, in the opinion of the Disciplinary Committee, makes them unfit to practise
- the Disciplinary Committee has found them guilty of disgraceful professional conduct.

10.5 Advertising by vets

By a recent change of rules, vets are now entitled to advertise their charges but they must indicate a range of prices and can offer cut-price deals in the High Street.

They are legally able to pay for advertisements in newspapers, magazines and local radio stations, but they must not knock on doors or make 'cold calls' to home telephones.

10.6 Client's responsibility to pay

If you are a persistent slow payer or bad debtor, your vet may refuse to treat your pet. Your vet also has a legal right to hold on to your pet until fees are paid, although, in practice, this type of action will be taken only in extreme cases.

11 INSURING YOUR PET

Your pet is as likely as any other member of your household to be involved in an accident or to suffer an unexpected illness. The potential benefit of having pet health insurance cover is becoming widely recognised. Veterinary professionals recommend such insurance because it allows them to do the best for a sick or injured animal without having to worry whether treatment costs can be afforded. It has to be remembered that serious accidents and diseases often result in long and sometimes expensive treatment. In addition, not all house contents insurance policies cover legal liability for damage or injury caused by pets, for example by straying into the road and causing an accident. Most pet insurance policies offer cover for such liability [otherwise known as third-party insurance]. Some policies may even help with the costs of advertising for a lost pet and posting a reward for its recovery.

A wide range of pet healthcare and insurance plans is available. Policies can cover a variety of costs such as for anaesthetics, operations, X-rays, laboratory charges, medicines and hospital care. Some even offer cover for complementary medicine and behavioural disorders. You may find a policy which will cover for your holiday cancellation because your pet needed emergency treatment.

Premiums usually vary and are sometimes less for cats than for dogs. There are a number of criteria which will affect the cost of the policy premium. These will vary depending upon the level of cover required, the age and state of health of the animal concerned, the area in which it lives etc.

As always the advice is to shop around for the best available cover for your pet and check whether costs for vaccinations, neutering etc. are included. As with humans, so with animals, there are usually restrictions imposed with regard to pre-existing illnesses. Most policies carry an excess.

It will also be useful to check the 'small print' regulations which govern insurance policies; see the chapter on *Goods and Services*, section 7.2.3.

There are many different options available and it is worth considering the conditions closely to suit you and your pet. If in doubt, your vet will have a selection of proposal forms and staff to help you in making your choice.

Discounts for elderly pet-owners are available from certain insurers. Some policies will cover kennelling if you are admitted to hospital. If a pet-owner suddenly dies and the animal needs immediate care while the deceased's affairs are being sorted out, the executor would have to ensure that the premiums are up to date and the policy is transferred into the name of the person who intends to take over the pet, e.g. a son or daughter (see also the chapter on *Death – Before and After*, sections 2.1.4 and 3.3.1). The Cinnamon Trust offers support in the event of the loss of a pet, as well as providing a service to take care of a pet in an emergency – e.g. if its owner is rushed into hospital (see DIRECTORY).

DIRECTORY
PETS

Association of Pet Behaviour Counsellors
PO Box 46
Worcester WR8 9YS
Tel. 01386 751151
www.apbc.org.uk

The Blue Cross *(Head office)*
Shilton Road
Burford
Oxon OX18 4PF
Tel. 01993 822 651 *(animal hospital)*
Also see local directories
www.bluecross.org.uk

British Horse Society
Stoneleigh Deer Park
Kenilworth
Warwickshire CV8 2XZ
Tel. 01926 707 700
www.bhs.org.uk

British Houserabbit Association
(Helpline) Tel. 01403 267 658

The Budgerigar Society
Spring Gardens
Northampton NN1 1DR
Tel. 01604 624549
www.budgerigarsociety.com

Cat Action Trust 1977
PO Box 1639
London W8 7ZZ
Tel. 020 8993 7041
www.cat77.org.uk

Cats Protection
17 Kings Road
Horsham
West Sussex RH13 5PN
Tel. 01403 221 900
(National Helpline) Tel. 01403 221 919
www.cats.org.uk

Cinnamon Trust
Foundry House
Foundry Square
Hayle
Cornwall TR27 4HE
Tel. 01736 757 900
www.cinnamon.org.uk

Cotton Tails Rabbit and Guinea Pig Rescue
Tel. 0117 986 6806

**Department of the Environment,
Food and Rural Affairs** *(DEFRA)*
Nobel House
17 Smith Square
London SW1P 3JR
Tel. 08459 33 55 77
www.defra.gov.uk
*For diseased animals, phone the local DEFRA
number and ask for Animal Health Division.
See also Pet Travel Scheme below.*

Governing Council of the Cat Fancy *(GCCF)*
4–6 Penel Orlieu
Bridgwater
Somerset TA6 3PG
Tel. 01278 427 575
www.gccfcats.org

Kennel Club
1–5 Clarges Street
London W1Y 8AB
Tel. 08706 066750
www.the-kennel-club.org.uk

National Association of Registered Pet Sitters
The Pulpits
Little Hereford
Ludlow SY8 4AU
Tel. 01584 711 534
www.dogsit.com

National Canine Defence League
17 Wakley Street
London EC1V 7RQ
Tel. 020 7837 0006
www.ncdl.org.uk

National Dogwardens' Association
c/o Tewkesbury Borough Council
Council Offices
Gloucester Road
Tewkesbury, Glos GL20 5TT
Tel. 01684 295 010
www.ndwa.co.uk

The National Pigeon Association
Bridge Villa
Main Street
Pollington
Goole DN14 0DW
Tel. 01405 869 516
www.zyworld.com/npa/index.htm

The Parrot Society
108b Fenlake Road
Bedford MK42 0EU
Tel. 01234 358922
www.theparrotsocietyuk.org

Pet Advisory Committee
1 Deans Yard
London SW1P 3NR
Tel. 020 7799 9811
ns.urbanity.co.uk/patrick/pac

PetLog
PO Box 263
Aylesbury
Bucks HP19 8ZH
Tel. 08706 066 751
www.petlog.org.uk

Petsearch UK
851 Old Lode Lane
Solihull
West Midlands B92 8JE
Tel. 0121 743 4133
www.ukpetsearch.freeuk.com

Pet Travel Scheme
DEFRA
Area 201
1a Page Street
London SW1P 4PQ
Tel. 0870 241 1710
www.defra.gov.uk/animalhealth/quarantine

Proteus Reptile Trust
5 Oakland Road
Handsworth
Birmingham B21 0NA
Tel. 0121 523 9500
www.proteus.uk.net

The Royal College of Veterinary Surgeons *(RCVS)*
Belgravia House
62–64 Horseferry Road
London SW1P 2AF
Tel. 020 7222 2001
www.rcvs.org.uk

The Royal Pigeon Racing Association
Reddings House
The Reddings
Nr Cheltenham
Glos GL51 6RN
Tel. 01452 713 529
www.rpra.org

Royal Society for the Prevention of Cruelty to Animals *(RSPCA)*
Wilberforce Way
Southwater
Horsham
West Sussex RH13 9RS
Tel. 0870 333 5999
www.rspca.org.uk
(Cruelty Helpline) Tel. 08705 555999

16   MOTORING

For many people, any encounter with criminal law is very likely to be in connection with the motor car. You could be fined for speeding on the motorway; experience a minor collision near home; or have to report a car theft to the police. You may not be involved directly in any such matter but be called as a witness to an accident at which you happened to be a bystander.

Most households today own at least one car and more and more families run two cars. As a result, our roads are becoming ever more crowded and hazardous. Traffic has to be kept moving while at the same time all road users – whether pedestrians or drivers – must be protected, and accidents prevented.

As well as endeavouring to ensure traffic movement and responsible driving, the law deals with all aspects relating to vehicle usage, from specifying seat belt requirements, vehicle maintenance, and the safe transportation of young children, to protection of our environment by encouraging the use of lead-free petrol and the control of harmful emissions.

Criminal incidents involving 'road rage' have been widely reported on by the media. More recently, the level of road congestion, particularly in city centres, has become the focus of debate. From 2003, congestion charges are to be introduced in central London in an experiment to restrict traffic. A legal challenge to congestion charging has recently failed. If the scheme is a success, other cities may follow.

Not surprisingly, then, the laws, rules, and regulations which govern both the motorist and his or her car are very numerous and far-ranging. European law has had its impact, too, as we can see in numerous sections in the course of this chapter.

Above all, however, the law relies on all of us to obey the rules on motoring, in our own interests. A moment's carelessness while driving can have disastrous consequences for ourselves as well as for others.

In this chapter we look at:
- what must be done before you go on the road
- vehicle checks
- buying a car
- company cars
- other motor vehicles
- disabled drivers
- accidents
- car theft
- offences and penalties – general overview
- dangerous driving offences
- careless driving offences
- drink and drug related offences
- speeding offences
- general offences
- parking offences
- cycling offences
- disqualifications for non-driving offences
- congestion charging.

Note: in general, the rules outlined in this chapter relating to motor cars are equally applicable to other vehicles which are used on-road or in public places.

1   BEFORE YOU GO ON THE ROAD

1.1   You must be licensed to drive

It is an offence to drive a car without a driving licence. You can obtain a driving licence when you are 17 or over and have passed the theory test and driving test (see section 1.1.1(b) and section 1.1.2). A compulsory basic training course is required to have been passed if a moped or motorcycle licence is required (see section 5.2 and section 5.3).

1.1.1   Provisional licence

You can apply to the DVLA for a provisional licence, with a completed application form and the fee, from six months before your 17th birthday. On this form you must declare any disability.

1.1.1(a)   Driving with a provisional licence

Once you hold a provisional licence, you must:

a) drive only with a driver who has been qualified for three years; the driver must be over 21
b) display two 'L' plates on your car
c) inform your insurers
d) not drive on a motorway.

Licences are determined by the type of vehicle that you intend to drive; for example, cars with automatic transmission are in a separate category from manual-transmission cars.

1.1.1(b)   Theory test

As a result of a European Directive, a theory test has been introduced for learner drivers.

The test, operated by the Driving Standards Agency, can be taken only after you are in possession of a provisional licence, and must be passed before you may take the on-road practical test. There are four types of written theory test – one each for learner motorcycle, car, lorry, and bus and coach drivers. Tests last for about 40 minutes and cover up to 12 topics, including driver attitude, traffic signs, the effects of alcohol, drugs and fatigue, and the environmental aspects of vehicles. The tests involve multiple choice questions.

Example:
You are reversing around a corner when you notice a pedestrian walking behind you. What should you do?

Mark one answer

• Slow down and wave the pedestrian across.
• Continue reversing and steer round the pedestrian.
• Stop and give way.
• Continue reversing and sound your horn.

You are required to answer correctly 26 of the 35 questions.

The fee for the theory test is currently set at £18.00. There is a national network of theory test centres readily accessible to candidates and you may select a test session during the working day, in the evening, or at the weekend.

If you fail the theory test, you can retake it within three days. You will have to pay the £18.00 fee again.

In addition, learner drivers have to take and pass a computer-based 'hazard-perception test' which uses film footage showing real road scenes and potential hazards. The virtual-reality test last 15 minutes. The scheme is intended to cut accidents on the roads as research has shown that one in five accidents is caused by drivers with less than a year's experience at the wheel. The hazard test includes scenes such as a lorry turning fast off a highway, children crossing the road under the eye of a lollipop lady, and a woman dashing to catch a bus. Introduced in November 2002, it will be an important new element of the current multiple choice theory test.

You will be assessed on how quickly you spot the dangers in 14 clips chosen at random.

You must pass both elements to pass your test. If you fail either the existing multiple-choice section or the new hazard-perception test you will fail the whole test, so do ask your driving instructor about it.

You can obtain a short instruction video and further information about the new theory test from the Driving Standards Agency (*www.dsa.gov.uk*).

1.1.1(c) A 'driver' is someone in control of a vehicle

The law takes a broad view in defining the 'driver' of a car. It depends on who has 'substantial control' of a vehicle.

☞ *You are a provisionally licensed driver. You are being driven by a friend in his car which breaks down. He gets out and asks you to steer while he pushes the car. A policeman comes up to you and asks to see your licence. Have you committed an offence?*

   The answer is 'yes'. You are a learner driver and there is no qualified driver in the car with you.

It is even possible for two people to 'drive' a car at the same time – for example a learner driver and his instructor in a dual-control car.

Even if you are not actually driving at the time, you are still a 'driver' until your journey is finished.

☞ *You leave your car on a hill, with the hazard lights and handbrakes on, in order to post a letter. To your horror, the car rolls down the hill when the handbrake is accidentally released, and your car collides with a wall. Fortunately, no one is hurt. You have been told that you should report the accident but, as far as you are concerned, you were not driving the car at the time of the collision.*

   In a similar case, the court held that the driver was still in the course of completing his journey, as indicated by the switching on of the hazard lights, and he remained the driver until he completed his journey.

Do take note: the duty to report an accident includes situations where the driver was not actually driving at the time (see also section 7.1 below).

1.1.2 You must take a driving test

Form DL26 (available from post offices) must be completed and sent to the Clerk to the Traffic Commissioners for your area in order to arrange a date for an on-road driving test.

Do note: You can also apply to book a test online at *www.dsa.gov.uk*.

If the examiner is satisfied that you:

- have sat and passed your written theory and hazard tests (see 1.1.1(b) above)
- have passed your off-road compulsory basic training course if the licence is for a moped or a motorcycle. (For full details see 1.1.3 below.)
- have passed the sight test, and
- are competent to drive on the road

you will be able to obtain a driver's licence. Your examiner will issue you with a form (D750) which must be filled in and sent to the DVLA, together with the appropriate fee and your driving test pass certificate.

The DVLA now only issue photocard driving licences. You will have to send a passport photograph, together with a signed declaration from 'someone of standing' e.g. a magistrate, doctor, minister of religion. You will also have to enclose your passport or birth certificate. If your present 'paper' licence needs renewal or you need a duplicate because your details have changed or your licence has been mislaid, you will be issued with a replacement photocard licence. You can contact the DVLA regarding the issue of photocard licences: tel. 01792 772 151.

Do take heed: from May 1999 candidates are not considered competent to drive if on their test they commit 15 minor driving faults or one serious fault.

Photocard licences have to be renewed every 10 years, until you are 70, in order to keep your photograph up to date. After that you must renew your licence every three years (see section 1.1.7 below).

The issue of a disability that occurs before your licence expires is dealt with in section 6.1, and the problem of a licensed driver reverting to learner-driver status in section 1.1.9 below.

Licences for heavy goods vehicles and buses normally last until your 45th birthday. If over 45 you are required to:

- provide a medical report form (Form D4) completed by a doctor, and
- pay for your examination by the doctor.

After that you need to renew your entitlement every five years until you are 65. After 65 you need to renew it each year.

Do note: there is no legal cut-off age for drivers. The responsibility for deciding when to stop driving rests with the individual where there is no medical condition involved (see the Department for Transport leaflet on Advice for Older Drivers which can be obtained from DFT Free Literature, tel: 0870 1226236, *www.think.dft.gov.uk*).

1.1.3   Motorcycle licence requirements

The requirements for a motorcycle licence are complicated and depend on:

- size of the machine (light or standard)
- age of the learner
- whether or not you have a car licence
- whether or not you wish to drive a moped.

For an outline of the requirements, see section 5.3 below.

For full details, you must contact the Driving Standards Agency (*www.dsa.gov.uk*).

1.1.4   Licence counterpart

A counterpart is issued with your new licence, detailing the category of car that you can drive, as well as all convictions, penalty points and disqualifications, if any. When ordered to produce your licence, you will have to produce the counterpart as well.

1.1.5   If you fail the test

The pass rate is about 50 per cent. If you fail you must wait one month before applying for another test. If you feel that the examiner did not conduct the test properly, you can appeal to a magistrates' court.

1.1.6   Approved driving instructors

A register is kept, under the Transport Act 1988, of approved driving instructors who must display a certificate in the car. There are also driving instructors' organisations which foster road safety and teaching standards.

1.1.7   Renewing your licence when aged 70 and over

When the age of 70 is approaching, you will be sent a computer-generated reminder to your last known address, together with a form for renewal. This form includes a medical declaration but it is not necessary for a doctor to complete it – merely you, the driver. This form is to be returned to the DVLA plus licence fee (£8.50). Your licence is then renewed for three years. This renewal process will be repeated at three-year intervals.

1.1.8   The Highway Code

This Code is issued by the Department of Transport.

Breach of the Code is not a criminal offence. However, if you are being prosecuted by the police – for example, for careless driving – and you have not followed the Code, your breach of the Code may be used as evidence against you in any civil or criminal proceedings.

1.1.9   Reverting to learner-driver status

If you pass your first driving test on or after 1 June 1997 and obtain six or more penalty points – including any that were incurred within three years of the latest conviction – in the two-year period immediately following your first successful driving test, your licence will be revoked by the DVLA.

To regain your driving licence you will then have to:

- obtain a provisional licence
- drive as a learner with 'L' plates and accompanied by an experienced driver who is over 21, and
- pass both the theory and practical test again.

Beware: passing the retest will not remove the penalty points from your licence, and if the total reaches 12, a court may disqualify you.

1.2   Your car must be licensed, too

There is an annual fee for the car licence that has to be obtained for any car used – or even kept – on a public road. The licence (the 'tax disc') must be displayed unless the car is kept wholly on private land. If a tax disc was in force for your vehicle on or after 31 January 1998 and you do not tax the vehicle because it will not be used or kept on a public road, you must declare this to the DVLA.

This can be done on your vehicle licence renewal reminder (V11). Alternatively, you can declare a Statutory Off-Road Notification (SORN) using form V890, available from the DVLA Customer Enquiry Unit (tel. 01792 772 134). If you fail to make a SORN declaration when you should, you may be fined £1,000. A SORN declaration is valid for 12 months unless you relicense, sell, permanently export or scrap the vehicle before the 12 months have expired. You will normally be sent a V11 reminder form by the DVLA when the SORN declaration is about to expire. A vehicle covered by a SORN declaration can be relicensed at any time at a post office or Vehicle Registration Office in the usual way using the relevant form, either V10 or V85.

Further, the making of a false declaration when a vehicle is actually used or kept untaxed on a public road could result in a fine of up to £5,000 and two years' imprisonment.

☞   *You have an old car that you do not drive stored on your land until such time as you decide how to get rid of it. Are you liable for road tax?*

     The answer is 'no', but a SORN declaration will be required as explained above. However, you would be liable if the car were parked outside your house on a public road even if you had no intention of using it.

Owners of untaxed vehicles can also be prosecuted and fined up to £1,000.

Disabled drivers may be exempt from paying the car licence fee. However they are still under an obligation to display the disc (see section 6 below).

1.2.1   Car-tax concessions for 'greener' cars

Cars registered before 1 March 2001 are taxed under a system based on engine size. However, cars first registered and licensed on or after that date are charged under the graduated vehicle excise duty system. That system, based on carbon dioxide emissions, is intended to encourage manufacturers and purchasers to seek more fuel-efficient cars. Prior to first registration on or after 1 March 2001, cars will have been allocated a CO_2 figure (shown in grammes per km) which is measured as part of the car's Type Approval Test. In general that CO_2 emission figure will remain fixed for the car's life, but a change in fuel type may affect the VED charged.

1.2.2   Number plates

Every car has a unique registration number. With effect from 1 September 2001 a new British Standard was introduced setting out the physical characteristics of the number plates. These include visibility, strength and reflectivity. The new plate is marked with:

a) the number of the British Standard (from 1 September 2001 this will be BS AU 145d)
b) the name, trade mark (or other means of identification) of the maker, and
c) the name and postcode of the supplying outlet.

Also from September 2001 there is an optional provision for the display of the Euro-plate within the UK. The Euro-plate incorporates the symbol of the European Union (a circle of 12 stars on a blue background) with the national identification letters of the member state below. Vehicles displaying that symbol no longer have to use the traditional oval-shaped national identifier sticker when travelling within the European Union. It is possible to apply to the DVLA for a particular mark.

Lines open three months before a new registration letter comes into force. Numbers and letters are not reserved in advance but are issued on a first come, first served basis. The fees for personalised number-plates start at £250 but increase with possible demand. The DVLA operate a Hot Line on 0870 6000 142 and you can also get their free booklet, *Registration Numbers and You*, from the Sale of Marks Team, DVLA, Swansea, SA6 7JL.

Very desirable combinations, such as MIL 2000, may be held back and auctioned.

Number plates can also be transferred on payment of a fee of £80.

Do note: from 1 January 2003 suppliers of number plates will be required by law to register their details with the DVLA.

If you wish to purchase number plates, you will need to provide:

- evidence that it is your car (e.g. by showing your logbook), and
- proof of your identity.

1.2.3   Car registration and transfers

The purchase of a new car is accompanied by a registration document giving particulars of the vehicle and the name and address of the registered keeper. This document accompanies any subsequent transfer of the car. Details of the transfer must be filled in on the registration document by you, and sent on to the DVLA (see below 1.2.3(b)). The newly named person then becomes the car's registered keeper.

1.2.3(a)   Distinction between keeper and owner of vehicle

The keeper and the owner of a vehicle may not necessarily be the same person. The keeper is the person whose name is on the registration document – this is often also the name of the owner but the distinction must be borne in mind, particularly if you are buying a second-hand vehicle from someone who is unknown to you (see *Buying a car*, section 3 below).

1.2.3(b)   Safeguarding the registration document

If you sell your car privately, do not part with the document until you have been paid in full and the DVLA has been informed. If you sell to a dealer, you must also make sure that you follow the correct procedure for transfer as detailed on the document itself.

If you carelessly hand over your registration document with your car to a new owner without registering the change and informing the DVLA, you may find yourself liable for someone else's traffic offences!

If the car is to be scrapped make sure that the registration document is returned to the DVLA and not handed over to the person taking it away as scrap.

Note of warning: do not retain the registration document in your car (see also section 2.4 below).

☞   *You have been tempted by a 'snip' of a second hand car, advertised in your local newsagents' and, on inspection, the car looks well worth the asking price. It is a private sale and the owner says that he has mislaid the registration document temporarily. What do you do?*

Do not be too tempted – it may well be that you are looking at a stolen car. If you wish to pursue the matter, write to the DVLA explaining your interest and asking if it can help with registration details. Only buy the car if the details of name and address match those which the seller gives to you (see section 3.2.1 below).

All these procedures serve more than one function: the DVLA is under a legal duty to supply the licensing particulars of any car on its register to a local authority or to the police in investigating offences.

Vehicle crime affects us all and new measures are being taken to tackling the problem (see INS 157 issued by the DVLA).

From April 2003 all cars that have been written off and/or scrapped due to accident damage and are subsequently repaired must undergo and pass a Vehicle Identity Check (VIC) before they can be returned to the road. The check will confirm the identity of the vehicle. A logbook will only be issued for the car if it has passed the check. If you purchase a car without a logbook or a vehicle identity check pass, you could find that you will be unable to register it or to tax it.

Important: the VIC does not confirm that the vehicle is roadworthy.

1.2.4   Insuring your car

It is an offence to drive a car, or to let others use a car when you are responsible for it, without insurance cover. Insurance is thus compulsory by law. Insurance can be negotiated either directly with the insurance company or through a broker. It is worth enquiring for competitive premiums.

The policy of insurance must be granted by an 'authorised insurer'. The certificate of insurance must:

- be in the prescribed form
- contain particulars of any conditions to which the policy is subject (e.g. for social and domestic use only), and
- be delivered to the insured driver.

You must fill in a proposal form which will require personal and vehicle details. There are two major categories of insurance – comprehensive and third party.

1.2.4(a)   Comprehensive insurance

Comprehensive insurance covers injury to other persons or damage to their property as well as damage to your own car. It may cover other risks such as legal fees or theft of your belongings in the car and certain personal injury claims.

1.2.4(b)   Third party

Third-party insurance is the minimum cover under the law and will cover damage to other drivers and/or their cars if you are involved in an accident for which your driving is responsible. It will also cover passengers in your car – again provided that your driving was responsible for the accident.

It will not cover damage to your car or personal injury to yourself, however.

For exclusion from third-party cover under the most stringent conditions see below, section 14.5.

1.2.4(c)   'No-claims' bonuses

The insurance companies are safety-conscious in their own interests and try to promote good driving standards through financial incentives, in particular through the 'no-claims' bonus. There are disincentives too – for example, a driver convicted of a drink/drive offence may not be able to claim for damage to his own vehicle under his particular policy.

Do take heed: drivers with a conviction for a drink/drive offence may not be able to obtain insurance and, if they do, can expect to have their premiums increased by at least 100 per cent.

1.2.4(d)   Legal expenses

Some insurers offer to cover legal expenses for an extra premium. In view of the restrictions on legal aid availability (see chapter on *The Legal System*) and the inherent dangers of driving a car, the premium may well be worth it.

1.2.4(e)   Scrutinizing the small print

Always scrutinise the details of your policy, particularly if someone else uses your car.

☞ *Your car is insured for your social and business use and for 'any named driver'. One of those named drivers happens to be your son, who asks if he can borrow the car while his own is out of action. He uses the car to pick up a client and take him to his office but on the way has a minor collision with another car. Will you be covered?*

It is most unlikely that you will be able to claim on your insurance. 'Business use' is usually restricted to the policyholder and you could also be committing an offence in the circumstances.

1.2.4(f)   Full and frank disclosure

As with all other insurance policies, you are under a duty to make a full and frank disclosure to your insurers. Full disclosure covers among other matters:

- named drivers
- previous convictions
- type of use
- involvement in an accident.

(See also chapter on *Goods and Services*, section 7.2.2.)

Note: the Press Office of the Association of British Insurers (51 Gresham Street, London EC2V 7HQ), has free leaflets available for information on car insurance and other insurance generally (see also DIRECTORY).

A database, intended to hold details of all insured vehicles, will be linked into the police national computer, giving the police ready access at the roadside to insurance details. Uninsured drivers will thus be more easily identified and speedily dealt with.

1.2.4(g) Disqualification

Any insurance is automatically invalidated for anyone who drives while disqualified.

☞ *You have been knocked over by a driver who was disqualified from driving after a series of drink/driving offences. What do you do?*

You apply immediately to the Motor Insurers' Bureau (see section 1.2.5 below).

1.2.4(h) Driving other cars

☞ *You have borrowed your uncle's car which is comprehensively insured for other drivers. You have a collision with another car. Neither driver is hurt but both cars are slightly damaged.*

In this case, your uncle's insurance cover would be sufficient to cover accidental damage claims to his car as well as to the other driver's car.

Further, most policies will cover a policy holder in person even if (s)he drives a car which belongs to someone else.

Do take note, however, that such cover would be limited in scope to third-party cover only, i.e. the damage to the other driver's car will be covered but not to a borrowed car.

1.2.5 The Motor Insurers' Bureau (MIB)

The Motor Insurers' Bureau was set up to provide cover against drivers who have caused an accident and have no insurance cover or who cannot be traced (the 'hit-and-run' driver).

All the motor insurance companies must belong to the MIB by law. It pays out the compensation which the court decides should go to an accident victim who would otherwise be deprived because of the driver's lack of effective insurance. The sum is limited to a quarter of a million pounds in respect of damage to property. There is a £300 excess.

The 'user' of a vehicle cannot claim compensation for any injuries. Plainly not every passenger could be defined as a person 'using the vehicle' and there had to be present some element of controlling, managing or operating the vehicle. For example could the journey be considered a joint venture between driver and passenger? It is a question of fact and degree for the judge. In one case, a pillion passenger knew that the motorcycle driver was uninsured and unlicensed, and had been warned not to go with the driver. However, she had not only agreed to travel pillion on the cycle but helped to bump start it; in those circumstances, the claimant was to be regarded as 'a person using the vehicle' and thus unable to claim compensation from the MIB.

So do take heed: the MIB's obligation has limitations. In particular it will not pay out to a victim of an accident who is driving a vehicle which itself is uninsured or where the victim knew, or ought to have known, that he was being driven in a car which:

* was uninsured
* was stolen
* was unlawfully taken
* was being used in connection with a crime
* was being driven by an under-age driver.

However, as in all cases, the outcome depends on the view that the court takes on the facts. In one case, decided by the House of Lords, the question was whether the claimant 'knew or ought to have known' that the driver of the car in which he was a passenger was unlicensed and uninsured.

☞ *Brian had gone to a late-night party. He was being driven home by his brother, Steve, who lost control of the car on a bend. As a result of the accident, Brian was very seriously injured. Steve had not passed a driving test and the car was uninsured. Brian had known that, in the past,*

Steve had driven without a licence. The question was how to construe whether Brian 'knew or ought to have known' that Steve was uninsured in these circumstances.

In a similar case, the claimant had been merely careless, their Lordships concluded (by a majority). He did not actually 'know' that the driver was uninsured and a mere failure to enquire 'with reasonable prudence' whether the driver was insured, was not a bar to his claim against the MIB.

There are also steps which a victim must take to establish all available facts, e.g. to exchange names and addresses where possible or to contact the DVLA if you were able to note the number of the other vehicle. Claims should be made using the MIB's application form, wherever possible, and be accompanied by documents which support your claim. Copies of the form can be obtained by post or telephone, or from the MIB website (see DIRECTORY). There are also very helpful notes for the assistance of claimants, available in question and answer form.

The MIB can negotiate or settle a claim without waiting for judgment to be given.

1.2.5(a)   Hit-and-run

Whether or not a driver had relevant insurance against which a claim for compensation might be made is clearly irrelevant where the victim is hurt by a driver who is unable to be traced having fled the scene of the accident.

☞ *While crossing the road at night in an otherwise deserted street you are knocked over by a driver who makes off at high speed. How can you seek recompense?*

Again, the MIB provides assistance: the Untraced Drivers' Agreement operates where there can be no judgment because the person responsible for the accident cannot be traced.

The MIB investigates the circumstances and decides how much compensation is to be given. You can appeal against the award under the Untraced Drivers' Agreement to an arbitrator who is chosen from a panel appointed by the Lord Chancellor.

Important note: compensation is only available where there is personal injury. There is no compensation available in respect of property damage so, for example, if you come out to your car in the morning, and the driver who has rammed into the back of it left no note to identify himself, you cannot seek compensation from the MIB.

1.2.5(b)   Joy-riders

Joy-riding offences have become increasingly common in recent years (see also *Car theft*, section 8 below). In such cases there may be no recompense for an accident victim from the joyrider who has caused the accident. The MIB can be approached by an innocent victim of an accident. What is the position if the victim is not 'innocent'?

☞ *You accompany your friend on a joyride and you know that he has taken the car without the owner's permission and that he failed his driving test. There is an accident and you are injured. Can you turn to the MIB?*

The answer is 'no': no payment will be made where the victim knows that the vehicle was stolen or the driver was uninsured. (See also the chapter on *Accidents*, section 3.2. where a victim of an accident has assumed the risk.)

Remember: if you are hurt in any accident, it is always advisable to go to a solicitor who specialises in personal injury cases. The Law Society has a list of solicitors who participate in their Accident Legal Advice Scheme (ALAS). (See also the chapters on *Accidents* and *The Legal System*.)

2   VEHICLE CHECKS

2.1   Maintaining your car

There are numerous regulations that require you to maintain your car in working and efficient order; they are vitally necessary in the interests of your own safety, as well as the safety of others.

☞ *Your car is parked outside your house but you have not driven it for a while; the battery is flat and you have no intention of driving it in the immediate future. A policeman on the beat looks at it and decides that it appears defective. He asks to test it. What do you do?*

He has the authority to test any vehicle on demand if it:

a) appears defective or

b) has been involved in an accident.

2.1.1   Offences

It is an offence to drive a car unless the following are in good working order:

- seat belts
- brakes and steering gear
- lights
- windscreen, windscreen wipers and washers
- demisters
- mirrors
- tyres (including spare)
- silencer
- exhaust system.

To be considered to be in good working condition, tyres must be correctly inflated and be free from certain cuts and other defects. Importantly, cars, light vans and light trailers must have a tread depth of at least 1.6 mm across the central three-quarters of the breadth of the tread and around the entire circumference; motorcycles, large vehicles and passenger-carrying vehicles must have a tread depth of at least 1 mm across three-quarters of the breadth of the tread and in a continuous band around the entire circumference; and mopeds should have visible tread.

2.2   Car telephones and alarms

As you must exercise proper control of your vehicle at all times, you should not use a hand-held telephone or microphone while driving. Use of a hands-free microphone is permissible while driving but not if it takes your mind off the road. Only in an emergency may you stop on the hard shoulder of a motorway to answer or make a call. A number of proposals have been put forward under which the use of hand-held, or both hand-held and hands-free, telephones would be prohibited by legislation. Recent research has shown that drivers who talk on the telephone react more slowly than normal drivers. However, the Department of Transport has indicated that while the subject is 'under review', there are no immediate plans to introduce a specific offence of using mobile phones while driving.

Car alarms must not sound continuously for more than five minutes. The mechanism must be in good repair.

Under the Noise and Statutory Nuisance Act 1993, noise from car alarms of cars parked in the street can be a statutory nuisance (see also chapter on *Neighbours*). If the vehicle is unattended, an environmental health officer can fix an abatement notice on the car. He or she can then either have the vehicle removed or open the vehicle, 'if necessary by force', in order to stop the noise. However, the EHO is obliged by law to leave the vehicle 'secured against interference or theft ... as effectually as he found it'.

2.3   The 'MOT' test

If a vehicle has been registered for more than three years, it is an offence to use it on a road without a current test certificate. The tests are carried out by examiners authorised under the Act at specified vehicle testing stations.

You should note that the holding of a current MOT certificate does not in any way excuse you if you are charged with a failure to maintain any of the parts specified in section 2.1.1 above. You should always keep windscreens, windows, lights, indicators, reflectors, mirrors and number plates clean and clear. Ensure too that your seat, seat belts, head restraints and mirrors are adjusted correctly before you drive.

2.4   Checklist summary

In order to drive and to take your car on the road you must have the following documents:

- driving licence
- car insurance
- registration document

- current tax disc
- MOT certificate (if your car is more than three-years-old).

Note of warning: do not keep your registration document in your car. Should your car be stolen together with that document, the car might be sold and resold many times with ease without the original thief ever attracting suspicion.

2.5   Seat belts

It is an offence to be a driver or front-seat passenger without wearing a seat belt unless a special exemption applies. Similarly, a rear-seat passenger must wear a seat belt (if fitted). Exemptions include the holders of medical exemption certificates, people making local deliveries in a vehicle designed or adapted for that purpose, and children in the rear of taxis with partitions. It is the responsibility of an adult passenger to wear any seat belt fitted.

☞ *You are a front seat passenger and have not been wearing a seat belt. Your driver is involved in a collision, which is entirely the fault of another motorist, and you suffer whiplash injuries.*

Two consequences follow:

a) You could be prosecuted for breach of the law.

b) You will certainly receive reduced damages from the other driver's insurance company because you are guilty of 'contributory negligence'. The degree of contributory negligence is usually assessed on a percentage basis, so you could lose half or more of the damages you might otherwise have obtained.

2.6   Seat belts and children

The following table sets out the legal requirements for the wearing of seat belts or appropriate child restraints. (The classification of what is an 'appropriate child restraint' is currently under question, but it is not expected that any new rules will do anything other than modify the present specifications and strengthen the current requirements.)

An appropriate child restraint is a baby carrier, child seat, harness or booster-seat appropriate to the child's weight.

You are advised that you should not let children sit behind the rear seats in an estate car or hatchback, and it is suggested that child safety locks, where fitted, are used when children are in the car. (See the Highway Code.)

Seat belt requirements

This table summarises the main legal requirements for wearing seat belts

	FRONT SEAT (all vehicles)	REAR SEAT (cars and small minibuses*)	WHOSE RESPONSIBILITY
DRIVER	**MUST** be worn if fitted		**DRIVER**
CHILD under 3 years of age	Appropriate child restraint **MUST** be worn	Appropriate child restraint **MUST** be worn *if available*	**DRIVER**
CHILD aged 3–11 and under 1.5 metres (about 5 feet) in height	Appropriate child restraint **MUST** be worn *if available.* If not, an adult seat belt **MUST** be worn	Appropriate child restraint **MUST** be worn *if available.* If not, an adult seat belt **MUST** be worn *if available.*	**DRIVER**
CHILD aged 12 or 13 or younger child 1.5 metres or more in height	Adult seat belt **MUST** be worn *if available*	Adult seat belt **MUST** be worn *if available*	**DRIVER**
PASSENGER over the age of 14	**MUST** be worn *if available*	**MUST** be worn *if available*	**PASSENGER**

Minibuses with an unladen weight of 2540kg or less

3 BUYING A CAR

For most people, the money they spend on their car is their biggest single investment after buying their house. The legal rule of *caveat emptor* (buyer beware) particularly applies. Because of the sums involved, if you are not sure about your position it should be considered a money-saver – and not an expense – to consult a lawyer if things go wrong.

3.1 Buying from a dealer

A dealer is someone who sells 'in the course of business'. If you buy a car from a dealer, either new or second-hand, you have certain basic protections under the Sale of Goods Act and other consumer legislation (see also chapter on *Goods and Services*).

3.1.1 Dealer's legal requirements

A dealer cannot get out of the legal requirements that:

- the car will be fit for its normal purpose
- it is of 'merchantable quality'
- it conforms to his description given to you
- he has the right to sell it.

Note: a private seller is not bound to you under the Sale of Goods Act (see below, section 3.2).

3.1.2 New cars

New cars are usually bought from a dealer who is franchised by the manufacturer. There are generally manufacturers' warranties that go with the car which can extend your legal rights but cannot replace them or curtail them.

☞ *You have bought a new car but are not happy with it. The car has broken down after only a short distance. What do you do?*

- Do not delay in contacting the dealer. Put your complaint in writing.
- Make no attempt to accept a car repair, but if you should arrange to do so, you can still return the car and claim your money back if the repairs are not satisfactory.
- Do not drive it again in the hope that the fault will 'sort itself out'.
- Return the car and ask for a replacement vehicle. Your contract is with the dealer so do not be fobbed off by being told to contact the manufacturer.

You would be advised to send all correspondence to the relevant trade association, if the dealer belongs to one (see also chapter on *Goods and Services*).

3.1.2(a) Repair of vehicle

Under the Sale and Supply of Goods Act 1994 you are not 'deemed' (considered) to have accepted a vehicle merely because you have asked for, or agreed to, its repair under an arrangement with the seller.

3.1.2(b) Delay: a note of warning

Acting fast is the critical factor – any delay may be taken in law to mean that you have 'accepted' the car under the contract.

However, should this happen and you have lost the opportunity to return the car but you are not satisfied with the repair, do not delay in making your dissatisfaction known to the dealer.

3.1.3 Second-hand car purchases

Second-hand car deals can present particular problem areas:

- meeting consumer law standards ('fitness of purpose' and 'merchantable quality', for example, are not easy to prove in the best of circumstances). Such proof becomes much more difficult to assess in second-hand car deals
- 'clocking' i.e. turning back the mileage clock
- stolen cars
- insurance write-offs that have been 'repaired' to look as good as new.

☞ *You have bought a second-hand car which looks absolutely perfect on the outside but the steering wheel comes apart the first time you take it out on the road. It transpires that the 'car' comprises two insurance write-offs welded together. What do you do?*

a) Follow all the steps outlined for the buyer of a new car above (i.e. do not delay in contacting the dealer; and put your complaint in writing).

b) Insist on your money back rather than a replacement vehicle.

c) Inform the Trading Standards Department of your local authority which can launch a prosecution under the Trading Standards Act. The dealer has also committed a criminal offence under the Road Traffic Act 1988 so you should also inform the police (see section 3.1.4 below).

The government is concerned to tackle cowboy car dealers by giving added powers to the courts, trading standards officers, and the OFT. In particular, it wishes to tackle car dealers who sell stolen cars, 'cut and shut' vehicles, and traders who clock mileages on used cars.

In order to make it harder for thieves to disguise the identities of stolen vehicles, the DVLA is to tighten the rules on applying for tax discs if the applicant does not have the licence renewal reminder. From February 2003, drivers will have to present their logbooks at the post office in lieu (of the renewal reminder).

From 7 April 2003 every car that has been written off or scrapped because of accident damage, and is subsequently repaired, must undergo and pass a Vehicle Identity Check [VIC] before it can be returned to the road. The logbook will then carry a note to show that its identity is confirmed. Also from 7 April where an owner decides to dispose of a car with significant, unrepaired, accident damage, there is a new obligation to return the logbook to the DVLA.

Warning: if you buy a car without a logbook or a VIC pass, you could find that you will not be able to register or tax it.

Take extra heed: the VIC confirms the identity of the vehicle but not that it is safe to drive. For details, please ask for leaflet INF 133, tel. 0870 240 6424. (See also section 1.2.3(b) above.)

3.1.3(a) Conforming to dealer's description

As noted in section 3.1.1 above, a vehicle must conform to a dealer's description. This is particularly crucial where a second-hand car is concerned. For example, if you make a purchase having been told of a specific defect you will have no redress should subsequent trouble arise out of that defect. However, that defence will not be available should the car subsequently reveal a fault unrelated to the defect told to you by the dealer.

☞ *You have purchased a car having been told by the dealer that the brake lights may be defective. You drive the car away only to find that the fuel injection system is faulty, as well as the brake lights. What can you do?*

You will be entitled to claim damages in respect of the faulty fuel injection system, but not in respect of the brake light failure.

A dealer may attempt a defence that any defect in a vehicle should have been noticed by you on inspection. That defence may be upheld in the case of an obvious defect, e.g. a dented wing, but will not necessarily be upheld where the defect is one which would not be likely to have been spotted by a lay person. However, to avoid complications of that nature, it is suggested that a person buying a second-hand car (whether from a dealer or privately) should seek an independent inspection/valuation from a body such as the AA or the RAC. As an alternative to incurring the cost of such an inspection, it is advisable to have another person with you at the time of purchase. That person will then be available as a witness to any specific descriptions made by the dealer. (It is unlikely that the dealer will be willing to provide a written declaration of his descriptions – and there may be all sorts of back-form conditions which restrict his right to make such statements.)

3.1.3(b) Waiver of customer's rights

It is common practice for a dealer to request a customer to sign a receipt for the vehicle on which there may be a provision stating that the car has been inspected and that the customer is satisfied as to its condition. That receipt will not secure the position of the dealer against a complaint about a non-obvious defect, but, if you must sign, it is wise to add a proviso to the effect that no defects are observable to you as a lay person.

3.1.3(c) Buying a car under an existing HP agreement

It is not uncommon for a person to purchase a car which is the subject of a hire purchase agreement.

☞ *You have bought a second-hand car. A hire purchase company writes to you to say that it is a repossessed vehicle under an existing HP agreement and asks for the car back. What do you do?*

You should be protected by law. Provided you bought the car in good faith, for value, and quite innocently, without knowing it was on hire purchase, you should be entitled to keep it. Do keep all the documentation in connection with the purchase and check that you make careful enquiries as to whether the car is subject to an existing HP agreement. You should obtain a written warranty that:

- the seller is true owner of the vehicle and
- that it is not subject to an HP agreement.

See also section 3.2 1 below.

If you are approached with information that the car which you have bought is still under an existing HP agreement, you should seek legal advice immediately.

See also the chapter on *Goods and Services* (section 4.7.1).

Note: the above protection does not apply to a dealer who has innocently purchased a car subject to a hire-purchase agreement. Dealers generally have their own recourse in that they can check on a nation-wide database network whether a car is on HP or not. The protection also does not extend to you if you purchased the car from somebody who stole it. In such a case the only redress will be against the thief who stole it – which may be poor redress indeed (see below, section 3.1.5).

3.1.4 Dealer's offences

A dealer can be prosecuted:

- if he makes false statements about the vehicle
- if he sells a car that is not roadworthy because, for example, the brakes or steering are in a dangerous condition. Under the Road Traffic Act 1988, authorised examiners can enter a dealer's premises and test whether the used cars offered for sale are roadworthy.

Recently the Department of Trade and Industry has clarified the powers of trading standards officers to inspect second-hand vehicles on garage forecourts. It confirmed that under the General Product Safety Regulations, such powers indeed existed to inspect vehicles as well as records. Officers can also seize and detain unsafe cars. The only exceptions are antiques and cars sold for repair.

3.1.5 Stolen cars

A vehicle cannot be purchased without the consent of the owner, regardless of the buyer's knowledge or intent.

☞ *You have bought a car that was in fact stolen. You have now been contacted by the police on behalf of its true owner. You bought the car in good faith and quite innocently. What do you do?*

You may have no option but to hand the car over to the police. The insurers of the car may have paid out the owner and may therefore settle with you for cash. But it still appears very unfair, as you then find yourself paying twice over. It is a question of which of two innocent parties should bear the loss – you, the buyer, or the true owner. At present the law favours the owner.

Note: the question of title to goods is currently under review (see also the chapter on *Goods and Services*).

Pilot projects are underway nationwide to deny serious and violent criminals the use of the roads. Automatic Number Plate Recognition (ANPR) systems scan registration numbers and check them to identify stolen cars and vehicles which have been involved in crimes. Once a suspicious vehicle is recognised it becomes the focus of targeted interception. There is evidence to show a strong link between road traffic offences and other criminal conduct, and the use of this technology is intended to make life safer for all of us.

3.1.6 Summary checklist

- It is perhaps better to buy from a dealer who is a member of a trade association with a Code of Practice. Such a Code has been drawn up by the Retail Motor Industry Federation. The Office of Fair Trading also has a leaflet on buying a used car (see DIRECTORY).

- Have a second-hand car checked by a professional.
- Take down in writing the seller's description of the car.

3.2   Buying privately

The buying and selling of cars on the private market is commonplace but it is important for a purchaser to realise that, in such transactions, he does not get the same legal rights as he would when buying from a dealer.

3.2.1   Seller's obligations

The only obligation on a private seller is that any particular specified by him must be true. There is no obligation on a private seller to make any particular specifications about the car, and a buyer has no promise that the car is of proper quality in relation to its price.

The Trading Standards Office suggest that a buyer purchasing a second-hand car from a private seller should have the car checked by an independent motor mechanic; test drive it; and ensure that the asking price can be met, taking in to account the insurance and running costs. The Office sets out a useful buyer's checklist: *www.tradingstandards.gov./uk.*

See advice in section 3.1.3(c) above that the buyer obtain a warranty from the seller that the car is not subject to an existing HP agreement.

3.2.2   Contrast with dealer's position

The legal requirements on a dealer (set out in section 3.1.1 above) are not applicable in relation to a private seller.

3.2.3   Complaints against a private seller

A complaint may be lodged against a private seller where evidence (of a witness or in writing) is available to show that the seller made a false statement about the car and that false statement is relevant to the buyer's complaint. In truth, a buyer's best line of defence is to protect himself prior to purchase by having an independent body carry out a vehicle check and valuation. It is possible to sue in respect of a false promise made by the seller, but in practice such an action is unlikely to prove rewarding.

3.2.4   Dealer posing as a private seller

A dealer – often one operating part-time – may sell a car pretending to be a private seller. In some instances it may be possible to spot that the individual is in fact a dealer by noting separate advertisements showing the same name or telephone number. Should you purchase a vehicle from someone who is in fact a dealer the normal dealer's promises are applicable (see section 3.1.1 above), and your buyer's privileges are not affected by the fact that the sale was represented to you as being of a private nature.

A dealer acting in this way is guilty of a criminal offence.

3.2.5   Car under existing HP agreement

The unwitting purchaser of a car subject to a hire purchase agreement where the sale is of a private nature may be protected in the same way as if the car had been purchased from a dealer. See the resultant position as outlined in section 3.1.3(c) above. (For misrepresentations in connection with HP transactions, see the chapter on *Goods and Services*.)

3.2.6   Stolen cars

The purchase in a private sale of a stolen vehicle affords no protection to the purchaser. The same position applies as when the car was purchased from a dealer (see section 3.1.5 above).

3.3   Buying at auction

Buying a car at an auction may enable one to save a good deal of money. However, the following practical considerations apply to restrict your ability to make a claim for legal remedy if the car proves to be defective:

- the auctioneer will almost inevitably exclude both himself and the person selling from liability for any defects. A dealer is not able to sell and to exclude his legal promises but there is no such restriction on an auctioneer

- generally, an auctioneer will not reveal the name of the seller – usually a dealer. In such a case the dealer might be traced only by applying to the person last named on the registration document to try to find out to whom the vehicle was sold. Often it will be the case that a purchaser of a defective vehicle at auction will be unable to find any person to sue.

When buying at an auction, you will be bound by the auctioneer's written conditions, which must be available to you before you buy. These may be posted on the wall or issued in a booklet or on other paperwork. Unfair conditions may be challenged, but it is best not to rely on any such right. The best course is to study those conditions before taking the risk of buying or selling at auction.

4 THE COMPANY CAR

It is estimated that more than two million people in this country drive company cars. The employer acquires the car (usually on a three-year lease) and pays the cost of repairs, road tax and insurance. Naturally the issues that most often arise concern the tax advantages and/or disadvantages to the employee of such an arrangement. By and large there has been a steady increase in tax on company cars.

4.1 The benefits

The general rule is that where a car is placed at the disposal of an employee or a director earning more than £8,500, it is taxable on a sliding scale. The scale is based on the original price of the car, its age and the level of business mileage. While petrol and portable telephones are also taxed, car parking facilities at the place of work are not.

4.2 Insurance

This is usually effected by 'block fleet' policies taken out by the employer (see also section 14.5 below). It is also the employer's duty to ensure that the car is insured.

☞ *You are driving a company car on company business and have a collision with another car. It transpires that the car you are driving is not insured. What can you do?*

There is a special defence for employees using vehicles in the course of their employment if they are quite unaware that the car lacks cover. In such a case, their employer could be prosecuted.

5 OTHER MOTOR VEHICLES

In general, the rules outlined in this chapter relating to motor cars are equally applicable to other vehicles which are used on-road or in public places. Accordingly, this section does no more than draw attention to particular requirements placed on drivers of vehicles which are outside the legal definition of a motor car.

5.1 Heavy goods vehicles

HGVs are subject to special rules concerning, among other things, laden and unladen weight, the fitting of tachometers (devices recording speed, mileage and hours driven) and speed limitations.

It is not practicable to detail these rules except to note that vehicles weighing over 7.5 tonnes, and all articulated vehicles, are subject to a maximum speed limit of 60 mph on motorways. Additionally, you must be aged 18 to obtain a licence to drive a medium-sized goods vehicle and aged 21 for entitlement to a HGV licence.

5.2 Mopeds

A moped is a vehicle of not over 50 cc with a maximum design speed of not over 50 kph. The kerbside weight is not to be in excess of 250 kilograms. To ride a moped, learners are required to be 16 or over; have a provisional moped licence; and complete a compulsory basic training course (CBT). The moped may not be driven on the road before those three conditions have been met.

To obtain a full moped licence you must first pass the theory test for motorcycles and then the moped practical test. Persons having a full car licence may ride a moped without 'L' plates, although it is recommended that a CBT course be completed before riding on the road. The following gives exemption from taking the theory test:

- full car licence

- full A1 motorcycle licence
- full moped licence, if gained after 1 July 1996.

If you ride a moped you, and any pillion passenger, must wear an approved safety helmet which must be fastened securely. Helmets are 'approved' if passed by the British Safety Standards Institute and thus carry a BSI seal of approval. It is advisable to acquire a new helmet to ensure a correct fit. In any case, it is not possible to be certain that a second-hand helmet has not been weakened in a collision or by having been dropped. Your pillion passenger must sit astride the machine on a proper seat and keep both feet on footrests.

Beware: a pillion passenger must not be carried until a full moped licence has been obtained.

It is an offence to ride a moped on any motorway.

5.3   Motorcycles

You may obtain a provisional licence to ride a motorcycle from the age of 17, but before the cycle may be ridden on the road, you must satisfactorily complete a compulsory basic training (CBT) course. This involves an off-the-road circuit designed to show whether you can control your vehicle properly. Having passed that test you may ride a motorcycle not exceeding 125 cc on the public road, with approved 'L' plates displayed at both front and rear, for up to three years. During that period you must pass a motorcycle theory test and then a practical test to obtain your full motorcycle licence, otherwise you will lose your provisional licence for a period of one year before you may reapply for a provisional licence.

If you have a full car licence you may, after satisfactorily completing a CBT course, ride a motorcycle of up to 125 cc, with 'L' plates, on public roads.

If you have a full moped licence and wish to obtain full motorcycle entitlement you must take a motorcycle theory test if such a separate test was not required when you obtained your moped licence, and then pass a practical motorcycle test. If your moped licence was obtained before 1 December 1990, you will need to complete a CBT course satisfactorily before riding a motorcycle as a learner.

When you pass a test on a motorcycle of between 75 and 125 cc, you obtain a light motorcycle licence (A1) which entitles you to ride a cycle of up to 125 cc with power output of up to 11 kW. If your test vehicle is between 120 and 125 cc and capable of more than 100 kph you will receive a standard (A) licence. That will restrict you to motorcycles of up to 25 kW for two years, after which you may ride any size of machine. That two-year restriction does not apply to riders over the age of 21 or to riders who attain 21 before that restriction would otherwise end. Such persons may obtain a licence to ride larger motorcycles where they:

- have successfully completed a CBT course
- pass a theory test, if required to do so
- pass a practical test on a machine with power output of at least 35 kW.

(To practise, you may ride a larger motorcycle, with 'L' plates, on public roads, provided that you are accompanied by an approved instructor on another motorcycle in radio contact.)

The rules regarding the wearing of helmets and carrying a pillion passenger are as for moped riders (see section 5.2 above). Note that it is illegal to carry more than one pillion passenger.

Take heed: it is also illegal to carry a pillion passenger, or pull a trailer with a larger motorcycle, until you have passed your full test.

5.4   Passenger service vehicles

Special rules apply to passenger service vehicles (including minibuses designed to carry eight or more passengers) and it is not appropriate to detail them here, beyond stating that following a series of fatalities, minibuses and coaches carrying three or more children have to be fitted with seatbelts.

Minibuses, PSVs and taxis require an MOT certificate as soon as they are one-year-old (not three years, as is the norm).

5.5   Tractors

You must be aged 17 or over to drive a tractor on the road. Road tax is payable if the vehicle is ever on a public road – even if doing no more than crossing it, e.g. from one field to another.

5.6 Electrically assisted means of transport

Electrically assisted pedal cycles having a speed not in excess of 15 mph, electric wheelchairs and invalid carriages are not classified as motor vehicles and no licence is required. However these, and other electrically assisted means of transport, such as powered skate boards, may be considered to constitute 'motorised vehicles'. Accordingly, improper use of them, e.g. while under the undue influence of drink or drugs, may result in the imposition of a fine or in the imposition of penalty points against one's driving licence (see sections 9 to 12).

6 THE DISABLED DRIVER

6.1 Declaration of disability

You must declare your disability to the licensing authorities when making your application for a driving licence or if there has been the onset of a disability since receiving your full licence.

In accordance with European Community legislation, driving licences must record any special vehicle controls which are needed to overcome the effect of any physical disability. If asked to do so by anyone in authority, for example, a police officer, the disabled driver must be able to demonstrate safe control of the vehicle, whether or not there have been special adaptations to the vehicle. If the disabled person is unable to do so, a prosecution may result. The DVLA have a Drivers Medical Branch which can be contacted at telephone number: 0870 600 0301.

6.2 Entitlements

Persons who are chronically sick or disabled qualify for certain benefits including parking concessions.

6.2.1 State benefits

Certain very severe illnesses may render you unfit to drive at all. You can receive driver-potential advice and assessment from the Mobility Information Service for a small fee (see DIRECTORY).

If you are able to drive, you should find out about your various entitlements. These include exemptions from excise duty and VAT, mobility allowance and parking facilities. (Three-wheeled invalid cars were phased out after having been found to be inherently dangerous.)

☞ *You sustained a serious leg injury in a sporting accident. You are dependent on your car for getting about, as a result. You have a full driving licence. What do you do?*

a) Inform the DVLA and your insurers.

b) Establish which kind of car you are able to drive – i.e. whether one with manual or one with automatic transmission. Advice of all kinds is available. For example under the MAVIS scheme in Crowthorne in Berkshire, there is a facility to try out various models of car and/or adaptations. Other organisations, such as Motability, give assistance with car purchase, as well as HP and leasing facilities (see DIRECTORY).

c) The DVLA will ask for further details of your medical condition. It will also ask for permission to consult your doctor and specialist, who must certify that you can still drive. You must also be able to provide information regarding your eyesight.

d) You may then receive a restricted licence, depending on your physical condition, e.g possibly limited to three-year revisions or to one that specifies that you must drive a car with 'controls which can all be correctly and conveniently operated'. If you feel that the licence is too restrictive, you are entitled to appeal.

e) You can apply for a mobility allowance, and car tax and road tax exemptions. Again this is subject to medical assessment.
The mobility allowance can go towards the cost of leasing or buying your car.

f) You can apply for a disabled person's badge if you are left with 'a permanent and substantial disability in walking'. This enables you to park on single yellow lines and in metered parking bays in certain circumstances. It can be withdrawn if it is abused (see below, section 6.3).

6.3 Use of disabled person's badge

It is an offence to display a disabled person's badge when driving a motor vehicle on the road, except where the badge is issued and displayed in accordance with the regulations.

An able-bodied person may display such a badge on his vehicle and avail himself of the parking concessions if he is transporting a disabled person provided that the disabled person's badge concession would be available for use on his or her own vehicle. These badges are also available for the transportation of disabled non-drivers. Parents may have one if they have a disabled child, for example.

☞ *You are transporting your disabled wife in your own car to do the shopping. She is registered disabled and generally displays a disabled person's badge on her own car. Today you want to purchase some large items which would not easily fit in her car and which she could not carry on her own. You both set out to do the shopping. Are you guilty of an offence when you park on the line outside the store you intend to visit, and display her badge?*

The answer is 'no', you are not in breach of any legal provisions. However, should you take your wife home and then drive alone to do some private business, using the badge to park in an otherwise illegal position, you are guilty of an offence and are liable on summary conviction to a fine not exceeding level 3 on the standard scale. (See section 9 below.)

6.4 Temporary disability

The above concessions are not generally applicable where you are suffering from a temporary disability, in particular if you are taking prescribed drugs or medicines. It is an offence to drive when so influenced. When taking prescribed medicines, ask your doctor if it is safe to drive. Similarly, ask your pharmacist if you are purchasing over-the-counter medicines.

However, if your mobility is seriously impaired on a temporary basis, e.g. if you are recovering from a major operation, you may obtain a disabled person's badge for a limited period.

6.5 Nature of disabled person's badges

As stated at 6.2.1(f) above, the possession of a disabled person's badge enables parking in some otherwise restricted areas. In addition many large stores and supermarkets set aside spaces dedicated to the use of disabled persons. Most of the latter still indicate that these are dedicated to orange badge holders, but the orange badges are being phased out and replaced by a blue parking card conforming to a European Communities model. This blue card has been issued in all cases occurring after 1 April 2000 and to all replacement cards issued after that date.

Accordingly all badges will have been replaced by the blue badge by 31 March 2003. The card carries a passport-sized photo of the holder and, when in use, it is to be displayed at the front of the vehicle in such a way that the front of the card is clearly visible for checking purposes. The blue card entitles the holder to the special local parking facilities available in each Member State. Misuse of the card may constitute a criminal offence in the country where such misuse occurs. Each card is issued for a three-year period and is then subject to renewal on payment of a small fee.

The issue of such cards does not affect proposals for eligibility or the current criteria of concessions in each Member State. Indeed, the UK government is considering a review of the disability badge scheme to tighten the eligibility criteria, and to deal more effectively with any abuse of the scheme.

7 ACCIDENTS

The cardinal rule is that you must report an accident to the police where it involves injury to another person, damage to another vehicle or to an animal (but not a cat!), property adjoining a street, or 'street furniture' which usually means a lamppost, bollard etc. You must also stop after an accident. See also the chapter on *Accidents*, section 1.1.

Do take heed: young men in the 17–24 age group are most at risk of being involved in a fatal accident either as victim or as a driver who kills.

7.1 Obligation to report an accident

If someone else is injured (including a passenger of yours) in an accident, you are required to stop and to produce your insurance details. If you cannot produce insurance details at the time of the accident, a report must be made to the police within 24 hours and insurance details must be produced to them within five days.

If someone else's property or animal is injured you are required to stop. If at that time you do not exchange your name and address, a report of the accident must be made to the police within 24 hours.

☞   *You are driving along a rather dark, narrow country road, with the car radio turned up, and you pass a car on your right. You think you might have heard a scraping noise but cannot be sure because of the noise of the music. The next day you notice a substantial dent to your car and realise that there was a collision with the other car. What do you do?*

You are under a duty to report the accident to the police within 24 hours.

Failure to report an accident thus arises once you become aware that it has happened. It also applies whether or not there was somebody else at the scene. For the penalties for failing to report an accident, see section 14.3 below.

7.2   No obligation to report an accident

However, you are not under an obligation to report to the police if:

- you have a collision with another car and no one is hurt, and you stop to exchange your name and address with the other driver, as well as registration and insurance details
- only your own car is damaged.

7.3   The immediate tasks after an accident

Irrespective of the legal liability to stop and exchange your name and address and/or insurance details (see sections 7.1 and 7.2 above), you should stop and check whether anyone has been injured and take the precautions outlined below.

☞   *You are driving along a quiet suburban street well within the speed limit. You notice out of the corner of your eye that some boys are kicking a football on the pavement. All of a sudden, one of them races after the ball into the road just in front of you. You swerve to avoid him and hit a car coming from the opposite direction. The boy is unhurt but the other driver appears quite dazed and both cars have been badly damaged. What do you do?*

   a) Call an ambulance as you have no way of ascertaining whether the other driver is suffering from shock and/or concussion.
   b) Call the police.
   c) Keep a cool head – the most difficult task of all!
   d) Make no admission as to any liability.
   e) Endeavour to take down witness details, as once the crowd which gathers at the scene drifts off, you are unlikely to be able to trace witnesses again.
   f) Try to make a preliminary sketch of the position of the cars.

7.4   After the event

   a) Write down all the details as you remember them.
   b) Inform your insurers whether or not you expect a claim.
   c) Hand in all the relevant documents at your nearest police station: licence (plus counterpart, if any), insurance, and MOT, within five days. If you could not give them to the police present at the time of the accident you must specify then which police station you intend to go to.
   d) Go back to the scene to take measurements, and even photographs.
   e) If the police inform you of any prosecution, possibly for careless driving (remember you did notice the boys out of the corner of your eye), you should contact a solicitor who specialises in road traffic offences, or seek other legal advice (see the chapter on *The Legal System*).

7.5   Insurance certificate and driving licence

It is advisable to keep your insurance certificate in your car at all times and not to drive without your driving licence. These precautions can reduce the inconvenience of having to attend at a police station to produce either document.

8   CAR THEFT

Car theft continues to grow and the Home Office has issued a list of the makes and models of cars most likely to be stolen. It is estimated that one in four drivers leaves his or her car unlocked. There are two separate offences that concern the taking away of vehicles under the Theft Act 1968.

8.1 Theft

This involves an intention – as with all theft – to deprive the owner permanently of his possession. Car theft is usually perpetrated by well-organised, professional thieves, and the cars are made to 'disappear' quickly – either literally by being transported out of the country, or by 'laundering' through other means. Stolen cars are often then used to carry out other crimes, or other car thefts.

The rule is that a thief can never become the 'owner' of the car, and so he cannot pass on title to the car to another person – even one who buys in good faith. Thus anyone buying a stolen car is liable to its true owner– if the owner can trace it.

The owner of a Mercedes Benz handed over his car and the log book in the course of an armed robbery when he was held up at gun point. He was also forced to write a 'receipt' for an alleged £46,000 so that it could look like a sale. The robbers then threatened to kill his family if he told the police. The Mercedes thereafter changed hands three times before the owner approached the police a month later. The court held that the successive new 'owners' had no title to the car.

8.2 Taking a vehicle without consent, or 'joy-riding'

This is usually carried out by juveniles. It is defined under section 12 of the Theft Act 1968. Because there is no intention to deprive the owner permanently of his car but to dump it at some point, it is categorised as a separate offence from theft. The large numbers of joy-riders occupy a great amount of police and court time and teenage joy-riders are an increasing hazard on the road.

8.2.1 'Aggravated Vehicle-Taking' Act

The 'Aggravated Vehicle-Taking' Act 1992 lays down an aggravated form of the offence of taking without consent, to meet the increasing danger from joy-riders. That includes driving the vehicle, or allowing oneself to be driven in the taken vehicle. The aggravated offence is considered to have taken place if at any time after the vehicle was taken (whether by the driver, the passenger or someone else), one or other of the following occurs:

- the vehicle is driven dangerously on a road or other public place
- an accident occurs in which any person is injured
- an accident happens in which there is damage to the vehicle or to any other property.

Where the aggravation relates to damage only, and the value of the damage is small, the offence is triable summarily in a magistrates' court with a maximum penalty of six months' immediate imprisonment or a fine of up to the statutory maximum, or both. On indictment, the maximum penalty is two years' imprisonment (or five years' if an accident results in someone's death). Thus the penal consequences depend on the consequential effects of the driving rather than the extent to which the defendant is culpable.

The aggravated offence carries a compulsory disqualification of a minimum of 12 months, and endorsement.

The youth of the defendant will not generally be taken to be a mitigating factor as the relevant provisions were introduced primarily to cover offences perpetrated by young persons.

8.3 Insurance notification

Should your car be stolen or taken without consent, it is important that you notify your insurer without delay. If the car is not recovered or is found smashed by joy-riders, your insurance company will provide your only form of redress.

The courts now have extended powers to convict persons on these charges. Powers relate only to conviction on criminal charges. No provision is made for the convicted person to make restitution to the aggrieved owner for damage to his car. (For the position on personal injury, see section 1.2.4 above.)

9 OFFENCES AND PENALTIES – GENERAL OVERVIEW

The Road Traffic Act 1991 introduced stiffer new penalties for a wide range of offences. The toughening up on the effective enforcement of traffic laws is well illustrated by the fact that no fewer than seven offences may attract a period of imprisonment. Additionally, many of the provisions have been redrafted to make it clearer when an action constitutes an offence.

Warning notice: Under the Police Reform Act, driving while disqualified (see further below) becomes an arrestable offence.

The principal particular offences will be considered in some detail in subsequent sections.

9.1   Alternative verdicts

It is possible in certain cases for a person charged with an offence to be convicted of a lesser one. This route will presumably be taken where the outcome of prosecution for the more serious offence is uncertain.

For example, you may be charged with dangerous driving. If it may be difficult to prove the this charge, your legal adviser may press for a reduction to the lesser, alternative charge of careless and inconsiderate driving.

9.2   Enforcement and technology

The prosecution may obtain a conviction by producing in evidence photographs taken from speed cameras and cameras situated at traffic lights. It is not necessary for such photographs to be backed up by eyewitness evidence. Where photographic evidence is not available you cannot be convicted of a speeding offence solely on the opinion evidence of one witness.

9.3   Driver identity

The owner of a vehicle will himself be guilty of an offence if he refuses to divulge the identity of the driver of his vehicle if that driver is suspected of having been involved in a serious offence.

An owner will not be convicted, however, if he can establish that he did not know and could not reasonably have been expected to know the identity of the driver. A company and its directors may also be found guilty of failure to disclose unless it can be demonstrated that failure to keep records of drivers was reasonable in the circumstances.

9.4   Interim disqualification

Where a magistrates' court refers an offender to the Crown Court for sentence or defers sentence for social inquiry etc., the court may disqualify that person pending his ultimate sentence. This power is exercisable only in cases where the offence is one which attracts a discretionary or mandatory disqualification from driving. In practice, it seems likely that an interim disqualification is more likely to occur where the offence is subject to a mandatory disqualification.

Credit will be given for the period of interim disqualification when it comes to the imposition of the sentence.

☞   *You are convicted on 1 March 2002 and placed under interim disqualification for an excess-alcohol offence. You appear for sentence on 31 March and are disqualified for 12 months. When will your disqualification order end?*

At midnight on 28 February 2003.

9.5   Newly qualified drivers

In an effort to cut down on accidents caused by newly qualified drivers, measures have been introduced which include:

- retesting of new drivers convicted of serious driving offences
- separate theory testing as part of the driving test.

For details, see sections 1.1.1(b) and 1.1.8 above.

9.6   Classification of penalties

Road traffic offences may lead to:

- imprisonment
- fines
- penalty points endorsed on your licence.

9.6.1   Penalty points

The penalty-point system is intended to deter drivers from unsafe driving since the accumulation of twelve or more points over a three-year period will result in a disqualification for a minimum period of six months, and for a longer period if the driver has previously been disqualified. Indeed you may lose your licence simply through committing a number of very trivial offences under the totting-up procedure.

If your disqualification results from an accumulation of twelve penalty points on your licence those penalty points will be removed from your licence.

However, if you are disqualified for a specific offence, e.g. dangerous driving, those previous unrelated penalty points will not be removed from your licence.

☞ *You have six penalty points, dating from January 2001 on your licence and on 1 June 2001 are disqualified from driving for a period of twelve months, having been convicted of careless driving. On 30 June 2002 you are convicted of driving without insurance and eight penalty points are awarded against you. Will you again be disqualified from driving?*

Yes. The court will take account of your original six points. You now have fourteen penalty points awarded within a three-year period and disqualification is applicable.

Note: the courts are most unlikely to hear favourably any argument to the effect that your business interests will be adversely affected by any disqualification imposed.

Note also: in a recent case, the defendant argued that his human rights had been infringed because he needed a driving licence for his work. His plea failed to gain a sympathetic hearing!

9.7   Penalty table

Offence   *Maximum penalties*

	IMPRISONMENT	FINE	DISQUALIFICATION	PENALTY POINTS
*Causing death by dangerous driving	10 years	Unlimited	Obligatory – 2 years minimum	3–11 (if exceptionally not disqualified)
*Dangerous driving	2 years	Unlimited	Obligatory	3–11 (if exceptionally not disqualified)
Causing death by careless driving under the influence of drink or drugs	10 years	Unlimited	Obligatory – 2 years minimum	3–11 (if exceptionally not disqualified)
Careless or inconsiderate driving	–	£2,500	Discretionary	3–9
Driving while unfit through drink or drugs or with excess alcohol; or failing to provide a specimen for analysis	6 months	£5,000	Obligatory	3–11 (if exceptionally not disqualified)
Failing to stop after an accident or failing to report an accident	6 months	£5,000	Discretionary	5–10
Driving when disqualified	6 months (12 months in Scotland)	£5,000	Discretionary	6
Driving after refusal or revocation of licence on medical grounds	6 months	£5,000	Discretionary	3–6

Penalty table *(cont)*

Offence   *Maximum penalties*

	IMPRISONMENT	FINE	DISQUALIFICATION	PENALTY POINTS
Driving without insurance	–	£5,000	Discretionary	6–8
Driving otherwise than in accordance with a licence	–	£1,000	Discretionary	3–6
Speeding	–	£1,000 (£2,500 for motorway offences)	Discretionary	3–6 or 3 (fixed penalty)
Traffic-light offences	–	£1,000	Discretionary	3
No MOT certificate	–	£1,000	–	–
Seat belt offences	–	£500	–	–
Dangerous cycling	–	£2,500	–	–
Careless cycling	–	£1,000	–	–
Cycling on pavement	–	£500	–	–
Failing to identify driver of a vehicle	–	£1,000	Discretionary	3

* Where a court disqualifies a person on conviction for one of these offences, it must order an extended retest. The courts also have discretion to order a retest for any other offence which carries penalty points: an extended retest where disqualification is obligatory, and an ordinary test where disqualification is not obligatory.

See section 10.5 below on re-testing requirements.

Do note: the Table above is not exhaustive of all driving offences.

10   DANGEROUS DRIVING OFFENCES

The offence of driving recklessly has been replaced by two offences:

- driving dangerously
- causing death by dangerous driving – or, as the Act puts it, causing death 'by driving a mechanically propelled vehicle dangerously on a road or other public place'. This attracts the most serious penalties.

The meaning of 'dangerous driving' is the same for both offences.

10.1   Meaning of 'dangerous driving'

A person is regarded as driving dangerously if:

- the way he drives falls far below what would be expected of a competent and careful driver, and
- it would be obvious to a competent and careful driver that driving in that way would be dangerous.

'Dangerous', in this context, means likely to cause either injury to a person or serious damage to property.

10.1.1   Dangerous driving covers state of vehicle

Driving will also be regarded as dangerous in circumstances where it would be obvious to a careful and competent driver that driving the vehicle in its current state would be dangerous. This extends to anything attached to or carried on or in the vehicle and the manner in which it is attached or carried.

☞ *A load of hay carried on your open-backed truck falls off and causes an accident to the vehicle behind you. The load was large but you had not tied it down in any way. You had given no particular thought as to whether the bales were likely to be stable. Could you be found guilty of dangerous driving?*

Yes. The jury could find that it would have been obvious to a careful and competent driver that there was a clear risk that the load might fall and cause death or injury. It does not matter that you did not consider that possibility.

10.2 The meaning of 'mechanically propelled vehicles' and 'public place'

10.2.1 Type of vehicle

Dangerous-driving offences extend to any mechanically propelled vehicle rather than being restricted to a 'motor vehicle'. So the offence could extend, for example, to dangerous driving of stock cars, scramble bikes and even a mechanical sit-on lawnmower. It would also extend to a vehicle which is being towed and could not be driven under its own motor power.

10.2.2 Type of place

The extension of the offence to driving not only on a road but also in a public place means that an offence may be committed in, say, a public car park or in a pub car park to which the public have access.

10.2.3 Exclusion: motor-sports events

There is an exclusion covering areas in which the driving occurs in accordance with an authorisation for a motoring event given under regulations made by the Secretary of State.

☞ *You are taking part in an authorised event and take risks which could very well result in damage to a fellow competitor or his vehicle. You collide with another vehicle causing damage to it. Can you be found guilty of an offence of dangerous driving?*

The answer is 'no'. The driving was undertaken in the course of an authorised motoring event. You could, however, be sued for negligence, depending on the circumstances.

10.3 Penalty for causing death by dangerous driving

The maximum sentence for causing death by dangerous driving is ten years' imprisonment and/or an unlimited fine. The offence is triable only on indictment [i.e. in a Crown Court].

The offence carries an obligatory disqualification period of not less than two years.

Alternatively, a charge could be laid for manslaughter caused by driving. However this step is likely to be limited to only the most serious of cases since, should there be an acquittal on that charge, an alternative verdict of committing the statutory offence would not be possible. In contrast, if there is an acquittal on a charge of causing death by dangerous driving, an alternative verdict of dangerous driving or of careless and inconsiderate driving may be reached. Should an offender have been convicted of causing death by dangerous driving within ten years preceding the current offence, the obligatory minimum disqualification period is three years.

10.4 Penalty for dangerous driving

The maximum penalty for dangerous driving is:

- on indictment (Crown court proceedings): two years' imprisonment and/or an unlimited fine
- on summary trial (magistrates' court proceedings): six months' imprisonment and/or a fine subject to the statutory maximum.

The offender must be disqualified for not less than 12 months.

If a person is found not guilty of dangerous driving, an alternative verdict of careless and inconsiderate driving may be brought.

10.5 Mandatory retesting

Where a person is disqualified for:

- manslaughter by driving
- causing death by dangerous driving, or
- dangerous driving

the court must order that person to be disqualified until the appropriate driving test has been passed. In such cases the test will be an extended driving test – not the standard 'L' test. The extended test will be approximately double the length of the standard test and will, in general, require the candidate to drive for an unspecified period on an unrestricted dual carriageway. Fees for the retest must be met by the offender and are approximately double those charged for a standard test. (For the definition of a 'restricted road', see section 13.1 below.)

11   CARELESS DRIVING OFFENCES

It is an offence to drive a mechanically propelled vehicle on a road or other public place without due care and attention, or without reasonable consideration for other persons using the road or place.

It is also an offence if death is caused by such careless driving when under the influence of drink or drugs.

The meaning of 'mechanically propelled vehicle' and 'public place' is discussed in section 10.2 above.

11.1   What constitutes careless driving?

There are no hard and fast rules of law and each case depends on its particular circumstances.

☞ *You signal that you intend to turn left and then turn right. Can you be convicted of careless driving?*

> The answer is 'yes', if you have taken no precautions to look behind you to see if any other vehicle was coming from behind. However, if you made certain that no other driver was to be inconvenienced or endangered by your action, you could escape conviction.

Other examples of careless driving include:

* crossing a white line
* failing to stop and look, at a T-junction
* edging on to a road when the view is obstructed
* reading a map etc in the car.

11.2   Penalties for careless or inconsiderate driving

An offence of this nature may only be tried summarily and, if convicted, the offender may be fined up to £2,500. Endorsement of one's licence is obligatory with penalty points in the range of three to nine. Disqualification is discretionary.

Do note: In addition to the possibility of criminal action being taken for careless driving, a civil action may be brought. For example, in one case a claim for personal injuries was upheld where it was found that a driver had been negligent in attempting to overtake a coach when it was unsafe to do so (see also chapter on *Accidents*, section 6.1.4(b)).

11.3   Death caused by careless driving when unfit through drink or drugs

For this offence to be founded it must be established:

a) that a death has been caused as a result of the defendant having driven without due care and attention or without reasonable consideration for other persons using the road or place, and

b) i.   at the time of driving the defendant was unfit to drive through drink or drugs, or

  ii. the defendant had consumed so much alcohol that the proportion of it in his breath, blood or urine at the time exceeded the prescribed limit, or

  iii. the defendant, within 18 hours after driving, failed without reasonable excuse to provide a specimen as required.

It is not necessary for the prosecution to show that the intoxicant caused the careless driving resulting in death. It is sufficient that there was careless driving resulting in that consequence and that the defendant transgressed one of the three provisions outlined above. If a person fails, without reasonable excuse, to provide a specimen, he is liable to be convicted as if he had provided a specimen which was over the limit. The prescribed legal limits are set out in section 12.2.1 below.

11.4   Penalty for careless driving when unfit causing death

The maximum sentence for this offence is ten years' imprisonment and/or an unlimited fine. There is an obligatory disqualification period of not less than two years. That minimum period is to be increased to three years where there has been a conviction for another such offence within 10 years of the commission of the current offence. Rehabilitation courses for drink/drive offenders are considered at section 12.7.

In two cases where the defendants, whose drunken driving caused three deaths, received very lenient sentences, the Lord Chief Justice issued guidance on sentencing policy. He stated that sentences should reflect society's abhorrence of these crimes and that sentences should punish the driver and deter others. In the worst cases, sentences up to the statutory maximum of ten years should be imposed.

A person found not guilty of careless driving causing death may nevertheless be found guilty of an offence of:

- careless and inconsiderate driving
- driving when unfit through alcohol and drugs
- driving with excess alcohol in breath, blood or urine, or
- failing to provide a specimen.

12   DRINK/DRIVING OFFENCES

The best advice is never to drink and drive. A drunken driver can be as dangerous to himself and others as someone out of control with a loaded gun. Never forget, for the safety of yourself and others, that

- the police can easily check the alcohol limits laid down by law, with simple tests
- it is a serious offence to refuse a test without reasonable excuse.

There are a number of offences which can be grouped under different categories, and these are outlined below.

12.1   Being under the influence

This offence covers driving, attempting to drive, or being in charge of a vehicle while under the influence of drink or drugs. In effect, it applies whenever you are unfit to drive, i.e. when your ability is impaired through drink or drugs.

The courts take a very broad view of 'being in charge' of a vehicle; at all times someone is generally assumed to have charge of a vehicle. You would have to show that you had handed over the vehicle to someone else's charge, or were so far from the car (e.g. at home in bed) that you had ceased to be responsible for it.

☞ *You know that you have had a great deal to drink so do not intend to drive. But you are walking with a slightly swaying gait to your car with your ignition keys in your hand when you are stopped by the police and asked to take a breath test. Have you committed an offence?*

The answer is 'yes', usually having ignition keys on you is sufficient proof that you are 'in charge' of your vehicle if you are also under the influence of alcohol.

12.2   Being over the limit

Being over the limit is an offence that entails driving, attempting to drive, or being in charge of a vehicle with excess alcohol in breath, blood or urine.

The alcohol in a pint of draught beer could bring you over the limit, depending on factors such as your sex, size, degree of fatigue etc., as well as the time that you have taken over your drink. There is no 'safe' amount of alcohol that you can drink!

12.2.1   Legal limits

- 35 microgrammes of alcohol in 100 millilitres of breath
- 80 milligrammes of alcohol in 100 millilitres of blood
- 107 milligrammes of alcohol in 100 millilitres of urine.

12.2.2   Asking to see a solicitor

It is advisable to request the presence of a solicitor in any circumstances where you have been asked to attend at a police station to give a specimen.

12.3   Refusing the tests

There are now three separate offence covering:

- failing to provide a specimen of breath, without reasonable excuse, for a breath test (at a roadside test)
- failing to provide a specimen without reasonable excuse for analysis or laboratory test (following the preliminary roadside screening)
- failure to give permission for a laboratory test of a specimen.

☞   *Your roadside test has proved positive and you have been taken to the police station where there was no breath analysis machine. You are asked to provide a sample of blood but say you have a phobia about needles because of AIDS. Can you be found guilty of 'failure to provide' a specimen?*

The answer can be 'yes', if the police can show that you have received injections in the past. Fear of AIDS may be considered a reasonable excuse provided you can show medical evidence of genuine phobia. Other safeguards for the motorist are outlined in section 12.5.

☞   *You are arrested after failing a roadside test. At the police station you are told of your right to consult a solicitor. You therefore refuse to provide a specimen until a solicitor is present, as you honestly believe that you are within your rights. You are then charged with having refused a specimen without reasonable excuse. You wonder if there have been other such cases.*

In a similar case, the court held that although a defendant was entitled to legal advice, he was not entitled to refuse to provide a specimen while waiting to see a solicitor. He did not have a 'reasonable excuse' for his refusal. What amounted to a reasonable excuse was narrow in scope.

12.3.1   Where the driver is incapable of giving consent

A significant new power to take blood samples from drivers without their consent came in to force in October 2002 under the Police Reform Act. Where there has been an accident, and a driver involved is incapacitated or unconscious, the police can ask a doctor to take a blood sample to help to decide if the driver should be prosecuted for drink or drug driving. The sample will not be analysed until the driver regains consciousness and gives his or her consent. However, refusing to allow the sample to be tested is punishable with up to six months' imprisonment. While medical practitioners have been given this power, they are not under a duty to take samples. A doctor could therefore refuse a request from the police if, for example, the procedure would be inadvisable in light of the person's medical condition. Doctors are also advised by the BMA to satisfy themselves that the driver is unable to give valid consent and does not otherwise resist the taking of the sample.

12.4   The motorist's safeguards

All the drink/driving offences exist to protect you and the public against drunken driving. There are also safeguards to protect the motorist – for example, the police cannot go in for random breath testing (see section 12.4.1 below). Whether the correct balance has been struck in the public interest between the police and the motorist arouses much controversy.

12.4.1   Random breath testing

Random breath testing is not allowed. You must have given the police 'reasonable cause to suspect' that you are over the limit, for example by driving erratically or by committing some motoring offence. You can also be asked to take the test if you have been involved in an accident.

12.5   Other safeguards

a) Only a uniformed policeman can ask you to take a roadside test.
b) You can only be asked to take another test if the first one is positive, i.e. the first test is taken purely as a screening device.

c) Any further tests can only be done at certain police stations by an officer specially trained for the purpose, or at a hospital.

d) You can ask to be told of your rights and ask to see the pro-forma police form. You can ask to see your solicitor or the duty solicitor.

e) You must give two specimens of breath and only the lower one is used. You will receive a signed printout of the result. If you are on the borderline the police must tell you that they can ask for the sample to be replaced by blood or urine. In the last resort, the final decision is that of the police unless there are medical reasons why you cannot give blood.

f) A specimen of blood must be taken by a doctor.

g) You must also receive a sample of either the blood or urine, clearly labelled, for your own private analysis.

h) If you are a sick person, specimens can only be taken with the doctor's permission.

Take note: the police have the right to detain you until it appears that you would not recommit the offence, i.e. until you have sobered up.

12.6 Penalties

A person convicted of a drink/driving offence is liable to a maximum term of imprisonment of six months and/or a fine of £5,000. An obligatory disqualification period of 12 months is also applicable. If found not guilty of an alcohol- or drug-related offence involving driving or attempting to drive, you may be found guilty of an alternative offence of being in charge of a vehicle when unfit to drive through drink or drugs or with excess alcohol in breath, blood or urine.

For repeat offenders or where the alcohol level is high the disqualification period may be longer than 12 months. For example, a second drink/drive offence in the space of 10 years will result in a minimum of three years' disqualification. Additionally, in some serious cases, the court must (in addition to imposing a fixed period of disqualification) order that the offender be disqualified until he or she passes a driving test. In other cases the court has a discretionary power to order such disqualification. The test may be an ordinary-length test or an extended test according to the nature of the offence.

12.7 Courses for drink/drive offenders

Rehabilitation courses are available throughout the country for persons convicted of a drink/driving offence. An offender cannot be compelled to attend such a course, but where he is given that option and completes the course successfully, his period of disqualification will be reduced. A qualifying offender must be at least 17-years-old and is required to meet the costs of the course. Further, the latest date for completion of a course must be at least two months before the last day of the reduced period of disqualification (e.g. in the case of a two-year disqualification which is reduced by six months, the specified date for completion must be within 16 months).

Rules are laid down regarding certificates of completion necessary to satisfy a court that the disqualification period may be terminated. However, the convicted person may also be required to resit a driving test before his period of disqualification is terminated.

12.8 The High-Risk Offenders Scheme

Drivers who are convicted of a drink/driving offence within ten years of completing their course, will be classified as high-risk offenders. The scheme also covers:

* those disqualified for having a proportion of alcohol in the body which equalled or exceeded
  i. 87.5 microgrammes per 100 millilitres of breath, or
  ii. 200 milligrammes per 100 millilitres of blood, or
  iii. 267.5 milligrammes per 100 millilitres of urine
* those disqualified for failing without reasonable cause to provide a specimen for analysis.

Under the High-Risk Offenders Scheme offenders are required to satisfy the Medical Advisor at the Driver and Vehicle Licensing Agency that they do not have a drink problem and are fit to drive, before their licences are returned.

The Agency will notify offenders covered by the Scheme what they need to do to apply for the return of their licence. There is a charge for applying for the restoration of the licence. A fee must also be paid for the necessary medical examination.

If you have any queries about the High-Risk Offenders Scheme please contact the DVLA on Swansea (01792) 782956 and quote the reference HRO/REHAB.

12.9 Defences

It has been consistently held that a defence against a drink/driving charge will not stand unless the driver was under reasonable immediate fear of his life or of serious injury. Thus, a man who claimed he had driven while over the limit to escape unwelcome homosexual advances was found to have no viable defence.

Similarly, a woman who claimed she feared violence from her boyfriend following an argument about another man did not have a good defence. However, she might have been considered to have a reasonable defence if she had driven the car to avoid violence if there was reliable evidence of his violent behaviour towards her.

Likewise, a driver failed in his attempt to rely on the defence of 'necessity' when he drove with excess alcohol in order to reach an all-night chemist to buy medicine for his ill daughter. It was held that the defence was available only if the consequences were inevitable and involved serious harm to the driver or someone for whom he was responsible. In this case the child was either not at risk of serious harm, or, if at risk of such harm, a bottle of medicine would not have alleviated that risk. In the event, the facts were not near the threshold of setting up the defence of necessity. There had to be proportionality between the offence and the perception of harm.

13 SPEEDING OFFENCES

You must not exceed the various speed limits laid down for motorways and all other public roads. Only in exceptional circumstances will a defence be available.

☞ *Your daughter has been unemployed but has at last found a job. She sets off in the morning only to return 30 minutes later to say that she has missed the bus and will be late for work. You drive her to work – racing to get there on time. You are stopped by the police for speeding and given a fixed penalty notice. Will the prosecuting authorities make an exception in your case?*

You could write a letter setting out the circumstances and it would then depend on the view that they take of the circumstances. In a case of genuine emergency, such as the need to rush someone to hospital, you would be more likely to get a sympathetic hearing.

The Department for Transport is undertaking a 'speed review' in light of its findings that excessive speed helps to kill around 1,200 people each year, and to injure over 100,000 more; in other words, speed contributes more to road casualties than any other factor.

13.1 Restricted roads

The general rule is that you cannot drive on a 'restricted' road at a speed exceeding 30 miles per hour. Restricted roads are defined as those where lamps are placed not more than 200 yards apart.

13.2 Who imposes limits

Other national speed limits are imposed by the Department for Transport while local limits are imposed by the local authorities. The motorway limit of 70 miles per hour is regulated separately, but all roads, without exception, are subject to speed limits.

13.3 Regulation of classes of vehicle

Different classes of vehicle are also regulated: for example a motor car drawing a trailer on the motorway should not exceed 60 miles per hour.

13.4   **Specified speed limits**

Type of vehicle	BUILT-UP AREAS*	ELSEWHERE Single carriageways	Dual carriageways	MOTORWAYS
	mph	mph	mph	mph
Cars & motorcycles (including car-derived vans up to 2 tonnes maximum laden weight)	30	60	70	70
Cars towing caravans or trailers (including car-derived vans and motorcycles)	30	50	60	60
Buses & coaches (not exceeding 12 metres in overall length)	30	50	60	70
Goods vehicles (not exceeding 7.5 tonnes maximum laden weight)	30	50	60	70†
Goods vehicles (exceeding 7.5 tonnes maximum laden weight)	30	40	50	60

These are the national speed limits and apply to all roads unless signs show otherwise.

The 30 mph limit applies to all traffic on all roads in England and Wales (only Class C and unclassified roads in Scotland) with street lighting unless signs show otherwise.

†*Limit is 60 mph if articulated or towing a trailer.*

Note: the 30 mph limit applies to all traffic on all roads with street lighting in England and Wales unless signs show otherwise. Local authorities have the power to vary speed limits within their areas. The authorities may impose speed restrictions on particular local roads permanently or temporarily, which may be effective in respect of only certain hours of the day; for example, near schools during recognised hours of school-related traffic.

13.5   **Photographic evidence of speeding**

Cameras have been installed for the detection of speeding. Photographic evidence from these cameras may be relied on by the prosecution without there being any corroboration by a witness to the offence. In some instances cameras which do not actually provide photographic evidence have been installed but, as the police move working cameras from site to site, it would be unwise to assume that at any time one particular camera is not functioning.

The police are to be given greater power to target motorists who are persistent offenders. Digital speed cameras are being installed, and an extra fine imposed on drivers caught speeding, to cover the installation costs.

13.6   **Penalties**

A person found guilty of a speeding offence is liable to a possible fine of £1,000 (£2,500 for motorway infringements) and may have his licence endorsed by between three and six penalty points (maximum three in cases of fixed-penalty offences). Furthermore, the court has a discretion to disqualify the driver.

14   **GENERAL OFFENCES**

There are a great number of offences which might be committed by a motorist other than those referred to in previous sections of this chapter. An overview of the more important of these is given below.

14.1   Causing danger to other road users

A person is guilty of an offence if he intentionally and without lawful authority or reasonable cause:

a) causes anything to be on or over a road, or
b) interferes with a motor vehicle, trailer or cycle, or
c) interferes (directly or indirectly) with traffic equipment in such circumstances that it would be obvious to a reasonable person that to do so would be dangerous.

'Dangerous', in this context, has the same meaning as in the offence of dangerous driving (see section 10.1 above).

☞   *You are fed up with heavy goods vehicles constantly taking the route past your home instead of using the nearby alternative dual carriageway. You presume this is being done to avoid traffic congestion problems on the dual carriageway. In desperation, after a sleepless night because of the roar of juggernauts, you build a temporary barrier at the nearby crossroads, hoping this will deter vehicles from turning into your road. You don't think this will be dangerous – merely a deterrent. Can you be charged with an offence of causing danger to other road users?*

Yes. You intentionally placed an obstacle on the road without lawful authority and it would be obvious to a reasonable person that this would constitute a danger. It is not necessary for you to have considered it dangerous.

14.1.1   Penalties

The maximum penalties for an offence of causing danger to other road users are:

• on summary trial, six months' imprisonment and/or a fine subject to the statutory maximum
• on indictment, seven years' imprisonment and/or an unlimited fine.

14.2   Vehicle construction and use offences

It is an offence to use, or cause or permit another person to use, a motor vehicle or trailer on a road where such use involves a danger of injury because of:

• the condition of the vehicle
• the purpose for which the vehicle is used
• the number of passengers carried or the manner in which those passengers are carried
• the load of the vehicle.

It is also an offence to contravene construction and use requirements as to brakes, steering or tyres, or weight requirements. These offences lead to a mandatory licence endorsement of three penalty points. The offender is also liable for discretionary disqualification, unless he can establish that he did not know, and had no reasonable cause to suspect, the existence of a defect.

The police operate non-statutory Vehicle Defect Rectification Schemes (VDRS) which allow for a vehicle which is found to be unfit to be repaired or scrapped within a certain time limit, on the basis that the driver will not then be charged with an offence.

There are a number of different schemes throughout the country but the only substantial differences are in the time limits for having the repair done or the vehicle scrapped, and in the offences that are covered.

14.3   Accidents

The requirements to stop at the scene of an accident and to report an accident are dealt with at section 7 above. A failure on either count can result in a maximum of six months' imprisonment and/or a fine of £5,000. Disqualification is discretionary but the offender's licence is to be endorsed with between five and ten penalty points. Disqualification is a likely outcome in the case of a 'hit-and-run' offence.

14.4   Licence violations

It is an offence to drive otherwise than in accordance with a licence. This is applicable regardless of whether the offender has no licence at all (possibly because he is under age and could not qualify for a licence) or whether the holder is driving a vehicle not covered by his licence or in a manner not permitted by his licence. For example, the holder of a provisional licence driving without 'L' plates or without an accompanying approved licensed driver would be committing an offence. An offence of this nature attracts a maximum fine of £1,000, discretionary disqualification, and penalty points in the range from three to six. Driving when disqualified or when not permitted to drive by reason of physical disability are more serious offences and are subject to a maximum period of six months' imprisonment and/or a fine of up to £5,000, with a discretion as to further disqualification; a licence may also be endorsed with up to six penalty points.

If you are a disqualified driver who has held a licence in the past and are entitled to hold a similar licence when the disqualification period has expired, you can drive legally after that period, even though you do not physically hold a licence, provided that an application for a licence has been received by the appropriate authorities and that you fulfil the general requirements for the grant of licences.

14.5   No insurance

It is possible to gain an exemption from third-party insurance but as this requires a deposit of not less than £500,000 with the Accountant-General this is an option unlikely to be invoked except by a body running a very substantial fleet of vehicles. The majority of road users will have no such exemption and commit an offence if driving without at least third-party insurance cover. An offence may result in a fine of up to £5,000, possible disqualification and endorsement of one's licence with penalty points ranging between six and eight.

14.6   No MOT certificate

You must have a current MOT certificate for any vehicle on a public road where one is required, i.e. when a motor car is three-years-old or more. Such a certificate is not needed for a vehicle held solely in a private place but must be available where, for example, the vehicle is parked on a public road – even if you have no intention of driving it. An offence can lead to a maximum fine of £1,000 but does not involve endorsement of your licence. Of course higher penalties may be attracted if, for example, use of the vehicle is considered to have constituted dangerous driving (see section 10.1).

14.7   Traffic signals

If you fail to stop at a red traffic light or at a stop sign, or ignore a traffic warden's instructions etc., it might be that you would find yourself charged with dangerous or careless driving (see sections 10 and 11), but the normal result will be that you will be issued with a fixed fine and have your licence endorsed by up to three penalty points. It should be remembered that photographic evidence of such a failure is sufficient without other witness evidence being supplied.

Temporary traffic lights set up at, say, an area of roadworks, must be obeyed in the same way as permanent lights.

14.8   Seat belts

If you fail to observe the seat belt requirements (see section 2.5), you are guilty of an offence punishable by a fine of up to £500. Penalty points are not incurred.

15   PARKING OFFENCES

Apart from parking restrictions on a yellow line, double yellow lines, red route or other designated parking-restricted areas, there are the offences of

- parking in a manner that obstructs other cars
- leaving your vehicle in a dangerous position.

15.1   Local authorities

Local authorities run their own parking schemes although the Department for Transport has overriding authority, for example in designating red routes in urban areas. Their objective in introducing and enforcing parking regulations is to maintain in urban areas a safe environment that tries to cater for the needs of all users of the highways, in particular those of residents, businesses and visitors. The task is a difficult one and becomes more so with every year as the volume of traffic increases and the demands made on available routes grows exponentially.

15.2   Taking parking offences out of the hands of the police – 'decriminalisation'

The Secretary of State is able to make orders under the Road Traffic Act 1991 accepting local authority etc. plans for permitted parking and special parking areas. As a result many local authorities have now taken over from the police the responsibility for parking enforcement in towns and cities.

Failure to observe parking provisions in such areas may not be considered criminal, providing the offence relates to a stationary vehicle. Usually, a Penalty Charge Notice ('ticket') will specify a fixed fine to be paid for the parking infringement. However local authorities also have the powers to clamp or tow away vehicles (see section 15.5).

15.3   Parking meters

Where parking meters are provided you are required to comply with the displayed conditions relating to payment and to duration of stay.

☞   *You have found an empty metered parking bay in a busy street. It still has one hour of unexpired time on the meter so you leave your car there and return an hour later. You then put in sufficient coins for another two hours. Have you committed an offence?*

The answer is 'yes'. You have two legal choices:

a) to remove your car before the end of the hour of 'free' time; or
b) to put in the coins on your arrival that would have brought you within the two-hour limit.

You cannot run an additional two hours' worth of parking time on to the existing unelapsed time shown on the meter.

15.4   Parking-ticket adjudicators

In London, local authority Parking Adjudicators are available to consider contested parking offence cases of the local authority (see DIRECTORY under the Parking and Traffic Appeals Service). Details of the National Parking Adjudicators' Service – that covers the rest of England and Wales – are also to be found in the DIRECTORY.

The procedure for dealing with parking appeals is set down in Schedule 6 of the Road Traffic Act 1991 and associated regulations. You will receive 21 days' notice of a hearing, which lasts about 20 minutes. Alternatively, you can submit your evidence in writing.

There are set grounds for appeal:

- the offence did not occur
- the vehicle was taken without the driver's consent i.e. it had been stolen and then parked illegally
- the driver had sold the car before the parking offence took place
- the car was rented and the driver accepted responsibility for parking fines in his contract with the company
- the driver is asked to pay the wrong amount or the order under which the parking ticket was made is not valid.

Note: the Adjudicator must only deal with the facts and the law, and has no power to take extenuating circumstances into account, but local authorities may do so in exceptional cases (e.g. where a man parks illegally in order to see his wife, who is about to give birth, into hospital).

Other factors which the local authority should consider are that:

- the parking meter was faulty
- the parking attendant has made an error in writing out the notice
- the vehicle had broken down
- evidence shows that the charge should be waived on compassionate grounds.

15.5 Wheel-clamping

Local authorities, which have taken up powers to enforce parking regulations (see section 15.2 above) can clamp and/or tow away vehicles that are in breach of parking restrictions; a fine must be paid for the vehicle's release.

The police also have the authority to clamp or tow away vehicles that contravene parking regulations in areas not covered by the local authority's parking order. They can also tow away from any area vehicles which cause an obstruction or are parked in a dangerous position.

It should be noted that illegal operatives are offering to release cars for less than the official fee. Do not be tempted to accept such an offer as the unofficial removal of clamps (usually by cutting the clamping device) is an illegal act and you could be charged as a party to the commission of the offence.

15.6 Clamping on private land

Landowners and their agents have resorted to clamping vehicles on private land and currently there are no regulations to control this activity. Local authorities too can use their enforcement powers to clamp those vehicles in their car parks and private estates, e.g. a local council housing estate, that contravene their parking regulations.

☞ *You parked your car in the private parking-ground of a block of flats when you visited a friend living there. A large notice was displayed stating that unauthorised cars parking in the area would be wheel-clamped, and that a clamped car would be released only on payment of a £40 fee. You returned to find your car clamped and unwillingly paid the fee for its release. You wonder what the legal position is, and whether you can claim your money back.*

It appears from case law that, where a notice has been prominently displayed warning drivers that unauthorised parking would entail clamping and that release would only be effected by paying a fee, you willingly took the risk by leaving your car there.

It thus seems that a private landowner has the authority to clamp vehicles on his land if there is adequate warning. However, he is not justified in

a) charging an unreasonable or exorbitant fee for unclamping
b) causing damage to the vehicle; or
c) detaining the vehicle after the owner has expressed a willingness to pay the fee.

Do note: it seems there must also be a means for an owner to communicate his offer to pay the fee without excessive delay.

It is unclear what level of charge would be considered unreasonable or exorbitant but it is worth bearing in mind that the fee for release of a vehicle that has been officially clamped for a parking offence is in the region of £100.

If you feel you have been unfairly treated by having been overcharged, or in any other way, you would be advised to pay the fine and then to seek legal redress or to take the matter up with your motoring organisation if you are a member of one.

In a recent case, a woman was forced by an attack of nausea to pull off the road and park on private land. She did not see the notice warning that any unattended vehicle would be clamped because the notice was attached to the wall of another bay in which a Range Rover was parked. When she returned to her car after a few minutes, she found that it had been clamped. She paid the £105 fee to have her car released and later brought an action, supported by the AA, for damages.

The Court of Appeal ruled that she was entitled to be repaid the £105 release fee, stating that the act of clamping the wheel of another person's car – even when that car was on private land – was an act of trespass on someone else's vehicle unless it could be shown that the driver had accepted the risk of his or her car being clamped. It had to be shown therefore that drivers saw and understood the significance of a warning notice so that they took on the risk willingly. It was essential that notices were placed in a position where they were bound to be seen, e.g. at the entrance to a car park.

15.6.1 Regularising clamping firms

Under the Private Security Industry Act 2001 clamping firms are to operate only with licensed clampers. An occupier of premises (for example the landlord of a block of flats) will be guilty of an offence if any unlicensed individual clamps, immobilises, or removes a vehicle on his property. An occupier will have a defence against any such offence if he can show either:

a) that he did not know and had no reasonable grounds for suspecting at the time that the individual in question was not the holder of a licence; or
b) that he had taken all reasonable steps to ensure that an unlicensed individual would not engage in any such conduct on his premises.

If found guilty of an offence, fines and/or imprisonment could follow.

A new body, the Security Industry Authority, will be set up under the 2001 Act to oversee the issuing of licences to individuals and suitable firms in order to outlaw cowboy clampers. The necessary regulations are expected to be in force by the end of 2003.

Contractors will have to apply for a licence to become approved contractors and will have to sign an undertaking that they will abide by the British Parking Association's Code of Practice and Code of Conduct (in preparation).

The Association acting for the Security Industry Authority will be responsible for managing and enforcing these codes to ensure that the service that the contractors and individual operators provide is carried out in a responsible, effective, and efficient manner. The Code of Practice will provide for an independent arbitration service in the event of a dispute between the clamping firm and an aggrieved motorist.

16 CARELESS OR INCONSIDERATE CYCLING

It is a summary offence to ride a cycle on a road without due care and attention or without reasonable consideration for other persons using the road. It carries a maximum penalty of a fine of level 3. 'Careless or inconsiderate' have the same meaning as for driving a vehicle – see section 11.1 above.

A legislative proposal would make it illegal to sell a new bicycle which does not carry a bell.

(For cycle paths and a code of conduct for mountain-bike riding and off road cycling, see the chapter on *The Countryside*, section 1.1.8(d).)

17 DISQUALIFICATIONS FOR NON-DRIVING OFFENCES

Magistrates have the power to remove licences from people who fail to pay fines, for up to 12 months.

There are Home Office proposals which would give magistrates' courts power to impose a driving disqualification for offences such as burglary and car theft. A ban from driving could be imposed for a set period determined by the court.

It is also suggested that men who default on an order to pay maintenance for their children under the Child Support Acts, could also lose their driving licences (see chapter on *Children (Part 1)*, section 2.2.3).

18 CONGESTION CHARGES

Every day commuters in cars suffer from the fact that there are too many vehicles on too few roads. In the cities, there is simply too little space for the traffic which is increasingly being generated. The economy and our environment suffers as a result.

In order to tackle the problem, a £5 charge will be imposed, from 2003, on a designated area of inner London where congestion charging will apply to non-authorised motor traffic.

For further information go to *www.cclondon.com* or call 0845 900 1234; or write to Congestion Charging, PO Box 2985, Coventry CV7 8ZR.

DIRECTORY
MOTORING

Association of Approved Providers of Drink Driving Training *(ADDAPT)*
c/o TTC
Grosvenor House
Central Park
Telford TF2 9TW
Tel. 01952 292246
www.ttc-uk.com

Association of British Insurers *(ABI)*
51 Gresham Street
London EC2V 7HQ
Tel. 020 7600 3333
www.abi.org.uk

Automobile Association Legal Services
Lambert House
Stockport Road
Cheadle
Cheshire SK8 2DY
Tel. 0870 550 0600
www.theAA.com

British Parking Association
2 Clair Road
Haywards Heath
West Sussex RH16 3DP
Tel. 01444 447 303
www.britishparking.co.uk

Disabled Drivers' Association *(DDA)*
Ashwellthorpe
Norwich NR16 1EX
Tel. 0150 848 9449
www.dda.org.uk

Disabled Drivers Motor Club
Cottingham Way
Thrapston
Northamptonshire NN14 4PL
Tel. 01832 734 724
www.ddmcc.org.uk

Disabled Motorists Federation
145 Knoulberry Road
Blackfell
Washington
Tyne and Wear NE37 1JN
Tel. 0191 416 3172

Driving Instructors Association
Safety House
Beddington Farm Road
Croydon
Surrey CR0 4XZ
Tel. 020 8665 5151
www.driving.org

Driver and Vehicle Licensing Agency *(DVLA)*
Swansea SA99 1BL
Tel. 01792 772 151
(Vehicle enquiries) Tel. 08702 400 010
(Licence enquiries) Tel. 08702 400 009

Financial Ombudsman Service
South Quay Plaza
183 Marsh Wall
London E14 9SR
Tel. 0845 660 902
www.financial.ombudsman.org

Institute of Advanced Motorists Ltd
IAM House
510 Chiswick High Road
London W4 5RG
Tel. 020 8994 4403
www.iam.org.uk

Living Streets
(formerly The Pedestrians Association)
31–33 Bondway
London SW8 1SJ
Tel. 020 7820 1010
www.livingstreets.org.uk

Mobility Advice and Vehicle Information Service *(MAVIS)*
O Wing
Macadam Avenue
Old Wokingham Road
Crowthorne
Berkshire RG45 6XD
Tel. 01344 661 000
www.mobility-unit.dft.gov.uk/mavis.htm

Mobility Information Service
National Mobility Centre
Unit B1
Greenwood Court
Cartmel Drive
Shrewsbury SY1 3TB
Tel. 01743 463 072
www.mis.org.uk

Motability
Goodman House
Station Approach
Harlow
Essex CM20 2ET
Tel. 01279 635666
www.motability.co.uk

Motor Insurers' Bureau
6–12 Capital Drive
Linford Wood
Milton Keynes MK14 6ST
Tel. 01908 240000
www.mib.org.uk

Office of Fair Trading
Fleetbank House
2–6 Salisbury Square
London EC4Y 8JX
Tel. 020 7211 8000
www.oft.gov.uk

National Parking Adjudicators Service
Barlow House
Minshull Street
Manchester M1 3DZ
Tel. 01611 834 1881
www.parking-appeals.gov.uk

Parking and Traffic Appeals Service
General Processing Office
PO Box 1010
Sutton
Surrey SM1 4SW
Tel. 020 7747 4700
www.parkingandtrafficappealsservicetcfl.gov.uk

Retail Motor Industry Federation
201 Great Portland Street
London W1W 5AB
Tel. 020 7580 9122
www.rmif.co.uk

RAC Legal Services
PO Box 700
Bristol BS99 1RB
Tel. 01454 208000
www.rac.co.uk

RAC Motoring Services
Great Park Road
Bradley Stoke
Bristol BS32 4QN
Tel. 01454 208000
www.rac.co.uk

Royal Society for the Prevention of Accidents
(ROSPA)
ROSPA House
Edgbaston Park
353 Bristol Road
Birmingham B5 7ST
Tel. 0121 248 2000
www.rospa.org.uk

Society of Motor Manufacturers and Traders Ltd
Forbes House
Halkin Street
London SW1X 7DS
Tel. 020 7235 7000
www.smmt.co.uk

The Vehicle Builders and Repairers Association Ltd
Belmont House
Finkle Lane
Gildersome
Leeds LS27 7TW
Tel. 0113 253 8333
www.vbra.co.uk

Veteran Car Club of Great Britain
Jessamine Court
15 High Street
Ashwell
Herts SG7 5NL
Tel. 01462 742818
www.vccofgb.co.uk

17 ACCIDENTS

In this chapter we look at the legal position where an accident has happened – not only traffic accidents, but any situation where people happen to suffer an injury to themselves or damage to their property. Such things can happen anywhere – for example, at home, in the street, at work or at school.

In some situations you may be satisfied with receiving an apology and an explanation. But as a result of news reports, lawyers' advertisements, and the general tendency in our modern world to look to the law to deal with such problems, most people are now aware that they may be able to claim compensation for some accidents.

This is a trend which is causing increasing problems for certain sectors of society. Due to some well-publicised tragedies, for example, schools may become reluctant to organise school outings; employers' liability insurers have warned that workplace compensation is 'buckling under the strain' of expectations of awards; while the proportion of NHS funding which goes on legal costs is proving to be a significant problem for the public purse. Indeed, alternatives are now being canvassed in the health section (see below, section 9).

Useful leaflets are available from the Community Legal Service on claiming compensation for personal injury, medical accidents and no-win, no-fee actions. Telephone the LSC Leaflet line on 0845 3000 343 or e-mail *LSCleafletline@direct.st-ives.co.uk*

If you hurt yourself or damage your property through your own carelessness, you will have no redress unless you have taken out insurance to cover this situation. For example: while gardening, you trip over a rake you had earlier forgotten to remove; in falling you injure your wrist, and also break your spectacles. Clearly your only recompense is to claim on a personal accident policy or household insurance.

If an individual is injured through someone else's fault, however, there may be a claim for damages in law. Compared with the example just given, if you have a similar fall due to an implement left lying by a council workman in your local park, you might well have a good claim for compensation.

The general rule is that you may be able to claim damages if:

a) you have been injured by someone's failure to take precautions against causing injury;
b) it was a situation where a reasonable person would have been aware of the risk of your being injured, and
c) he or she would have taken precautions to avoid the risk.

The same applies if your property or possessions are damaged or destroyed.

In fact, as we shall see, the law provides patchy and not necessarily consistent protection. For example, an accident at work is likely to give more comprehensive rights to compensation than an accident in someone's home, even though both accidents may be equally disruptive and painful.

It is important to be aware that while it is possible to outline the general rules, the result of any individual case will always depend on the particular facts and circumstances, and the view which a judge will take of all the details and perhaps the history of the situation.

You should also be aware that going to court can be expensive and the outcome uncertain. It can also take time; accident victims have complained of having to wait inordinately long for the compensation which they are eventually awarded.

Further, if you are contemplating legal action, you should take account of the fact that what used to be called legal aid is no longer available for most personal injury cases. In some cases, car and household insurance policies may provide for assistance for legal costs. Accidents at work may give you rights to benefits or to trade union help not available for other types of injuries. Finally, a solicitor may agree to take on your case on the basis that if you win compensation, you will give him or her an uplift of their usual fees to cover costs. (This is dealt with in the chapter on *The Legal System* and below in sections 1.1.2 and 11.6.)

Useful information is contained in leaflet No. 17 put out by the Community Legal Service (formerly the Legal Aid Board), available on-line from *www.legalservices.gov.uk* or tel. 0845 3000 348.

Do note: personal injury claims generally are now being funded under a conditional fee agreement between client and solicitor. See sections 1.1.1 and 1.1.2 below, and the chapter on *The Legal System*, section 3.4.

In this chapter we look at:

- when an accident happens
- when you can sue
- defences to a claim of negligence
- occupier's liability
- accidents in the street
- railway, bus or coach accidents
- accidents at work
- accidents involving children
- medical accidents
- accidents and sport
- claiming compensation.

1   WHEN AN ACCIDENT HAPPENS

1.1   What to do after an accident

If you think you may be able to lodge a claim for an accident, act promptly. People involved in accidents are hurt, upset, angry and confused. It is difficult to keep a cool head but, if you can, do remember to do the following (or if too injured, ask someone else to help):

a) Take the names and addresses of any witnesses to the accident. After a traffic accident, call the police if anyone is injured.
b) Ask your doctor or hospital casualty department to examine your injuries and to keep a detailed record for later use.
c) Take measurements and photographs of the scene of the accident, of visible injuries and of property damage as soon as possible.
d) Write out a full narrative, recording the date, the time and the weather conditions if relevant. Include a sketch plan where appropriate.
e) Inform your insurers if you think you may be covered for the type of accident.
f) Make a note of details of torn clothing, broken spectacles, taxi rides, medical expenses, etc. as all these additional losses and expenses can form a claim for 'special' damages (see *Claiming compensation*, section 11 below).
g) Make enquiries to see if similar accidents have happened at the same site.

Some solicitors give you a first interview free under a scheme known as *Accident Line*. Their names can be obtained by telephoning Freephone 0500 19 29 39, or by writing to Freepost, PO Box 61, London NW1 7QS.

Do note: funding for personal injury claims has undergone significant changes (see immediately below, section 1.1.1).

1.1.1   Personal injury claims

i. Personal injury claims for up to £1000 can now be pursued in the small claims courts.
ii. Personal injury claims over £1000 will now generally be conducted on a 'conditional fee' basis (see 1.1.2) so that community legal funding [formerly legal aid] will not be available.

There are certain exceptions where claims for personal injury will be funded – provided, of course, that claimants qualify on both the 'means' and 'merits' tests for community legal funding (for details see the chapter on *The Legal System*, section 3.1). If you think that you may be eligible for funding you can apply only to those firms of solicitors which have been vetted and accredited by the Legal Services Commission [formerly the Legal Aid Board] and are therefore under contract to the Commission.

What are these exceptions?

- Claims involving clinical negligence, for example a claim against a hospital trust where a patient was wrongly diagnosed and/or improperly treated.
- Claims that have a wider interest and would benefit people in addition to the claimant, e.g. a case which would involve a new point of law.
- Claims where there is serious wrongdoing alleged against a public authority, e.g. where the claimant alleges personal injury suffered at the hands of the police during the course of an arrest.
- Claims where personal injury is suffered and which arises out of a housing claim, e.g. where a tenant alleges the landlord's consistent failure to repair a broken staircase and, as a result has suffered a fall with concomitant injuries.
- Claims which are very expensive so that there may be some help in topping up the conditional fee agreement, e.g. where the conditional fee agreement for a personal injury claim may set a ceiling of £25,000 but the costs are expected to double that. In such a case, some community legal funding may be available provided that all the other criteria which are laid down are met.

1.1.2   Conditional fees

Outside of the community legal service funding, solicitors can offer a service whereby they will take up claims on your behalf and will not charge fees if the case does not succeed. However, because you will still be liable for fees incurred by the other party to the action, great care has to be exercised in pursuing any such option.

Because of these risks, there are ground rules for the 'conditional fee' scheme [i.e. the 'no win, no fee' scheme] whereby:

a) the person who succeeds in the action can recoup the cost of the solicitor's additional charges (the 'uplift') from the other side, including insurance he or she may have taken out to cover the costs if he or she loses;

b) defendants to an action can now also take out insurance against the possibility of losing the action provided that they can persuade both a solicitor and the insurer that their case for the defence will stand up in court.

You can now take out 'after the event' insurance to cover some, if not all, the legal costs involved.

You should also be able to get an immediate bit of help, known as Legal Help, [formerly the Green Form Scheme] which is also only available from solicitors' firms that have a contract with the Legal Services Commission [formerly the Legal Aid Board].

So if you do think that you have a claim, seek advice promptly.

Remember, too: that delay may result in your claim lapsing (see section 2.1 below on *Time limits*).

2   WHEN CAN YOU SUE?

The law does not regard a duty to take care as being owed to everyone in the world. The test is a test of 'reasonableness'. Was it reasonably foreseeable that someone else would get hurt by a failure to take care? That is the question to be asked. If the risk of harm to another person is remote it is unreasonable to impose a duty of care on the person who might otherwise be at fault because of careless behaviour. This will depend on the circumstances of the incident.

Thus to prove negligence, the victim must show that:

- it was reasonably foreseeable that harm would result from a failure to take care
- there was a duty of care owed to him or her
- the duty was not discharged
- damage or injury resulted.

Even if all these criteria can be established, the person at fault may still have a defence to the claim (see section 3 below). If the injury or damage is pure happenstance or 'Act of God', of course no remedy is available – it is for this type of incident that insurance must have been obtained in advance if compensation is to be available. See also section 3.3 below.

☞ *You are a spectator at a car rally which takes place in bad weather conditions over rough terrain. You are standing beside a hairpin bend, near the track, when the driver of the lead car swerves and his car's bumper gives you a glancing blow on your legs. You are treated immediately for a surface wound, but your right leg gives you considerable pain thereafter. You want to know whether you can sue the rally organisers.*

Each case always depends on the circumstances.

The rally organisers quite clearly have a duty of care towards spectators who attend their events. The question of whether they failed in their duty in this case depends on the facts: if a judge finds that they employed an inadequate number of stewards to supervise the spectators in bad weather conditions which made driving more hazardous, then you would probably have made out your case.

If, however, you stationed yourself in a dangerous spot by standing too near the track, you might have contributed to your own misfortune, in other words your damages could be considerably reduced because of your own 'contributory negligence'. See *Defences to a claim of negligence,* section 3 below.

If it was the case of a driver who, acting in the heat of the moment, misjudged the distance, there may be no fault on anyone's part.

The law also assumes that people will take reasonable precautions for their own safety. When a visitor to Lyme Regis who walked on the Cobb (the old harbour wall) slipped on a patch of algae, and fell, the local council was held to be not liable, since the visitor was well able to assess the obvious danger of slippery, algae-covered stones.

2.1 Time limits

The law lays down time limits within which you must begin legal proceedings. You are strongly advised to take legal advice on this.

If an injury is caused by deliberate assault, the time limit is six years.

In cases of personal injuries or death caused by negligence, there is a three-year time limit, which runs from the date of the injury or the date when the victim knew of this (whichever is the later). If you are going to take legal steps to claim damages, you must commence them before this period expires, and should therefore act as soon as you can after the event.

☞ *A workman was exposed to noxious dust over a period of years. As a result he contracted silicosis.*

This was a case in which he was suffering damage long before he knew of it so the three-year period began to run only from the date on which he could reasonably have been expected to become aware of his illness.

☞ *A claimant was advised by a community worker in 1991 that his deafness might be caused by working in a mill and that he should consult a doctor and a solicitor. He had immediately seen a solicitor who had obtained a legal aid certificate initially limited to the obtaining of a medical certificate. Did the claimant's knowledge of the injury relate from that date?*

No. Where expert evidence beyond the scope of a layperson was necessary to establish the cause of the injury, the mere fact of seeking a medical opinion did not mean that the claimant could know the cause of the injury.

There are exceptional circumstances where even shorter periods apply.

Although, the courts have power to extend time limits, they will only do so in exceptional circumstances.

A patient whose condition deteriorated after an operation inferred that the operation had not been a success but had nothing to alert him to the fact that he had actually been injured in the course of the operation. The three-year limitation period for making a claim commenced only from the date on which it was discovered that the actual operation involved a medical accident.

It is in your interests, therefore, to act promptly, otherwise you may lose your chance of compensation for good.

Children can bring a claim for personal injury in their own right within three years of their 18th birthday. Children under 18 must sue through their parent or guardian, who will bring an action on their behalf.

In the case of dependants suing because of the death of a breadwinner (see section 11.5 below) the three years run from the date of the death.

The Law Commission has proposed that the law on limitation periods should be made simpler and fairer. It proposes changes to the law which would make it 'modern and cost effective'. At the moment, serious anomalies arise – in particular in the limitation periods for injury to persons, which are shorter than in cases which involve property damage. The proposals envisage shortening the time period to three years from the date of the claimant's knowledge of the injury. To date, no action has been taken in relation to the Commission proposals.

Claims against airlines arising out of international travel may be subject to a shorter time limit under international agreements. In all cases, act promptly to find out what limits could apply to you.

2.2 Civil and criminal

The aim of civil proceedings is to compensate the victim. The aim of criminal proceedings is to fix blame and allocate punishment.

However, in recent years the distinction between civil and criminal proceedings has become somewhat less significant in this regard because a criminal court now has the power to order a convicted offender to pay compensation to his victim. For claims over £1,000 which result from criminal injury, a claim can also be made to the Criminal Injuries Compensation Board. The compensation ordered on a criminal case will be on a limited scale for criminal injury, with a tariff scheme that applies fixed awards for injuries.

Criminal proceedings are often completed much more speedily than civil cases and usually at no financial cost to the victim. Even if you intend to bring civil proceedings for damages as well, the fact that the offender has been convicted in a criminal court will often assist you in proving your claim. For example, if you were involved in a car accident as a result of another driver's dangerous driving, the fact that the driver has been successfully prosecuted for dangerous driving would assist you in bringing a claim for damages where you need to prove that he had been at fault. The amount awarded in the civil courts has no upper limit.

2.3 Alternative sources of compensation

Because of the limitations imposed by the law on claiming damages, as well as the time and the expense involved, the main protection against accidents comes from insurance:

a) To take care of ourselves, we take out life policies, personal accident insurance, health policies, household and all risks policies, etc.

b) To take care of others, we take out liability policies (compulsory third party insurance for your car serves the same function).

For details of insurance after the event, see chapter on *The Legal System*, section 3.4.3.)

2.3.1 Important changes

The procedures for claiming damages have undergone a radical overhaul:

a) Conditional fees: in the general run, you must now enter into a conditional fee agreement with your solicitor when you sue for damages for personal injury (see section 1.1.2 above);

b) Funding is to be withdrawn for most personal injury cases and the conditional fee agreement takes its place;

c) in simple cases of minor injury, a claim of up to £1,000 can be made in the small claims court (see also the chapter on *The Legal System*, section 4).

d) the costs of legal action, usually to a pre-set limit, is now being underwritten by some insurance policies. For example, it may be an 'add-on' to your motor insurance policy or to your general household cover; you may be able to take out 'after the event' insurance (i.e. after an accident) to cover costs (further details are found in the chapter on *The Legal System*).

Before you consider going to court, however, do investigate any speedier route for immediate assistance – for example:

- an occupational sick pay scheme or pension scheme that may provide benefits for work accidents
- social security benefits – information can be obtained from your local benefits office or Citizens' Advice Bureau
- the use of alternative dispute resolution, i.e. a negotiated settlement, as a way of dealing with your claim.

2.4 Group action for compensation

Where a number of claims arise from the same cause it may be possible to speed up the claims process by pursuing a group action rather than having to pursue cases individually through the courts. Just such arrangements were entered into for the thousands of compensation claims from former British Coal mineworkers suffering from respiratory diseases.

2.5 Claims where the defendant is no longer in existence

By the time that the existence of an injury is identified (see 2.1 above) the defendant may no longer be in existence. This is particularly the case where a claim is made in regard to negligence of a former employer who has gone out of business. In an attempt to overcome this problem, a Code of Practice was issued in November 1999 to assist employees in tracking down their former employer's insurer. The Code commits insurers to make a thorough search, when requested, of records of policies issued to any such employer. (From 1969 employers have been required to insure their liability to employees for injury or disease sustained during their employment.) This voluntary Code should assist employees who fall ill with employment-related conditions which have taken a long time to develop, and who encounter problems in finding their employer's insurer, often after the employer has ceased to trade. Under the Code, insurers are required, as from November 1999, to keep records of all policies issued for a period of 60 years.

3 DEFENCES TO A CLAIM OF NEGLIGENCE

Even if you can establish that someone else was legally at fault in causing you harm, he or she may have a successful defence to your claim. This can have the effect of preventing you from recovering any damages at all or, with less drastic effect, of reducing the amount you can recover. The most common defences are:

- contributory negligence
- voluntary assumption of risk
- unavoidable accident.

Take note: only one of these defences need apply.

3.1 When the victim contributes to the accident

The wrongdoer may argue that although the harm was caused partly by his or her fault, your lack of care also contributed to the accident. If that can be proved, your damages will be reduced proportionately.

☞ *In a council-run sports club, the gym mats were negligently placed too close to the wall. The staff failed to warn users or to supervise the use of the mats. A keen athlete did a somersault on the mats and permanently injured his spine against the wall.*

Although the council was liable for the negligence of its employees, the athlete had to bear a significant responsibility for his injuries as he was an intelligent and experienced sportsman and had been showing off to his friends when he should have been taking more care of himself. His damages were reduced proportionately.

The extent to which an injured person will be considered to have contributed towards the damage which occurred will be a question of fact in each case. The relevant negligence of both parties must be taken into consideration. In one case army officers organised a social function for off-duty soldiers, with a lorry to take them back to barracks at the end. One soldier fell off the lorry on the way back and was injured. He sued the Ministry of Defence for compensation. The court held that rowdy behaviour and drunkenness was foreseeable and should have been guarded against by the officers organising the social function, but the soldier was held to have been 75% to blame for his injuries because he was an adult who should have appreciated the risks he was running arising out of his own behaviour. The damages he was awarded were accordingly reduced by 75%.

In other circumstances, although aware of a danger, you may find yourself in a 'no choice' situation. For example, in another case, a tenant complained to his landlord that a steep flight of stairs from his flat to the street was badly lit and lacked a handrail. The landlord, who was responsible for maintenance, did nothing to improve the situation. One evening, the tenant fell on the stairs and injured his leg. The landlord was held liable to compensate the tenant.

3.2   When the victim took the risk

If you agree to run a risk and then an accident does indeed occur, you may not be able to make a claim.

☞   *You and your friend decide to test your 'hot hatch' cars in a race on an open road. The cars collide. What is your position ?*

Even if your friend was to blame for the collision, it would be unlikely that your claim against him would receive a sympathetic hearing in court!

☞   *You persuade your friend to give you a ride on his newly purchased motor bike, although he warns you that he is not yet proficient and that you come on it at your own risk.*

You probably could not hold him liable for any resulting accident.

Similarly, you are assuming the risk if you accept a lift from a driver knowing he is probably too drunk to drive safely, or knowing that he is uninsured. (See also the chapter on *Motoring*, section 1.2.5, where the victim of an accident who knows that a driver is drunk or uninsured cannot generally claim compensation from the Motor Insurers Bureau.)

However, when someone is engaging in a business which entails a risk of injury or property damage, they may ask customers to sign a form, or they may put up a notice exempting the organisers from liability. Even if you have seen the notice or signed such a form, the attempted exemption is invalid in law if an accident involving personal injury results from the organisers' negligence.

☞   *You decide that you wish to learn horse-riding and approach your local stables. You are asked to sign a form exempting the management from liability. Your horse bolts in the road on your second lesson and you fall off, suffering a broken wrist. Afterwards, you learn that the horse has been unruly before.*

You are not prevented from making a claim by having signed the exemption clause. Contracts cannot generally exclude liability for death or injury caused by negligence

See also section 2.4 on 'the small print' regulations and unfair contract terms in the chapter on *Goods and Services*. See also chapter on *Pets*, section 4.6.

3.3   Unavoidable accident

Where an accident occurs because of something or some situation which could not have been foreseen and against which precautions could not have been taken, this is a complete answer to a claim for compensation. An example would be a traffic accident which took place because of a driver's sudden heart attack.

It is always a question of fact whether or not an accident was foreseeable. For example, it might be assumed that being injured by another golfer's ball when you are playing on the links would be seen as an unavoidable accident. However, where a golfer attempted a difficult shot which, in order to succeed, had to clear a coppiced hazel, the likelihood of deflection of the ball on to a player on a nearby fairway was found to have been foreseeable.

4   OCCUPIER'S LIABILITY

The vast majority of accidents happen in the home. Whether you can sue anyone depends on the cause of the accident and whether or not the accident happened in your own home or in someone else's. This section deals with accidents which result from the actual state of the premises although, of course, accidents happen in the home for all sorts of other reasons – for example, a faulty cable on a vacuum cleaner could cause a nasty shock (see chapter on *Goods and Services*, section 6).

4.1   Who is an occupier?

The fundamental rule is that persons in control of premises – whom the law calls *occupiers* – must exercise a reasonable degree of care to ensure that their premises are reasonably safe for others to use. Accordingly:

- a local authority is responsible for schools, libraries and streets
- shopkeepers, hoteliers, publicans etc. are responsible for their business premises
- other authorities in charge of premises also owe a duty of care, for example, the airports authority for airports, the health authority or hospital trust for clinics and hospitals.

Two important points to remember:

a) Although called an 'occupier', it is the person or body in control or in charge of the premises who is liable; it need not be the person in 'occupation' of the premises in the everyday meaning of the word.

b) 'Occupier's liability' also means that as a private householder, you are responsible for the safety of those who come into your house or flat. (See section 4.3.1 below.)

4.2   What are premises?

'Premises' has a very extended meaning; the term does not just apply to buildings. Even parks, seawalls, housing estates, bridges, railway lines, cranes and lorries have been held to be 'premises' for the purposes of occupier's liability.

4.3   Who can claim?

Only persons who suffer physical injury or damage to property can claim. For example, A and B visit a department store. A trips on loose carpet, sprains her ankle and tears her coat. B has her purse stolen from the fitting room while trying on a dress. The shop owner, as occupier, is responsible for A's loss and injury but not for B's.

The occupier can be liable even if the injury is caused *indirectly* by the dangerous state of the premises. In one case a police officer successfully sued Reading Football Club when he was injured by a lump of concrete thrown during violence at a football match. The club, as 'occupier' of the ground, was responsible for the fact that to its knowledge the premises were not in good repair so that the terrace could be broken up to form missiles, and it was known that visiting fans would contain a violent element.

4.3.1   Responsibility towards those you invite

The occupier's primary responsibility is to any person who comes into the premises:

- as a guest
- to do a job (e.g. to repair the washing machine); or
- for some other lawful purpose, such as to read the meters.

4.3.2   Responsibility towards those you do not invite

The liability for harm suffered on property even extends to:

- authorised ramblers
- children tempted by some attraction (such as a pond or 'conker' tree)
- 'trespassers' – which includes people innocently straying from the highway
- undesirables, for example someone who is on the property for an unlawful purpose such as burglary or vandalism.

The extent of the duty diminishes with each category. Thus the duty owed to someone who trespasses on to your property has been defined as 'humanitarian' only. In other words, you cannot allow a real danger to exist on your property as a deterrent to others without taking certain steps to indicate the situation. For example, if you own a vicious dog which you allow to roam loose over your property, without warning notices, and it savages someone who strays on to your land, you would still be liable to pay the victim compensation.

A person who enters on to another's land because he is exercising his 'right to roam' under the Countryside and Rights of Way Act (see chapter on *The Countryside*) is not a 'visitor'. The Act provides that the landowner will not be liable to such a member of the public for any injuries the latter sustained which are caused by dangers which are natural features of the land, or by any plant, tree or shrub, or by ditches, ponds and streams even if they are not natural features.

If there is a danger on your property of which you are aware, e.g. an abandoned mine shaft, you must protect yourself by putting up warning notices, by surrounding it with a fence, and by actively discouraging trespassers. Where experience shows that warning notices are being disregarded, more will need to be done – for example, you might have to fence off the danger.

4.3.3   Problems with children

As an occupier you may be responsible for children tempted to trespass on your property. It has been said repeatedly that children's ingenuity in finding unexpected ways of doing mischief to themselves and others should not be underestimated. In one case a small boat had been abandoned on council-owned land. Two 12-year-old boys decided to repair it in the fanciful hope of being able to sail it, and in the course of attempting to jack it up one boy was badly injured. The court ruled that the council was liable because they knew of the risk that the boat would attract children who would meddle with it at the risk of injury, even though the precise way in which the accident occurred – leading to more serious injury – was not foreseen. (See also section 8 below.)

Do remember: that young children may not be able to see or to read warning signs, and that they may be expected to be less careful of their own safety than adults.

4.4   Accidents in the home

4.4.1   Accidents involving yourself

If you spill gravy on your kitchen floor and then slip and injure yourself, you can blame no one else. If, however, your neighbour slips on the gravy, you may be responsible as occupier of the premises – most household insurance policies do carry an occupiers' liability clause protecting you against liability for such accidents. *You are advised to check your policy on this!*

Warning note: statistics issued in November 1999 show that most accidents happen in the home, with some 220,000 each year involving children.

The Department of Trade and Industry has produced information on avoiding slips and trips. See their website at *www.preventinghomefalls.gov.uk* or contact the Health Information Service on 0800 66 55 44.

4.4.2   Accidents involving visitors

You are under a duty to ensure that your premises are safe for those you may invite or permit to enter. Uneven garden paths, for example, could mean you are responsible for resulting falls by your friends, neighbours, postmen or delivery men, etc.

☞   *Your local horticultural society has asked you to arrange an 'open day' for members of the public to visit your garden on behalf of a charity. A close friend warns you that when she arranged a similar open day, one of the visitors tripped over a bit of loose paving in the garden path. She says that she has been receiving letters from a lawyer threatening legal action as a result of the accident. What should you do?*

If you are planning to have large numbers of strangers on your property, e.g. if you are having a fete or opening your garden for charity to members of the public, first check with your insurers to establish that you are adequately covered against an accident. (Under the National Gardens Scheme you would be covered by a group liability policy.)

The danger to visitors may arise not only from the state of the property. If you keep a vicious dog that bites, you could be liable to pay damages to someone bitten by it. You could also incur criminal responsibility under the Dangerous Dogs Act (see chapter on *Pets*, section 3.5).

4.4.3   Accidents in your rented home

You are responsible for the state of the premises whether you own your home or live in it as a tenant. However, your landlord is generally responsible for the safety of the common parts, such as lifts and stairs, and is liable not only to you but to your family and other visitors.

Manchester City Council was fined the maximum £25,000 when faultily installed heating in council flats caused the death by carbon monoxide poisoning of one of the tenants. His dependants could also claim compensation from the Council.

A business landlord is liable in the same way as a residential one.

See also the chapter on *Landlords and their Tenants*, section 2.1.3.

4.5   Accidents on someone else's property

4.5.1   Private premises

See sections 4.3 and 4.4 above.

Health and Safety Regulations impose criminal sanctions on employers and proprietors who put at risk the safety of their employees or members of the public on their premises (see also section 7 below).

4.5.2   Public premises

☞ *You have reserved a book at the local library and have received a card to say that the book is waiting for collection. When you arrive, there are trails of melted snow in the entrance hall of the library from other visitors but no mats have been laid to cover the slippery floor. You fall and injure yourself. A friend advises you that you ought to sue the local authority but you are not sure of the legal position. The library building is generally well looked after. What is the position?*

Your friend may be right, but whether the authority is liable in those circumstances will be a matter of fact and degree.

The cause of the danger could be a major problem such as a design defect in the building itself or it could be a simple matter of failure to replace light bulbs. In other words, it does not depend on the occupier's personal 'fault'. But as in all these cases, it is a matter of degree. The emphasis is on the word 'reasonable', i.e. the occupier of premises has a duty to take reasonable care to see that his or her premises are reasonably safe for others to use.

4.5.3   Safety for persons

The primary duty of an occupier is to take care to see that the premises are safe for those who come on to them. But adults are expected to have some care for their own safety, especially in the case of those who could be expected to be aware of special dangers – for example, an electrician would be more aware of faulty wiring than the householder. (See section 4.6.2 below.)

4.5.4   Safety for property

Moreover, the premises have to be reasonably safe not only for people but also for their property, provided that the loss or damage to property results from the state of the premises and not from some other cause.

☞ *While staying in an hotel, you hang your clothes and put your suitcase in the wardrobe. Because of a leaking roof, the cupboard is flooded and your belongings are ruined.*

The hotel is liable to pay compensation. (However, this may be limited to a woefully inadequate maximum of £100 in total per guest under the Hotel Proprietors Act 1956, if the hotel has a notice to that effect; see also chapter on *Goods and Services*, section 9.1.5.)

A different rule applies if the loss of your property took place through the negligence of an employee of the hotel. For example, the £100 maximum will not apply if a chambermaid forgets to lock the door behind her and your clothes are stolen.

4.6   Defences to a claim

Apart from showing 'reasonable care', there are other defences to a claim for accidents under occupier's liability. Only one of these defences must be proved:

a) An independent contractor was responsible

b) Special risks were taken

c) Adequate warning was given.

4.6.1   The independent contractor

If the hazard was caused by an independent contractor, it is generally the contractor and not the occupier who will be held responsible.

☞   *After taking recommendations you carefully select a firm of electrical contractors to rewire your house. Unbeknown to you, they do their work negligently. You then call in a carpenter to erect some bookshelves and he suffers a severe shock when he plugs an electric drill into a socket. He threatens to sue you. You want to know whether you are liable.*

Even though you are the occupier, you probably have no liability in this case. In law it is the electrical firm which ought to be sued.

4.6.2   Specialists and special risks

An occupier is not liable for special risks if he or she employs someone with their own special expertise but who has an accident nonetheless.

☞   *A window cleaner balances his foot on an ornamental trellis attached to an outside wall of your house. The trellis gives way and he falls.*

You are not liable. It was his job to know that an ornamental trellis would not be strong enough to support his weight. If, however, while going upstairs inside your house, the window cleaner tripped on a loose stair carpet, you would be liable.

4.6.3   Giving adequate warning

An occupier may be able to discharge his duty of care by giving adequate warnings of the danger. For example, a supermarket employee may stand beside a spillage, warning customers away, until staff can clean it up.

If the danger is exceptional, a mere warning notice will be entirely inadequate so warning lights, notices or fencing off dangers may be appropriate in particular circumstances.

Notices which attempt to exclude a business's liability for death or personal injury are ineffective in law. Even for property damage, a notice may be ineffective if unreasonable. A company which runs a parking garage can protect itself by a notice stating that it will not be responsible for damage to or theft from cars but that will not absolve it from gross negligence.

☞   *You leave your car in a parking garage where you have to hand over the car keys to the staff who then park the car for you. Your ticket states that your car is left at your own risk. There is a notice to the same effect. A member of staff drives your car so negligently that he rams it against a concrete bollard. The garage proprietor denies liability and points to the clauses on the ticket.*

You should not take 'no' for an answer in these circumstances. Take legal advice as you may have a very good claim for the damage to your car.

5   ACCIDENTS IN THE STREET

Many of us have tripped on a pavement, got up a bit shaken and a bit bruised, and then walked on. If however, you fall because of a broken, uneven or loose paving stone or because of a hole in the road, and you have the misfortune to hurt yourself or damage your belongings (e.g. spectacles), the local highway authority may be at fault. It is harder to prove that a highway authority, rather than another driver, caused an accident.

5.1   Highways

5.1.1   What is a highway?

Take note: a 'highway' comprises the road which you cross (the carriageway) and the pavement which you walk on (the footway).

5.1.2   Highway authorities

Local highway authorities are:

- county councils in non-metropolitan areas
- metropolitan borough councils outside London
- London borough councils within London
- district councils or parish councils for unclassified roads, footpaths and bridleways.

(Motorways and trunk roads are the responsibility of the Highways Agency.)

All these authorities maintain highways at public expense and keep a list of the highways in their area. This information is particularly important if you fall far from where you live and you have to ascertain which highway authority is involved. You can write – or inquire in person – and should not be charged for the information.

Note, however: that the maintenance of local roads may have been delegated to private contractors under the Local Authorities (Contracting Out of Highways Functions) Order 1999. Contracting out may also have occurred in relation to trunk road schemes. In such cases it may be necessary to ascertain who was the relevant private contractor.

Nonetheless, in the first instance you are strenuously advised to establish the relevant local authority. Consult your local library for a map of the area or write to the local authority Surveys Department which also keep maps. You can then address your claim to the Insurance Department of the appropriate local authority.

You can also establish in which neighbourhood a particular street is to be found at *www.neighbourhood.statistics.gov.uk*.

If the accident was caused by a mains cover or ongoing repairs, the appropriate organisation to claim from may be the utility companies (e.g. British Telecom, Transco or the water companies).

As always, in circumstances in which you think you have a claim, take legal advice.

5.1.3   Dangers beside the highway

Passers-by can also be endangered by what happens beside the highway. A pile of rubble or a trench adjoining a footpath could cause injury to someone who is not keeping strictly to the path, and the contractor responsible will be held liable for such injuries. Liability will depend on how near the danger was to the highway. This depends on the circumstances and is not a simple matter of measurement.

5.1.4   When the local highway authority is liable

The authority is only responsible for dangers arising from the condition of the highway. Not all accidents in the street are attributable to this. (See section 5.1.7 below.)

The liability of a highway authority is based on lack of due care, so that if it could not have known of the danger it would also have a good defence.

☞ *Some building work is going on in the next-door property and a lorry tips its load of bricks on to the pavement, cracking some flagstones. You have a bad fall as a result. What is the position?*

The local highway authority is not expected to be aware of an incident such as this as soon as it happens. Regular inspections and maintenance (of which a register will be kept by the authority) may demonstrate its reasonable care. You would probably have to take the matter up with the building contractor involved as responsible for your accident.

5.1.5   Maintenance

A local highway authority's duty is to repair the highways in its area and maintain them in a reasonable condition. What is reasonable is a matter of degree. A reasonable person using the highway would expect:

- some degree of unevenness in a pavement
- to take some heed of where he or she walks
- more holes in a road than in a pavement.

Tripping incidents vary greatly – there is no general rule that an uneven pavement will invariably be a danger; it will depend on the court's view of the particular facts.

The extent of the duty also depends on the type of highway; it is reasonable for a highway authority to devote more resources to the repair of a busy shopping street than to an unfrequented footpath.

In a case where a branch of a tree belonging to a council and adjoining a public highway fell on a vehicle injuring the driver, the council was found to have failed in its clear duty to make inspections. There had been sufficient indication to warrant a proper inspection of its condition prior to the time of the accident. The council, in pruning the tree in the past, altered the tree's natural state and created a potential danger through decay, which they allowed to persist or continue.

Remember: although maintenance involves clearing away standing snow or ice and providing extra protection in bad weather, e.g. by gritting or salting roads, again the duty is a matter of degree.

☞ *You slip because of a puddle of water on the pavement. You feel that you were not at fault and would like to take the matter up with your local highway authority. Have you any case?*

It is unlikely that the highway authority would have a duty to clear purely temporary hazards such as those caused by rainwater puddles, unless the gullies or sewers were permanently blocked because of lack of repair. For instance, in one case the court held that there is no duty on the highway authority to remove accumulated mud or snow on a road.

Whether a highway is out of repair is a matter of the circumstances in each case. It is reasonable to expect walkers on unmade country paths to look out for uneven surfaces, projecting roots or stones, whereas users of a main road can expect a higher standard of maintenance. In the words of a judge, all such cases are 'fact-sensitive'.

In each case, therefore, it will be a question of fact whether the authority had taken all reasonable steps. A motorist, injured when his car skidded on ice, failed in his claim, despite the evidence showing that the council were aware of the forecast conditions but had not ordered out their gritting vehicles in time for them to have completed their rounds by the time the frost was sufficient to form dangerous icy patches on the roads. Otherwise, no highway authority could avoid from time to time being temporarily in breach of such a duty.

The duty to maintain extends to the provision of adequate lighting to be kept in working order.

5.1.6 Warning signs
Failure to erect signs warning of a dangerous bend in the road will not usually make the highway authority liable for an ensuing accident. But where a motorist's view was restricted by a high bank on land adjoining the highway, the authority was held by the House of Lords to be negligent in failing to erect signs.

5.1.7 Objects in the street
Where an accident has been caused by something falling into the street, negligence is usually present. Materials do not normally fall from building sites unless someone has been careless; walls do not collapse unless there has been dangerous neglect of repairs.

☞ *You are injured by a piece of guttering which falls from the roof edge of a building. You want to take the matter further but do not know whether to approach the highway authority or the building owner.*

The 'occupier' is liable (see *Occupier's liability*, section 4 above) unless there was some other cause for which he is not responsible (e.g. there had been underground subsidence at the foundations, or the guttering had been vandalised by a trespasser).

The same principle applies to trees.

☞ *A large beech tree growing in your next-door neighbour's garden topples over onto the roadway, damaging your car. Your neighbours deny all responsibility. What is the position?*

Your neighbours are liable if they knew or should have known the tree was diseased or otherwise dangerous, but not if they could not have known that fact, e.g. if there was only below-ground damage to the roots. There is no duty to have experts examine trees unless there has been some cause for concern about their safety.

5.1.8   Danger created by others

Danger may have been created by necessary work on underground mains or cables. Gas, electricity or water companies responsible for such excavations must take precautions to prevent danger to passers-by. If the body responsible has put up warnings, this may be sufficient to discharge its duty to take all reasonable care. The warning must also be adequate. The utility company will be liable to compensate owners of property in the street which are damaged by their activities. For example, a water company laying a new water main would be liable for damage caused to your sewer.

5.1.9   Handicapped persons

An 'adequate' warning must take into account the fact that certain passers-by can be particularly vulnerable to hazards in the roads.

☞ *A trench in the street, excavated by the electricity company, was protected by signs and lights which warned ordinary pedestrians of the danger, but gave inadequate warning for persons with a visual handicap.*

A court decided that it was reasonable for the company to have had such people within its consideration. It should have anticipated their presence and done more to protect them against the danger it had created.

Do note: under the Disability Discrimination Act 1995, service providers, e.g. shops or restaurants, public service vehicle operators, landlords and certain occupiers, will be required to make actual physical adjustments to their premises so that they are both safe and accessible for use by the disabled. Educational establishments are also about to be subject to these requirements, e.g. to make certain that there are toilet facilities available for the disabled. See the codes of practice at *www.drc-gb.org.uk.*

6   RAILWAY, BUS OR COACH ACCIDENTS

6.1   Operator's duties

Whether we travel by bus, coach or train, those in charge of operations are under a duty to use reasonable care and skill to ensure our safety. Their duty of care applies to our possessions too.

6.1.1   Insurance

All carriers have compulsory third party insurance cover for their liability. (If you have accident cover or all risks property insurance you may also be able to claim against your own insurers.)

6.1.2   Exemption clause

Statements on a ticket or on other notices which try to limit or avoid the operator's liability for death or personal injury are ineffective in law. They can, however, reasonably impose limits on their liability for lost or damaged property.

6.1.3   To whom is the duty owed?

The duty is owed to all passengers irrespective of the terms under which they travel.

☞ *You and your four-year-old son take a 'Runabout' coach trip from London to Nottingham. The company is privately run. Your son is allowed to travel free as a special concession. The coach is involved in a collision on the M1 due to the driver's negligence. Your son is thrown forward on to the seat in front of him and breaks his nose. Your hold-all, containing your camera, comes crashing down from the rack above your head and your camera is damaged beyond repair. The company dispute liability on the grounds that your son did not pay for his fare.*

They also point to a limitation of liability clause on your ticket and state that you can only recover £50 on your camera. What is your position ?

The operating company's duty of care is owed to all passengers, even those who have not paid for their journey (e.g. elderly passengers on a free bus pass) or reduced-price passengers (e.g. children). However, you might be bound by the limitation of liability on damage to property. (See also the comments on unfair contract terms, sections 2.4 and 7.2.3, in the *Goods and Services* chapter.)

6.1.4   Scope of the duty

The operators of the service will be liable if the accident results from failure to ensure that the vehicle is in a safe condition and is driven safely.

However, an operator will not necessarily be liable for an accident which happens to you after you have alighted, even if that was not at a recognised bus stop, for example. If, say, the regular stopping place was blocked and the bus driver allowed passengers to leave the bus at another spot which was by traffic lights and intrinsically safe, the carrier would be unlikely to be held liable if you then suffered an accident while crossing the road against the traffic lights.

A taxi driver was held not to have owed a duty of care to an inebriated passenger who was set down close to, but on the other side of the road from, his stated destination and near a pedestrian crossing. In that case it was found that the danger had been caused by the passenger's own action in consuming too much alcohol.

6.1.4(a)   Safety of vehicle

The vehicle must be *reasonably safe* for its purpose. This means that vehicles must be regularly maintained and inspected. With the break-up of British Rail into different operators, it may not be easy to establish which one is responsible for failures in equipment, track, servicing, inspection etc. Do take legal advice.

6.1.4(b)   Safe driving

The vehicle must not be driven negligently. Operators are liable for the unsafe driving of their employees. In some cases negligence is obvious (e.g. where there has been a collision between trains).

☞   *You sat upstairs on a bus with your elbow projecting from the open window. The driver pulled away from the kerb too close to a pole, and your arm was badly injured.*

The operators would be liable for their employee's negligent driving.

In another case a woman was in the process of boarding a train which started with a jolt, so that she fell between the platform and the moving train; she lost both her legs as a result, and recovered full damages from British Rail.

Note: it is negligent for a driver:

- to jolt the vehicle when starting
- to move off without checking to see if passengers are attempting to board or alight from the vehicle
- to disregard the safety of standing as well as of seated passengers.

6.1.4(c)   General safety

A safe system must be in operation. However, victims can experience difficulties in pinpointing the blame in practice where responsibility for safety is split between various bodies – as vividly illustrated by recent railway disasters.

6.2   Occupier's liability

Like any other occupier, bus and rail authorities are also responsible for the safety of their premises:

- platforms must be at a reasonable height for train-users
- stations must be kept in a safe condition, e.g. floors must be safe and there must be proper lighting.

Failure entails liability not only to passengers but to other persons on the premises, such as someone meeting a friend off a train or coach, or merely visiting the station to shop or to use a toilet.

6.3   Defences available to operators

Where your own lack of care has contributed to the injury, your damages will be reduced proportionately (see section 3 above). It has been held to be contributory negligence for a passenger to try to board a moving bus, or to try to close an open carriage door while the train is in motion.

6.4   Ships, aircraft, hovercraft

The liability of those who operate other forms of transport such as ships, aircraft or hovercraft, and their premises (hoverports, airports, etc.) is similar to the above.

It has been held that a certifying authority and its inspector who certified a light aircraft as fit to fly owed a duty of care to a passenger. They did not have to be proved to be directly responsible. A passenger about to be taken up in an aircraft was entitled to assume that it had met the applicable safety requirements and that proper care had been taken in checking that safety requirements had been met. There are international conventions limiting the level of compensation, which may differ according to random variables such as where you embark and disembark, so always insure before you travel.

Lately, incidents of 'air rage' have occurred aboard aircraft. If you are hurt as a result of such an incident, you may have a claim against a person who has caused the disruption. Also such a person may be found guilty of the offences of:

- endangering the safety of the aircraft
- being drunk in an the aircraft
- acting in a disruptive manner.

These offences are already liable to a maximum penalty of up to two years' imprisonment and/or a fine of £5000.

The offences of smoking in an aircraft where prohibited, and of failing to obey the aircraft commander, e.g. with regard to the use of electronic equipment such as a mobile phone, are liable to a maximum fine of £2,500.

A survey carried out by the Civil Aviation Authority on behalf of the government shows that 'air rage' is still a rare occurrence but it regards any such incident as unacceptable and not to be tolerated.

6.5   Accidents abroad

If you have an accident abroad, your rights and liabilities will depend on the law of the foreign country where the accident occurred. Always advise your travel insurers as soon as possible, and in serious cases contact the nearest British consulate. If you booked through a package offered by a UK travel company you may be able to claim compensation from them for certain kinds of accidents, e.g. unsafe hotels or touring coaches. (See the chapter on *Goods and Services*, section 9, and the chapter on *The Legal System*, section 3.6.4.)

7   ACCIDENTS AT WORK

Liability for the safety of a workforce depends on a complex interaction between employers' liability for negligence and a growing number of statutory regulations which have imposed extra, and in many cases stricter, duties on them.

Accidents at work are extremely common – in fact, nearly 50 per cent of claims for personal injury going through the courts annually concern work accidents, and the number of fatal injuries is rising fast – the Health and Safety Commission recorded a 34% rise in 2000–2002! Apart from the misery and pain involved for the victim and his family, work accidents cause other immense and untold costs: firms lose productivity and can even go out of business; insurance premiums go up; the National Health Service, on already stretched resources, has to provide treatment and facilities to cope with those who are hurt; and social security has to support employees who can no longer work in either the short or the long term.

Take note:

- small firms have a worse record of accidents than big firms
- retail and service industries are just as accident-prone as heavy industry.

Employers should always remember: that victims of work accidents, even of quite minor accidents, are increasingly ready to litigate.

7.1   Before an accident occurs

If you are an employer, it is your legal responsibility to assess what potential harm your employees or others might face in the workplace, to decide on the necessary safety precautions, and consistently to maintain these to a reasonable standard. Apart from facing claims for damages from injured employees, your business might be shut down and the management fined for breach of safety regulations. If you are an employee, the failure of your employer to take proper care is putting you at risk.

☞   *You have complained several times to your boss that the lift in the office building seems unsafe. He has taken no notice. While you do not wish to keep bothering him about it, you do not want to run the risk of injury. What do you do?*

If you believe that you are exposed to an unreasonable risk of injury, you should consult your trade union if you have one. You may also find it useful to get in touch with the Health and Safety Executive which is responsible for safety standards. Its inspectorate not only gives advice but also has enforcement powers (see DIRECTORY at the end of the chapter).

The duty of care owed by an employer to take reasonable steps to avoid employees' exposure to a foreseeable risk of injury extends to psychiatric damage as well as physical injury, although a certain level of anxiety or stress in some occupations is normal.

If you try to conceal from your employer the stress your job is putting on you, you are less likely to be able to get compensation for a breakdown than if you have told them about the adverse effect work pressures are having on you.

If any danger is so extreme that you leave your job, you could take your case to an employment tribunal. In a recent case, a tribunal decided that an employer had 'dismissed' his employee when she left her job because she felt that security was still too lax after a robbery. If you are dismissed or otherwise victimised because you have complained about serious safety risks at work, you would also have a good case for taking the employer to a tribunal. Indeed the Public Interest (Disclosure) Act 1998 was passed to protect employees who 'blow the whistle' against their employers where they report dangerous working conditions, among other issues. Any dismissal as a result is automatically unfair under the Act (see also below, and the chapter on *Working for a Living (Part 2)*, section 4.6).

7.1.1   Employer's liability insurance

- By law employers must take out insurance to cover themselves against employees' compensation claims. (It is a criminal offence not to do so.) As insurance premiums are rising steeply at present, this is presenting a major problem for employers – some even having been driven out of business because they cannot afford the cover, as insurance companies have become reluctant to insure those in dangerous businesses.
- An employer is also likely to have taken out a public liability policy. That covers the risks of injury to or damage to property of other persons such as customers, contractors or their employees working on the policy-holder's premises. It may also cover the intake of noxious emissions or pollution.
- If the employer's business involves known risks (for example, it may be concerned with chemicals), the insurance company will inspect and insist on compliance with extensive safety precautions to minimise accidents.

Employers beware:

- any failure to observe insurers' precautions can affect the validity of the insurance cover
- any failure to take these precautions is also a factor in assessing an employer's liability to an injured employee

- uninsured costs in most work accidents are four times those of insured costs, in overtime, legal costs, delayed production etc.

Employers are actively encouraged to take preventive action beyond their insurance and statutory obligations. Advice is offered by the Health and Safety Executive in the hope that employers will appreciate that safety measures are very much in their own interests.

Employees note: remember that you too can take out your own accident insurance cover.

7.2   When an accident occurs

In the short term, an injured employee is entitled to statutory sick pay for up to 28 weeks if still employed, and if out of work, to some form of sickness benefit. If still unable to work after six months, a claim could be made for long-term invalidity or disablement benefit.

Take note: obtaining these benefits does not dis-entitle an injured person from also claiming compensation in the form of damages from the employer. (See, however, section 11.1 below.)

Check your occupational sick pay or pension scheme as well for benefits.

If you have taken out your own insurance policy against accidents, any amount received from your own insurer would not be deducted from damages from your employer – provided you have paid the premiums yourself.

Make sure that your accident is brought to the immediate attention of your employer. This must be done in writing. Even if you appear not seriously hurt at the time, you may suffer long-term harm and may need to make a claim at a later stage. Any firm employing more than ten workers must keep an accident record book.

7.2.1   Industrial illnesses

An employee can contract a work-related illness which cannot be classified as an 'accident'. If the employer was at fault, no distinction between an occupational disease and an accident needs to be drawn for the purposes of claiming damages from the employer.

Although entitlement to industrial injuries benefit depends on proof that the victim suffered an 'accident', an employee who becomes ill due to work conditions may nevertheless be able to claim damages from his employer if the latter were at fault, e.g. where a doctor contracts TB after treating patients with the disease, or where the pressures of the work lead to a stress-related illness. [Some prescribed diseases are compensatable by social security benefits under the Social Security (Industrial Injuries) (Prescribed Diseases) Regulations 1985. Stress disorder is not so prescribed.]

☞ *Colin contracted occupational asthma after working in a paint-spraying unit of his employer's factory. He claimed damages from the employer. Its own company doctor had recommended that Colin be moved from this work because of his particular susceptibility to the illness, even though he knew of this himself. The employer argued that it was for Colin as a responsible adult to decide whether to take the risk of continuing in his job.*

    In a similar case the court held that where the risk of serious harm was known to the employer, he had a duty to protect Colin from himself and should have moved or dismissed him for his own good, even though he wanted to keep his job. As they had negligently failed to follow their own doctor's advice, they were liable in damages. (Colin's contributory negligence in remaining in this employment was not argued in this particular court case. If it had been, it would have reduced his damages proportionately. See 3.1. above.)

    If an employee has been exposed to the danger of illness by more than one employer over the course of this working life, e.g. by exposure to asbestos, and he contracts an asbestos-related cancer, he can recover compensation from all the employers even though it cannot be proved in which period of employment he actually contracted the disease, because all the employers exposed him to a risk to which he should not have been exposed.

7.2.2   Scope of employer's liability

The duty of an employer is to take *reasonable* care to prevent injury to people or their property at the workplace. The duty is a duty of care, it is not an absolute duty. The duty of care has various aspects, including:

- the provision of safe arrangements and working methods
- the provision of safe work premises and access to them
- the provision of suitable materials and equipment, and training and supervision as to their use
- the provision of competent staff.

There are also duties owed not only to members of staff but also to visitors to the premises, independent contractors working on the premises, and neighbours. However, some types of work are inherently hazardous. An employer who has taken proper precautions is not liable for all injuries; for example, if a dustman is injured by broken glass poking from a refuse bag he could not claim compensation from his employers.

Do note: the Disability Discrimination Act 1995 has imposed additional statutory duties on employers to take reasonable steps to make their premises both safe and accessible for disabled employees. These include training and working methods; see immediately below and chapter on *Working for a Living (Part 1)*.

7.2.3 Safe arrangements, training and working methods

The employer must plan to ensure that the method of carrying out the work does not expose employees to unreasonable risks. Employers have been held liable not only for physical but also for psychological injury as a result of excessive work loads or unreasonably long working hours. The employer has a duty to provide training about hazards and the methods for their prevention. There may need to be a regular educational programme, bringing home to employees the particular steps they should take to reduce the risk of injury.

In one case two youngsters were sent to an engineering firm to gain work experience. They were told to clean a large machine using rags and paraffin and in so doing their overalls became soaked with paraffin. When they stood next to the stove, their overalls burst into flames. The company was held liable for their injuries, as it had failed in its duty to set up a system which ensured supervision of inexperienced workers and kept management informed of workplace practices.

If the use of a safety device or a change in the distribution of the work between employees would avoid known hazards, an employer's inertia in not providing or introducing these might give rise to liability. The general standards and practice of the industry as a whole may be relevant in determining whether the risks were known before the accident.

Particular instructions as to the method of carrying out the work or warnings of the dangers given to the employee may be sufficient to discharge the employer's liability, but it is not enough to issue instructions unless adequate steps are also taken to see that they are observed.

However, as in all cases of negligence, the facts of a particular situation will determine what is reasonable. If an employee has some autonomy in determining how the work is done, an employer may be exonerated from blame, particularly if the employee is skilled or experienced, unless there is reason to believe the dangers are being ignored or they are hidden ones.

☞ *A librarian was required to stack shelves from a trolley full of books. She could select the number of items to place on the shelves at any one time. While lifting a load she injured her back, and was eventually obliged to give up the job.*

Her employer was not liable to her for the injury, because practice has shown that where employees have control over the size of their loads and the way they choose to lift them, it should constitute an effective system for avoiding excessive strains.

By contrast, a social worker who injured her back lifting an elderly, 15-stone client whom she found halfway out of bed and in a distressed state, was able to claim damages from her employer.

It is not only the weight of a load, of course, which can affect the risk of injury – the objects may be slippery, sharp or hot; by regulations, employers must design systems of work on ergonomic lines when requiring manual operations of all kinds.

7.2.4 Safe work premises

Employers are liable if they fail to provide a safe workplace for staff, including the means of access to the workplace and places to which they are sent out to work. In one case, a firm was held liable for an employee's injuries which resulted from a failure to grit an adjacent car park in icy weather. Other examples arise where illnesses are caused by micro-organisms in heating and ventilation systems. These have been widely reported in recent years. The employers were liable when three workmen died after being sent to clean a dangerous gas-filled sewer with no training or protective equipment. The structure and fittings of the premises must not themselves cause a risk of injury; uneven, greasy or debris-covered floors, inadequate lighting, loose carpets, are obvious examples. Failure to provide fire extinguishers where inflammable chemicals are dealt with would be another example.

Safety standards for the place of work may rise with time, as knowledge accumulates about particular hazards. Employers are expected to be aware of government and HSE publications warning of particular risks.

7.2.5   Suitable materials and equipment

Equipment must be safe and suitable for the job in hand. The employer must ensure that it is regularly inspected and maintained, and that those who use it are adequately trained.

If the job is sedentary, safe seating must be provided. There is a growing awareness of the importance of muscular and other strains involved in today's high-tech offices. Prolonged use of VDU units can involve eye and muscle strain, as well as hazards to pregnant women. In all cases, equipment must be checked to see that it is suitable for safe use. There are also regulations requiring guards to be fitted to dangerous parts of machines, protection against equipment overheating, stability of equipment etc.

If the task is hazardous or the machinery, e.g. paper guillotines, dangerous, then training must be given. Protective safety equipment must be made available.

Remember: even when personal protective equipment, e.g. gloves, goggles, safety harnesses, has been provided, employers will be liable if they fail to insist on their use.

By regulation, employers are also required to meet certain standards for the comfort and welfare of their employees, such as heating and ventilation, which go beyond pure safety measures.

7.2.6   Competent staff

☞ *One of your work colleagues is known to be a practical joker. One day, he pulls away your chair as you are about to sit down – as a result, you land on the floor. You suffer more than mere social embarrassment, as you hurt your back badly. What can you do?*

> Theoretically, you could sue your colleague but as he is probably not worth suing, you could pursue a claim against your employers. They would be liable in damages if they knew of your colleague's propensity for horseplay and had taken no steps to warn him against silly behaviour.

The same principle applies if you suffer an injury because a fellow-employee is inexpert, given to outbursts of temper, or drinks too much.

A worker in a canteen was injured when struck on the head by a raw potato thrown by a fellow employee. She was awarded substantial compensation by the Criminal Injuries Compensation Board. The employer was also civilly liable to pay damages.

An employer's liability extends beyond problems posed by fellow-employees and can include dangerous actions of a third party on the work premises.

☞ *Your employer engages a firm of heating engineers to install gas heaters in your office. They do the work negligently, with the result that an appliance explodes, injuring you.*

> Your employer is liable to you.

7.3   Safety legislation

The negligence liability of an employer is heavily overlaid with statutory duties flowing from Acts of Parliament, statutory regulations, and increasingly, EU Directives. All these have imposed more and more duties on employers to safeguard their employees' health and safety.

The Health and Safety at Work, etc. Act 1974 imposes a general duty on employers to ensure, so far as is reasonably practicable, the health, safety and welfare at work of all employees. The Provision and Use of Work Equipment Regulations 1998 require employers to ensure that work equipment is maintained in efficient working order and in good repair. This is an absolute liability, and does not depend on proof of fault or negligence. The Health and Safety at Work Regulations 1999 make it clear that an employer has no defence in criminal proceedings for a contravention of health and safety regulations by sheltering behind the actions of a subordinate employee, i.e. the employer's duty is not delegable.

There are regulations under the Act which cover particular industries or workplaces, e.g. the use of lead in the potteries industry or the wearing of protective helmets in the construction industry. There are a large number of measures designed to control particular types of hazard, such as the use of computers, electrical dangers, risks of eye injury, hazardous levels of noise. Important among these are controls on substances hazardous to health, including chemicals, dust, micro-organisms and noise. The Health and Safety Executive publishes guides to help employers comply with regulations, including those which give effect to a comprehensive EU Directive on the management of health and safety, providing for risk assessment in the workplace, higher standards of care, and the taking of precautionary measures in the work place.

Offices are also covered by legislation and regulations, which deal with such matters as the provision of adequate lighting, heating, cleaning, first aid facilities, sanitary facilities, seating for sedentary work, and safe lifts, and also the protection of non-smokers from tobacco smoke.

A draft code of practice on smoking in the workplace is currently under consideration but no timetable for its implementation is yet finalised, as the impact of such a code on the hospitality industry is still being investigated. In the meantime, the Health and Safety Executive has a leaflet (Leaflet INDG 63) on *Passive Smoking in the Workplace* which can be downloaded from *www.hse.gov.uk/pubns/indg63.pdf*.

The prevention of repetitive strain injury – especially for those regularly using computers and word processors – is also covered by statutory regulations. Repetitive strain injury has been held to be a physical rather than a psychogenic condition.

Where different parts of office premises are occupied by different firms and companies, it is the owner of the premises who is responsible for the safety of the common parts of the building, including entrance hall, stairs, passages and toilets.

Almost all of these legal duties imposed on employers are enforced either by the Health and Safety Inspectorate or by the local authority environmental health officer (although fire precautions are enforced by the local fire authority). There is the sanction of criminal proceedings against the employer and/or the power to bring work to a halt until safety measures are introduced.

Directors of companies have even been convicted of manslaughter after people died because of the way the businesses were operated. There are also proposals for a new offence of corporate killing, aimed at ensuring that more companies and individuals face criminal proceedings for management failures that result in death. In 1996 proposals were put forward for a new criminal offence of 'corporate killing', under which companies could be prosecuted where death results from management failures causing incidents such as the sinking of the P & O ferry *Herald of Free Enterprise* (which killed 192 people in 1987). Despite several other tragedies since, such as the major rail disasters at Southall, Ladbroke Grove and Paddington, no legislative action has yet been taken to enact the proposals into law.

From the point of view of an injured employee's claim for damages, the claim can be based on breach of statutory duty. The victim's task of establishing liability is made simpler in such a case, because negligence need not be shown.

The employer's duty to take the prescribed safety measures is usually absolute – for example, to fence moving parts of machinery in a factory. It would not be any defence for an employer that it was too expensive to take such steps.

Note: the statutory duties may be phrased in unqualified terms, or may be expressed as a duty to take all reasonable practicable steps. Each case will have to be considered individually.

7.4 Contributory negligence

Employees have a duty to co-operate with the employer to take care for their own and others' safely.

☞ *You are sent by your firm of chartered surveyors to survey the roof of a three-storey block of flats. You have telephoned to the main office for additional assistance as you realise, once on site, that the task is too much for a single person. In the meantime you decide to explore the roof – as far as possible – by examining the loft. You fall through and are injured.*

You may be found by the court to have contributed to your own misfortune in this particular case – even if your employers were also negligent in having sent you to do a task without proper assistance.

Employees who put their colleagues or members of the public at risk by carelessness or by disobeying safety instructions lay themselves open not only to the (possibly theoretical) claim for damages jointly with their employer but also, of course, to disciplinary charges and even dismissal. Criminal charges are also a possibility.

See also the example in section 7.2.6.

7.5   Staff at risk from the public

A new concern for employers and their employees arises from the fact that staff can be at risk from members of the public – as highlighted by the tragic case of Suzy Lamplugh, an estate agent who kept an appointment with a 'client' and was never seen again.

Employers can be held liable if they fail to take all reasonable steps to prevent and guard against the likelihood of risk to their employees. They are under a duty to carry out appropriate risk assessments and brief their staff accordingly. They must also provide appropriate aftercare for a staff member injured in a violent incident.

They may not be liable for accidents occurring on other premises for which they cannot take responsibility. For example, employees sent to work on a building site in Saudi Arabia who were injured there could not hold the employer in Britain liable as he could not control daily events there. His responsibility was only to take reasonable steps to ensure the safety of the employees on his own or other premises where they were directed to work.

However, the exact position regarding overseas personal injury claims is not totally clear. In one case the House of Lords allowed a plaintiff, employed by a Namibian company and injured in Namibia, to bring a claim against parent companies in the UK who were not his employers. The circumstances were somewhat unusual as the plaintiff could not fund his claim in Namibia but was able to pursue the case in England on a conditional fee basis. For legal aid abroad, see the chapter on *The Legal System*, section 3.6.4.

Certain groups of employees are particularly vulnerable in their dealings with the public. Social workers, nurses, benefits staff, bus and van drivers and schoolteachers have been threatened, abused and physically assaulted in the course of their duties. A parent who punched his child's headteacher was recently sentenced to nine months' imprisonment for the assault. In an effort to combat assaults against NHS staff, magistrates have been given power to impose exemplary maximum fines for any such acts of violence up to a maximum of £20,000. The right to claim civil compensation in these cases works in tandem with the criminal law.

Employees who are victims of criminal assault may be able to receive compensation from the Criminal Injuries Compensation Board (see also above, section 2.2).

7.6   Amount of fine

Under the health and safety at work legislation there is an exemplary maximum fine of £20,000 for breach of general duties under sections 2 to 6 of the 1974 Act where the offence is dealt with summarily. When imposing fines for breaches, the court should look at how far short of the standard the defendant fell in failing to meet the 'reasonably practical' test. A deliberate breach with a view to profit seriously aggravates the offence.

Further, the size of the company and its financial strength or weakness do not affect the degree of care required in matters of safety. Other matters relevant to sentence are the degree of risk and extent of the danger created by the offence; the extent of the breach, e.g. whether it was an isolated incident or continued over a period; and the defendant's business and the effect of the fine on the business. Where the defendant is a company, a fine should be large enough to bring home the message, not only to the managers but also to the shareholders. Where death is the consequence the penalty should reflect public disquiet at the unnecessary loss of life.

The Public Interest Disclosure Act 1998 is intended to protect workers 'who blow the whistle' about dangers and hazards in the workplace. Among other work situations, it is intended to protect an employee who reports a situation where there is a danger to any member of the public (e.g. an operator of machinery in an amusement park) or a danger to fellow workers. Disclosure should be made to the Health and Safety Executive or to some other regulatory body. The employee must act in good faith and believe that the allegations are substantially true. The organisation Public Concern at Work (see DIRECTORY) offers free legal and practical advice to persons concerned about malpractice in their workplace (see also chapter on *Working for a Living (Part 2)*, section 4.6).

8   ACCIDENTS INVOLVING CHILDREN

The law recognises that children are vulnerable and unpredictable and that what is an obvious danger to an adult may be an allurement to a child.

Primarily it is the legal responsibility of parents, or of others who have charge of the child – even temporarily, such as a childminder, baby-sitter or teacher – to see that they are safe. Their safety involves both taking precautions at home (having safety gates on stairs and childproof containers for medicines) and taking particular care of children out of doors. Older children are expected to take some care for their own safety, e.g. when crossing the road.

8.1   An accident caused to a child

8.1.1   Precautions and safety measures

Note the safety regulations designed to protect children against accidents – for example, regulations covering the flammability of clothing and the safety of toys or nursery equipment. Check that any toy or equipment you buy carries a BS, BSI or CE mark which mean that safety standards are being complied with. There is no need to wait until an accident actually occurs.

☞ *You buy your three-year-old child an expensive boxed doll. On the box it states that it is suitable for a child of 36 months and over but has no other mark. The hand of the doll comes away from its arm and could be easily swallowed – even by a three-year old. You think the toy is not safe and should not be on the market. What can you do?*

Inform the safety standards officer of your local authority who will take the matter up with the manufacturers and retailers. Standards officers have enforcement powers in addition to their investigative duties.

The Department of Health and the DTI frequently run campaigns aimed at improving the safety of children and reducing the risks of accidents, e.g. by encouraging the wearing of bicycle helmets; drawing attention to potential dangers in the garden – such as drowning in ponds, burns from barbecues, and accidents from unsecured slides and swings – and to dangers in the home, such as unsecured medicines and other household chemicals. 'Blitz' campaigns often warn of accidents that are most likely to occur on specific dates, e.g. the hazards from fireworks on bonfire night.

(Advice on safety can also be obtained from the Child Accident Prevention Trust and the Royal Society for the Prevention of Accidents, see DIRECTORY.)

8.1.2   Parents and other carers

If other people look after your children while you are at work, it is not always easy to establish whether they are properly qualified to do so.

☞ *You leave your toddler with a childminder while you go out to work. The child gets hurt on a swing. You are sure it was an avoidable accident and that the minder was just not taking due care. Have you any redress?*

You must complain to your local authority which keeps a register of childminders who have been vetted by its own staff. You can also sue the childminder on the child's behalf.

The Children Act 1989 lays down guidelines for the registration by the local authority of all persons who look after children under eight on domestic premises, for gain, for more than two hours per day (see also chapter on *Children (Part 1)*).

8.1.3   Road accidents

Damages for a child hurt in a road accident will be reduced by the extent to which its own carelessness contributed to any injury.

☞   *You are driving your car during rush-hour in a busy road at about 20 mph. An 11-year-old boy, without looking, runs into the centre of the road to retrieve a ball, and is struck by your car. The child suffers a broken arm. You feel that you were not altogether at fault for the accident.*

   In a similar incident, the driver was held only 25 per cent to blame for the accident. The court felt that the child's blameworthiness, even taking account of his age, was considerably greater.

Where a four-year-old ran quickly into the road into the path of an oncoming car, the driver was held not liable for her injuries. His attempt to avoid her was all that a prudent motorist could have done in the circumstances.

8.1.4   School trips

Although most school trips cause no problems, there have been some horrifying accidents reported. Regulations requiring seatbelts on minibuses have been in force since 1997 (see section 5.4 in the *Motoring* chapter). Many buses involved in school runs similarly have seat belts fitted, but in some instances coaches used for ferrying children to and from school are also used for public service bus work and do not have belts fitted. Pressure groups are calling for this anomaly to be removed. Organisers of activity holidays for children have to be licensed and need to comply with safety regulations (see section 9.3 in the *Goods and Services* chapter).

However, no other legal requirements appear to be in place. The Department for Education and Skills issues only guidelines, and now require education authorities to carry out adequate risk assessment of the trip. Local education authorities do impose fairly rigorous standards on school governors and headteachers, where the schools themselves are responsible for organizing expeditions, covering such matters as staff/pupil ratios on such trips, the experience and qualifications of supervisory staff, whether they have undertaken an exploratory visit to the centre etc. Health and safety regulations would also apply if things went wrong in this country on a school trip. However, at least one of the schoolteachers' unions currently advises its members not to go on school trips, because parents no longer accept that genuine accidents can occur when other people are in charge of their children.

If your child is to go on a school trip, try to find out in advance what is the extent of the school's plans and risk assessments. Do also try to establish whether there is insurance in place, both for the costs if the operator goes out of business and for any illness or accident which might occur during the trip. Even if you are asked to sign a consent slip, this does not alter the position on claiming compensation, because the school and education authority cannot legally exclude liability for personal injuries.

8.2   When a child causes an accident

8.2.1   Parents' liability

In general, parents are not liable for the damage that their children cause, although they may feel moral responsibility, e.g. to pay for the replacement of a neighbour's window broken by their son's cricket ball.

In the rare case where the child has personally got assets, he or she can be sued for compensation. In one case a 10-year-old boy was sued for the cost of repairs to a car which knocked him down through the boy's own fault.

Note: an award of damages can be enforced when a child starts earning if this takes place within six years of judgement.

But it does happen that parents are personally negligent in not properly controlling their children. The fault is then theirs in failing to prevent an accident. In the case of a young child accompanied by an adult, it could be that the adult would be held wholly or partly responsible. For example, a driver who sees a little girl walking with her mother might reasonably expect the mother to prevent the child from running into the road. A parent who does not control children in a car, to the detriment of other road users, will also be held responsible.

☞ *You have picked up two of your son's school friends for the school run and the three boys are being very rowdy in the back seat of your estate car. They unwind the car windows and start throwing conkers on to the road. Unfortunately, one hits the windscreen of an oncoming car so that the driver is distracted and has a minor accident. He complains that you were to blame for the accident and that it was your duty to control the children in the car in the interests of other road users. Is he correct?*

The answer is 'yes'.

In one case, a lorry driver was killed when he swerved to avoid a four-year-old who had wandered out on to the street from his local authority nursery school. The authority was held negligent in failing to supervise the child. The driver's widow was awarded damages against the LEA.

A parent's liability for a child's actions is also related to the danger involved.

☞ *A father allowed his 13-year-old to use a bow and arrow and fire it in the garden, even after his son had injured a neighbour's pet with it. Then another child got hurt in a similar incident.*

It is likely that a court would view the father's actions as negligent in light of the fact that there had already been one incident. On the other hand, it might take the view that the result would probably have been the same even if the father had repeatedly warned his son to take care when using the bow, as children cannot be expected to be obedient to instructions 100 per cent of the time.

8.2.2 Liability of other carers

When a child causes an accident while in the care of others, the same principles apply. In the 'school run' example above, the mother is equally responsible for the accident whether the offending conker was thrown by her son or by one of the other children.

8.3 Children at school

8.3.1 Safety of premises and equipment

A local education authority is responsible for taking reasonable care for the safety of a child at a maintained school. The governing body of a fee-paying school owes the same duty of care to its pupils. All maintained schools have a governing body, which is incorporated and is therefore a legal entity, that can be sued. A lawyer might advise parents, however, that the LEA should also be joined in any action. A governing body is required to have insurance cover against accidents on school premises. The duty of care requires the school to provide safe premises, just as the occupier of any other premises must.

☞ *Heavy swing doors with a powerful spring are installed in a primary school. A small girl catches her hand in the door and it is crushed.*

The school (or education authority) is liable, as such doors are unsuitable for a school for this age group.

Playgrounds, sports facilities and school buses are also required to be suitably designed and safely maintained. The child's safety at school must also be safeguarded by the provision of suitable materials and equipment (e.g. round-ended rather than pointed scissors should be provided for younger children), and by a reasonable level of supervision. This does not mean constant supervision, although obviously more supervision is required the younger the child or the more dangerous the activity. It is not unreasonable for the duty to supervise to be delegated in appropriate circumstances to unqualified staff such as dinner ladies, or to prefects or monitors.

After several tragic accidents where children have died or been injured on school trips, the government has issued guidelines to ensure greater safety. Copies are available from the Department for Education and Skills (*www.info.dfes.gsi.gov.uk*).

8.3.2 Security

Security in schools is a growing concern and schools are increasingly being seen as responsible for the protection of both children and staff. The Government has provided funding for schools where the maintenance of a secure environment is most needed. If damage occurs and there is shown to have been inadequate security measures in place, it is very likely that the authority would be held liable. For example, it might be considered that a school with a number of entrances and exits should have installed a CCTV system covering all entrances; or that a school that had suffered a number of problems from trespassers should have installed an electronically controlled reception area or a system of identification cards required for entry onto the premises.

On the question of children's safety on activity holidays, see chapter on *Goods and Services*, section 9.3.

8.3.3   Negligent supervision

Schools are responsible for the negligence of the staff in failing to protect pupils' safety. For older children, warnings about dangerous substances or practices may be a sufficient discharge of the teacher's responsibility to safeguard his pupils.

Where a teacher warned pupils in a chemistry lesson about the dangerous nature of a chemical, he was held not to be negligent when one of the pupils carelessly spilt some of the chemical on another pupil, causing burns. On the other hand, where a teacher had left an unmarked container of the dangerous substance in a position where pupils could get at it, he was held to have been negligent.

Provided there is a reasonable level of supervision, a school may not be liable if a child is hurt during playground games or organised sports activities.

☞   *A pupil was severely injured by a head-on tackle during a school rugby match. Some degree of instruction had been provided.*

   In that case, the school was not liable, and was found not negligent in failing to insure the pupil nor in failing to advise his parents to take out such insurance.

In another case, a referee was found negligent when a 17-year-old player was injured. The Central Council for Physical Recreation arranges bulk insurance through schools to cover this type of accident.

The usual course of events if a pupil alleges negligence against a school is for the injured pupil to sue the school together with the controlling local authority, alleging a lack of reasonable supervision or a lack of adherence to reasonable safety precautions. Whilst a pupil is at school, each teacher acts *in loco parentis* and is expected to adopt the standards which would be expected of a reasonable caring parent.

This does not expect the behaviour of the teachers to be exemplary in foreseeing and taking precautions against all hazardous situations. For example, a teacher was held not negligent in leaving two four-year-old children unattended for 10 minutes while she was giving first aid to another child. In a later case where two 15-year-olds were engaged in a play sword-fight using plastic rulers and one was partially blinded by a fragment of snapped off plastic, the school and the teacher were found not to have been negligent. Instead the claim was pursued against the pupil who had allegedly caused the injury. It was held that both girls had been negligent by participating in horseplay which in its latter stages was becoming dangerous. Also both must have appreciated that it was dangerous and that physical injury was foreseeable although the precise injury might not have been foreseen. The case makes it clear that a child's behaviour is to be judged objectively according to the standard of an ordinary prudent and reasonable child of that age.

8.3.4   Claims against children

☞   *You are a teacher on playground duty. A pupil with a history of aggressive disruption throws a cricket ball with all his force at you and fractures a cheekbone. You want to know whom to sue.*

   You can claim damages from the education authority for failing to protect you from the risk of such an injury.

8.4   Children and occupier's liability

Premises must be reasonably safe for children, and that means taking into account the fact that children are less able to take care of themselves than adults.

☞   *Your four-year-old is injured when she slips between the bars of an air vent in a walkway in a shopping centre. It is clear that such an accident could not have happened to an adult or an older child. Would that be a factor in assessing the safety of the premises for the purposes of liability?*

The answer is 'no'.

A two-year-old girl, when visiting the zoo, put her hand through the bars of a cage, where a chimpanzee grabbed it and bit off two fingers. The zoo was held at fault and responsible for the width of the cage bars.

A playground manager (such as the local authority) will be liable if a child is injured by:

- unsafe or defective equipment
- unsuitable surfaces, or
- hidden dangers.

☞   *A toddler is badly cut by pieces of glass concealed in a sandpit in a public park.*

The local authority which manages the playground can be held liable to pay her compensation.

☞   *A tree has been planted in a public park with attractive but poisonous berries. A child eats the berries and becomes ill.*

The local authority which owns the park is liable as its officials should have realised the berries presented a dangerous attraction to children.

8.4.1   Children as 'trespassers'

The question of children who trespass on land and who then get hurt is a vexed problem for the courts. There might be liability to children who trespass in certain circumstances:

a) if there is a hidden danger on the land, or an allurement which tempts children to use it even without permission (e.g. a ramp suitable for skateboarders to practise stunts), and
b) if the occupier knows that children trespass on the land and lets them do this,
he may be regarded as having given them 'permission' and will be liable if they are injured.

However such liability will be limited to damage of a type which might reasonably have been foreseen. Where the line is to be drawn can be difficult, and there is no fixed point in a scale of probability. As one judge put it, in cases of children, their ingenuity in finding unexpected ways of doing mischief to themselves and others should never be underestimated. (See also section 4.3.3 above.)

9   MEDICAL ACCIDENTS

Under the general rules of negligence, professional persons, such as doctors and dentists, must exercise a *reasonable degree* of skill so as not to cause foreseeable injury to their patients.

Medical accidents can and do occur without anyone to blame. A simple and routine operation can go disastrously wrong because the patient reacts badly or does not recover properly. Such patients are as much victims of medical accidents and can suffer just as much as in cases where negligence is proven. Yet they cannot recover compensation because they cannot point to a doctor and say 'It is his fault'. Negligence claims are eating up increasing amounts of the NHS budget – as much as £4 billion pounds (6% of the annual budget in 2001–02) was quoted by the government when announcing plans in 2002 to reform the system. It is thought the plans will introduce:

- capping of the legal costs of claims
- a no-fault scheme for birth injuries
- the replacement of lump-sum compensation awards by fixed annual payments to victims.

Mediation between patients and hospital trusts is also being considered, as in many cases the legal costs at present exceed the compensation awarded by the courts.

If you were being treated by the NHS, you should in the first instance use the NHS complaints procedure. (Private hospitals are required by law to have their own complaints procedures.)

Information on how to complain should be provided in hospitals and GPs' surgeries. Sometimes, a full explanation of treatment and circumstances will enable you to understand what has happened and why. If you are not satisfied with this, you could turn to the Health Services Ombudsman (see DIRECTORY). If you still wish to claim compensation, legal action may be contemplated.

9.1   Difficulties of proving negligence

In all cases, liability to pay compensation is based on lack of due care. In some cases, this is beyond argument, as when, for example, a dentist pulls out a sound tooth.

In other cases, medical accident victims may have great difficulty in proving negligence.

9.1.1   Standard of care required

Remember: a doctor or dentist is not to be judged by the highest professional standards but is required to exercise the skill and care of the average competent practitioner in his or her field.

However, it is no longer the case that a doctor escapes liability for negligent treatment just because he or she presents evidence from a number of medical experts that the treatment or diagnosis accorded with sound medical practice. The experts would also have to show that the doctor's opinion was responsible and reasonable in balancing the comparative risks and benefits of a particular course of treatment.

Self-regulation of doctors by their own body, the General Medical Council, has been coming under increasing criticism in the wake of recent medical scandals. The General Medical Council has been accused of not taking action even when doctors should have been suspended from practice for breach of the criminal law. Increased action to discipline doctors and to call for their immediate suspension is expected for serious professional misconduct. The GMC's record with regard to checking on doctors' under-performance, being slapdash in record-keeping, or not examining patients properly is also under scrutiny.

9.1.2   Establishing cause and effect

It can be very difficult to establish cause and effect, because:

- patients have to prove that the doctor failed to practise an acceptable standard of professional skill
- the courts have tended to be protective towards doctors for fear of 'opening the floodgates' to litigation
- it may be difficult to establish that it was the doctor's or hospital's negligence which resulted in the injury.

This is a particular problem where the negligent conduct is said to be a failure to treat or to diagnose.

☞   *Your 15-year-old son fell off his bike and was taken to casualty, where the doctor in charge diagnosed a knee injury. In fact the boy had also injured his hip, as was discovered when he returned to the hospital some days later. By that time the hip joint had become deformed. You would like to sue on your son's behalf but have taken a second opinion from a consultant orthopaedic surgeon who says that the deformity would have resulted from the original fall even if the damage to the hip had been diagnosed on the first visit to casualty.*

The courts would hold that if the same result would have followed, irrespective of the treatment, you could not recover damages in negligence. Whether or not the courts would take such a view would depend on the facts in light of expert and other evidence. But a doctor's negligent failure to undertake proper investigative procedures – if early diagnosis would have led to a cure – would be the basis of a claim against the doctor.

A patient suffered extreme pain and fear because she was awake during an operation. The court held the anaesthetist had not been negligent because he had used an accepted anaesthetic technique which was approved by a responsible body of medical opinion even though it carried a small risk of the patient's awareness during the operation. In another case, however, the patient recovered damages.

Note: if you think you have a claim, take legal advice. Medical negligence is a specialised and difficult area. Seek out a solicitor who specialises in medical negligence cases, and always act promptly. Time limits may seem ample (three years in the usual cases) but all such matters can take an inordinately long time to process.

9.2   Defences to negligence

9.2.1   Medical knowledge at the time of an accident

Practitioners are expected to apply the medical knowledge current at the time of treatment. You would have to show that the treatment was known to have risks or to cause serious side effects at the period when it was actually used on you.

9.2.2   Adequate information provided

The doctor's negligence may consist in failing to provide information to the patient or in failing to obtain the patient's consent to treatment. In the case of a treatment which in itself carries with it some risk of harm or side-effects, it is a good defence for the doctor to show that the patient was informed about the risks and consented to run them. This again is a question of degree.

☞ *You underwent pain-relieving surgery on an arthritic joint. The doctor did not warn you that there was a risk that the joint might fuse. What is the legal position?*

> The House of Lords has held that a doctor was not negligent when he did not warn a patient of a one per cent risk of partial paralysis from pain-relieving surgery. However, if there had been a ten per cent risk or more, their Lordships said, a patient should be told of it so that the patient has full knowledge of any unfortunate consequences (i.e. in legal terms, could give 'informed consent'). If a substantial body of doctors would not have regarded it as necessary to warn the patient, failure to do so will not be regarded as negligent in law.

If no or insufficient information is given, the patient may be able to sue – therefore, for example, pregnant women suffering from epilepsy should be warned about the danger that anti-convulsive drugs prescribed to control the condition may cause serious birth defects. In another case, despite persistent questioning from a patient advised to undergo spinal surgery, the doctor failed to warn her adequately of the risks involved. He was held liable in negligence as her condition worsened after the operation and the judge accepted that she would not have proceeded with surgery 'there and then' but would have sought a second opinion. He also refused to accept that the worsening of her condition would have happened in the course of time in any event.

However, good professional practice has tended over the years towards a greater degree of frankness, with more respect being paid to patient autonomy. Patients are likely to be better informed and more ready to ask questions, while the courts also are less willing to accept medical practice and judgement than has been the case in the past.

9.2.3   No consent given

If no consent at all has been given to a particular procedure the doctor is clearly liable, e.g. in cases where women who consented to an abortion or bladder operation found a hysterectomy had been performed on them as well.

9.2.4   Other factors

Doctors have also been held to be negligent for:

*   failing to investigate the patient's medical history before administering further treatment, or
*   failing to provide adequate information so that those responsible for subsequent treatment are duly informed.

☞ *You were discharged from hospital after surgery. The surgeon failed to inform your GP that your condition required continued monitoring at home. Your recovery from the operation is greatly prolonged as a result.*

> The hospital is liable.

9.3   Who is responsible

9.3.1   NHS treatment

For NHS treatment the health authority or self-governing hospital trust is responsible for any proven lapses in skill or care of its employees. It will not matter whose fault or error caused the accident – whether a senior consultant or junior doctor, nursing sister or student nurse. A consultant who works part-time in the hospital is also a member of staff for this purpose.

☞ *You were treated by an inexperienced house officer when you attended a casualty station after an accident. In fact he even told you it was his first day on the job. You now feel you were incorrectly treated. Will his inexperience be relevant to establishing liability?*

An inexperienced doctor would not be excused from negligence on account of his lack of skill. The health authority is under a duty to ensure adequate staffing so that there is proper supervision of trainees.

In fact, junior doctors in training constitute the largest single group of high-risk doctors as far as claims are concerned. The excessively long working hours of junior doctors and the inadequate conditions under which they often work constitute a special problem over which the trainees themselves have no control, but for which their employers can be held responsible.

9.3.2   Private treatment

In the case of a fee-paying patient, the doctor must be sued personally. If the injury was caused by negligent nursing care the private hospital is sued. The National Care Standards Commission became operation in April 2002. It is responsible for inspection of private nursing homes (see DIRECTORY).

All doctors carry insurance under special schemes (see DIRECTORY).

9.4   General non-medical safety in hospitals

Security is a growing problem in hospitals. Numbers of people wander in and out of hospital premises for all sorts of reasons, but there have been some horrific cases of injuries to patients in hospitals from outsiders.

As far as responsibility for the actions of its own staff is concerned, a hospital is liable for a patient's physical safety – even apart from the treatment administered. Cases include a patient who was scalded by being given too hot a bath, and an inadequately supervised child patient who fell out of a window.

Hospitals are also responsible for the safety of their premises, like any other 'occupier' (see section 4.1 above).

9.5   Emergency services

In a recent case where the ambulance service was slow in responding to a doctor's call so that there was a dangerous delay in getting the patient to hospital, the service had to pay compensation for the resulting deterioration in the patient's condition. On the other hand, in claims against the fire brigade, the court held that there was no common law duty of care to the public at large to answer a call for help. 'If therefore they fail to turn up, or fail to turn up in time, because they have carelessly misunderstood the message, got lost on the way, or run into a tree, they are not liable.'

Clearly therefore the law in this area is still in the process of development.

9.6   Complementary medicine

There is a growing recognition, even in the medical profession, that practitioners of complementary medicine have a role to play in a patient's wellbeing. Osteopaths, chiropractors, acupuncturists and others are also governed by the general rules of negligence, i.e. they must use a reasonable degree of skill so as not to cause foreseeable injury to their patients.

Take note: practitioners of complementary medicine are not required to be as skilled as qualified doctors. They must be reasonably skilled and use such care as one would expect from an ordinarily competent person in their particular field. Although they are not required by law to be registered, many of them are registered by their own organisations, which lay down training standards to give a level of competence patients should expect.

Check: to see that a practitioner is registered.

☞ *You have a trapped nerve in your neck and are in a great deal of pain. A friend recommends you to a masseur. He examines you, looks at your X-rays and agrees that your neck condition is very serious. He then proceeds to give you a strenuous massage. Your condition worsens. Has the masseur breached his duty of care?*

If practitioners of complementary medicine undertake treatment for a serious condition when they knew or should reasonably have known that they were not competent to deal with it, they could be liable for recklessness or negligence.

Note: unlike doctors, alternative therapists are not always obliged by law to obtain insurance cover. Responsible therapists will have done so. Even though many of the techniques used are 'non-invasive' (i.e. are unlikely to do any harm) you should always check with their umbrella organisations with regard to the insurance position.

Legislation is to be introduced requiring all doctors and dentists to have professional indemnity cover. This may be extended to include pharmacists and opticians.

The Medicines Control Agency has a website devoted to safety information on herbal remedies, See *www.gov.uk/ourwork/licensingmeds/herbalmeds/herbalsaftey.htm*. A European Union directive harmonising and regulating standards in relation to food supplements and traditional herbal medicinal products is in the pipeline and is expected to become law in 2004.

9.7 Veterinary medicine

A vet owes the same duty as a doctor to discharge his duties with a reasonable level of competence and care. As vets also frequently provide medication, they are responsible if the products are unsafe or unfit for their purpose. (See also the chapter on *Pets*, section 10.)

☞ *You are a farmer who asks the vet to inoculate your herd of cattle against summer mastitis. Unknown to the vet the serum used is defective.*

He is liable to compensate you for losses in the herd (although he will be able to claim reimbursement from the suppliers).

There may be more difficulties about calculating compensation if the animal is not a working animal but a pet. Distress at the loss of a much-loved cat may not be compensatable even if due to maltreatment, although damages for inconvenience, refund of expenses etc., will be claimable.

The Office of Fair Trading is currently investigating the high prices charged for veterinary medicines, after complaints by both farmers' groups and individual consumers that prices are substantially higher in the UK than in other European countries.

10 ACCIDENTS AND SPORT

Public attention, as never before, has been focused on the subject of accidents and sport. Mass disasters, such as those at the football fields of Bradford and Hillsborough, have led to direct government intervention in matters of public safety and crowd control. Far-reaching legal issues have been raised by these events for which the ordinary rules of negligence have seemed inadequate.

Note, however: that you may have no claim for damages at all if you have consented to run the risk of some degree of injury, as, for example, where the sport is an inherently dangerous activity, such as skiing or hang-gliding. Novices should ensure there is adequate supervision and/or qualified instructors.

If you engage in such sports regularly, personal accident insurance can be arranged through the governing body of the sport, as an ordinary personal accident policy may not cover you. Always tell your insurer before embarking on a dangerous sport.

In all cases it is a matter of degree. You may have consented to run some risk of injury but you will not have consented to negligence on the part of others, such as the employment of an unqualified instructor or failure to maintain a ski lift properly.

Some reports show that rugby players have a risk of serious injury or death three to four times greater than that of players in other team games such as football, hockey or cricket.

At first sight it might seem that someone indulging in the professional sport of boxing has consented to all the attendant risks, but this is not necessarily so. Thus the British Boxing Board of Control was liable to meet a claim for damages in respect of a professional boxer fighting in a contest where the Board had failed to provide an appropriate system of medical assistance at the ringside. The boxer had accepted the risk of injury at his opponent's hand but not the risk of the Board's failure to work out carefully its governing rules.

In another case a professional footballer injured in a tackle by another professional player succeeded in his negligence claim. He was able to establish that a reasonable professional player would have known that there was a significant risk that, in the circumstances, serious injury would result.

A professional jockey was seriously injured while riding in a race when his horse shied at the penultimate hurdle because two other riders took his line on the bend and left him with no room. The judge stated that the other riders were guilty of lapses of care and that every contestant in a lawful sporting event did owe a duty of care to avoid causing injury. However the prevailing circumstances would also depend on the contest, and the rules which regulated it, among other matters. The stress of the race, and the measures needed to win also had to be taken in to account in the context of a fast-moving contest. It was not possible to characterise momentary carelessness as negligence in this particular case.

Thus it is clear that each case depends on the particular circumstances.

10.1.1 Occupier's liability

The general rule is that of occupier's liability (see section 4.1 above): anyone who is injured by unsafe sports premises can claim compensation from the persons in control of the premises. So those who offer sports facilities to members of the public must take all reasonable steps to ensure that the facilities provided are reasonably safe for ordinary use.

☞ *Your local public swimming baths offer a heated outdoor pool. You take a dive into the pool from the diving board and suffer head injuries as a result. It transpires the diving board has been sited at a part of the swimming pool where the water was insufficiently deep for diving.*

   In a similar case the local authority was held liable.

Do take note: each case turns on its facts.

☞ *A student, together with two friends, climbed over a locked fence at his college pool in the early hours of one morning. There was a warning notice outside to say that use of the pool was prohibited between 10 pm and 6.30 am. The water level of the pool was low and it contained chemicals. He took a running dive and struck his head on the bottom of the pool, sustaining very severe injuries. The appeal court held that the student had trespassed on the premises at night and had taken the risk of danger upon himself.*

   In this case, the college had removed the diving board some years before the accident. The court also went on to point out that 'it was a danger common to all swimming pools' that there might be insufficient water to accommodate a dive as pools have no uniformity in shape, size or configuration. That was a danger 'obvious to any adult and indeed to most children who were old enough to have learnt to dive'.

   However, a case somewhat similar on its facts went the other way. An 18-year-old went to a park run by the local authority which included a lake where swimming and diving were prohibited with warning signs stating: 'DANGEROUS WATER: NO SWIMMING'. The claimant was aware of the notices but standing thigh deep in water, he dived, hit his head on the bottom and suffered catastrophic injury. On his appeal, the Court of Appeal stated that the local authority were aware that there was widespread flouting of their warning notices against swimming in the lake. It was their duty as occupiers, therefore, to take protection against these risks, for example by planting vegetation so as to deter public access to the water.

So yet again, the decisions themselves demonstrate that there are no hard and fast rules, and each case turns not only on its facts but on the view that the court takes of those facts, the legal precedents, and the circumstances which surround them.

☞ *An aerobics class is held in the hall of an adult education institute. You become a member of the class but you injure your back when you slip on the polished floor of the hall.*

   The local education authority which runs the institute could be liable to compensate you, as although you voluntarily undertook the risks inherent in brisk exercise, you were entitled to assume that the premises were reasonably fit for the purpose of aerobics.

The degree of care which such occupiers or organisers of sports events must show will vary with the circumstances. Dangerous sports or especially vulnerable participants (e.g. children, the disabled) are entitled to expect a greater degree of care, and more steps to be taken for their safety.

The directors of an outdoor activity centre were jailed in 1994 for unlawful killing through gross negligence when four young people drowned as a result of inadequate precautions for their safety.

10.1.2 Outside the sports facilities

Clubs or other occupiers of sports halls or grounds may be liable for accidents which occur beyond the boundaries of their premises.

☞ *You are cycling along a road and are struck on the forehead by a ball which has been hit by a golfer from a golf course which adjoins the road. You learn that the course has been laid out with a hole in such a position that balls are frequently driven into the road.*

You can claim damages for injury from the club (and also from the player if he can be identified).

Note: if the incident had not been usual, but had been wholly exceptional, the club would not have been liable.

In a recent case a family whose home bordered a village green where cricket matches were customarily played obtained an injunction to prevent such games from taking place, after they proved that they and their property were regularly in danger from cricket balls.

Increasing criminal law controls have also been introduced to curb violence by supporters at sports events, especially soccer hooligans. For example, the 1989 Football Spectators Act allows offenders to be ordered to report at police stations on match days.

10.2 Spectators

A spectator at a sporting activity may have a claim against a participant who has injured him, such as a competitor at a motor rally who drives so recklessly that his car leaves the track and plunges into the crowd.

However, misjudgement in the heat of the moment need not be negligence.

☞ *You are a competitor in a gymkhana. You gallop your horse so fast round a corner that it swings off the track and injures a spectator. The spectator sues you personally as well as the organisers. What is your position?*

In a similar case, the court held that the rider was not liable to the injured spectator.

Note: a victim's damages will be reduced if his own lack of care contributed to his injuries.

10.3 Injuries on the sports field

A failure to observe the rules of a sport, even if this causes injury to another player, does not necessarily give rise to liability. There would have to be negligence. As we have seen, a want of judgment in the heat of the game does not necessarily amount to absence of due care. Participants in contact sports will be taken to have consented to run the risk of injuries incidental to the game (see *Foul play*, section 10.3.1 below).

☞ *Before an ice hockey match-players are warming up on the ice. A player who has not yet put on his safety helmet suffers a head injury when another player's practice shot at the goal ricochets off the goal post.*

In a case with these facts, the court decided that as shots at goal are a normal part of warming-up, the injured player had no claim.

If a player's misjudgement or recklessness while playing causes injury to another player, both civil and possibly criminal liability will follow. A mere error of judgement is not so serious: if a reasonable player would not have realised he risks causing significant injury to another player, this may be classified as a mere error of judgment. It is different with severe cases of misjudgment, recklessness, or deliberate actions – here the player responsible may be held liable both to criminal charges and for paying compensation to the victim.

10.3.1   Foul play

Concern has been voiced in many quarters at the increasing levels of deliberate violence on the sports field. Foul play can amount to a criminal assault, as well as giving rise to civil claims for damages, and there are several cases where players have been sent to prison for such incidents. In the criminal law there is no difference, said one judge, between mugging an old lady in the street and mugging an opponent on the playing field.

☞   *During a club rugby match your jaw is fractured by an off-the-ball punch from a player from the opposing team.*

    Apart from criminal liability, you can sue for damages for assault and can also claim from his club, which may be liable for his conduct.

    Many clubs now carry insurance to protect players against injuries.

Remember: if you are injured by the deliberate violence of anyone – on or off the field, whether player, referee or spectator – you can also lodge a claim for compensation from the Criminal Injuries Compensation Board see above, section 2.2).

Any sporting organisation such as a football club can apply to court for an injunction to keep known offenders from entering their premises, in order to prevent misbehaviour.

10.4   Defences to a claim

You may be taken to have voluntarily run the risk of injury (like a spectator at a cricket match who is injured in the course of play when the batsman hits a six) as long as the danger is incidental to the ordinary course of the sport or game. In a decided case this defence was successful even against a six-year-old claimant who had been taken to a match by his father.

Contributory negligence may also be raised as a defence e.g. if in order to take action photographs, a spectator positions himself in a spot where injury is foreseeable.

11   CLAIMING COMPENSATION

11.1   A note of warning

The aim of damages is to compensate a victim of an accident, but he may not in fact get as much as he has lost, partly because compensation will always be in money – which cannot compensate for e.g. the loss of a limb – but also because the law limits the type of losses which can be included in the calculation.

Damages are not awarded to punish the person whose fault caused the accident, although there may separately be a criminal prosecution arising out of the same facts.

Note: court actions in the High Court are always lengthy, risky and expensive processes. If other ways of obtaining compensation are available, particularly if the amount claimed is not large, these should always be considered in preference – e.g. settlement out of court, arbitration, etc. See section 2.3 above, and also the chapter on *The Legal System*. The 'small claims court' cannot award more than £1000 damages for personal injuries (although the limit is £5000 for other types of claim).

Legal aid was abolished for accident victims in April 2000. Claimants who cannot afford to pay lawyers for private help will have to find a solicitor prepared to take the case using a conditional fee agreement (see chapter on *The Legal System*).

If you do get damages, but have also received certain social security benefits, such as disability allowance, provided that these are paid as a direct result of the accident, your compensation will be adjusted accordingly. The money recovered will then be paid direct to the Department for Work and Pensions. For details of this, contact the Compensation Recovery Unit, Customer Services, Room M0135, Durham House, Washington, Tyne & Wear, NE38 7SF.

11.2   General damages

11.2.1   Property damage

When property is damaged, the compensation will be the cost of repairs or the amount by which the value of the property is diminished by the accident. If beyond repair, the cost of replacing it or its pre-accident market value will be awarded.

11.2.2   Personal injuries

The damages awarded to compensate the victim will include:

- financial loss, e.g. loss of earnings, medical costs
- an amount given to compensate for pain and suffering
- an amount given to compensate for temporary or permanent impairment of the ability to engage in his usual activities before the accident, such as sport.

Compensation for pain and suffering and for impairment of abilities is known as 'non-pecuniary loss'.

The amount of damages is determined by judges, who have developed a tariff of conventional awards to cover the range of possible injuries. For example, the conventional range of awards for quadriplegia is around £120,000 to £150,000; for moderate brain damage £40,000 to £65,000; for complete loss of sight in one eye £22,500 to £25,000 and for minor whiplash injuries it is up to £3,500.

The Law Commission issued a Report in April 1999 concluding that awards for non-pecuniary loss for serious personal injury were too low. Since that date, the Court of Appeal has issued new guidelines that awards for damages in these cases should be increased. Proposals for periodical payments rather than single lump-sum awards are under consideration by the government.

11.3   Special damages

Expenses actually incurred by a victim are sometimes called special damages, e.g. medical expenses, costs of nursing assistance, costs of disablement aids. These can also be claimed from the wrongdoer.

In all cases the court will take into account the nature of the claim.

☞   *Your BMW was damaged in an accident which was not your fault. You were told that the repair would take eight days. You needed the use of a car for work and hired another BMW for the required days at a cost of £1,350. You want to establish your position.*

   In a similar case, the court held that the hire of an expensive car in the circumstances was not reasonable, and awarded £340, the cost of hiring an ordinary saloon car.

11.4   Nervous shock

The damages awarded to the victims of an accident will include an amount to compensate for psychological suffering. The fact that the victim suffered no tangible physical injury is irrelevant. Damages will also be awarded for psychological injuries which result in physical symptoms (such as a heart attack or a miscarriage) or in psychiatric illness.

For example, in one case a policewoman who suffered post-traumatic shock after a colleague unlawfully discharged a pistol in her presence was entitled to recover damages from the chief constable for her resulting psychiatric injury as she was more than a mere bystander and could be said to have been 'involved' in the incident.

On the other hand, this does not necessarily apply to 'secondary victims' no matter how severe their psychological suffering. For example, the relatives of some of those killed in the Hillsborough football stadium disaster failed to get damages even though they had seen TV news broadcasts of the horrifying events.

However severe the distress which an accident causes to the victim's family or friends, it is not something for which compensation can be claimed. If the shock of seeing the accident, hearing about it or seeing the victim shortly afterwards causes actual psychiatric illness, however, those in a close relationship to the victim, e.g. spouse or parent, may be awarded damages for their own mental injury.

Due to international agreements, persons who suffer psychological or mental illness as a result of air travel are unable to recover compensation from the airline.

11.4.1 Proposals for change

The Law Commission has drawn attention to the anomalies arising under the current rules governing who can claim damages for negligence where a person suffers a recognisable psychiatric illness as a result of another person's death, injury or imperilment. Examples of the arbitrary and unjust nature of the current recovery procedure were given as follows:

- A mother was told about a car accident which happened close to her home in which one of her children was killed and others seriously injured. She rushed to the hospital and saw her family within two hours of the accident. She was able to recover damages for the resulting psychiatric illness she suffered because she saw the immediate aftermath of the accident. But the relatives of those who died at the Hillsborough football stadium disaster, some of whom saw the tragedy unfold on live television and later went to the stadium to identify the deceased, were not able to recover damages because they were not close to, and did not perceive with their unaided senses, the accident or its immediate aftermath.

- A father who suffered psychiatric illness on the death of his son three days after the boy was injured in a road accident was unable to recover damages from the negligent driver. He had gone directly to the hospital and had sat at his son's bedside in intensive care for the three days before the child's life support system was turned off. He was unable to recover damages because he did not see the immediate aftermath of the accident and his illness was not 'shock-induced'. Had his son died within a few hours of arrival at the hospital and the father had then seen his body, he would probably have been able to recover damages.

In a subsequent case, a mother who spent three days at her son's bedside witnessing the tragic end of his life was able to recover damages for the grief which she had to endure.

Among other recommendations, the Commission proposed that:

- the restrictions based on closeness to the accident and direct perception of it should be removed
- the requirement for a close tie of love and affection should be retained.

As yet there have been no legislative moves towards implementing these proposals of the Commission.

11.5 Fatal accidents

Where someone is fatally injured in an accident, his dependants can bring an action against the person who was at fault. The claim is strictly for the loss of the financial support of which they were deprived by the victim's accidental death, and the extent of that support will have to be proved. The loss of services which can be valued in money terms, such as those which spouses provide for each other, is compensatable – it is not necessary to show that the survivor incurred increased expenditure or a reduced income.

The legal definition of dependants who can bring such an action includes not only spouse and children, but also close relatives, ex-spouses and cohabitees who lived with the deceased for more than two years.

Only one action can be brought, for the benefit of all the dependants together, and the damages will be divided among them in proportion to the support they have lost. Proceedings must be started within three years from the date of death or from the date of knowledge of the dependants.

Where the dependants include a spouse or child of the deceased, a claim for damages for bereavement can be included. The parents of an unmarried child victim can claim a fixed sum of £10,000 for bereavement. Parents of children who were over 18 when they died cannot make a claim under this heading, except for funeral expenses.

11.5.1 Fatality of the wrongdoer

Where the person whose fault caused the accident was himself fatally injured, the claim can be brought against the estate.

11.6 Free legal advice

The Law Society runs a helpline for people injured in an accident and wishing to consider a claim through the courts (Freephone 0500 19 29 39).

If you do need to sue, for all claims – not just personal injury – you may be able to agree with a lawyer that if you lose the case you do not have to pay costs, while if you win the lawyer may get a mark-up over and above his usual fees for taking on the risk of the case under a conditional fee agreement (for more details on the scheme, see chapter on *The Legal System*, section 3.4). Solicitors are not free to choose the extent of the mark-up they would require to take on the risk. In one case the client and the lawyer had agreed the latter would take on the case for a 60% mark-up on fees. The Court of Appeal reduced this to 20% in that case. Subsequently a 5% mark-up was stated to be adequate in simple cases.

The solicitor must agree the mark-up with the claimant beforehand and the claimant can take out insurance to cover the costs of having to pay the losing side. Insurance policies can also cover the cost of the policy itself and the mark-up.

Take heed: insurance may not cover *all* the costs involved.

It is also open to a defendant in a case to obtain insurance to defend the action against him and to enter into a conditional fee agreement with a solicitor who would be willing to take on the case.

Do take note: whether as claimant or as defendant, you would need to have a strong case to persuade your solicitor that it will be worth his or her while to fight your corner.

11.6.1 Unqualified advisers or 'claims assessors'

There are unqualified advisers who offer to process claims of people who have suffered personal injury. They are not regulated by any legal rules or codes of conduct.

Do note however: Claims management companies (unlike claims assessors) generally employ solicitors, who are of course subject to professional and public codes of conduct and must carry professional indemnity insurance.

DIRECTORY
ACCIDENTS

Action for Victims of Medical Accidents *(AVMA)*
44 High Street
Croydon CR0 1YB
Tel. 020 8686 8333

Association of British Insurers *(ABI)*
51 Gresham Street
London EC2V 7HQ
Tel. 020 7600 3333
www.abi.org.uk

British Acupuncture Council
63 Jeddo Road
London W12 9HQ
Tel. 020 8735 0400
www.acupuncture.org.uk

British Association for Accident and Emergency Medicine
The Royal College of Surgeons
35–43 Lincoln's Inn Fields
London WC2A 3PN
Tel. 020 7831 9405
www.baem.org.uk

British Association for Immediate Care *(BASICS)*
Turret House
Turret Lane
Ipswich
Suffolk IP4 1DL
Tel. 01473 218407
www.basics.org.uk

British Chiropractic Association
Blagrave House
17 Blagrave Street
Reading
Berkshire RG1 1QB
Tel. 0118 950 5950
www.chiropracticuk.co.uk

British Homeopathic Association
15 Clerkenwell Close
London EC1R 0AA
Tel. 020 7566 7800
www.trusthomeopathy.org

British Medical Association
BMA House
Tavistock Square
London WC1H 91P
Tel. 020 7387 4499
www.bma.org

Centre for Accessible Environments
Nutmeg House
60 Gainsford Street
London SE1 2NY
Tel. 020 7357 8182
www.cae.org.uk

Child Accident Prevention Trust
4th Floor
18–20 Farringdon Lane
London EC1R 3HA
Tel. 020 7608 3828
www.capt.org.uk

Criminal Injuries Compensation Authority
Morley House
26–30 Holborn Viaduct
London EC1A 2JQ
Tel. 020 7842 6800
www.cica.gov.uk

Dental Protection Ltd
33 Cavendish Square
London W1G 0PS
Tel. 0845 608 4000
www.mps.org.uk

Disability Information and Advice Line *(Dial UK)*
St Catherine's
Tickhill Road
Doncaster DN4 8QN
Tel. 01302 310123
www.dialuk.org.uk

General Osteopathic Council
Osteopathy House
176 Tower Bridge Road
London SE1 3LU
Tel. 020 7357 6655
www.osteopathy.org.uk

General Dental Council
37 Wimpole Street
London W1G 8DQ
Tel. 020 7887 3800
www.gdc-uk.org

General Medical Council
178 Great Portland Street
London W1W 5JE
Tel. 020 7580 7642
www.gmc-uk.org

Health & Safety Executive *(HSE)*
Daniel House
Trinity Road
Bootle
Merseyside L20 3TW
(Infoline) Tel. 08701 545 500
www.hse.gov.uk

Health Service Ombudsman *(England)*
11th Floor
Millbank Tower
London SW1P 4QP
Tel. 020 7217 4051
www.ombudsman.org.uk

Health Service Ombudsman *(Wales)*
5th Floor
Capital Tower
Greyfriars Road
Cardiff CF10 3AG
Tel. 02920 394621
www.ombudsman.org.uk

The Medical Protection Society
33 Cavendish Square
London W1G 0PS
Tel. 0845 605 4000
www.mps.org.uk

MIND
Granta House
15–19 Broadway
Stratford
London E15 4BQ
Tel. 020 8519 2122
www.mind.org.uk

The National Care Standards Commission
St. Nicholas Building
St. Nicholas Street
Newcastle upon Tyne NE1 1NB
(Helpline) Tel. 0191 233 3556
www.carestandards.org.uk

NHS Direct
Tel. 0845 46 47

Nursing and Midwifery Council
23 Portland Place
London W1B 1PZ
Tel. 020 7637 7181
www.nmc-uk.org

The Patients Association
PO Box 935
Harrow
Middlesex HA1 3YJ
Tel. 020 8423 9111
www.patients-association.com

Personal Injury Panel
The Law Society
Ipsley Court
Redditch
Worcestershire B98 0TD
Tel. 020 7242 1222
www.training.lawsociety.org.uk

Public Concern at Work
Suite 306
16 Baldwin Gardens
London EC1N 7RJ
Tel. 020 7404 6609
www.pcaw.co.uk

Royal Pharmaceutical Society of Great Britain
1 Lambeth High Street
London SE1 7JN
Tel. 020 7735 9141
www.rpsgb.org.uk

Royal Society for the Prevention of Accidents
(ROSPA)
ROSPA House
Edgbaston Park
353 Bristol Road
Birmingham B5 7ST
Tel. 0121 284 2000
www.rospa.org.uk

Victim Support
Cranmer House
39 Brixton Road
London SW9 6DZ
Tel. 020 735 9166
www.victimsupport.org

18 THE LEGAL SYSTEM

Like all the other aspects of the law which we discuss in this book, the legal system is undergoing profound changes.

Within both branches of the legal profession – the solicitors and the barristers – there has been a generalised, if sometimes grudging, acceptance that reform and change were needed. Thus debate is now over the pace of change and the type of reform rather than the necessity for it.

At the same time, the legal system is under scrutiny by the public as never before. Clients want to know about costs, about efficiency, about where and how to complain if they are dissatisfied with the way their case is handled. Restrictive practices within the legal profession, which once may have looked arcane and somewhat endearing, are now often simply seen as unacceptable.

The demand for change has been kept up by pressure groups both from within and without the profession. Enlightened judges and lawyers realise that yesterday's concepts sometimes have little relevance in today's world. The famous 'reasonable' person in English law was typified as 'the man on the Clapham omnibus'. How relevant is such a concept when it may be a woman on the bus? Or a Kosovan refugee? How do we ask for consensus on values and behaviour in a pluralistic society where ethnic groups comprise not only the native-born but also recent arrivals whose view of the concepts of the common law may not coincide with those of the man on that Clapham bus? However, their expectations from the legal system and their requirements for justice have to be met too.

It was hoped that some of these testing questions would be answered by one of the most striking changes of legislation in recent years, namely, the incorporation into English law of the European Convention of Human Rights, known as the Human Rights Act 1998 (see below, section 6). Its impact on our judicial system and our perceptions of our rights and the redress we can expect for our wrongs was expected to be far-reaching. After two years, however, the Act has not so far led to the numbers of challenges and revolutionary change that were forecast before its introduction. It has also not led to the 'floodgates of litigation' which the pessimists predicted.

Nonetheless, what is clear is that the Act's most striking impact has been in the outlook of both lawyers and judges, who now must study all cases in light of the Convention. The Act thus has established itself as not merely a part of our legal framework, but as a defining tenet of our law (see below, section 6).

Another development destined to have maximum impact is the introduction of the Freedom of Information Act 2000. Due to its complexity, it is being introduced in phases and will not be fully in force until 2005. The government claims to be moving from the UK's traditional culture of secrecy to a more modern concept of open, and therefore more accountable, government. However there are a number of exemptions from the operation of the Act and the width of those exemptions is causing some concern. More immediately, in other areas, the government is also playing a leading role in bringing about change.

A Community Legal Service (has been set up to bring together a partnership of solicitors' firms (under contract to the Legal Services Commission) advice agencies and the voluntary sector in order to deliver targeted legal advice at local level. The Community Legal Service Fund, administered by the Legal Services Commission, replaces the former Legal Aid Board, and now provides publicly funded legal services for people who are entitled to them. Legal aid had grown to a costly £1.4 bn a year. The Commission has therefore set priorities at both national and local levels with the intention of targetting its resources on where the need is greatest.

Another great change is that, as from April 2000, more and more legal work is funded from sources other than by the taxpayer. Certain types of cases have been withdrawn from public funding altogether – in particular, run-of-the-mill personal injury cases – and are now litigated, if at all, under conditional fee agreements (CFAs) paid for, where possible, by insurance cover. Matrimonial disputes, however, and matters involving the criminal law are still publicly funded provided the criteria for public funding are met.

The rules for conducting cases have also undergone a radical revision. New procedures were introduced in April 1999 for cases to be assigned to 'tracks' according to the size of the claim (see section 3.6.3 below). The early evidence is that this case assignment, together with the fact that judges are taking an active role in case management and time schedules, is streamlining and speeding up the judicial process. Alternative forms of solving disputes are also actively encouraged where possible. Complaints that the legal profession's charges to their clients are 'inflated' and 'unwarranted' are still being voiced. All these issues are briefly dealt with in the course of this chapter.

This chapter deals more specifically with the legal system and how to cope with it through an understanding of its structures. It outlines the steps you need to take in making a claim in the small claims court. *Your day in court* (see section 5 below) deals with court appearances as claimant or defendant, being called upon as a witness, or having to act as a juror.

It must be noted that not all the present reforms have met with unequivocal approval. While it is easy to dismiss criticism as mere self-interest on the part of the legal profession, serious concern must remain until the new systems have proved themselves in practice. The government has set high and estimable targets in promising greater access to justice for the vulnerable. On the other hand, while the tightening-up of criteria for receiving funded legal advice may cut down on those who abused the old system in the past it may not always be helpful to the deserving in the present; the number of solicitors' firms offering publicly funded help has shrunk, in some cases by half, because of the contractual rates on offer; some of the newer facilities, e.g. law on the Internet (see section 1.1.5 below) cannot – by their very nature – always reach the most needy.

There is little evidence and some scepticism so far on how well conditional fee agreements are serving the public; and the cutbacks in the number of appeals may defeat the cause of justice in some cases rather than further it.

These are the doubts which have been raised; one can only hope, in the interests of all of us, that they do not materialise.

In this chapter we look at:

- seeking advice
- dealing with the legal profession
- expense and delay
- bringing a small claim
- your day in court
- the Human Rights Act 1998
- the courts
- the judges
- sources of law
- reforming the law.

1 SEEKING ADVICE

There are certain major problems to overcome in seeking advice – apart from a psychological reluctance: the cost, the delay, and the complexity of dealing with the law. These are not fanciful – they are real anxieties for anyone with an everyday legal problem. Strenuous efforts are now being made to deal with these three main concerns of the person in the street who may need advice.

First and foremost, in seeking advice on how best to cope with any matter which may involve the law, you must consider the seriousness of the issue which you are facing, the kind of advice which you think you may need, and the type of advisor who, you think, can best help you.

Is your query of a general nature or do you need specialist legal advice, for example in a case of medical negligence? Even for specialist advice, you may consider approaching the voluntary sector, as some organisations have panels of lawyers who are experts in a particular sphere. Then again, your local advice agency may have experience in dealing with certain issues such as benefit applications or immigration matters, while the expertise of your high-street firm of solicitors may lie in other areas of the law, such as conveyancing.

Obviously other factors come into your considerations: the questions of cost, what help is available locally, and whether there are other ways of sorting out a problem – for example, by alternative dispute resolution or by using a trade organisation to assist you. Some of these matters are already discussed in the preceding chapters – see for example, *Working for a Living, Accidents,* or *Divorce.* The Directories which are attached to the chapters also provide help at hand in your quest. The Lord Chancellor's Department has inaugurated an online advice service which is intended to be the first port of call, *Just Ask* (*www.justask.org.uk*) which, as well as giving other information, lists advisors by locality.

This chapter, in particular, focuses on locating sources of legal help and directs you to information and outlets which can be of use.

It must be stressed that there is much information and advice readily available and, as we can see, advice is not necessarily confined to the solicitor's office or the barrister's chambers. The Community Legal Service has been set up as a means to this end (see 1.1 below); a good deal of law can be found on the Internet where new sites are being set up daily; advice agencies, which have been audited for quality, are being publicly funded; government departments put out helpful booklets; the voluntary sector endeavours to meet people's need to understand and deal with their problems by providing a range of free leaflets and other information (Age Concern, for example, issues helpful booklets), while mediation of all kinds is being actively encouraged. As stated above, some of these sources have already been referred to in the text. They are dealt with in greater detail below.

1.1 The Community Legal Service

From April 2000 the Community Legal Service made access to legal advice available to the public through the creation of local networks of legal services, with the intention that these would be based on local needs and priorities, and would deal with matters which most affect people's everyday lives, such as debt problems, housing, or entitlement to benefits. Priority categories to be targeted include public law, mental health and community care.

A key part of the Community Legal Service (CLS) was to bring together the funders of advice services (including the Legal Services Commission which replaces the former Legal Aid Board, and the local authorities) with advice providers – solicitors and advice agencies – in community partnerships. A CLS 'Quality Mark' identifies legal advisors who provide advice and information and have met its auditing and quality control standards.

A CLS directory lists a wide variety of advisors for each area. The directory is available in libraries, or enquiries can be made by telephoning 0845 608 1122 (Minicom number: 0845 609 66 77; open 7 am–11 pm on Mondays to Saturdays and 7 am–10 pm on Sundays).

Those who do not qualify for legal advice funding but still want to see a solicitor at their own expense can opt to use a CLS quality-marked lawyer.

1.1.1 Advice agencies

The present trend is to extend the use of advice agencies as a means of settling disputes without resorting to the law.

Their role has become increasingly enhanced under the present scheme for advice and assistance, which is being funded by the Legal Services Commission. Advice agencies are governed by rules of confidentiality and other professional safeguards. They also carry professional indemnity insurance, as do solicitors' firms.

Note of warning: as with all reforms, undesirable consequences sometimes also follow. Early morning queues form outside these centres which have difficulty in coping with the amount of work that would previously have been channelled through the legal aid system. With the best will in the world, only so much can be achieved by hardworking advisors in helping needy clients who present a range of problems in the course of a working day.

A second note of warning: it would appear that unqualified people, using the opportunities offered by the 'no win, no fee' or conditional fee agreements (see section 3.4 below), have been calling themselves 'legal advisors'. However, they do not carry insurance and are not governed by codes of professional conduct (see chapter on *Accidents*, section 11.6.1).

1.1.2 Law Centres

Law Centres offer legal advice and all have contracts with the CLS after having been audited for quality assurance. Their offices are usually in the local high street. There are about 52 law centres in England and Wales, found in inner city areas in the main, and generally funded by local authorities. They are run by lawyers and advice workers and tend to specialise in social welfare law, for example housing and immigration. Specialisations may vary from one area or centre to another. If a law centre is not able to take on a case itself, it can usually refer you elsewhere.

1.1.3 Legal advice centres

Legal advice centres are staffed by volunteer lawyers who offer free advice and assistance, the type of legal advice depending on the particular centre. They can also assist in pursuing claims in tribunals and small claims courts; they can help with form-filling, and will write letters on behalf of their clients. If they are unable to help you directly, the staff can point you towards other sources of advice or refer you on to a local solicitor who specialises in your type of problem, e.g. housing, or problems associated with claiming benefits.

These centres are usually run by church groups, charities, etc., so check if there is one in your vicinity. Many are members of the Federation of Independent Advice Centres (see DIRECTORY).

1.1.4 Citizens' Advice Bureaux

You can also obtain advice from a Citizens' Advice Bureau (CAB) – run by the National Association of Citizens' Advice Bureaux (NACAB). Offices are to be found throughout the country. These are financed by grants from central and local government. CABx deal with all sorts of queries and they are often the first port of call for the public for free advice. Trained staff are able to offer help with a range of issues such as consumer queries, debt, repossession, etc.

An advice worker will help you to establish your legal position. If there is a difficult problem, you may be referred elsewhere or to a solicitor, law centre or legal advice centre for assistance in sorting it out. There is no charge for advice from a CAB and there are lots of leaflets available. Addresses can be found in the local telephone directory or on the Internet at *www.nacab.org.uk*.

These responsibilities emphasise the role of the Citizens' Advice Bureaux in seeking to ensure that people do not suffer because they are unaware of their rights or are unable to express them effectively. The Citizens' Advice Bureaux are also influential in endeavouring to ensure that social policy goals are met at a national and local level. The CABx also have a website where you can find advice on an extensive range of subjects including employment, welfare, family, consumer and housing matters. It is *www.adviceguide.org.uk*.

The NACAB website also offers a range of information in easily accessible format at *www.Adviceguide.org.uk/nacab* (see also immediately below).

1.1.5 The Legal Internet

If you have access to a computer, you may be able to get advice from websites – often without charge. These sites may be provided by professional firms, but many are provided by government bodies, such as the Lord Chancellor's Department.

The 'Just Ask!' website (see above) is part of the Community Legal Service project. It is intended to be the initial enquiry point for people wishing to find legal information and help via the Internet. 'Just Ask!' provides co-ordinated access to 400 online legal information and help websites thtough its Advice Search feature. It also features an electronic version of the CLS Directory, updated daily, containing over 15,000 entries. The directory enables users to locate, either locally or nationally, legal service providers that can assist with particular queries.

If you are happy with using this medium, you may save yourself both time and trouble in accessing information relevant to your situation. However, you should note that the information given will usually be of a general nature and may not relate to your particular circumstances or answer your specific concerns.

Self-help law can assist you in formulating the nature of your problem even if you have to seek help elsewhere. For example, some of the sites have question-and-answer fact sheets which can be very helpful in trying to identify basic rights, e.g. in employment law.

Other information is available on the Internet too. Again it depends on the kind of information which you are seeking. For example, you may want to draw up a simple will. You will find the forms which you require, together with instructions on how to fill them in, on websites. These services often involve payment of a fee (usually quite modest) but may also demand a modicum of expertise in downloading etc.

You can also find the forms that you will need in court – for example, to initiate a claim in the small claims court or to start possession proceedings against your tenant. The website run by the Lord Chancellor's Department, under its court service (see *www.open.gov.uk/lcd/lcdseafr.htm*) allows you to fill in the form on-screen and then submit it for processing.

Legal publishers have large databases of information on which one can do in-depth research on most topics or pinpoint a piece of legislation or particular case which you need to find – e.g. a case in family law which deals with a non-molestation order. Some of these facilities are free but many are by subscription only. Solicitors' firms can also be found on the web with a range of services on offer.

Note of caution: despite the prevailing enthusiasm for information technology as a means of solving problems, on-line services have their limitations for clients in legal difficulties.

The reasons for this are not hard to see. A legal problem may have several ramifications. For example, a divorce can involve family, taxation, and conveyancing issues. Even a seemingly simple problem, such as a dispute over a bill, can entail scrutiny by an advisor of lengthy correspondence between the parties before helpful advice can be given.

Another warning note: most legal sites on the Internet carry disclaimers, which should be read with care.

1.2   Alternative dispute resolution

More and more emphasis is being placed on solutions to conflict outside the courts through mediation rather than confrontation. The generic term is *Alternative Dispute Resolution* (ADR). As we see immediately below, ADR can take many forms.

1.2.1   In-court arbitration – the small claims procedure

This is used when a money claim does not exceed £5,000 (see *Bringing a small claim*, section 4 below); and where a personal injury claim or a housing disrepair claim are under £1000.

1.2.2   Out-of-court arbitration

This can be used when the parties agree by contract to have any dispute between them settled by arbitration; for example, landlord and tenant may agree that an arbitrator should fix a new rent. Generally speaking, the arbitrator's decision is final and binding on the parties although the process takes place out of court.

Other forms of out-of-court arbitration are more informal; for example, you may have a complaint about some goods you purchased, and an arbitration service is provided by the relevant trade organisation which has set up a scheme to deal with common complaints. Again, generally speaking the arbitrator's decision is final. You can still insist on your right to resort to the law under limited circumstances, such as if an arbitrator can be shown to have been biased, or his decision is totally unreasonable on the facts, or wrong in law. Thus in consumer contracts, a clause that insists on arbitration will be considered reasonable under the 'small print regulations' if, in the light of all the surrounding facts, it is shown to be fair, e.g. where the arbitrator is independent (see the chapter on *Goods and Services*, section 2.4).

Ombudsman services are another form of arbitration which can be very helpful in sorting out a dispute, such as where you feel your bank has unfairly deducted a sum from your account and your written complaints to your branch manager and senior managers have not resolved your disagreement. An application to the Financial Ombudsman Service, in such circumstances, will assist in clarifying your position – hopefully, in your favour.

1.2.3 Mediation

Mediation was envisaged as an integral part of the Civil Procedure Rules (CPR) landscape. However uptake in the UK has not been as great as originally envisaged. It is still relatively new in the UK and is still viewed with a degree of suspicion.

The benefits are clear in that it offers a quick and cost-effective forum in which you can retain control of your dispute while reaching a sensible solution and preserving your existing relationship. It is a voluntary procedure which is confidential and without prejudice.

Mediation in divorce proceedings is being widely encouraged as a way to settle issues such as disputes over the matrimonial home, or questions concerning the welfare and future well-being of children of the relationship. Public funding can be available for mediation of these disputes and is dealt with in the chapter on *Divorce* (see section 2.2.1).

The use of trained mediators is also being encouraged in areas such as neighbourhood disputes (see the chapter on *Neighbours*, section 2.2.5) and bullying in schools.

Lawyers themselves are being increasingly trained in the use of mediation techniques in addition to conducting their usual negotiations (see section 2.2 below), so it is unjustified to regard a lawyer's approach to a problem as necessarily confrontational.

Note of warning: publicly funded help may be refused for disputes which are regarded by the Legal Services Commission as amenable for resolution through mediation.

1.3 ACAS

The Advisory, Conciliation and Arbitration Service (ACAS) was set up to act as mediator in industrial disputes. It normally deals with large disputes between trade unions and management, but also deals with individual employer and employee disputes.

Every application to an employment tribunal is also first sent to ACAS to determine whether there is any possibility of a negotiated settlement.

An ACAS arbitration scheme was launched in May 2001 as a voluntary alternative to the employment tribunal procedure for the resolution of unfair dismissal disputes in the form of arbitration. It is non-legalistic and far more flexible than the traditional model of employment tribunals and courts.

Note: It only applies to cases of alleged unfair dismissal and its decision is final with limited opportunites to appeal. By embarking on the arbitration procedure, you waive the right to go to an employment tribunal.

1.4 Commissions to assist in discrimination cases

1.4.1 Equal Opportunities Commission

The EOC was set up to work towards the elimination of sex discrimination in the employment field and to promote equality of opportunity between men and women.

1.4.2 Commission for Racial Equality

The CRE was similarly set up to work towards the elimination of racial discrimination and to promote equality of opportunity and good relations between persons of different racial groups.

1.4.3 Disability Rights Commission

A Disability Rights Commission (DRC) began its work in April 2000 to oversee the implementation of the Disability Discrimination Act. The DRC is empowered to work towards eliminating discrimination against disabled people and to keep under review the workings of the Act.

The DRC has set up a conciliation service to resolve disputes between disabled clients and providers of services in regard to access to goods and services. A second conciliation service has been established to help disabled children and adults in the education system.

Many of these issues are also looked at in the chapters on *Working for a Living*.

1.4.4   Functions of the Commissions

The Commissions have power to assist individuals in bringing cases under the Race Relations Act, the Sex Discrimination Act and the Disability Discrimination Act. They can conduct formal investigations into alleged instances of discrimination. They may also apply to the court for a decision on whether certain types of unlawful discrimination have occurred. They can take action on behalf of an alleged victim of discrimination and they handle individual complaints as well as acting on a referral basis, e.g. from a trade union.

Do take note: an approach for assistance to one body is not exclusive of another source of help. For example, 40 per cent of applications brought under the Disability Discrimination Act in the employment field.have been resolved through ACAS.

1.5   Specialist groups and organisations

Certain organisations listed in the Directories at the ends of chapters in this book offer help to their own members. Others (such as Victim Support) may offer advice to members of the general public. These groups and organisations may be in a position to refer problems to their own legal departments (for example, if you are a member of the RAC, you may be able to approach their legal department in the event of an accident).

In certain other cases, an organisation may put you in touch with a solicitor in your area who is a specialist in a particular field – an example would be an organisation such as Action for Victims of Medical Accidents (see DIRECTORY at end of the *Accidents* chapter). They may also give information about fees payable.

Do note: not all the organisations listed in the directories are in a position to give help in this way.

1.5.1   Trade unions

Many employees are members of a trades union which will assist them in the event of a dispute at work or other problems involving the workplace, for example, threatened redundancy. The TUC also has a wide range of leaflets available (see their website: *www.tuc.org.uk*).

1.5.2   Free Representation Unit

The Free Representation Unit was set up by members of the Bar. It deals only with cases which are referred to it by other advice agencies, such as a Law Centre or a CAB. Its representatives, who are qualified barristers, act on a voluntary basis in the various tribunals, for example employment, immigration or social security tribunals. A representative only takes on a case after representation in a particular case has been authorised by the FRU's committee.

Note: the FRU does not accept referrals direct from members of the public.

1.5.3   Free property advice

The Royal Institution of Chartered Surveyors (RICS) runs a voluntary advice service on property matters for those unable to obtain professional assistance in the normal way. Chartered surveyors give their advice on a voluntary basis after having problems referred to them by a CAB. The service is not means-tested but the CAB will decide on eligibility.

Most large towns and rural areas have such a service. To find out if there is one in your area and whom to contact, get in touch, in the first instance, with your nearest CAB.

RICS also runs a dispute resolution service (see Property Law DIRECTORY at end of chapter on *Buying and Selling your Home*).

1.5.4   CAFCASS

The Children and Family Court Advisory and Support Services for England and Wales (CAFCASS) has brought together the Family Court Welfare Service (FCWS, currently part of the Probation Service), the Guardian ad Litem and Reporting Officer service (GALRO, currently run by local authorities), and the children's branch of the Official Solicitor. It is established under the Criminal Justice and Court Service Act 2000 to provide a more child-focused service, pooling the experience and expertise of the three services, focusing on representing the needs, wishes and feelings of children in family proceedings.

2 DEALING WITH THE LEGAL PROFESSION

For many people, however, their local or family solicitor remains the immediate person to approach when confronted by a legal problem. Moreover, the government's emphasis on mediation, use of the Internet, or advice and other agencies, is not likely to change this perception overnight.

Furthermore, when you approach a legal advice centre, after having discussed your problem, your advisor may consider that it is best that you see a lawyer and direct you to one under a local referral scheme. Greater use of the referral system is one of the aims of community partnerships, at local level, so that people's needs for legal advice can be better met.

2.1 Local referral schemes

Under the local referral scheme, run through their local Law Society, solicitors act in conjunction with local advice agencies (such as Law Centres and Citizen's Advice Bureaux). Each local scheme, available in most but not all areas of the country, decides which type of law it intends to cover within a broad framework of 'personal matters'.

An initial interview, which may be low cost or free, is intended to diagnose the problem and discuss the issue of fees, as well as assessing the client for eligibility for Community Legal Service Fund contributions (which replaced civil legal aid from 1 April 2000). If you wish to establish whether a solicitor's firm offers a free or low cost first interview you must either ask at a CAB or contact the firm direct to establish what services they provide. The advice is to 'shop around' in order to find out what is available locally for your purposes.

Do not forget: the Legal Aid Board itself has been succeeded by a new body, the Legal Services Commission.

2.2 Solicitors

In England there are basically two kinds of lawyers: solicitors and barristers.

The range of topics in this book are but an indication of a High Street solicitor's work. This work includes 'contentious' (related to the word 'contest') and 'non-contentious' business.

However, most of the work never involves the courts, that is, most solicitors' work is non-contentious. This involves such standard legal tasks as, for example, the drawing up of a will or seeing to the conveyancing on a house purchase. Solicitors see a great deal of their work as a form of 'mediation' in any event. They conduct negotiations which, in many instances, can lead to a settlement out of court. These negotiations are usually conducted by 'without prejudice' correspondence.

Contentious work concerns a contest between two parties and involves litigation (going to court). Contentious work can be criminal, or matrimonial or other civil work (for instance a claim for damages for a personal injury, or a boundary quarrel between neighbours).

Solicitors do all the preparatory work in a case and will, where necessary, brief barristers for it.

Solicitors usually practise in partnership although some are sole practitioners. They are all members of the Law Society which looks after their interests.

The Law Society publishes a regional directory of its members. This gives information on the types of work which solicitors' firms offer. These directories are available in local libraries and Citizens' Advice Bureaux.

Until recently, solicitors have not appeared in the higher courts as advocates. Instead they have had to instruct a barrister to appear for their client (see *Barristers*, section 2.3 immediately below). However, solicitors now have the right to appear in higher courts after suitable training. In fact just under 1,600 solicitors out of a profession of nearly 80,000 have been given the status of solicitor advocates, the majority of whom have higher rights of audience in the criminal courts. From April 2000, the overriding duty of a solicitor who acts as an advocate is to act with independence in the interests of justice – this overrides his duty to you as his client.

Solicitors should inform their clients of how much they will charge (see *Costs – keeping clients informed* below, section 3.5). They are also obliged to have a complaints-handling procedure within their own firms.

Solicitors, under their professional obligations, should also provide the following information to clients:

- the name of the person who has the routine conduct of the client's affairs
- who to approach in the event of any problem with the service
- how the client's affairs are progressing.

Solicitors will also negotiate with you a conditional fee agreement in suitable cases (see section 3.4 below). Such agreements are now available for all civil proceedings and not just for cases which involve personal injuries. Your solicitor will also advise you on insurance cover in the event that you do not win your case and have to pay the costs of the defendant (see also below, section 3.4). Standard form 'no win no fee' agreements between solicitor and client have been drawn up by the Law Society.

Before you go to see a solicitor do first establish the following:

1) Whether the firm has experience in dealing with your type of problem
2) Whether there will be a charge for an initial interview or whether it will be free
3) Whether you need disabled access (The Disability Discrimination Act 1995 places solicitors under a duty not to discriminate against disabled clients but it is important to check in advance)
4) Whether you have all the documents that will be needed for your first appointment (it cannot be overstressed that you should take all the paperwork relevant to your claim)
5) Whether you have details of your income and expenditure to enable the solicitor to ascertain eligibility for public funding (take any earlier public funding certificates along with you)
6) Whether, if you are changing solicitors, you have details of your previous solicitor who may still hold your papers
7) Whether, if you have suffered a personal injury as a result of an accident, you have all the details to hand to take with you (see Chapter on *Accidents*, section 1.1, which provides a list of steps to take after an accident).

Remember: many proceedings have strict time limits; for example, an application to an employment tribunal must be made within three months. So once you have instructed a solicitor, who then asks you for further information, do give it as soon as possible to avoid delay. Also make sure you give him or her any correspondence which has passed between you and the other party.

Finally, do not make any decisions in connection with the case without discussing it with your solicitor first.

2.3 Barristers

Barristers are advocate lawyers who appear in the higher courts (see section 7 on the court structure). When they appear in court, they are briefed by their instructing solicitors. Until recently, barristers had a monopoly of the right to represent clients in the higher courts (the 'right of audience').

Barristers are known as Counsel and traditionally have had no direct dealings with the public – hence someone with a legal problem is not usually able to consult counsel, but barristers do advise solicitors in consultation on points of law. However, the Bar Council has approved a range of proposals to give a wider variety of individuals and organisations direct access to the services of a barrister, hopefully reducing the cost of legal services.

It is generally accepted that these rules will involve changes in the way barristers work, and the following proposals have been put forward:

- The new regime should be implemented cautiously, with restricted direct access subject to a review after two years
- Direct access should only be possible in restricted areas of criminal and family work, notably for advice and in a very few court matters where, at present, it is clear that the additional role of the solicitor is not necessary in the interests of the client
- There should be no direct access in immigration work
- There should be mandatory training for all barristers wishing to work on this basis
- Barristers who have been in practice for less than three years should not be permitted to undertake the work except with an experienced leader

- It should be mandatory for barristers to send a clear client-care letter dealing with exactly what he or she is and is not able to do, the likely fees to be charged and other information that you as a client will need.

The rules need to be approved by Lord Chancellor and are expected to come into effect in 2003.

Barristers are mostly self-employed and work in offices called *chambers*. Each set of chambers employs a clerk who negotiates the barristers' work and sets their fees.

The Access to Justice Act 1999 has extended the rights of audience for employed barristers – for example those employed in the Crown Prosecution Service will be able to conduct cases in court instead of having to brief their colleagues in chambers.

Also barristers employed in solicitors' firms will be entitled to have direct dealings with clients.

Litigants can also act for themselves without instructing solicitors or counsel (see section 2.7.4).

2.4   *Pro bono* work

Both solicitors and barristers do take on cases free of charge in the public interest as well. This work, known as *pro bono* work, is being actively encouraged by the Bar Council and the Law Society.

2.5   College of Law advice centre

The College of Law runs a free legal advice system. It is by appointment only and the client's problem must be in an area of law that is of educational benefit to students (see DIRECTORY at the end of this chapter for details).

2.6   Other legal personnel

2.6.1   Legal executives

Legal executives work in solicitors' offices and deal with routine legal work. They qualify as legal executives after passing examinations set by their own Institute, plus five years' work experience. They sometimes work under the supervision of a solicitor but also carry out many tasks on their own, specializing in a particular area of law, e.g. wills and probate, or conveyancing. They are bound by a strict code of conduct. The Institute of Legal Executives provides an information pack on training requirements (see DIRECTORY). The Institute of Legal Executives is in the process of making an application for permission for its members who have met suitable training requirements, to conduct litigation before the courts.

2.6.2   Licensed conveyancers

These are persons who are trained and licensed to undertake property conveyancing. They are then allowed to compete with solicitors in conveyancing work.

The Council of Licensed Conveyancers oversees disciplinary matters. All licensed conveyancers must be insured so that clients are protected in transactions undertaken on their behalf. The Council publishes a booklet giving details of current training requirements (see the chapter on *Buying and Selling your Home*, and the property law DIRECTORY at the end of that chapter).

2.6.3   Accident Line

This service offers callers a free advice session on Freephone 050019 29 39 for personal accidents.

2.6.4   Duty Solicitor Scheme

If you are arrested – or even if you are just being questioned by the police – you are entitled to the free advice and assistance of a solicitor.

You may also ask to see your own solicitor or to see a local solicitor from a list which the police should provide to you.

Duty solicitors are available on a voluntary rota basis to provide assistance and cover if you have to go to court in all except minor cases, e.g. a traffic offence. The solicitor may also represent you. You must ask to see the duty solicitor as soon as possible by informing a court official or the police.

Note: A Criminal Defence Service was introduced on 2 April 2001 (see below, section 3.3.1).

2.7 Complaints about legal services

2.7.1 Solicitors

If you have a complaint about your solicitor, you should first contact the complaints-handling machinery within the firm, so that complaints are tackled at source. If you are still not satisfied, complaints can be taken to the Office for the Supervision of Solicitors with a panel of lay members and with a structure more independent of the Law Society.

All solicitors must carry professional indemnity insurance which will protect a client against fraudulent malpractice.

2.7.2 Barristers

The traditional immunity of barristers, which protected them from claims of negligence in relation to their presentation of a case in court, has now been removed by the House of Lords. Likewise solicitor advocates also enjoy no such immunity.

A modest increase in public complaints against barristers was recorded in the 2001 annual report of the Bar Council's Independent Complaints Commissioner. The public can now receive compensation of up to £5,000 for losses which no longer have to be recoverable at law.

The Commissioner has expressed concern about the impact of extending direct access to the Bar on complaints handling. He sees potential for an increase in complaints given the barrister's wider area of work and responsibility.

New 'fitness to practise' rules, improved in July 2001, mean a barrister can be suspended for reasons of ill health.

2.7.3 Legal Services Ombudsman

If you feel that the professional body itself has not dealt satisfactorily with your complaint, you can apply to the Legal Services Ombudsman, who will investigate the matter.

You can contact the Office of the Legal Services Ombudsman either by writing or by telephoning (see DIRECTORY for details). You will be sent an application form which asks for information about your complaint against the lawyer concerned. The form also asks you to say why you are not happy with the professional body's handling of your complaint.

Normally you must apply to the Ombudsman within three months of receiving the professional body's decision. If you miss that deadline, the Ombudsman will not normally consider your case. The deadline may be extended only if there are 'special reasons' for doing so, i.e. circumstances outside your control that prevent you referring your case to the Ombudsman in time. An example might be the serious illness of you yourself or of a close family member.

Also, if you can show that the professional body failed to inform you in writing about your right to refer your case to the Ombudsman, or about the three-month deadline, then the Ombudsman might consider that to be a 'special reason'. If your allegations are particularly serious, or they raise issues of unusual sensitivity or importance, a decision might be made to consider your case anyway. The services are entirely free of charge.

There is no right of appeal against a decision of the Ombudsman, although the decisions are subject to judicial review.

2.7.4 Litigants in person

Every year people choose to represent themselves without using a barrister or a solicitor. Generally speaking, about half the litigants to the small claims courts and the tribunals are litigants in person (LIPs) – indeed these were set up for people to conduct their own cases without resort to the costly employment of lawyers.

Permission to appeal is becoming harder to obtain, particularly if you wish to appeal to the Court of Appeal, and with the advent of conditional fee agreements for most civil litigation, it would appear that the number of litigants in person is in marked decline in the higher courts.

Remember: contact your CAB or advice agency in the first instance if you wish to act for yourself. While some cases may be straightforward, in other instances the legal issues may be complicated and you may be advised against tackling them unaided. There is a range of leaflets available to assist you (see also section 5.2.3 below).

2.8   Complexity of the law

It is not just the layperson who sometimes finds the law, and the language which lawyers use, impenetrable. Judges also complain that a body of law which affects us all – for example, in the employment or taxation fields – will be difficult to interpret because of its complexity.

Sometimes, issues cannot be simplified. Sometimes, however, lawyers are correctly accused of using difficult language and arcane phraseology for its own sake.

In order to overcome these difficulties, Latin phraseology is being phased out from court proceedings and documentation, and judicial language is being altered – for example, a plaintiff is now referred to as a claimant.

It is also encouraging that many of the leaflets presently being put out by various departments and organisations bear the 'Crystal Mark' of clarity approved by the Plain English Campaign.

The Legal Services Commission (which has replaced the Legal Aid Board) makes its advice leaflets available in several languages. This is also the case with the information provided by the Community Legal Service on its 'Just Ask!' website (see above, section 1).

3   FUNDING LEGAL PROCEEDINGS

The question of lawyers' fees and costs in litigation are being tackled in a number of ways.

As we have seen above, there are many avenues to explore in seeking advice on everyday legal problems which need not necessarily lead you to be very much out of pocket.

The fact of the matter is that – in theory – we should all be entitled to access to justice. In fact, often it has been only the very rich or the very poor who could afford to pursue their claims.

The extension of claims which can be made to tribunals and the small claims courts is intended to provide part of an answer. The other is a greater emphasis on other means to settle disputes (see section 1.1.1 above, on advice agencies). Allocating cases to the lower courts (see section 3.6.2 below) is another means of trying to cut down on the cost of going to court.

However perhaps the most far-reaching changes have come about in the way that litigation is presently funded. The Legal Services Commission (LSC) funds a range of legal services for those who meet its eligibility criteria. Always discuss with your solicitor, who must be under a contract with the LSC, whether you are entitled to public funding and at what level (see below section 3.1.1). The services cover the following:

- *Legal Help* – initial advice and assistance with legal problems (the former 'green form' scheme).
- *Help at Court* –a solicitor or adviser can speak on your behalf at certain court hearings, without formally acting for you in the whole proceedings.
- *Approved Family Help* – the provision of advice in family disputes, including assistance through negotiation or otherwise. This includes not only legal help, but also the issuing of proceedings and securing representation where necessary to obtain information from another party, or to obtain a consent order.
- *Family Mediation* – mediation for a family dispute, including finding out whether mediation appears suitable or not (see also chapter on *Divorce*, section 2).
- *Legal Representation* – provides legal representation so that you can be represented in court if you are taking or defending court proceedings (formerly civil legal aid).
- *Support Funding* – provides partial funding of very expensive cases which are otherwise funded privately under a conditional fee agreement (see also chapter on *Accidents*, section 1.1.2).

3.1   Publicly funded legal services [formerly 'legal aid']

Thus the former legal aid system has been replaced by two new schemes to secure the provision of publicly funded legal services for people who qualify. The Legal Services Commission (LSC) runs both schemes. The schemes are:

1) a community legal service fund for civil and family cases and
2) a criminal defence scheme for people suspected or accused of crime.

LSC funding does not generally cover personal injury claims or cases arising out of the carrying on of business or partnership. Also excluded are boundary disputes between neighbours and actions for libel and slander.

The Legal Services Commission gives top priority to child protection cases and cases where a person is at risk of loss of life or liberty. The Commission also gives high priority to the following:

- other cases involving the welfare of children
- domestic violence cases
- cases alleging serious wrong-doing or breaches of human rights by public bodies; and
- 'social welfare' cases, including housing proceedings and advice about employment rights, social security entitlements and debt.

There are two hurdles which a would-be applicant for legal funding must overcome:

- meeting the financial tests imposed (the 'means' test) and
- fulfilling other criteria (the 'merits' test) which has been tightened up. These criteria include your chances of success in pursuing your claim, a cost/benefit analysis, and/or establishing to the satisfaction of the LSC that the type of case you are concerned with deserves funding, i.e. it is a case of high rather than low priority.

Since 2 April 2001 only organisations with a contract with the LSC have been able to provide advice or representation funded by the LSC. For family cases and specialist areas like immigration and clinical negligence only specialist firms are funded to do the work.

Note: Claims for personal injury other than clinical negligence are not usually funded by the LSC. Such cases can instead be pursued under 'conditional fee agreements' between solicitors and.clients (see section 3.4 below, and the chapter on *Accidents*, section 1.1.2).

3.1.1   Qualifying for Community Legal Service funding – financial considerations

Your solicitor will be able to tell you if you qualify for Community Legal Service funding and, if so, to what extent you qualify. Eligibility is based on your capital, income and dependants. Factors to be taken into account include:

- your savings
- your income
- your partner's income
- your dependants
- your property
- your possessions.

If you are on a low income with limited capital you may qualify for free funding. On the other hand, you may qualify for partial funding only. People on benefits such as income support may have automatic eligibility.

3.1.2   Initial legal help

For initial legal help you will qualify if your gross income is £2,250 per month or less and your disposable income is £611 per month or less and your disposable capital is £3,000 or less.

3.1.3   Help at court

Help at court is provided by a solicitor or advisor who can speak for you at certain court hearings, e.g. to apply for an adjournment in eviction proceedings, without having to act for you in all the proceedings.

The same means test as above applies.

3.1.4   Higher funding levels

If you need to go to court , your solicitor may advise you to apply for a higher level of funding for full legal representation, in which case there are other criteria to be met in terms of capital and income. For most types of legal representation your gross income must be £2,250 per month or less, your disposable income must be below £695 per month and your capital must be below £8,000.

For example, you might have reasonable grounds for claiming damages but the amount involved is small enough to be dealt with by the county court as a small claim, which does not require you to have legal representation. An application for legal representation would be refused, but if you qualified financially you might be able to obtain legal help.

3.2 Qualifying for Community Legal Services Funding – priority considerations

You must satisfy the tests set out in the Funding Code for funding from the Community Legal Service Fund. Less stringent tests apply to higher-priority cases (see above). However, it will now be harder for lower-priority cases, such as money claims, to get funding. Stringent examination must show that the cost of pursuing a claim does not outweigh the end result. Further, the Commission can decide not to fund a case where there may be an alternative way to settle the dispute (see above, section 1.2 on *Alternative dispute resolution*).

You may also be able to fund your case by entering into a conditional fee agreement, and/or by special insurance cover arranged for the purpose. Sometimes legal costs are already included in your car or household insurance policy as an 'add-on' to your existing cover.

A useful leaflet, *A Practical Guide to Community Legal Service Funding by the Legal Services Commission* (August 2002) is available (LSC leaflet Line: 0845 3000 343).

3.3 A note of warning – the 'statutory charge'

Remember: if you are successful in legal proceedings, you may be asked to make a contribution to your solicitor's bill. It would therefore be wise to check with your solicitor whether it is worth going ahead with your case. The importance of this note of warning cannot be over-stressed.

Where you gain money or property with the help of LSC funding, you may have to repay all or some of your legal costs [called the 'statutory charge']. In such circumstances, the funding acts as a loan – many people forget that they may have to pay towards their solicitors' bill even in the event of a positive outcome to their claim. LSC funding may put the client in the same position as a fee-paying client.

For example, if your solicitor receives £750 for you and his/her bill is £100, you will receive £650.

A helpful leaflet, *Paying Back the Legal Services Commission* is available (LSC Leaflet Line: 0845 3000 343).

The statutory charge does not apply if the money or property recovered consists of either maintenance payments, or payments up to £3,000 in a matrimonial property settlement.

Suppose, for example, you are a married woman and do not work. You petition your husband, who has moved in with another woman, for divorce. As you are living apart from him, his income does not count towards your financial qualifications for legal funding, which you obtain. You seek a cash settlement against him and are successful. If the amount which you recover is over £3,000, you may have to pay back to the LSC a contribution towards your funding.

Note: your solicitor will not be able to pay you the money from your cash settlement until he or she has cleared the statutory charge.

3.3.1 Criminal Defence Service

The Criminal Defence Service (CDS) administered by the Legal Services Commission replaced the old system of criminal legal aid on 2 April 2001. The aim of the CDS is to secure the provision of advice, assistance and representation, according to the interests of justice, to people suspected of a criminal offence or facing criminal proceedings. The Legal Services Commission provides these services through contracts with lawyers in private practice and by providing them through Public Defenders (employed directly by the Commission). Firms are audited against the contract to ensure they continue to meet quality assurance standards. For the name of a contracted firm in your area phone 0845 608 1122 (calls charged at local rate and open from 7 am – 11 pm Mondays to Saturdays and 7 am – 10 pm on Sunday).

Duty solicitors are available at police stations and magistrates' courts and offer free legal advice.

Contracted offices have been checked thoroughly to see that they meet certain standards and provide a quality service. The CLS logo is a mark of quality and will be displayed in the window of contracted solicitors' offices.

When you find a solicitor, make sure that what you tell him/her about your finances and your case is accurate. There are penalties for deliberate false statements about capital and income and you may have your public funding taken away if you give a solicitor wrong information about your case. Keep in touch with your solicitor about your case and be guided by his/her advice. You must immediately tell him/her if your finances change or if you change your address.

Courts no longer have to conduct a means test before granting representation. Instead, at the end of a case before any court other than a magistrates' court, the judge has power to order a defendant to pay some or all of the cost of his or her defence.

In some cases you will have to satisfy a means test in order to receive advice and assistance from a solicitor.

'Advice and assistance' covers help from a solicitor including giving general advice, writing letters, negotiating, getting a barrister's opinion and preparing a written case. It enables people of small or moderate means to get help from a solicitor. It does not cover representation in court. If you have to go to court your solicitor may advise you to apply for representation, or in some cases, advocacy assistance.

Advice and assistance is available in England and Wales and applies only to questions of English law. It does not cover the law of Scotland or Northern Ireland, nor that of any other country. There are similar schemes in Scotland and Northern Ireland. If you want to find out about these schemes contact the Scottish Legal Aid Board or the Northern Ireland Legal Aid Department (see the contact details in DIRECTORY at the end of this Chapter under the Scottish Legal Aid Board and the Law Society of Northern Ireland).

3.4   Conditional fee agreements

Taking legal action can be a costly as well as a stressful business. If you find you need to use the courts you will need to decide how to pay for your case. If you do not qualify for help from the Community Legal Service Fund, you may already have legal-expenses insurance as part of some other insurance policy which will cover your costs. Alternatively, you may want to consider a conditional fee agreement.

Until just under a decade ago English law did not allow lawyers to take on cases on a speculative basis. The conditional fee system was introduced at the same time that legal aid eligibility was being cut. It was intended thus to counterbalance a possible denial of access to justice for a broad range of persons.

Under the conditional fee system, lawyers charge an uplift on their fees (which was proposed to be up to 100 per cent but has been generally 25 per cent) if you win your case. The loser still pays the winning side's costs but does not pay his or her own solicitor for their services. Hence, the uplift – to compensate your solicitor for having taken on a risk in the first place.

It was thought that the question of what is a suitable uplift on solicitors' fees had been settled when the Court of Appeal decided that solicitors could charge a 20% success fee in 'straightforward' road traffic cases. However the issue was considered again and the court decided that a figure of 5% was more appropriate in cases where there was a minimal risk of losing, so the present situation is in a a state of uncertainty. The Access to Justice Act 1999, which came into force on 1 April 2000, allows courts to order that a successful litigant should recover the success fee payable under a conditional fee agreement from the losing party. It also allows the cost of any insurance against the risk of losing the case to be recovered in the same way. This makes it easier for membership organisations, such as trade unions or motoring organisations, to underwrite litigation on behalf of their members.

3.4.1   Agreement with your solicitor

If the nature of any case is suitable for a conditional fee agreement, and the client is able to arrange such an agreement, free legal representation will not be granted.

Note: to qualify for a conditional fee agreement, you will have to convince your lawyer that your case is strong enough to justify the lawyer and/or insurer taking the risk.

Where it is appropriate to settle a case, it will be in the opponent's interest to do so in order to avoid having to meet the claimant's legal fees as well as any success fee and insurance premium that is recoverable.

The Solicitor can draw up a conditional fee agreement with the client and advise on insurance cover. The Law Society has drawn up a model fee agreement. There are also regulations determining a checklist which the solicitor must go through with the client. These include the following:

- the circumstances whereby the claimant may have to pay costs and disbursements (see below)
- other alternatives to finance the claim
- the advantages of any particular contract of insurance
- other liabilities.

Do note: the above list is not exhaustive.

Be warned: a 'no win, no fee' agreement removes some of the uncertainty and financial risk of taking legal action, but not all of it. Remember it is only an estimate. The final cost may be higher if, say, the case takes longer than expected, or as happens in some cases, the judge may order you to pay some of the defendant's costs. You will also have to pay the solicitor's expenses, known as 'disbursements', e.g. for an expert's report. To cover your legal costs, you will generally be advised to take out insurance (see section 3.4.3 below).

Defendants – take heed: while defendants can seek a solicitor to enter into a conditional fee agreement (and possibly even obtain insurance cover as well), this may not be easy to find, as a defendant is not generally making a money claim in the first place but merely trying to block one made against him or her.

3.4.2 Personal injury cases

Most personal injury cases are removed from the scope of the Community Legal Service fund. It is considered that most of these can be funded through conditional fee agreements. Some funding remains available for investigative costs where disbursements exceed £1,000 or the solicitor's fees exceed £3,000. Further funding is available where the disbursements exceed £5,000 or the total lawyers' fees exceed £15,000. (For the exceptions where personal injury cases can still be publicly funded, see chapter on *Accidents*, section 1.1.1).

3.4.3 Legal-expenses insurance

To protect yourself from big legal bills you can take out insurance to pay the other side's legal costs and expenses for you both. There are two main types of insurance to cover such expenses.

Before-the-event insurance is mainly sold together with other insurance (e.g. household insurance) and cannot usually be purchased once a problem exists. It will cover your costs only if the insurer takes the view that you have a strong case and will normally pay for your solicitors' fees and expenses, court fees and the other party's legal costs. But it will not cover any compensation you have to pay if you lose the case.

After-the-event (ATE) insurance can be taken out once a dispute has arisen to cover court costs and the other party's costs if you lose. In some cases ATE insurance stands alone to cover all or most of the costs. However it may be used together with a conditional fee agreement with your solicitor (see above section 3.4.1) You may be able to recover all or part of the premium from the other party if your case is successful so long as the court is satisfied that it was reasonable to take out the policy in the particular circumstances of the case.

3.5 Costs – keeping clients informed

Lawyers are supposed to tell their clients in advance about the possible level of charges and how costs are likely to be calculated.

The best possible approach to avoid future conflict is to ask for the information to be provided in writing. Indeed the solicitors' professional written standards require that solicitors 'give clients the best information possible about the likely level of charges'.

In fairness to the profession, not all legal fees are calculable in advance, however. Unforeseen problems may arise. For example, you may have written to your next-door neighbour complaining of a leak from a common drainpipe. He may do nothing about it and you eventually instruct your solicitor to write on your behalf. If your neighbour then seeks evidence from a builder by affidavit [sworn evidence] or an expert's report from a surveyor, you may have to counter by supplying your own evidence from another expert and another builder. In no time at all, the costs begin to snowball.

Therefore:

- you must ask your solicitor for a periodic statement of expenses to date
- you can instruct your solicitor to set a ceiling on the amount you are prepared to spend
- your solicitor should also keep under review the question of whether costs will outweigh the benefit derived from pursuing your case further. In other words, at what point does it becomes advisable to drop a claim altogether? Or, in the example above, would it not be cheaper to effect the repairs yourself?

3.5.1   Costs in court

The legal expenses payable for the services of a solicitor and barrister in court are known as costs. In a court action the losing party usually has to pay the costs of the successful party. In legal parlance 'the costs follow the event'. The thrust of much of the present reforms is to prevent the unnecessary running-up of excessive litigation costs.

Thus, certain rules have been introduced to allow the courts greater freedom in how costs are awarded:

i.   Courts may now award costs at different stages in proceedings, and alter the shares of costs to be awarded against parties.

ii. In deciding what order to make, the court must have regard to all the circumstances – in particular the conduct of the parties – so that even if you win your case, the court can decide not to reward you with an order for costs, in other words, costs may not follow the event.

The court will make such an order for all or part of the costs against the winning side if this has:

- not followed the correct procedures before commencing the action
- exaggerated the value of the claim so that the case was allocated to the wrong track (see below, section 3.6.2)
- been unco-operative with the other side
- not tried to settle the claim where appropriate
- pursued a particular allegation unreasonably.

Barristers' fees are negotiated between solicitors and the barristers' clerks.

3.5.2   How the court calculates the charges – 'taxation of costs'

The court also controls the amount of costs by way of a procedure called 'taxation of costs'.

So even if you win a case, and your opponent is ordered to pay your costs, do not necessarily expect to be paid in full. Even as a winner, you can end up out of pocket. For example, the taxing master of the court might think that your solicitors overcharged on their hourly rate, or that they took too many hours to prepare the case. After taxation of costs, you will then have to pay the shortfall between what your solicitors charged you and what has been allowed by the taxing master.

Another note of warning: costs sought under conditional fee agreements can also be taxed.

3.6   Pressures of time

3.6.1   Delay

There is no question that pursuing a legal remedy – no matter how just your cause – can be very time-consuming. Procedures are unwieldy and slow of their very nature; lawyers are often hard-pressed and can only give their limited time to your case. Of course for every person who approaches a lawyer, his or her problem is the most pressing of all. But multiply this factor by the number of clients and it is not surprising that we sometimes feel we are not getting the attention our problem deserves.

At the same time, court business is also under tremendous pressure. You can speed things up by taking all steps to make sure that your case is heard in the right 'track', which depends largely, but not exclusively, on the amount of the claim (see immediately below).

3.6.2 Allocation of tracks

It is for the judge to decide to which track a case should be allocated after studying the nature of the case and the representations made to him by both sides. You must give your views in a questionnaire (Form N150 'allocation questionnaire'). Apart from the amount in dispute, the judge will also take into account the timetabling and evidence necessary to deal justly with the case.

The defendant will also fill in the questionnaire and you are expected to agree and co-operate with the other side as far as possible.

3.6.3 The amount in dispute

There are three tracks available, as follows:

The small claim: This is an available route if your claim is no more than £5,000, except in the cases of personal injury claims and housing repair claims, which can be pursued under the small claims track only if they are under £1,000.

The fast track: You may pursue a 'fast track' for claims between £5,000 and £15,000. Under the 'fast track' scheme, there is a fixed five-hour (maximum of one day) hearing, a limit on legal costs, and a guaranteed court date within six months. Expert evidence is limited to a written evidence only (see section 5.10.5 below).

The multi-track: This is for claims over £15,000. You can only start a claim in the High Court if it is for more than £15,000.

Penalty Notice!: if you exaggerate your claim so that a case is allocated to the fast track when it should have been heard in a small claims court, or is allocated to the multi-track when it should have been heard under the fast track scheme, you can have all or part of your costs refused, even if you win the case (see section 3.5.1 above).

3.6.4 Legal funding abroad

Many foreign countries have legal aid schemes which may be more limited than local schemes. England and Wales have an agreement with some European countries that they can pass on applications from people seeking legal aid for civil proceedings in those countries. The countries covered by this agreement are: Austria, Azerbaijan, Belgium, Bulgaria, Czech Republic, Denmark, Eire, Estonia, Finland, Greece, Italy, Lithuania, Luxembourg, The Netherlands, Norway, Poland, Portugal, Spain, Sweden, Switzerland and Turkey. Although each country decides the application under its own rules, you can make your application in England or Wales.

The LSC will pass on your application on to the relevant authority in the foreign country. You can, if you qualify financially, get legal help from a solicitor to help you with the application, including obtaining any necessary translations.

If you need legal aid outside these countries you should approach the United Kingdom representative (embassy/consulate) of the country concerned for information.

4   BRINGING A SMALL CLAIM – ARBITRATION PROCEEDINGS

Small claims hearings are part of the general court system in the county court. They enable you to take your own case to court by using a simple, straightforward procedure. If your claim is £5000 or less it will generally be treated as a small claim. Claims over that amount may also be dealt with as a small claim but then the court and the defendant have to agree to this. The judge may think it is better for both parties to have the case dealt with in the small claims court if neither of you have solicitors since the rules in the small claims court are more suited to people acting without the assistance of legal representatives. Personal injury claims of up to £1000 can be heard, and housing disrepair claims for the same amount. Other matters between landlord and tenant may include rent arrears or return of deposits. Possession proceedings are heard in the county court. (See also section 3.6.2 above.)

Small claims are heard by a district judge under a simplified procedure in a private room. The judge acts as an arbitrator. You can ask for your case to be taken out of the small claims court of you can show that:

a) it involves a difficult question of law;

b) the facts are complicated;

c) it involves fraud; or

d) you have agreed with the defendant that it should not be heard in the small claims court.

Do take note: you will also find it helpful to read section 5 below – in particular, on the steps necessary to prepare yourself for a court appearance, see section 5.5.

4.1 Procedure in outline

To bring a claim in the small claims court you have to go through the following procedure:

a) Fill in the court form stating the amount claimed, why it is being claimed and who the claim is against. Many legal centres and other bodies will help with form-filling. You must also state why you consider the small claims track to be the most appropriate one for your case.

b) Take the completed form to your local county court. The staff there will go through the form and ensure that it is properly completed. You will have to pay a filing fee and they will retain the form to start your case moving.

c) Within two weeks or so the court will send a summons to the person against whom you are claiming (the defendant). The defendant must send back a defence within 14 days. If he or she fails to do so you may be entitled to a ruling in your favour without the matter going any further. The court will be able to tell you if that is the case.

d) If the defendant does send in a defence, you will be told what steps you have to take for the hearing [the 'directions']. For example, the judge may order each party to exchange any documents such as invoices or letters on which you rely to prove your claim.

e) If the case has to go to court it will probably do so within about three months from the time you fill in the form.
The judge will supervise the proceedings and each party will tell his or her side of the story. The judge then usually makes a ruling at once, having heard all that you have to say.

f) If you win, you will be entitled to claim some expenses you have incurred in bringing the claim, e.g. you may be allowed up to £200 from the defendant for an expert witness if the judge had agreed to your using an expert, and you will be able to claim back the court fee. In addition you can claim not more than £50 per day each for you and any other witness, and/or travelling and overnight expenses.

An amount of £260 for legal fees is allowed only where you have claimed an injunction or an order for specific performance (for a definition of these terms see section on *Equity*, 9.2 below).

Note: you may find that the other side has legal representation even though you yourself are pursuing a claim in person. However, if you lose, you are not obliged to pay their costs other than those outlined above.

Do remember: winning in the small claims court is just the first step. Enforcing your claim can be much more difficult.

The law allows only very limited grounds to appeal against the judge's decision. You can only bring an appeal in a small claims court if you have good reason to show that there was either:

• a mistake of law or
• a serious irregularity in the way the hearing was conducted (see also section 5.9 below).

4.2 Using new technology

It is now possible to make a money claim to recover a debt over the Internet for a fixed amount under £100,000. A guide to the online service is to be found at *www.courtservice.gov.uk/mcol* or try the helpdesk at 0845 6015935.

5 YOUR DAY IN COURT

The average law-abiding citizen probably hopes that the nearest he or she will ever get to viewing court proceedings is by watching a courtroom drama on TV. However, clearly circumstances might arise which entail your having to attend an actual court hearing. For example, you may have to pursue or defend a claim; you may be called as a witness in someone else's case; or you may be called for jury service.

What you should do is considered below in outline. Appearances in court can be unnerving and the surroundings are often forbidding. Proceedings can seem unnecessarily inflexible and anachronistic.

Understanding the procedure may go some way in assisting you to prepare yourself so that you feel less at a loss in a difficult, and sometimes even traumatic, situation – for example where you are a defendant in eviction proceedings and fear you may lose your home. Do always establish whether there is a duty solicitor present in court if you do not have your own legal assistance. Law Centres and other agencies also administer such schemes as does the Legal Services Commission (see sections 3.1 and 3.3.1). Be certain to ask the court officials beforehand to establish that you will receive such assistance on the actual day of your hearing. See also below for Witness Support services (section 5.10.9).

The truth is that the general public do not find the courts user-friendly. In a very real sense, of course, the formality is there to serve a purpose. We are meant to be in awe of the law. Furthermore, certain technical rules which govern court proceedings, for example, the laws of evidence, are intended to be a genuine safeguard to litigants.

But given that people's liberty, property, or even their own children, can be removed from them by court proceedings, the public are entitled to a greater degree of consideration and understanding than they sometimes receive. Alas, certain judges and court administrators still seem to forget that they are there to serve the public and not vice versa.

5.1 The adversarial system

If a matter cannot be resolved out of court it goes to trial and is supervised by a judge. The parties and their lawyers present the two sides of the story and the judge ensures that the rules are adhered to. He or she then decides who wins the case on the basis of the evidence and the strength of the arguments presented by each party.

This system is known as the 'adversarial' system.

5.2 Litigation as a last resort

All litigation is a gamble. There is never any certainty as to the outcome. No matter how convinced you are of your own case, you must never forget your opponent is equally convinced of the rightness of his or her own cause.

You must not forget, either, that the role of the judge is to stand back and take an impartial and objective view of the case including all the facts and surrounding circumstances as well as the law in relation to those facts. Even if you feel that justice is on your side, the judge's view of the dispute may not be the same as yours – for example, the judge's interpretation of a tiny provision in a statute may be fatal to your case.

5.2.1 · Before you make a claim

Issuing a claim is a last resort and should only be undertaken once all other ways of settling a dispute have been explored.

If for example you want to claim money which is owing to you, do first write a letter to the other side stating how much is owing and what it is for, and set a date for the return of the money. Head your letter 'without prejudice' and include a warning that you may go to court to recover the money if the deadline is not met. Keep a copy of the letter and of any further correspondence.

Warning: before you start any court action do consider whether you are likely to get your money back even if you win a judgment in your favour. If the debtor is unemployed or bankrupt or have no money of his or her own and no personal possessions of any value, you may have difficulty recovering any part of the debt. Alternatively they may be able to pay off the debt by instalments if you are prepared to wait.

5.2.2 Insolvency

It is worth finding out in advance whether your debtor is likely to be able to pay. You can contact the Insolvency Service (see DIRECTORY), providing the full name of the person or company and their last address. They should be able to tell you whether the person is bankrupt. If it is a company, it may be in compulsory liquidation in which case it has probably stopped trading and will have neither money nor assets.

5.2.3   Help for potential litigants

The Court Service publishes a comprehensive series of leaflets explaining the basic court procedures, from making a claim to enforcement procedures. They include guidance for those wishing to pursue civil claims as litigants in person which fall outside the scope of the small claims court.

The leaflets are specifically aimed at litigants in person and use plain English in a question and answer format. Some leaflets are available in Welsh. They are all available free from any county court office or from the Court Service website at *www.courtservice.gov.uk*. Advice agencies such as the Citizens Advice Bureaux also supply some Court Service leaflets to their customers. The telephone number of the CAB at the Royal Courts of Justice is 0845 120 3715.

5.3   Claimant or defendant – when you are 'a party to the proceedings'

In general your legal advisor will give you instructions on what you should do and what you can expect.

5.3.1   Court information

You can also enquire by:

- calling into the court office between 10 am and 4 pm (4.30 pm in the Royal Courts of Justice) any weekday and speaking to a member of the court staff
- telephoning the court any weekday
- writing to the court; or
- if the matter is urgent, sending a fax to the court.

Information is also available on the Court Service website:
see *www.courtservice.gov.uk/cs_home.htm#notices*. The website carries the day's listings [the 'cause list'] for the Royal Courts of Justice.

The Court Service Customer Service Unit can be telephoned on 020 7210 2269.

You can write to the Court Service Unit, The Court Service, Southside, 105 Victoria Street, London SW1E 6QT. Information is also available on an audio cassette from the Court Service Unit.

In all cases, tell the court your claim number and the date of your hearing if you have one.

Do pay heed: court staff cannot give you legal advice or answer questions regarding the likely success of your case or the evidence you will need. Legal advice of that kind should be sought from a solicitor, a law centre, or other advice agency. However, court staff can tell you about court forms and procedures.

5.3.2   Disability

If you have a disability which makes going to court or communicating difficult, you must contact the court.

If the court Customer Service Officer cannot help, contact the Court Service Disability Helpline on 0800 358 3506 between 9 am and 5 pm weekdays. Your call will be free. If you are hard of hearing, you can use the Minicom service on 0191 478 1476.

5.3.3   Preliminary hearings

These take place:

- to decide what must be done to prepare your case for final hearing (i.e. a 'case management conference')
- to consider any other application you or the other side have made (an 'interlocutory' application) for example, for an adjournment
- if there is a decision to be made on the allocation of a case track (see section 3.6.2 above).

5.3.4   Legal Terms

Basic charges – The hourly rate that most solicitors charge to do your legal work.

Claim – How much you are asking for in damages.

Conditional fee agreement – A way of paying for your case, also known as 'no-win, no-fee' (see above section 3.4).

Counterclaim – When someone sues you in response to your suing them.

Community Legal Service Fund – What used to be called legal aid. A fund of government money to help people in certain circumstances who are unable to afford to pay for a legal case themselves (see above, section 3.1.1).

Damages – The money you win, either in court, or, if you settle, out of court.

Disbursements – Payments made by the solicitor above and beyond the basic charges, to work on your case. These may include court fees, accident-report fees or expert witness fees, as well as paying for a barrister to argue your case if it goes to court.

Legal-expenses insurance – Insurance taken out to protect against financial loss as a result of going to court (see above, section 3.4.3).

Success fee – The amount that your solicitor will add to your bill if you win your claim (by prior agreement).

5.4 Do you need to call witnesses?

If you wish to call a witness to give evidence in support of your claim or defence, your witness will be required at a final hearing. Witnesses are not needed at a preliminary hearing. As a general rule claimants and defendants must choose their own witnesses and arrange for them to be present on the appointed day.

An information leaflet for witnesses is available from any county court office and you will find it useful to read that yourself before giving it to your witness.

5.4.1 The unwilling witness

If your witness is unwilling to come to the hearing, you can issue a witness summons by completing Form N20 which is available free from any court office. You must issue that summons at least seven days before the date of the hearing and it must reach the witness [be 'served'] at least four days before the hearing. A fee is payable and court staff will be able to tell you how much this is. You can obtain a leaflet on fees from any county court.

When you issue a witness summons you will have to pay the witness's expenses in travelling to and from the court and compensation for loss of time in attending court. (The witness leaflet gives more information about witness expenses.)

5.5 Preparing for the hearing

Before your case comes up for hearing you need to ensure that you, and any witnesses, know the time and date of the hearing, where the court is, and how to get there. Every court has its own information leaflet which tells you about its location and facilities.

If the hearing is the final hearing, make sure that you have done everything to prepare your case. In particular, ensure that you have sent all requested documents to the court.

You should have ready all the documents ('evidence') you want to use at the hearing. It will help if you have them in the order you wish to use them, and have copies to give to the judge.

Make a note of what you want to say. This will help make sure that you do not forget anything.

5.6 Settling the dispute

If at any time before the hearing, you agree to settle your dispute, you must let the court know immediately. Write to the court and to the defendant confirming that the dispute has been settled, giving your claim number and the date of any hearing. If you do not tell the court that your dispute has been settled, you may have to pay the other side's costs.

5.7 The hearing day

You should make sure that you arrive in good time for your hearing. Proceedings can entail delay so do take that into account in making your arrangements, e.g. for a babysitter.

5.7.1 Public or private hearing

The hearing may be 'in public' or 'in private' [i.e. 'in chambers'].

Members of the public are allowed to be present at a hearing in public, if there is sufficient room. However, generally only the parties to a case, their witnesses and legal representatives are present at a hearing in private.

It is for the judge to decide whether a hearing is to be in public or in private, but cases involving a person's finances or family proceedings are usually heard in private.

5.7.2 Swearing an oath

You (and any witnesses) will normally be asked to swear [take an oath] that what is said or used in evidence to prove your case is true. The oath is sworn on the Bible but members of particular religious groups can choose to swear on their own holy book.

Affirmation: if you object to being sworn, you can give a promise to tell the truth (called 'affirming').

5.8 The hearing

At the hearing the judge will usually want to hear first from you because you are the person who started the case, i.e. you are the 'claimant'. It is then the turn to speak of the person who disputes your claim, the 'defendant'.

When you are giving evidence, you may only refer to notes you have made if the judge has given you permission to do so, unless your claim is being heard in the small claims court.

You, or your lawyer, will be given an opportunity to speak and to put questions to the defendant and any witnesses. The judge may also ask you some questions.

If you want to ask any questions, remember to ask only one at a time. Do not interrupt the judge or another witness.

Always bear in mind: your court time is limited so you must be well prepared, and speak briefly and to the point.

It will be useful, particularly if you have no legal representation, to make a note of the statements made by the defendant and their witnesses and of the judge's decision and the reason for it.

5.8.1 The decision

The judge will normally tell you about the decision reached after all the evidence has been given. A written copy will be sent to you and the defendant after the hearing. This may order either you or the defendant to do something, e.g. pay money or give up possession of a house or flat to a landlord.

In some cases, the judge may need more time to arrive at a decision and you will be sent a notice telling you the time, date and place where the decision will be given.

5.9 Appeals

If you do not agree with the judge's decision, you may have a reason to appeal against it ['grounds of appeal']. This means that a more senior judge will look at your case and decide if the original decision was right.

If you want to appeal, you must act quickly. If you find yourself on the losing side you must apply for *permission* to appeal within strict time limits which start on the day the judge makes a decision, or shortly afterwards. Permission to appeal is almost always necessary and granting it is by no means automatic. The time you have will depend on the type of order you are appealing against. Court staff will tell you what this is. You may also have to pay a fee.

Warning: if you wish to appeal against a judicial decision, there must be recognised legal grounds for your appeal. It is not just a matter of finding yourself on the losing side and feeling deeply unhappy with the outcome. In addition the court will also weigh up whether your appeal has a real prospect of success, or whether there is some compelling reason why your appeal should be heard.

The notes you have made at the hearing will help those advising you to decide whether you do have grounds for an appeal.

If you lose your appeal you will probably have to pay the other party's costs.

Do remember: with regard to the Court of Appeal, the tests are even stricter: for permission to be granted an appeal must raise an important point of principle or practice or there must be some other reason to hear the appeal, e.g. a miscarriage of justice in a criminal trial.

See Form 201 'Routes of Appeal' issued by the Court Service, Civil Appeals Office Registry, Room E307, Royal Courts of Justice, Strand, London WC2A 2LL, Tel. 020 7946 6409, which sets out the routes of appeal from 2 May 2000 onwards.

5.10 Being a witness

You may be called upon to be a witness in a civil or criminal case.

5.10.1 Being a witness in a civil case

There are two classes of witnesses who may be called to give evidence in a civil case – a 'witness of fact' and an 'expert witness'. You may be asked to appear as a witness of fact because, for example, you have seen an accident take place, and are able to say how it happened. You may be asked to act as an expert witness because you have a special qualification or skill (you are a doctor, surveyor, builder etc.), and can give a professional opinion (a 'report'), about a victim's injuries, the conditions of the road on which an accident took place, whether roofing was waterproof etc.

5.10.2 Refusal to be a witness

If you are asked to be an expert witness, you can refuse to appear. It is for you to decide whether you can spare the time from your work or business to prepare a report and, perhaps, go to a court hearing.

If you are asked to be a witness of fact, you can also refuse, but you can be made to act by the issue to you of a witness summons (Form N20) (see above, section 5.4.1). That form tells you that you must go to court to act as a witness, and when and where to attend. If you do not go when you are told, you will be 'in contempt of court' and could be fined up to £1,000.

If, therefore, you have prior arrangements such as a booked holiday, which affects you availability on a particular date, you must let the court know as soon as possible.

Warning: think carefully before you make an application to be excused. If your application is refused you may have to pay the costs of the issue of the witness summons.

5.10.3 The procedure

First you will be asked about your statement (or your report if you are an expert witness) by the lawyer acting for the person who asked you to be a witness. You may then be cross-examined by the opposing party's solicitor or barrister. The judge may also want to ask you some questions. If you need to refer to your papers, ask the judge if you may do so.

5.10.4 Giving evidence as a witness of fact

The court will decide whether your evidence is to be given in writing, or to be spoken, or both. Your written evidence should be contained in a 'witness statement'. That statement should be in your own words and should contain:

- your full name, address and occupation
- a statement of whether the details in it are made from your own knowledge; and
- a signed statement of truth – i.e. 'I believe the facts stated in this witness statement are true' – followed by your signature.

Warning: if you knowingly give false information in your statement and you have verified it with a statement of truth, you may be liable to a fine or imprisonment.

5.10.5 Giving evidence as an expert witness

Usually your evidence as an expert witness will be limited to your written report. If you do have to give evidence in person, the claimant who asked you for your report will tell you when and where to attend or will serve you with a witness summons (Form N20).

Your written report is addressed to the court.

Note: your duty is to help the court with all matters within your expertise. That duty overrides any obligation you may have to the party instructing you or paying for your report.

Sometimes the opposing party in a case will accept that your report should be used as evidence. If this happens, you may not have to go to the court hearing. Otherwise you will be told the date and place of the hearing.

Do take note: you must have the judge's permission to use an expert witness if your case is heard in the small claims court (see section 4 above) or under the fast-track procedure (see section 3.6.3).

5.10.6   Claiming expenses – the expert witness

You should be paid expenses by the person who asked you to act as an expert witness. These include the following:

- the cost of your travel to and from the court
- the cost of overnight accommodation (if this is necessary)
- a reasonable amount to compensate you for any wages or income you may lose when you go to court; and
- a reasonable amount for the time you have spent in preparation.

Note: there is no fixed amount for preparing an expert report. It is for you to decide how much your time is worth. You should agree an amount before you agree to write the report.

5.10.7   Being a witness in a criminal case

If you are called as a witness in a criminal trial there may be some delay before the case will be heard. However, the Crown Court aims to have the first hearing within six weeks of receiving the case and to start most trials within 16 weeks of when the case is received. Difficult cases, such as murder or rape trials, may be delayed by upwards of a year. You should be kept informed as to when the case is likely to be heard.

If you are witness for the prosecution, you will be summoned by the Crown Prosecution Service.

5.10.7(a)   Waiting at court

Not all court buildings have separate waiting areas for witnesses. However, if you wish to wait apart from the other side's witnesses, ask the court staff to arrange that for you.

Generally, you should not have to wait more than two hours, but delays can happen if, for example, an earlier case takes longer than planned.

5.10.8   Travel expenses and allowances

If you are a defence witness, the court will give you a claim form and explain what expenses and allowances you can claim. Your expenses will be paid within five working days from receipt of your claim.

If you are a prosecution witness, you must get your claim form from the Crown Prosecution Service representative. That representative will explain what expenses and allowances you can claim and give you a pre-paid envelope in which you can return your completed claim form.

5.10.9   The Witness Service

The Witness Service is run by the independent charity Victim Support, and helps witnesses, victims and their families before, during and after the hearing. Trained volunteers in every Crown Court centre in England and Wales give free and confidential support and practical information about court procedures. The Witness Service will normally get in touch with you before the court hearing to offer their help. The help they offer includes:

- arranging for you to visit the court before the hearing
- arranging for someone to go with you into the courtroom if you have to give evidence; and
- giving you the chance to talk over the case when it has ended and to get more help or information.

See DIRECTORY under Victim Support for contact details.

5.10.10 **Child witnesses**

There is an increasing tendency to accept the evidence of children, which recent research has shown is not more inaccurate than that of adults. The judge can decide whether or not a young child should be permitted to give evidence.

5.10.10(a) **Taking an oath**

The evidence of a child under 14 must be given unsworn, and over that age the judge must ascertain whether or not the child really understands the meaning of the taking of an oath.

5.10.10(b) **Assisting the child witness**

The judge has power to clear the court when a child is to give evidence and may permit the evidence to be given from behind a screen. A child can also give evidence by means of a live television link.

Child witnesses can find the experience of giving evidence very stressful. Cases generally involve children who have themselves been victims of crime or who have witnessed crimes of violence committed against others. Children can be called as witnesses for either the prosecution or the defence.

The judge may also allow a social worker or relative to sit by the child to assist him or her in not becoming too nervous while giving evidence. The role of the 'adult supporter' can involve liaising with both the prosecution and the defence before the trial, as well as with the police, local authorities and the Crown Prosecution Service, in order to try to minimise the trauma for the child witness.

The NSPCC has produced a *Child Witness Pack* which is intended for children, parents and their carers to assist in understanding trial procedures. The Children's Legal Centre has available a leaflet, *Being a Witness*, which tells children what to expect at court. It is intended for children of eight and over, but should be read together with an adult familiar with court procedure.

Also, where a child is required to give evidence in a Crown Court, the court staff will:

- arrange to have the case heard as soon as possible
- provide a Child Witness Officer or Witness Support Officer to make sure everything runs smoothly
- make sure that someone meets children and their companions when they come to court, and takes them to a private waiting area away from the defendant; and
- answer questions about how things are done in court.

Sometimes the judge will let the child give evidence using a 'TV link'. If he does, arrangements can be made for the child to see the TV link equipment before the trial.

See Family Law DIRECTORY on page 109.

5.11 **Jury Service**

At present the jury's principal duty is to give a verdict in criminal cases, and, occasionally, findings of fact at coroners' courts (see below, section 7.6). Very few civil cases involve juries, the most usual being libel trials. The tradition that a jury consists of twelve persons reaches back into history, but is no longer always carried out in practice. A county court jury must consist of eight persons and a coroner's jury must consist of not less than seven and not more than eleven persons. In other courts juries may consist of any number of persons, not above twelve, provided there are at least nine.

Plans are afoot for a fundamental overhaul of the jury system. Sir Robin Auld has produced a massive report with 300 recommendations for changes to the criminal court system following widespread consultation with lawyers, judges, academics, crown prosecutors, magistrates and others in the system. The suggested changes would mean a substantial number of defendants losing the right to choose to be tried by jury instead of by magistrates. But there would be a new right for defendants charged with serious offences to choose to be tried by judge alone, rather than by judge and jury. The judge also recommends a complete rethink on jury eligibility so that groups who are now ineligible, such as lawyers and clergymen, or those who are automatically exempted, such as doctors, nurses and soldiers, would be eligible to sit on juries in the future.

The report also recommends a dramatic reduction in the number of self-employed and professional people who manage to get themselves excused from jury service. A Home Office study in 1999 found that two out of three people called for jury service avoided it and it is suggested that those excused for genuine reasons such as illness should have their service deferred, rather than being let off completely.

5.11.1 Who can serve as a juror?

You are normally qualified to serve as a juror if you are:

- on the electoral register for parliamentary or local government elections
- between the ages of 18 and 70; and
- ordinarily resident in the UK for any period of at least five years since the age of 13.

These conditions also apply to coroners' juries.

For those deemed ineligible or disqualified, or who may be excused, see immediately below.

a) Ineligible persons are:
- members of the judiciary
- others involved in the justice system, such as barristers and solicitors, probation officers, prison officers and the police
- the clergy
- the mentally ill.

b) Disqualified persons are:
- those who have served a prison term or a youth custody term, been given a suspended sentence, have served a community service order, or have been placed on probation or on bail.

Stipulations apply to both the severity of the sentence and the time since it was imposed.

c) Persons who can be excused as of right are:
- those over 65 years of age
- members and officers of the House of Commons and House of Lords
- MEPs
- members of the National Assembly for Wales and the Auditor General for Wales
- full-time serving officers of any of the armed forces
- doctors, nurses, midwives, veterinary surgeons, veterinary practitioners, dentists and chemists
- practising members of religious societies or orders, the tenets of beliefs of which are incompatible with jury service.

Note: The Auld Report has proposed that professional people, including lawyers, should no longer be automatically exempt from jury service (see above, section 5.11). Present juries, it was felt, are no longer representative of the population generally and can comprise a too high proportion of the unemployed.

d) Persons who may be excused are:
- Those with good reason.

If you are summoned for jury duty, you may be able to satisfy the court officer that there is a good reason why you should be excused, such as that you run a one-man business. If your reason is not accepted, you do have a right of appeal to the court, or one of the courts, to which you have been summoned. You must give written notice of your appeal stating why you wish to be excused from service.

e) Persons with previous jury service

If you have served on a jury previously, you will be excused if you can satisfy the court that:

- you have served, or attended to serve, within two years of your present summons, or
- you have been excused from further service for a period which still has time to run.

5.11.1(a) Deferral of jury service

If you are summoned for jury service, you must show that there is a good reason why your summons be deferred. Such 'good reason' might be that you have pre-booked a holiday abroad or that you or your partner are expecting a baby. If your request for deferral is refused, there is a right of appeal to the court, or one of the courts, to which you have been summoned.

5.11.2 Being summoned for jury service

The Lord Chancellor, using electoral registers, is responsible for the issuing of summonses to potential jurors.

You will receive your summons either by post or by hand delivery. When you attend, you may be asked some questions to establish whether you are qualified for jury service.

If you receive a summons to attend as a juror and require further information, you should be able to receive this from your local Crown Court. Before the actual hearing, you and your fellow jurors may also be shown a video, which will clarify the relevant points of court procedure for you.

Do log on to *www.juror.cjsonline.org*. This site takes you through what you can expect during jury service, and explains the stages and procedures that you will encounter in court.

5.11.3 Failure to attend

If you fail to attend, or are unfit for service by reason of drink or drugs, you will be liable to a fine. You will not be liable to a penalty if you can show there was a valid reason for your failure to comply with the summons or for not being available when called on to serve (for example in a case of genuine illness).

5.11.4 Offences

It is an offence to make a false statement or to get someone else to make a false statement on your behalf in order to try to evade jury service. It is also an offence to sit on a jury when you are not eligible to do so.

Any such offence is punishable on summary conviction.

5.11.5 Swearing-in of the jury

Once in the jury box, each juror will be sworn in separately. If you object to being sworn you are permitted to make a solemn affirmation rather than taking an oath.

The form of the oath in criminal trials is: 'I swear by almighty God that I will faithfully try the defendant(s) and give (a) true verdict(s) according to the evidence'. The following words are used for the affirmation: 'I do solemnly, sincerely and truly declare and affirm that I will faithfully try the defendant(s) and give (a) true verdict(s) according to the evidence'.

5.11.6 Death or incapacity of a juror

If, in the course of a criminal trial, a juror dies or is discharged as being incapable of continuing to act, or for any other reason, the jury remains properly constituted so long as its members are not reduced to below nine. However, the court may discharge the jury where it sees fit to do so.

5.11.7 Misconduct of jurors

A jury may be discharged or a new trial ordered if, after being sworn, any juror is guilty of misconduct. Misconduct includes talking to someone or receiving evidence about the case out of court; determining a verdict by lot or, if the jury is unable to agree, 'splitting the difference'.

Misconduct or impropriety by a juror may result in either that juror, or the entire jury, being discharged.

5.11.8 Bias

If a juror is biased then he or she, or the entire jury, may have to be discharged. The test to be applied by the court is whether, having regard to the circumstances, there is a real danger of bias, which may include:

- deliberate hostility towards the defendant
- inadvertent knowledge of the defendant's bad character
- alleged racism
- acquaintance with prosecution witnesses; or
- a close connection with the case in some way.

5.11.9   Giving the verdict

Do note: in a criminal case, the jury may acquit the defendant at any time after the close of the prosecution case.

The jury is entitled to communicate with the judge after it has retired. In criminal cases any such communication must be read out in open court.

General verdicts in criminal cases are findings of 'guilty' or 'not guilty'. In civil cases general findings relate to whether the jury has decided in favour of the claimant or the defendant, with the amount of the assessed damages, if the finding is for the claimant. A jury's verdict on the issue before the court must be given in open court in the presence of all the jurors and, preferably, in the presence of the defendant.

5.11.10   Discharge of the jury

After you have given your verdict, the judge will discharge you. If the case has been exceptionally long or difficult, you may be exempted from further jury service for a period of years. You and your fellow jurors cannot be recalled to rectify the verdict and there must be a new trial if the court considers that injustice has been done. Nor can you or your fellow jurors be asked questions in order to determine whether the jury's verdict was one which was supported by the evidence produced.

5.11.11   Payment of jurors

A person who serves as a juror is entitled to receive payments by way of allowance:

- for travelling and subsistence; and
- for financial loss incurred because of jury service, up to the 'relevant amount'.

5.11.11(a)   The 'relevant amount'

The relevant amount is calculated in accordance with rates determined by the Lord Chancellor. As these rates alter regularly, you should ask an official of the court for the amount which applies at the time you are called for jury service. It is likely that, if you are self-employed, the allowance for loss of earnings will fall short of the amount of your loss.

5.11.12   Offences against jurors

It is contempt of court to use or threaten violence, or even to use threatening or abusive language, in or near the courts, to a juror.

Intimidation of jurors is becoming more frequent, and any threat should be reported as soon as possible to a court official. Often the best person to speak to will be the usher who is in charge of you and your fellow jurors.

It is also an offence to corrupt or influence a juror and, similarly, for a juror to allow him or herself to be bribed.

Note: you will be guilty of contempt of court if you:

- obtain
- disclose, or
- solicit

any particulars of statements, opinion, arguments, or votes cast by members of a jury in the course of their deliberations in any legal proceedings.

From time to time, calls have been made to allow academic research into the manner in which juries have reached their verdicts, but, to date, any such request has been sternly refused.

6   HUMAN RIGHTS

The purpose of the Human Rights Act 1998 was to incorporate the European Human Rights Convention into UK law. Since the Act came into effect on 2 October 2000, the Convention rights have been enforceable in the UK courts. Until then, people had to take a case to the European Court in Strasbourg, and even then only when domestic remedies had been exhausted. That process was both costly and time-consuming. This represents a wholly new and radical departure for our legal system. Judges have greater power than before to determine moral and social issues and public bodies are open to a different kind of challenge from members of the public.

For example, until now, a local authority's decision to close down a school could only be judged in terms of the legislation which governed their powers under the education and local government legislation. Now such a decision would have to be examined to see whether it might also have infringed our rights. Another example involves the NHS: if a health authority decides that a very expensive treatment is beyond its current resources, a patient who needs the treatment could raise a claim that his or her human rights are being breached.

6.1 How the Act works

If you think that a public authority has breached your Convention rights, you may:

a) take the authority to court;

b) rely on the Convention rights in the course of any other proceedings involving a public authority, e.g. judicial review, criminal trial, care proceedings, housing possession proceedings.

If you take the direct route as in (a) above, you must bring the proceedings within a year or less of the act complained of, but a court may allow an extension if that is considered fair in the circumstances.

If a court finds that Convention rights have been breached, it may award whatever remedy seems to it to be appropriate. This could include damages. However, damages will take into account the awards made by the European Court of Human Rights, which tend to be modest.

The court is obliged to try to consider existing law – so far as it is possible to do so – in such a way so as to make it conform to your rights under the Convention.

If the court finds, however, that your rights have been breached but that the public authority acted within the law of the land, it cannot change the law or find the case in your favour. The court will then issue a declaration of 'incompatibility'. In other words, it states that the law of the land is incompatible with your rights under the Convention. It will then be for Parliament to change the law accordingly (see also *Note*, below).

Proceedings can be brought only by the person who has suffered from a breach of the Convention rights as a result of the actions of a public body, i.e. the victim. Interest groups, such as trade unions, cannot bring proceedings directly unless they meet the victim test, but they are able to assist persons bringing cases.

There is no definition of what constitutes a 'public authority' but it is likely to include the following:

- government departments
- local authorities
- the NHS
- police, prison and immigration officers
- public prosecutors
- courts and tribunals
- non-departmental public bodies
- any person exercising a public function.

Note: a public authority will not have acted unlawfully under the Act if, as a result of a provision in a statute, it could not have acted differently.

6.2 Appeals to the European Court of Human Rights in Strasbourg

You can still take a case to the European Court of Human Rights but you will first have to show that you have tried all the legal routes open to you in the UK.

7 THE COURTS AND THE JUDGES

It is usual in legal books to outline the court system by starting at the top, i.e. the House of Lords, and then working downwards through the various levels and structures. However, in everyday legal situations, if we have to go to court at all, we usually appear in the lower courts. For that reason, the outline below follows that pattern.

7.1   Tribunals

Tribunals are informal courts within the civil legal system which deal with cases in specialised areas. They consist of a lawyer acting as chairman, sometimes sitting with lay members, who will probably have experience in the field in which the dispute has arisen.

They include employment tribunals dealing with disputes between employers and employees, especially concerning unfair dismissal or discrimination (see sections 1.4.1 and 1.4.2 above on the Equal Opportunities Commission and the Commission for Racial Equality; see also the chapter on *Working for a Living (Part 2)*).

Tribunals are intended to be simple and easy to use but they often involve complicated areas of law. It is thus becoming more common for lawyers to be engaged to argue points of law. Conditional fee agreements can be entered into between solicitor and client in most civil cases and insurance cover may be arranged for representation. The layperson acting for him- or herself against a lawyer briefed by an employer could be severely disadvantaged (see above, section 2.7.4).

Other tribunals cover such areas as immigration, rent and other land assessment, social security, immigration and mental health. The Medical Appeal Tribunal hears appeals against refusal of claims for mobility allowance and other injury-related benefits. (See the chapter on *Children (Part 1)*, regarding the Child Support Appeal Tribunal, section 2.2.1.)

7.1.1   Employment Appeals Tribunal (EAT)

The EAT hears appeals from employment tribunals. It comprises a High Court judge and two lay members with knowledge of industrial relations, e.g. trades union officials etc.

7.2   Magistrates' courts

Magistrates' courts are the lowest courts in the criminal justice system although their jurisdiction is being extended. They also have a civil jurisdiction in family matters dealing with, for example, maintenance and adoption. In addition, they are responsible for granting liquor licences for restaurants, betting shops and casinos etc.

7.3   Crown courts

The crown court is a more senior court which deals with criminal cases heard by a judge and jury. It also acts as an appeal court where the judge sits with some lay magistrates to hear the appeals.

7.4   County courts

County courts are situated all over England and Wales; they are presided over by a circuit judge and have the power to hear all but the most important civil cases. Fast track cases are allocated to the county courts, i.e. money claims between £5000 and £15,000, and also repossession cases, most landlord and tenant disputes, disputes over wills, and bankruptcy and the winding up of companies.

They also have jurisdiction over family matters with power to grant divorces and make orders concerning property and children.

Cases may be transferred from the county courts to the High Court if a complex issue arises which needs a ruling by a High Court judge. A case may also be transferred back again to the county court as necessary.

7.5   Court of Protection

Relatives can apply to the court for a receiver to be appointed where there is a person incapable of taking care of his or her own property. The court issues a Guidance Note with notes for personal applicants, and notes for solicitors. The forms include a medical certificate and a certificate listing family and property. The court also registers enduring powers of attorney. (See also the chapters on *Death – Before and After* and on *Growing Old*.)

7.6   Coroners' courts

A coroner must hold an inquest if a death is not due to natural causes.

An inquest is not, strictly speaking, a trial – it is an investigative procedure. However, there may be witnesses who are called and, in certain circumstances, a jury. Juries are usually summoned if someone has died in custody or in connection with an arrest.

Although relatives may be represented by a lawyer, legal aid is not generally available. However exceptional funding may be available if there is

- a significant wider public interest in the client being represented at the inquest
- the client is a member of the deceased's immediate family and in the light of the circumstances of the death, funded representation is required to assist the coroner in conducting a thorough investigation and determining the facts.

7.7   The High Court

The High Court sits at the Royal Courts of Justice in London and at other centres throughout England and Wales. It is divided into three sections: Queen's Bench, Chancery and Family. Multi-track cases are allocated to the High Court (see section 3.6.2 above).

7.7.1   Queen's Bench Division

This is the biggest of the three divisions. Its work covers general civil claims for damages in tort (breach of duty) and contract.

Within the QBD there are specialist courts:

- the Commercial Court, which deals with commercial matters
- the Admiralty Court, which deals with shipping disputes
- the Divisional Court, which deals with judicial reviews (see section 7.7.4) and appeals from the magistrates' courts on points of law.

7.7.2   Chancery Division

This division deals with disputes concerning matters such as tax, land mortgages, property, trusts etc. It also deals with wills.

There are specialist courts within the Chancery Division:

- the Companies Court, which deals with company matters, e.g. winding up, directors' disqualifications, administrations etc.
- the Patents Court, which deals with disputes concerning copyright, passing off etc.

7.7.3   Family Division

The Family Division, as the name suggests, deals with family matters, particularly disputes in divorce proceedings. It also has jurisdiction over wards of court, and deals with adoption orders (See the chapter on *Children (Part 2)*).

7.7.4   Judicial review

Judicial review is the process for reviewing administrative decisions by e.g. government departments, local authorities etc. The court can examine the legal and procedural elements of such a decision but is not entitled to rule on its merits.

Judicial review is being increasingly used to challenge decisions of government departments and is known as 'the citizen's weapon'. Cuts in social services budgets have prompted challenges under this procedure, to – for example – the closure of old people's homes.

7.8   Court of Appeal

This court hears appeals from the county court, High Court and Crown Courts. Permission to appeal must be granted and this is used as a filtering process to weed out appeals which have little prospect of success. In addition, appeals must generally involve an important point of legal principle.

The Court of Appeal is divided into the criminal and civil divisions and is situated at the Royal Courts of Justice in London. The Lord Chief Justice presides over the Criminal Division. An appeal is usually heard by three judges known as Lords Justices. However some appeals are heard by two judges if the case is considered appropriate.

7.9 House of Lords

The Lords of Appeal in Ordinary (the Law Lords) are the legal members of the House of Lords and form the highest court in England. The House of Lords hears not only English appeals but also Scottish civil, though not criminal, appeals. Generally the House of Lords hears only appeals on points of law of general public importance. Permission has to be obtained to pursue such an appeal, either from the Court of Appeal or from the House of Lords itself.

7.10 Privy Council

The Judicial Committee of the Privy Council hears appeals from what remains of the Colonies, and from those former British territories which have chosen to keep it as their final Court of Appeal, including New Zealand, Trinidad and Singapore.

The Privy Council is made up mainly of those Law Lords who sit in the House of Lords. However, sometimes a judge from one of the Commonwealth countries is also invited to sit.

7.11 Court of Justice of the European Union

The European Court of Justice (ECJ) is the court of the European Union sitting in Luxembourg. It was set up under the EC Treaty to interpret European Community law which applies to all the Member States of the European Union. It has jurisdiction over Member States on matters concerning Community law. Its judgments on the interpretation of this law are final and take precedence even over House of Lords' decisions.

There are 15 Judges, one from each Member State. There are also six Advocates General who assist the judges of the court by delivering an opinion in open court after written and oral submissions. The Court of Justice, when giving its ruling, usually follows the outcome suggested by the Advocate General although the court is free to disagree with the opinion. There is also the Court of First Instance established to relieve the Court of Justice of some of its heavy case load.

A national court may refer a question to the ECJ where it considers that interpretation of EU law is necessary before it can make a decision on a case before it. A court is required, however, to refer a question to which there is no answer under national law.

The ECJ gives general guidance in its rulings but it is for the national courts to apply its interpretation of EU law to the specific case giving rise to the reference.

The court is made up of a judge from each Member State of the Council of Europe, and each judge gives a separate decision.

8 THE JUDGES

There have been increasing calls for more openess in the selection procedures of the nation's judge. The present system has been described by the first Commissioner for Judicial Appointments, who is charged with scrutinising it, as 'opaque, unduly slow' and, moreover, that 'equal treatment of candidates cannot be demonstrated'.

8.1 Magistrate

A magistrate sits in the local magistrates' court (see section 7.2 above) and hears a range of matters including minor criminal cases and many family proceedings. Magistrates are chosen by the Lord Chancellor from applicants within the local community. They are also known as Justices of the Peace. Three magistrates usually sit together to hear cases and they are advised on the law by a magistrates' clerk who is a qualified lawyer.

A very comprehensive website can be found at *www.magistrates-association.org.uk/mags.assn/* which gives details of the courts, and advises on how to become a magistrate etc.

There are also some full-time magistrates who are known as stipendiaries. These are legally qualified people who sit alone to hear cases. They are found mainly in the big cities.

8.2 District judge

A district judge sits in the county court and hears 'minor' cases such as small claims (see section 4 above). District judges also decide on some preliminary questions which might arise in other cases.

8.3   Circuit judge

A circuit judge sits in both the county courts and the Crown Courts in the six areas around England and Wales known as circuits. Circuit judges are mostly former barristers although a few are former solicitors.

8.4   Official referee

An official referee is a circuit judge nominated to sit as a High Court judge to deal with cases which need a detailed examination of documents and accounts or scientific investigation. Official referees deal particularly with cases involving the construction industry.

8.5   Master

A master is a senior judicial officer who hears minor cases and rules on preliminary issues in the Chancery Division and the Queen's Bench Division of the High Court.

8.6   High Court judge

A High Court judge sits in the High Court in London and in centres around England and Wales and hears the more serious cases.

Once appointed as a High Court judge a person might be selected as one of the judges who sit in the Court of Appeal and hear appeals from the lower courts on points of law only.

The Lord Chief Justice is the senior judge in England who sits in the Criminal Division of the Court of Appeal and presides over the Queen's Bench Division of the High Court.

The Master of the Rolls is the senior civil law judge who presides over the Civil Division of the Court of Appeal.

8.7   The Law Lords

The Law Lords are the most senior appeal judges. They sit in the House of Lords. There are ten of them and they sit in groups of five to hear appeals.

The House of Lords is expected to act to some extent in the role of a constitutional court, in order to construe legislation to conform with the Human Rights Act 1998 insofar as that is possible. Where it is not possible, it can call on Parliament to make speedy changes to the law to establish conformity (see also section 6 above).

8.8   The Lord Chancellor

The Lord Chancellor is the head of the judiciary, as well as a senior member of Cabinet, a dual role which has been the subject of criticism He oversees the administration of justice and endeavours to promote law reform. He is also responsible for the appointment of judges, who are now appointed after public advertisement but still chosen, generally, from the senior ranks of the Bar.

The Lord Chancellor's Department endeavours to provide a fair system of justice and oversees the Community Legal Services' funding system and the passage of much legislation through the courts.

9   SOURCES OF LAW

9.1   Common law

The basis of English law is known as the 'common law'. This means that it is a system of law which has been built up over the centuries by decisions of judges in particular cases. Reports of these cases are published in the Law Reports. Cases decided in the higher courts are more influential than those in the lower courts. Where decisions differ, decisions in the higher courts overrule those from the lower courts.

9.2   Equity

The strict rules of law are influenced by a discretion which the courts have, to ensure that the rules are applied fairly. This is called the 'equitable jurisdiction' or 'equity'. Over the years rules have also evolved to lay down when the discretion can be exercised. Just because a rule works unfairly in a particular case does not mean the courts can modify its operation, however.

Certain court procedures are known as 'equitable remedies' – the most common instance being an injunction. For example, a court may make an order (or grant an injunction) to stop you from using a footpath in a dispute with your neighbour over a right of way. Another equitable remedy is an order for specific performance – for example the court may order your landlord to carry out repairs to your flat.

9.3 Statute

Statute law is made up of Acts of Parliament. The Government normally introduces a Bill suggesting new rules to be followed on a particular topic, which has to pass through both Houses of Parliament. It then receives the Royal Assent and becomes law.

9.4 Precedent

This is the system whereby decisions made by a court in one case are applied to cases where similar issues arise. The House of Lords has the final word on any point of law and the decisions of the Court of Appeal overrule decisions of the lower courts etc.

9.5 European Community Law

European law is contained in Regulations, Directives and Decisions. A Regulation is binding on all Member States directly. A Directive affects all the Member States but it is for the individual Members to achieve the aim of the Directive by taking whatever measures are necessary. A Decision is binding in all its aspects upon those to whom it is addressed. Thus decisions do not require national implementing legislation. A Decision may be addressed to any or all Member States, to enterprises or individuals.

9.5.1 Conventions

As we have seen with the incorporation of the European Convention of Human Rights in to UK law (see above, section 6), the need to conform with international obligations can have a direct impact on the legal system at the national level. This can only be expected to grow, with increasing 'globalisation' of justice.

10 REFORMING THE LAW

Contrary to popular impression, the law is not static. It moves with the times as we have seen again and again throughout this book.

However, it needs certainty too. We cannot have our legal system in a continual state of flux. We must know – as far as possible – that our actions which are legal today will not be made illegal tomorrow. This should be kept in mind when charges of 'being out of date' are levelled at the law. As always a line must be drawn between certainty and reform. As always, too, the position of the line will have proponents and opponents.

Change comes from many sources as we will see below.

10.1 Who makes the law

10.1.1 Parliament

In the United Kingdom, there is no written constitution. Parliament has the right to make or change any law and the courts must then enforce it. In theory this right is unfettered except by international obligation.

In practice, of course, MPs are answerable to their own constituents and so they endeavour to ensure that the legislation which they pass will reflect a broad consensus. Sometimes they may fail to gauge public opinion correctly, such as with the Poll Tax, and the law may become unworkable. Sometimes, there may be an over-hasty reaction to public opinion, and the law may not be as carefully considered as it might have been. An example, in some eyes, is the Dangerous Dogs Act which was passed in response to attacks on children by pit bull terriers (see the chapter on *Pets*). Ultimately, though, it is to Parliament that we must all turn – whether judge or layperson – for reform of those areas of the law that are in the most pressing need of change.

Further, under the Human Rights Act 1998 Parliament must change a law as speedily as possible where a claimant's human rights have been breached but the court has found that the public authority acted within the existing law [known as a 'declaration of incompatibility' (see section 6.1 above)].

10.1.2 The precedents

Again contrary to popular impression, judges themselves continually keep the law under review. The whole system of common law and precedent depends on judge-made law although judges will say that their task is only to interpret the law and not to 'make' it. A striking example of judge-made law is the House of Lords' decision that a man can be guilty of marital rape. This single decision overturned a very different, centuries-old, judicial perception of the laws governing the relationship between husbands and wives.

Once a definitive decision has been given in the House of Lords, it then binds all the other courts – unless reference is made to the European Court of Justice or the Court of Human Rights.

10.2 Who advises on changes to the law

10.2.1 Law Commission

The Law Commission advises the Government on law reform. It is headed by a High Court Judge seconded from his or her duties for the purpose, usually for a period of three years.

The Commission's function is to make proposals for updating and reforming the law. Throughout the book, we have mentioned proposals put forward by the Law Commission – for example, on proposed changes to the current rules on claiming damages for psychiatric illness as a result of someone else's death or injury (see the chapter on *Accidents*, section 11.4.1).

10.2.2 Royal Commissions

The government will appoint a Royal Commission to examine a particular area of law in the light of a pressing need for such an investigation. After a series of miscarriages of justice in the criminal justice system for example, a Royal Commission on Criminal Justice was appointed under Lord Runciman, with wide terms of reference.

10.2.3 Pressure groups

The importance of groups keeping up pressure on the government for change in the law cannot be overemphasised. Such groups can be formed by concerned members of the public or can come from within the legal system itself.

10.2.3(a) Within the legal profession

In a sense, of course, no one is more likely to be aware of anomalies in the legal system than those who deal with it as part of their everyday business.

There are many groups within the profession, both solicitors and barristers, who have a fundamental concern with changing the law. Official bodies such as the Law Society and the Bar Council may reflect this concern to a greater or lesser degree. Other groups are formed by members of the professions, such as the organisation called *Justice*, which investigates complaints of wrongful conviction.

10.2.3(b) The public at large

Pressure groups within the public at large can spring up to meet an immediate need and to make their voices heard quickly and effectively. A single issue can unite a group of people who can launch an effective campaign on matters diverse, such as nursery places, pension-splitting on divorce, parking zones, or protection of a wild habitat.

However, there are also many long-standing groups which work consistently over decades towards changes in the law in their particular sphere of interest. An example is an organisation such as the Ramblers Association which has consistently campaigned for what it regards as the proper enforcement of the laws concerning the right to roam (see the chapter on *The Countryside*).

DIRECTORY
THE LEGAL SYSTEM

Academy of Experts
2 South Square
Gray's Inn
London WC1R 5HT
Tel. 020 7637 0333
www.academy-experts.org

The ADR Group *(Alternative Dispute Resolution)*
Grove House
Grove Road
Redlands
Bristol BS6 6UN
www.adrgroup.co.uk

AIMS
(Advice, Information and Mediation Service)
AGE Concern (England)
Astral House
1268 London Road
London SW16 4ER
www.ageconcern.org.uk/aims

Bar Pro Bono Unit
7 Gray's Inn Square
London WC1R 5AZ
Tel. 020 7831 9711
www.barprobono.org.uk

Chartered Institute of Arbitrators
12 Bloomsbury Square
London WC1A2LP
Tel. 020 7421 7444
www.arbitrators.org

Children and Family Court Advisory and Support Services for England and Wales *(CAFCASS)*
13th and 14th Floors
Archway Tower
2 Junction Road
London N19 5HQ
Tel. 020 7210 4400
www.cafcass.gov.uk

The College of Law Legal Advice Centre
14 Store Street
London WC1A 7DA
Tel. 020 7291 1230

Community Legal Service Directory
Tel. 0845 608 1122

Council for Licensed Conveyancers
16 Glebe Road
Chelmsford
Essex CM1 1QG
Tel. 01245 349599
www.conveyancers.gov.uk

Court Funds Office
22 Kingsway
London WC2B 6IE
Tel. 020 7947 7648
www.courtservice.gov.uk

Crown Prosecution Service
50 Ludgate Hill
London EC4M 7EX
Tel. 020 7796 8000
www.cps.gov.uk

District Land Registries National Searches
Tel. 01752 636 666

Federation of Independent Advice Centres *(FIAC)*
4 Deans Court
St Paul's Churchyard
London EC4V 5AA
Tel. 020 7407 4070
www.fiac.org.uk

The Free Representation Unit
4th Floor, Peer House
8–14 Verulam Street
London WC1X 8LZ
Tel. 020 7831 0692
www.fru.org.uk

General Council of the Bar
3 Bedford Row
London WC1R 4DB
Tel. 020 7242 0082
www.barcouncil.org.uk

The Insolvency Service
21 Bloomsbury Street
London WC1B 3SS
Tel. 020 7637 1110
www.insolvency.gov.uk

The Institute of Legal Executives
Kempston Manor, Kempston
Bedford MK42 7AB
Tel. 01234 841000
www.ilex.org.uk

Justice
59 Carter Lane
London EC4V 5AQ
Tel. 020 7329 5100
www.justice.org.uk

Law Centres Federation
Duchess House
18–19 Warren Street
London W1P 5LR
Tel. 020 7387 8570
www.lawcentres.org.co

The Law Commission
Conquest House
37–38 John Street
Theobalds Road
London WC1N 2BQ
Tel. 020 7453 1220
www.lawcom.gov.uk

The Law Society
113 Chancery Lane
London WC2A 1PL
Tel. 020 7242 1222
www.lawsociety.org.uk

The Law Society of Northern Ireland
Legal Aid Department
Bedford House
16–22 Bedford Street
Belfast BT2 7FL
Tel. 02890 246 441
www.nilad.org

Legal Action Group
242 Pentonville Road
London N1 9UN
Tel. 020 7833 2931
www.lag.org.uk

Legal Aid
(see Legal Services Commission)

The Legal Services Commission *(England)*
85 Gray's Inn Road
London WC1X 8TX
Tel. 020 7759 0000
www.legalservices.gov.uk

The Legal Services Commission *(Wales)*
Marland House, Central Square
Cardiff CF1 1PF
Tel. 02920 647 100
www.legalservices.gov.uk

LSC Leaflet Line
St. Ives Direct, Edenbridge
Kent TN8 6HF
Tel. 0845 3000 343

Liberty
21 Tabard Street
London SE1 4LA
Tel. 020 7403 3888
www.liberty-human-rights.org.uk

Lord Chancellor's Department
Selborne House
54–60 Victoria Street
London SW1E 6QW
Tel. 020 7210 8500
www.lcd.gov.uk

(for **Small Claims Procedure***)*
Civil Operations
Southside
105 Victoria Street
London SW1E 6OT

Mediation UK
Alexander House
Telephone Avenue
Bristol BS1 4BS
Tel. 0117 904 6661
www.mediationuk.org.uk

Mediation Wales
3 Alexandra Gate
Fford Pengan, Tremofa
Cardiff CF24 2UD
Tel. 0292 0415353
www.mediationwales.org.uk

National Association of Citizens' Advice Bureaux
115–23 Pentonville Road
London N1 9LZ
Tel. 020 7833 2181
www.nacab.org.uk

Office of the Legal Services Ombudsman
3rd Floor, Sunlight House
Quay Street
Manchester M3 3JZ
Tel. 0161 839 7262
www.olso.org

Office for the Supervision of Solicitors
Victoria Court
8 Dormer Place
Leamington Spa
Warwickshire CV32 5AE
Tel. 01926 820 082
www.oss.lawsociety.org.uk

The Scottish Legal Aid Board
44 Drumsheugh Gardens
Edinburgh EH3 7SW
Tel. 0131 226 7061
www.slab.org.uk

Solicitors Pro Bono Group
113 Chancery Lane
London WC2A 1PL
Tel. 020 7929 5601
www.probonogroup.org.uk

Supreme Accounts Office
Room E01
Royal Courts of Justice
Strand
London WC2A 2LL

Useful legal websites
Conveyancing – www.e-conveyancing.gov.uk/
Employment Law Guide – www.emplaw.co.uk
European Court of Human Rights –
www.echr.coe.int
Gateway to the Criminal Justice System –
www.cjsonline.org
The Home Office – www.homeoffice.gov.uk
The Lord Chancellor's Dept – www.lcd.gov.uk
The Legal Services Commission –
www.legalservices.gov.uk
Low pay issues and workers' rights –
www.lowpayunit.org.uk
Office of Fair Trading – *consumer issues* –
www.oft.gov.uk
Online guide to human rights law –
yourrights.org.uk
Online magazine – www.spr-consilio.com
Online legal dictionary – www.duhaime.org
Radio 4 Programme Law in Action –
www.bbc.co.uk/factsheets/lawinaction

Office of the Legal Services Ombudsman –
Enquiries can be e-mailed to:
enquiries.olso@gtnet.gov.uk

INDEX